Acadamh Ríoga na hÉireann   An Chartlann Náisiúnta

An Roinn Gnóthaí Eachtracha

Cáipéisí ar Pholasaí Eachtrach na hÉireann

Imleabhar V

1937 ~ 1939

EAGARTHÓIRÍ

Catriona Crowe

Ronan Fanning

Michael Kennedy

Dermot Keogh

Eunan O'Halpin

Royal Irish Academy   National Archives
Department of Foreign Affairs

Documents on Irish Foreign Policy

Volume V

1937 ~ 1939

EDITORS
Catriona Crowe
Ronan Fanning
Michael Kennedy
Dermot Keogh
Eunan O'Halpin

First published in 2006 by
Royal Irish Academy
19 Dawson Street
Dublin, Ireland

A catalogue record for this title is available from the British Library

ISBN-10: 1 904890 21 0
ISBN-13: 978 1 904890 218

Publishing consultants
Institute of Public Administration, Dublin

Design by Jan de Fouw
Typeset by Carole Lynch
Printed by ColourBooks, Dublin

Contents

Editors

Ms Catriona Crowe
(Senior Archivist, National Archives)

Professor Ronan Fanning MRIA
(Professor of Modern History, University College Dublin)

Dr Michael Kennedy
(Executive Editor, Documents on Irish Foreign Policy Series,
Royal Irish Academy)

Professor Dermot Keogh MRIA
(Professor of History, University College Cork)

Professor Eunan O'Halpin MRIA
(Professor of Contemporary Irish History, Trinity College Dublin)

Editorial Assistant
Ms Sanchia O'Connor (Royal Irish Academy) (to September 2005)
Dr Kate O'Malley (Royal Irish Academy) (from October 2005)

Editorial Advisory Board

(In addition to the Editors)

Ms Anne Barrington (Department of Foreign Affairs) (from June 2004
to September 2005)

Mr Patrick Buckley (Royal Irish Academy)

Mr Karl Gardner (Department of Foreign Affairs) (August 2005 to July 2006)

Mr Tony McCullough (Department of Foreign Affairs) (from August 2006)

Ms Alma Ní Choigligh (Department of Foreign Affairs) (to August 2005)

Mr Adrian O'Neill (Department of Foreign Affairs) (from September 2005)

Ms Miriam Tiernan (Department of Foreign Affairs) (to July 2006)

Abbreviations

The following is a list of the most commonly used abbreviated terms and phrases in the volume, covering both documents and editorial matter. Other abbreviations have been spelt out in the text.

DFA   Department of Foreign Affairs collection, National Archives, Dublin
DT S   Department of the Taoiseach, S series files, National Archives, Dublin
NAI   National Archives, Dublin
TD   Teachta Dála (Member of Dáil Éireann)
NAUK   The National Archives (formerly the Public Record Office), Kew, London
UCDA   University College Dublin, Archives Department

Preface

The National Archives Act, 1986, provides for the transfer of departmental records more than thirty years old to the National Archives of Ireland for inspection by the public, unless they are certified to be in regular use by a Department for administrative purposes, or unless they are certified as withheld from public inspection on one of the grounds specified in the Act. The bulk of the material consulted for this volume comes from the records of the Department of Foreign Affairs (previously the Department of External Affairs) and the Department of the Taoiseach, all of which are available for inspection at the National Archives of Ireland at Bishop Street in Dublin. Other material comes from the holdings of the University College Dublin Archives Department and The National Archives, Kew, London. The Department of Foreign Affairs documents in the National Archives of Ireland have been made available to researchers since January 1991.[1]

The concept of a multi-volume series of documents on Irish foreign policy was put forward in 1994 by the Department of Foreign Affairs. Mr Ted Barrington, then the Political Director of the Department of Foreign Affairs, brought the proposal to a meeting of the Royal Irish Academy's National Committee for the Study of International Affairs of which he was then a member. The then Tánaiste and Minister for Foreign Affairs, Mr Dick Spring, sanctioned the proposal, which was also welcomed by the Director of the National Archives of Ireland, Dr David Craig, whose permission was necessary for the publication of material in his care. The Royal Irish Academy agreed to become a partner in the project when Council approved its foundation document on 3 April 1995.

The main provisions of that document are:

- that the project's 'basic aim is to make available, in an organised and accessible way, to people who may not be in a position easily to consult the National Archives, documents from the files of the Department which are considered important or useful for an understanding of Irish foreign policy';
- that an Editorial Advisory Board, comprising representatives of the Department, of the Academy and of the National Archives, in addition to senior Irish academics working in the fields of modern history and international relations, would oversee decisions on publication;
- that the series would 'begin at the foundation of the State and publish volumes in chronological order' and that the basic criterion for

---

[1] The Department of Foreign Affairs was known as the Department of External Affairs from December 1922 to 1971. From January 1919 to December 1922 the Department was known as the Department of Foreign Affairs or the Ministry of Foreign Affairs (see DIFP Volume I for further details).

the selection of documents would be their 'use or importance in understanding the evolution of policies and decisions'.

These arrangements found public expression in the 1996 White Paper on foreign policy, *Challenges and Opportunities Abroad* (16.48), which provided that–

> As part of the Government's desire to encourage a greater interest in Irish foreign policy, it has been agreed that the Department of Foreign Affairs, in association with the Royal Irish Academy, will publish a series of foreign policy documents of historic interest. It is hoped that this initiative will encourage and assist greater academic interest in the study of Irish foreign policy.

Provision for the project was first included in the Department's Estimates for 1997 and a preliminary meeting of what became the Editorial Advisory Board, in Iveagh House on 10 April 1997, agreed that an assistant editor should be appointed in addition to the editors nominated by the National Committee for the Study of International Affairs: Professors Ronan Fanning, MRIA, Dermot Keogh MRIA and Eunan O'Halpin MRIA. Dr Michael Kennedy was appointed in June 1997 when work began on the selection of documents. Dr Kennedy was in January 1998 designated executive editor, and is responsible for the direction and day-to-day running of the Documents on Irish Foreign Policy (DIFP) project. At the December 2003 meeting of the DIFP Editorial Advisory Board the important contribution of the National Archives to the DIFP project was officially recognised and the National Archives formally became a full partner to DIFP. Accordingly, Ms Catriona Crowe, Senior Archivist at the National Archives, who had attended meetings of the editors since June 1997 and who was de facto a fifth editor of DIFP, was formally appointed an editor of the DIFP series.

The first volume, *Documents on Irish Foreign Policy I*, covering the period 1919 to 1922, was published in November 1998 in the run-up to the eightieth anniversary of the founding of the Department of Foreign Affairs in January 1919. Subsequent volumes have been published at two-yearly intervals with Volume V being published in November 2006.

Introduction

This volume of selected documents, the fifth in the Documents on Irish Foreign Policy series, covers the development of Irish foreign policy from 1 January 1937 to 1 September 1939.

The volume opens in the aftermath of the passing by the Oireachtas of the Executive Authority (External Relations) Act of December 1936 in a period where the future direction of British-Irish relations was the dominating factor in Irish foreign policy. Throughout 1937 Eamon de Valera, the President of the Executive Council (Taoiseach from 29 December 1937) and Minister for External Affairs, and Malcolm MacDonald, the British Dominions Secretary, together with their senior officials sought to resolve outstanding differences between Britain and Ireland. The receipt in Dublin in November 1937 of a British memorandum on aspects of relations between the two countries in time of war was the catalyst facilitating the commencement of full inter-governmental negotiations in London in January 1938.

The negotiations led to the conclusion of a tripartite Anglo-Irish agreement in April 1938 encompassing the removal of barriers to British-Irish trade, the resolution of the dispute over the land annuities question[1] following a lump-sum payment by Ireland to Britain, and provisions for the handing over of the three British defended anchorages in Ireland[2] to Irish control. De Valera had hoped for movement during the talks towards the ending of partition, but these hopes were in vain.

The probability of a major European war gained strength during the year 1938 and the Irish government and administration seriously anticipated the outbreak of conflict from the time of the Sudeten crisis of August-September. The likelihood of war increased over the next twelve months and Irish missions abroad continually reported local opinions of war and peace and rumours of imminent conflict. By August 1939 most missions were reporting that the outbreak of war was only a matter of days away. The volume ends on the morning of 1 September 1939 when a telegram from the Irish Chargé d'Affaires in Berlin was received in Dublin containing the words 'hostilities expected immediately'.[3] Irish military preparations for such a conflict were begun too late and as a result the state was almost defenceless when the conflict finally started; despite crippling deficiencies in equipment, weapons and organisation, Ireland would try to defend itself against any invader, but resolved to remain neutral. Volumes VI and VII of *Documents on Irish Foreign*

---

[1] This issue had arisen in 1932 when Fianna Fáil had refused to hand over to Britain payments due under loans advanced to Irish farmers to buy out their holdings under the terms of a series of Land Acts running from the 1880s. See DIFP IV for details for how the annuities question had developed from 1932 to 1937, in particular documents Nos 18, 38, 57, 66, 70, 73, 78, 81, 85, 88, 89, 120, 126, 136, 137, 138, 140.

[2] The 'Treaty Ports' of Cobh, Berehaven and Lough Swilly retained under the defence annex to the Anglo-Irish treaty of 1921.

[3] See below No. 357.

Policy will cover the course of Irish foreign policy during the Second World War.

* * *

The resolution of outstanding issues in British-Irish relations, ultimately achieved through the April 1938 Anglo-Irish Agreements, and Irish perspectives on the final years of peace in Europe before the outbreak of the Second World War are the central themes in this volume.

In order to discuss the shape of British-Irish relations following the enactment of the External Relations Act and in view of the imminent introduction of a new Irish Constitution, *Bunreacht na hÉireann*, de Valera and MacDonald met in London on 14 January 1937. There were differences of opinion during the discussions, but the talks contributed to the development of mutual trust and goodwill between the two men and set the basic agenda of defence, economic and financial issues that were ultimately to be addressed through the 1938 Anglo-Irish Agreements.

Before the two could meet again British-Irish differences arose over the coronation of King George VI and the Imperial Conference of 1937. Dublin protested over the wording of the oath to be taken by the King at his coronation on 12 May 1937, leading to Ireland adopting an attitude of detachment and protest towards the coronation ceremony. Ireland also refused to attend the Imperial Conference in London. De Valera turned down a British suggestion that British-Irish negotiations would take place in the wings of the conference.

The Dáil approved *Bunreacht na hÉireann* on 14 June and it was carried by referendum on 31 July. Although the new Constitution did not come into effect until 29 December the way was now clear for de Valera to move towards trying to resolve the remaining, non-constitutional differences with Britain.

De Valera and MacDonald built upon their January talks by meeting in Geneva on 15 and 16 September 1937 while both were attending the Assembly of the League of Nations. Dublin then used the receipt of a memorandum in November 1937 from the Dominions Office on control of food supplies and the imposition of censorship in time of war as the catalyst to initiate full-scale intergovernmental talks with Britain.

De Valera, accompanied by Minister for Finance Seán MacEntee, Minister for Industry and Commerce Seán Lemass and Minister for Agriculture James Ryan, travelled to London for the first governmental-level British-Irish discussions since 1932 and the talks opened on 17 January 1938. The first plenary session concluded on 19 January. Further plenary sessions were held on 23 February and on 3 and 4 March. After this the talks broke up into official-level discussions.

On 22 April the negotiations were concluded and financial, trade and defence agreements were signed in London on 25 April. The annuities question was resolved through a lump sum payment of £10 million by Ireland to Britain, Irish goods were given preferential access to British markets and a tariff commission was established to review tariffs at set intervals, and the three Treaty ports were to be returned to Ireland, a process to be completed by autumn 1938.

Even before the handover of the ports had been completed a much more sensitive area of British-Irish contact had been initiated. In late August and in October 1938 officers from the military intelligence branch of the Defence Forces (G2) accompanied by the Secretary of the Department of External Affairs, Joseph P. Walshe, and the Irish High Commissioner in London, John Dulanty, began secret talks with the British security services on co-operation and counter-espionage in time of war. Though documents relating to these talks can be found in British archives, no documents were found in Department of External Affairs archives. Nor were any documents found relating to the follow-on visit to Dublin in July 1939 by Percivale Liesching of the Dominions Office, though the visit is well documented on the British side. The absence of material on these meetings is probably due to the sensitivity surrounding British-Irish security co-operation. However it is also likely that any records of these discussions were destroyed in Dublin in May 1940 in a move undertaken to eliminate sensitive material in anticipation of a German invasion of Ireland.[1]

As a result of the troubled international climate Dublin attempted in 1938 to initiate talks with the government of Northern Ireland on areas of mutual concern in wartime. Through the Secretary of the Department of Industry and Commerce, John Leydon, exploratory official-level talks on cross-border co-operation began in April 1938, with the approval of Leydon's minister, Seán Lemass. These talks came to an abrupt halt in October 1938 after de Valera, in an interview in the London *Evening Standard*, outlined his views on a federal solution to partition.[2] Leydon attempted to reconvene discussions in November 1938, but the interview had soured the atmosphere and the possibility for meaningful talks on cross-border relations slipped away.

Beyond relations between Ireland, Northern Ireland and Britain the collapse of collective security and the failure of the League of Nations following the Italian invasion of Abyssinia had a fundamental impact on Irish foreign policy. The League had been a cornerstone of the State's international relations since Ireland joined in 1923 and de Valera had shown considerable support for the League since 1932. But the failure of the League to counter Italy's aggression in Abyssinia and its inability to place international law at the core of international relations led Dublin to realise that the League was now of little practical value to Ireland in protecting the State in the event of war. De Valera continued to support the principles upon which the League was founded, but was increasingly of the opinion that neutrality was now the best possible course for Ireland, an option given more substance following the return of the Treaty ports in 1938.

As President of the Executive Council/Taoiseach and Minister for External Affairs, Eamon de Valera was the dominant intellectual force behind Irish foreign policy in the late 1930s. Strengthened by the vigour of de

---

[1] A full account of the destruction of documents in May 1940 can be found below in Appendix 1.

[2] See also Maurice Moynihan (ed.), *Speeches and Statements of Eamon de Valera* (Dublin, 1981), pp 358-62.

Valera's robust approach to Ireland's international relations, the Department of External Affairs consolidated its power during this period. Though it remained small in size, its position in the Irish administrative system was now one of complete control over all aspects of Ireland's external interests. It had triumphed in the turf wars with the Department of the President,[1] with a truce holding between Walshe and the Secretary of the Department of the President, Maurice Moynihan, over the limits of the jurisdictions of their departments.

External Affairs and the Department of Industry and Commerce developed a close working relationship in the late 1930s, a situation due in large part to the need for both departments to work together on trade aspects of the 1938 Agreements and also owing to the personal relationship between Walshe and John Leydon, the Secretary of the Department of Industry and Commerce. In addition, Frederick Boland, Assistant Secretary at External Affairs from 1938, had spent from 1936 to 1938 heading the foreign trade section at Industry and Commerce and this deepened the working relationship between the two departments.

By contrast, the relationship between External Affairs and the Department of Finance remained functional. James J. McElligott, Secretary of the Department of Finance and head of the Irish civil service, maintained his close relationship with the Treasury in London as can be seen below in his handling of the financial aspects of the 1938 Agreements.[2]

The structure and personnel of the Irish diplomatic service remained relatively static in the period covered by DIFP Volume V. De Valera remained Minister for External Affairs and Walshe remained Secretary of the Department of External Affairs. De Valera's tactical reliance on Walshe to implement his grand strategy of Irish foreign policy continued as Walshe undertook high-level missions to London and the Vatican on de Valera's behalf in 1937 and 1938.

The Irish High Commissioner in London, John Dulanty, remained the central figure after de Valera in all aspects of British-Irish relations. Twenty-one documents printed below, mainly confidential reports on British-Irish relations written by Dulanty, come from files found in the autumn of 2005 in the basement of the Embassy of Ireland at Grosvenor Place in London. An almost complete set of confidential reports covering Dulanty's years as High Commissioner (1930-49) make up a sizeable portion of this collection. Until their discovery few of Dulanty's pre-1941 confidential reports had been located. It was assumed that they had been destroyed as part of a haphazard destruction of material in the Department of External Affairs on 25 May 1940 that was undertaken to remove sensitive documents in anticipation of an imminent German invasion of Ireland.[3] For the period covered by DIFP

---

[1] See DIFP Volume IV, particularly No. 251 and No. 325.
[2] See McElligott's letters to MacEntee below of No. 131 (20 Jan. 1938), No. 134 (24 Jan. 1938) and No. 135 (25 Jan. 1938).
[3] A full account of the destruction of these documents in May 1940 can be found below in Appendix 1.

Volume V the sequence of confidential report files from this new collection is incomplete. Only the files for 1937 were located.[1]

The senior staff of most missions abroad remained unchanged between 1937 and 1939. Dulanty remained in London, Francis (Frank) Cremins in Geneva, Charles Bewley in Berlin, William J. B. Macaulay at the Holy See, and Leopold Kerney in Madrid. In Paris Art O'Brien retired in 1938 to be replaced by Seán Murphy, ending Murphy's eleven years as Assistant Secretary at Headquarters, and in the same year Robert Brennan was moved to Washington. Michael MacWhite left Washington to establish Ireland's only new foreign mission in the period covered by this volume when he was posted as Minister to Italy in mid-1938. Though John Hearne was appointed High Commissioner to Ottawa in June 1939, he did not take up office until September 1939, after the period covered by DIFP Volume V.

The most problematic of these staff members was Charles Bewley, Minister Plenipotentiary at Berlin. Known for his anti-Semitic views and his admiration of the Nazis, Bewley had by 1937 'gone native' in Germany and made no attempt at hiding his virulent anti-Semitic and pro-Nazi outlook. The sentiment in Bewley's despatches was reinforced by a clash of beliefs with de Valera and of personalities with Walshe.

Much of Bewley's reporting to Dublin from January 1937 to January 1939 was destroyed in May 1940, while virtually all the records of the Irish Legation in Berlin were lost when British bombing during an air raid in November 1943 destroyed the premises. Consequently, there are large gaps in the sequence of Bewley's reports in this volume. There is very little in the volume on Irish relations with Germany in 1937 save some correspondence on the new Irish Constitution and on the nature of British-Irish relations. What is clear from a further document covering concerns over the Berlin Legation accounts is that Dublin was aware of Bewley's unsuitability to remain in Berlin.[2]

The reader will be left largely in the dark as to the exact contents of Bewley's reporting through 1938, but a report on Kristallnacht has survived owing to the fact that it was filed separately from the files that were destroyed.[3] The topics covered by Bewley's missing 1938 reports, as recorded in the register of incoming letters in the Department of External Affairs, have been reproduced as an appendix to this volume in order to give some impression as to other themes covered.[4]

Bewley was informed of his recall on 27 February 1939 and told that his period as head of mission in Berlin would end on 31 July 1939. He replied to Walshe on 10 March that he was not prepared to take up a post in Dublin, but was instructed to report to the Department of External Affairs on 3 August. He failed to report as ordered and was given until 11 September to explain

---

[1] A comprehensive search of the embassy was carried out for the missing files for 1938 and 1939 without success.
[2] See document No. 105 (26 Nov. 1937) below.
[3] See document No. 249 (9 Dec. 1938) below.
[4] See Appendix 1.

his absence, having been judged to be absent without leave from 3 August. Bewley submitted his resignation on 11 September, de Valera considering it retrospective from 3 August.

William Warnock temporarily replaced Bewley in Berlin. It had been anticipated that Thomas J. Kiernan would replace Bewley and the agreement of the German government for Kiernan's appointment was obtained. The outbreak of the Second World War prevented Kiernan's appointment and Warnock remained in Berlin until 1943.

A direct consequence of the decline of the League of Nations was the change in the role of Frank Cremins, Irish Permanent Delegate to the League. Cremins had replaced Seán Lester at Geneva in 1934. Lester served in Danzig as League High Commissioner to the Free City, returning to Geneva in 1937 as Deputy Secretary General of the League. As the power of the League declined, Cremins' reports to Dublin focused to a greater extent on the power struggle in Europe between totalitarianism and democracy. Cremins' reports on European affairs, in particular those on German expansion and Nazi foreign policy, and those of Michael MacWhite from the newly opened Irish legation in Rome on Italian foreign and domestic policy, provide a counterbalance to Bewley's biased reporting from Berlin, in particular during the last months of peace in Europe in 1939.

Owing to the destruction of documents there are considerable gaps in confidential reporting from missions for 1938 and 1939, in particular from London, Washington and Berlin, but other apparent gaps and absences in the material reproduced below, in particular from Paris, the Holy See and Madrid are due to the indifferent quality of reporting. Art O'Brien in Paris proved unequal to the task of reporting on European affairs from the French capital, though his annual reports from Paris do show the heavy level of activity at the Irish Legation.[1] Much of his confidential reporting was devoted to summaries of newspaper articles and is not suitable for publication. The Irish Minister to the Holy See, William J. B. Macaulay, whilst being an ably informed insider where Vatican affairs were concerned, did not report in significant detail on wider European affairs. Leopold Kerney, Minister to Spain, was out of necessity largely concerned with the civil war in that country.

The Irish Minister to Spain was something of a thorn in Dublin's side in so far as he sought Irish recognition of Franco prior to the Nationalist victory in the civil war. Dublin maintained that diplomatic relations were with states, not their governments, and de Valera and Walshe sought not to take sides in Spain, supporting instead the continuing work of the International Non-intervention Committee. Kerney nevertheless continued to needle Dublin to recognise Franco as head of state. In February 1939 Dublin finally recognised the Burgos government as the de jure government of Spain and Franco as head of state. Kerney's work in Spain, whether from Saint Jean de Luz, San Sebastian or Madrid, required him to keep in close contact with the warring parties in order to seek the release of Irishmen interned by both sides. The repatriation of minors was of considerable concern to Dublin, but the

---

[1] See documents No. 94 (4 Oct. 1938) and No. 229 (7 Oct. 1939) below.

greatest portion of Kerney's time was devoted to seeking the release of Frank Ryan. Despite ongoing contacts with the Spanish authorities Kerney's efforts proved unsuccessful and Ryan remained in custody.

At Headquarters the most important change to the small high-level group of de Valera, Joseph Walshe, Seán Murphy, Sheila Murphy and John Hearne, that ran Irish foreign policy was the return of Fredrick Boland to External Affairs in 1938 as Assistant Secretary on Seán Murphy's departure to Paris as Minister. As a technocratic career civil servant Boland was an important counterbalance to Walshe's mercurial and at times overzealous nature. The appointment of John Hearne as High Commissioner at Ottawa resulted in the promotion of Michael Rynne to the position of Legal Adviser. Thus the group of Walshe, Boland, Rynne and Sheila Murphy, de Valera's most senior foreign policy advisors during the Second World War, was in place before the conflict broke out. Further down the ladder of diplomatic rank, the late 1930s saw the rise of John Belton, of William Warnock, of Con Cremin, who would later become Secretary of the Department, and of Denis Devlin, though Devlin's career would be cut short by his death from leukaemia in 1959.

Walshe's role as Ireland's most senior foreign policy expert remained unchallenged in the run-up to the Second World War. In the documents printed below the reader will be aware of lengthy periods where Assistant Secretary Seán Murphy stood in for Walshe; this is evident in particular in Murphy's signature of letters for Walshe and his undertaking of matters in British-Irish relations normally reserved to Walshe alone. In the aftermath of the 1938 Agreements Walshe took a long period of leave during which he travelled to Egypt and Sudan. This trip was a long holiday, but only in part; Walshe was also engaged in a semi-official capacity, meeting officials in both countries on de Valera's instructions. Two of his letters to de Valera have been printed in this volume, giving an insight into Walshe's unusual personal relationship with de Valera.

The relationship between de Valera and his most senior advisers is further to be seen in the documents below in the marginal notes and annotations to documents. Sheila Murphy, Walshe's Private Secretary, circulated documents sent to the Secretary, to Assistant Secretary Seán Murphy and his successor Frederick Boland, John Hearne and, following Hearne's departure to Ottawa, to his successor Michael Rynne. Their initials are to be found on many documents. The additional annotation 'Read to President', or after December 1937, 'Read to Taoiseach', show how de Valera's poor eyesight made it easier for documents requiring a decision from him to be read to him and the notations give the reader an insight into which documents Walshe and others considered to be of important enough to bring to de Valera's attention.

Though External Affairs remained a small department through the 1930s, this volume shows the energy within the Irish diplomatic service and among the makers of Irish foreign policy in the last years of peace in Europe before the outbreak of World War Two. The senior figures managed the development of policy under de Valera's direction and a number of talented junior diplomats were rising through the system. Developing British-Irish relations as relations between two sovereign states remained at the core of Irish foreign policy between 1937 and 1939. War brought a wider challenge, that of proving sovereignty through independence of action, and exercising independence of action through practical neutrality. This would require not simply good relations with London, but skilful and inventive diplomacy with belligerents on all sides in the Second World War.

Records of the Department of Foreign Affairs, and other archival sources
Until the passage of the National Archives Act (1986), government departments in Ireland were under no compulsion to release their archives. The Department of the Taoiseach, however, has voluntarily released material since the mid-1970s. The Department of Foreign Affairs records have been released on an annual basis since 1991.

In the late 1920s the Department of External Affairs established a numerical registry system for filing its papers. Under this system a list of subject categories corresponding to the main areas of the department's work was drawn up and each subject category was assigned a unique number code. For example the number code 26 was allocated to files and papers dealing with the League of Nations. Individual files within each number category were assigned a unique sub-number. File 26/95 deals with the Irish Free State's candidature for the League of Nations Council in 1930. This registry and filing system, known colloquially as 'number series' files, was further developed in the mid-1930s. The existing two-digit prefixes had the number 1 added to them with, for example, the previous 26 series becoming the 126 series and so on. A further development took place in the late 1930s with the 1 being replaced by a 2, thus 126 became 226.

The most sensitive information held by the Department of External Affairs was kept in the Secretary's Files series. This collection began in the 1920s, with files being designated S with a number following (not to be confused with the separate Department of the Taoiseach S Series files.). In later years A and P series were created, as well as a PS series for the Private Secretary to the Secretary. These series were held under lock and key in the Secretary's office and were only made available to lower ranking officials under certain conditions. The S Series was a target for widespread destruction during the wartime invasion scares of 1940.

Material generated in Irish missions abroad is held at the National Archives in Dublin in the Embassies Series collection. For the late 1930s this material covers the missions in London, Washington, Geneva, Brussels, the Holy See, Paris, Berlin, Madrid and Rome. Due to weeding and wartime destruction the Embassies Series is very patchy for the inter-war years. The collections for Madrid and Paris are the most complete. The archives of the Irish Legation in Berlin were almost completely destroyed after a bomb hit the chancellery during an air raid in 1943. Unfortunately, the majority of files of the Irish Embassy in London (Irish High Commission from 1923 to 1949) were shredded in the 1950s. Similarly, very little survives from the Washington Embassy for the period covered by this volume. Where files do survive there is an understandable degree of overlap with Headquarters' number series files.

The main files from the Department of the Taoiseach (known from 1922 to 1937 as the Department of the President of the Executive Council, or simply 'the Department of the President') are known as the 'S-files' series. They begin at S1 and progress numerically (S1, S2, S3 etc.) in a roughly chronological order. In contrast to the 1920s, when foreign policy matters appeared regularly on the agenda of the Executive Council and Cabinet, with de Valera as President of the Executive Council and Minister for External Affairs there was a tendency for the members of the government to leave foreign policy decisions solely to him.

Readers of Volume V will notice that both Executive Council minutes and Cabinet minutes are published. While in common parlance the Executive Council (as the Government of the Irish Free State was known from 1922 to 1937) and the Cabinet are considered to be the same body, there was a difference between the two. The Executive Council (from 1938 referred to as the Government) was the term given to members of the Government meeting under the functions devolving upon it by provision of the Constitution or the law. The Cabinet was the name given to the Government meeting to decide matters of policy as the main policy-making organ of the State. The distinction between Government decisions and Cabinet decisions was abolished with the commencement of the Eighteenth Government on 9 March, 1982.

The editors have reproduced four documents from The National Archives, Kew, London. The first document (No. 51) is a facsimile of the letter from John Dulanty to Malcolm MacDonald enclosing a copy of the 1937 Constitution; the second (No. 104) is the original top copy despatch sent by de Valera to MacDonald on 24 November 1937 which initiated what became the negotiations leading to the 1938 Anglo-Irish Agreement; the third document (No. 239) is the original of a letter from de Valera to MacDonald sending MacDonald best wishes on his return to the Dominions Office on 31 October 1938; and the final document (No. 355) is de Valera's note dated 31 August 1939 to Neville Chamberlain indicating that Ireland intended to remain neutral in the event of war.

Editorial policy and the selection of documents
The Executive Editor is responsible for the initial wide choice of documents. These documents are then assessed periodically by the five Editors in order to select the most appropriate documents for publication. Documents are prioritised in terms of importance on a one to five scale and are processed by the Editors in geographical and thematic tranches. The documents in this volume are presented in chronological order based on date of despatch. The text of documents has been reproduced as exactly as possible. Marginal notes and annotations have generally been reproduced in footnotes; annotations have however sometimes been reproduced in the body text when to have reproduced them as footnotes would have reduced the clarity of the document from the reader's point of view. Where possible the authors of marginal notes have been identified. There have been no alterations of the text of documents nor have there been any deletions without indication being given of where changes have been made. Nothing has been omitted that might conceal or

gloss over defects in policymaking and policy execution. With the exception of twenty one documents from files which were located in the London Embassy in the autumn of 2005 and which were released to the public in 2006, all material reproduced was already open to the public at the relevant repository.[1]

At some points in the text the footnotes refer to documents that were 'not printed'. Either the document referred to could not be found or the document was either routine or repeated information found elsewhere in the documents selected and so was not printed. Where it was impossible to decipher a word or series of words, an ellipsis has been inserted or the assumed word inserted with an explanatory footnote. Spelling mistakes have been silently corrected, but capitalisation, punctuation, signatures and contemporary spelling have in the main been left as found in the originals and have been changed only where the sense is affected. Additions to the text appear in square brackets. Original abbreviations have been preserved and either spelt out between square brackets or explained in the list of abbreviations. Where a sender has signed a document, either in original or copy form, the word 'signed', in square brackets, has been inserted. A similar practice has been followed with initialled or stamped documents, with the word 'initialled' or 'stamped' inserted in square brackets as appropriate. In all cases without an insertion in square brackets, the signature or initials were typed on the original document and are reproduced as found. Where an unsigned copy of a letter is reproduced, the words 'copy letter unsigned' have been inserted in square brackets. The Editors have at all times tried to confirm the identity of the senders and recipients of unsigned letters, and in cases where identity is impossible to establish a footnote has been inserted to that effect. In correspondence, English was the working language of Irish diplomats. It is evident from the archives that written communication in Irish was only used for documents of symbolic national importance, although Irish was the spoken language of a number of diplomats, particularly Joseph Walshe, and many officials were bilingual.

In the weeks leading up to the outbreak of the Second World War foreign missions were instructed to send 'situation reports' to Dublin in Irish on the likelihood of war breaking out as seen from their particular post.

In correspondence, the Irish language was otherwise more commonly used for salutations and in signatures. In many cases there was no consistent spelling of Gaelicised names and in the DIFP volumes many different spellings of the same name and salutation in Irish occur. These have not been standardised and are reproduced as found.

---

[1] The guidelines of the Department of Foreign Affairs state that

There may be no alteration of the text, no deletions without indicating the place in the text where the deletion is made, and no omission of the facts which were of major importance in reaching a decision. Nothing may be omitted for the purpose of concealing or glossing over what might be regarded by some as a defect of policy.

However, certain omissions of documents are permissible to avoid publication of matters that would tend to impede current diplomatic negotiations or other business.

In addition, the above guidelines are to be interpreted in conjunction with the obligations laid out in the National Archives Act (1986) and the Freedom of Information Act (1997), the provisions contained in which are to be regarded as taking precedence.

The authors of the documents reproduced tended to refer to Britain as 'England' or made no distinction between the two geographical entities and the Editors have not thought it necessary to insert (sic) at all relevant points throughout the volume.

Acknowledgements
The editors would like to thank all those who were involved in the production of Volume V of the Documents on Irish Foreign Policy series. The assistance of the following is particularly acknowledged.

At the Department of Foreign Affairs: Dermot Gallagher, Secretary General of the Department; Anne Barrington; Susan Conlon; Alma Ní Choigligh; Stephen Dawson; Brendan Fitzpatrick; Karl Gardner; Clare Hanratty; Andrée Kearney; Christina McCormack; Nuala ní Mhuircheartaigh; Daithí O Ceallaigh, Ambassador to Great Britain; Aidan O'Hara; Adrian O'Neill; Miriam Tiernan and Maureen Sweeney.

At the Royal Irish Academy: Dr Michael Ryan and Professor James Slevin (successively Presidents of the Academy); Patrick Buckley, Executive Secretary of the Academy; Dr Howard Clarke, Secretary of the Academy; Dr Úna Uí Bheirn, Eagarthóir of the Academy's Foclóir na Nua-Ghaeilge; James McGuire (Managing Editor) and Dr James Quinn (Executive Editor) of the Academy's Dictionary of Irish Biography; Sanchia O'Connor and Dr Kate O'Malley.

At the National Archives: Dr David Craig, Director, for his generosity in providing access to the facilities and collections; Ken Hannigan, Keeper; Mary Mackey and Tom Quinlan.

At the University College Dublin Archives (School of History and Archives): Seamus Helferty; Ailsa Holland; Professor Michael Laffan; Kate Manning; Dr John McCafferty and Orna Somerville.

At The National Archives, London: Natalie Ceeney, Chief Executive of The National Archives, and Paul Johnson, Manager of the National Archives Image Library. We thank The National Archives for permission to reproduce the image on p. 62 from material in its care.

At the Institute of Public Administration: Declan MacDonagh; Eileen Kelly; Hannah Ryan and Tom Turley.

We would like to thank the MacWhite family for permission to consult and reproduce material from the papers of Michael MacWhite held at the University College Dublin Archives.

We would also like to thank Commandant Victor Laing of Military Archives, Cathal Brugha Barracks, Dublin; Helen Litton, and Maura O'Shea.

Catriona Crowe
Ronan Fanning
Michael Kennedy
Dermot Keogh
Eunan O'Halpin

23 June 2006

List of Archival Sources

National Archives

Department of Foreign Affairs
2003 release (2003/17 series)
2006 release (2006/39 series)
Confidential Reports
    119 Series
    219 Series
Embassies Series
    Geneva Embassy (League of Nations)
    London Embassy
        Spanish Civil War Non-Intervention Series
    Madrid Embassy
    Paris Embassy
Letter Books
    Berlin 1936-1937
    Rome/Madrid 1936-1937
Number Series Files
    Pre-100 Series
    100 Series
    200 Series
Secretary's Files
    A Series
    S Series

Department of the Taoiseach
S Files
Cabinet Minutes
Executive Council Minutes (to 29 December 1937)
Government Minutes (from 29 December 1937)

Department of Finance
E Series Files

University College Dublin Archives

Eamon de Valera papers (P150)
Seán MacEntee papers (P67)
Michael MacWhite papers (P194)

The National Archives, Kew

Dominions Office (DO 35)
Prime Minister's Office (PREM 1)

Biographical Details

This list gives priority to the main Irish ministerial, diplomatic and administrative figures who appear in the text. Key foreign figures have also been identified, but generally in less detail. Minor figures, or people who receive only an occasional mention, have been identified in the text in footnotes.

Aiken, Frank (1898-1983) TD; educated at Christian Brothers School, Newry; succeeded Liam Lynch as Chief of Staff of the IRA (April 1923) and issued the cease-fire orders which ended the Civil War; Minister for Defence (1932-39); Minister for Lands and Fisheries (June-November 1936); Minister for the Co-ordination of Defensive Measures (1939-45); Minister for Finance (1945-48); Minister for External Affairs (1951-54 and 1957-69); Minister for Agriculture (March-May 1957); Tánaiste (1965-69).

Avenol, Joseph (1879-1952) Secretary-General of the League of Nations (1933-40).

Baldwin, Stanley (1867-1947) British Conservative politician; Prime Minister (1923-24, 1924-29 and 1935-37); Lord President of the Council (1931-35).

Batterbee, Sir Henry (Harry) (1880-1976) Assistant Under-Secretary, Dominions Office (1930-38).

Beary, Michael, Assistant Secretary, Department of Defence.

Bewley, Charles Henry (1888-1969) Educated at Park House, Winchester and New College, Oxford; called to the Bar in 1914 and to the Inner Bar in 1926; Trade Representative to Germany (1921-23); Minister to the Vatican (1929-33); Minister to Germany (1933-39).

Boland, Frederick H. (1904-1985) Educated at Merchant Taylor's School, London, Catholic University School, Dublin, Clongowes Wood College, Trinity College Dublin, King's Inns, Dublin, Harvard University, University of Chicago and University of North Carolina; entered Department of External Affairs (1929); Junior Administrative Officer (1930-31); First Secretary, Paris Legation (1932-34); Head of the League of Nations Section of the Department of External Affairs (1934-36); Principal Officer in charge of foreign trade section, Department of Industry and Commerce (1936-38); Assistant Secretary, Department of External Affairs (1938-46); Secretary, Department of External Affairs (1946-50); Ambassador to Great Britain (1950-55); Permanent Representative/Ambassador to the United Nations (1956-64).

Brennan, Robert (1881-1964) Educated at Christian Brothers School, Wexford; Sinn Féin Director of Publicity (1918-20); Under-Secretary, Department of Foreign Affairs (7 February 1921-21 January 1922); organiser of the Irish Race Conference (Paris, January 1922); anti-Treaty propagandist during the Civil War; General Manager, the *Irish Press* (1931-34); Secretary,

Washington Legation (1934-38); Acting Chargé d'Affaires, Washington (March-September 1938); Minister to the United States of America (1938-47); Director of Broadcasting, Radio Éireann (1947-48).

Chamberlain, Neville (1869-1940)   British Conservative politician; Chancellor of the Exchequer (1923-24 and 1931-37); Prime Minister (1937-40); Lord President of the Council (1940).

Craig, Sir James (later **1st Viscount Craigavon**) (1871-1940)   MP (Westminster and (from 1921) Northern Ireland parliaments) (1906-40); leader of the Ulster Unionist Party (1921-40); first Prime Minister of Northern Ireland (1921-40).

Cremin, Cornelius 'Con' (1908-1987)   Educated at St Brendan's Killarney, University College Cork, and at Athens, Rome, Munich and Oxford. Third Secretary, Department of External Affairs (1935-37); First Secretary, Paris (1937-43); Chargé d'Affaires ad interim, Berlin (1943-45); Chargé d'Affaires ad interim, Lisbon (1945-46); Counsellor, Headquarters, Dublin (1946-48); Assistant Secretary, Department of External Affairs (1948-50); Minister Plenipotentiary / Ambassador to France (1950-54); Ambassador to the Holy See (1954-56); Ambassador to Britain (1956-58); Secretary, Department of External Affairs (1958-63); Ambassador to Britain (1963-64); Ambassador to the United Nations (1964-74).

Cremins, Francis T. (1885-1975)   Clerical Officer, General Post Office (1900-22); Higher Executive Officer, Publicity Department, Department of External Affairs (1922-25); Higher Executive Officer, Department of Lands and Fisheries (1925-29); Head of League of Nations Section, Department of External Affairs (1929-34); Permanent Representative to the League of Nations (1934-40); Chargé d'Affaires at Berne (1940-49).

Cudahy, John Clarence (1887-1943) Served in the United States Army during the First World War; Ambassador to Poland (1933-37), United States Minister to Ireland (1937-40) and United States Ambassador to Belgium (1940).

de Mamblas, Viscount José (Pepe) Oxford-educated former head of the Cultural Relations section of the Spanish Ministry of State; appointed in February 1937 by the Nationalist Government to liase with the British and Irish diplomats.

de Valera, Eamon (1882-1975) TD; born in New York, brought to Ireland in 1885 by an uncle; educated at Bruree National School, Co Limerick, Christian Brothers School, Charleville, Co Cork, Blackrock College, Co Dublin, the Royal University of Ireland, Dublin, and Trinity College Dublin; teacher of mathematics at Rockwell College, Co Tipperary and Blackrock College, Co Dublin; Commandant of the Third Battalion of the Dublin Brigade of the Irish Volunteers during the 1916 Rising; imprisoned in England (1916-17); elected for East Clare (July 1917), elected President of Sinn Féin (October 1917); imprisoned in England (1918-19); returned unopposed for East Clare and elected for East Mayo in the 1918 General Election, also elected for North Down (1921-27) and South Down (1933-38) to the Parliament of Northern

Ireland; President of Dáil Éireann (1 April 1919 – 9 January 1922); whilst in America from 11 June 1919 to 23 December 1920 de Valera referred to this post as 'President of the Irish Republic'; opposed the Treaty; served with the Third Dublin Brigade of the Republican Forces during the Civil War; announced re-organisation of Sinn Féin (January 1923); arrested by Irish Free State troops and imprisoned (August 1923-July 1924); TD for Clare (1923-59); resigned Presidency of Sinn Féin (March 1926), founder of Fianna Fáil (May 1926); became leader of the opposition in Dáil Éireann (August 1927); President of the Executive Council and Minister for External Affairs (1932-37); President of the Council of the League of Nations and Acting President of the Assembly of the League of Nations (1932-33); Taoiseach and Minister for External Affairs (1937-48); Minister for Education (September 1939 – June 1940); Minister for Local Governnment (August 1941); Taoiseach (1951-54 and 1957-59); President of Ireland (1959-73).

Drummond, Sir (James) Eric (later **16th Earl of Perth**) (1876-1951) Secretary General of the League of Nations (1919-33); British Ambassador to Italy (1933-39).

Duggan, George Chester (1885-1969) Chief Secretary's Office, Dublin (1908-14); Ministry of Shipping, London (1914-18); Superintending Clerk, Finance Division, Chief Secretary's Office, Dublin (1919-21), transferred to the government of Northern Ireland (1921), Assistant Secretary, Ministry of Finance, Belfast (1922-25); Principal Assistant Secretary and later Senior Assistant Secretary, Ministry of Finance, Belfast (1925-39); Ministry of War Transport, London (1939-45); Comptroller and Auditor General of Northern Ireland (1945-49).

Dulanty, John W. (1881-1955) Born in Liverpool; educated at St Mary's School, Failsworth, and Manchester University; joined British Civil Service (1914); successively Examiner, Board of Education, and Principal Assistant Secretary, Ministry of Munitions; Assistant Secretary to the Treasury (1918); awarded CB and CBE; Managing Director of Peter Jones Ltd (1919-26); Irish Trade Commissioner in London (1926-30); Irish High Commissioner in London (1930-49); Irish Ambassador to Britain (1950).

Eden, Anthony (1897-1977) British Conservative politician; Minister for League of Nations Affairs (1935); Secretary of State for Foreign Affairs (1935-38); Secretary of State for Dominion Affairs (1939-40); Secretary of State for War (1940); Secretary of State for Foreign Affairs (1940-45 and 1951-55); Prime Minister (1955-57).

Elliot, Walter (1888-1958) British Conservative politician; British Secretary of State for Agriculture (1932-36); Secretary of State for Scotland (1936-38) and Minister for Health (1938-40).

Fisher, Sir Warren (1879-1948) Permanent Secretary to the Treasury and Head of the British Civil Service (1919-39).

Franco Y Bahamonde, Francisco (1892-1975) Spanish general; head of insurgent government in Spain (1936); Chief of State (1936-75).

Harding, Sir Edward J. (1880-1954) Assistant Secretary, Colonial Office (1921-25); Assistant Under-Secretary, Dominions Office (1925-30); Permanent Under-Secretary, Dominions Office (1930-39).

Hearne, John Joseph (1893-1969) Educated at Waterpark College, Waterford, and University College, Dublin; called to the Bar (1919); Assistant Parliamentary Draftsman (1923-29); Legal Adviser, Department of External Affairs (1929-39); called to the Inner Bar (1939); High Commissioner to Canada (1939-49); Ambassador to the United States of America (1950-60).

Hempel, Edouard (1887-1972) German Minister to Ireland (22 June 1937-8 May 1945).

Hoare, Sir Samuel (1880-1959) British Conservative politician; Secretary of State for Foreign Affairs (1935); First Lord of the Admiralty (1936-37); Home Secretary (1937-39); Lord Privy Seal (1939-40).

Hyde, Douglas (1860-1949) Irish language scholar; co-founder and President (1893-1915) of the Gaelic League; member of Seanad Éireann (1925-38); President of Ireland (1938-45).

Inskip, Thomas Walker Hobart (later **1st Viscount Caldecote**) (1876-1947) British Conservative politician; Minister for Co-ordination of Defence (1936-39); Secretary of State for Dominion Affairs (January-September 1939); Lord Chancellor (1939-40).

Kerney, Leopold Harding (1881-1962) Irish Consul, Paris (1919-22); Irish Republican Envoy in Paris (1923-25); Commercial Secretary, Paris Legation (1932-35); Minister to Spain (1935-46).

Lemass, Seán (1899-1971) TD; educated at O'Connell Schools, Dublin; took part in the 1916 Rising and the War of Independence; opposed the Anglo-Irish Treaty; interned during the Civil War; elected to Dáil Éireann (1924); founder member of Fianna Fáil (1926); Minister for Industry and Commerce (1932-39, 1941-48, 1951-54 and 1957-59); Minister for Supplies (1939-45); Tánaiste (1945-48, 1951-54 and 1957-59); Managing Director, *Irish Press* (1948-51); Taoiseach (1959-66).

Lester, Seán (1888-1959) Educated at Methodist College, Belfast; news editor of the *Freeman's Journal* (1916-23); joined the Department of External Affairs (1923); head of Publicity Office (1923-25); head of the League of Nations Section (1925-29); Irish Free State Permanent Representative to the League of Nations (1929-34); League of Nations High Commissioner in Danzig (1934-37); Deputy Secretary General of the League of Nations (1937-40); Secretary General of the League of Nations (1940-46).

Leydon, John (1895-1979) Educated at St Mel's College, Longford, and St Patrick's College, Maynooth; entered the British Civil Service (1915) serving in the War Office and the Ministry of Pensions; returned to Ireland (1923); Assistant Principal Officer, Department of Finance (1923-27); Principal

Officer (1927-32); Secretary, Department of Industry and Commerce (1 May 1932-1939 and 1943-55); Secretary, Department of Supplies (1939-46).

McCauley, Leo T. (1895-1974) Educated at St Columb's College, Derry, and University College, Dublin; lecturer in classics (University College, Dublin); Department of Finance (1925-29); transferred to the Department of External Affairs (1929); Chargé d'Affaires, Berlin (1929-33); Chargé d'Affaires, Holy See (1933-34); Consul General, New York (1934-46); Assistant Secretary, Department of External Affairs (1946-49); Ambassador to Spain (1949-54); Ambassador to Canada (1955-56); Ambassador to the Holy See (1956-62).

MacDonald, Malcolm (1901-1981) British Labour politician; Parliamentary Under-Secretary, Dominions Office (1931); Secretary of State for Dominion Affairs (November 1935-May 1938 and October 1938-January 1939); Minister for Health (1940-41); son of James Ramsay MacDonald, Prime Minister of Great Britain (1924, 1929-31 and 1931-35).

McDunphy, Michael (1890-1971) Educated at O'Connell Schools, Dublin; Assistant Secretary to the Provisional Government (1922) and to the Executive Council (1922-36); Secretary to the President (1937-54); Director of the Bureau of Military History (1947-57).

McElligott, James J. (1893-1974) Educated at Christian Brothers School, Tralee, and at University College, Dublin; entered the Civil Service in 1916 as a first division clerk, dismissed after seeing active service in the 1916 Rising; imprisoned in Stafford Jail; joined the staff of the *Statist* in London in 1919; Acting Editor (1920); Managing Editor (1922); returned to Ireland in 1922 to take up position as Assistant Secretary, Department of Finance (1922-27); Secretary, Department of Finance (1927-53).

MacEntee, Seán (1889-1984) TD; educated at St Malachy's College, Belfast, and Belfast Municipal College of Technology; took part in the 1916 Rising; elected for South Monaghan (1918-21); took part in the War of Independence; opposed the Anglo-Irish Treaty; took part in the Civil War; founder member of Fianna Fáil (1926); Joint-Treasurer of Fianna Fáil (1926-32); Minister for Finance (1932-39 and 1951-54); Minister for Industry and Commerce (1939-41); Minister for Local Government and Public Health (1941-48); Member of the Council of State from 1948; Minister for Social Welfare (1957-61); Minister for Health (1957-65); Tánaiste (1959-65).

MacMahon, Peadar (1893-1975) General Officer Commanding, Curragh Training Camp (1922-24); Chief of Staff of the Defence Forces (1924-27); Secretary, Department of Defence (1927-58).

MacWhite, Michael (1882-1958) Served in the French Foreign Legion (1914-18); Secretary, Irish delegation to Paris Peace Conference (1920); Irish Representative to Switzerland (1921-23); Permanent Representative to the League of Nations (1923-28); Irish Minister to the United States of America (1928-38); Irish Minister to Italy (1938-50).

Macaulay, William J. Babbington (1892-1964) Educated privately; Royal Navy (1914-18); Inland Revenue (1918-25); Secretary, Irish Legation, Washington (1925-30); Consul General, New York (1930-34); Minister to the Holy See (1934-40).

Moynihan, Maurice (1902-1999) Educated at Christian Brothers School, Tralee, and at University College, Cork; entered the Department of Finance (1925); Secretary to the Government (1937-48 and 1951-60); Secretary, Department of the Taoiseach (1937-60); Governor of the Central Bank of Ireland (1961-69); brother of Seán Moynihan (Secretary to the Government (1932-37) and Assistant Secretary, Department of Finance (1937-52)).

Murphy, Seán (1896-1964) Educated at Clongowes Wood College and University College, Dublin; solicitor; Secretary, Irish mission to Paris (1920); Representative of the Irish Free State in Paris (1923); Administrative Officer, Department of External Affairs (1925-27); Assistant Secretary, Department of External Affairs (1927-38); Minister to France (1938-50); Ambassador to Canada (1950-55); Secretary, Department of External Affairs (1955-57).

Murphy, Sheila Geraldine (1898-1983) Dáil Éireann publicity department (1921-22); Secretariat of the Provisional Government (1922-23); Private Secretary to the Irish High Commissioner in London (1923-26); Private Secretary to Secretary, Department of External Affairs (1926-46); Archivist, Department of External Affairs (1933-46); Second Secretary, Political and Treaty Section, Department of External Affairs (1947-49); First Secretary, Cultural Relations Division, Department of External Affairs (1949-51); First Secretary, Political Division, Department of External Affairs (1952); First Secretary, Irish Embassy, Paris (1952-59); Counsellor and Head of Economic Section, Department of External Affairs (1960-62); Assistant Secretary, Department of External Affairs (1962-64).

Nunan, Seán (1890-1981) Born in London; member of the Irish Volunteers, fought in the 1916 Rising; Clerk of Dáil Éireann (1919); Secretary to Eamon de Valera (1919-21); Registrar of the Dáil Éireann loan in the USA (1919-21); Consul General, New York (1932-38); First Secretary, London (1938-41); Consul General, Washington (1941-46); Consul General, New York (1946-47); Minister to the United States of America (1947-50); Assistant Secretary, Department of External Affairs (1950); Secretary, Department of External Affairs (1950-55).

O'Brien, Art (1872-1949) Educated at St Charles' College, London; President of the Gaelic League in London (1914-35); President of the Sinn Féin Council of Great Britain (1916-23); co-founder of the Irish Self-Determination League of Great Britain and Vice-President (1919-22), President (1922-24); Sinn Féin Representative in London (1919-22); opposed the Anglo-Irish Treaty; Managing Editor, *The Music Trades Review* (1924-35); Minister to France (1935-38); Deputy Chairman, Mianrai Teo from 1939.

O'Ceallaigh, Seán Thomas (1883-1966) TD; educated at O'Connell Schools, Dublin; took part in 1916 Rising; Ceann Comhairle (Speaker) of Dáil Éireann

(1919); Irish representative to the Paris Peace Conference (1919) and representative in Paris (1919-22); opposed the Anglo-Irish Treaty; Sinn Féin Envoy to Italy; Sinn Féin Envoy to the United States of America (1924-26); founder member of Fianna Fáil (1926); Minister for Local Government and Public Health (1932-39); Tánaiste (1937-45); Minister for Finance (1939-45); President of Ireland (1945-59).

Ó Cinnéide, Padraig Educated at Belvedere College, Dublin, and University College, Dublin; Higher Executive Officer, Department of Justice (1922-27); Assistant Principal Officer, Department of Finance (1927-32); Chief Clerk of the Land Commission (1932-37); Assistant Secretary to the Cabinet (1937-47); Assistant Secretary, Department of Health (1947); Secretary, Department of Health (1947-59).

O'Donovan, Colman John (1893-1975) Educated at St Aloysius' College, Glasgow; Second Class Clerk, India Office (1913-16); Intelligence Officer, Dublin Brigade of the IRA (1920-21); Assistant Trade Representative, Brussels (1922-26); Department of Industry and Commerce (1926-30); First Secretary, Irish Legation, Washington (1930-33); First Secretary, Irish Free State Legation, Berlin (1933-35); First Secretary, Irish High Commission, London (1935-38); Irish Legation, Holy See (1938-40); Chargé d'Affaires, Holy See (1940-42); Chargé d'Affaires, Irish Legation, Lisbon (1942-45); Department of Local Government (1945-50); Minister to Belgium (1950-53).

O'Duffy, Eoin (1890-1944) Chief of Staff of the IRA, Sinn Féin Deputy for Monaghan in Dáil Éireann (1921); supported the 1921 Treaty; Assistant Chief of Staff of the National Army and General Officer Commanding South Western Command (1922); Commissioner of an Garda Síochána (1922-February 1933); leader of the Blueshirt movement (1933-36); President of Fine Gael (September 1933-February 1934); led an Irish Brigade to Spain to fight (1936-37) under General Franco during the Spanish Civil War; collaborated with the Nazis during the Second World War.

Pope Pius XI (Achille Ratti) (1857-1939) Ordained 1879; Nuncio to Poland (1919-21); Cardinal and Archbishop of Milan (1921); elected Pope Pius XI (1922-39).

Pope Pius XII (Eugenio Pacelli) (1876-1958) Cardinal Secretary of State (1930-39); elected Pope Pius XII (1939-58).

Robinson, Monsignor Paschal (1870-1948) Papal Nuncio to Ireland (1930-48).

Roche, Stephen Anselm (1890-1949) Educated at Blackrock College, Co Dublin, and Trinity College, Dublin; Assistant Secretary, Department of Justice (1926-34); Secretary, Department of Justice (1934-49).

Ruttledge, Patrick Joseph (1892-1952) TD; educated at St Muredach's College, Ballina, St Enda's School, Dublin and Trinity College Dublin; solicitor; took part in the War of Independence; opposed Anglo-Irish Treaty; took part in the Civil War; acting President of the Republic while de Valera was imprisoned (1923-

24); Minister for Lands and Fisheries (1932-33); Minister for Justice (1933-39); Minister for Local Government and Public Health (1939-41).

Ryan, Frank (1902-1944) Educated at St Colman's College, Fermoy, and University College, Dublin. Interned during the Civil War; editor of *An Phoblacht* (1929-33); founder member of Republican Congress (1934). Fought on the Republican side in the Spanish Civil War (1936-37), was wounded, and recuperated in Ireland; returned to Spain and was captured by Nationalist forces, 1 April 1938; sentenced to death, later commuted to 30 years hard labour. In August 1940, with the connivance of the Irish minister in Madrid, Leopold Kerney, Ryan was secretly released into the custody of German military intelligence. A plan to land him and the IRA's Sean Russell in Ireland by U boat in August 1940 collapsed when Russell died at sea. Ryan died in Dresden.

Ryan, Dr James (1891-1970) TD; educated at St Peter's College, Ring, Co Waterford, and University College, Dublin; medical doctor; took part in the 1916 Rising; opposed the Anglo-Irish Treaty; founder member of Fianna Fáil (1926); Minister for Agriculture (1932-47); Minister for Health and Social Welfare (1947-48 and 1951-54); Minister for Finance (1957-65); Member of Seanad Éireann (1965-69).

Rynne, Michael Andrew Lysaght (1899-1981) educated at Crescent College, Limerick, Our Lady's Bower, Athlone, Clongowes Wood College, University College, Dublin, and King's Inns; Assistant Legal Adviser, Department of External Affairs (1932-36); Head of League of Nations Section, Department of External Affairs (1936-39); Legal Adviser, Department of External Affairs (1939-50); Assistant Secretary, Department of External Affairs (1951-53); Ambassador to Spain (1954-61).

Scott, William D. (1890-1966) Inland Revenue (1910-20); Chief Secretary's Office Dublin (1920-21); Assistant Secretary, Ministry of Finance, Belfast (1921-24); Permanent Secretary, Ministry of Commerce, Belfast (1924-44); Head of the Northern Ireland civil service (1944-53).

Simon, Sir John (1873-1954) British Liberal politician; Foreign Secretary (1931-35); Home Secretary (1935-37); Chancellor of the Exchequer (1937-40).

Stanley, Edward Montagu Cavendish (Lord Stanley) (1894-1938) Deputy Chairman of the Conservative Party (1927-29); Parliamentary and Financial Secretary to the Admiralty (1931-35); Parliamentary Under-Secretary for Dominion Affairs (1935-38); Secretary of State for Dominion Affairs (May-September 1938).

Thomas, James Henry (1874-1949) British trade union leader and Labour politician; Colonial Secretary (1924); Secretary of State for Dominion Affairs (1930-35); Secretary of State for the Colonies (1935-36).

Twomey, Daniel R. (1886-1968) Secretary, Department of Agriculture (1934-47).

Walshe, Joseph Patrick (1886-1956) Educated at Mungret College, Limerick, and University College, Dublin; former Jesuit seminarian and teacher at Clongowes Wood College; solicitor; served on the Irish delegation in Paris (November 1920-January 1922); Secretary to Dáil Ministry of Foreign Affairs (February 1922-August 1922); Acting Secretary, Department of External Affairs (September 1922-August 1927); Secretary, Department of External Affairs (August 1927-May 1946); Ambassador to the Holy See (May 1946-September 1954).

Warnock, William (1911-1986) Educated at High School, Dublin and Trinity College, Dublin; Third Secretary, Department of External Affairs (1935-38); First Secretary, Berlin (1938-39); Chargé d'Affaires ad interim, Berlin (1939-43); First Secretary, Department of External Affairs, Dublin (1944-46); Chargé d'Affaires en titre, Stockholm (1947-50); Envoy Extraordinary and Minister Plenipotentiary to Switzerland (1950-54); Assistant Secretary, Department of External Affairs (1954-56); Envoy Extraordinary and Minister Plenipotentiary to the Federal Republic of Germany (1946-59); Ambassador to Germany (1959-62); Ambassador to Switzerland (1962-64) and, concurrently, Ambassador to Austria (1963-64); Ambassador to India (1964-67); Ambassador to Canada (1967-70); Ambassador to the United States of America (1970-73); Ambassador to Switzerland (1973-76).

Wilson, Sir Horace John (1882-1972) Chief industrial advisor and unofficial personal adviser to Stanley Baldwin and Neville Chamberlain (1935-40); Permanent Secretary to the Treasury and Head of the British Civil Service (1939-42).

Wood, Edward, Viscount (later **1st Earl Halifax**) (1881-1959) British Conservative politician; Viceroy of India (1926-31); Lord Privy Seal (1935-37); Lord President of the Council (1937-38); Foreign Secretary (1938-40); British Ambassador to Washington (1941-46).

List of Documents Reproduced

1936

1937

Documents on Irish Foreign Policy, Volume IV, 1937–1939

Documents on Irish Foreign Policy, Volume IV, 1937–1939

1938

1939

Documents on Irish Foreign Policy, Volume IV, 1937–1939

1936

No. 1 NAI 2006/39

*Memorandum by John W. Dulanty of an interview given by Eamon de Valera
to Joseph P. Walshe and John W. Dulanty*

DUBLIN, 16 December 1936[1]

The President gave an interview this morning to Mr. Walshe and myself.

I said that I had the instructions for the coal-cattle pact, and I understood that I was to seek for a renewal of the existing coal-cattle pact. To this the President agreed, but said that paragraph (v) of the instructions meant first that we could not even seem to be asking for concessions on a general trade agreement. If a favourable opening presented itself, I was to begin tentatively on the question of a general trade agreement. I said that I had not seen the Minister for Industry and Commerce, but, in view of the President's statement, I knew now what my general line was in talking to the British.

On the political situation, the President said he was glad that I had been here during the recent difficulties about the King, because it had enabled me to get the home reactions on the question. As it appeared to me, the position was to see what could be done on these economic questions and on the ports. As a beginning to a settlement on the lines of a united Ireland, I was to make it as clear as possible that there was not to be any interference in our internal affairs from any outside source, notwithstanding any symbols that might have been handed down from the past.

Mr. Walshe thought that it would be a good thing to emphasise in any conversations with the British that they ought to appreciate that, in our recent legislation, we had really been assisting the British, and, if they were intent upon a general settlement they ought to see that we had done no more than carry out intentions which the Government had explained clearly well in advance.

The President entirely agreed, and said that he thought the thing to do was to fix up outstanding matters between the Saorstát and the United Kingdom on such questions as the economic difficulty, and then start with proposals for a United Ireland. He was not unaware that this might present political difficulties for the British, but the British were never to be misled

---

[1] This document is one of twenty-one reproduced in this volume from file NAI 2006/39 which contains confidential reports and high-level correspondence between Dulanty and Dublin and which was located in the Irish Embassy in London in the autumn of 2005. Though outside the immediate chronological scope of DIFP Volume V, the editors judge the document to be of such importance that they have included it in the volume.

into thinking that anything short of a United Ireland meant a really satisfactory settlement. The British ought to see that An Saorstát represented their wing and their back door.

The President also thought that what the Dáil had done last week was really of very great assistance to the British. It was important to make clear to the British that last week's events in no sense represented a manoeuvre but really a help to them.[1]

I said that I doubted whether the Dominions Secretary or any of his colleagues who were properly informed could regard last week's events in the light of a manoeuvre. There was, in the first place, the President's own public statements that, in the new Constitution, the King would have no part or lot on the internal affairs, but would be retained for the external functions which he was at present discharging. This had been emphasised almost *ad nauseam* by me in conversations with Mr. MacDonald and the leading British civil servants whom he had directed to discuss matters with me. Over and over again, I had explained that, whilst I was not in a position to present them with the details of the new Constitution, they could accept as definitive the intentions of An Saorstát to establish a Constitution on the above-mentioned lines, namely, no participation of the King in internal affairs, but the continuance of the King's existing functions in external affairs.

Mr. Walshe quoted from the London evening paper 'The Star', and referred also to this morning's leader in the 'Irish Times' which he thought indicated a nearer approach to acceptance of the new position than had appeared before.

I mentioned that, through a personal friend of mine in the Treasury, Mr. S.D. Waley, I had secured some figures, not yet quite complete, showing the financial relations between the Six Counties and Great Britain. The President said that he had given directions for some enquiries on the same matter, and he asked that he should be furnished with the figures that I had confidentially obtained, not that he would use them publicly, but that they might be helpful to him as a check on the figures which he had already received.

---

[1] On 11 December 1936 King Edward VIII abdicated. On the same day de Valera introduced the Constitution (Amendment No. 27) Bill 1936 and the Executive Authority (External Relations) Bill in the Dáil. The former ended the functions of the British monarch in relation to the internal affairs of the Irish Free State. The latter gave authority for the continued exercise by the monarch, on the advice of the Executive Council, of functions relating to the external relations of the Irish Free State.

1937

No. 2 NAI DFA 227/87

Memorandum on non-intervention in the Spanish Civil War from Maurice
Moynihan to Joseph P. Walshe (Dublin)

DUBLIN, 1 January 1937

With reference to Mr. Murphy's[1] letter of the 30th ultimo with enclosures in regard to matters arising out of the Agreement regarding Non-intervention in Spain, I have to inform you as follows:-

A. *Supervision of Spanish Land and Sea frontiers.*
It was agreed that the Government should contribute towards the cost, estimated at £620,000 per annum, of the proposed scheme of supervision over the land and sea frontiers of Spain and the Spanish dependencies, the operation of which would be dependent on its acceptance by the two parties in Spain.

It was decided, however, that when communicating this decision to the General Committee an inquiry should be made as to how the officers of the International Committee of Supervision are to be recruited.

B. *Prohibition of exports to Spain.*
In connection with the proposal to extend the present scope of the prohibition of exports to Spain to cover all classes of arms and war material, it was decided that a reply should be sent to the effect that as the types of arms and war materials covered by the proposal are not manufactured in the Saorstát, it would not appear necessary that any definite prohibition should be instituted in Saorstát Éireann.

[signed] M. O'MUIMHNEACHÁIN
a.s. Rúnaí

No. 3 NAI 2003/17/181[2]

Confidential report from John W. Dulanty to Joseph P. Walshe (Dublin)
(No. 1) (Secret)

LONDON, 4 January 1937

Mr. Malcolm MacDonald telephoned yesterday saying that he would like to have a conversation with me that day before leaving for nine or ten days in

---

[1] See DIFP Volume IV, No. 416.
[2] This file was formerly numbered 'S. 42' in the External Affairs Secretary's Files series.

the North of Scotland. I spent about an hour and a half with him at his home in Hampstead in the late afternoon.

He said he would like me to assure the President of the British appreciation for the assistance which the Saorstát Government had given them in a difficult situation arising out of the abdication.

Twice previously he had had at the last minute to cancel visits to his constituency, the last occasion being owing to the abdication. His next visit unfortunately was fixed for the coming week. He was leaving Euston that night for a tour of his constituency in the North of Scotland. If it had been at all possible to get out of this engagement he would gladly have done so because of his anxiety to speak to the President.

Mr. MacDonald said that he had curtailed his holiday in order to have an opportunity of studying our two Acts on the Constitution and the official reports of the debates in the Dáil last month. He had not yet completed this study nor had he had, owing to the Christmas holidays, an opportunity of consulting certain members of the Cabinet. He hoped that the President would agree to informal conversations taking place between representatives of both sides. His own idea was that Sir Horace Wilson, Sir Grattan Bushe[1] and Sir Harry Batterbee might talk to Mr. Walshe, Mr. Hearne and myself. I reminded Mr. MacDonald of a fairly recent conversation when he made the same suggestion and when I said that I thought that as a first step the British ought to let us have, in whatever form they considered appropriate, a statement of the points on which they wished to have further information. I did not see how the President could authorise representatives of his to go into conference, however informal, without some idea being given beforehand of the matters to be discussed.

He said that he was most reluctant to put anything on paper at all at this stage. *In addition to the Fisher letter,[2] recent* experience had shown in other matters how easily misconceptions of the written word could arise. I then said that they must have some idea of the questions on which they were anxious to secure further information and if that were the case couldn't he at least tell me so that I could let my Government know. He said that his own examination was not yet complete and before the conversations began he wanted the assent of certain of his colleagues in the British Cabinet to the questions which he proposed for exploration. Owing to his absence from London as well as that also of his colleagues, this consultation would not be possible until the week beginning Monday, the 11th January.

Trying first by one question and then another to ascertain a little more of the difficulties, which for my own part I believe Mr. MacDonald honestly feels, I at last ascertained from him that there would be no discussion at all on our first Bill.[3] On the constitutional structure which we had decided upon

---

[1]   Sir Henry Grattan Bushe (1886-1961), Assistant Legal Adviser, Colonial/Dominions Office (1919-31), Legal Adviser, Dominions Office (1931-41), Governor of Barbados (1941-6).

[2]   Words in italics are a later handwritten insertion by Dulanty. See DIFP Volume IV, Nos 358, 359, 361, 362, 363, 370, 372, 373, 374.

[3]   The Constitution (Amendment No. 27) Act (1936).

for our own internal affairs there would not be any question. The conversations which he was most anxious to get started would be concerned wholly and solely with our second Bill governing the relationship between An Saorstát and the other member states of the British Commonwealth.[1] Though I made no pretence to an informed appreciation of constitutional matters, I thought I was right in saying that, shortly put, the functions of the King in relation to our external affairs would continue as heretofore, and that the position created by our second Act far from being of an ambiguous or complicated character was really simple.

Mr. MacDonald again urged that I should represent to the President on Tuesday next the great importance which he, Mr. MacDonald, attached to the proposed talks. At the two meetings in the Grosvenor Hotel[2] the President he thought had accepted his suggestion of conversations, adding of course with some emphasis that the British must not think there was any final solution between the two countries to be reached whilst Ireland was divided as it was now. He had informed the British Cabinet of the President's attitude and conversations had in fact taken place. He could say for his part that these conversations had been distinctly helpful. He did not want to add to his present difficulties with certain of the British Cabinet and he was afraid that if we did not at least make an attempt by these informal conversations to clear up constitutional points his task in the British Cabinet would be harder.

An ideal procedure from his point of view would be to have the suggested talks in the week beginning 11th January; then, with the results of these talks before them, the President and he could have a meeting on Mr. de Valera's return through London.

He pointed out that in addressing the Ard Fheis in November last the President had said that the terms of co-operation between the Irish people and any other people must be mutually agreed upon, and that if some scheme of co-operation were decided upon, the Irish people not ready to accept dictation from anyone equally had no right to tell other people what those terms of co-operation must be. There must be mutual agreement and co-operation. It was this offer of co-operation on the part of the President which Mr. MacDonald was most anxious to accept and work out to the full value for both parties.[3]

As on a former occasion Mr. MacDonald said that he felt, speaking for himself, there was a very good chance of getting rid of the difficulties between the two countries, and he was anxious the moment he could get the Constitution matter out of the way to go forward to the work of expediting a settlement.

My own impression is that Mr. MacDonald honestly believes that he can carry through the British Cabinet and the British Houses of Parliament a

---

[1] The External Relations (Executive Authority) Act (1936).
[2] From late March 1936 de Valera and MacDonald had met informally in de Valera's rooms at the Grosvenor House Hotel, Park Lane, on a number of occasions when de Valera was passing through London en route to Dublin from continental Europe.
[3] This paragraph has been highlighted by insertion of a line down the left margin and with the marginal note: 'Irish Press report in cover of file'.

large measure of settlement. At the same time there can be no doubt that he is excessively cautious and obviously genuinely apprehensive of making a wrong step. If the situation be properly handled he has high hopes of a *real advance on the road to*[1] settlement but the least slip he feels may easily make the problem more difficult, if not for the present insoluble.

[signed] J.W. DULANTY
High Commissioner

No. 4 NAI DFA London Embassy, Non-Intervention Committee Series

Letter from John W. Dulanty to Francis Hemming (London) (Copy)
LONDON, 4 January 1937

Dear Mr. Hemming,
I am now in a position to inform you that the Government of the Irish Free State would be prepared to contribute towards the cost – estimated at £620,000 per annum – of the proposed scheme of supervision of the land and sea frontiers of Spain as set out in Paper N.I.S. (36) 205, provided that all the other Governments represented on the Committee are prepared to participate in the scheme and that the scheme is accepted by the two parties concerned in Spain.

Yours sincerely,
[copy letter unsigned]

No. 5 UCDA P150/2183

Letter from Joseph P. Walshe to Eamon de Valera (Zurich) (Secret)
DUBLIN, 9 January 1937

Dear President,
I hope by the time you receive this letter we shall have heard good news about you. The Press, both English and Irish, state that Dr. Vogt[2] will be able to let you come home very soon. I do not want to worry you with official matters, but I know you would prefer to be kept fully informed of things which are really important. You may consider that the following points require an early decision:-

(1) Conversations between ourselves and certain British Civil Servants concerning the position of the King as established under the recent Act.
The High Commissioner has told me that you were undecided at the time of leaving London as to whether or not these conversations should take place. It seems to me that the desire of the British to have these conversations is an indication that there is something in the Act which they regard or would like

---

[1] These words have been handwritten by Dulanty above a number of words that have been so heavily crossed out that they are illegible.
[2] Professor Dr Alfred Vogt, Director of the University Eye Clinic, Zurich, an eye specialist whom de Valera had been visiting for treatment since early 1936.

to regard as incompatible with membership of the Commonwealth. On the other hand, they may want a definite assurance that the prerogatives of peace and war would still be exercised by the King. I feel that assurances of this kind are not for Civil Servants to give. We should have to say that the King's functions are exclusively confined to those set out specifically in the Act. We could not, for instance, say that he was an executive organ here, lest that expression might be used by Mr. MacDonald in the House of Commons. As you said to me some short time ago, it would be impossible for us to suggest a formula to be used in the House of Commons which would satisfy both our people and the extreme Tory Wing. Moreover, the whole suggestion of con-versations is very like interference in our affairs, and if the British are really as well disposed towards us now as they say they are, they themselves on examining the Act and your statements in the Dáil should be able to find a formula which will not create difficulties for us. Moreover, it would not be expedient to tell them that Article 1 of the Constitution is going to disappear. If we did, they would be very likely to come to conclusions as to our inten-tions which would not be justifiable but might be used against us.

To sum up, I think, if you have no objection, that we should instruct the High Commissioner to discourage in every possible way this idea of con-versations and to repeat to the British that they are, in our view, entirely unnecessary.

(2) The procedure to be adopted should the Pope[1] die in the near future.
All the news from Rome indicates that, while the Holy Father may linger on even for some weeks, his death cannot be much longer postponed. A clot may get to the heart at any moment, and we want to be ready for the emer-gency. The procedure I have suggested to the Vice-President is this. A telegram would be sent in your name to Cardinal Pacelli.[2] The Vice-President would at once call on the Nuncio,[3] and then on the Archbishop.[4] He would enquire from the Archbishop when the Solemn High Mass would take place and inform him that the Cabinet would, of course, attend officially. Mr. Macaulay[5] has informed me that as at present arranged the Vatican do not expect any special foreign representatives to attend the funeral, though the situation would be different with regard to the Coronation of the new Pope, which would take place ten days after the funeral. The Vatican, however, said that owing to their special relations with the Italian State the King or the Crown Prince and Mussolini would undoubtedly be present. I have spoken to the Nuncio about the inexpediency in the new circumstances of Italy alone among States being represented. He was simply horrified when he heard that the Vatican had come to such a decision. If the other Catholic States of the

---

[1] Pope Pius XI.
[2] Cardinal Eugenio Pacelli (1876-1958), Cardinal Secretary of State (1930-39), elected Pope Pius XII (1939).
[3] Monsignor Paschal Robinson (1870-1948), Apostolic Nuncio to Ireland (1929-48).
[4] Archbishop Edward J. Byrne (1872-1940), Roman Catholic Archbishop of Dublin (1921-40).
[5] William J. B. Macaulay, Irish Minister to the Holy See.

world are not represented at the funeral, the old accusation of the 'Italian mission' will become stronger than ever. The Nuncio is anxious that we should do something in a discreet fashion to prevent the Vatican making such a regrettable blunder. I have spoken about this with the Vice-President, and he agrees that I should say to Macaulay that we, as a Catholic State in direct communication with the Holy See, would find it very strange if some representative from this country other than the Head of our Diplomatic Mission did not attend the funeral of the Holy Father. We can, of course, say nothing about the general principle, but I am also asking Macaulay to talk to his colleagues from Portugal, Poland and Belgium and to sound them in a discreet way as to what their views are with regard to representation. This discreet line of action will not do any harm, and it may do a great deal of good.

(3) The Form of Declaration to be made by the King at the Coronation.
The High Commissioner gave you the form now suggested by Great Britain, i.e.:-
'Will you solemnly promise and swear to govern the peoples of Great Britain, Ireland, Canada, Australia, New Zealand and South Africa, of your Empire of India and of your Possessions and Territories beyond the Seas, according to the Statutes in the Parliament agreed on and their respective Laws and Customs?'
The High Commissioner told me that you seemed inclined to accept this form as a way out but had not given any final decision. The British now want a reply from all the States of the Commonwealth before the end of this month, as they say that the complete programme of the Coronation will have to be published, including the words used by the King in this Declaration. Before you went away you discussed with me the possibility of a solution which would consist, as far as we are concerned, of sending an advice in due course to the King, together with a form drawn up by us relating to his observance of our laws concerning his functions. He would sign the form, and there should then be no need for the inclusion of Ireland in the Coronation Declaration. Would you think of letting me send the British a despatch pointing out that it would be entirely inappropriate for Saorstát Éireann to be included in a declaration made by the King before the Archbishop of Canterbury and relating almost entirely to the maintenance of the Church of England? It is the first opportunity that we have had of objecting to a purely sectarian declaration made by the King, who is in some form or other King in several countries whose religion differs entirely from that of the majority of the people of the United Kingdom. The simplest solution, as far as we are concerned, would be to get all mention of Ireland withdrawn, but if we cannot do so we should insist on the reference to religion being made general. For example, the King could say that he would govern the peoples of the countries concerned according to the laws and in conformity with the religions thereof. The occasion is a very historic one, and we might possibly be criticised for having missed the opportunity of at least protesting against the one-sided character of the King's Declaration.

I hope it will not be too much trouble for you to tell Mr. Devlin[1] generally what you would like me to do about these matters.

I remain, dear President, with great respect and esteem,

Yours sincerely,
[signed] J.P. WALSHE

The[2] news of your very early return came as a very pleasant surprise on Saturday morning. I did not send on this note as I was doubtful about its arriving in time to catch you in Zurich. However I think you may wish to have it in London. If you are coming through immediately I will postpone all action until you arrive home.

The least we must get the British to do is to separate the declaration about governing etc. from the completely different question of the established religion of England.

He could make the first declaration outside the religious service proper and the second as part of the religious service.

The use of 'Ireland' in conjunction with Canada, Australia etc. in these circumstances might be a political gain for us. We could possibly use it as a recognition of the essential unity of our country.

Everything of course depends on what attitude you find over there when talking with MacDonald and the extent to which you consider it worth while making any concession at all in this matter.

J.P.W.
11th January '37.

No. 6 UCDA P150/2349

Handwritten report by John W. Dulanty on talks between Eamon de Valera and Malcolm MacDonald (London)

LONDON, 14 January 1937

Early in the evening conversation with the President on the 14th January Mr. MacDonald referred to those confidential observations of the President's during the morning of that day (on the new Constitution) which were meant for him alone and not, as yet, for the British Cabinet. On exactly the same basis of strict confidence he wished to explain that they had been considering the question of a private talk with Lord Craigavon.

As he had already told us, his hope was that his colleagues would say that, so far as they were concerned, we had satisfied the requirements – albeit to a minimum degree only – of Commonwealth membership.

Now whether or not that decision was reached the British were very anxious to avoid as much as ever possible controversial attacks on questions between Great Britain and us by the Six County Government and its supporters. They had therefore considered making representations privately to Lord Craigavon. How far they could succeed with this gentleman they could

---

[1] Denis Devlin (1908-1959), third secretary, Department of External Affairs.
[2] Handwritten postscript.

not say. They were however convinced that it would be of no avail for *them* to talk to anyone else in the Northern Cabinet. Craigavon was by a long way more open to reason than were his colleagues.

They had however learnt lately that Craigavon would next week sail for New Zealand and would be away for several months. In these circumstances Mr. Baldwin had asked him to call at Downing St when passing through London. Friends of many years standing they seldom or never missed seeing each other whenever Lord Craigavon came to London and it was thought that no special significance would be attached to their coming together again.

Mr. Baldwin would first suggest avoidance of political controversy in the hope of persuading Lord Craigavon to his view and then try to get him similarly to persuade his Cabinet. That done and provided the atmosphere of the talk was favourable he was resolved to open up with Craigavon the question of a United Ireland.

This part of the conversation finished with an exhortation from Mr. MacDonald that the strictest secrecy should be observed with regard to it.

No. 7 NAI 2006/39

> *Memorandum of aspects of the discussion between Eamon de Valera and*
> *Malcolm MacDonald by John W. Dulanty[1]*
> LONDON, 14 January 1937

Mr. MacDonald said that he would do his best to let us see a draft of any answer he would make in the House of Commons on Tuesday next.[2] It could only be a partial answer since the Cabinet would not have reached a decision on our recent legislation until next Wednesday. He hoped that the Cabinet's decision would be that what we had done and were intending to do was not incompatible with full membership of the Commonwealth. In the event of that decision being reached would the President prefer to communicate with the other member states of the Commonwealth on his recent legislation or would he prefer that the United Kingdom Government should send the texts of legislation and intimate at the same time that so far as the relations with the other member states of the Commonwealth were concerned there had been no change? The President said he would like to think about that question but he thought the United Kingdom Government might send the Acts. On the principle that there had been no change it was perhaps hardly necessary for him to communicate with the other member states. Mr. MacDonald said he wanted the whole of the States of the Commonwealth to accept and then he could get ahead with the ports and other questions.

I suggested that if the British Cabinet decide as Mr. MacDonald hoped the discussion on the ports and other questions need not wait until the views of the Dominions had been obtained. With this Mr. MacDonald agreed.

---

[1] This document is a draft of sections of points (27) to (33) of No. 8 below. Although there are similarities between the documents, the differences in wording are such that the inclusion of both texts is warranted.

[2] 19 January 1937.

Mr. MacDonald was inclined to think that he should say next Tuesday in the House of Commons that the Irish Free State remained a full member of the British Commonwealth and refer to his conversations with Mr. de Valera in London. The President said that the British could have if they wished good relations. He, Mr. de Valera, would not bother his head for a moment as to any doubt as to that possibility.

The President said that in the matter of Defence care must be taken by the British that they must not look for entry into our ports at any time except on our invitation and with our goodwill. Our attitude as he had already explained was that we would not allow our territory to be used as a base of attack on Britain but we could not be in any war just because Britain was at war. We could only be at war when our interests were jeopardised.

Mr. MacDonald agreed and said that General Hertzog and other Prime Ministers had laid it down that their country was only at war when their Parliament so decided.

Mr. MacDonald said that the use of our ports would be absolutely vital to them if they were at war but he quite saw that a proposal that they the British must have our ports when they wanted them would be quite impossible of agreement for us. The President thought that the ports as an example of things being allowed to settle themselves – there was no chance of settlement if the British made the occupation by them of our ports a condition to any agreement.

The President said that Mr. MacDonald would of course have to consider his own answers but he thought that any answer based on statements which the President made in the Dáil would be quite acceptable to us.

Mr. MacDonald again said he would try to let me have the draft answer.

No. 8 NAI 2003/17/181

Confidential report from John W. Dulanty to Joseph P. Walshe (Dublin)
(No. 5) (Copy) (Secret)[1]

LONDON, 15 January 1937

(1) On Monday the 11th January Mr. Malcolm MacDonald telephoned to me asking whether it would be possible for him to call on the President when he was passing through London on his return home from Zurich. I conveyed this request to the President on his arrival in London at half-past eleven on the night of Wednesday, 13th January. The President said he was prepared to see Mr. MacDonald then but as that could not be arranged Mr. MacDonald said he would call on the President at the Grosvenor Hotel at half past ten o'clock the following morning, Thursday, the 14th January.

(2) Mr. MacDonald began by conveying the warm thanks of Mr. Baldwin and the other members of the Cabinet for the help they had received from the Government of An Saorstát in the difficult situation which suddenly confronted the British Government in the recent abdication crisis. He under-

---

[1] Marginal note by Sheila Murphy: 'As revised by President'.

stood how difficult it was to get Parliament together in such a short time and to face the difficulties following thereon.

(3) Mr. MacDonald said he was glad to avail himself of the opportunity which this meeting provided of asking the President if he could oblige him with further information on certain points in connection with the Executive Authority (External Relations) Act 1936.

(4) The President said he was of course ready and willing to oblige Mr. MacDonald with any information. As on previous occasions he had expressed his willingness to co-operate with a view to establishing good relations between these two neighbouring States, but there was one point which it was incumbent on him to make clear to the British Government, namely, that the real solution lay in the establishment of an All-Ireland Republic on terms of active goodwill and co-operation with the United Kingdom Government. In any case the closer we approximate to that position the more satisfactory the result. If that could not be achieved at present, he had to repeat what he had said on so many former occasions, the immediate next step was to secure a united Ireland.

(5) Mr. MacDonald said that he and his colleagues were in no doubt as to the President's mind on these matters and they knew that from the President's point of view no immediate arrangement short of a united Ireland would be regarded as a settlement.

(6) Turning to the Executive Authority (External Relations) Act, Mr. MacDonald read Clause 3 of that Act and asked whether the Act contemplated An Saorstát having a full membership of the community of nations forming the British Commonwealth of Nations, or a membership – such as an associate or partial membership – short of the full membership. His own interpretation was that reading that Clause together with Clause 1 of the present An Saorstát Constitution full membership was meant.

(7) The President replied that so long as the association continued full membership was intended even though at the present moment instead of enjoying any advantage An Saorstát suffered grave disadvantages from such association. The President added that if we had association it must be with all its advantages.

(8) He felt that he ought to let Mr. MacDonald know that it was not his intention to include Article 1 in the new Constitution and proceeded to explain his reasons for this. The President had promised that the new Constitution would not contain any reference to the King.

(9) Mr. MacDonald thought that such an omission presented difficulties since it appeared to him that the doubt as to whether we contemplated full membership would be increased. He appreciated the President's reasons for the proposed omission from the new Constitution and enquired whether it would be possible to amend the Executive Authority (External Relations) Act 1936 in such a way as to make clear that we intended full membership.

(10) The President feared that the difficulties in the way of an amendment of the Act precluded the possibility of his entertaining that suggestion.

(11) The Union of South Africa, Mr. MacDonald said, were anxious to have another declaration made which would make clear to the world the

co-equality of each of the member states of the Commonwealth. It would be helpful from his point of view if and when such a declaration was made An Saorstát could be associated with it in such a way as to dispel any doubt about our being full members.

(12) The second question Mr. MacDonald said they would like to ask was whether we had it in mind that in our external affairs the King should perform no other functions than those indicated in Clause 3. He conceded that the functions where described were the only functions which he could think of at the present time. It was possible however that since the Commonwealth was a dynamic and not a static organisation other functions might be added at some later date. Supposing that in such circumstances in the future the other member states increased these functions, would we agree to do likewise?

(13) The President said that he would like to consider that matter further, but his immediate reaction was that Clause 3 as it stood covered all that was necessary. Was Mr. MacDonald thinking of the contingency of a declaration of a state of emergency or a state of war?

(14) Mr. MacDonald said he was not.

(15) The President continued that he thought it was likely that the Government of An Saorstát would use the King as a medium or organ by which a state of war would be declared.

(16) Mr. MacDonald asked whether it would be right for him to tell his colleagues that we would be willing to allow the King to do for us whatever it might be decided he should do for the other States of the Commonwealth. The President said that would be a matter for consideration when such a question arose.

(17) Mr. MacDonald said that he understood from the official reports of the Dáil Debates that the King's title in An Saorstát remained unchanged.

(18) The President agreed that the title remained unchanged.

(19) The Executive Authority (External Relations) Act 1936 the President emphasised did no more than record in a Statute the precise extent to which the King at present exercised functions for Saorstát Éireann.

(20) After thanking the President for the foregoing information Mr. MacDonald said that the Constitution (Amendment No. 27) Act 1936 dealing as it did with the internal affairs of An Saorstát was clearly the concern only of the people of An Saorstát. Absolute freedom in internal affairs was of course one of the bedrock principles of the Commonwealth, but it was equally clear that the principle of active co-operation between the member states was similarly essential. It seemed to him that An Saorstát had shown the will to co-operate by putting through the legislation which had been the subject of his enquiry that day. There was however a further principle of the recognition of the Crown as a symbol of co-operation or association of the Commonwealth. He was most anxious to avoid any words which might suggest that he was 'pushing the Crown' at us but if they had not recognition of the Crown he did not see how the Commonwealth could continue. Membership of the Commonwealth was clearly the requisite condition for the mutual advantages which the several States enjoyed in the form of trade and other preferences. Expressed in another way, he thought non-recognition

of the Crown would put us in precisely the same position as a foreign state. The President said that he quite conceived a republic being a member and that co-operation was the essential link.

(21) If a foreign country took the United Kingdom to, say, the Hague Court on a question of Imperial Preference or Most-Favoured-Nation Clause they wanted to be in a position to prove that any State to which they gave special trade preferences was in the fullest sense a member of the Commonwealth and therefore entitled to such advantages.

(22) The President replied that so far as An Saorstát was concerned the advantages referred to were conspicuous by their absence. Our people as he had previously stated had no sentiment or feeling for the office of King. We did not want the Crown but if the other nations in the Commonwealth did want the Crown as a symbol of their co-operation we were accepting that position.

(23) Mr. MacDonald referred to the words 'so long as' which occurred in Clause 3 and asked whether it would be accurate to say that so long as An Saorstát was associated with the other nations at present forming the British Commonwealth we would accept the Crown as a symbol.

(24) The President said he was not sure of the precise origin and history of the phrase and he would therefore like to give the point further consideration. The functions which the symbol had been performing and still performs for us would be continued. That fact he thought constituted adequate recognition.

(25) After informing Mr. MacDonald of his present intention with regard to the omission of Article 1 of the present Constitution the President then gave an exposition in general terms of the new Constitution which he hoped to get placed on our Statute Book. He could not say exactly what attitude might be adopted by his own political organisation or his colleagues in the Executive Council. His objective was to place before the Irish people a Constitution for their acceptance, an acceptance which would be in the completest sense free and unfettered and in no way imposed by an authority outside that of the Irish people themselves. He wished to bring about a situation as clear of political trouble as he could make it so that the two countries could co-operate in act and deed rather than mere words. The two Acts passed in December last and the Constitution now under consideration and in process of construction had as their single aim the removal of obstacles to that co-operation. He had spoken in this way about the new Constitution in view of Mr. MacDonald's assurances that he also was most anxious to bring about the best possible relations between the two countries and he thought it well therefore that he should know now what his (the President's) intentions were. These remarks however he wished to be taken by Mr. MacDonald as personal and confidential to himself and not at present for the members of the British Cabinet since the Constitution was only in process of construction and had, as he had explained, not been submitted to the Executive Council. This reservation did not however apply to the proposed omission of Article 1 of the present Constitution. He thought that the British Cabinet should be informed of that intention.

(26) Expressing his gratitude for the exposition of the Constitution Mr. MacDonald said he would treat this as meant for him alone but would inform his colleagues about Article 1.

At this stage Mr. MacDonald having to leave for a luncheon engagement said the President's explanations had been so helpful that he would greatly value a further conversation if that could be arranged. It was agreed that Mr. MacDonald should return later in the day.

On his return during the evening of the same day the conversation was resumed.

(27)[1] Mr. MacDonald stated that he would inform the British Cabinet at its meeting on Wednesday the 27th January of the information which the President had been good enough to give him. Clearly he could not say what the decision of the Cabinet would be but he hoped that they would share his view that what we had done in our recent legislation and were intending to do in the new Constitution was not so far as they were concerned incompatible with full membership of the Commonwealth. In the event of that decision being reached would the President prefer to communicate with the other member states of the Commonwealth on the subject of his recent legislation or would he prefer that the United Kingdom Government should send the texts of our legislation and intimate at the same time, if the British Cabinet so decided, that so far as they were concerned the legislation was not incompatible with full membership of the Commonwealth? It was not material he thought whether they or we forwarded the Acts and he would do whatever the President wished.

(28) The President said that he would like to consider that question but, at the moment, he thought that there was no objection from his side in the Acts being sent by the United Kingdom Government. On the principle which he had emphasised earlier in the conversation that there had been no change in the situation so far as external relations were concerned it was perhaps hardly necessary for him to communicate with the other member states.

(29) Mr. MacDonald repeated the assurances he had frequently made to me in the past few weeks that as soon as the British Cabinet had taken the view that, so far as they were concerned, the principle of our membership was not in question he hoped to secure similar decision from the other members of the Commonwealth, and, that done, to resume at the earliest possible moment the discussion on such matters as the ports, financial settlement, and a trade agreement.

(30) I suggested that if the British Cabinet decided as Mr. MacDonald hoped the discussion on the ports and other questions need not wait until the views of the Dominions had been obtained. With this Mr. MacDonald agreed.

(31) On the question of Defence, the President said that the British must not seek entry into our ports except on our invitation and with our goodwill. We were not imperially minded and had no imperial interests. What our people really wanted was a position of neutrality. The nearer we approximated to that position the better. In our own interests we would not allow our territory to be

---

[1] See above No. 7 for an earlier note by Dulanty on this section of the talks.

used as a base of attack on Britain but obviously we could only be at war when our interests were jeopardised and the Dáil had so decided. It would be fatal he thought even to appear to insist upon occupation of the ports in any circumstances except by our free invitation, or to make the use of our ports by the British a condition in any settlement.

(32) The use of our ports Mr. MacDonald thought would be absolutely vital to them if they were at war but he agreed that any proposal that the British could require the use of these ports whenever they wanted them would be quite impossible for us. His personal view was that an arrangement about the ports could be made. He was not nearly so easy in his mind about the financial settlement on which of course depended a full trade agreement.

(33) Whilst not wishing to be contentious the President did not conceal his surprise to hear that a financial settlement would present such difficulty as was suggested since it appeared to him that on that question we had an unassailable case.

(34) On the question of the form of the Oath to be taken by the King at the Coronation Mr. MacDonald explained that the Government of the Union of South Africa wanted the Oath to be changed in such a way as to provide for each member state to be named individually. The United Kingdom Government had deliberately refrained from consulting us because they felt they would only cause the President embarrassment, but they had explained to General Hertzog[1] that to name the Irish Free State specifically would present difficulties for us. Their efforts to get some collective formula accepted all round had not succeeded. On the contrary, Australia and Canada had now joined with South Africa in pressing for separate mention of each member state. As a possible way of meeting the difficulty he was disposed to suggest the repeating of the King's title where the word 'Ireland' would be used and the use of the words 'Irish Free State' thereby avoided.

(35) This question the President explained had not been before him until immediately prior to his leaving Dublin for Zurich. He was impressed by the great difficulty thus presented. Our attitude to the Crown being so fundamentally different from that of Britain or possibly of certain other member states it would be clear to Mr. MacDonald how completely unsuitable the whole Coronation procedure was for us. Was it not possible to lift the Oath completely out of what was avowedly a sectarian service? Whilst he did not wish to suggest the suppression of any act of religion whether of worship or devotion he could not regard the ritual under which the head of one particular denomination in England administered the Oath in the midst of that denomination's service as anything but impossible for our people. Although it did not seem possible at this moment that his Government could take part in the ceremony like the other member states he still felt he should say that the Oath should be a secular proceeding divorced from the proposed service.

(36) Mr. MacDonald said he would consult the Archbishop of Canterbury and see if it was possible to do anything on this question which he agreed was beset with great difficulties.

---

[1] General James B. M. 'Barry' Hertzog (1866-1942), Prime Minister of South Africa (1924-39).

(37) The fact of Mr. MacDonald's visit to the President having appeared in the London newspapers it was decided to issue a communiqué. I submitted the following draft:

> Mr. Malcolm MacDonald, M.P. called on Mr. de Valera, the President of the Executive Council of the Irish Free State, at his Hotel in London today when informal discussions took place on a number of matters affecting the relations between the two countries.

which was approved.

(38) Mr. MacDonald again expressed his appreciation of the help which the two meetings had been to him. The conversations, informal but frank he ventured to think on both sides, had clarified the position in his mind.

(39) In saying good-bye to Mr. MacDonald the President reminded him of the view which he had expressed on a previous occasion at the Grosvenor Hotel, namely, that even if an acceptable settlement were reached a good deal of time would have to elapse before really cordial relations could be established.[1] Our people could not be expected to lay aside in a day the memories of centuries.

(Signed) J.W. DULANTY
High Commissioner

No. 9 NAI DT S9449A

> *Despatch from Eamon de Valera to Malcolm MacDonald (London)*
> *(No. 11) (18/73) (Copy)*
> DUBLIN, 19 January 1937

Sir,

With reference to your despatch No. 145 of 9th December, I have the honour to request you to be so good as to inform the Italian Ambassador in London[2] that my Government have learned with much pleasure of the desire of the Italian Government to institute diplomatic relations with Saorstát Éireann, and that the proposal to establish a Legation at Dublin is entirely agreeable to them.

I should be grateful if, at the same time, you would kindly convey my apologies to the Ambassador for the unavoidable delay in replying to his enquiry.

I have the honour to be,
Sir,
Your most obedient,
humble servant,
EAMON DE VALERA
Minister for External Affairs

---

[1] See above No. 3.
[2] Count Dino Grandi (1895-1988), Italian Ambassador to Britain (1932-39).

No. 10 NAI DFA 5/249

Confidential report from John W. Dulanty to Joseph P. Walshe (Dublin)
(No. 6) (Secret)

LONDON, 19 January 1937

I send herewith a small brochure giving the Form and Order of the Coronation in 1911.[1]

As I mentioned on the telephone yesterday the Archbishop of Canterbury is proposing to bring the Litany immediately after the Preparation and to let the Entrance into the Church remain as it is but to bring the Oath, which previously followed the Sermon (well on into the course of the Church of England service), immediately after the Recognition.

Apparently the Archbishop thinks that this change would have the effect of putting the Oath immediately in front of the beginning of the Church of England service proper.

When Mr. Malcolm MacDonald told me of this last evening I said to him I felt sure my Government would not regard that as satisfactory. Even though no Church of England hymn was sung or C of E prayer said before the Oath was taken it could not seriously be contended that the Litany and the singing of the Psalm did not form an integral part of the Coronation service, and the proposed position with regard to the Oath was really from our point of view as unsatisfactory as before. Surely it was possible for the Oath ceremony to be performed at the entrance to the Abbey. Mr. MacDonald said in view of earlier conversations with me he had put this point to the Archbishop who had said that he felt it would be impossible to have this ceremony at the door so to speak behind the backs of the whole assembly and away from the main centre of the Abbey where the Coronation had taken place all though the centuries.

Mr. MacDonald repeated that if we had any further suggestion to make he would see the Archbishop and endeavour to meet our wishes.

J.W. DULANTY
High Commissioner

No. 11 NAI 2003/17/181

Memorandum by Joseph P. Walshe on a phone conversation with
John W. Dulanty (London)

DUBLIN, 25 January 1937

Questions in the H of Coms on the Conversations of the 14th January.[2]

At 10.20 on the 'phone this morning, the high Commissioner told me that the following question was being put to the Secretary for the Dominions by Ross, M.P. for Derry:[3]

---

[1] Not printed.
[2] Handwritten heading by Walshe.
[3] Major Sir Ronald Deane Ross (1888-1958), Ulster Unionist MP for Londonderry (1929-1951).

Question:

Whether the conversation with Mr. de Valera covered matters affecting the interests of Northern Ireland and, if so, whether he had consulted the Government of Northern Ireland thereon.

The following was the answer which Mr. MacDonald was to give:-

'In the course of our recent conversation, Mr. de Valera expressed his wish that steps should be taken towards the establishment of a United Ireland. The matter was not further discussed, however; the second part of the question does not therefore arise.'

I informed the President immediately of the terms of the reply and he directed me to suggest the following reply:

'In the course of our recent conversation, Mr. de Valera laid stress upon the fact which he has so frequently emphasised in public statements, that it was only on the basis of a united Ireland that really cordial relations between the peoples of the two countries could be established. The detailed part of the conversation dealt with issues immediately in dispute between us other than that of a United Ireland. I have already informed the House that all these conversations were informal in character and did not constitute negotiations.'

~~In the course of a further conversation with the High Commissioner.~~[1] The High Commissioner came back on the 'phone at 11.20. He had been talking to Mr. MacDonald. Mr. MacDonald wanted the answer put as briefly as possible and to prevent as far as possible awkward supplementary questions being asked. He therefore wished to keep to his original reply but on pressure from the High Commissioner he agreed to say instead of 'Mr. de Valera expressed his wish' that 'Mr. de Valera strongly urged that steps etc.' I repeated to the High Commissioner the President's chief objection was to the second sentence in Mr. MacDonald's reply, that is, 'the matter was not, however, discussed further.' On speaking further with the President on the matter, he suggested that this sentence should be replaced by 'no scheme for a united Ireland was discussed'. That change, together with the use of 'strongly urged' would make the reply relatively satisfactory.

The High Commissioner will be unable to see Mr. MacDonald again before two o'clock but he thinks that he will be able to secure his agreement for the change. Mr. MacDonald has gone to a meeting of the Cabinet which is unlikely to end before that time.

The H.C. eventually succeeded in persuading Mr. MacDonald to adopt the suggestion in last par[agraph] but one hereof.[2]

J.P.W.
25th January, 1937.

---

[1] This fragment has been crossed out by Walshe.
[2] This sentence is handwritten.

No. 12 UCDA P150/2179

Confidential report from John W. Dulanty to Joseph P. Walshe (Dublin)
(No. 10) (Secret)

LONDON, 25 January 1937

I saw Mr. Malcolm MacDonald for a few minutes at the end of the British Cabinet meeting today, which meeting I understand was concerned solely with the examination from their point of view of the two constitutional Acts passed by our Government in December last.

Mr. MacDonald said that what he had to say was at the moment informal and confidential and asked that I should give this interim message to the President himself.

He said that the United Kingdom Government's tentative view was that the recent Irish Free State legislation should not be regarded as having altered fundamentally the position of the Irish Free State as a Dominion.

They would decide for themselves but obviously they could not decide for the other partner Governments in the Commonwealth. In view of the President's agreement with Mr. MacDonald that the latter should circulate to the partner Governments our recent Acts, he, Mr. MacDonald, would now circulate them to the other partner Governments and inform them that the United Kingdom Government were of opinion that the Acts should not be regarded as containing any fundamental change in the position of the Irish Free State as a member state of the British Commonwealth.

The United Kingdom Cabinet were however seriously concerned about the possibility of Article 1 of the Constitution being dropped out of the new Constitution and of its not appearing anywhere else. It would make their position very much more difficult and they hoped that the President might see his way either to maintain that Article in the Constitution, or, if he could not for the understandable reason which he gave to Mr. MacDonald, make a fresh clause in Act 2. All that would appear to be needed was an amending one clause Bill adding to the existing Act and saying that the Free State was a co-equal member of the community of nations known as the British Commonwealth. He was afraid that some constitutional provision of this kind was vital from the point of view of the United Kingdom Government.

They would be glad if we could see our way to revise our wording of clause 3, section 1 of Act No. 2 so that our recognition of the Crown as a symbol of the association should be brought into line with that of the other member states of the Commonwealth.

The United Kingdom Cabinet also felt that our reference in Act No. 1 to the King as an 'organ' would hurt their people very much on what was a really susceptible point.

Mr. MacDonald concluded this short conversation by emphasising that his remarks were strictly confidential and must, pending the receipt of replies from the partner Governments, necessarily be tentative. The

President he thought would see that the foregoing suggestions, though informal and tentative, were put forward in a friendly spirit.

[signed] J.W. DULANTY
High Commissioner

No. 13 NAI 2003/17/181

Confidential report from John W. Dulanty to Joseph P. Walshe (Dublin)
(No. 11) (Secret)[1]

LONDON, 27 January 1937

(1) The conversation with Mr. Malcolm MacDonald which formed the subject of my Secret minute No. 10 of the 25th January[2] was of less than five minutes duration. The discussion at the meeting of the United Kingdom Cabinet that day was so protracted that he had to hurry to the House of Commons where he was in fact late with his answers to questions.

(2) In these few minutes Mr. MacDonald told me, necessarily briefly, the decision of the Cabinet that morning. That decision appeared to me to be of such importance that I saw him again today in order to ensure that I had correctly reported his conversation. For this purpose I read to him my Secret minute No. 10. He agreed with it but said that there were one or two explanations which he would like to make.

(3) In the first place he said that he had described the United Kingdom Cabinet's view as tentative because he wanted to make clear that in their view the question of the effect of this legislation was of common concern. He did not wish the word 'tentative' to be regarded as though they wished to re-examine the question. They had no such wish unless one of the other Governments raised some new point.

With regard to the closing sentence of the first paragraph on page 2 of the secret minute he said that whilst he had used the word 'vital' when speaking to me, he thought than on reflection instead of that sentence he would prefer the following: 'the United Kingdom Cabinet attached very great importance to this and hoped that Mr. de Valera could see his way to meet them.'

Further, Mr. MacDonald said that the suggestions which the United Kingdom Cabinet put forward as described in the Secret Minute under reference were put forward informally. By that he meant, he said, that the Cabinet appreciated that the President would wish to be free to say that any alterations which he felt able to make were not made as a result of representations from the United Kingdom or any other Government.

[signed] J.W. DULANTY
High Commissioner

---

[1] Marginal note by Seán Murphy: 'Read to P.[resident], 29/1/37, S.M.'.
[2] See above No. 12.

No. 14 NAI 2006/39

> *Letter from Seán Murphy to John W. Dulanty (London)*
>
> DUBLIN, 30 January 1937

I send you herewith text of a Statement which it is thought you might make verbally to Mr. MacDonald in connection with the suggested modification of the Coronation Oath.

[signed] SEAN MURPHY

With[1] regard to the proposed modification of the Church of England part of the oath the President thinks that Mr. Mac's original suggestion to insert after 'Protestant Reformed Religion' the words 'where established by law' is much better than the modification you mentioned to me on the telephone.

[initialled] SM

[STATEMENT]

The Minister for External Affairs appreciates the efforts made by Mr. MacDonald to meet some of the difficulties in relation to the Coronation Ceremony, and in particular his efforts to have the secular part of the Oath removed from the Church of England Service proper. He fears, however, that the mere separating of that promise scarcely does this when the solemn confirmation of it with all the other promises is made at the culminating point of the Church of England Service. It is only right that Mr. MacDonald should know that the attitude of the Government of Saorstát Éireann towards the Coronation as a whole can only be one of detachment and protest, so long as our country is partitioned and the religious service implies discrimination (to put it mildly) against the faith of the majority of the people of this country.

No. 15 NAI DT S9177

> *Memorandum on non-intervention in the Spanish Civil War from*
> *Seán Murphy to Eamon de Valera (Dublin)*
>
> DUBLIN, 2 February 1937

President,

At the meeting of the International Non-Intervention Committee in London on Thursday next, the Government representatives will be asked to state whether their Governments agree

(1)   to an extension of the Non-Intervention Agreement under which each Government agreed not only to prevent the export to Spain and the Spanish Dependencies of arms and war material but also the recruitment in, the departure from, or transit through, their respective countries of persons proposing to proceed to Spanish territory for the purpose of taking service in the present war;

---

[1]   Handwritten postscript by Murphy.

(2) to put into operation measures designed to secure such an extension of the Agreement on as early a date as possible in February, 1937, that date to be settled in agreement by the International Committee, provided that the other governments concerned agreed to take similar action;

(3) to the institution of a system of supervision of the land and sea frontiers of Spain, to be operated outside Spain.

This scheme is in substitution of the earlier scheme of supervision the cost of which was estimated at £620,000. The new scheme is estimated to cost £898,000 per annum. Governments who have already agreed to contribute towards the earlier scheme are asked to agree to make contributions to the present scheme on the same basis.

(4) to make a contribution of 20% of the amount of the annual contribution at once, in order to provide for the preliminary expenses of the scheme.

The amount payable by the Saorstát in this connection would be something short of £2,000.[1]

I have discussed with the Department of Justice the steps it would be necessary to take in order to prevent Saorstát nationals from taking part in the present conflict in Spain. The Department of Justice agree that it would be better to confine the necessary legislation to the present Spanish crisis. In doing so, the reason for bringing in the Bill is because we are members of the International Committee, and such a step is considered necessary in the interests of international peace. The Department of Justice think that a Bill of general application brought in at this moment might be regarded as an attempt to put through general legislation on the occasion of a particular crisis. They feel also that a general Bill would require much more careful consideration than the time at our disposal will allow. Another reason for confining the Bill to the present Spanish situation is the need for including in the Bill certain prohibitions against the export of war material which is not already covered by existing legislation.

Your direction is sought as to whether the High Commissioner may be instructed to inform the Non-Intervention Committee that[2] the Saorstát Government is ready to take the necessary measures to prohibit the enlistment, recruitment, departure from or transit through Saorstát Éireann of persons proposing to proceed to Spanish territory for the purpose of taking service in the present war, provided all the other Governments represented on the Non-Intervention Committee take similar action; that he may also inform the Non-Intervention Committee that[3] the Government of Saorstát Éireann is prepared to contribute towards the revised scheme for the supervision of the land and sea frontiers of Spain at the new estimate of £898,000 per annum, and that they would make available 20% of the Saorstát's annual[4] contribution to this scheme as soon as it may be required.

[signed] SEAN MURPHY

---

[1] Handwritten marginal note: 'See Finance'.
[2] The sentence from this point until the word 'action' has been underlined by a reader.
[3] The sentence from this point until the end of the document has been underlined by a reader.
[4] The word 'annual' is a handwritten insertion.

No. 16 NAI DT S9177

*Extract from the minutes of a meeting of the Cabinet
(Cab. 7/389) (Item 2)*
DUBLIN, 2 February 1937

SPANISH CIVIL WAR: Non-intervention.
It was agreed that the High Commissioner in London should be instructed to inform the Non-Intervention Committee
(a) that the Government of Saorstát Éireann were ready to take the necessary measures to prohibit the enlistment, recruitment, departure from or transit through Saorstát Éireann of persons proposing to proceed to Spanish territory for the purpose of taking service in the present war, provided that all other Governments represented on the Non-Intervention Committee took similar action;
(b) that the Government were prepared to contribute towards the revised scheme for the supervision of the land and sea frontiers of Spain, the estimated cost of which would be £898,000 per annum;
(c) that the Government would make available 20% of the Saorstát's annual contribution to this scheme when required.

No. 17 NAI DFA 227/87

*Extract from a memorandum on non-intervention in the Spanish Civil War
from Seán Murphy to John W. Dulanty (London)[1]*
DUBLIN, 3 February 1937

[matter omitted][2]
With regard to the question of naval supervision in paragraph (e) of the questionnaire,[3] the Government of Saorstát Éireann are prepared to agree to whatever system is regarded by the International Committee as the most effective for the purpose.
With regard to the suggested prohibition of the transit of volunteers through Saorstát Éireann, the Government feel that it would be extremely difficult to enforce the prohibition in this matter. This aspect of the question is not one of much importance so far as Saorstát Éireann is concerned, as it is very unlikely that foreign volunteers will pass through Saorstát Éireann in transit to Spain.

[stamped] (Signed) SEÁN MURPHY
Rúnaí

---

[1] Marginal annotation: 'Sec[retar]y'.
[2] The matter omitted repeats the text of the Cabinet minute above (No. 16).
[3] Non-intervention committee Secret Paper N.I.S.36 (290), not printed.

No. 18 NAI DFA Letter Books Rome/Madrid 1936-37

Letter from Joseph P. Walshe to Leopold H. Kerney (St Jean de Luz)
(41/104)

DUBLIN, 15 February 1937

I am directed to inform you that representations have been received in the Department from the parents of four boys under 21 years of age who have joined the O'Duffy Brigade and are now in Spain. Particulars of the four cases and of the circumstances in which the boys left for Spain without the consent or knowledge of their parents are attached. Except in the case of John O'Connor we have no information about any of the boys since they left Ireland.

The Minister wishes you to make an urgent appeal to General Franco's Authorities to allow the boys to return to their homes on the ground that they are minors and are in Spain against the will of their parents.

On receiving a copy of the letter written by John O'Connor to his mother we asked the British Foreign Office to take action through their Ambassador in Lisbon, with a view to securing the return of the boy to Ireland. As, however, it is unlikely that O'Connor remained more than a few days in Lisbon, it is quite possible that the Ambassador will be unable to give any assistance. You should, therefore, include O'Connor's case in you representations to the Franco Authorities.

I also enclose particulars of a boy named Thomas Woods,[1] who left for Spain on the 11th December with a party under Frank Ryan who were going to join the International Brigade. Will you please approach the Spanish Government Authorities for information regarding this boy and make similar representations regarding his return to his home.

Should you succeed in securing the release of any of the boys you are authorised to repatriate them on the usual conditions. Please keep us notified by wire of any information you may obtain about them.

[stamped] (Signed) J.P. WALSHE
Rúnaí

---

[1] This refers to Tommy Woods (referred to incorrectly as 'Wood' in the original of No. 18) who was a 17-year old from Dublin's north inner city. He secretly joined the International Brigade on 11 December 1936. Because he was a minor, his parents, through the Department of External Affairs, attempted to have him repatriated in spring 1937. Kerney failed to ascertain Woods' whereabouts. Woods had in fact died in Andujar Hospital as a result of wounds received in battle in Córdoba on 29 December 1936. The circumstances of his death did not become apparent until July 1937.

No. 19 NAI DFA 227/4

Code telegram from the Department of External Affairs to William
J.B. Macaulay (Rome)
(No. 3) (127/20) (Copy)
DUBLIN, 12.15 pm, 16 February 1937

Please[1] wire immediately any further information available re intentions of Vatican concerning recognition of Franco.

ESTERO

No. 20 NAI DFA 227/4

Code telegram from William J.B. Macaulay to the Department of External Affairs
(Dublin) (No. 1) (127/20) (Copy)
ROME, 16 February 1937

Your telegram No. 3.[2] No definite information available. Trend of events towards recognition, probably after capture of Madrid.

Saorstát

No. 21 NAI DFA 227/87

Memorandum by the Department of External Affairs on the Spanish Civil War
(Non-Intervention) Bill (Dublin)
DUBLIN, 18 February 1937

SPANISH CIVIL WAR NON-INTERVENTION BILL 1937[3]

The object of this Bill is to give effect to the Agreement reached at the International Non-Intervention Committee on the 17th February, that the Governments who are parties to the non-intervention policy should, as from midnight on February 20th/21st, 'extend the Non-Intervention Agreement to cover the recruitment in, the transit through or departure from, their respective countries of persons of non-Spanish Nationality proposing to proceed to Spain or the Spanish dependencies for the purpose of taking service in the present Civil War.'

It will be remembered that in August of last year on the initiative of the French Government the International Non-Intervention Committee was established. The Government of Saorstát Éireann became a member of that Committee in the belief that the policy of ~~the~~ Non-Intervention ~~Committee~~[4]

---

[1] Marginal annotation: 'PSS. File with you'. Sheila Murphy was Private Secretary to the Secretary.
[2] See above No. 19.
[3] This memorandum formed the basis of a speech by de Valera in Dáil Éireann during the second stage of the debate on the Spanish Civil War (Non-Intervention) Bill, 1937 (See *Dáil Éireann, Parliamentary Debates*, vol. 65, cols 598-601, 18 Feb. 1938).
[4] The words crossed out in this document have been crossed out in the original.

was best in the interests of Spain itself as well as in the interests of European peace. The Governments represented on the Non-Intervention Committee decided, towards the end of September, to prohibit the exports of arms and ammunition to Spain from their respective countries. It is common knowledge that the prohibition of export has not been strictly adhered to. It is also well-known that during the last 3 or 4 months considerable numbers of volunteers from various countries have joined the armies of the two parties in Spain. No matter what side in the present conflict one's sympathies may lie, and there can be ~~no~~ little doubt on which side is the sympathy of the ~~vast~~ majority of the people of this country, there must be a general desire to see the present conflict in Spain brought to a speedy conclusion. The Governments represented on the Non-Intervention Committee realising that so long as arms and ammunition were imported into Spain, and that volunteers from various countries could join the ranks of either party, the present war in Spain was likely to continue almost indefinitely. Apart from the fact that the continuance of the war would entail increasing loss of life and property, the presence of foreign volunteers in Spain greatly increases the danger of an international incident which might seriously affect the peace of Europe.

The Governments represented on the Non-Intervention Committee accordingly agreed that they would prohibit their nationals from taking part in the Civil War on either side. They also agreed to a system of supervision of the land and sea frontiers of Spain in order to prevent the exportation of arms and ammunition to that country.

The Government of Saorstát Éireann have agreed to the proposals of the Non-Intervention Committee because they believe it is the only contribution the Saorstát can make towards bringing the present conflict in Spain to an end, and preventing that conflict from spreading beyond Spain, and thus endangering the peace of Europe. The Government of Saorstát Éireann also believe that the Spaniards should be left to settle their ~~own internal~~ differences, and to work out for themselves ~~what particular~~ the form of government ~~is~~ most suited to their ~~national~~ needs.

It is for these reasons that the Dáil is being asked to pass the present Bill. It is quite clear from the text of the Bill itself what steps it is proposed to take and I do not feel that any explanation of the various sections is called for. There is one section, however, to which I should like to draw particular attention; I refer to section 10 which gives power to the Executive Council to prevent the export from Saorstát Éireann of articles which, in its opinion, are implements of war, or war material. Deputies will be aware that by section 17 of the Fire Arms Act, 1925 the export of arms and munitions from Saorstát Éireann is prohibited unless licensed by the Minister for Justice. The Fire Arms Act, however, does not cover all implements and material of war. The International Non-Intervention Committee are anxious that the prohibition regarding the export of arms and war material should cover all classes of arms and war material. They have, accordingly, requested all Governments represented on the Committee to take steps to prohibit the export of all types of war material. As Saorstát Éireann does not manufacture arms or war material it is unlikely that this section will have to be used, but the power to prohibit the export of such material is taken in order to carry out the request of the Non-Intervention Committee for uniformity regarding the classes of material prohibited in the various countries.

No. 22 NAI DT S9628

> *Memorandum on the Spanish Civil War (Non-Intervention) Bill by*
> *Michael MacDunphy (Dublin)*
> *(S9628)*
>
> DUBLIN, 19 February 1937

There is no record of either the scheme of this Bill or its text having been either submitted to or approved by the Executive Council, or of authority being granted for the introduction of the Bill in the Dáil.

Neither did this Department receive from any source any official intimation, written or verbal, in regard to it. This Department received its first intimation regarding the Bill from the press reports of the morning of the 18th instant.

As a result of subsequent enquiries it was ascertained that following the decision of the Executive Council of 2nd instant to adhere to the proposal of the Non-intervention Committee in London steps should be taken to prevent the despatch of volunteers to Spain etc., the Department of External Affairs on the 9th instant wrote to the Department of Justice stating that the Minister for External Affairs was anxious that a Bill should be prepared to give effect to that decision and asking that Department to prepare the necessary measure.

The Bill was duly prepared and was introduced in the Dáil without being submitted to the Executive Council either for approval or for authority for its introduction, this being in direct conflict with the regular procedure.

No. 23 NAI 2006/39

> *Letter from John W. Dulanty to Sir Harry Batterbee (London)*
>
> LONDON, 19 February 1937

My dear Batterbee,

In the course of a conversation with Mr. Malcolm MacDonald on the 4th February I mentioned certain points in connection with the Coronation ceremonial which you and I had already discussed. I had some days previously intimated to Mr. MacDonald that Mr. de Valera was appreciative of the efforts which had been made to make the Coronation Oath less objectionable to the people of the Irish Free State but that the Government's attitude must be one of detachment and protest so long as partition remained, and further, so long as the religious part of the Oath together with the King's declaration of faith represented an affront to the religious beliefs of an overwhelming majority of our people.

You joined us and explained the position at that moment of:

(1) The High Constable of Ireland
(2) The High Steward of Ireland
(3) The Ulster King of Arms

(4) The Dublin Herald

(5) The Standard Bearer of Ireland

(6) The Archbishop of Dublin

in relation to the coming function.

On (1) the information from the Earl Marshal's Office was that the time for making a claim before the Court of Claims had now gone by and the presumption therefore was that the claim had lapsed.

On (2) you stated that this office had been held for 350 years by the family of the Earl of Shrewsbury and that the claim for this Coronation had been accepted by the Court of Claims. The Earl of Shrewsbury had been authorised to carry a white wand. Since the office of High Constable of Ireland would not be filled on this occasion the further question would arise as to whether the High Steward of Ireland should attend as such. It was suggested in the Earl Marshall's Office that it would seem somewhat anomalous if the High Steward were present at the Coronation when no person was present as High Constable of Ireland.

Petitions in respect of (3) and (4) had passed the Court of Claims but to neither of these petitioners had any functions been assigned.

Mr. MacDonald took the view that whilst not overlooking the tradition behind these several offices it could not be denied that they were now anachronisms. If the King asked Mr. de Valera for formal advice and Mr. de Valera advised against such participation in the ceremony then he doubted whether the King could invite these gentlemen in the respective capacities named.

Knowing that I was shortly crossing to Dublin Mr. MacDonald asked me to obtain Mr. de Valera's views informally. By 'informally' he meant that if Mr. de Valera so wished he could say later that there had been no official representations made on these matters.

Accordingly I spoke in this way to Mr. de Valera on my recent visit, who, after emphasising that our position with regard to the Coronation was one of detachment and protest, said that he regarded the whole ceremony as being in no sense legal but simply traditional.

The offices were now anachronisms and corresponded in no way to present-day realities. He was clear that there should be no High Constable of Ireland and no Bearer of the Standard of Ireland. He did not see how any of the suggested officers could discharge functions, however merely decorative and ceremonial as they might be, as representing the people of Ireland. But in cases where it was proposed that officers should attend in virtue of the fact that they would be discharging functions as the descendants of those who formerly acted in the same capacity he would be disposed not to cause difficulty by raising objection.

On (5) Mr. de Valera thought that there need be no objection to the attendance of the Archbishop of Dublin. He was an ecclesiastic who stood in a different position from that of the officers named above. He thought that the correct procedure would be for the Archbishop of Canterbury to transmit his invitation through Mr. Malcolm MacDonald to me when I would forward it to Mr. de Valera who would hand it to the Archbishop.

Yours sincerely,

[copy letter unsigned]

No. 24 NAI DFA 5/249

Confidential report from John W. Dulanty to Joseph P. Walshe (Dublin)
(No. 13) (Secret)

LONDON, 19 February 1937[1]

Last evening I went to a meeting of High Commissioners in Mr. MacDonald's room at the Dominions Office, but on finding that the business for discussion was the arrangements for an Empire youth rally at the Coronation I asked Mr. MacDonald to excuse me since my Government were not interested and I could, obviously, contribute nothing to the discussion. He agreed.

I had, however, a few minutes conversation with him in which I once again reminded him that our position on the Coronation was one of detachment and protest, quoting the words of the statement which I had made orally to him in accordance with the Department's minute of the 30th January.[2] Further, if the President were questioned in the Dáil about the Coronation or the Oath the answer he would make would be similar to the above-named oral statement. Mr. MacDonald said he quite understood that but he hoped that the word 'protest' could be avoided. It would materially help him and others who were working towards a settlement if the use of that word could be avoided.

He referred to the intended omission of Article 1 from the proposed new Constitution and said he got the impression from his talk with the President in the Grosvenor Hotel[3] that the President himself intended to give further consideration to this point. I said that I thought there was no hope of my Government having *as he, Mr. MacDonald, had suggested*[4] an amending Act to the second of the two Constitution Acts passed in December last. Mr. MacDonald said that he would be grateful if the President could see his way to send me a draft of whatever provision it was proposed to make in this connection in the new Constitution. He was of course not making this suggestion with any idea of United Kingdom approval. The draft could be shown by me privately to Sir Harry Batterbee so that it would be possible to say there had been no communication even of an informal character with the British Government. He thought it possible that they might be able to make suggestions which would meet their difficulties and which suggestions he though the President would be ready to consider. On these matters, as both he and the President were already aware, the form would be of high importance.

I said that I would communicate his request to the President.

[signed] J.W. DULANTY
High Commissioner

---

[1] Marginal note: 'Recd 23rd J.P.W.'.
[2] See above No. 14.
[3] See above Nos 3, 7 and 8.
[4] The words in italics have been inserted by hand by Dulanty.

No. 25 NAI 2006/39

Confidential report from John W. Dulanty to Joseph P. Walshe (Dublin)
(No. 14) (Secret)
LONDON, 25 February 1937

I enclose herewith an Aide Memoire[1] undated which I received this morning from the Dominions Office in which it will be seen that the British naval authorities indicate the possibility of vessels belonging to the Limerick Steamship Company being molested by Spanish warships acting in the interests of the Spanish Insurgents.

The Dominions Office state they are making inquiries as to whether ships belonging to any other member states of the Commonwealth are likely to be in Spanish waters. They do not think there is much likelihood of this but if such possibility exists the Dominions Office would make suggestions similar to those contained in the Aide Memoire to the other member states.

[copy letter unsigned]
High Commissioner

No. 26 NAI 2006/39

Letter from John W. Dulanty to Joseph P. Walshe (Dublin)
(Secret)
LONDON, 26 February 1937

I send herewith an undated and Secret note on the Irish Brigade in Spain which I received this morning from the Dominions Office. Sir Harry Batterbee explains that the British were in the habit of getting information about certain happenings, by which remark I understood him to convey that this was a report of the British Secret Service.

[copy letter unsigned]
High Commissioner

[Enclosure]
The Irish Brigade
(Secret)

1. On the 25th January there was a total of 641 non-commissioned officers and other ranks belonging to General O'Duffy's Irish Brigade on Spanish territory. (This figure is based on the ration strength). Most of them had been brought to Spain in the 'Argulia' ex Liverpool about the 5th December, 1936, the 'Ardeola' ex Liverpool 12th December, and a German ship which sailed from Ireland about the same time and was later picked up and escorted to Lisbon by a German destroyer. Other groups, each between ten and forty volunteers, had reached Spain by other routes.

---

[1] Not printed.

2. The majority of the members of the Irish Brigade were landed at Lisbon whence they proceeded to Caceres. At Caceres the Brigade was inspected by General O'Duffy, after which all were required to sign enlistment papers (printed in Spanish and therefore understood by very few) agreeing to serve as legionaries in the Spanish Foreign Legion for a period of six months or the duration of Spanish hostilities, whichever happened to be longer.

3. At Caceres they were equipped in uniforms of German manufacture consisting of inferior quality khaki-coloured German pattern tunics and khaki forage caps. German pattern shrapnel helmets were issued. No underclothing was issued and the men suffered from cold.

4. Complaints about the food were made from the first day, and despite promises, little had been done to improve rations. Pay was at the rate of three pesetas per day.

5. German Mauser rifles manufactured in Spain under licence and Hotchkiss machine guns were issued at Caceres and training immediately commenced. Difficulty was experienced with the Hotchkiss, owing to overheating and seizing of the breech-block.

6. The Brigade was formed into the 13th Tercio of the Spanish Foreign Legion and this designation was still borne, although consideration was being given to changing the number to the 15th Tercio, thirteen being unlucky.

7. In general, the Brigade was composed of a poor type of soldier, deficient in physique and character. There were at least two lunatics in the ranks.

8. Most of the officers were ill-trained and inefficient.

9. The Sergeant Major was an ex-soldier of the British Army who had seen service in India. He was efficient, but was supported by inexperienced sergeants of a bad type. Some of the corporals had served in the British or Irish Free State armies and a few alleged they had held commissions.

10. There was continual talk of the arrival of reinforcements and it was proclaimed that the total strength would ultimately be five thousand men. On the 21st January a further detachment of 500 men was expected. None arrived, however, and it was subsequently admitted by the Officers that they had not left Ireland. It was now generally realised that few, if any, further reinforcements would arrive.

11. In view of the many serious complaints against uniforms, rations, service conditions, unclean barracks, etc., all letters written by the men to their families and friends were now strictly censored and very few letters got through. Of twenty letters written by one member of the Brigade to his family in Ireland not a single one reached the addressee.

12. Up to the 25th January the Irish Brigade had seen no fighting. On that date it was announced that the Brigade was to leave for the Malaga front.

13. General O'Duffy had then only visited his force on two occasions: the first being on the day of arrival and the second being some two weeks later when he addressed his men on the subject of their enlistment. Amongst other things he said that if any man had enlisted with an object other than religion and a willingness to fight for the Catholic cause he

should immediately say so when he would be given his passport and sent back to Ireland. Some two hundred men applied for repatriation under this promise but none was given his passport or allowed to leave Spain.

No. 27 NAI CAB 1/7

> *Extract from the minutes of a meeting of the Cabinet*
> *(Cab. 7/395) (Item 4) (S9618)*
> DUBLIN, 11.00am to 1.30pm, 26 February 1937

CORONATION DAY: Suggested appointment as a Holiday
It was decided that Wednesday, 12th May, 1937, the date of the Coronation of King George VI, should not be appointed as a Bank Holiday or as a Public Holiday.

No. 28 NAI 2006/39

> *Confidential report from John W. Dulanty to Joseph P. Walshe (Dublin)*
> *(No. 16) (Secret)*
> LONDON, 3 March 1937

It will be recalled that I sent a Secret minute on 2 November 1934 about the question which had been raised by the British Home Office of taking special precautions at the ports to prevent the admission of dangerous or undesirable aliens in connection with the wedding of the Duke of Kent and the Silver Jubilee Celebrations in 1935.

Sir Edward Harding now informs me that the British Home Office in connection with the Coronation propose about the middle of April to take measures similar to those which were taken in November 1934 – as set out in the letter of Sir Ernest Holderness to me of the 2nd November 1934 and enclosed with the above Secret minute – and they hope that we will be prepared as in 1934 to take similar measures in An Saorstát.

May I give a reply on the lines of your Secret minute of the 9th November 1934?

[copy letter unsigned]
High Commissioner

No. 29 NAI 2006/39

> *Confidential report from John W. Dulanty to Joseph P. Walshe (Dublin)*
> *(No. 17) (Secret)*
> LONDON, 6 March 1937

(1) As the Department is aware the British King on his accession sees as a matter of courtesy the whole of the Diplomatic Corps and the High Commissioners. On receiving his invitation and after communicating with Dublin I called on King George VI at Buckingham Palace on the 4th March last.

(2) He began the conversation on purely personal points such for example as his enquiry about my having been in commercial life etc. He talked about one of my sons whom he had seen riding in a point-to-point race and then went on to talk about his own children and the pains that he and the Queen took to prevent their eldest child being spoilt through the attention, unavoidably excessive, which was paid to her.

(3) The late King George, he said, had always had a quiet but real admiration for Mr. de Valera because the news which reached his father from various sources about the President went to show that however you may differ politically you had to admire the President's rare gift of natural good manners. Both in Geneva and in London he said the President had widely established this reputation.

(4) For some time his talk was a lamentation on the decay of good manners. He could think of certain people in the public life of this country about whose great ability there could be no doubt. He had not met them and he did not want to meet them because from all he had heard they were utterly devoid of good manners. He had sometimes thought after talking with an agricultural labourer that the labourer was superior in manners to many of the people in modern society. He was ready to acquit most people of the charge of intentional mannerlessness because he supposed the rush, the hurry, and the worry of modern life gave people no time to think, so that this deplorable absence of manners might well be due more to the lack of thought than to the lack of goodwill. It was odd too, he reflected, that outstanding ability often went with a complete lack of the team spirit, 'For example,' he said, 'look at Mr. Churchill, one of the ablest men in this country, but he is like the cat that walks alone; he must go off and do things on his own without any real attempt at co-operation with his fellows'.

(5) The King said that he was very glad to hear that the President had had some conversations with Mr. Malcolm MacDonald. The latter had given him an account of these conversations and he greatly hoped that the difficulties between the two peoples might soon be cleared away.

(6) The conversation turned then on the subject of the Coronation and the King expressed his regret that the President would not in present circumstances be able to attend. Without embarking on any contentious talk I thought it well to say that until recently in Ireland the King and nearly all associated with the monarchy had been a kind of stage property of the old Unionist political party – to which observation he gave surprisingly quick and ready assent. It was indisputable that the history of the two peoples consisted almost entirely of one story – the story of the attempt by the British, sustained unbroken through the centuries, to subdue and to possess Ireland. It was similarly an accepted historical fact to say that an equally unbroken resistance by us had defeated that attempt. How could it be thought then that our people could in the nature of things have the same feeling for the King that the English had. Their attitude was of course not towards the King personally but towards his office of the titular head and front of a foreign system which they had only lately broken down. Here again the King made no demur or contested in any way what I had said. He remarked that he

quite understood the present position but he would like to know whether the relations between the two peoples need always be as they were now. I answered that both in private and in public the President had consistently expressed his wish and the wish of the nation to live on terms that should exist between good neighbours, but that our people must be entirely free and unfettered in their choice of what those relations should be. We, no less than any other self-respecting people, must be the masters of our own destiny.

(7) He told me that he had read with interest the two Constitutional Acts passed by the Dáil just before Christmas. The only comment he said he wished to make was that he did not like being called an 'organ'. It was bad enough to be called an 'instrument' but he would prefer being called an 'instrument' because 'organ' seemed to him not altogether a happy description. This was said laughingly.

(8) Reverting to the Coronation the King gave an amusing account of his rather exhausting part in it. 'How would you like' he said, 'to pass through throngs of people for four and a half hours and to know that all the time thousands and thousands of people were staring at you. Hang it, you can't keep smiling all the time. It is fatiguing too because, as I said to my wife, all that is to happen throughout this long ceremony happens to me – everybody else gets off scot free. I have to dress and undress three times and I have to be not only word perfect but I have also to be foot perfect because if I turn to the left instead of the right the whole show will get hopelessly tangled up.'

(9) I enquired about the health of the Queen and the Princesses. He said they were well, but in a jocular manner observed that according to the newspapers he himself was rather ill and had only two years to live. 'According to some of them I am consumptive, I stammer incessantly, I am a dull dog, and in short a complete wreck.' All this was said with a humorous light in his eye and was no more than pleasant raillery against the newspaper gossip. In the 40 minutes conversation he stammered three times – one being barely noticeable and the others ...[1]

(10) He asked to be remembered to the President whom he hoped some time he might meet and I was to say that if at any time he could be of help to An Saorstát he was at our service.

(11) Whereas the late King George was inclined to be rather brusque, the Duke of Windsor to be slightly over-anxious to please, the present King seemed to me to be simple, frank, free from affectation, and to have neither the brusqueness of his father nor the touch of the cinema star that marked his brother. The view is generally held by those who have knowledge of and contact with the Court that of the late King George's sons the present King, although in no way brilliant, is from the point of view of character and a sense of duty the best of the lot.

[copy letter unsigned]
High Commissioner

---

[1] This sentence is handwritten and the final six words are indecipherable.

No. 30 NAI 2003/17/181

Confidential report from John W. Dulanty to Joseph P. Walshe (Dublin)
(No. 18) (Secret) (Copy)

LONDON, 6 March 1937

Mr. Malcolm MacDonald told me last evening that he had now heard from each of the other member States of the Commonwealth on the subject of our two Constitutional Acts. He had been much disappointed at the delay in getting these replies – the last one, received that morning, had been obtained only after his sending urgent cables pressing for an immediate reply. As he had not yet been to his colleagues with these replies he was not in a position to give me any details.

He was, however, anxious to let the President know in a purely informal manner that certain of these other States were troubled about the omission thus far of the former Article 1 from the new Constitution. They were also concerned, some of them, about Section 3 sub-Section 2 (a) (here I quote from memory) and, further, about the use of the word 'organ'.

He was telling me this now before he had approached the British Cabinet in order to acquaint the President informally at the earliest possible moment of the reactions of the other member States.

Mr. MacDonald proposes to continue his correspondence with the other member States in the hope of 'getting the constitutional question solved and out of the way immediately'. It would be an immense help towards this end if the President could see his way to make some kind of substitution for Article 1. Could the President have a clause – he could not pretend to give the wording – to the effect that unless some Act were passed later to the contrary An Saorstát would continue its existing membership of the Commonwealth group? In this way or some similar way it might be possible to deal with the point that we wanted a Constitution which would not need alteration in the event of certain contingencies later.

With the constitutional question out of the way he would press for the continuance of the exploratory talks about Defence, Financial Settlement and Trade Agreement. He did not wish to be too optimistic but he still thought we could advance a long way, possibly to a settlement, on these matters before the Imperial Conference began on 14 May next.

After making it clear that I had no instruction from my Government on the matter I said that unless the British bestirred themselves and reached a position vastly different from that of to-day on the questions Mr. MacDonald had mentioned there was no likelihood of the President or his colleagues attending the Conference. This remark depressed Mr. MacDonald who argued that we were present at the Ottawa Conference[1] and as some advance he thought had been made between us since 1932 there was a case for the President trying to co-operate by attending the Conference. I reminded him

---

[1] See DIFP Volume IV, Nos 9, 20, 21, 49, 56, 57, 69, 89, 90, 91, 93, 97, 98, 100, 102, 103, 104, 111, 116.

that what are called the Annuity or Special Duties on our exports were put on whilst our Ottawa Delegation was on the high seas *en route* for the Conference and that in other respects the position between us to-day was different from that when my Government decided to attend the Ottawa Conference.

(Signed) J.W. DULANTY

No. 31 NAI DFA Madrid Embassy 19/4

Extracts from a confidential report from Leopold H. Kerney to Joseph P. Walshe (Dublin)
(S.J.19/1) (Confidential) (Copy)
ST JEAN DE LUZ, 6 March 1937

[matter omitted]
Ireland and Spain.
De Mamblas asked me to enlighten him as to the true position in Ireland, and I understood clearly that my remarks would be the basis of some report by him. He mentioned the names of O'Duffy, Belton[1] (he made a note of this name, which was not familiar to him) and McCullagh;[2] he had seen in a hotel in Salamanca an open letter to President de Valera published in pamphlet form. I explained, confidentially of course, the position as regards each of the three; I sketched the history of the first two, their position in Irish public life, I explained their attitude and their policy. I informed him of the rather violent attack on the President by O'Duffy in an opposition newspaper in connection with the legislation following the decisions of the non-intervention committee. De Mamblas expressed the fear that O'Duffy's attitude might have an adverse effect on the decisions of the Irish Government. I assured him that there need not be the slightest apprehension on this point and that the Government's attitude would not be influenced one way or the other by anything O'Duffy might say or do. I told him that the Government's first duty was of course to safeguard Irish interests; that they did not feel that they could just at this stage set a headline by giving to the Franco régime an official recognition, which would in any case be of no material and of but slight moral advantage to Spain; that our attitude was uninfluenced by and independent of that of England; that the President himself had stated that there was no doubt as to the direction of the sympathies of the majority of the Irish

---

[1] Patrick Belton (1884-1945), Fianna Fáil and Fine Gael TD for various constituencies, including Dublin County (Fianna Fáil) (June to September 1927), Dublin North (Fine Gael) (1933-7). Left Fine Gael about 1935 to form and then lead the Irish Christian Front, which supported General Franco. Rejoined Fine Gael and was elected for Dublin County in 1938. Belton continued to hold strong pro-Fascist views and was expelled from Fine Gael in 1940.

[2] Francis McCullagh (1874-1956), Irish-born retired British army officer, the author of many books including accounts of the revolutions in Russia and Mexico. He was in Spain as war correspondent of the London *Daily Mail*. His *In Franco's Spain, being the experiences of an Irish war-correspondent during the great civil war which began in 1936* was published in London in 1937.

people; that I had no doubt myself as to where the sympathies of my Government were, although I had not discussed this question officially at home; that recognition by the Vatican would be a very desirable preliminary step; that my personal opinion was that recognition by some important Catholic country such as the Argentine or Brazil might have a repercussion in Ireland.

[matter omitted]

I reminded de Mamblas that, notwithstanding the links of history and religion that existed between the two countries, there was a very strong democratic spirit in Ireland, and therefore there would be a disposition amongst the Irish people generally to look askance at any regime in Spain which might appear to be imposed on the people following on what might by some be believed to be a purely military revolt. I believed, therefore, that it was of the utmost importance that it should be made clear that there was democratic approval for the re-introduction of the monarchy. He said that the reaction against the excesses committed under the Republic was so great that there had been a tremendous swing over of opinion in favour of the monarchy.

Semi-official Representative of Franco in Ireland.
De Mamblas asked me about the Spanish Legation in Dublin, and told me incidentally that Aguilar[1] was not in high favour because his resignation had been too long delayed. He asked me how we would view the presence in Dublin of an unofficial or semi-official representative of Franco; he asked me to ascertain your views in the matter. I told him that, if there were to be such a representative, his position would be a delicate one and the greatest tact, caution and care would be necessary because there was no doubt but that the opposition would make every effort to utilise this gentleman's presence for their own advantage, thereby creating difficulties for the Government. Would you please advise me as soon as may be as to your attitude in this matter, as I expect de Mamblas to raise this question again at some early future date.

In conclusion, I would call your attention to the fact that, though the Church in Spain came out definitely on one side in the civil war, the Vatican has endeavoured to remain outside and above the contending parties; compare this with Franco's desire to keep Don Juan from appearing to take sides. And I also express the fear that the 'cleaning up' operations during the Regency will involve much bloodshed, and possibly many acts of personal vengence which the new régime may not be able to (I hesitate to say willing) to prevent.

[copy letter unsigned]
Aire Lán-Chómhachtach

---

[1] Alvano de Aguilar Gomez Acebo, Spanish Minister in Dublin (Dec. 1935-Sept. 1936).

No. 32 NAI DFA Madrid Embassy IP 3/6

Letter from Joseph P. Walshe to Leopold H. Kerney (St Jean de Luz)
(141/14) (Secret)

Dublin, 6 March 1937

Reports are being received in Ireland that the soldiers of the 15th Tercio (Irish Brigade) of the Foreign Legion are to a large extent discontent with their lot. They complain of the bad food, poor clothing and of their treatment generally.

They are said to be poor in physique, and with exceptions, bad soldiers.

General O'Duffy is said to have visited his men only on two occasions.

Could you ascertain whether there is any truth in these reports. Please, in any case, send home any information you can obtain about the 15th Tercio as well as about the progress of the War in general.

[signed] J.P. Walshe
Rúnaí

No. 33 NAI DFA Madrid Embassy IP 3/6

Letter from Leopold H. Kerney to Joseph P. Walshe (Dublin)
(S.J.51/1) (Secret) (Copy)

St Jean de Luz, 8 March 1937

Referring to your minute 141/14 of 6th inst.,[1] I will be on the look-out for any information I can gleam[2] regarding the 15th bandera of the Tercio; I cannot count on any reliable impartial testimony as regards conditions there from any of my friends on Franco's side, but I will try to get hold of some more independent observer.

There passed through here recently a Norwegian journalist, Axelbergh I think was his name, who has been contributing articles to the 'New York Times'. He had left before I knew he was here. I am told that he referred in a conversation to O'Duffy, and expressed the opinion that he was a 'queer fellow'; that in some bar or hotel in Salamanca he was *in the habit* of calling round him any journalists he saw, standing them drinks and telling them yarns, with the injunction not to repeat them but, apparently, with a contrary intention. This statement, for whatever it may be worth, was not given for the sake of pandering to any particular prejudice.

[copy letter unsigned]
Aire Lán-Chómhachtach

---

1   See above No. 32.
2   'glean'?

No. 34 NAI DFA 119/17A

Code telegram from the Department of External Affairs to Leopold H. Kerney
(St Jean de Luz) (No. 1)[1]

DUBLIN, 5.40 pm, 8 March 1937

Your reports received. Please go to Salamanca to explore the situation close at hand and to secure material for a full report to enable the government to come to a decision about the recognition of the authorities there. See all authorities and all others who may be able to give information. Also continue efforts to secure early return of youths whose cases have already been referred to you.

ESTERO

No. 35 NAI CAB 1/7

Extract from the minutes of a meeting of the Cabinet
(Cab. 7/398) (Item 4) (S9704)

DUBLIN, 9 March 1937

SPANISH CIVIL WAR: Shipping Bill
Authority was given for the preparation and introduction of a Bill to give effect to the international agreement regarding Non-Intervention in the Spanish Civil War regarding Merchant Shipping, subject to submission of the text to the Executive Council for approval.

No. 36 NAI DFA Secretary's Files S64

Letter from Michael MacWhite to Joseph P. Walshe (Dublin)
(Confidential)

WASHINGTON, 10 March 1937

A Chara,
Before the expiration of another week eight years will have elapsed since I presented my letters accrediting me as Minister Plenipotentiary from the Saorstát to the President of the United States of America.

Soon after my arrival in this country I discovered that for one reason or another the Saorstát Legation did not occupy a very important place either in the estimation of the Administration or in that of the other Diplomatic Missions of which there are fifty-four in this capital. It was to a large extent ignored by them as well as by many of our own people. Some of the latter regarded it as an adjunct of the British Embassy. It had few, if any, contacts with Irish societies or with those Catholic educational institutions which are directed mainly by persons of Irish birth or antecedents whose sympathies are of so much interest for us and it was not in very high standing with the Catholic Hierarchy of America. The circumstances under which I entered upon my duties were not therefore of the most favourable kind.

---

[1] Marginal note: 'PSS. File with you. Copies also on files 127/20 and 41/104'.

As the primary duty of a Minister Plenipotentiary is to safeguard the interests of his nation and, at the same time, to uphold its prestige and maintain it on a level equal, if not superior, to that of other States, I set about, after a brief survey, to overcome the difficulties that stood in the way. It became necessary for me at the outset to emphasise that I represented a country and not a party. It took a little while for some of our own people to realise this as a purely diplomatic mission was something to which they were unaccustomed. It was imperative to avoid intrigues and cliques so as not to become the instrument of either individuals or parties, which is not an easy matter as those acquainted with conditions in this country can readily understand.

Little by little, I established contacts with outstanding representatives of our race some of whom were not always in accord with the policy of the Government of the day. As the occasion presented itself I visited some of the principals among the Catholic Hierarchy including the four Cardinals and was most cordially received by all of them. I have met them frequently since, either at the Catholic University or at other functions, and I flatter myself no little at the disposition they always manifest towards me.

During my time here I have been the guest of many Irish Clubs and Associations, and, in addition, have delivered addresses at half a score Universities and Colleges. Some of these have bestowed on me the highest honours permitted by their Charters. I have also lectured for Federal and State Bar Associations and various cultural and civic organisations. Everywhere, I have been welcomed with the utmost cordiality and kindness.

In my relations with the Administration I have always insisted on the independent status of the Saorstát and demonstrated why separate consideration should be given to our problems, irrespective of how Great Britain may be affected thereby. Sometimes my listeners were not very sympathetic nor were they always willing to be convinced against their ingrained prejudices, but time and circumstances and continued effort have forced them to modify their attitude and render them more sympathetic to our views.

American newspapers have frequently repeated the time-worn bogey that the Irish are a quarrelsome and thriftless people who are governed either by malice or hatred, or both, in their attitude towards England. Some of them have even suggested that the Saorstát Government was not entirely blameless in this respect. To reply to these charges to the Editors would only provoke an insidious repetition of them, as they would always have the last word, but individual newspaper men are, as a rule easy to approach, and are not impervious to certain kinds of argument. It required a little time, however, to convince those who were brought up in an anti-Irish atmosphere that the members of our Government were honest, capable and serious-minded Administrators who applied the most intelligent and efficient methods to the solution [of] problems which were the outcome of centuries of oppression and misgovernment. I brought to their attention repeatedly the fact that, in regard to our National finances, no country in Europe had a more enviable reputation than ours; and that during the last five years no State of equal size and population had progressed in industrial development to anything like the same extent. Even our Social Security Services outdistanced by far those of the United States with all its resources.

In the field of International relations and World peace I called attention to the many praiseworthy contributions we have made. That the stand taken by President de Valera on the Manchukuo affair, on the Italo-Ethiopian dispute and in regard to the Civil War in Spain, was inspired by the highest principles of diplomacy and statesmanship and had, in the eyes of the European nations, added to the prestige of both his country and himself.

On the question of the Land Annuity dispute and the Penal tariffs that ensued I experienced no little difficulty in getting State Department and other officials to see the justice of our case. English news agencies had been able to disseminate, effectively and in advance, the British viewpoint of the issues involved, and in this country British propaganda rarely or ever falls on deaf ears. Some would like to attribute the stand taken by the Government to the 'old hatred' of England, but they have a better appreciation of the rights and wrongs of the case to-day and a clearer understanding then heretofore of the policy of the Saorstát not only in her relations with Britain but with the outside world as well.

In the social life of this capital where wealth counts for so much our role, notwithstanding our slender resources, has not been altogether insignificant. In the beginning, I found it necessary to bring the representatives of other nations to a realisation of the political existence of the Irish Free State. Almost the first step in accomplishing this was by forcing them and the people of the circles in which they moved to acknowledge that we, ourselves, socially existed. Money is not in itself a means to this end; tact and savoir faire are also necessary. We began by entertaining Cabinet Ministers and other high officials of the Administration, and were the subject of their hospitality in return. We did the same with Ambassadors and other Envoys, so much so, that within a short time one could meet at our Receptions almost everybody of weight and influence in the political, diplomatic and social life of Washington. Although we have no Legation residence, which is a considerable disadvantage, our social functions are, admittedly, the envy of many of the more elaborate Embassies and Legations here.

After this brief survey you will, I am sure, realise that without expanding facilities it is scarcely possible to extend our contacts or increase the prestige of the Legation beyond the present level. It is, in fact, a matter of surprise to me that popular interest has been maintained so long. It is well known that after a certain lapse of time a Chief of Mission, in whatever capital he may be, comes to be taken for granted. Once that point is reached he cannot hope to make headway against the indifference that long association inevitably produces. There is novelty and attraction in new Envoys and a renewal of public interest in their new environment for the country they represent. That is the reason why, in my opinion, no Ambassador or Minister should, unless in very exceptional circumstances, remain more than five or six years accredited to the same country.

For the reasons set out here it would be in the interests of the Department and of the Public service that I be transferred to a Post nearer home. As I understand there is to be a vacancy in Paris in the near future, I respectfully

submit that my seniority in the diplomatic service of the Saorstát and the efficiency with which I have performed the duties associated with my rank, over
a period of sixteen years, entitles me to the Minister's first consideration for
this appointment. It is, I am sure, unnecessary for me to recall my activities
at Geneva where it is generally recognised that I laid the groundwork for the
election of the Saorstát to a seat on the Council of the League of Nations, and,
in other ways, advanced her status and prestige.

I have a background of a military character which is not without its
advantages in France and have had friendly and close relations with two or
three former Ambassadors who now reside in the French capital. Many
members of the Paris Diplomatic Corps are old acquaintances of mine. I am
aware that certain difficulties have been encountered by Saorstát Ministers in
the establishment of closer contacts in French diplomatic and official circles
but these can hardly be regarded as being insurmountable. Tact and experience should be helpful in overcoming them. To have been for eight years a
Minister in the United States carries a certain amount of prestige in France
and a long acquaintanceship with American diplomats in Paris cannot but be
helpful. It is not difficult to foresee how this may be made to serve as a level
for strengthening and enlarging our official contacts with the French
Government. Both my wife and myself speak tolerably good French and
know France from one end to the other.

There are other reasons of a more personal character, though by no means
insignificant, why I should like to be appointed to Paris. I have a son[1] whom
I want to have educated in the Saorstát and brought up in a manner befitting
an Irish citizen. He attends Castleknock College at present. As the
Departmental regulations do not permit me to return to Ireland each year
except at a financial sacrifice I can ill afford, he must at considerable expense
come over here for his Summer holidays. Besides, were he to contract a
serious illness while at Castleknock neither his mother nor myself could get
to him in time to be of any comfort or service. My wife has also contracted
Sinus trouble while in this country. Local Health authorities report that this
complaint is, for some undetermined cause, endemic in the District of
Columbia. Like myself, she finds the climate here very exhausting, and quite
recently was sent by her Doctor to Bermuda in order to avoid a complete
breakdown.

I shall be obliged if you give this matter your most serious consideration
and bring it to the attention of the Minister at your early convenience.

Mise, le meas,
[signed] M. MacWhite

---

[1] Eoin MacWhite (1923-72), who later served in the Department of External Affairs including as Ambassador to Australia (1964-7) and the Netherlands (1967-72).

No. 37 NAI 2006/39

Letter from Joseph P. Walshe to John W. Dulanty (London)
(135/157)

DUBLIN, 18 March 1937

With reference to your Secret minute No. 16 of the 3rd instant[1] concerning the precautionary measures which will be taken in Great Britain in connection with the Coronation, you may assure the Dominions Office that arrangements will be made here to ensure the exercise of special vigilance at all Saorstát Éireann ports from the middle of April.

[signed] J.P. WALSHE
Rúnaí

No. 38 NAI DT S9735A

Extract from the minutes of the Executive Council (Dublin)
(C. 7/351) (Item 5)

DUBLIN, 23 March 1937

ITALY AND THE SAORSTÁT: Exchange of Diplomatic relations.
1. *Italian Legation at Dublin*
   The establishment of an Italian Legation at Dublin and the appointment thereto of Signor Romano Lodi Fé as Envoy Extraordinary and Minister Plenipotentiary was approved.
2. *Saorstát Legation at Rome.*
   The creation of a Saorstát Legation at Rome and the appointment thereto of an Envoy Extraordinary and Minister Plenipotentiary was approved.

No. 39 NAI 2003/17/181

Confidential report from John W. Dulanty to Joseph P. Walshe (Dublin)
(No. 23) (Secret)

LONDON, 23 March 1937

Confirming my telephone conversation with the Secretary on the 16th, I saw Mr. Malcolm MacDonald at his request in the House of Commons on that day.

He told me that he had sent fairly long cables on Tuesday of last week to the Dominions on the subject of our Constitutional Acts. His hope was that these other States would take the same line that the United Kingdom Government had taken, namely that the amendments to our Constitution were not incompatible with membership of the Commonwealth. In view, however, of the disappointing delay which he had experienced in getting replies from the Dominions on this question he would not give a date when he thought that position would be reached. At the outside, however, he

---

[1] See above No. 28.

hoped the United Kingdom Government would have replies to their cables in about a fortnight, – that is about the 29th March.

Assuming that agreement was reached with the other States, what did I think our position would be in regard to resuming conversations on the questions of defence, financial settlement, and trade agreement? I said that I had no instructions on the matter but I thought it likely that our position would be that which was outlined at the Grosvenor Hotel conversations with the President on the 15th January last when it was agreed that discussions on these questions might proceed before the views of the other Dominions had been obtained.[1]

Mr. MacDonald enquired whether the President would be ready to send Defence experts for the discussion on the ports etc. I said that the President whilst willing to send experts later would not consider it either necessary or desirable to send them until the general principles of our relations with Britain on defence had been determined. I reminded him that the previous conversations had not been really satisfactory from our point of view and I hoped that if they were resumed it would be on the basis of the United Kingdom representatives being able to put forward fairly definite statements. He reminded me that when they last tried to put definite statements in writing the result was not happy. I said that if they had a definite policy with regard to such a matter of defence it was surely not difficult to express it with better results than was the case with the Fisher letter.[2] He said that he would see what could be done in this regard.

Mr. MacDonald next said that he hoped on the question of financial settlement we could see our way to make some proposal. I told him that our position with regard to the annuities was clear. Throughout the conversations with the British officials I had been instructed to say that on this question we had no proposal to make since it appeared to us our position there was unassailable. Mr. MacDonald said he was quite sure the President would not think he was trying to manoeuvre so as to get some political advantage when asking for this proposal. His difficulty was that he doubted whether he could get his people to move at all unless we put forward some suggestion. I reminded him that we had months ago said on the ports that we were ready to remove any fears the British might have by putting our defences in such order as would provide against:-

(a) an attack on Britain through our country, or
(b) a common attack on both countries,

that our aim was to make our country safe for our own people and that we were willing at the same time to see that a free Ireland was not a source of danger to Britain. A condition precedent however to all this suggested defence provision of ours would be a financial settlement. Without that the money would not be available.

Mr. MacDonald said he thought when we got down to close consideration we would find that the defence provision would not cost a great deal. In

---

[1] See above Nos 3, 7 and 8.
[2] See DIFP Volume IV, Nos 358, 359, 361, 362, 363, 370, 372, 373, 374.

giving that opinion, which was his own merely, he was bearing in mind the relative strengths of the British and Irish exchequers.

Turning to the question of the arrangements for the Coronation he mentioned that they had got rid of the Lord High Constable of Ireland and also of the Dublin Herald attending the Westminster Abbey ceremony. They were trying to do the same with regard to the Ulster King-At-Arms but there the difficulty was that he was still functioning in that capacity and they were doubtful whether they could prohibit his attendance. The Lord High Steward of Ireland would attend in virtue of the fact that he would be discharging functions of the descendants of those who formerly acted in the same capacity. It was on this basis it will be recalled that the President told me informally he would not cause difficulty by raising objection.

With regard to the Standard Bearer of Ireland, Mr. MacDonald said they were in this difficulty. The Irish Standard was simply one of the quarterings of the Royal Standard and the bearing of the Royal Standard would be incomplete without the standard for each of the quarterings. I pointed out that this was not an hereditary office and whilst it was called a Standard of Ireland it could hardly be said to be representative of the Irish people. Its significance appeared to me to be merely historical and if the President were approached formally on the matter and decided to advise the King against the bearing of such a Standard the question would be settled. Mr. MacDonald said that he had had that point in mind already but the Royal Standard and its quarterings were matters of ancient royal prerogative. He hoped that in the circumstances we would not raise objection to this. I said I thought such a course might present real difficulties for us but Mr. MacDonald suggested that since the President had not been formally or officially approached he hoped he (the President) would regard himself as being free of the question.

[signed] J.W. DULANTY
High Commissioner

No. 40 NAI DFA 119/33

*Extracts from a report on the work of the High Commissioner's office
from March 1936 to March 1937 by Colman O'Donovan
to Joseph P. Walshe (Dublin)*

LONDON, 31 March 1937

[matter omitted]

POLITICAL AND ECONOMIC

2. In the sphere of international politics the year under review was no less notable than its predecessor, the outstanding event being the Civil War in Spain, and the setting up of the non-Intervention Committee with the double aim of preventing the conflict from spreading to other areas and bring it to an end with all possible speed. In common with the other countries in Europe (with the exception of Switzerland) the Saorstát was represented on the Committee and it fell to this office to keep the Government informed of the Committee's discussions and decisions and

to arrange for the taking by the Saorstát Government of the measures agreed upon by the Committee. In addition, when Land and Sea Observation schemes were established with a view to preventing the arrival in Spain of war materials or non-Spaniards proceeding to that country to take part in the conflict, the office made arrangements through the Department for the recruitment of personnel for the two schemes and later for the despatch of the selected officers to this posts.

3. Other activities of the office arising out of the trouble in Spain included the making of arrangements for the evacuation of Saorstát nationals in the early days of the conflict and efforts to secure the repatriation of under-age Saorstát nationals who at a later date joined up with one or other of the contending parties.

4. The Coal-Cattle arrangement came up for renewal in the month of January last and, following negotiations which have been reported on by Confidential Despatch, was enlarged in certain important respects. Arising out of this arrangement discussions took place with the appropriate British authorities regarding coal and cement prices.

[matter omitted]

9. One of the most important events of the year in the politico-economic sphere was the conclusion of the Trans-Atlantic Air Service Agreement. Current developments in this connection are followed through our representation on the ad hoc Committee which has been set up to receive reports of progress and to deal with the various matters arising for decision between the Governments concerned. This office has also been engaged in obtaining information in regard to airport design and construction in this country and elsewhere and other matters of interest in connection with the establishments to be set up in the Saorstát for the operation of the transatlantic service.

10. Of unique importance, though of short duration, was the constitutional crisis of December last. For many months previously arrangements had been proceeding for the Coronation of Edward VIII and industry had been experiencing something like boom conditions in working to satisfy the enormous demand for pottery and other articles commemorating the event. In little more than a week the crisis was resolved and Edward VIII passed into history. Even the Coronation programme was undisturbed and the present King was crowned with every appearance of popular enthusiasm on the day already fixed for the Coronation of his brother. Though the Government of the Saorstát took no part in the proceedings this office was affected by the event through having undertaken the distribution of 3,000 seats on official stands made available to visitors from the Saorstát.

[matter omitted]

SECRETARIAT

20. The work of the Secretarial side of this office ranges over a wide variety of subjects which it is neither necessary no practicable to enumerate in this Report. The registration of nationals under the Irish Nationality and

Citizenship Act continued during the year and brought with it enquiries on such complex questions as the position of Irish nationals in this country in regard to compulsory military service.

21. In connection with the consideration of applications for military service pensions much new work has been thrown on the office, the assistance of which has been invoked in many hundreds of cases for the purpose of ascertaining the facts in regard to the medical history of applicants during periods of political imprisonment in this country or Northern-Ireland or service in the British Army or Navy, and of obtaining particulars of any wound or other pensions received as a result of such latter service.

22. Another activity which increased considerably during the past year was the making of arrangements in suitable cases for the repatriation of Saorstát nationals who had become public charges in this country, the cost of transfer being in all cases borne by the public institution concerned here. The increase of such cases is doubtless a natural consequence of the growth of emigration from the Saorstát to this country which has been observable during the year. Various aspects of this question have been referred to in the press of both countries and the ecclesiastical authorities here have been in consultation with the Office in regard to the measures to be taken to ensure the welfare of Irish girls coming to this country to enter domestic service.

23. The ordering of stores of various kinds for the Department of Defence and the making of arrangements for their delivery and, where necessary, inspection, has figured prominently amongst the activities of the Secretariat. In addition attendances by officers of the Defence Department at various courses of Instruction at the War Office or Air Ministry establishments were arranged and facilities obtained for a study on the spot by officers of the same Department of the organisation of anti-air raid services in this country. Enquiries were also undertaken and visits to suitable centres arranged in connection with the project of establishing a Small Arms factory in the Saorstát, and the training of personnel of the Saorstát Aeronautical Engineering staff.

[matter omitted]

No. 41 NAI 2006/39

Letter from Seán Murphy to John W. Dulanty (London)
DUBLIN, 1 April 1937

The President does not wish to express any views on the proposal that the Irish Quartering of the Royal Standard should be carried out at the Coronation Ceremony. It should be clearly understood however that the carrying of the Irish Quartering does not in any way associate Saorstát Éireann with the Coronation Ceremony.

[signed] SEÁN MURPHY
Rúnaí

No. 42 NAI 2003/17/181

Letter from Seán Murphy to John W. Dulanty (London)
(Secret) (Copy)
DUBLIN, 1 April 1937

The President has carefully considered the question of letting Mr. MacDonald have the text of the Article of the new Constitution referred to in our conversation today. He feels that in all the circumstances, and in particular in the interest of the relations between the two countries, the new Constitution should be framed by the representatives of the Irish people solely in the interests of this country and without any consultation with any member of the British Commonwealth. For that reason he thinks it better not to send Mr. MacDonald the draft of the Constitution or the draft of the Article in question. You can inform Mr. MacDonald, however, that provision is being made in the new Constitution for the continuance of the position created by the Executive Authority (External Affairs) Act, and that in fact that Act will be continued. You may also inform him that there will be no article in the new Constitution corresponding to Article 1 of the present Constitution and there will be no mention of the King.

It is essential that the President should be able to say, if the question is asked, that the Constitution has been framed without any consultation with the British Government and that the latter are not in any way responsible, whether by way of suggestion or otherwise, for anything that appears in the Constitution.

(Sgd.) SEÁN MURPHY
Rúnaí

No. 43 UCDA P150/2419

Handwritten report from Joseph P. Walshe for Eamon de Valera (Dublin)
ROME, 22 April 1937

Secretary's report on his visit to Rome April 1937

The President

I arrived in Rome by air on Saturday 17th April about 4.30 p.m. having left Dublin by the Holyhead boat the previous evening.

Macaulay arranged an interview with Monsignore Pizzardo the Assistant Sec. of State for midday Sunday.

Monsignore Pizzardo received us with his usual cheerfulness, and when I explained the object of my visit he said that he saw no difficulty in getting the desired approval. This, as things happened, proved to be excessive optimism. He arranged an interview for us with the Cardinal S. of State[1] for Tuesday. Meanwhile I left with him, for the Cardinal's information, the first three sections of Art 45.[2] The Cardinal was most amiable. He kept us over an

---

[1] Cardinal Eugenio Pacelli.
[2] Article 45 of the new Irish constitution then being drafted.

hour well into lunch time as he did also on the two following days. I gave him an exposé of the background historical and religious in which the new Constitution came to be written, and I emphasised particularly the aspect of the 'appeasement' which you desired to bring about not only amongst our own people of all religious and political beliefs but also between our people and the British people. He was deeply interested in all I had to say about the aims you had set before you to accomplish, and he asked me endless questions.

I thought it well to say at a very early stage that you fully realised that the sections of the Constitution under discussion did not correspond with the complete Catholic ideal. You would like to have the approval of the Vatican in so far as it could be given. At any rate you wished to have the satisfaction of having let the Card. Sec. and the Holy Father see the sections relating to the Church before putting them before Parliament. Card. Pacelli expressed his great joy that you had done so. You should understand that whatever he and the Holy Father might say they were in the fullest sympathy with you and the Govt. in your difficulties, and thus appreciated how great a task it was to achieve anything like the Catholic ideal in the special circumstances. Nevertheless he would say with complete frankness and friendliness what he felt bound to say – though of course that would not detract from his good wishes and those of the Holy Father to you in your task. He said that he had had a preliminary chat with the Holy Father, but would of course see him again the following (Wednesday morning) in order to repeat to him the aperçu historique which I had just given him. He felt however that the 'special position' given to the Catholic Church had no real value so long as there was not a formal acknowledgement of the R.C. Church as the Church founded by Christ. Moreover its importance was based on numbers only (as far as the text was concerned) and the realisation given to the other churches mollified any advantage which might have been derived from exclusive recognition. He thought we should use the word 'tolerates' in regard to them. He could see no juridical consequence flowing from the text used which could confer advantages on the Catholic Church not equally conferred on the other bodies. Ireland was *the* Catholic Country of the world, and he thought we should have made a very special effort to give to the world a completely Catholic Constitution. I told him that I quite realized how important the form of the Constn was in the mind of the Vatican, but from what I had already said he would agree that we had abstained from using the forms in order to be able to keep the realities. In our case the full Catholic framework would destroy absolutely the building which we desired to construct. We had to take the long view in order to reconcile the most hostile religious opinions, and to get all our people to work for our common country.

Catholic forms in the rigid sense incorporated into our Constitution now would defeat that purpose, and would also certainly defeat the purpose which he and the H.F. had in mind, namely the establishment of permanent peace in our country, and peace with G.B. (an almost exclusively protestant country). Above all they would hinder the growth and influence of the Catholic Church in Ireland and Great B. and would revive all the old accusations of intransigence and intolerance. In real truth, in our Constitution, we were being more Catholic than the Church because we were assuming the ultimate success of the aims of the Church, while the Cardinal's suggestion might well destroy all chance of ever attaining them. The Cardinal all the time insisted that he was talking as a Church man must talk and he never once departed during all our conversation from his attitude of the greatest possible friendliness. From the beginning he made me feel free from any sense of embarrassment whatsoever, and he encouraged me to be as frank with him as he was with me. I think that I did not omit any explanation or argument which could reasonably be offered. But it became clear at a very early stage of our conversations that we should not succeed in getting any expression of approval of the text from the Vatican. From the nature of things they have to stake their full claim, and formal or indeed informal approval was not to be given to a text which did not come down completely on the side of strict Catholic doctrine. The Cardinal told me with a smile but quite truthfully that according to the strict teaching of the Church we were heretics to recognise any church but the one true church of Christ. Again I reminded him of the danger of seeing only the form and he assured me at once that the Church would not take an heresy too seriously. It did not shake him when I contrasted the expressly Xtain[1] character of the new Const. with the liberalism (continental sense) of the old though he recognized the great change for the better. He promised to have a long talk with the Holy Father and to obtain his blessing for Govt. for having done so well in such difficult circumstances. It was clear when saying this that the Cardinal did not realize that the Holy Father was going to adopt the negative attitude which he made known to me the following day. Indeed he gave me the very clear impression that having said all *he* could say, he was going to get the Pope to bless the Govt. for the effort they had made to meet the Catholic view point – without making any reference to the Const.

I need hardly therefore say that I was very disappointed when I received from the Cardinal yesterday the exact text of the words used by the Holy Father, 'Ni approvo ni non disapprovo; taceremo'. And the Cardinal did not leave me any doubt as to the meaning. I had asked him to ensure at least that the H.F. would not disapprove. The answer was: 'I do not approve, neither do I *not disapprove* we shall maintain silence'. I tried to translate the evil out of this double negative but the Cardinal held me to the sense. He went on to show that the H.F. was doing quite a lot in saying that he would maintain silence. It was an attitude of complete neutrality. He might have taken the text without bearing in mind all the implications of the explanations I had given, because the text after all was what counted, but he refrained from disapproving. He would not say 'I approve' and while he would not say 'I do not disapprove' he took the middle position of keeping silence. So argued the Cardinal and while he clearly wanted to give us a crumb of consolation he had to maintain that the Pope went to the extreme limit to which his position allowed him to go.

---

[1] 'Christian'.

On the question of marriage which they regard as one of the supreme tests of the Catholicism of a State the Cardinal said we were also heretical. Cases of nullity and of 'ratum et non consummatum' (in the case of marriages celebrated in the Church) are within the Exclusive domain of the Church and must be formally declared so to be.

I told him of the difficulties of taking that attitude in a country of mixed religions where divorce was forbidden to all. The non-Catholics could justifiably complain that a way of escape lay open to Catholics which was not available for them. I touched lightly on the difficulties 'ratione scandali' which could arise from cases in which evidence relating to defective intention for example might satisfy the ecclesiastical but not the lay mind. The Cardinal pointed out that the Yugoslav Govt. had recently concluded a concordat with the Holy See formally accepting the full Catholic doctrine. I suggested that as the Concordat was the subject of very serious quarrels between the Orthodox Church and the Govt. the latter might not be able to ratify it against the will of the majority of their people, and that in the end it may prove to have been a grave mistake to insist on the full pound of flesh. The Cardinal admitted this, but he seemed to regard the displeasure of the Orthodox Church with a certain amount of satisfaction.

I insisted again and again that we regarded the fundamentally sound position of the Church in the hearts of the people as an infinitely greater safeguard for Catholic doctrine than forms in any documents whether constitutions or Concordats – and that that conviction was never absent from your mind when drawing up the constitution. The Holy Father and he the Cardinal, would realize, as our State evolved – that we had acted in the best interests of the Church as well as of the people.

At the Cardinal's request we went back again to see him today Thursday. He told me how very ill the Pope had been and that there were several ministers accredited to the Vatican whom he had never seen and who would be annoyed if they heard – and they would hear – that he had given a private audience to me. However there were some people whom in the normal course he had to see on Saturday – and he would like Mr. Macaulay and myself to come with them. He would be able to give us his Blessing and perhaps say a word to us.

The Cardinal then asked me about the Coronation and our attitude regarding it. I explained to him our general attitude and also the particular objection we had to the continuing anti-catholic character of the ceremony as stated publicly by you. I took the opportunity of saying that there were rumours in Ireland that the Legate was to attend the ceremony at Westminster, but that we naturally did not believe it. He assured me with great emphasis that they never had contemplated allowing the Legate to be present. 'If that happened' he said, laughing heartily, 'your Govt. would certainly be plus Catholique que l'eglise' and they would be right. Attendance as a spectator was of course permissible even for a Legate but the 'ratio scandali' was an all sufficient and compelling reason for abstention.

I thanked the Cardinal for his great kindness. He asked to be warmly remembered to you and to thank you for your courtesy in having sent me.

I wish to add that the position of influence with the Cardinal which is held by Mr. Macaulay and his wife and the great friendship which he has for them made my task very easy and pleasant. The Cardinal's attitude from the first moment, and I must repeat that, could not have been more friendly.

The Cardinal on Tuesday expressed himself as very pleased that you intended to use the 'full official title of the Church' which he compared carefully with the title in the text of the Lateran Treaty.[1] He said that the H.F. would of course also be very pleased. I did not ask him a second time about the title as he was clear beyond misapprehension the first time. I am sorry that my telegram was not sufficiently clear about this point. 'Other Christian Churches' he could not formally approve, but let it go without taking any responsibility for it. He thought 'Bodies' would be more appropriate. Again I had to explain that in using the word 'Church' we were following the local custom and doing only what ordinary courtesy required. We did not intend to imply and nobody in our country would regard us as attempting to imply that there was any Church in the strict sense other than the one true Church. He gave me a long and very interesting discourse on the oneness of the Church and the impossibility of having a plurality of them and he quoted a good deal from an encyclical of the present Pope (6 Jan 1928) which immediately struck me as being a superb and very beautiful statement of the position.

To conclude this scanty and hastily written report I want to express my great regret at not having been able to do what I was sent out to do. But I have learned a great deal about the attitude of the Holy See to such matters and I can assure you, most confidently, that at the back of their adherence to rigid forms and dogmas there is very sincere respect, and even gratitude for the extent to which you have been able to go in making our Constit. Catholic, notwithstanding the very great difficulties which they understand better than they pretend to understand them. I will of course amplify this report viva voca on my return.

J.P.W. 22nd April 1937

No. 44 UCDA P150/2419

*Code telegram from the Department of External Affairs to
Joseph P. Walshe (Rome) (Copy)*
DUBLIN, 22 April 1937

Reference my telegram April 21st[2] President also anxious to know whether official title of Church approved by the Pope. Your telegram No. 5[3] says that Pacelli gratified by title.

ESTERO

---

[1] The Lateran Treaty of 11 February 1929 (modified in 1985) regulated the relations between Italy and the Vatican City. It provided a solution to the 'Roman Question' which had arisen in 1870 when Rome was incorporated into the Kingdom of Italy. Under the treaty, the Italian state renounced all claims to Vatican territory and the Vatican City, recognised the Italian state and became an independent sovereign state. A concordat to the treaty defined the rights of the two states in the realms of education and spiritual matters.
[2] Not printed.
[3] Not printed.

No. 45 UCDA P150/2419

Code telegram from Joseph P. Walshe to the Department of External Affairs (Dublin)
(Copy)

ROME, 23 April 1937

Your telegram about official title.[1] Approved by Pope. It is 'The Holy Catholic Apostolic and Roman Church'.

WALSHE

No. 46 NAI 2003/17/181

Minute signed by Seán Murphy (for Joseph P. Walshe) to
John W. Dulanty (London)
(Secret) (Copy)

DUBLIN, 24 April 1937

I send you herewith memorandum to be handed to Mr. MacDonald in reply to the memorandum which he handed to you on the 3rd April.[2] The memorandum has the same informal character as Mr. MacDonald's.

Copies of Mr. MacDonald's memoranda are enclosed.

(Signed) SEÁN MURPHY
Rúnaí

[Enclosure][3]

1. The Government of Saorstát Éireann (to be known after the passing of the Constitution as 'Éire') have received the Note handed by Mr. MacDonald to Mr. Dulanty on the 3rd April setting forth the attitude of the Governments of the United Kingdom, Canada, Australia, South Africa and New Zealand on the recent Constitutional legislation of Saorstát Éireann. The Government of Saorstát Éireann note that the Governments of Canada, the Commonwealth of Australia, New Zealand and the Union of South Africa are prepared to treat the Irish Free State legislation in question as not affecting a fundamental alteration in the position of the Irish Free State as a Member of the British Commonwealth of Nations. They note further that the United Kingdom Government, in reaching the same conclusion, have formulated three propositions. The Government of Saorstát Éireann do not wish to enter into a controversy as to the precise meaning and implications of these propositions. They would like to point out, however, that the acceptance of (ii) and (iii) as they stand would seem to imply that in certain vital aspects of their Constitutional development no further evolution of the individual States of the Commonwealth is possible.

2. With regard to the first proposition, it would be impossible for any Government in Saorstát Éireann to express an unqualified desire to remain a

---

[1] See above No. 44.
[2] MacDonald's memorandum not printed.
[3] Marginal notes: 'Approved by President S.M., 23/4/37.'; 'Handed to Mr. MacDonald by Mr. Dulanty on 27 April, 1937' (by Sheila Murphy).

Member of the British Commonwealth of Nations whilst Ireland remains a partitioned nation. On the other hand, the Government of Saorstát Éireann would regard the removal of the inequalities of the Treaty position and the acceptance of the association of Saorstát Éireann with the Commonwealth in a manner consistent with Ireland's history and aspirations as definite steps towards the desired unity and the establishment of friendly relations between Ireland and Great Britain.

3. With regard to a departure from the provisions of the Articles of Agreement mentioned in paragraph 2 of the United Kingdom Government's Note, it need only be said that the evolution in the status of the Members of the Commonwealth which has taken place since the Articles of Agreement were signed has created an entirely new situation; these Articles of Agreement have been gradually replaced by legislation in the Irish Parliament based on declared principles of co-equality. It is on the basis of these principles also that the new Constitution about to be presented to the people has been drawn up. The Articles of Agreement postulated control of the Irish Parliament by the British Parliament. Until that situation was ended no approach to a final settlement between the peoples of the two countries could be made.

4. The Government of Saorstát Éireann fully endorse the hope expressed by the United Kingdom Government that there may be a fuller development of co-operation in all matters of common concern between them, and they share the belief that such co-operation would be in the mutual interests of both peoples.

No. 47 NAI 2003/17/181

Confidential report from John W. Dulanty to Joseph P. Walshe (Dublin)
(No. 25) (Secret)[1]

LONDON, 26 April 1937

In accordance with the arrangement already notified to the Department I met at the British Treasury Sir Warren Fisher, Sir Horace Wilson, and Sir Edward Harding, on the 23rd instant. Sir Warren Fisher enquired what had taken place in the conversations after he had had to drop out of the talks last Autumn.[2] Sir Horace Wilson said that he and Sir Harry Batterbee had had conversations with me which turned on the constitutional aspect. Until the questions on that had been resolved it had not been possible to discuss even in a tentative way questions of defence, financial settlement, and trade agreement.

In answer to Sir Warren Fisher I explained the main provisions of our two Constitutional Acts of December last and gave a summary of what had passed between the President and Mr. MacDonald in London in January last.[3] (Sir Edward Harding was away on tour in Australia and New Zealand when the President and Mr. MacDonald met.)

---

[1] Marginal note by Joseph P. Walshe: 'Recd. in the Depart. 29th April 37'.
[2] See DIFP Volume IV, Nos 358, 359, 361, 362, 363, 370, 372, 373, 374.
[3] See above Nos 3, 7 and 8.

Sir Warren Fisher repeated what he had said last Autumn about the paragraphs dealing with defence in his letter.[1] This letter he said he had signed against his better judgment. Whilst of course nobody could force him to sign the letter he had signed it because he felt that unless a letter of some kind issued conversations were not likely to begin. He asked me again to assure the President that neither he nor his colleagues wished on this matter of defence to assume what I had myself described as a 'master and servant relationship' instead of that of free equals. The United Kingdom would be glad to consider the question of defence. If his letter were not satisfactory would I tell him in what particular respect or respects it failed? I expressed surprise at this question because our position had been made crystal clear when the President talked to Mr. MacDonald on the 15th January last.[2] The position then clearly defined by the President was that the ports were Irish and not British ports. The British had no right there. They ought to leave and not seek to return except on our invitation and with our goodwill. We were not imperially minded nor had we any imperial interests. The nearer we could get to a position of neutrality the better. The President had made it clear that in our own interests we would not allow our territory to be used as a base of attack on Britain, but obviously we could only be at war when our interests were jeopardised and the Dáil had so decided. Our first aim must always be to make our country safe for our own people but we would see to it that a free Ireland was not a source of danger to Britain.

I recalled that months ago I had told these gentlemen that we were ready and willing to remove any fears the British might have by putting our defences in such order as would provide against:
(a) an attack on Britain through our country, or
(b) a common attack on both countries.

If the British genuinely wanted to meet us what they must avoid was even the appearance of insisting upon occupation of the ports in any circumstances except by our free invitation. In this, as in other matters, the true basis of co-operation was the mutual interests of both parties. It would from our point of view be fatal for the British to endeavour to make the use of our ports by them whenever they wanted a condition of any settlement.

Sir Warren Fisher said that he could well understand the President's point of view and he did not think that the British Government would press for the use of our ports whenever they wanted them. Sir Horace Wilson also recognised the difficulties from our point of view but he hoped that we would see that if England were at war with a European power the fact that Ireland – apart entirely from any Commonwealth connection – was an immediate and valuable source of strength to England for food and possibly other supplies would mean that England's enemies would inevitably attack Ireland. Even if the war were in Asia, with for example Japan, enemy ships coming through the Panama Canal and travelling at the great pace which modern vessels have achieved could easily jeopardise England's trade routes for supplies of

---

[1] See DIFP Volume IV, Nos 358, 359, 361, 362, 363, 370, 372, 373, 374.
[2] See above Nos 3, 7 and 8.

food and munitions. He thought that something could be done to meet the President's difficulty about prior assurance. The United Kingdom had understandings with Dominions and certain foreign countries of a mutual and reciprocal character. Avoiding entirely the idea of assurances or undertakings from us and aiming solely at a mutual reciprocal understanding could we not suggest some form of words which would not infringe our sovereignty and at the same time meet Britain's requirements by allaying their fears about the use – even though against our will – of Irish territory by enemy forces attacking Britain. I said that I would put this suggestion before my Government. Speaking for myself, I thought that some understanding such as that which I believe existed before 1914 between Belgium and France might have a suggestive value for the proposed formula.

[signed] J.W. DULANTY
High Commissioner

No. 48 NAI DFA Secretary's Files S1

Letter from James J. McElligott to Seán Murphy (Dublin)
DUBLIN, 27 April 1937

Dear Murphy,
With reference to your note of yesterday's date[1] about the Parliamentary Question put down by Deputy O'Neill regarding the amounts withheld from Great Britain and the yield from the British special duties on Irish Free State produce, the total amount so collected by the British in the four years to which the Deputy refers was £19,382,229 of which £9,794 was due to the Isle of Man, leaving £19,372,435, the amount referred to by the Deputy, available for the British Exchequer. The figures for the first three years have been taken from the British Finance Accounts and for 1936/37 from the Statement of Revenue and Expenditure laid before the British House of Commons by the Chancellor of the Exchequer[2] when opening the Budget this year.

We *estimate* the amount withheld from the British in the same four years at £19,314,162, as compared with the Deputy's figure of £19,309,668. Firm figures are available for all the items except Land Annuities, which, as you are aware, were revised by the Land Act 1933 and it would involve a very considerable amount of time and labour in arriving at the figure which would be paid to the British under that head if the annuities had not been revised and the dispute had not arisen. I think, however, that the estimate I have given above is sufficiently close for all practical purposes.

The Deputy has ignored the financial year 1932/3 during which the dispute started. In that year the amount withheld was £4,771,617 and the amount paid into the British Exchequer (i.e. ignoring the Isle of Man) in that year, on foot of the special duties, was £2,514,084. If these figures are added to the ones I have given for the subsequent four years you will see that from the commencement of the dispute up to the 31st March last instead of there

---

[1] Not printed.
[2] Neville Chamberlain.

being a credit balance in favour of Britain there has been a fairly substantial deficit.

Yours sincerely,
[signed] J.J. McELLIGOTT

No. 49 NAI 2003/17/181

Confidential report from John W. Dulanty to Joseph P. Walshe (Dublin)
(No. 26) (Secret)

LONDON, 28 April 1937

In accordance with the Department's Secret minute of the 24th April[1] I handed yesterday to Mr. MacDonald the informal memorandum enclosed with that minute which was a reply to the informal memorandum which Mr. MacDonald handed to me on the 3rd April.

After reading the memorandum through Mr. MacDonald said it would obviously be necessary for him to study it carefully and later consult with his colleagues.

Subject to this further study and consultation he thought that the document might be regarded as satisfactory but he was not easy in his mind about that portion of paragraph 1 of our informal memorandum which referred to (ii) and (iii) of Mr. MacDonald's informal memorandum. He thought the question which his colleagues would be certain to press on him would be this: leaving aside for the moment the question of what might or might not be the evolution of the Commonwealth in time to come did (ii) and (iii) of his informal memorandum describe the position as it existed today from the Irish Free State point of view?

No comment was made by Mr. MacDonald on (1) of his informal memorandum, namely, about An Saorstát desiring to remain a co-equal member of the British Commonwealth of Nations.

In view of the fact that he had communicated to the other Member States of the Commonwealth the terms of his informal memorandum Mr. MacDonald thought he should communicate the terms of our informal memorandum in reply. I said it would be necessary obviously for me to obtain the President's instruction. Perhaps you will let me know what reply should be made on this point.

Mr. MacDonald asked if I could tell him whether there was still a chance of our Government sending a delegation to the Imperial Conference. I said that I had no information beyond that contained in the President's statements in the Dáil from which the obvious deduction was that we would not have a delegation at the Conference. At this Mr. MacDonald seemed disconcerted. He recognised he said that the conversations in the Grosvenor Hotel with the President were frank and unrestrained on both sides and were subject to modification in the light of later reflection.[2] There had however been no

---

[1] See above No. 46.
[2] See above Nos 3, 7 and 8.

doubt about the President's sharing his (Mr. MacDonald's) wish for co-operation. He also understood the President to say that there would be much greater chance of co-operation so soon as the constitutional questions had been resolved. With that end in view he, Mr. MacDonald, had got his colleagues in the Cabinet and the other Member States of the Commonwealth to adopt the view they had adopted and now the Imperial Conference presented a splendid opportunity for co-operation. Our delegates need not worry about the Coronation ceremonies but they could make their valuable contribution to the discussions at the Conference and, more than all, beside the Imperial Conference there would be the invaluable opportunity of discussion and consultation between his Government and ours on the matters outstanding between us. He would entreat the President to consider the chance which this Conference offered possibly of solving defence, financial settlement, and trade agreement. I asked about the unity of Ireland. He said that was a question they were quite ready to consider but he did not think there was the same chance of reaching a very early settlement on that as on the other matters he had named.

[signed] J.W. DULANTY
High Commissioner

No. 50 NAI 2003/17/181

Confidential report from John W. Dulanty to Joseph P. Walshe (Dublin)
(No. 28) (Secret)[1]

LONDON, 30 April 1937

At Mr. Malcolm MacDonald's request I saw him in his office this evening. Mr. MacDonald said that he had seen in the newspapers a report of replies made by the President to questions in the Dáil as to whether the Government of Saorstát Éireann would be represented at the forthcoming Imperial Conference. He had had however no official communication. On the 27th March of last year the Prime Minister of the United Kingdom had communicated with the Member States of the Commonwealth and invited their agreement to the holding of the Conference in May of this year. All that the United Kingdom Government had received in reply thereto was a short note stating that the Government of Saorstát Éireann had no comment to make on the proposal to hold the Conference.[2]

The United Kingdom Government naturally would like to know whether the President intended to send a delegation. They had to decide on the circulation of important secret documents which were to be discussed at the Conference and he did not see how he could circulate these confidential papers to us if we did not propose to attend. There were other minor details of organisation such as the reservation of seats at the Conference table on which they could not proceed until they knew definitely and officially what our intentions were.

---

[1] Marginal note by Sheila Murphy: 'Original letter on File S.2.'
[2] See DIFP Volume IV, No. 392.

I said that I would get instructions on this matter. I did however remind Mr. MacDonald of a conversation some time ago when I said that unless the United Kingdom Government bestirred themselves to reach a solution on all questions outstanding between them and us we did not see how any Government in Dublin could send a delegation to the London Conference.

Mr. MacDonald did not dispute this but he thought it was reasonable to expect us to inform them officially whether or not we were coming to the Conference. He sincerely hoped that we might be. It was scarcely possible to exaggerate the importance of the discussions which would take place in London this month. The United Kingdom Government would make the fullest and frankest statements about the European situation, particularly their relations with Germany and Italy, and also the fullest information would be given as regards the position in the Far East in their relations with Japan. Geneva he thought would be child's play compared with the far-reaching importance of the discussions on international politics and the dispositions of the United Kingdom forces for defence.

He referred again to the conversations with the President in January and said that it was due in large measure to personal contact with the President on that occasion that he had secured the assent of his colleagues to the view that our December Constitutional Acts did not bring about any fundamental alteration in our association with the Member States of the Commonwealth.

He had told his colleagues that he had understood from the President that when the constitutional question was resolved there would be much greater possibility of co-operation between the two countries. Mr. MacDonald thought that he had got the Cabinet to accept, though reluctantly, our December Acts and now there was a unique opportunity for co-operation of which the President apparently was refusing to avail himself.

I said that I was present at all the Grosvenor Hotel talks and there was certainly no ground for suggestion that if the Constitution problem was solved the President would attend the Imperial Conference. What the President said still held. There were opportunities for co-operation entirely apart from the Imperial Conference as Mr. MacDonald himself had shown in the importance which he attached to the secret informal conversations between myself, Sir Warren Fisher, and Sir Horace Wilson.

Mr. MacDonald thought that our abstention from the Conference would have a prejudicial effect on the minds of the other statesmen. My rejoinder to that was that differences between ourselves and the United Kingdom were limited to the political relations of these two islands and did not directly involve Canada, South Africa, or any other of the Member States. The fault for the division of our country could not be laid at their doors and I did not see how they could accept responsibility in any of the other questions such as the ports, financial settlement or trade agreement at present outstanding between us.

Mr. MacDonald agreed but went on to say that we could make an effective contribution on the discussions of vital interest to each member of the group, and then over and above those group questions the United Kingdom people and ourselves could, apart from the Conference, get to grips on the ~~se other~~[1] Irish-English[2] questions.

I said that I would communicate these views and give him a reply as soon as possible on the question of our attendance or non-attendance at the London Conference.

No. 51 NAUK DO 35/890/12

> *Letter from John W. Dulanty to Malcolm MacDonald (London)*
> LONDON, 1 May 1937

See facsimile of this document on page 62.

No. 52 NAI DFA 227/87

> *Letter from John W. Dulanty to Francis Hemming[3] (London)*
> *(Secret) (Copy)*
> LONDON, 1 May 1937

Dear Mr. Hemming,
I am writing with reference to your letter of the 5th instant, No. E.A.C./736,[4] to inform you that the Government of the Irish Free State would favour the extension of the Non-Intervention Agreement in such a way as to secure the co-operation of non-European countries.

Yours sincerely,
(Signed) J.W. DULANTY

No. 53 NAI DFA Paris Embassy 19/34

> *Code telegram from Art O'Brien to the Department of External Affairs (Dublin)*
> *(No. 54) (Copy)*
> PARIS, 19 May 1937

Yesterday Saturday evening at Concours Hippique Captain Lewis[5] won first individual prize Coupe Cavalerie Française. At distribution prizes the military band instead of playing Irish national anthem put on a very bad gramophone record of 'O'Donnell Abu' to amazement of all diplomatists and teams present. That a military band at an international show is ignorant of national anthem of an invited guest nation, and gives instead bad gramophone record of another air is a public insult which no country would or should tolerate. The insult is rendered inexcusable by fact that invitation was accepted through French Government intermediary many weeks ago. Appropriate

---

[1] The letters 'se' and the word 'other' have been crossed out in the original.
[2] The designation 'Irish-English' has been inserted by hand by Dulanty.
[3] Secretary to the International Non-Intervention Committee.
[4] Not printed.
[5] Captain John Lewis, Army Equitation School, Irish Defence Forces.

10

HIGH COMMISSIONER
FOR IRISH FREE STATE

33-37 REGENT ST,
LONDON, S. W. I.

SAORSTÁT ÉIREANN

1st May, 1937

Dear Secretary of State,

I beg to hand you herewith a copy
of the Draft Constitution *of the State of Éire*.

Yours sincerely,

[signature]

The Right Honourable Malcolm MacDonald, M.P.,
Secretary of State for Dominion Affairs
Dominions Office
S.W.1

action would be to withdraw our team from remainder of Concours unless public apology be made by radio announcement at Concours, by statement to the Press, by letter from Foreign Office and also Ministry of War. Do you authorize me to proceed on those lines or do you wish for more drastic action. I think this procedure will be successful. I have already verbally advised Chef du Protocole that a very strong written protest will be lodged with Foreign Office to-morrow. Have also advised President of Concours that if similar incident occurs to-day I and my guests will demonstratively retire at once and our team will ride out of the ring. Minister of War verbally expressed regret to Captain Corry[1] this morning, but Captain said matter was diplomatic and that Irish Minister would deal with it. I am awaiting your urgent reply ENDS

EIREANN

No. 54 NAI DT S9092A

Extract from the report of the interdepartmental committee[2] set up to examine the establishment of a short wave broadcasting station

DUBLIN, 12 May 1937

[matter omitted]
(1) *The utility of a Short Wave Station*
In the present stage of technical development of radio science the chief function of a Short Wave Broadcasting Station in the Saorstát would be to serve listeners in distant extra-territorial regions. At present the principal sphere of usefulness of Short Wave broadcasting is for news and the spoken word, as limitations of the transmitting medium render it difficult to receive music with the fidelity necessary for its complete enjoyment. Listeners within the Saorstát would not be catered for by a Short Wave Station and such a Station would, in consequence, not induce an increase in the number of wireless licences held here or lead to an augmentation of Broadcasting revenue. Therefore, in considering the question of the establishment of a Short Wave Station, it has to be recognised that, in respect of the expenditure which would necessarily be incurred, there would be no set-off in the form of additional revenue, unless sponsored programmes were permitted and we are not in a position to anticipate that such permission would be given. Even, however, if sponsored programmes were permitted they could not be relied upon for regular and permanent income.

The main object of a Station whose field of service would lie wholly in distant countries would, we assume, be to serve as a vehicle for National propaganda. It could be employed to reach people of our race abroad when it is desired to keep in touch with affairs in the motherland, or foreigners whom it is considered desirable to win to a particular point of view on political or commercial matters; also, and perhaps most important of all, it could

---

[1] Captain Dan J. Corry, Army Equitation School, Irish Defence Forces.
[2] The committee was comprised of representatives of the Department of External Affairs, the Department of Finance and the Department of Posts and Telegraphs.

be used for countering propaganda of an unfavourable nature which, either openly or in veiled form, is a not uncommon feature of news broadcasts of outside origin. There is scope too for the dissemination of programmes reflective of the artistic and general cultural standards of the country. For these purposes Short Wave broadcasting is the most effective instrument at the disposal of the State. There are, however, technical difficulties which we deal with in paragraphs (3) and (4) below.[1]

Then weighing the need for a Short Wave Broadcasting Station it is of interest to note that, apart from the wealthier countries, such small countries as Bulgaria, Czecho Slovakia, Hungary, Norway, Poland, Yugoslavia, etc. have already erected Short Wave Broadcasting Stations.
[matter omitted]

No. 55 NAI DFA Madrid Embassy IP 3/6

Confidential report from Leopold H. Kerney to Joseph P. Walshe (Dublin)
(S.J. 51/1) (Confidential)
St Jean de Luz, 12 May 1937

I called on the Duchess of Tetuan yesterday in San Sebastian, where she is now living; she had just returned from Salamanca, where she spent the last few weeks and where she was a guest of Fr. McCabe[2] at the Irish College. O'Duffy went to meet her there. She was anxious to see him; she is well disposed towards O'Duffy and not inclined to criticise him but she thinks him somewhat 'fantastique'. She asked me to treat confidentially any information which I picked up in the course of my conversation with her.

There has been friction between O'Duffy and General Yagüe.[3] The Duchess believes that a couple of the Spanish liaison officers (of whom I understand there are about 5 in all) are largely responsible for this state of affairs, because of their propensity for carrying tales to headquarters. O'Duffy is perfectly satisfied with the conduct of his men, but the Spanish military authorities are definitely of opinion that they are very undisciplined and are much given to drinking; the Duchess says there have even been some cases of shooting amongst themselves. The lack of discipline led to a demand on the part of the military authorities that a Spanish officer (a commandant or major) should be put in charge of them, presumably under O'Duffy's generalship. Yagüe made this demand and Franco approved of it. O'Duffy refused flatly. This is the big difficulty that has arisen; my personal opinion is that it is a convenient difficulty and is a pretext rather than the real cause for O'Duffy's recent decision, unless the proposed appointment meant in reality the shelving of O'Duffy.

The Duchess, who is if anything prejudiced in favour of O'Duffy and his men, made every effort to bring about some agreement between O'Duffy and

---

[1] Not printed.
[2] Father Alexander McCabe, Rector of the Irish College in Salamanca.
[3] Colonel Juan de Yagüe Blanco (1891-1952), commander of the Tercio under which the Irish Bandera were to form.

the military authorities; she is concerned at the harm which may be done to Irish prestige by O'Duffy's departure; Spanish newspaper readers in Franco's territory are not yet aware of this impending event. The 'bandera' was not engaged in any actual fighting, but had had continuous service near the front, and needed a rest. The men were badly clothed and needed new uniforms. A proposal was made that they should be transferred from General Yagüe's control to that of General Mola[1] on the Santander front, that they should be supplied with new uniforms, that they should be given three weeks' rest and that they should have a Spanish officer in charge of them. There was agreement on the first three points but not on the last, and on this last point both O'Duffy and the Spanish General Staff are equally unyielding.

The present position is that the 'bandera' has been disbanded and that the men are stationed in Caceres pending the completion of the arrangements by the Spanish authorities for their embarkment at El Ferrol (the naval base near Corunna[2]); I do not know whether the ship will transport the men direct to Ireland or via Liverpool.

The Duchess thinks there were not more than about 650 men in O'Duffy's 'bandera'; one of the men had a leg amputated; she thinks, but is not sure, that this man is a minor. She says that O'Duffy was constantly with his men, but that he was criticised for giving orders direct to the men rather than through their officers and that his manner was not that of a general. She quotes General Yagüe as saying that the worst possible Irishmen had been sent to Spain and that it would be a good riddance to pack them all into aeroplanes and send them over to the 'Reds'.

The Duchess says there are 3 or 4 Irish volunteers ill in hospital at Salamanca, one of these suffering from tuberculosis; she visited them. If there are any wounded or sick who are unable to travel, I presume that the Spanish authorities will care for them whilst in hospital, but that, if and when they are discharged as cured or incurable, the question of their repatriation at public expense will arise for consideration.

Aire Lán-Chómhachtach

No. 56 NAI DFA Paris Embassy 19/34

Confidential report from Art O'Brien to Joseph P. Walshe (Dublin)
(E19/34)

PARIS, 14 May 1937

Incident of National Anthem – Concours Hippique Paris 1937
I attach hereto copy of my telegram No. 54[3] which was dispatched to you in code on Sunday last, the 9th of May. In reply to this telegram, you telephoned

---

[1] General Emilio Mola Vidal (1887-1937), Military Governor in Pamplona (Feb. 1936), one of the leaders of the 1936 army revolt. During the Spanish Civil War Mola was commander of the Army of the North. He was killed on 3 June 1937 when his aircraft crashed during bad weather.
[2] Coruña.
[3] See above No. 53.

me on Monday the 10th, instructing me that you would be satisfied if an apology were made over the loud speakers at the Concours Hippique at some appropriate time during the competitions on Tuesday the 11th of May (N.B. There were no competitions on May the 10th) followed by the playing of the correct National Anthem at some appropriate time during the competitions.

I attach also hereto a copy of my telegram No. 55 dispatched to you in code on Tuesday the 11th of May,[1] giving the results of my interview with the Foreign Office and the arrangement agreed to thereat.

These two telegrams give a general impression of what exactly happened, It is, however, perhaps as well that I should enlarge on the text of those telegrams to some extent in order that the whole course of events may be clear to you.

On Saturday evening the 8th of May, Captain Lewis won the first individual prize in the competition for the Coupe de la Cavalarie française. Following the usual procedure, the winners rode into the ring in order of place and when the first prize was announced, to the amazement of all present who were acquainted with the Irish National Anthem, instead of hearing the military band play Amhrán Na bhFiann, we heard the air of O'Donnell Abu very badly rendered on a bad gramophone record. At the time, I happened to be standing and was caught unawares. The Belgian Ambassador and other diplomats in the special boxes looked round to my box and seeing me standing, they also stood. Captain Lewis was also taken unawares and was at the salute.

This incident happened at about 11.30 p.m., right at the end of the Concours. It was consequently too late to take any action that evening.

I went then from the Concours to the Polish Embassy where a soirée was being held and almost the first person who I met there was M. de Fouquiéres, the Chef du Protocole. I took the opportunity of relating to him immediately what had happened and making a protest at what I considered a very serious discourtesy both to Ireland and to the Irish team. I informed M. de Fouquiéres that I would be sending a letter of protest to the Foreign Office early on Monday morning the 10th of May.[2] M. de Fouquiéres was very much upset at the incident and expressed to me at once his personal regret and told me that the matter would receive immediate and careful attention.

On Monday morning the 10th of May, I sent a letter addressed to M. Yvon Delbos,[3] Minister of Foreign Affairs, copy of which I attach hereto.

In the meantime on Sunday morning the 9th of May, I had a meeting with Captain Corry, the chef d'équipe, and having discussed the whole matter with him I informed him of what I thought should be done in the event of a repetition of this incident during the course of the competitions on Sunday afternoon. Captain Corry and the other members of the team were to attend on that same morning at the Ministry of War in order to be presented to the

---

[1] Not printed.
[2] Not printed.
[3] Yvon Delbos (1885-1956), French Radical politician and Minister for Foreign Affairs (1936-8) in the Popular Front governments.

Minister. After the reception had taken place, the Minister of War asked for Captain Corry especially and expressed to him his personal regret for what had happened. Captain Corry after the reception came to see me again and informed me of what had happened.

On that day (Sunday), I arrived at the Concours a quarter of an hour before the start and saw the Marquis de Juigné, President of the Comité of the Concours. I made a very firm protest to the Marquis and told him that should there be a recurrence of the same incident during the course of the afternoon, whilst I disliked to make any demonstrative protest, I would, nevertheless, feel obliged to retire at once from the Concours with the guest from my special box and that the Irish team would ride out of the ring. I informed the Marquis that it being a Sunday I was not able to take the matter up with the Foreign Office until the following day and that, although the incident was a diplomatic one and would have to be reported to the Foreign Office, I was making matters clear to him immediately as the chief authority at the councours, in order to avoid any unpleasant contre temps during the day. The Marquis de Juigné was, I found, extremely upset at this incident. He informed me that several weeks back when he had known the teams that would compete, he had immediately sent a list of the countries concerned to the Etat-Major de Paris, informing them that at some time during the course of the concours, it would be necessary for the military band to play the National Anthems of all these countries and that, consequently, the military band supplied by the Army authorities should have the scores of all the national Anthems and should be prepared to play any of them at a moment's notice. The Marquis de Juigné received a reply from the Etat-Major stating that everything was in order. He, himself, and his committee were, therefore, also taken completely by surprise when they heard instead of the strains of the military band a bad gramophone recording of an air which, they knew, was not the National Anthem.

The Marquis de Juigné told me that he himself had made the strongest of protests with the military authorities and that he had even threatened to resign his position as President of the Concours, unless the military band were made in some way answerable to them. Later on that same afternoon, the Marquis de Juigné came to see me again. He told me that, in the meantime, he had seen the General en Chef de l'Etat-Major who had sent for the band master responsible. The band master explained that when he had been given a list of the countries whose National Anthems he would have to play, he found he had the scores of all of them with the exception of that of Ireland. He consequently went to the Garde Républicaine, thinking that they would have the scores. The Garde Républicaine, however, told him that they had not these scores and after this, he did nothing and, apparently on his own responsibility and in a moment of confusion, when called upon to play the Irish National Anthem, he turned for help to the gramophone and put on the first Irish record he came across.

Later again on Sunday afternoon, when I arrived at the Legation, a Captain from the Etat-Major called to see me in company with the Chef d'Orchestre. He started by giving me a long apology from the Etat-Major for what had happened and concluded by asking if the Legation could let him have the band score of our National Anthem as, having hunted all over Paris, they found that they could not obtain it and on the other hand, they were informed that the playing of it might be required the same evening. I informed the Captain that all I could give him was the Anthem with words and piano accompaniment. They had evidently anticipated this position and he pointed out to me at length the difficulty which the chef d'orchestre would have in arranging an orchestration in time for 11.00 o'clock that same evening. He suggested in the circumstances that should the Irish team win, they would put on a gramophone disc of the proper air of the anthem, it being understood that that would be for that evening only and that by Tuesday (i.e. next day of competitions) they would be ready to play the air on the military band.

I expressed to the Captain my regret that I could not accept this alternative and that our National Anthem must be played in exactly the same manner as the National Anthems of every other country, i.e. by the military band that was there for the purpose. As he seemed rather insistent in pressing his alternative of the gramophone record, I too had to be more insistent and I informed him that unless the Anthem was played as I had demanded, I would be regretfully obliged to retire from the Concours and that the officers of the team would similarly retire. Eventually after further discussions, the Chef d'orchestre agreed that he would have an orchestration ready by 11 o'clock that evening.

Later again on that Sunday evening and whilst I was still at the Legation, I had a telephone call from the Information bureau of the Telephone services stating that they had an urgent inquiry for the music of the Irish National Anthem and they asked if I could help them. I stated that I assumed that their enquiry came from a military source and that in that case, I had already dealt with the matter.

On my return to the Concours that evening, the same captain from the Etat-Major called at my box again, conveying all the regrets for the incident and asking if I would receive General Daudin, Chef de l'Etat-Major de la Région de Paris. I replied that I would be delighted to receive the General who, then, came along to the box. He again made all apologies and expressed great regret. I thanked him for his visit and for his expressions of regret but I was obliged to tell him that the matter could not rest at that as I had been obliged to report it to my own Government and to the French Foreign Office.

Again the Marquis de Juigné called upon me before the end of the performance and our conversation was very much on the same lines.

On Monday morning the 10th instant; I sent off my letter to the Minister of Foreign Affairs, copy of which is attached hereto.[1]

About mid-day, I had my telephone conversation with you in which you advised me that you would be satisfied with a suitable apology and a suitable playing of the National Anthem.

At about 8.00 p.m. on that Monday evening, M. Bargeton, Directeur de la Section Politique de Ministére des Affaires Etrangéres, telephoned to me

---

[1] Not printed.

personally and asked if I could receive him immediately. I had to tell him that I was in the middle of dressing to leave for an important official dinner and eventually, it was agreed that I would call upon him at 10.00 the next morning, Tuesday the 11th inst.

At 10 o'clock on May 11, Tuesday, I accordingly called upon M. Bargeton who started by expressing the sincere regret of his Government and his Department for what had happened, but in continuing, he was rather inclined to minimise the affair, treating it as an unfortunate but still explicable incident. He went on to suggest as a solution which they hoped I would accept, that the Gouverneur Général de Paris, would call upon me and personally make his apologies for what had happened and that, afterwards, the Irish National Anthem should be played in its proper turn at the competitions in the afternoon when all the teams would arrive in the ring for presentation to the President of the Republic who was attending the Coupe des Nations competition on that afternoon. I told Mr. Bargeton that I thought he was treating the matter rather too lightly and that the solution which he suggested could not be satisfactory. Since the Legation had no direct relations with the French army, we could not look upon them as primarily responsible and that in these circumstances, whilst an explanation from the army would make clear the error of the army band, an apology from the Army authorities cold not be sufficient to give satisfaction to a complaint of a diplomatic nature and which, in effect, was a serious lack of courtesy from one nation to another when all the circumstances were taken into due consideration. Mr. Bargeton would not accept this point of view – he said he considered that he matter was not actually diplomatic and that it was merely a minor regrettable accident. Mr. Bargeton was rather inclined to show some annoyance and impatience, however I brought him back to a more proper view of the incident by asking him to consider what would happen if a similar incident were to occur in regard to a French team visiting Ireland.

Although this seemed to bring him to a better realisation of the seriousness of the matter, he was still disinclined to agree to my suggestion (put forward in my letter to the Minister of Foreign Affairs) for an apology to be given over the loud speakers publicly at the Grand-Palais and for the proper playing of the air at a later period. He thought this would be giving too much prominence to the incident and would reflect upon the Government and the organisers of the Concours. Finding that I was so insistent and as he himself had been brought to see the matter in rather a different light, and, nevertheless, feeling that he was in a difficulty, M. Bargeton suggested asking M. Lozé of the Protocole to join us. I accepted this willingly. M. Lozé is the Sous-Chef du Protocole, acting as Chef of the Protocole during the absence of M. de Fouquiére at the Coronation in London. When M. Lozé joined us, M. Bargeton explained fully to him the position which we had reached and subsequently I also gave my view to M. Lozé of the position and what I thought should be done and which I considered they could quite easily do. After further lengthy discussion, it was finally agreed that prior to the commencement of the Coupe des Nations competition, an announcement would be made over the loud speakers at the Concours so that all might hear, expressing regret and apologising for the incident of last Saturday and stating that the Irish National Anthem would be heard later on, played by the military band. As this arrangement covered your requirements, I accepted it, stating that in my view it was the minimum solution for such an incident and that my Government had behaved very generously in agreeing to this minimum solution. I thought it well also at this stage to point out the much more serious consequences which would have followed if the same incident occurred in regard to some of the other teams competing at the concours. (N.B. I had in mind for instance Germany.)[1]

I told M. Bargeton and M. Lozé that I would arrive at the Concours at a quarter to two so that I might be certain to hear the announcement when given out at two o'clock. I attach hereto a copy of the actual words of the announcement as agreed to and as given over the loud speakers.[2]

Unfortunately the effect of this announcement was lost to a very great extent by the fact that after I had left them at 11.45 in the morning, it was suddenly decided at about 12.30 to advance the hour for starting the competitions to 1.30 p.m. instead of 2 o'clock.

No notice was given to me of this change of time. It was only conveyed to the competing teams at the last moment. Very few of the public or representatives of the Press were present. Whether this change of time was purposely made to decrease the effect of the announcement, I am not able to say. At the time of the commencement of the Coupe des Nations, our National Anthem was played in its due turn when our team rode into the ring. It was played by the military band and in all the circumstances, it was fairly good, but the military band itself was not a very good one and in fact did not even play the Marseillaise very well.

At the moment of writing, I have not received any written acknowledgement or reply to my letter of the 10th of May addressed to Mr. Yvon Delbos, Minister of Foreign Affairs, but M. Lozé has told me over the telephone this afternoon that a reply will probably follow shortly. I will, of course, communicate the contents of this reply to you whenever it is received.

Aire Lán-Chomhachtach

No. 57 NAI DFA Madrid Embassy IP 3/6

Letter from Joseph P. Walshe to Leopold H. Kerney (St Jean de Luz)
(Secret)

DUBLIN, 14 May 1937

I have your interesting report of 12th instant concerning General O'Duffy.[3]

It is most important that we should have the earliest possible definite information about the date of General O'Duffy's departure from Spain. Please make every effort to discover the date, and inform the Department by cypher.

[signed] J.P. WALSHE
Rúnaí

---

[1] The sentence in brackets is handwritten by O'Brien.
[2] Not printed.
[3] See above No. 55.

No. 58 NAI DFA 119/21

Annual report from Michael MacWhite to Joseph P. Walshe (Dublin)
(108/36)[1]

WASHINGTON, 19 May 1937

During the fiscal year 1936-37 the services of the Legation and of the various Consulates have been employed to a greater extent than heretofore. The demands on the Legation for information regarding political, economical, educational, and social developments in the Saorstát have been considerable. A custom has developed here in schools and colleges to devote a day or even a week to the study of different European countries and amongst these Ireland seems to occupy a very prominent place. This is to some extent due to the fact that a large number of teachers are of Irish extraction. A number of schools have made a special display of Irish tourist literature but owing to the limited supplies we receive from the Irish Tourist Association, we are not always able to satisfy the demands.

The number of visitors to the Saorstát during the year showed an appreciable increase. 11,172 seem to have landed in Free State ports. The number of passports issued by the Consulates and the Legation was 2,128, of renewals 1,636, and of visas 7,408 (see annex A)[2]. Documents legalized totalled 1,063 and there were 528 registrations under the Nationality and Citizenship Act. Cash receipts amounted to approximately $91,000. Due to the reduction in the visa fee, the receipts for the current year are not likely to amount to more than one-third of this sum.

In addition to the foregoing, a considerable number of estates were handled and important sums of money were remitted to heirs through the Department of External Affairs, and through local Solicitors acting for the parties concerned. Some of this money would have been lost to the heirs in Ireland either in the form of exaggerated legal dues or through being diverted to other channels if the Consuls had not been active in their interest.

Many enquiries respecting the finding of markets for Irish products have been received. The demand for our whiskies and woollens is gradually increasing, and there is undoubtedly a market here for many other Saorstát products if only our manufacturers were sufficiently enterprising. They should, in their own interests, make a study of the American markets and of the system of marketing prevailing here. The American purchaser is very discriminating and the way in which the goods are presented to him is of considerable importance.

Annexed hereto are reports from the different Consulates giving their activities during the year.[3]

[signed] M. MACWHITE

---

[1] Marginal annotation by Sheila Murphy: 'Seen by Sec[retar]y'.
[2] Not printed.
[3] Not printed.

No. 59 NAI 2003/17/181

Confidential report from John W. Dulanty to Joseph P. Walshe (Dublin)
(No. 31) (Secret)[1]

LONDON, 20 May 1937

I have just returned from Mr. MacDonald's office. He said that he had asked me to call because he had now almost finished his own examination of our draft Constitution and there were two points about which he would like to be clear. The first was with reference to our second Act in December last (External Relations). He understood from the President during the London conversations in January[2] last that the Irish Government intended to let this second Act stand side by side with the Constitution. It would not be embodied in the Constitution but would be, so to speak, supplementary to it.

The second point was that he understood that the President intended to make it as difficult to change materially the External Relations Act as it would be to change materially the Constitution itself.

He would be glad to know whether what he understood from the President to be the position on these two points in January last was the position today. May I be informed at an early date what answer should be given to Mr. MacDonald?

Our draft Constitution had been sent to each member of the United Kingdom Cabinet but the heavy list of Coronation engagements and the work of the Imperial Conference, in addition to the normal Departmental duties, had left scant time for adequate study of so important a document. He had put other matters aside and given himself up to a careful study of the draft. He hoped to be able to have the views of his colleagues in about a fortnight's time when he thought it likely that the United Kingdom Cabinet would have some comment to offer. My impression was that he anticipates difficulty with his colleagues.[3]

The business of the interview finished at this point and the conversation became, as it often does at the end of an interview, rather general. Mr. MacDonald walked to the door of the Dominions Office with me. He is always manifestly careful to avoid saying anything which might appear to disturb the relation of mutual trust and goodwill which he feels exist today[4] between himself and the President. He said that, speaking personally and privately, he was sorry that the President had suggested that if a Saorstát delegation had been sent to the London Conference they would have been in a position of humiliation.

I pointed out that what the President had said was that he did not think we should be expected to run the risk of a recurrence of Ottawa. Even now, despite all that Mr. MacDonald himself had said, the two countries were still not in the position of making agreements. The coal-cattle pact, its renewals

---

[1] Marginal annotation by Joseph Walshe: 'Recd 22nd May bag. J.P.W., 22nd May'.
[2] See above Nos 3, 7 and 8.
[3] This sentence is handwritten.
[4] These two words have been handwritten by Dulanty over crossed out words.

notwithstanding, had not reached the stage of agreement but was still merely an unwritten understanding – and one from which it could not be denied the British were considerable gainers. It was of course true that the President had said both in private to Mr. MacDonald and in public that he was ready when circumstances allowed to co-operate and be on the[1] terms of good neighbours with Britain. The draft Constitution, whatever Mr. MacDonald's diehard colleagues might say, was a step in the right direction since it was saying once and for all certain things that in fairness to our people the President had to say. Attendance at the London Conference was, after all, not the one and only form of co-operation.

But, Mr. MacDonald rejoined, it must be clear to the President that the Ottawa position of their declining to enter into agreements with us had now been abandoned. The conversations with the President in January last, the frequent talks he had had with myself, the meetings which he had arranged for Sir Warren Fisher and Sir Horace Wilson to meet me[2] were all proofs, he submitted, that they were anxious to reach agreement. He recalled that the plan for the Warren Fisher meetings he had pushed forward with, he thought, the President's concurrence, with the sole object of reaching a point where Ministers of both Governments could meet in the confident hope of arriving at agreements. Speaking entirely for himself he said there was some risk that 'The Times' report of the President's speech might be misleading because the ordinary reader might infer that the British had sent an invitation in humiliating terms to the Irish Government. So far from that being the case they would have welcomed a delegation from Ireland and would have treated that delegation in all matters on precisely the same basis as the other Member States of the Commonwealth. We could have contributed to the discussions or refrained. We could have agreed to enter into arrangements which might be suggested or we could have declined. We would have had, he continued, complete and absolute freedom at every point of the proceedings, and his own personal regret was that neither Mr. de Valera nor any member of his Government should not have met and discussed these questions of common concern with the other Member States of the Commonwealth. Our presence there instead of prejudicing the settlement of the questions outstanding between Ireland and England would, he thought, have helped forward their solution.

Mr. MacDonald's observations on the Imperial Conference were, I believe, intended to be strictly private, as distinct from the two points on which he sought information in the ordinary diplomatic way.

[signed] J.W. Dulanty
High Commissioner

---

[1] This word has been inserted by hand by Dulanty.
[2] The words 'to meet me' have been inserted by hand by Dulanty.

No. 60 NAI 2006/39

Handwritten letter from Joseph P. Walshe to John W. Dulanty (London)
(Secret)

DUBLIN, 21 May 1937

My Dear John,

An official letter on the constitution and its consequences would take some time to get to you as the President is very busy with his preparations for the Committee stage.

Here however are some unofficial considerations which you could certainly use in your chats with the Dominion Ministers or others whose good will you want to secure.

(1) The constitution marks a completely new stage in our relations with G. B. It is not the final stage of the long process of reconciliation. Only the unity of Ireland will bring that. But for the first time we have written down for ourselves by ourselves the fundamental law which is to govern the whole corporate existence of our people. In that fundamental law we have *freely* provided for the King. True he does not occupy the same formal position as in the other States of the Commonwealth, but that does not detract one iota from the essential fact that he is King of Ireland and is definitely declared so to be by Act 58 of 1936 (12th December). The law can be changed at any time if the people desire it. But the position in South Africa is juridically precisely the same. Our President, however, has special powers of holding up Bills and should the Dáil suddenly take the revolutionary step of repealing 58 of 36 the Senate and the President would undoubtedly make sure that the issue would go to the people by way of referendum. The very fact that the King's position is specifically secured by an Act of Parliament makes it infinitely more secure than if it were secured by some external agency. For the first time in our whole history we have of ourselves accepted the King's position. If the British are wise they will let things be.

(2) Co-operation now becomes possible. We have put it beyond the legal power of the British to regard us as their ***,[1] their thing. If they respect our absolute right to dispose of ourselves they have us as their friends for ever. I believe that it is for them a much more important turning point than it is for us. For them it is a great opportunity lost through allowing old prejudices to blind them. As far as we are concerned we are not going to be deterred by what can only be another example of England's desire to dominate over us.

The P. said on Thursday that we had a common interest in the defence of this country – that we should call upon their aid and accept it in a struggle against a foreign aggressor. Nothing so important has been said with approval since the establishment of the Saorstát. Doesn't that solve the whole defence question? Fisher's statement about the money being a big difficulty

---

[1] One word illegible.

seems grotesque before the acceptance by the strongest Irish Leader of our times of such a principle. Do get them to see light on this point. Why will they be blind where we are concerned and so farseeing when they are dealing with purely foreign peoples. From the propaganda point of view alone agreement with us on this vital issue (with all the implications in America and Commonwealth) would be worth millions. Who is the enemy in their camp? Is it Harding? Or is it some politician. I must let this rough note go. The formula will reach you definitely in a few days.

Yours
J.P.W.

No. 61 NAI DFA Paris Embassy 19/34

Confidential report from Art O'Brien to Joseph P. Walshe (Dublin)
(P 19/34) (Confidential)

PARIS, 2 June 1937

New American Minister to Ireland

Further to recent correspondence re the above, the American Ambassador in Paris came in to have an aperitif with me this morning and we had a very long chat about a variety of matters, some others of which I will deal with in separate minutes.

In the course of our chat, Mr. Bullitt[1] referred to Mr. Cudahy who has been nominated as American Minister to Ireland. Mr. Cudahy and Mr. Bullitt are very old and intimate friends. At the time that I first wrote to you about the above, I assumed, from the fact that Mr. Cudahy was going as Minister to Ireland, that he was at present Minister in Poland. I find, however, that this is not the fact and that Mr. Cudahy is actually Ambassador in Poland. He has, however, always expressed his desire to be appointed as Minister in Ireland. Mr. Bullitt was in the United States at the time that the recent appointment was made. Mr. Bullitt was then spending a fortnight with the President and he saw the cables which passed in the matter. The President offered Mr. Cudahy a choice between two other Embassies by way of promotion in position, leaving the choice to Mr. Cudahy who, however, replied that rather than be appointed as Ambassador elsewhere, he would still prefer to be nominated as Minister to Ireland and that if the President wished to do him a favour he would be glad that this should be taken into consideration. Mr. Cudahy, therefore, in order to fulfil his ambition as being Minister to Ireland, is taking the very unusual course of going back in rank from Ambassador to Minister. I think Mr. Bullitt was anxious that I should let our Minister of External Affairs know this in order that it might be appreciated how great a desire Mr. Cudahy had to go to Ireland.

Mr. Bullitt said that the Minister will find Mr. Cudahy a very charming man and he is quite certain that he will be very much in his element in

---

[1] William Christian Bullitt (1891-1967), United States Ambassador to the Soviet Union, 1933-6; United States Ambassador to France, 1936-40.

Ireland. I understand that Mr. Cudahy is not actually of Irish birth but is of Irish descent in the first generation.

[copy letter unsigned]
Aire Lán-Chómhachtach

No. 62 NAI DFA Madrid Embassy 19/4

Handwritten confidential report from Leopold H. Kerney to Joseph P.
Walshe (Dublin)
(S.J. 19/1) (Copy)

St Jean de Luz, 7 June 1937

Unofficial Visit from Spanish Government Official

Some little time ago I had a visit from Francisco de Arano, agent in Valencia for the Irish Iberian Trading Co., Ltd., Dublin. He had an aged mother and two elderly sisters in Franco's territory and appealed to me to try to get them out of Spain. I made enquiries and ascertained that there would be no objection to furnishing them with the necessary permits. Arano's mother and sisters were subsequently allowed to cross the French frontier. On 3rd June I received a visit from Francisco AYALA, who handed me a letter of introduction from Arano in which he was described as a high official of the Ministry for State. AYALA told me that his father (since dead) and 3 brothers (non-combatants) were prisoners in Burgos, where he had also 2 young brothers, 12 and 14 years of age; their mother was in Perpignan. AYALA hoped that I might be able to secure permission for these 2 minors to leave Spain.

I pointed out to AYALA that all I could do would be to enquire whether a permit to cross the frontier would be granted, and, as his name was known to Franco's people (so he admitted), it seemed almost certain that no satisfactory reply would be obtainable, and my position was such that I could hardly insist or bring any pressure to bear; I advised him to make use of the good offices of the International Red Cross as in this way I thought he was more likely to meet with success. It is not desirable to court failure in a matter of this kind, nor is it prudent to prejudice my standing with Franco's people by taking too close an interest in families associated with the other side.

So far the visit was clearly of a personal nature and I informed AYALA that I did not propose to report his visit officially; he thought, however, that it might be as well to do so. I asked him why my few letters to Valencia had remained unanswered; he thought they might have gone astray in the post, but admitted that there was a certain feeling against the Diplomatic Corps non-resident in Spain. I told him that, from their point of view, it was scarcely to their advantage that, in reply to questions in the Dáil, it had to be stated that representations to Salamanca had received attention whereas communications to Valencia had met with no response. I reminded him that the Irish Government's attitude had been very correct throughout and that the Government had not yielded to the clamour for a breach of diplomatic relations with Spain, but that public opinion was somewhat inflamed, Ireland being a predominantly Catholic country, and prejudiced, even prior to the civil war, by the destruction of churches in Spain. AYALA's attitude was that the Catholic Church in Spain was identified with the enemies of the Republic, but that this was not so in the Basque country (Euzkadi) where there had been no excesses. As to the future of religion in Spain, he said that Valencia had given definite promises to the Basques that there would be full freedom for the practice of all religions but without any special privileges for the Catholic religion; he thought the restoration of freedom of religion, with the assistance of Basque priests, would precede the end of the war.

The next point I raised was the prevalence of disorder and anarchy as, if the choice were to be between disorder and order, there could be no doubt as to where the sympathies of the outside world would go. He said that a complete change had taken place and that order had been definitely established, that the upheaval caused by the war had made disorder inevitable, but that now they had a disciplined army and police and ordered conditions of life existed; he was very emphatic on this point and begged me to go to Valencia for a few days to judge for myself. He said that the recent troubles in Barcelona were deliberately provoked by the U.G.T. (socialist labour syndicate)[1] for the purpose of putting an end to the State of anarchy for which the C.N.T. (anarchist labour syndicate)[2] was responsible. He reminded me of the fact (which is quite true) that there had been a strange sympathy on this occasion in the nationalist press for the anarchists in Barcelona.

As to the military position, I expressed the opinion that, so long as the initiative of military operations was not in their hands, the belief was generally entertained that there was a definite superiority of their adversaries who alone had made any forward movements. He replied that the initiative was now passing into their hands, both on the Bilbao front and elsewhere, and that there would soon be a big improvement in this respect.

I concluded the conversation by regretting that I had not been notified of the change of Government in Valencia; AYALA thought the official advice might have been sent to Madrid. He promised to send me a copy of the Diplomatic list which I need.

[copy letter unsigned]
Aire Lán-Chómhachtach

No. 63 NAI 2003/17/181

Confidential report from John W. Dulanty to Joseph P. Walshe (Dublin)
(No. 34) (Secret)

LONDON, 10 June 1937

I should be glad to have at as early a date as possible the suggested formula which it will be remembered Sir Warren Fisher suggested we might draw up,

---

[1] Unión General del Trabajodores.
[2] Confederación Nacional del Trabajo.

and also a reply to the two questions specifically put to me by Sir Malcolm MacDonald[1] – see my Secret minute No. 31 of 20th May.[2]

[signed] J.W. DULANTY
High Commissioner

No. 64 NAI DFA London Embassy, Non-Intervention Series files

*Letter from Colman O'Donovan to John W. Dulanty (The Dolphin Inn,
Thorpeness, Suffolk)*

LONDON, 15 June 1937

Dear High Commissioner,
In the course of a telephone call to-day Joe Walshe said that they had had a communication from the Valencia Government asking for our consent to the appointment of a Chargé d'Affaires in Dublin. They have replied that though they value the maintenance of relations with the Spanish people they do not wish at the present moment to take any action which might be regarded in some quarters as interference in Spanish affairs and have suggested that as the post has now been vacant for more than a year it might continue so for the present. In other words, they have turned down the request though they have been very polite about it. Joe Walshe thought you would like to know of this as it represents a new stage in the course of our relations with the Spanish Government.

There is no news yet of a resumption of Non-Intervention Meetings. It looks as if the two sides in Spain will accept the proposals that have been submitted to them in the matter of guaranteeing the safety of the patrol ships and I think it is expected that when this acceptance comes to hand a meeting of the Committee will be held, in which Germany and Italy would take part.

No. 65 NAI 2006/39

*Confidential Report from John W. Dulanty to Joseph P. Walshe (Dublin)
(No. 36) (Secret)*

LONDON, 17 June 1937

General Hertzog told me today that from the point of view of South Africa the Conference just finished was the most satisfactory Imperial Conference which he had attended. This was his fourth Conference. I asked what particular feature or features of the Conference afforded him such satisfaction.

He said that there was a marked improvement in the general attitude of the United Kingdom Government towards the other members of the Commonwealth. He thought more than at any other Conference the United Kingdom Government had accepted the conception of 1926 and all that it implied, whether actual or potential. There was no trace at any time of the

---

[1] Marginal note by Joseph P. Walshe: 'No reply at present. Despatch later. J.P.W. 11th June 37'.
[2] See above No. 59.

United Kingdom wishing to assume any attitude other than that of complete equality with the other Governments.

General Hertzog said that he had had a farewell conversation this morning with Earl Baldwin and had told him that although he came to this Conference not without misgiving he was going away feeling happier about the reality of the co-equality of the Governments in the Commonwealth than he had ever felt before.

The talks on defence had been very illuminating. The British, as far as he and his colleagues could see, had shown the completest frankness and candour in discussing world, and particularly European, affairs.

He did not think he could say that any real progress had been made on economic questions. The pivotal question in the economic sphere was the trade relations between the United Kingdom and the United States which were now under discussion. He hoped that these discussions would produce a satisfactory agreement because he felt that it was of immediate and obvious importance to all the countries in the Commonwealth. In reply to my enquiry he said that this was the view taken at the end of the Conference by Canada, South Africa, Australia, and New Zealand – the two last named had in the earlier stages of the Conference shown reluctance to take the line adopted by the others but in the end had agreed. The position was now that all the Governments were prepared to make some sacrifice to achieve the objective of a United States-United Kingdom trade agreement.

In answer to his questions I gave him a brief outline of the position of the President in relation to the British Commonwealth.

Although Ireland had not been mentioned in any of the discussions, General Hertzog had talked privately with Mr. Malcolm MacDonald who made no concealment of his desire to reach an early settlement with the President, and further, admitted that in his view the United Kingdom people in the last few years had made mistakes in dealing with Ireland.

He asked me to convey his best wishes to the President. He doubted whether his Government could ever do much in the way of helping Ireland in the clearance of her difficulties with England, but if they could not help directly they would certainly never hinder.

[copy letter unsigned]
High Commissioner

No. 66 NAI 2006/39

Letter from Joseph P. Walshe to John W. Dulanty (London)
DUBLIN, 19 June 1937

I am directed by the Minister for External Affairs to instruct you to purchase (through what seems to you to be the most appropriate channel) the Mace of the old Irish House of Commons, which is to be sold at Christie's on the 22nd June, for a sum not exceeding £3,000:0:0: inclusive of commission and other incidentals, if any.

Of course the Minister hopes very much that the Mace will not go to anything like this price and he wishes you to continue your good offices to keep the price as low as possible.

[signed] J.P. WALSHE

Mace bought for £3,000 by Bank of Ireland.[1]

No. 67 NAI DT S9311

Letter from W.A. Honohan[2] to Maurice Moynihan (Dublin)
DUBLIN, 25 June 1937

With reference to your minute (S.9311) of the 24th instant,[3] I am desired by the Minister for Finance to transmit herewith, for the information of the President, a statement in triplicate showing the amounts withheld by the Government from the British Government and the sums collected by the British Government by means of special import duties on Saorstát products, in each of the years 1932/33, 1933/34, 1934/35 and 1935/36 together with the estimated amounts in respect of the year 1936/37.

[signed] W.A. HONOHAN
Rúnaí Aire

[Enclosure]

FINANCIAL RELATIONS WITH GREAT BRITAIN

	Amount withheld by Saorstát	Amount collected by Great Britain in Special Duties on Saorstát Exports	Excess of amount withheld over duties collected
	£	£	£
Year 1932-33	4,764,767	2,515,003	2,249,764
Year 1933-34	4,905,859	4,555,238	350,621
Year 1934-35	4,845,206	4,694,594	150,612
Year 1935-36	4,800,000	5,421,515	- 621,515
Year 1936-37 (Estimate)	4,750,000	4,709,000	41,000
TOTALS	£24,065,832	£21,895,350	£2,170,482

---

[1] Marginal note by Dulanty's Secretary, Miss M.E. (Bessie) Foxe, 26 June 1937.
[2] William A. Honohan, junior administrative officer, Department of Finance.
[3] Not printed.

No. 68 NAI DFA 126/37

Extract from a letter from Francis T. Cremins to Michael Rynne (Dublin)
(Ass./18)

GENEVA, 23 July 1937

Dear Michael,
[matter omitted]
It is, as I have said, much too early to formulate any views as to what will happen at the Assembly, or as to whether the Assembly will be an important meeting or not. With the Spanish situation as it is, and the varying Sino-Japanese situation, and the general unrest in Europe, coupled with the progress in re-armament, and the danger of incidents, anything may happen between this and September, and grave questions may therefore arise. I know that in connection with all these things you will be wondering whether the Minister ought to come or not. In regard to the Minister's coming, I stated my views last year, and I have little to add or to subtract from them in regard to this year. After all, all the important Foreign Ministers come to the Assembly, if only to meet and talk with each other, and they find it of advantage to do so, and, even in private conversations, our Minister would have much to contribute in the dangerous position to which European politics have been brought, when a great part of Europe and elsewhere may be within measurable distance of finding itself another Spain. The Minister's views that unless the real difficulties in connection with the 'vanquished States' – political and territorial – and not merely the economic difficulties, are tackled and disposed of, the alternative is almost certain war, when everybody will lose, could not be too often rubbed home. Even the question of the economic difficulties is as you know making slow progress, as witness the proceedings as the Raw Materials Committee.
[matter omitted]

No. 69 NAI 2003/17/181

Confidential report from John W. Dulanty to Joseph P. Walshe (Dublin)
(No. 37) (Secret)

LONDON, 26 July 1937

Mr. MacDonald told me to-day that both the British Prime Minister and himself were of opinion that it would be extremely helpful to them if he (Mr. MacDonald) could have one or two fairly full conversations with the President.

He would willingly cross over to Ireland where, he says, he is practically unknown but as that might present difficulties to the President he would not suggest that course.

If the President intended to go to Geneva or even to Zurich Mr. MacDonald would be glad to go and stay at some place convenient to either of those towns where it would be possible, he felt sure, for the President and him to meet without the fact of their meeting becoming public. He knew, of course, how essential it was for the meeting to be held in the strictest secrecy.

I told Mr. MacDonald that thus far I had not heard of any intention of the President to visit either of these places, but that I would in accordance with his request place the suggestion before Mr. de Valera.

Any date after the 20th September or possibly even after the 12th would be convenient to Mr. MacDonald.

[signed] J.W. DULANTY
High Commissioner

No. 70 NAI 2006/39

Confidential report from John W. Dulanty to Joseph P. Walshe (Dublin)
(No. 38) (Secret)

LONDON, 26 July 1937

When I was last in Dublin the President said it would be well to make discreet inquiry on the subject of the forts in the north of Ireland because rumours had reached him that a certain amount of activity had been observed on Lough Swilly.

I have made discreet inquiry and I am told by the Dominions Office that the position is as follows:-

At Forts Lenan and Dunree on Lough Swilly the only works now in hand for which the War Office have given approval and have allotted funds are:-

(a) *At Fort Lenan:*
  (i)   Construction of a squash court (half the cost borne by the R.A. Games fund) ... £800
  (ii) Construction of sanitary annexes
  (iii) Provision of boilers, etc. for hot water for ablution rooms ... } £750

(b) At Fort Dunree – as for (ii) and (iii) above ... £1,200

[copy letter
unsigned]
High Commissioner

No. 71 NAI 2003/17/181

Letter from Seán Murphy (for Joseph P. Walshe) to John W. Dulanty (London)
(Secret) (Copy)

DUBLIN, 30 July 1937

With reference to your secret No. 37 of the 26th July,[1] I am directed to state that the President is not at the moment able to say whether the discussions at Geneva will be sufficiently important to warrant his attendance at the League Assembly.

Apart from this consideration he cannot see at present whether his engagements here would allow him to go to Geneva even if that were desirable.

He agrees that a meeting in Dublin would be out of the question.

---

[1] See above No. 69.

The President would be very pleased to have a discussion with Mr. MacDonald in the event of his going to Geneva. The ground was very fully covered at previous discussions and it is to be hoped that if further discussions take place some definite proposal will be put forward.

I am to request that you may inform Mr. MacDonald accordingly.

(Sgd.) SEAN MURPHY
Rúnaí

No. 72 NAI DFA 227/4

Confidential report from William J. B. Macaulay to Joseph P. Walshe (Dublin)
(M.P. 19/37) (Confidential)

ROME, 12 August 1937

An Rúnaí,

The position of Franco's Envoy to the Holy See appears to be rather ambiguous. The Cardinal Secretary told me that this Chargé d'Affaires would be merely in charge of the Embassy and representing Franco without Letters of Credence and would be received by the Cardinal Secretary, in fact he was received on Tuesday. The Holy See still insists that this does not mean recognition of Franco – apparently because Letters of Credence have not been accepted. It is natural to conclude that the Holy See is waiting for more definite evidence of Franco's ultimate success before recognising him diplomatically.

I am informed on excellent authority that the letter sent by the Cardinal Primate of Spain to all the Spanish Bishops for their signature was drafted by Franco, or on his behalf, and is merely a propaganda weapon. Some of the Bishops refused to sign it including the Bishop of Vittoria in exile here. The idea is that when this letter or declaration has been signed by all the Spanish Bishops it will be sent to all the Bishops throughout the world and released to the Press by them in their several dioceses. The Italian Press has already referred to this forthcoming document as an example of the unity of the Church in Spain and an indictment of the Reds.

The Vatican has now reached a point as regards Germany where all hope of reconciliation is practically abandoned as indicated by the Holy Father's pointed reference recently to Cardinal Mundelein. The fact that Franco has to accept assistance from Hitler is deplored. The Holy See will make no further overtures to Germany, they are beginning to think they have been too long-suffering already.

His Holiness' health remains fairly good considering how ill he had been. It is said that he will remain at Castelgandolfo until very late in the year.

[signed] W. J. B. MACAULAY

No. 73 NAI DFA 126/37

Extract from a memorandum on the Eighteenth Ordinary Session of the League of Nations Assembly by Michael Rynne to Seán Murphy

DUBLIN, 16 August 1937

Assistant Secretary
re Eighteenth Ordinary Session of the Assembly, 13th September, 1937
[matter omitted]
4: There remains one other question on the existing Agenda which may be considered as of particular interest, at any rate to Saorstát Éireann. This is item 13 which relates to the civil and political status of women. As will be recalled, Mr. Hearne was Rapporteur for this question when it was last down for discussion by an Assembly (First Commission of the 16th Assembly, 1935) and this country, both before and since that time, has played a prominent part in the movement to secure the equality of the sexes. At the present time our policy with regard to the position of women in the State may be considered to have been defined anew in the Constitution of 1937. Hence even if, in certain quarters, there was no suggestion that our policy had undergone a change, we might still be expected to inform the League of recent developments and to continue to display a special interest in the subject of women's rights.

Obviously, however, this question is one that requires not only delicate handling, but very expert knowledge of the many issues involved, as well as a thorough familiarity with the present law and policy of this country in regard to women. It might, therefore, be desirable to include the Legal Adviser to the Department in the Delegation to this Assembly, especially if the Minister feels that a formal statement of Saorstát Éireann's policy concerning women ought to be made at the next Assembly.
5: In the event of the Legal Adviser being one of the Delegation it might be practicable for us to take a definite line in a few of the more technical (legal) matters which are likely to come up in the First Committee. Chief of these is the question of the measures proposed during the last year for the international suppression of terrorism, concerning which a diplomatic conference is going to be held in November next.
6: Naturally, it is still rather early for a decision as to whether the Minister should or should not be advised to head the delegation to the Assembly. According to Mr. Cremins, there is always the possibility of an important international affair, such as the Sino-Japanese outbreak or the Spanish conflict, being brought up at the session. Also the fate of Palestine may be more nearly decided by September. But difficult questions, such as those of Spain, China and Palestine are essentially matters that the Great Powers prefer to settle out of the Assembly, which, since 1935, is tending to become more and more formal and ineffective. Apart from this general opinion, it would seem unwise to attempt any forecast of the final agenda of the Assembly at the moment.

So long as we have nothing to go on but an agenda of a purely technical, administrative character, of no political interest whatever, it is suggested that we should not recommend the Minister to attend the Assembly, or even to appoint another member of the Government to go there. We ought, moreover, indicate that there is no immediate prospect of securing the promise of the Chairmanship of any important Committee for the Head of the Irish Delegation.

This is a matter, however, that might be further explored in the coming weeks, if the Minister so directs.

7: In conclusion, it is well to add that there seems to be a chance of the Eighteenth Assembly recognising Italy's position in Ethiopia either by way of the exclusion of an Ethiopian Delegation by the Credentials Committee, or following on a general discussion to be initiated, perhaps, by the Council meeting which immediately precedes the Assembly.

8: Although it would be helpful at this stage to know the Minister's general attitude on the subject of heading the Delegation, it is, of course, clear that he may wish to await further information of a more hopeful kind. In the event of such information being received early next month, a further minute will be immediately submitted.

No. 74 NAI DT S10133

> *Extract from the minutes of a meeting of the Cabinet*
> *(Cab. 8/5) (Item 8)*
> Dublin, 17 August 1937

WORLD'S FAIR, NEW YORK, 1939: SAORSTÁT participation.
It was decided that the Saorstát should participate in the New York World's Fair to be held in New York in 1939.

No. 75 NAI DFA 126/37

> *Letter from Michael Rynne to Francis T. Cremins (Geneva)*
> *(126/37) (Personal and Confidential) (Copy)*
> Dublin, 19 August 1937

Dear Frank,

I delayed replying to your semi-official letter (Ass./18) of the 23rd July[1] until your return from leave, as I was awaiting something to go on regarding the probable composition of our Delegation. As matters now stand, I cannot give you anything really definite, only general surmises, as follows:

(1) *Minister.* On the basis of the Agenda, dated 5th May last, there is no argument whatever for the Minister's attending the Assembly, but very much the contrary. The Minister has been so advised. As regards the prospects of the Italian Empire, Spain, China and Palestine coming up at the Assembly, our sentiments are mixed. Some of these prospects are definitely discouraging, some are more inviting. The various possibilities of each have been discussed with the Minister. But, *notwithstanding all this, please take note that the Minister*

---

[1] See above No. 68.

may very well attend the Assembly, at least for portion of the time, and therefore make any preparations you may think appropriate to such an eventuality. If you can do it without arousing hopes or suspicions, endeavour to find out whether there would be an important Chairmanship going – for instance.

(2) *Secretary*: The Secretary is still away on leave, and I have no reason (and probably no right!) to anticipate his mind on the matter of the Delegation, but, if the Minister were to attend the Assembly and if Palestine was to loom large on the Agenda, there's no knowing but the Secretary might also attend. He will be just back from the scene of action and should be fully equipped with the 'low-down' on the whole Jew-Arab situation.

(3) *Legal Adviser*: If the two foregoing do not go to Geneva this time, or even if they do, there is every chance of our having John Hearne with us. At any rate, I have been pressing in that direction and, all other things being equal (the rush for the Senate Bill, etc.), the interested parties do not seem to see any strong objection. Obviously, from the point of view of Saorstát Éireann the status of women is still a live issue (or at any rate a lively one!), and only John could do it justice. Also we are supplied with some elaborate, mostly negative, views on Terrorism and there are doubtless other legal questions on which we might take a line. Calendar Reform has been given a great deal of thought here, and we are still considering it actively, but I suppose that might not fall to John, being in another Committee.

(4) *Myself* – You have always with you.

(5) *Warnock*[1] – I think he will be along, even if the party is so big that it includes Captain Brennan,[2] Miss O'Connell[3] and Sheila Murphy.

That's all I will say for the present, but will let you know immediately anything definite is decided on. Meanwhile prepare for the best and expect the worst – I am assuming you hope for a descent in force.

Concerning the Assembly generally there is not much to add. We have promised the Aga Khan (by personal letter from the Minister) our support for the Presidency, whereat he was so pleased that he presented us with a new Cup. We are holding up our Status of Women observations until John can get the Minister to approve them; they may not be circulated until we get to Geneva. We are preparing some notes here as usual and have left a large number of blanks in the text pending a line from you to tell us the prospective new Council Members, etc., etc. In future, it will be well to have these notes prepared by yourself about this time of year, after your holidays. One result of having them overhanging us here is that they interfere with holidays (mine are postponed until November!) and, of course, are not so good as those that could be done by someone who is whole-time on the League. As I am sure you will agree, the only valuable or interesting bits that occur in these annual notes are the portions supplied (generally at the last minute) by the Permanent Delegate! Since you were running the show from the home-front both the importance of the League and the work of the Department

---

[1] William Warnock, Department of External Affairs.
[2] Captain Seán Brennan, de Valera's Aide de Camp.
[3] Kathleen O'Connell (1888-1956), de Valera's Private Secretary (1919-56).

have undergone considerable changes. In consequence, I find myself suddenly confronted three weeks before an Assembly with a lot of documents, mostly, it is true, of minor importance, but with which I am practically unfamiliar and which have to be mastered *tant bien que mal* in a rush. During the rest of the year there is no question, of course, about what must be done and what may be delegated. The days are past when the 'League Section' was a specialised branch full of maps and French newspapers – and Peace! However, you may have seen we are advertising for more Cadets and so may yet hope to be able to spread out existing work, especially during the summer months.

Afraid this letter has become more egoistic than 'personal', but I may not have time to write you much unofficially before we meet. However hard the Assembly flops, I'll be glad to see you again.

Good wishes,
Yours,
[unsigned]

No. 76 NAI DFA 126/37

Extracts from a letter from Francis T. Cremins to Michael Rynne (Dublin)
(Ass. /18) (Personal and Confidential)
GENEVA, 24 August 1937

Dear Michael,
Many thanks for the information contained in your semi-official note of the 19th August.[1] Glad to hear that the possibilities are good, although the probabilities may eventually fall short of them.
[matter omitted]
As regards a Chairmanship, or one of the other seats on the General Committee, it will as I indicated be difficult to get any idea about this until the Assembly actually meets, as the whole procedure is altered by the new Nominations Committee, which will be appointed only when the delegates are here. The difficulty is naturally increased by the uncertainty whether the Minister will attend or not. There is in fact no one here who would venture to commit himself in regard to any of the posts falling to be filled by the Nominations Committee. If the President were actually on the spot, or notified as coming, I would hope that something could be done when the nominations are being considered, but otherwise, as you will understand, it would be very difficult to get anything on which you could place any reliance. I will however keep the matter in mind. The Aga Khan has already long since been notified in the Press as heading the Indian Delegation, and he is probably in a position to prepare the ground with some individual Governments. So far here I have heard of no other candidate for the Presidency. The most interesting chairmanship for the President would be that of the Sixth Committee, but he had that only two years ago.

---

[1] See above No. 75.

As regards the notes, I feel satisfied that it would be a great mistake from your own point of view to rely on notes supplied to you for a knowledge of the subjects on the agenda. It is the knowledge acquired from the reading, out of which the notes are prepared, which counts, not the notes themselves, which would naturally be somewhat superficial. Especially if the Minister is on the Delegation a detailed knowledge of each subject by the person or persons who will be always at his hand is essential. I found this, and so did Fred Boland, and I am certain that you will find it too. I can fill in all the local stuff as usual, but, especially if the Minister is there, you would be lost without a detailed knowledge of each question. What, for example, could Mr. Warnock know about the agenda unless he went into the questions himself and prepared his memoranda? I'm sorry of course about the leave difficulty, but after all the memoranda could be started in May or June, when the Agenda is circulated, and done gradually. Moreover, in regard to the bigger political questions you would have access to supplementary information which would not be so easily available here. We can talk about the matter when you come out.

I am delighted to hear that John also will be coming. I hope you are hurrying up that memorandum!

I am looking forward to seeing you.

Best wishes,
Yours sincerely,
[signed] F.T. Cremins

No. 77 NAI DFA 126/37

> *Letter from Michael Rynne to Francis T. Cremins (Geneva)*
> *(Personal) (Copy)*
>
> Dublin, 26 August 1937

Dear Frank,

Please excuse my air of impatience if I write you so soon after my last (19th August)[1] to ask for some quick information on the forthcoming Assembly's agenda. One of my reasons lies in the fact that I am liable at any moment to be put through the third degree on the matter. A few days ago, the President asked me what was going to happen, and, when I told him all that was in your recent minutes, he didn't seem quite satisfied. I fear it sounded too vague and negative. It is not enough to say the Assembly *might* be postponed and that an Ethiopian delegation *might* turn up and that the Sino-Japanese dispute, 1937, is *not* up, etc., etc., – or at least not for the President. He wants something more definite to go on, as he seems in the mood for taking definite decisions. One such (regarding Iran's candidature for the Council) I send you in today's bag. Always between ourselves, I think there is a good chance of his going to Geneva (better now than when I last wrote), and I would like to be well-supplied with the dope. So please endeavour to write us officially

---

[1] See above No. 75.

in the next few days, telling us everything you have found out lately. Especially mention whether rumours of a postponement are still rife in Geneva: the President is very against any postponement, which shows he is seriously thinking of going. Also, we want to know as exactly as possible what to expect in regard to the Negus. Possibly we may hear something on this from another source, but there's nothing to hand as yet. Other minor matters requiring elucidation are:-

1) the probable decision concerning Spain's continued membership of the Council

2) the likelihood, if any, of that country being represented by a Franco delegation, assuming that Santander is the beginning of the end;

3) the possibility of Spain, China and Palestine getting on to the agenda as precise 'items', as distinct from their being dragged into a general discussion on the Secretary-General's report. (We note Iraq's intentions about Palestine. How will they be phrased?).

4) All you know of the procedure likely to be followed re Palestine as a result of the Permanent Mandates Commission's recent report.

5) Anything you may have to say, supplementary to what we can find in documents, about Item 9 Emigration, Item 10 Housing, and Item 11(a) Nansen Office. This is, of course, of minor importance, so, unless something comes to your mind, without entailing special research, don't bother. Please send us an advance copy of the revised agenda when writing.

Yours, in haste,
[copy letter unsigned]

No. 78 NAI DFA 126/37

Confidential report from Francis T. Cremins to Joseph P. Walshe
(Ass. /18) (Confidential)

GENEVA, 31 August 1937

I have to state for the information of the Minister that the position in regard to the rumours of postponement of the Assembly remain as they were when I last reported on the question, i.e. no one has taken any steps to propose postponement. It may be taken that the Assembly will open on the date fixed, the 13th September, 1937.

There is no definite information here at the Secretariat or amongst my colleagues (I have discussed the matter with Mr. Walters[1] and others) as to whether H.M. Hailé Selassié will send a delegation to the forthcoming Assembly. The general impression is, however, that such a delegation will be sent. Dr. Riddell (Canada) tells me confidentially that such an impression prevails in London, and that the British Foreign Office expects that there may be a good deal of trouble at the Assembly in connection with the Ethiopian question. He had some information also that the British were thinking of

---

[1] Francis 'Frank' P. Walters (1888-1976), Under-Secretary General and later Deputy Secretary General of the League of Nations.

arranging, if possible, a meeting of Dominion representatives in London before the Assembly with a view to explaining and exploring the situation.

The first question that will come up, if an Ethiopian delegation is sent, is the question of the Credentials, on which I have already fully reported. Mr. Walters expresses the opinion and so does Dr. Riddell, that on that question the Credentials Committee are likely on the facts of the position as they exist this year to decide against the Ethiopian credentials. The matter would in that case go to a vote in the Assembly, and no one at this stage can give any reliable forecast of the result of the vote. There will undoubtedly, it is thought, be much opposition to voting an Ethiopian delegation out of the Assembly. The position is in fact much the same as it would have been in May last – at the Special Session – except that it is considered probable that a greater number of States would now be prepared to support the Credentials Committee, if they reported as indicated, in view of the developments in the International situation, and especially of the efforts at entente between Great Britain and Italy. The Anglo-Italian pourparlers, if in any measure successful, are likely to be followed by Franco-Italian pourparlers. Much will depend on the state of these conversations.

The other question is that of recognition of the Italian conquest of Ethiopia. I am informed that there is no question whatever of such recognition being accorded by Great Britain, and undoubtedly such a question would stand no chances whatever in the Assembly. Signor Mussolini has stated in fact that he would not expect it. I enquired if there is any likelihood that the Polish Declaration at the Special Session will be followed by similar Declarations at the coming session. No information as to this is so far available, nor is it known whether any State is likely to make a definite proposal of recognition, although this is regarded as by no means impossible. Egypt has been mentioned in the Press as likely to do so.

The Polish Legation here state that they have no information so far and no instruction. The Minister will not however return to Geneva until about the end of this week.

[signed] F.T. CREMINS
Permanent Delegate

No. 79 NAI DFA 126/37

Confidential report from Francis T. Cremins to Joseph P. Walshe
(Ass./18) (Confidential)
GENEVA, 4 September 1937

With reference to the forthcoming session of the Assembly, and on the assumption that the President will as always participate in the general debate, I have to suggest that amongst the subjects to which he could if he approved refer might be the following. (This minute does not purport to give a text for a statement but merely a possible general line, not necessarily consecutive, as it occurs to me.)

1) The dangerous international situation, and the deterioration since the previous Assembly.

2) Spain.
3) Sino-Japanese dispute.
4) Mr. Cordell Hull's declaration of the 16th July, and American efforts to promote peace.[1]
5) Palestine.

In the present international situation, I think that a purely political statement is called for. This could be a development of the President's last speech, which is even more applicable this year than it was when delivered, in view of the deterioration in the situation.[2] The conflicts in Spain, in the Mediterranean, and in the Far East, are no doubt the immediate causes of the present dangers, but the real underlying cause is the general malaise in Central Europe which is the result of the Peace Treaties of 1919, and of the will during the past 17 years on the part of some of the States which won the war to continue the penalties and effects of the Treaties to new generations in the vanquished States. This malaise involves practically 80 or 100 millions of people in Europe. If it did not exist no single State would have ventured to run counter to the principles of the League in the way to which we are in recent years becoming accustomed. To that malaise the present competition in armaments can be traced, but collective security can never be assured by an apparent preponderance in armaments, for, as we can see, new factors continually arise, new weaknesses are discovered, which upset the balance. Effective protest is in any case not possible while some particular State, if interfered with in what it sets itself to do, can hold out the threat of a new world war infinitely more disastrous to civilisation than the last. The Governments of the Great Powers and of other Powers closely concerned can still avoid the danger of a new world war, but they must be prepared to make sacrifices if their peoples are to be spared it. These sacrifices would, however, be of little moment, whatever they might involve – and I have in mind even the return of some territories – in comparison with those which their peoples will be called upon to bear, in defence of the errors of 1919, if war ensues. That is obvious from our knowledge of the Spanish struggle, and of the struggle commencing in the Far East, to the horrors of which gas warfare has mercifully not been added. It is understood of course that any attempt at settlement should necessarily form part of a general settlement, including measures of disarmament. Without limitation of armaments confidence in the future would not be possible.

The difficulties of promoting a just peace now, after the errors and missed opportunities of so many years, are evident, but would they not be accentuated a hundredfold after another general war? What sort of peace, whoever wins – and it is evident that the side with the greatest resources must win,

---

[1] Cordell Hull (1871-1955), United States Secretary of State (1933-44).
[2] A reference to de Valera's speech to the special session of the Assembly of the League of Nations on 2 July 1936 concerning the withdrawal of sanctions imposed on Italy following her invasion of Abyssinia in October 1935. This speech is published in Maurice Moynihan (ed.) *Speeches and statements by Eamon de Valera 1917–73* (Dublin, 1980), pp 282-5 and in *Peace and War: Speeches and Statements by Mr. Eamon de Valera on International Affairs* (Dublin, 1944), pp 54-9.

which should be a warning to States whose judgement may be warped by a sense of permanent injustice, or to those who may be tempted to carry threats too far – can be expected after another prolonged war? Will the next generation have to face another catastrophe as a result of it?

Degeneration in the organisation of peace is obvious. Instead of a body of States reasonably armed, and bound together by treaty to settle disputes peacefully and to protect each other against aggression, all the major States and many of the smaller ones feel themselves forced to compete with their neighbours in armaments. Instead of States cultivating friendship with their neighbours, the old policy of making friends with next-neighbour-but-one is too often pursued, (e.g. France-Russia; Germany-Japan; Russia-China; Russia-Czechoslovakia; Germany-Italy; etc.), the result being a vicious policy of encirclement which settles nothing and renders distrust and eventual strife inevitable.

The League has suffered because it was used to guarantee treaties which were too repressive to be borne, and regional arrangements in Europe will fail because it is useless to ask States to guarantee situations which they themselves consider to be unjust. It is clear that all arrangements for collective security must be ineffective unless they have as base a just arrangement.

One looks in vain on the Agenda of the Assembly for a reference to the dangerous international situation which exists today? What sort of situation will exist when the next Assembly meets if the Great Powers do not get together with a definite will to measure and find solutions, not in respect of this or that symptom, but of the underlying problems. Between States which are over-armed peace is at the mercy of incidents, or of agents-provocateurs. In view of the dangers, the Assembly should not separate without demanding in the name of all the people that the Great Powers, which are responsible for the present situation, should proceed to deal with the root cause of the malaise in Europe. These are matters for Statesmen and not for soldiers, and it is only too obvious now that they cannot be allowed to drift indefinitely. Moreover, it is manifest that attempts at economic appeasement are not enough. Greater prosperity in the present situation only means greater facilities for re-armament. These are the facts of the situation, and they should be faced by Statesmen with the courage with which statesmen and peoples will face war. No problems should be regarded as being beyond the power of governments to solve peacefully. At the stage we have now reached, it seems fundamentally a question of plotting the sacrifices and the relief from the burden of armaments which a general political and territorial settlement would entail against the sacrifices which war would involve whether it is won or lost. There is no doubt of the choice which peoples, if they had their way, would make.

A sympathetic reference to Mr. Cordell Hull's initiative of July could be worked in, and also perhaps a reference to the Inter-American Conference of Buenos-Aires (mentioned in Chapter 2 of the Secretary-General's Report – A.6.1937). Views also on Spain and on the Japanese attack on China could be expressed if desired, and the question of Palestine could be referred to if the Minister wishes to express any views, or any hopes of a just and peaceful settlement of that problem.

Perhaps also a reference to the peaceful settlement of the Sanjak problem by the Council might be made. The Iraq-Iran dispute is also being settled peacefully by the parties themselves.

The power of the Press for good or evil, in regard to the promotion of goodwill, is a subject that might deserve a paragraph.

Perhaps the question of a reference to religious persecution in Germany and the absurd promotion of a German God might be considered.

[signed] F.T. CREMINS
Permanent Delegate

No. 80 NAI 2003/17/181

> *Letter from Seán Murphy to John W. Dulanty (London)*
> *(Secret) (Copy)*
> DUBLIN, 4 September 1937

With reference to my secret minute of the 30th July[1] I am directed by the President to inform you that he is going to Geneva to the League Assembly. He is leaving Dublin on the morning boat on Thursday, 9th September, staying that night in London and leaving for Paris on the morning of Friday, the 10th. A further minute will be sent to you regarding the President's journey.

The President wishes that you should inform Mr. MacDonald that he is going to Geneva. As regards the venue for the suggested meeting it is thought that somewhere near Zurich might be the most suitable, as a journey to Zurich by the President would not give rise to speculation. However, the President has an open mind on this matter and he will be prepared to meet Mr. MacDonald at any place and time mutually convenient.

It would be well if you were able to let the President know on his way through London whether Mr. MacDonald has any suggestion to make regarding the venue and the date of the meeting.

(Sgd) SEAN MURPHY
Rúnaí

No 81 NAI 2006/39

> *Confidential report from John W. Dulanty to Joseph P. Walshe (Dublin)*
> *(No. 40) (Secret)*
> LONDON, 7 September 1937

Mr. Eden asked the High Commissioners to meet him at the British Foreign Office last evening. Of the High Commissioners there were only Mr. Jordan aand myself present, the other High Commissioners being on the Continent on leave prior to proceeding to Geneva. There were also present:

Mr. Ilsley, Canadian Minister for Finance and a Delegate to the Assembly

Mr. Stirling, Secretary to the Australian Delegation at Geneva

---

[1] See above No. 71.

Dr. Gie, Union of South Africa Minister at Berlin and Delegate to Geneva
His Highness The Aga Khan, and Sir Denis Gray (India Office), Delegates
to Geneva

Mediterranean

The British Foreign Secretary said that his Government in agreeing with the
proposal of the French Government for a conference on the recent submarine
attacks in the Mediterranean had suggested that the Conference should be
limited to Mediterranean powers only. They wished to avoid the risk of a
fruitless political wrangle. The French Government however insisted upon
the Black Sea powers – Russia, Romania and Bulgaria – being included. The
British had to agree to this but had pressed for Germany to be included so as
to make the attendance of Italy more likely. It seemed to him that the
Germans had behaved better than Italy in the Spanish conflict and it was
interesting to note that the French were hoping that the Germans would
attend the Conference. As yet it was not known which powers were accepting the invitation. The intention was to hold the Conference at Nyon, near
Geneva, on Friday next, 10th September.

It was the British hope to keep the discussion to technical rather than
political grounds. He thought his colleagues in the British cabinet would
agree to his proposals that this conference should decide that the recent submarine activities in the Mediterranean in sinking ships without warning represented a grave abuse of that weapon, and that these sinkings were contrary
to international engagements. He would try to get a resolution requiring both
parties to the conflict in Spain to keep their submarines when submerged
within the limits of their territorial waters. Outside the territorial waters the
submarines should be required to have surface movements only. The British
Admiralty experts were looking into this and relative points on the submarine question but he hoped to obtain decisions more or less on these lines at
the Conference.

(After the meeting, speaking to me alone Mr. Eden told me in strict confidence that following upon the discharge by the British of the depth charge a
certain European nation summoned its submarines to their respective bases).

There was no reference at this meeting to the telegrams which the United
Kingdom Government had sent on Monday last to us and other partner
Governments about instructions to the Masters of merchant vessels. It seems
reasonable to assume that the British will defer their final decision on the last
mentioned point until the resolutions of the International Conference are
reached.

The Far East

Mr. Eden said that the Japanese had stated that they did not wish to interfere
with foreign shipping but they were very anxious to avoid the abuse of the
unjustifiable use of neutral flags. The United Kingdom, the United States,
and France, all agreed with this view since it would mean a far less difficult
position than if the Japanese Government declared a state of war and exercised its belligerent rights at sea. The British Foreign Secretary then outlined

the proposals contained in the telegrams which I sent to the Department on Saturday last. The United States were extremely anxious that the British should proceed on these lines. They have a very big trade with China and would want the minimum interference with their shipping. Again, China is now the largest export market for Germany and that country also would prefer the British proposals to a declaration of a state of war by Japan.

A copy of an ad interim reply by the Japanese Government to the British Government's communication on the shooting of the British Ambassador was handed to Mr. Eden during the meeting and he immediately read out its terms. After reciting that they took all steps for the British Ambassador's comfort and their tendering of sympathy at the appropriate diplomatic points the Japanese Government said that they were conducting investigations into the incident. They had as yet found no evidence which showed that the shooting was done by any of their forces. They were prosecuting these investigations with all speed and would communicate again when they had reached a conclusion.

The British manufacturing resources are theoretically available to either party in the Far East for the supply of munitions. Actually this does not mean a great deal since there is little margin of armament production available outside the production of munitions for Britain itself. The British have however accepted some orders from the Chinese for aeroplanes, and the United States are executing considerable orders for aeroplanes also for the Chinese.

The information in the British Foreign Office is that the Japanese are rather seriously concerned at the strength of the Chinese resistance. (The opinion in financial circles in the city of London is that if China can put up a good defence for six months the position may become critical for Japan since it may be difficult if not impossible for her to continue this vast expenditure on warfare and at the same time continue under-selling her competitors in the markets of the world. This is City opinion, not Whitehall.)[1]

Abyssinia
It seemed as though the meeting was finished when I enquired what line the United Kingdom Government were proposing to take at Geneva with regard to Abyssinia. Mr. Eden said that he thought the only question on this subject which would come before the League would be as to whether Abyssinia existed as an independent sovereign State with a Government in being and whether she was therefore competent for membership of the League. Their information was that the Italian forces were now in effective military occupation of the whole of Abyssinia save for one small section in the South West. The Italians had not of course had time to set up an effective civil administration. It would seem that there was now no Abyssinian Government as such since the two deputies who tried to carry on the Government after Hailé Selassie's departure had now escaped into Kenya. In his view the question of recognition of Italy in Abyssinia and the title of its King would be for the powers individually though on this he was not stating a final opinion. He

---

[1] The last sentence is handwritten by Dulanty.

had been interested to learn from Mr. Walters of the League Secretariat in Geneva that the expectation was that no Delegate from Abyssinia would attend and when Mr. Eden asked why that opinion prevailed he was told that it was because of the suggested forthcoming conversations of Lord Perth with Mussolini.

I suspect, and it can of course be no more than a suspicion, that the British are probably looking for an appeasement in the Mediterranean as a result of the Conference on Friday if Italy can be induced to attend, which is now less sure after the Russian incident. If such appeasement be achieved and if the British Ambassador at Rome should be successful in the proposed con- versations – these proposed talks it will be recalled, were the subject of warm commendation both by the British Prime Minister and the Duce – in securing an improvement in the general European situation some form of recognition of the Italian conquest might be agreed to by the British as a part of a general European settlement.

During the talk on Abyssinia a protracted and somewhat tiresome dis- cussion was started by Mr. Jordan. He wanted to know what his position was if he at Geneva opposed any recognition of the Italian conquest in Abyssinia and the British Ambassador at Rome conveyed as he put it the British Commonwealth recognition of that conquest. Was not the British Ambassador at Rome the King's Ambassador and was he not, as such, since New Zealand had no Minister in Rome, the representative of the King in his capacity as King of New Zealand? Without waiting for Mr. Eden to answer this question I said that Lord Perth clearly represented only the Government of the United Kingdom and cited Washington, Paris, and Berlin as foreign government capitals where we, together with other partner Governments, had our own Ministers. In the case of Tokyo, should the British Government decide to recall their Ambassador it was perfectly open for the Canadian Government if they so wished to retain their Minister in that city. Mr. Malcolm MacDonald accepted this and after some rather desultory talk Mr. Eden said that he did not think the New Zealand Government had any responsibility for the British Ambassador in Rome. Although it should hardly be necessary the discussion seemed to make it incumbent on me to emphasise the obvious fact that we went to Geneva as a sovereign independent State.

[copy letter unsigned]
High Commissioner

No. 82 NAI 2003/17/181

Confidential report from John W. Dulanty to Joseph P. Walshe (Dublin)
(No. 41) (Secret)

LONDON, 7 September 1937

Last evening I conveyed to Mr. Malcolm MacDonald the intimation con- tained in your Secret minute of 4th September.[1] He seemed very pleased at the acceptance of his suggestion of conversations with the President.

---

[1] See above No. 80.

We spoke of the various points at which a meeting might be arranged but it is unnecessary to report that part of the talk because when Mr. Walshe (please see Mr. Walshe's separate note of this meeting – enclosed herewith)[1] and I paid a courtesy call on him today Mr. MacDonald stated that he is going to Geneva on Monday next as a member of the United Kingdom Delegation. Before the Summer vacation Mr. Eden had asked him to join the Delegation but he had declined because he did not wish to be engaged in Geneva if there was a possibility of the President being agreeable to a meeting somewhere other than Geneva. Yesterday Mr. Eden had repeated his request pointing out that the United Kingdom Delegation was undermanned in that it contained only himself and Mr. Walter Elliot, who as an individual minister[2] was less concerned with Geneva than Mr. MacDonald. Mr. MacDonald was doubtful about going since it might look as though he had suddenly put himself into the Delegation on learning that the President was to be in Geneva. As the result of a talk between Mr. Chamberlain, Mr. Eden, and himself he had now decided to go and he thought that it would be possible to arrange a meeting or meetings in some convenient place outside Geneva.

Yesterday I reminded Mr. MacDonald of the lengthy conversations which had already taken place at the Grosvenor Hotel,[3]and I suggested that if real progress was to be made he should be prepared to leave generalities and formulate however tentatively their proposals for dealing with the questions outstanding between the two countries.

His reply to this suggestion, which reply he more or less repeated today to Mr. Walshe and myself, was that at the Grosvenor Hotel much the biggest part of the talk turned on the Constitution when the President was good enough to expound what his intention and objective were. That conversation had been of immense value to him, (Mr. MacDonald). It had enabled him to go to his colleagues and explain precisely what was in Mr. de Valera's mind. There were still a few points on the Constitution where some difficulty remained for his Government notably its relation to the Six Counties. The other questions of Defence, Financial Settlement, and Trade Agreement, had scarcely been touched upon; he wished to give the President the whole of his mind on these questions and in return to be informed of the whole of the President's mind. His hope then was to return to London after about a week in Geneva, consult with his colleagues here and in the light of those discussions to have a further talk in London with the President on his way home from Geneva when he hoped progress would be made.

Mr. Walshe has joined me whilst I was dictating this report and has handed me his note of the subsequent part of the conversation. It is therefore unnecessary for me to go over the same ground.

[signed] J.W. DULANTY
High Commissioner

---

[1] Handwritten marginal note by Dulanty. For Walshe's note see below, No. 83.
[2] 'Minister' is a handwritten insertion by Dulanty, replacing the word 'Member'.
[3] See above Nos 3, 7 and 8.

No. 83 NAI 2003/17/181

Handwritten letter from Joseph P. Walshe to Seán Murphy (Dublin)
LONDON, 7 September 1937

Dear Seán,

Will you please read this for the President.

I went with the H.C. to see MacDonald at 12.30 today. Batterbee and Harding were both away.

I asked him what idea he had about the conversation to take place with the President.

He said that the last conversation had cleared the air and expected that further progress might be made now. The first conversations would naturally be exploratory, but he would report to his colleagues and it might be possible to reach some element of finality in a further conversation [on] the President's way back to Dublin.

MacDonald had just been asked to form part of the British delegation to Geneva as the Ministerial strength was a little low. He was still hesitating and a little worried lest the Press should say that he went to G. at the last moment because the President was going. And he thought that publicity of that kind might worry the P. I assured him that it would not. In any case if MacD. was a member of the B. delegation there would be nothing strange in his meeting the P. occasionally in Geneva whereas a special ad hoc journey to Zurich or some other place other than Geneva would – if it became public – cause much more embarrassment to both sides.

MacDonald thought the British would have to object to 3 + 4 of the Constn.

We were really declaring the 6 counties to be within the jurisdiction of the Dublin Parliament, part indeed of an existing state.

The six counties were part of the U.K. and the British had just as strong reason to object as if France or some other country declared part of the U.K. to be under her jurisdiction. I said it would be very unfortunate to raise that issue. 3 + 4[1] constituted a claim to the unity of the Irish Nation – it was a national matter of the utmost importance to us. His example did not introduce any element of parity. It was an undeniable fact that the Irish nation was one; and it followed that the assumption that the whole country should be one jurisdictional area was perfectly justifiable – and even essential – in such a fundamental document. The President's idea in drawing up the Constn. was to satisfy the greatest possible number of our people and to provide a basis on which normal relations with G.B. could be established. 3 + 4 were essential to the whole fabric of the Constn. and the whole object of the Constn. would fail without them. MacD. thought that feeling in the Six Counties was much worse since the passing of the Constn. To that I replied that the feeling was only transitory. If as the President most sincerely hoped the Constn. brought about a certain degree of contentment and enabled him

---

[1] At this point Walshe had written '2' before '3', but had crossed '2' out.

to make some arrangement with G.B. the six county people would forget the Constitution and think only of the fact of the existence of better relations. The momentary worsening of feeling in the Six Counties – if his information was correct – was to be reckoned with as an inevitable stage in our progress towards better relations.

MacD. went on to say that he wished the President would not believe that the British wanted to perpetuate partition, or that they could put an end to it. Only the attitude of our Govt. towards the six counties could do that. I said that I felt sure that, given favourable conditions, the President would do everything possible to bring about good feeling – a favourable settlement of our quarrel was, of course, an essential preliminary.

He did not commit himself to any exact proposition on the financial question. He thought the President believed that there could be a complete settlement – if we spent just a few hundred thousand a year more on defence. He knew that the President would agree to nothing until it was quite clear that they were going to leave the ports. That they were ready to do, but they must be quite sure that the invitation would come to them if G.B. were attacked. Ireland was an absolutely essential element in their defence system and we could not expect them to leave themselves exposed to attack through hesitation on our part. My answer was that we had to safeguard our sovereignty first of all, but we were quite conscious of the fact that in modern warfare an attack on either of our countries might constitute a danger to both. He should speak further to the President about the 'invitation' issue. The President realised how important it was and had given it very serious thought.

Though MacD. would not say that a considerable advance on the question of Defence expenditure would make them abandon their claim to the annuities I did get the impression that it was still the best line of approach in present circumstances.

The H.C. and I can give the President a better idea of the atmosphere of this conversation when we meet on Thursday evening but these points may be of some use in the President's immediate consideration of the matter.

Yours,
J.P.W.

No. 84 UCDA P150/2495

Memorandum prepared by the Department of Finance for the Department of External Affairs on sums claimed by the British Government as due from the Irish Free State[1]

DUBLIN, 13 September 1937

In compliance with the request from the Department of External Affairs this morning for an estimate in the briefest possible terms of the capital value of

---

[1] Marginal note by Sheila Murphy: 'Note prepared by D/Finance for President's information September 1937'.

the sums claimed by the British Government as due from the Irish Free State, other than Land Purchase Annuities, the following statement, which is required this evening, has been prepared. It will be understood that the figures given in this statement are necessarily approximate and in some cases, e.g., pensions, little more than guesses.

2. The main heads of the British claim, other than Land Purchase Annuities, relate to pensions and these may be grouped under the following heads – Civil Service (including Inland Revenue and Customs and Excise but excluding Post Office which continue to be collected), R.I.C., and Judicial Pensions, with Allied Services and Audit Services. These pensions are, for obvious reasons, a declining charge but the rate of decline cannot be estimated in view of our lack of information as to the age composition of the various bodies of pensioners. Further, the fixing of the date on which the capital value of the various items in dispute, other than Land Purchase Annuities, is to be assessed is a matter of some difficulty. Payments have been withheld since 1932 but the British have endeavoured to effect recovery by means of penal duties. Up to the 31st March, 1937, the total of such duties collected by them was 21.9 million pounds as compared with a total of 24.1 million pounds withheld, leaving what they regard as a deficit of 2.2 million pounds. If we exclude altogether Land Purchase Annuities and the kindred figure of Bonus and Excess Stock charges, the total amount withheld up to 31st March last has been 8.6 million pounds which is 13.3 million pounds less than the sums collected by the British under the penal duties.

3. In the following table the 1st April, 1937, is assumed as the date for the necessary capital calculation, which is made on the basis that any sums due under the respective heads have been discharged up to that date.

4. A further assumption has had to be made as regards the rate of interest and here 4% has been taken. The lower the rate of interest assumed the greater, of course, will be the capital liability and the figure mentioned is as high as we can go. The British will probably regard it as excessive and consider something between 3% and $3^1/2$% as the maximum justifiable.

5. It should be pointed out that no reference has been made in this Memo, to counter-claims against the British e.g. in respect of over-taxation, currency and coinage, Road Fund and other items set forth in the statements presented in October, 1932, by the Free State to the British Government.

6. In view of the foregoing it will be understood that the following estimates of the capital value of the amounts withheld from the British Government, other than Land Purchase Annuities, cannot be advanced as firm figures except in the case of item V., Local Loans Fund Annuity, and must, accordingly, be used with caution.

	Claim in 1936–37	No of years payments assumed	Capital Amount
	£		£
I. Civil Pensions (including Inland Revenue and Customs & Excise, but excluding Post Office)	75,958	5	340,000
II. R.I.C. Pensions	986,684	12	9,265,000
III. Judicial Pensions	11,774	5	55,000
IV. Pensions – Allied & Audit Services	2,372	10	15,000
V. Local Loans Annuity	600,000	Term unexpired	4,540,000
VI. Railways & Marine Works Annuities	2,867	—	20,000
TOTAL	£1,679,655	—	£14,235,000

No. 85 NAI DFA 126/37

Telegram from John J. Hearne to the Department of External Affairs (Dublin)
GENEVA, 14 September 1937

President de Valera selected by nominations committee as a vice president of the 18th assembly and unanimously elected in plenary session this afternoon. Will therefore be a member of general committee which consists of the president of the assembly eight vice presidents and chairman of assembly committee. The general committee controls the procedure and supervises the whole work of the session.

For Information Bureau
HEARNE

Recd. at my home – informed Press, but found out they had recd. the information in full from Reuters and were publishing it.

J.P.W.
15/9/37[1]

---

[1] Handwritten note by Walshe.

No. 86 UCDA P150/2349

Memorandum by Eamon de Valera of informal conversations with
Malcolm MacDonald
GENEVA, 4.10 pm to 6.50 pm, 15 September 1937

Mr. MacDonald said he was anxious to have another informal chat on the matters in dispute between the two countries. The previous discussions in the Grosvenor[1] had been very helpful to him and enabled him to understand matters which he would not otherwise have been able to understand and put him in a position to explain them similarly to his colleagues. There were matters in regard to the new Constitution which he would like to come back on, but it was better to leave that over for a subsequent talk. He wished to take up at the moment the three or four problems – the financial dispute, the treaty ports and defence, trade and partition.

With regard to the latter, he said that I had repeatedly stated that without a settlement of the partition problem it would not be possible to have between the two countries that goodwill and co-operation which both of us desired. On partition he just wished to repeat what he had said before – that they could do nothing to force the North to join with the South. They could see no way in which the ending of partition could be brought about in a short period of time, and that if progress was to be made it was necessary to turn to the other questions.

Finance and Defence could perhaps be linked together, as I had suggested, but the British Government regarded the annuities as due on the foot of Mr. Cosgrave's agreement in the Ultimate Financial Settlement.[2] He did not think they could go before their people and ask them to forego repayment of that debt. On the other hand, I had repeatedly, he said, committed myself in public to the statement that not one single penny of the land annuities would be paid. There were also other monies withheld – Local Loans, Pensions, etc. I had not committed myself in regard to them in the same way, but he feared payment of these alone would not satisfy the British public or the British Government could not take the responsibility for urging a settlement on these lines.

With regard to Defence, they were advised by their military and naval experts that our ports were necessary for them for the purpose of defending their food supplies in time of war and that whilst they would be quite ready to hand over the ports they would want to be assured that an invitation to use these ports would be forthcoming in time of need for the purpose indicated.

On my side I made it clear that my commitment in regard to the annuities was definite and that I could not possibly recede from it. I asked him, if he, himself, had ever made himself acquainted with our case on the annuities. I gave him a rough idea of the basis of our position; said I was perfectly satisfied that the monies were not due and that as a private individual I would

---

[1] See above Nos 3, 7 and 8.
[2] See DIFP Volume II, No. 385.

not pay monies to which I regarded myself as having such a right and that as a public representative I would regard it as a duty to oppose the payment of them whether in office or not in office. If there was to be a financial settlement the payment of these monies would have to be excluded.

With regard to the other monies, I had not examined the merits of the case as I had with the land annuities. I felt justified in retaining them because of the fact that I regarded the land annuity payments that had been made as having been wrongfully paid and that we were entitled to be given credit for them and they would more than counterbalance the amounts due on the other payments even if on the merits these were found to be due to Britain. That was why I had not therefore felt obliged so far to examine the merits in detail. The land annuities had been specifically given to Ireland, North and South, by the 1920 Act, and the British Parliament had taken on itself the exclusive liability of meeting the interest and security fund of the stock.

Mr. MacDonald reverted to the old position that they had Mr. Cosgrave's agreement and that they regarded us as bound by that. It would not be fair that they should suffer even if from the point of view of Irish procedure Mr. Cosgrave was acting ultra vires. The matter of Irish procedure was something in which they had no concern. I put it to him that if there was a departure from universal custom of States there should be some provision in the constitution or custom of a particular State to warrant it. After all Ireland was not an unknown State with procedures with which they were not aware, etc. Mr. MacDonald repeated the difficulty they would have with the parliament and people; whilst I insisted that the present Irish Government could not consider the payment of the annuities, but we would I thought be able to consider a compromise on the other payments particularly if the payments were to be made by way of defence. He said that his defence experts were of opinion that the bringing up to date of the existing ports and the treaty ports would not involve expenditure of much over half a million pounds. I pointed out, and he agreed, that it was the continuing expense, the upkeep that mattered. The present strength of our army was probably much too low for purposes of adequate defence. We would have to increase the strength of the regular army and provide for the training of a Volunteer force. The upkeep of some ships and aeroplanes would be an additional cost, and our people were already taxed to the utmost. I would require to go into the matter in detail as regards our defence requirements, and in that we would have to take the advice of the British or some other great power that had experience as to what our requirements would be. I would also have to examine in detail the financial items.

Mr. MacDonald asked could we put experts or officials to continue conversations, and I thought it would be of no use. These were negotiations obviously for principals.

We discussed the advantages to Britain of a complete settlement with Ireland. It would change the attitude of the Irish people throughout the world towards Britain if the old quarrel was definitely settled. He thought the settlement of partition was out of the question. I said our aim must be then to make the other settlements, it being understood that they could only be partial in the hope that the making of them would prepare the way for the ultimate settlement. Before he left he had quite definitely my views on the following matters:

1. That the ending of partition was absolutely necessary for the good relations we both desired.
2. That we could not consent to paying a penny of the land annuity money.
3. That we could not consent to any commitment to invite the British to our ports when they might desire the use of these ports for the defence of their supplies in time of war.
4. That the line to pursue for a solution was to find how our increased commitments in regard to defence (so as to make good the policy of preventing a foreign power from using our island as a basis of attack against Britain) would be held to equate the payments on which a compromise could be made.

I indicated that I was willing to meet representatives of their Government for the purpose of hammering out the financial agreement once the main lines were fixed and that it was certain that an agreement could be arrived at.

We agreed to resume the discussion at 4 tomorrow (the 16th) when he wished to take up some points in the Constitution, and I agreed to lunch with Eden and himself on Saturday to hear from Eden the position in regard to international affairs.

No. 87 NAI DFA 227/4

Letter from William J. B. Macaulay to Joseph P. Walshe (Dublin)
(M 10/37)

Rome, 16 September 1937

I shall be glad to be informed what attitude I am to adopt towards 'the Chargé d'Affaires of Spain' who has announced to me his reception by the Cardinal Secretary of State and his presentation of his Letter of Credence.

I do not see how I can acknowledge this communication at all in view of our relations with the Valencia Government.

[signed] W.J.B. Macaulay

No. 88 UCDA P150/2349

Memorandum by Eamon de Valera of informal conversations with Malcolm MacDonald

Geneva, 17 September 1937

I have already had two very long conversations with MacDonald on Wednesday and Thursday afternoons (Sept. 15th and 16th).[1]

The discussion ranged over the new Constitution, the External Relations Act, Partition, the Treaty Ports and Defence, Financial dispute and Trade.

---

[1] See above No. 86.

In regard to the Constitution, MacDonald put forward the British point of view in regard to these matters, whilst I put forward our point of view. The net results appear to me to be the following:

NEW CONSTITUTION: At the time the Constitution is about to come into effect the British will make some formal protest in regard to Articles 2 and 3. Their point seems to be that they do not want to appear to be acquiescing in our claim put forward in these Articles. I pointed out that we would have to reply fairly stiffly on that matter and there could of course be no question of any change.

PARTITION: I again emphasised that this was the most fundamental and vital question in regard to the relations between the two countries; that no agreements on other matters could bring about the good relations both he and I desired so long as partition lasted. Settlement on the other matters would help to make the solution of partition itself easier perhaps by improving the relations and securing the good-will of Great Britain. MacDonald insisted that they could do nothing about partition which could only be ended by ourselves winning over the North. The British would do nothing to stand in the way. I pressed him on whether they desired partition or not. He said they did not desire it 'for its own sake'. They were committed to the North. I asked if they would publicly state that so far as they were concerned they would desire partition to end. He could not promise that such a ~~settlement~~[1] statement would be made. His steadfast view was that the partition solution would have to wait. I said we would therefore have to consider definitely a campaign to inform British and world opinion generally as to the iniquity of that whole position.

THE PORTS: They were ready, he said, to hand over the treaty ports at once if they could be guaranteed an invitation to use them in case of a war when they would need them to protect their essential supplies. He said it was the definite view of the military and naval experts that these ports were necessary to them. I pointed out that public opinion in Ireland would not stand for any such guarantee. Such a guarantee would in effect mean that we were merely holding and maintaining the port defences for their use. MacDonald said he would go into the matter again, that if the military and naval view remained unchanged it was possible that the British Government would prefer to leave things as they are and maintain their rights under the 1921 treaty. I pointed out the danger of that situation from our point of view and their point of view, and we would have to claim the recognition of our complete sovereignty over our ports. I pointed out that our sovereignty over our own territorial waters would not preclude the British vessels from operating immediately outside the territorial limits and questioned the soundness of the military and naval men's views and said that at any rate the wider considerations should be held sufficient to have these views overridden. He admitted that they could override them, but they were bound to take the experts views very seriously into consideration.

---

[1] All words struck through in this document are words deleted in a similar fashion in the original.

GENERAL DEFENCE: On this he said that they appreciated and regarded it as of great value my public statement that our territory would not be allowed to be used by any foreign power as a basis of attack upon them. I said that that principle should be the bedrock on which our defence relations to each other should be built. An independent Ireland would have ~~no~~ a direct interest in the maintenance of the inviolability of its territory and of its independence. The moment all threats from Britain had ceased and good relations were established an attack on Britain's security would indirectly be an attack upon us. In case of a common attack it would be of incalculable importance to Britain to be able to feel that our part of the general front was safe. It would be our duty to set about putting ourselves in such a position that that would be true. Our resources of course were limited, but we were a people of natural military gifts and I felt that if the burden of the tariffs were removed our people could be induced to bear a fair burden of taxation. To set our defences in order we would need equipment and expert advice. A considerable portion of the equipment would have to be purchased from abroad; the advice would have to come from the experts of some great power. If we had come to a settlement with Britain, naturally so as to provide for the case of our operating side by side it would be advisable to have our equipment or organisation and our defence measures generally the same as those of Britain and part of a common scheme. Towards preparations of this sort the Government could hope to win the support of public opinion generally, although the aim might be misrepresented, but no public opinion could be secured for expenditure or preparation if it was thought that the aim was simply to assist Britain. The aim must clearly be to defend the independence of our own country, but that I repeated would be of incalculable value to Great Britain in a time of stress. The influence of a satisfied Irish opinion at home and in America should not be lost sight of by the British Government. The position of Canada and a number of other considerations made it important that Britain in a time of war should be supported by the active good will of the people of the United States. Irish opinion played an important part in that matter.

FINANCIAL DISPUTE: MacDonald adverted to the fact that I had committed myself definitely to not paying a single penny of the land annuities. They regarded these monies as due to them on the basis of the Cosgrave agreements. To them Cosgrave was the head of a responsible government capable of entering into binding contracts. They should not be penalised because there was some domestic procedure which he did not follow. I replied that neither should we be penalised because an agreement was signed which had no proper authority behind it. In our opinion the money was not due. I referred to the 1920 Act and asked MacDonald if he had made himself acquainted with the details of our case. He made it clear that he had not. I suggested he should try to understand that case. So far as we were concerned I was so satisfied that the monies were not due that under no circumstances would I, as a private individual, agree to pay away monies to which I had such an obvious right. MacDonald said he felt that the British Government would be unable to face their Parliament and people with the proposition that these payments should be entirely remitted.

Discussing the other withheld payments I agreed that there was a possibility of compromise in regard to them. I had not examined the merits of the British claim in regard to these, because I was satisfied generally that the annuity payments which had been wrongfully made would more than cover any claim which the British could advance in their regard. MacDonald said he understood that my suggestion in our talks in London had been that the increased cost of our defence forces incurred by the taking over of the ports and the modernising of their equipment should be regarded as meeting the British financial claim. He had made enquiries he said and was informed that about half a million pounds would be the total cost of modernising defences of the defence of the treaty ports. I told him that it was not the first capital cost that mattered but the continuing charge. Our present army would have to be considerably increased, both the standing army and our volunteer forces. We would need some coast patrol vessels, and also a number of aeroplanes. The annual cost of maintenance of these could hardly be less than a million pounds, and our taxation was already an extremely heavy burden, particularly because of partition, the general depression and the result of British tariffs. It would be extremely difficult to increase it to any appreciable extent. The exact amount of the cost could only be discovered when we went into detail.

Ex-Service Pensions.[1]

TRADE: I pointed out that a trade agreement would be necessary in relation to any settlement of the financial dispute. I thought the trade settlement would present no difficulty. I pointed out that of course we could not forego the right of protecting our own industries, but that we would have need of considerable capital, equipment and goods which it would be quite uneconomic for ourselves to produce. In any case we would have either directly or indirectly to purchase in order to secure payment for what we ~~want~~ sell. The ideal for our country [was] not to have all its eggs in one basket, but to have a balancing trade with two or three large countries, but if the countries we would like to purchase from us were unable to do so, well we could not buy from them.

The conversations ended with a full realisation by MacDonald that we desired to be on friendly terms with England, were animated with no ill-will towards them, but that our desire was to clear away the ground and prepare a foundation on which cordial relations and friendly co-operation would be possible. I agreed to have lunch with himself and Eden at the Bois on Saturday next, the 18th inst., so that Mr. Eden might give an account of the international situation. MacDonald repeated what he had said at the beginning that the conversations in London had been of great value to him, that these conversations he hoped would be of similar value, that he would report to the Prime Minister when he got back, might possibly then have a discussion with the Cabinet Sub-Committee and then if they could find a basis, put forward proposals to us. I thought that discussions by civil servants would be of no use as the questions were essentially ones which

---

[1] There appear to have been no notes taken on this subject at this point.

would have to be decided by principals. I thought a delegation of British Ministers could meet ~~ourselves~~ ours either in Dublin or in London to hammer out a settlement finally, but that any such meeting would be worse than useless unless there was a reasonable prospect that a settlement could be made.

Notes:

At the outset of our discussion Mr. MacDonald said that he was very glad to have the opportunity of further discussion, that his last talk in London had been extremely helpful and made it possible for him to explain clearly to his colleagues the purpose aimed in the new Constitution.

=========================

DEFENCE Note

The British would in their own defence be compelled, if we did not do it, to make provision for the defence of our area if we were not strong enough ourselves to resist an attack on our territory by another power. We would naturally be only too glad to invite them to assist. The need of the unity of Ireland in any satisfactory defence. At present no general strategic plan possible.

The development of food possibilities of Great Britain and then of our country as a defensive measure.

No. 89 NAI DFA Letter Books Berlin 1936-1937

Letter from Joseph P. Walshe to Charles Bewley (Berlin)
(105/45)[1]

DUBLIN, 23 September 1937

Your report No. 31/29 of the 16th September[2] concerning the leading article in the 'Irish Press' of September 10th, 'The Origin of a Libel', simply illustrates the difficulty created for other countries by Germany's attitude towards aspects of life and beliefs which profoundly affect them all. Your remarks about the semi-educated character of the person who wrote the article are quite irrelevant, and they deprive your report of the objective detachment without which no report is of any value. The 'Irish Press', in condemning this particular pictorial representation of Ireland's attitude towards Communism, was reflecting the views of the vast majority of the people of this country. It would be unfortunate if a paper which is known to have affiliations with the political party in power could give expression to no views about foreign countries which might be unpalatable to their rulers. Foreign countries like Germany which offend against the good feelings of other nations by their persecution of Christians and Jews and generally ignore the sentiments of nations other than their own cannot expect the world Press, even when it does happen to represent the views of

---

[1]   File 105/45 'Articles in the Irish Press uncomplimentary to Germany' was renumbered 214/8 and was later confidentially destroyed on an unknown date.
[2]   Not located, file destroyed.

Governments, to ignore its fundamental duty of formulating the view of the average man in the country concerned.

As has already been suggested to you, the actions or views of newspapers or of the Government in this country should not be regarded as *ipso facto* wrong because they happen to be in conformity with opinion in the neighbouring country, and the Minister is still at a loss to understand how this frequent community of view in international matters between this country and Great Britain can in any way prevent our Ministers abroad from pursuing their task of obtaining the fullest recognition for Irish nationality. In this matter the Minister would be glad to have some constructive suggestions from you as to what really should be your work in Germany in order to promote our interests in other than purely commercial circles. If official Germany continues to insult actively the most sacred beliefs of the people of this and the other Christian countries of the world, there may easily be a movement here in favour of closing down our Mission in Berlin. No doubt, in conjunction with other Representatives in Berlin, you have from time to time informed the Foreign Minister how impossible it is to secure a better tone towards Germany in the Press or in public opinion so long as the German Government openly vilifies the tenets which are common to us all.

When Herr von Kuhlmann[1] was here, I had a frank conversation with him on this whole issue, and after he had made some complaints similar to yours about the attitude of our Press, I explained to him the growing dismay in this country and amongst our people the world over at the attitude of Germany towards the Christian religion. If official Germany chooses to brand Ireland as a country which is indifferent to the growth of Communism, she must expect some retort of the kind you complain of at least so long as her zeal to keep Communism out of Europe is accompanied by a teaching which retains the very worst element in that creed.

[copy letter unsigned]
Rúnaí

No. 90 NAI DFA 227/4

Code telegram from Joseph P. Walshe to William J. B. Macaulay
(No. 11)
DUBLIN, 4.35 pm, 27 September 1937

Your M 10/37 of 16th September.[2] You should treat Chargé d'Affaires as you would the representative of a fully recognised State.

ESTERO

---

[1] Dr Wilhelm von Kuhlmann, German Minister Plenipotentiary and Envoy Extraordinary to Ireland (1934-6).
[2] See above No. 87.

No. 91 NAI DFA 105/46

Letter from Charles Bewley to Joseph P. Walshe (Dublin)
(43/33)

BERLIN, 28 September 1937[1]

Having regard to the fact that the new Constitution will shortly come into effect, I shall be glad if you will ask the Minister for instructions on the following points.
1. Should I communicate officially to the Foreign Office the official alteration of the name of the state from Saorstát Éireann to Éire?
2. What further explanations should be given as to the effect of the Constitution on the relations of Éire to Great Britain?
3. In the event of questions being put to me on the general relations of Éire to Great Britain, what general line should be taken?
4. In the event of inquiries as to Éire's probable position in the case of a war between Germany and Great Britain, what should be the attitude adopted?

[signed] C. BEWLEY

No. 92 NAI DFA 105/46

Letter from Joseph P. Walshe to Charles Bewley (Berlin)
(105/46) (Secret) (Copy)

DUBLIN, 1 October 1937

In ~~reply~~[2] reference to the questions put in your minute of the 28th instant,[3] I am directed by the Minister to reply as follows:-
1) You will receive instructions in due course.
2) Only such as are obvious from the articles of the Constitution.
3) The relations between the two countries are improving since the removal of Mr. Thomas.[4] Great Britain's new determination not to seek to interfere in our affairs is creating a better atmosphere for a settlement of the more outstanding questions between the two countries. But the fact remains that only the removal of partition can open the way for the final political settlement.
4) No doubt, this type of enquirer will meet with the treatment he deserves at your hands.

[stamped] (signed J.P. WALSHE)
Rúnaí

---

[1] Marginal note: 'Sec[retar]y'.
[2] The word 'reply' has been crossed out and 'reference' has been inserted instead.
[3] See above No. 91.
[4] James H. Thomas.

No. 93 UCDA P150/2807

Extract from a speech given by Eamon de Valera at the Eighteenth Ordinary Session of the League of Nations

GENEVA, 2 October 1937

[matter omitted]

When on the initiative of the French and British Governments some twelve months ago, the non-intervention policy was agreed upon, and the Non-Intervention Committee was set up, my Government rejoiced. We believed in the policy of non-intervention, because that policy respected the right of the Spanish people to decide for themselves how they should be governed and who should be ~~the governors~~[1] the rulers – a right held particularly precious by our people because of their long struggle to get it acknowledged in their own regard. We believed in the policy of non-intervention also, because we were satisfied that, if left to themselves, the Spanish people would quickly secure a decision on the matters in dispute, and such conflict as there might be would be freed at least from the exasperation and bitterness, the callousness and cruelty which outside interference inevitably brings in its train, and which unfortunately it has brought in its train in the conflict now being waged. Moreover, we were convinced that foreign powers were unlikely to participate in the conflict through any love of the Spanish people, through any desire for the improvement of their social conditions or any regard for their civilisation or traditions. Their participation was much more likely to be prompted by selfish motives which might ultimately lead to the destruction of the great Spanish nation, or at least the loss of valuable portions of the national territory. Finally, we know that intervention on one side of the dispute would inevitably provoke counter-intervention on the other, leading to a fatal competition which could only result in a general European disaster.

With such convictions, Mr. President, it is obvious that our Government would greatly desire to be associated with those parts of the resolution which would confirm the policy of non-intervention. We deplore the interventions and counter-interventions which have bid fair to make Spain a cockpit for every European antagonism.

The people of Ireland are far from being indifferent to some of the issues at present being fought out in Spain, but the Irish Government is determined to adhere to the policy of non-intervention and steadfastly to advocate it as the best for Spain and the best for Europe. It would be a misrepresentation, therefore, of our Government's position to suggest, as I believe the second part of paragraph (7) does, that we are included in the States meditating a change of attitude. We have given no indication of such a change. If, as was suggested in the Sixth Committee, the intention of that sub-paragraph is merely to record a fact, then the record should be accurate. The fact to be recorded is, not that the members of the League which are parties to the

---

[1] These words have been crossed out in the original of this document.

Non-Intervention Agreement are meditating the termination of the policy of non-intervention, but that certain of those parties are meditating that course. I know that the withdrawal of some of the parties to the Non-Intervention Agreement can bring that agreement to an end so far as its effectiveness is concerned, but I want to emphasise that the Irish Government will not be one of those to take any share in that responsibility, and I want to make it clear beyond any possibility of misunderstanding that our Government are not being committed to any policy or action which might result from the termination of the Non-Intervention Agreement.

There is a danger, in the present condition of Europe, that the League of Nations, as it now is, may degenerate into a mere alliance of one group of States against another group. That would be the end of our hopes for a real League, and I consider that the smaller States of the League in particular[1] should resist from the beginning every tendency in that direction.

To conclude: With the greater portion of the resolution we are heartily in agreement, particularly with those parts which affirm the rights of the Spanish nation, with that part which expresses the hope that the diplomatic action initiated by certain powers will be successful in securing the immediate and complete withdrawal of the non-Spanish combatants from Spain, and with that part which urges the Council of the League to be ready to seize an opportunity that may present itself for securing a peaceful solution of the conflict. Being unable, however, to accept the text of the resolution as a whole, or *as I understand* to secure the necessary changes in that text, the Irish Delegation *have no alternative but to* abstain from the vote.[2]

No. 94 NAI DFA Paris Embassy 19/34

Confidential report from Art O'Brien to Joseph P. Walshe (Dublin)
(P. 19/34) (Copy)

PARIS, 4 October 1937

Conditions at the Legation during the past few months
It will no doubt be of interest to you and the information may also be very useful in formulating a view with regard to the calls upon a Minister's time in Paris, if I give a brief account of some activities during the past months.

From the beginning of May onwards, the calls upon my time for diplomatic functions, social functions and visitors, have been such that it is only with the very greatest difficulty that I have been able to find sufficient time to deal with the administrative work of the Legation. The International Exhibition in Paris has, of course, been chiefly responsible for this abnormal state of affairs. Firstly every pavilion that was opened had an inaugural ceremony to which all members of the Diplomatic Corps were invited. These inaugural ceremonies took place for the most part in the morning at any time

---

[1] Handwritten insertion: 'in particular'.
[2] Words in italics are handwritten insertions by de Valera.

between 9 and 11.30. In addition, each national pavilion had an evening reception in connection with its opening to which all the Diplomatic Corps were invited. These receptions took on a variety of characters and were held at any time between 9 p.m. and midnight. Again over 200 International Conferences of one sort or another have been held in Paris or will have been held from the beginning of May to the end of October. To a few of these, as you know, we have sent delegations. In connection with nearly every one of these international Conferences, the Members of the Diplomatic Corps have been invited, always to the two séances d'ouverture et de clôture and, in a great number of cases, to evening receptions and dinners or luncheons and afternoon functions, garden parties, etc.

Of course it would have been physically impossible to accept all these invitations, but to even attend to a minimum of them has been a very great strain.

Since about the middle of June, there has been a continuous flow of visitors from Ireland calling at the Legation with the request to see the Minister and in nearly every case, on account of the position which the callers held, or on account of the introductions which they brought, or because they were formerly associated with me or again because they were old friends, either personal or in the movement, it has been incumbent upon me to see them. In a very large number of cases, it has further been incumbent upon me to entertain them at luncheon, dinner, or otherwise. The number of visitors has seldom been less than 3 or 4 a day and, on many occasions, the number has been from 8 to 10 during the day (N.B. This does not, of course, include visitors who come to the Chancery for consular or business purposes).

Miss O'Briain and I were calculating the other day that for the past three months, we have only had a meal alone on about 12 occasions.

In addition to the above, there has, of course, been a number of delegations calling at the Legation to whom I have given varying attention and entertainment. Altogether it has been a very strenuous and trying season and from a personal point of view, I should be very sorry indeed if the Exhibition were continued next year, i.e. if it still continued to be as big an attraction as it has been on the present occasion for two years in succession, it would demand very great physical endurance.

[copy letter unsigned]
Aire Lán-Chómhachtach

P.S. – Owing to the state of affairs above-indicated, many reports on recent events have remained in abeyance. I am now clearing a number of these up and will continue to do so during the first days of my leave.

No. 95 NAI DFA 105/46

Letter from Charles Bewley to Joseph P. Walshe (Dublin)
(43/33)

BERLIN, 7 October 1937

I beg to refer to my minute of 28th September[1] requesting you to ask the Minister for instructions on the points therein contained, and your minute dated 1st October.[2]

1. I note that instructions will be sent me with regard to the official communication to the German Foreign Office of the alteration of the name of the State from Saorstát Éireann to Éire.

2. You state that only such further explanations should be given to the German Foreign Office as are obvious from the articles of the Constitution. I presume that the succinctness of this answer was due to your anxiety to reply promptly to my question, for which I am duly grateful. At the same time, I must point out that 'obvious' is a purely relative term, and that I have had no indication from you what are considered its 'obvious' effects. I shall be glad of instructions on this point.

3. I note that I am to state in response to inquiries that relations of Éire to Great Britain are improving since the removal of Mr. Thomas, and that Great Britain's new determination not to seek to interfere in our affairs is creating a better atmosphere. I am of course more than pleased to hear of this new development, of which I had seen no mention in the Press and which the Department now mentions to me for the first time. As I had, in response to inquiries about Great Britain's interference in our affairs, been in the habit of referring to the British penal duties on Irish goods, the British occupation of Irish ports, and similar matters, I shall be obliged if you will inform me what instances I should give illustrating Great Britain's new determination not to seek to interfere in our affairs.

4. You state that no doubt the type of inquirer who wishes to know about Éire's probable position in the case of a war 'will meet with the type of treatment he deserves' at my hands. I am sorry that I do not altogether apprehend your meaning. The question of the right of Éire to remain neutral in wars in which Great Britain is concerned is one which greatly interests foreign opinion, which cannot be expected to be familiar with the constitutional position. I should have thought that it would be proper to inform inquirers that Éire has an absolute right to remain neutral under the Constitution, and that the question how it would make use of such right could naturally only be determined according to the circumstances at the time. I shall be glad to hear from you whether such an answer should be given.

[signed] C. BEWLEY

---

[1] See above No. 91.
[2] See above No. 92.

No. 96 NAI DT S10297

Extract from the minutes of a meeting of the Cabinet
(Cab. 8/18) (Item 4)
DUBLIN, 26 October 1937

EXTERNAL GREAT SEAL
The question of what alteration, if any, should be made in the External Great Seal and its associated Seal, the Signet Seal, in connection with the coming into operation of the new Constitution, was considered.

Decision in the matter was left to the President.

No. 97 NAI DT S2485A

Memorandum on external seals by Joseph P. Walshe to Eamon de Valera
DUBLIN, 26 October 1937

THE PRESIDENT
External Seals
We use three Seals on documents signed by the King, as hereafter set out:-
(1) *The External Great Seal* on Ratifications and Full Powers
(2) *The Signet Seal* on Exequaturs (which enable Foreign Consuls to exercise their functions here) and on Commissions (appointing our Consuls abroad).
(3) *The Fob Seal* on the back of the envelope enclosing Letters of Credence or Recall.
The External Great Seal and the Signet Seal have two separated faces, one face bearing the usual national emblem and the other the effigy of King George V. The Fob Seal has, of course, only one side, which bears the King's Arms with the modification that the Harp is carried in two quarters instead of one.

The question at issue is whether we shall keep the King's effigy as it is or have a new effigy cut for George VI. If we leave the effigy in its present form the two sides will contradict each other, as the Irish emblem will bear the superscription 'Éire' according to the new Constitution (December 29th 1937) and the other side will carry the effigy of a King who died in January 1936.

Inasmuch as we have deliberately maintained the King for specific external purposes in order to gain a definite national end, and inasmuch as we legally created George VI King in December 1936, it would seem more logical to put his effigy on the Seal.

[initialled] J.P.W.

No. 98 NAI 2003/17/181

Confidential report from John W. Dulanty to Joseph P. Walshe (Dublin)
(No. 43) (Secret)
LONDON, 30 October 1937

Last evening Mr. Malcolm MacDonald asked me to see him for a few minutes. I accordingly went to the Dominions Office.

Mr. MacDonald said that he would like me to explain to the President that owing to his being somewhat suddenly included in the British Delegation to the Nine Power Conference[1] he had been compelled to put aside the work he had been doing on the question of the relations between our two countries. He said he was much disappointed at this interruption. The President, he said, would probably be thinking that it is now some time since our last conversation and that some word from him, Mr. MacDonald, was now due if not overdue. He assured me that the moment he was free from the Nine Power Conference he would resume without delay his work which had been unavoidably interrupted.

At the conclusion of his interview with the President in the Grosvenor Hotel on the last occasion[2] Mr. MacDonald I feel sure had the definite intention of putting forward proposals after the necessary discussion with the United Kingdom Cabinet. He said to me yesterday, however, that he was not sure whether there would be any proposals to put forward or not. There might be proposals he said but on the other hand there was the equal probability that his colleagues would decide to let matters remain as they were.

[signed] J.W. DULANTY
High Commissioner

No. 99 NAI DT S10325A

Extract from the minutes of a meeting of the Cabinet
(Cab. 8/20) (Item 5)
DUBLIN, 2 November 1937

AIR NAVIGATION: Arrangements with the United States
The President, as Minister for External Affairs, submitted for consideration the text of a proposed reciprocal Arrangement to be made between Saorstát Éireann and the United States of America, to govern the operation of civil air craft of the one country in the other, pending the conclusion of a Convention between the two countries.

The intention was that the Arrangement should come into force on the 27th November, 1937.

The Arrangement was approved.

---

[1] On 7 July 1937 Japanese troops clashed with Chinese forces near Beijing. The fighting quickly spread to other parts of China. In a further incident, the killing of two Japanese marines at a Chinese military airfield near Shanghai resulted in a Japanese invasion of the city on 11 August 1937. As a result of an appeal made to the League of Nations by the Chinese government in September 1937 the signatory states of the Nine-Power Treaty of 6 February 1922 (under which Britain, France, Italy, Japan, Portugal, and the United States signed two treaties which guaranteed the territorial integrity and administrative independence of China), with the exception of Japan, met in Brussels on 3 to 24 November 1937 to begin negotiations to end the war in China. Without Japanese participation, the talks collapsed.

[2] See above Nos 3, 7 and 8.

No. 100 NAI 2006/39

Confidential report from John W. Dulanty to Joseph P. Walshe (Dublin)
(No. 46) (Secret)

LONDON, 6 November 1937

I enclose a note[1] giving the salient points of Dr. Mahr's recent Presidential address on the Pre-History of Ireland to the Society of Antiquarians of London. The address which seemed to me to be wide and comprehensive in its scope was highly creditable in regard to the activities which centre round our National Museum. From the attentive way in which it was received by the audience and from a conversation which I had later with the Keeper of the British Museum I could see that Dr. Mahr carried considerable weight with the Antiquarian Society which consists of the leading archaeologists here.

I had some conversation with Dr. Mahr on the day following the lecture and I gathered that he feels his work in the National Museum is handicapped not owing in any way to the Department of Education but to the fact that the administrative machinery, particularly the financial side, is insufficiently elastic for his work, more particularly on its research development. He is very anxious to start a new Archaeological Survey of Ireland. I understand that both the material and the men being available it would not be a very expensive thing and it would definitely put the country upon the scientific map of Europe. Dr. Mahr said that he would very much like to see the President. He recalled that only a few years ago the President honoured the Celtic Congress in Dublin with an important speech in which he said that he would promise every support to any sound scheme which could be put forward in the line of Celtic research.

Both the Minister for Education and the Secretary for Education are I understand in sympathy with Dr. Mahr's project. If it could be arranged for the President to send for Dr. Mahr it would greatly help the latter to put succinctly his proposals.

[copy letter unsigned]
High Commissioner

No. 101 NAI DT S10336

Handwritten letter from Joseph P. Walshe to Maurice Moynihan (Dublin)
enclosing a memorandum on the coal-cattle pact negotiations

DUBLIN, 10 November 1937

Dear Maurice,
Here is the note on what happened at the Coal-Cattle Pact negotiations.
I hope it may be of some use.

Yours sincerely,
[signed] J.P. WALSHE

---

[1] Not printed.

[Enclosure]
Negotiations for Coal-Cattle Pact

First Pact

Tentative discussions started between the High Commissioner and Mr. Thomas in October 1934.

Negotiations for a Trade Agreement were proceeding at the same time in Berlin.

Instructions were issued to the High Commissioner on the 7th December[1] to agree in principle to a Coal-Cattle Arrangement on a £ for £ basis.

On the 14th December Mr. Twomey went to London to discuss with Mr. Street of the British Ministry of Agriculture[2] the proportions of the different categories of cattle to be exported by us.

The first Coal-Cattle Pact was announced on the 3rd January 1935.

Second Pact

The High Commissioner received an *Aide-Mémoire* approved by the Executive Council in December 1935.[3]

On the 30th December a Coal Order was made here prior to the completion of the detailed Arrangement with Great Britain.

On the 22nd January Mr. Leydon and Mr. Twomey went to London to discuss with officers of the Board of Trade and the Department of Agriculture those matters of the Arrangement relating to their respective Departments.

It was emphasised by Mr. Dulanty that there was no British delegation as such, and he advised that Mr. McElligott should not go with the other two officials.

Instructions were issued by the President on the 3rd February for the High Commissioner and the two officers assisting him.

The Second Pact was announced on the 17th February 1936.

Third Agreement

On the 7th December 1936 Mr. Dulanty was instructed to outline to the British the general character of our needs for the coming year.[4]

On the 22nd December the High Commissioner received from Overton of the Board of Trade[5] a proposal that the existing Arrangement should continue, and that discussions should take place for detailed adjustments within the general framework.

On the 3rd February 1937 the British replied to the High Commissioner's suggestions, and on the 25th February the announcement of the completed

---

[1] See DIFP Volume IV, No. 246.
[2] Arthur William Street (1892-1951), civil servant, Principal Assistant Secretary, Ministry of Agriculture and Fisheries, London (1936-8).
[3] See DIFP Volume IV, No. 309.
[4] See DIFP Volume IV, Nos 391, 393, 407, 415.
[5] Sir Arnold Edersheim Overton (1893-1975) Assistant Secretary of the Board of Trade and later Permanent Secretary of the Board of Trade (1941-5), Minister in Charge of the Middle East Office, Cairo (1945-7), Permanent Secretary, Ministry of Civil Aviation (1953-63).

Arrangement was made in the Dáil. No official from this side accompanied the High Commissioner on this occasion.

[initialled] J.P.W.

No. 102 NAI 2006/39

Confidential report from John W. Dulanty to Joseph P. Walshe (Dublin)
(No. 49a) (Secret)

LONDON, 18 November 1937

I called at Archbishop's House, Westminster, to-day to offer congratulations to His Grace the Archbishop on his elevation to the Cardinalate.

Dr. Hinsley told me that he received a telegram about 11 o'clock on Tuesday night from Cardinal Pacelli informing him of the Holy Father's decision, but enjoining upon the Archbishop strict secrecy for the present. That was the reason, Dr. Hinsley explained, that although he sat next to me at lunch on Wednesday he had made no reference to it nor had he mentioned it to Dr. Amigo who was also present at the lunch. On Wednesday evening, however, there was a throng of reporters and photographers at Archbishop's House. He telephoned to the editor of the Osservatore Romano who informed him that it had been made public in Rome.

Dr. Hinsley said he was gratified that I was the first layman and, what was especially pleasing to him, an Irishman who had called personally. He said that his mother belonged to a large family of Ryans of Tuam. She and her uncle came over to Yorkshire during the famine time and for many years he had tried to find out whether there were any members of his mother's family still living near Tuam. Only recently a Mr. Stephen Ryan of Tuam called on him and the Archbishop was satisfied that his mother's family was still living in Ireland. His mother's youngest sister, he told me, was one of the Sisters of Mercy in Tuam, and died recently aged 102.

He said that all through his life Ireland and its position in the world had been ever present to his mind and if there was ever any opportunity of his being of service to the Irish people he would be most willing to do such service.

Dr. Hinsley asked me to convey his cordial greetings to the President and his final words at the interview were: 'My blessing to Ireland'.

[copy letter unsigned]
High Commissioner

No. 103 NAI CAB 1/8

Extract from the minutes of a meeting of the Cabinet
(Cab. 8/28) (Item 6) (S10389A)

DUBLIN, 23 November 1937

RELATIONS WITH GT. BRITAIN: Suggested Governmental conference
The President submitted for consideration a draft of a despatch[1] which he proposed, in his capacity as Minister for External Affairs, to send to the

---

[1] See below No. 104.

British Government in reference to discussions between officials of the two Governments in regard to economic and other measures to be adopted in time of war.

He proposed to point out that such measures would depend fundamentally upon the relations existing between the two countries on the outbreak of war, and that the steps to be taken in preparation should be guided by a just appreciation of what those relations were likely to be.

If the Irish Government had to envisage a continuance of the existing strained relations between the two countries their plans should obviously be very different from those appropriate to a situation in which there would exist between the two peoples a feeling of mutual trust and a disposition to co-operate in matters regarded by both as of common concern.

This being the case the Government were satisfied that piecemeal discussions between Civil Servants on the economic and other aspects of the situation which would arise in the case of a major war could achieve no useful purposes until some prior understanding in principle had been reached between the two Governments.

The Irish Government considered it essential, therefore, that members of the two Governments should meet as soon as possible to consider all the important matters involved, and they would be glad to have an early intimation of the views of the British Government on this proposal.

The issue of a despatch by the President to the British Government on the lines suggested was approved.

No. 104 NAUK DO 35/891/4

Despatch from Eamon de Valera to Malcolm MacDonald (London)
(No. 126) (Secret)

DUBLIN, 24 November 1937

Sir,
I have the honour to refer to two documents recently received by the High Commissioner from your Government, one an Aide-Mémoire in relation to censorship in time of war, and the other a note suggesting discussions on the control of food imports and exports in time of war.[1]

2. For some time past the Government of Saorstát Éireann have been considering how best to protect the people of this country from the dangers to which they will be exposed in the event of the outbreak of another European war.

3. The measures that will in that event be necessary must depend fundamentally on the relations that will exist between our two countries at the time, and the steps to be taken in preparation now ought consequently to be guided by a just appreciation of what these relations are likely to be.

4. If the Irish Government has to envisage a continuance of the present strained relations between the two countries, their plans should obviously be

---

[1] Not printed.

very different from those appropriate to a situation in which there would exist between the two peoples a feeling of mutual trust and a disposition to co-operate in matters regarded by both as of common concern.

5. This being the case, the Government of Saorstát Éireann are satisfied that piecemeal discussion between civil servants on the economic and other aspects of the situation that would arise in the case of a major war can achieve no useful purpose until some prior understanding in principle has been reached between the two Governments.

6. My Government consider it essential, therefore, that members of the two Governments should meet as soon as possible to consider all the important matters involved, and would be glad to have an early intimation of the views of your Government on this proposal.

I have the honour to be,
Sir,
Your most obedient,
humble servant,
[signed] EAMON DE VALERA
Minister for External Affairs

No. 105 NAI DFA Berlin Letter Books 1936-1937

Letter from Seán Murphy (for Joseph P. Walshe) to Charles Bewley (Berlin)
(A. 41) (Copy)

DUBLIN, 26 November 1937

I am directed by the Minister to refer to your minute of the 22nd No. 25/33 relative to accounting matters[1] and to state the suggestion of justification for this Department's minute of the 1st July last is not understood.[2] The direction contained in that minute was based on the principle that, except in very exceptional circumstances, the Legation should not for any period be in charge of a non-national.

The Minister directs me to request you to furnish the accounts asked for in the Department's minute of the 15th[3] instant together with an explanation regarding the irregular encashment of the Imprests issued to you in respect of rent.

The Minister further directs me to inform you that minutes in reference to accounts should be acknowledged as soon as possible after receipt as the Accounting Officer must be in a position to explain to the Comptroller and Auditor General the cause of any delays in the furnishing of his monthly account of expenditure.

I am further to point out the tone of your minute under reply and your general attitude in relation to accounts show a complete lack of responsibility as Sub-Accounting Officer and I am accordingly directed to inform you that the monthly account of the Legation must in future be furnished to the

---

[1] Not located.
[2] Not located.
[3] Not located.

Department within 14 days of the end of the month to which the account relates.

[stamped] SEÁN MURPHY
Rúnaí

No. 106 NAI 2006/39

Confidential report from John W. Dulanty to Joseph P. Walshe (Dublin)
(No. 50) (Secret)

LONDON, 29 November 1937

Lord Hartington[1] told me on Friday afternoon last that the report of the British Inter-Departmental Committee on Migration to Great Britain from the Irish Free State was now finished.

They feel that they ought to publish the report now. It will be remembered that a number of questions have been put by members of the British Parliament asking when this report will be published.

The British Government felt however that if we were about to publish the report of our Inter-Departmental Committee on the same question they, the British, would be willing to consider holding their own report so that it might be published along with ours. I thanked Lord Hartington for the suggestion but said I doubted whether the report of our Committee would be ready for some little time yet.

Lord Hartington further said that if there were any phrases or forms of expression in their report which we would like to see modified he would be willing to consider this. The facts as stated in the report would of course have to stand. I have now received and enclose a copy[2] of the report in question dated 25th November. It will be observed that the Committee see no reason to interfere with the present system of recruiting certain types of labour from Ireland for work in England.

[copy letter unsigned]
High Commissioner

No. 107 UCDA P150/2179

Confidential report from John W. Dulanty to Joseph P. Walshe (Dublin)
(No. 51) (Secret)

LONDON, 1 December 1937

This evening I saw Mr. Malcolm MacDonald in response to his request. It is known that the death of his father[3] has deeply affected him and he looked ill and depressed.

The British Cabinet, he told me, had that morning decided, with practically no discussion, to accept in principle the suggestion made in our

---

[1] The Under-Secretary of State for Dominion Affairs.
[2] Not printed.
[3] James Ramsay MacDonald (1866-1937), British Labour politician; Prime Minister (1924, 1929-31 and 1931-35 (National Government).

Despatch No. 126 of 24th November last.[1] Details of time and other arrangements would be considered later.

His first reaction was that we might arrange a meeting before Christmas to be followed by meetings in the Parliamentary recess, but on reflection he thought that it would be a better plan to hold a meeting during the Parliamentary recess, say in the first week of January when two or three days might be held in reserve for continued discussion. During the recess[2] there would be less pressure on him and his colleagues but I was to understand that this view did not bar a meeting before Christmas if the President so wished. He would keep himself free, but at this moment he could not speak for the movements or engagements of his colleagues. To prevent misleading reports in the newspapers, it might be well to agree upon a short notice to the press announcing in advance the suggested meeting between Ministers of the two Governments.

He asked whether the President would come himself. I said that he would. Had I any idea as to whether the President, since he was suggesting the Conference, would come forward with proposals of his own. I said that I doubted whether the President would put forward proposals. Our despatch indicated clearly our reason for the suggested Conference.[3]

Mr. MacDonald said that the proposal to hold a Conference came to him as a bolt from the blue. The attitude of the President on the question of Conferences had always been that it was a mistake to confer publicly before you had a reasonable ground for thinking that agreement would be reached. Mr. de Valera had said, and he agreed entirely, that to hold a Conference which produced nothing left both parties in a worse position than if no Conference at all was held. That was why he had adopted the plan of conversations with Sir Warren Fisher, Sir Horace Wilson, and myself in the hope that some scheme could be agreed upon before Ministers met. He wondered therefore whether I could tell him why the President, with his views about a Conference, made the suggestion.

I repeated that I thought the Despatch told its own story. He would remember that he had a number of exploratory talks with the President and that when I met him on the 6th November (see my Secret report No. 41 of 7th November)[4] I had then suggested that the time had arrived 'to leave generalities and formulate, however tentatively, proposals for dealing with questions outstanding between the two countries.' Conversations in Geneva and London had followed, but so far no results, positive or negative, had been achieved.

Mr. MacDonald pointed out that whilst it was true that thus far nothing had emerged from their side it would be untrue to say nothing had been done. At the close of the last London meeting he had asked the President

---

[1] See above No. 104.
[2] The text from this point until the words 'keep himself free' has been highlighted by a line drawn along the left hand margin of the page.
[3] See above No. 104.
[4] See above No. 82. Report No. 41 was sent on 7 September 1937.

whether, as a result of these several informal conversations, he had any pro-posals to put forward. The President's reply was that he had not. He had explained fully what he thought should be done and if the British had any proposals he would give them careful consideration. Mr. MacDonald then began work on the questions outstanding between the two countries, to which subject priority had been given over any other, and he recalled that he had informed me that this work had been interrupted by his having to join the Nine Power Conference at Brussels, but as soon as he was free he would take it up again. He had been in London for two days in an interval between meetings of the Brussels Conference and had done practically nothing else but work on this question, having discussions with Mr. Neville Chamberlain and Sir John Simon. It would therefore be seen that he had not been idle. I said I appreciated this but he would remember that he had told me on the 29th October (see my Secret Report No. 43 of 30th October)[1] that there might be proposals, but equally that there might not be. Mr. MacDonald not only accepted this but said that that was still the position. My own impression is that they meant to put forward proposals and that Mr. MacDonald was safe-guarding himself by this qualification.

I said that the world situation, and more particularly the European situ-ation, being what it was my government could not be expected to wait indef-initely. There were various contingencies that might arise. One was that we might find ourselves in the situation in which it was incumbent upon us to provide for the protection of our own people from the consequences following upon a European war. That provision clearly could not be made in a few weeks or a few months and no Government worth the name could face its people if they had omitted to make adequate provision for such a contingency. Proof of that could be seen in the feverish activity of the British themselves – not to mention other European states – in the war preparations which were being pushed forward with maximum energy whilst we merely talked and waited. I was not an expert in defence but it seemed to me that we had more to give to the British than the British had to give to us, but if they had in contempla-tion an arrangement for defence on the basis of mutual interest the sooner we reached conclusions on that matter the better for both of us.

I told Mr. MacDonald that, speaking for myself, I had no doubt about his own sincere desire to reach a settlement. Having regard to what he had told me about his work on this question since the last London conversation I asked whether it would not be possible for his Government to bring forward the proposals on which I gathered he had been working.

Mr. MacDonald said that it seemed likely that his side would say that they could not at the Conference put forward any proposals, at any rate in the first instance. He thought it might be well to have what he called 'a canter over the course', where not merely defence but other questions might be surveyed. If the opening conversations on both sides were not pitched in too high a key, if the language were not too uncompromising and the conversations contained the promise of an approach to a settlement then he thought – though here

---

[1] See above No. 98.

again he was making no promise – they might in a later stage of the Conference be prepared to put forward proposals. He was, speaking for himself, most anxious that the atmosphere of the conference from the moment it began should be one in which, whilst admitting of a full statement of the case from both sides, a settlement should be possible.

Did he know, I enquired, what Ministers would be selected from their side? He said that this matter had not been discussed but he thought it was almost certain that Sir John Simon would be one. Who the other would be he could not at present say.

I left Mr. MacDonald (who, as I have observed, looked ill and depressed) with the feeling that whilst he welcomed the suggestion of a Conference of Ministers seemed to have some doubts about its outcome unless there was, on both sides, a firm purpose and intention to achieve a result.

[signed] J.W. DULANTY
High Commissioner

No. 108 NAI DFA 105/46

> *Letter from Joseph P. Walshe to Charles Bewley (Berlin)*
> *(Copy) (Secret)*
>
> DUBLIN, 2 December 1937

Your minute of the 13th November No. 43/33 relating to your instructions as to the change in the name of the State has been received.[1]

It would naturally be an opportunity for a visit by you to the Secretary of State. No doubt you have already had conversations with officials of the Foreign Office on the general purport of the new Constitution. The Minister assumes that your visits to the Foreign Office are relatively frequent and that you talk with the officials or with the Secretary of State about current matters. The obvious points on which explanations are asked for by Ministers accredited to this Government relate chiefly to the new position of the King and the position of the President of Ireland. These and any other explanations, which are clear from the text itself or from the text in the light of the President's speeches, you are in a position to give without special instructions. It would be useful to have a report on your conversation with the Foreign Office.

When informing the German Government of the change of the name of the State, you should not emphasise the Irish form. The change of name would not, of course, have the same political or national significance if 'Éire' were to be used by foreigners. As you are aware, it is the hope of everybody in this country that the use of 'Ireland' to describe the Twenty-six Counties will have a definite psychological effect in favour of the unity of this country on both Irish and foreign minds.

---

[1] Not printed. Bewley's minute of 13 November can be found on file NAI DFA 247/14; it repeats the request for instructions given in his reports of 28 September 1937 (No. 91 above) and 7 October 1937 (No. 95 above).

When talking on Constitutional matters with German officials you will be careful not to exaggerate what you describe as 'freedom from domination by England'. As you say in another report (7th October 1937),[1] the tone of which the Minister has some difficulty in understanding, the British still impose penal duties on our goods, still occupy our ports and still maintain our country divided. These things are not being changed by the Constitution, but the latter does represent the maximum effort of the Irish people to provide themselves with their own fundamental law and to secure for themselves complete internal sovereignty within the Twenty-six County area. If you are asked by a German official or by the Secretary of State what Ireland's position would be in the case of a war between Germany and Great Britain, you should naturally reply that such an event was too terrible to contemplate, and you must refuse to discus what our attitude would be. If, on the other hand, you are asked what Ireland's position would be if England were at war with Power X, there would be no reason why you should not reply in the form set out in your paragraph 4. The Minister would like you to be very careful to remember in all you say to German officials regarding our political position that they would have no scruple in repeating your statements to the British Ambassador or his officials if they thought the slightest advantage could be obtained thereby for Germany. The general atmosphere, notwithstanding the continuance of several really bad factors in our relations with Great Britain, is better, and – as I told you once before – that improvement began with the elimination of Mr. Thomas. It is hoped that an approach to a solution of the major difficulties, with the exception of Partition, between ourselves and Great Britain may be found during the next few months. And as the goodwill of important British officials would be a useful factor in obtaining a better settlement, the Minister desires our Representatives abroad to be careful to maintain relations of a relatively friendly character with the Heads of the British Missions.

It is noted in one of your reports that you speak of having seen the British Ambassador for the first and the last time. While there is no need to pay very much attention to the person or opinions of the British Ambassador, he should generally be regarded as a person whose influence could be used against us, and as realists governing a very small country the Government desire to avoid anything which might militate in the smallest degree against their securing to their people the best possible settlement with Great Britain. In this connection, it would be useful for the Minister to know what your precise relations are with the present British Ambassador in Berlin, and whether your relations with him or the Chargé d'Affaires are different from your relations with British officials in Rome. What is the extent of the British Ambassador's influence with the German Government?

The Minister would like to have a long comprehensive report from you going back over the international events of the past few months in relation to Germany, and also setting out generally, though comprehensively, the present position of the Churches in Germany. Press reports here tend to indicate

---

[1] See above No. 95.

that the Christian religion (Protestants and Catholics) is continuing to suffer persecution in Germany, and that there is a real danger of the new State succeeding in eliminating the practice of formal religion, at least, from the lives of the new generation.

(Signed) J.P. WALSHE
Rúnaí

No. 109 NAI 2006/39

Confidential report from John W. Dulanty to Joseph P. Walshe (Dublin)
(No. 52) (Secret)
LONDON, 3 December 1937

In view of the position indicated in my Secret Report No. 51[1] of the 1st December it would appear that it will probably be necessary to proceed with the negotiations for renewal and amendment of the Coal-Cattle pact independently of the suggested Conference of Ministers.

If this view be correct full particulars of the proposals from the Departments of Agriculture and Industry and Commerce should obviously be available immediately.

The Trading Account on the Coal-Cattle pact for the current year will, it is anticipated, show a monetary advantage on our side of the account of about £500,000 – chiefly due to the rise in the price of cattle. It would not be unreasonable to think that the British will probably use this as a factor in resisting any proposals of ours which may mean a loss of revenue to them. I think therefore the Department of Industry and Commerce should make as strong a case as is possible of our purchases other than coal – notably the contracts for machinery such as those for the National Oil Refinery which had been placed with Great Britain.

[copy letter unsigned]
High Commissioner

No. 110 UCDA P150/2179

Memorandum by Maurice Moynihan on John W. Dulanty's conversation with
Malcolm MacDonald
DUBLIN, 3 December 1937

RELATIONS WITH BRITAIN
Mr. Dulanty's Conversation with Mr. MacDonald
Report read by President at meeting of the Executive Council on 3rd December, 1937.

PRESIDENT:
With reference to the matter referred to above, I wish to submit for your consideration the following views:

---

[1] See above No. 107.

1. We should not try to have a Conference earlier than the time suggested by Mr. MacDonald, viz: in January, during the British Parliamentary recess. To do so would suggest undue eagerness on our part.
2. There should be no further private conversation between you and Mr. MacDonald between now and the proposed Conference.

    Both you and Mr. MacDonald appear to have said already everything that usefully can be said in such private informal conversations. Furthermore, it would be impossible to conceal from the public the fact of Mr. MacDonald's visit here or your visit to London, or to deceive the public as to the purpose. The whole thing would have almost a furtive air. It could have no useful result that could be announced, unless the definite settlement of arrangements for a formal Conference. The knowledge that there had been a conversation coupled with silence as to its outcome could only create disappointment.
3. The proposed Conference should be publicly announced beforehand, and should be of a formal character.

    This is best in the national interest. Informal private, or semi-private conversations could go on forever without any degree of ~~normal~~ moral[1] constraint on the British to contribute to a successful result. Once there is a formal Conference, with due publicity, either a settlement must result or each side must be prepared to justify from its own point of view the failure to reach a settlement.

    Whether a formal Conference succeeds or not, it will have value from our point of view. If it succeeds, the value is obvious. If it fails, it will have failed presumably because the British did not agree to any settlement which we would consider reasonable or honourable, and that position can be explained to the country.
4. I take it that at any formal Conference you will lead the Irish Delegation.

[initialled] MOM

No. 111 NAI DT S9240

> *Letter from Seán MacEntee to Eamon de Valera (Dublin)*
> DUBLIN, 10 December 1937

Dear Mr. President,[2]

In accordance with the decision of the Executive Council a preliminary meeting of the Secretaries of the various Departments concerned with the terms of the Coal-Cattle Pact for 1938 with the United Kingdom met in my Department yesterday; Industry and Commerce, Agriculture and External Affairs, as well as Finance, being represented. At the outset of business a rather marked difference of opinion revealed itself as to the scope of the deliberations of this informal Committee; some members taking the view that we should try to secure as many amendments, in our favour, to the existing

---

[1] The word 'moral' is a handwritten insertion replacing the word 'normal'.
[2] Marginal note: 'Submitted to President who reserved decision pending discussion with Secretary D/E.A. M O M 11/12/37'.

arrangement as possible, and others the view that we should not ask for any major change or concession but only for minor modifications. Those who held the former view stressed the fact that simply to seek minor alterations now would be considered as implying satisfaction on our part with the present state of affairs, and that, in any event, we should go ahead now as if nothing else but the Pact was in contemplation; while those who held the latter said that the British would be likely to refuse any concession other than a relatively small one, and that this refusal would re-act upon us later. The issue raised, which was supported by other arguments that I need not enter into, is so fundamental that I feel the best course to pursue now would be for *you* to see, if you can possibly spare the time, the Secretaries of the four Departments interested, and hear their opinions, and then give them a direction as to their future course of action. I hope this suggestion will commend itself to you.

Yours sincerely,
[signed] Seán MacEntee

No. 112 NAI 2006/39

Confidential report from John W. Dulanty to Joseph P. Walshe (Dublin)
(No. 54) (Secret)

London, 16 December 1937

Mr. Malcolm MacDonald told me last evening that he got a shock when he opened 'The Times' and found a report that our Government had decided to recognise the King of Italy as the Emperor of Ethiopia.

The Irish Free State was at present a member of the British Commonwealth of Nations. He had understood from the President that he was willing to co-operate with the Commonwealth on international matters of common concern. It might well be that the President took the view that this was not a matter of common concern and therefore consultation was unnecessary. That was not his (Mr. MacDonald's) view but the President was perfectly free to take that view if he wished. But even on that basis he thought that the President might have told him, not as a matter of consultation but merely as a matter of information, what he proposed to do.

I enquired what precisely was the advantage which Mr. MacDonald attached to our telling him merely as a matter of information. He said that he thought it was not a desirable position for him when lobby Correspondents could tell him of a matter such as this and of which he had no knowledge. He remembered the President's attitude in Geneva on the question of Palestine. The President had then said that if he had known that the question of the partition of Palestine was to come up at the meeting in the form in which it did he would certainly before the meeting have told Mr. Eden and Mr. MacDonald what his views were. That was a perfectly understandable position, but here we were taking up a position on a matter on which we could not fail to know that Britain and other members of the Commonwealth had views, and clearly their difficulties in this matter are increased by the line which the Irish Free State Government had taken.

The setting up of an Irish Legation in Rome, I pointed out, had been before my Government for a very long time and I felt sure the Irish Government could not defer action any further without appearing to be discourteous to the Italian Government who had, as Mr. MacDonald was aware, appointed a Minister in Dublin some months ago.

I was still not clear, I told him, about his contention that we should have communicated our intentions as a matter merely of information. A reference of that limited character clearly shut out any question of action or even of comment by them, what then was the difficulty for them?

He would recall the President's definite attitude on the question of reference about our Abdication legislation just about a year ago, and also the matter of our new Constitution. On neither occasion of those incomparably more important matters was any reference made to the British even on the simple basis of information. Not only was this procedure right and proper from our point of view but it seemed to us that it had advantages for the British.

Mr. MacDonald's rejoinder was that they kept us well informed by Foreign Office Secret reports and by their own cables. When I suggested that these documents usually related to questions already resolved or actions already taken Mr. MacDonald said that was not so. They informed us well in advance of their intention to appoint an Agent to General Franco. They informed us well in advance of their intention to allow General Franco to search ships flying their flag but only if no British man-of-war were near. (At this point of the conversation Mr. MacDonald appeared to be suggesting that they could have given orders about the search of our ships as well as their own. I immediately corrected this.) He went on to say that not entirely but largely because of our refusal to let British naval officers board and search our ships they, the British, abandoned the plan for their own ships. This was an example of the value of information before the event. From time to time Canada, South Africa, and other partner Governments had made comments or suggestions on the cables sent by the United Kingdom Government and very often that Government had modified its action in the light of these suggestions.

If the United Kingdom or any other Partner Government took action on some international matter which we felt we were concerned, we would he felt sure show keen dissatisfaction.

What he was sorry about was that it would give the Dictators a big lift – a help which he felt might be repugnant to the President's own feelings.

He was as he had frequently informed me, anxious to get as good a political atmosphere as was possible for the projected conversations in the near future. He was afraid that certain of his colleagues whose approach to our question was different to his would be disposed to think that we were ready to co-operate with the other members of the group when we wanted something or when in some other way it suited us, but that on an occasion such as the present when co-operation would be welcomed by all the members of the group we were rather determined to go our own way and show no disposition to be helpful. From that point of view he thought our action had been singularly unfortunate.

Taking up his reference to proposed conversations I said that if he and his colleagues were prepared to take the right line with us conversations such as that we were now agreed upon would come to a sharp and welcome end.

[copy letter unsigned]
High Commissioner

No. 113 NAI 2006/39

Confidential report from John W. Dulanty to Joseph P. Walshe (Dublin)
(No. 55) (Secret)
LONDON, 16 December 1937

Mr. MacDonald told me this evening that since our conversation of Wednesday night he had read the newspaper reports of the debate in the Dáil from which he had learned that the recognition which the President proposed to give in respect of Ethiopia was merely a de facto recognition. From the point of the European situation this was, he thought, less serious than the position he had envisaged in the previous evening's conversation. He went on to make a point of the fact that if we had given them earlier information he would not have misunderstood the situation.

He asked me when I thought the Minister might begin to function in Rome. I said my information was that he would probably take up duties early in the New Year and in any even not later than the first week in February.

Mr. MacDonald said, talking confidentially to me, his main aim was to prevent trouble for us and trouble for himself. He thought that the political repercussion in certain quarters here would make for difficulty with him and the other members of the Cabinet who were of his view.

Later today Mr. MacDonald telephoned to me directing me to read an article which appeared in the 'Manchester Guardian'. He also referred to notes in the 'Daily Telegraph' and the 'Daily Mail', excerpts from which are enclosed herewith. I asked him if he had seen the letter in the 'Scotsman' from Professor Berriedale Keith. He said he had not. I gave him a summary of the latter and asked him what his Constitutional Advisors would think of the suggestion that we should direct a Commission consisting of the Chief Justice, the President of the High Court, and the Chairman of the Dáil, to act in place of the King. Mr. MacDonald laughed at the suggestion and said that as far as he could find Professor Berriedale Keith cut very little ice in this country. I said that might or might not be so but I thought it was most unfortunate that the Press of this country on subjects the beginnings of which they did not understand should be allowed to carry on a campaign of misunderstanding which was destructive of the goodwill he, Mr. MacDonald, was so anxious to build up.

I told him that after my conversation with him last evening I was reading about the conquest of India. I found it was an historic fact beyond any kind of dispute that a woman – Queen Victoria – called herself on the bidding of a Jew named Disraeli 'the Empress of India'. There was no reference either on the basis of consultation or simple information to the three hundred and fifty million people concerned. Whether Mr. MacDonald failed in wit to respond with the obvious reply of 'other times other manners' or memory, I cannot say. All he did was to enquire whether I was 'grousing' about our not being consulted, and if I were he would take advice from the Secretary of State for India, – all this of course jocularly.

[initialled] JWD
High Commissioner

No. 114 NAI DT S10436A

Extract from the minutes of a meeting of the Cabinet
(Cab. 8/38) (Item 3)

DUBLIN, 21 December 1937

INTERNATIONAL CONVENTION ON BROADCASTING IN CAUSE OF PEACE, 1936: *Accession of Saorstát*
Authority was given to the Minister for External Affairs to arrange for the accession of Saorstát Éireann to the International Convention concerning the Use of Broadcasting in the Cause of Peace, which had been signed at Geneva on 23rd September, 1936.[1]

No. 115 NAI 2003/17/181

Confidential report from John W. Dulanty to Joseph P. Walshe (Dublin)
(No. 57) (Secret)

LONDON, 28 December 1937

I spoke to Mr. Malcolm MacDonald on the telephone at Lossiemouth yesterday and asked him to let me have this evening instead of to-morrow morning the advance copy of the statement which he had told me the British Government would issue in the press of the 30th December on our Constitution. Mr. MacDonald promised to let me know later in the day. He telephoned to me last evening and said that he had instructed Sir Edward Harding to meet Mr. Walshe and myself this evening at 5 o'clock and hand to us the statement in question.

Accordingly Sir Edward Harding saw Mr. Walshe and myself at this Office this evening and handed to me the accompanying statement dated 29th December.[2]

He explained that the typed inset portion of the statement only would be handed to the Pres, that is to say, without the first and final paragraphs.

Sir Edward Harding said the Secretary of State had asked him to supplement the statement in the following sense:-

---

[1] Handwritten marginal note by Nicholas Nolan (Department of the Taoiseach): '*Note*: The Irish Instrument of Accession to the above-mentioned Convention was deposited with the League of Nations on the 25th May 1938 – see Treaty Series, No. 4 of 1938. NS Ó N [Nioclás Ó Nualláin], 30.1.52'.

[2] Not printed.

First, Mr. MacDonald did not wish the third paragraph of the statement to be regarded as in any sense provocative. It represented the considered view of the United Kingdom Government on a matter affecting a part of the United Kingdom, and it would be necessary for any United Kingdom Government to define its attitude on such a matter. Secondly, he did not wish the statement as a whole to be regarded as a prelude to any rigidity of attitude on the part of the Ministers who would represent the United Kingdom at the January meetings. On the contrary he hoped, as he knew Mr. de Valera hoped, that these meetings would be the beginning of a real improvement in the relations between the two countries.

[signed] J.W. DULANTY
High Commissioner

No. 116 NAI DFA Paris Embassy 19/34

Extract from a memorandum by Art O'Brien, on the recognition of the King of Italy as Emperor of Abyssinia, to Joseph P. Walshe (Dublin)
(P19/34) (P5/1) (Copy)

PARIS, 31 December 1937

Friends of Ireland on the continent have been very much interested and elated by the decision to appoint a Minister to the Quirinal accrediting him to the King of Italy as Emperor of Abyssinia. That fact that we have not on this occasion waited for England to make the first move has created a very satisfactory impression. Even our best friends were a little surprised that we should have made this move independently, and they are gratified by this illustration of our cutting away from dependence on England in our foreign relations. It would be to them a further gratifying step if we proceed now to recognise the Franco Government in Spain without waiting for England to do so in the first instance, as she will undoubtedly before very long. The remark has been made to me that here also it is a question of the recognition of a de facto situation.

In an article which appeared in l'Action Française of the 26th inst. advocating the recognition by France of the Italian Sovereign as Emperor, much prominence is given to Ireland's decision in the matter. The writer, relying on an article in regard to that demarche which appeared in the Manchester Guardian and to which much prominence has been given in the Belgian and French press, stresses the point that England will shortly accord official recognition of the King of Italy as Emperor. The article is another instance of the publicity which Ireland's decision in this matter has received in the continental press.

Most of the newspaper articles which have come to my notice deal with the question of Irish recognition of the King of Italy (as Emperor) from the point of view of European politics generally; the matter is treated as one of first rate importance, and has had a considerable effect on opinion here because of the fact that it shortly preceded (and is by some brought into line with) the publication of the representations with a view to recognition made by the Netherlands Foreign Minister to the Oslo Powers.
[matter omitted]

1938

No. 117 UCDA P150/2183

Letter from Joseph P. Walshe to Eamon de Valera (Dublin)
DUBLIN, 3 January 1938

AN TAOISEACH

On reaching London by plane on Monday, the 27th December, I immediately got into touch with the High Commissioner and explained to him the extreme necessity of getting immediate information as to the contents of the Note which the British were to hand to us on the 29th (Constitution Day). Although Mr. MacDonald had assured him that there was nothing which would cause us serious difficulty in the Note, nevertheless only we ourselves could be the judges of that, and a preview of the Note might be the means of preventing a breakdown of the negotiations for a conference in January.

The High Commissioner phoned to Mr. Malcolm MacDonald, told him I was in London, and repeated what I had said about the Note. Mr. MacDonald agreed to let us have the Note at 5 o'clock on Tuesday, the 28th, instead of 10 o'clock on the following morning. Mr. MacDonald phoned Sir Edward Harding and instructed him accordingly. Sir Edward Harding invited the High Commissioner and myself to lunch on Tuesday. We had a very long conversation, in the course of which he said that I must remember that there could be no change made in the Note, as it was a Cabinet decision. I suggested that no Cabinet opinion[1] decision could be regarded as final unless Ministers were in the fullest possession of all the facts relating to the matter under consideration at the time the decision was taken, and that if there was something in the Note which in our view would prevent the January meeting I should emphasise in the strongest manner that he should get in touch by phone with all the Ministers concerned so that the necessary modification could be introduced. He then gave me the gist of the Note, and we discussed the main points for some time. I urged strongly on Harding that nothing in the form of the Note should give the slightest impression that the British Government or Parliament had any right whatsoever to interfere with the Constitution. He assured me the form was absolutely correct in this sense, and when a few hours later he brought the actual text to the High Commissioner's Office I could not frankly say that there was any assertion of a right in the British Government or Parliament to do so.[2] As you know, Sir, I telephoned the entire text of the Note and of a statement made by Sir

---

[1] The word 'opinion' has been crossed out in the original.
[2] The words 'to do so' have been crossed out in the original.

Edward Harding to us on behalf of his Minister, reiterating the latter's desire that the Note – especially the third paragraph – should not be regarded as in any way provocative.

I went to see Sir Edward Harding by appointment on Wednesday afternoon and had some three hours' talk. My main endeavour in this and my subsequent talk with Sir Edward Harding was to obtain from him a frank statement of the British minimum demands. I realised very soon that there is now a genuine desire on the part of the British for a complete understanding with us.

Sir Edward Harding said that the Treaty had indeed become a damnosa hereditas in the relations between the two countries. He went so far as to admit that Mr. Thomas had delayed the settlement of our difficulties and he expressed the belief that, if for the last few years we had had here a British High Commissioner, it would have been of very great help. However, he concurred generally when I told him that a settlement would have been impossible until our State, its Constitution and its laws were exclusively founded on the expressed will of the Irish people without any taint of interference or pressure from the British side. As far as the Twenty-six Counties were concerned, we had now come out of the mountains into the plain, and the way towards a settlement had become much easier. It was of fundamental importance that at the coming conference his Minister should not make any attempt to obtain any amendment of the Constitution – that, in other words, our negotiations as far as politico-constitutional matters are concerned should be based on the irrevocability of the Constitution.

We then turned to the broad lines of the settlement to be reached between us. My first anxiety was to find out what their stand was to be on the Annuities issue. I came back to the point as often as I could without appearing to show unreasonable curiosity. I am quite convinced that the British have made up their minds that it would be impossible for you, owing to your very frequent public utterances, to pay a penny of the Annuities. They are facing up to the difficulties of the conference in a realist mood, and they are ready to make the necessary sacrifices to obtain a settlement, but it was equally clear to me that there will have to be a cash payment on our side in relation to the other outstanding financial matters.

As far as I could gather, the line to be adopted is this. They will ask us to pay the pensions at present being paid in Ireland by them amounting to about £700,000. Further, they will demand a capital sum of some £7,000,000 to cover the local loans. With regard to the sum of approximately £250,000 at present being paid to pensioners who have left Ireland and are resident all over the world, they will propose that we should pay a capital sum of some £3,000,000. It is my impression that we have no chance of forcing the British to forgo the payment by us of the monies payable in this country and of the capital sum of £7,000,000 for the local loans. There will, however, be a sporting chance of getting the British to forgo the capital sum of £3,000,000 in substitution for pensions paid abroad in consideration of (though not as payment for) the modernising works which we should have to undertake immediately in the forts at present manned by the British. The British estimate of the cost of these works is a little under £1,000,000, but I think there is a real basis for argument here.

Sir Edward Harding could not have been stronger on the difficulties which his Government would have to face in Parliament if they were not able to show that the bargain was a reasonably good one for them. Their difficulty in putting over the forgoing of the Annuities payments would be insurmountable if they had not some substantial concessions to show in finance and in defence.

The position with regard to defence is slightly more complicated. Sir Edward Harding at first adopted the attitude that their forces should have the right to come into our ports in a grave emergency. That for them was the really important point. I explained to him that here we were dealing with a matter that concerned in the most vital fashion our national sovereignty. No Government in this country could give the right in such an unqualified manner to the British forces. But could not our mutual difficulties be solved in another way? We must assume that a major European crisis meant the coming to a head of the struggle for world power between Germany and Great Britain, and that in the course of such a struggle the danger to our country, owing to its geographical position and to the fact that it was a source of food supply for the British, was as real as it was to Great Britain herself. That being the case, it would be our duty to defend our shores by every means against an invader, whether as you, Sir, have frequently said, an attack was made directly on us for the purpose of seizing part of this island or on us for the purpose of using this island as a stepping-stone in an attack on Great Britain. But we quite recognised that the pressure of an invading force or of attacking planes might very soon become overwhelming for the forces which would be at our disposal. British aid would then have to be called in. What was supremely important was to recognise from the beginning that the forts and all our territory were exclusively ours, and that arrangements made to defend them in time of war would have to depend on our goodwill and complete and formal consent. I do not fear that we shall have any serious difficulty in finding a formula which will give us the completest sovereignty over every inch of our territory and which will, at the same time, satisfy the British that we shall co-operate with them when the two islands are being subjected to a common menace. I shall endeavour, in the light of my conversations with Harding, to draw up such a formula in the course of the next day or two.

I understand from certain remarks of Sir Edward Harding that one of the things which has made the British military people most suspicious of us is the fact that we have from time to time made public statements that we intended to declare our neutrality when a major crisis occurred. I remember only vaguely such statements, but I think some members of the Labour Party have made statements of the sort in recent times. Indeed, I may say at this point that I came away from my first week's conversations with the Permanent Head of the Dominions Office more convinced than ever that all statements in relation to external affairs should be made exclusively by you, Sir, and that casual remarks made by prominent public men on the

Government side could easily give rise to suspicions which render our relations with our principal 'external affair' more difficult. Sir Edward Harding
was quite frank in telling me what the obvious consequences would be of a
declaration of neutrality on our part at a moment when the British people
were in the very gravest danger from a powerful European enemy or group
of enemies. They would be obliged in their own vital interests (and no doubt
they would say it was also in our vital interest) to come in and occupy this
country and carry out functions which we as their 'most natural ally' (no
irony was intended, and I did not take him up on the expression) should
carry out. The British at the conference would generally argue that our
defence was a matter for ourselves, and that we could not claim financial
concessions from them because we were doing what any normal State considered it its duty to do. They are not, for instance, subsidising directly or
indirectly Australia, South Africa or Canada in defence matters. However, Sir
Edward Harding admitted that our defence interested them in an entirely
different manner, and he thought that as far as the material of the port
defences was concerned our expenditure could be taken into account.

On the trade side I think they will ask us to withdraw or reduce some of
the duties which hit them most heavily, or to increase our trade with them.
Sir Edward Harding was inclined at one moment to think that some of the
penal duties might have to be left in operation by them in order to satisfy
Parliament that they were getting some fraction of the Annuity payments. I
told him that a threat of that kind could only have one result, namely, to put
an end to the negotiations at once. A war of whatever nature must end as a
whole. There could be no half-measures. Obviously we should be ready to
drop our penal duties and to make a reasonable trade agreement with them.
Of course we expected to get a free market for agricultural produce in Great
Britain, and I believed the Minister for Industry and Commerce could find
the means, with their help, of diverting some of our external trade to the
advantage of British merchants. I did not think that, once the broad principles had been determined with fairness to both sides, there would be any
serious difficulty when we reached the stage of detailed discussion between
the Ministers concerned.

On the issue of the unity of Ireland, Sir Edward Harding adopted the now
stereotyped attitude of the British that it is very largely, if not exclusively, a
matter between ourselves and the Six Counties. I disagreed very strongly
with him on that point. They, at any rate, have no intention of making any
suggestion about unity at this conference, but I think that apart from the restatement of the principle which you, Sir, will have to make, something
might be gained by definitely suggesting a common purpose in pursuance
of which there could be a meeting between the two Governments once or
twice a year. The British would, I believe, be prepared to help us in bringing
about that first step towards unity if they were asked to do so. No doubt their
Right Wing political affiliations make it very difficult for them to make a
suggestion themselves.

To conclude this very summarised note, I should like to repeat my opinion that the British seem to seriously desire a settlement and that they are

ready to meet us in a friendly spirit with the intention of coming as far as possible along our path. I also wish to suggest that I should go back to London to continue my talks with Harding at the beginning of next week. I think, having discussed all these matters with you and having reached a more definite view as to what we can and what we cannot accept, it might be possible through Sir Edward Harding to bring the British closer to our view, or at least to ensure that there will be no real hitches in the early days of the conference through want of a proper understanding of each other's position.

[initialled] J.P.W.

No. 118 NAI DT S10389A

> Extract from the minutes of a meeting of the Cabinet
> (G.C. 1/2) (Item 5)
>
> DUBLIN, 7 January 1938

RELATIONS WITH GREAT BRITAIN: Suggested Governmental Conference
The Taoiseach adverted to a report which he had previously made with reference to the reply which had been received from the British Government arising out of the decision taken at the meeting of the Cabinet held on the 23rd November last,[1] approving of the issue of a despatch to that Government proposing an early conference between members of the two Governments.[2]

Approval was given for the sending of a delegation consisting of the Taoiseach, the Minister for Industry and Commerce, the Minister for Finance and the Minister for Agriculture, to a conference to be held in London on Monday, 17th January, 1938, for the purpose of discussing the various outstanding questions at issue between the two countries.

It was decided that any agreement which might be reached by the representatives of the Irish Government would be subject to the approval of the Government as a whole.

No. 119 NAI DT S10336

> Letter from Joseph P. Walshe to Maurice Moynihan (Dublin)
>
> DUBLIN, 11 January 1938

With reference to your minute (S.10336) of the 10th instant, I attach herewith a suggested reply to Deputy Norton's question.[3] If the Deputy presses the point about consulting with the Dáil beforehand in relation to revocation of duties, it might be better to let the Minister for Industry and Commerce or the Minister for Finance explain the machinery for the imposition and revocation of duties. The really important point, as far as the Minister for External Affairs is concerned, is that the Government's position in relation to the

---

[1] See above No. 103.
[2] See above No. 104.
[3] Not printed.

making of agreements with foreign countries without prior consultation with the Dáil should not be compromised.

[signed] J.P. WALSHE
Rúnaí

No. 120 UCDA P150/2487

Memorandum from Maurice Moynihan to Eamon de Valera (Dublin)
on the possibility of the restoration of the six counties
DUBLIN, 13 January 1938

Conference with British Ministers, January 1938.
Restoration of the Six Counties

It is, I think, unlikely that the forthcoming Conference will include in its direct results

(a) the restoration of the Six Counties, or

(b) the detachment of any portion of the present Six County territory and the addition of such portion to the area within our jurisdiction, or

(c) the setting up of any authority having functions of an advisory or other character in respect of the whole of the 32 Counties.

2. There is perhaps some remote possibility of achieving the setting up of some joint authority having advisory functions, if that would fall in with your policy. I take it, however, that failure to achieve (a), or (b), or (c) would not be regarded by you as necessitating by itself a breakdown of negotiations in regard to finance, trade and defence.

3. It was provisionally agreed at the meeting of the Government on Friday last, the 7th instant,[1] in regard to which I have already given you some notes, that any agreement which does not include the restoration of the Six Counties will not be regarded as disposing completely of the matters at issue between Ireland and Great Britain. An understanding of this nature clearly and publicly expressed and assented to by both parties to the Conference appears to be a necessary concomitant of any agreement that may now be reached. You may consider that failure to reach such an understanding would justify from our point of view a complete break-down of negotiations.

4. The understanding might cover the following points:

(1) The British Government to accept and publicly to recognise the position of the Irish Government that while the question of partition remains unsettled, the matters at issue between the two countries cannot be regarded as disposed of completely.

(2) Both sides to recognise that there is no question of coercing the majority in the Six Counties into any settlement of the partition problem.

---

[1] See above No. 118. This matter does not appear in the agreed minutes.

(3) The British Government to express themselves as being favourably disposed towards Irish union and as being prepared to do everything within their power by peaceful and friendly means to encourage it.

5. The prominence which has been given to partition, not merely in relation to the forthcoming Conference, but generally in statements of the Government's policy, seems to make it imperative that some such declarations as those at (1) to (3) should be made in conjunction with any agreement, particularly an agreement including clauses in relation to defence.

6. As a matter of tactics at the Conference, I would suggest that a full discussion of partition ought to come last, so that so far as possible we may know where we stand in regard to trade, finance and defence before the matter which may be regarded as containing the greatest danger to the success of the negotiations is reached. It will be impossible to keep partition altogether out of the earlier discussions, because all four questions are to a considerable extent interdependent, but I think the greatest possible light should be obtained on the British intentions regarding trade, finance and defence before all the cards are put on the table regarding partition.

[signed] M. O'Muimhneacháin

No. 121 UCDA P150/2491

Various rough notes and press releases kept by Eamon de Valera during negotiations in London

LONDON, 17-19 January 1938

Mr. de Valera said that in the view of his colleagues and himself the ending of Partition and the restoration of the unity of Ireland was the essential foundation for the establishment of real understanding and friendship between the peoples of the two countries ~~and that so long as Partition continued friendship and cooperation could not be complete~~.[1]

In reply the representatives of the United Kingdom said that so far as they were concerned there could be no alteration in the relations between Éire and Northern Ireland which had not the consent of the latter.

You ask me what are my hopes for the future relations between the peoples of Ireland and Great Britain. I have always said that I desired to establish friendly relations ~~with Great Britain~~ between the two peoples. That is still my desire and hope. But the historic Irish nation has been artificially divided. At least a third of the population of that part of Ulster which has been cut off from the nation – and *remember that third*[2] are resident immediately across the line which separates that part from us – want to be with us as citizens of a united Ireland.

---

[1] These words and others below have been crossed out in the document.
[2] Handwritten insertion by de Valera reproduced in italics.

We have no wish to coerce into a united Ireland our fellow-countrymen in the Northeast who differ from us. But we do ask them and all their friends to consider whether it is not their duty to play their part in bringing about a united Ireland, *which is so essential now*[1] not merely for the betterment of relations ~~amongst~~ *between* ourselves in Ireland but for the establishment of friendly relations with Great Britain and for the promotion of peace in the world.

I appeal to people of Irish origin in Britain, America and all over the world to give us their aid. The partition of the motherland must be a source of pain and sorrow to all of them. Through their combined influence we can, with God's help, within a *reasonably* short time bring that partition to an end.

Given to Paramount News and March of Time at about 12.30 midnight.

Practically nothing to add to the agreed press communiqué.

A few weeks adjournment to enable experts on finance and trade matters to complete their detailed examinations. Preparations for trade agreements invariably take a long time.

Throughout the three days meetings the discussions have been frank and friendly, each side appreciating the view of the other.

At nine o'clock Mr. Malcolm MacDonald is calling here to see me on a few matters in connection with the experts' examination.

No more information to give about the question of partition.

January 19th, 1938

No. 122 NAI DT S10389 (Annex)

> *Minutes of the conference between representatives of the United*
> *Kingdom and Ireland*
> *(Secret) (I.N. (38) 1st Meeting) (Copy)*
> LONDON, 2.45 pm, 17 January 1938

PRESENT

UNITED KINGDOM	ÉIRE
The Rt. Hon Neville Chamberlain, M.P., Prime Minister.	Mr. Eamon de Valera, Prime Minister and Minister for External Affairs.
The Rt. Hon. Sir John Simon, G.C.S.I., G.C.V.O., O.B.E., K.C., M.P., Chancellor of the Exchequer.	Mr. Sean F. Lemass, Minister for Industry and Commerce.
The Rt. Hon. Sir Samuel Hoare, Bt., G.C.S.I., G.B.E., C.M.G.,	Mr. Sean MacEntee, Minister for Finance.

---

[1] Text in italics in this document represents handwritten insertions by de Valera.

M.P., Secretary of State for
the Home Department.

The Rt. Hon. Malcolm MacDonald, Dr. James Ryan,
M.P., Secretary of State for   Minister for Agriculture.
Dominion Affairs.

THE FOLLOWING WERE ALSO PRESENT:

The Rt.Hon. Sir Thomas Inskip,   Mr. J. W. Dulanty, C.B., C.B.E.,
C.B.E., K.C., M.P., Minister for   High Commissioner for Éire.
Co-ordination of Defence.
(For part of time)

The Rt. Hon. Oliver Stanley,
M.C., M.P., President of the
Board of Trade.
(For part of time)

The Rt. Hon. W.S. Morrison, M.C.,
K.C., M.P., Minister of
Agriculture and Fisheries.
(For part of time)

Secretaries   Sir R.B. Howorth, K.C.M.G., C.B.
                Mr. C. N. Ryan, D.S.O., M.C.
                Mr. W.D. Wilkinson, D.S.O., M.C.

MR. CHAMBERLAIN said that he and his colleagues were very glad indeed
to welcome Mr. De Valera and his colleagues to London. Since the Meetings
held in 1932[1] it could truthfully be said that the relations between the two
countries had not been impaired and that the conditions for reaching a
better understanding were more favourable now than they had been. The
forthcoming discussions would take place on a footing of complete equality
and without any conditions. United Kingdom Ministers were very anxious to
reach a satisfactory agreement on the various outstanding questions. There
were a number of topics requiring examination and perhaps Mr. de Valera
would be good enough to indicate his ideas as to the order in which these
topics could most profitably be discussed.

MR. DE VALERA thanked Mr. Chamberlain for his welcome and said that
he and his colleagues had come to London with the same intention of
endeavouring to reach agreement on the outstanding issues between the two
countries. As regards subjects for discussion Mr. Chamberlain would no
doubt remember a Note[2] which he (Mr. de Valera) had addressed to him
mentioning the questions of censorship and food supply and control in time

---

[1] See DIFP Volume IV, Nos 136, 137, 138 and 140.
[2] See above No. 104.

of war. The Government of Éire had recently given careful consideration to the position of their country in the event of the outbreak of a major war. So long as the various important outstanding problems remained unsettled between the two countries there was a very real and serious danger that if Great Britain became involved in a major war the situation in Éire might not be very different from what the situation in the South of Ireland had been in 1914 when Mr. Redmond[1] found himself faced with difficulties which proved beyond his control.

Of these major problems he would mention the question of Partition. In the view of the Government of Éire there should never have been any partition at all, and also there should be no coercion of the minority in Northern Ireland. It would be difficult to exaggerate the dangerous possibilities inherent in these factors of the situation. Secondly, there were parts of the country which by every test should be within the jurisdiction of the Government of Éire but which, in fact, were subject to the jurisdiction of the Government of Northern Ireland. Thirdly, there was the problem of the presence of British troops in certain Éire ports.

These, among other considerations, would make the position of the Government of Éire one of great difficulty in the event of the outbreak of a major war. Moreover, that Government would be gravely handicapped by its inability to make any proper plans in advance. It would be realised how difficult it would be for the Government of Éire to impose taxation for increased Defence, which taxation in present circumstances their people could not, in fact, bear. If the position was envisaged in which Great Britain was involved in hostilities and Éire was perhaps indirectly involved, clearly the necessary preparations could not be made unless the people were enthusiastically behind their Government in supporting the necessary Defence measures.

If it was possible to secure a satisfactory settlement of all the outstanding differences between the two countries he (Mr. de Valera) was satisfied that it would be possible to secure such enthusiasm and support throughout Éire for Defence measures as would make the country so strong that no Power would venture to attack her. He need hardly point out how advantageous this would be to Great Britain. In this way not only would Éire be in a position to preserve her independence but she would be able effectively to prevent any enemy of Britain from using her as a base from which to attack the United Kingdom.

There were certain vital and fundamental considerations. In the first place the unity of the whole of Ireland must be secured, and the present state of affairs in the six Counties under which one section of the population, which was armed, was able to coerce another section, must be terminated. Secondly, the Government of Éire must obtain complete sovereignty over the ports

---

[1] John Redmond (1856-1918), MP (1880-1918), leader of the Irish Parliamentary Party (1900-18) which campaigned for Home Rule (domestic self-government for Ireland within the United Kingdom). Home Rule was granted by the Third Home Rule Bill of 1912 (passed in 1914), but its implementation was suspended due to the outbreak of the First World War. The demand for Home Rule was overtaken by events following the 1916 Easter Rising.

now held by the United Kingdom in their country; and thirdly in order that Éire might be able to find the necessary money for rearmament she must be relieved of the burden of the present special duties, etc., which the United Kingdom had imposed upon her.

He hoped that the Conference would open with the idea of securing improved relations between the two countries instead of, as in the past, each country being a source of irritation and annoyance to the other. There was no need for him at the moment further to particularise his point of view as he had already spoken to Mr. MacDonald and had explained his attitude fully to him.

MR. CHAMBERLAIN said that it was evident that the questions which would have to be discussed ranged over a fairly wide field and would have to be taken in some kind of order. All the questions were closely connected with one another and he hoped that in the course of discussion it would be possible to construct a general picture and to see how far it was possible to reconcile the points of view of the two Governments.

PARTITION

As regards the question of partition the position so far as the United Kingdom was concerned was simple. The United Kingdom Government regarded partition as a matter which would have to be discussed between the Governments of Éire and Northern Ireland. The Government of the United Kingdom would not in principle be disposed to object to any arrangement which might be freely and voluntarily entered into between the two Irish Governments, but it must be clearly understood that they would impose no sort of pressure or coercion on Northern Ireland in the matter. He could not too strongly emphasise that an agreement freely and voluntarily entered into between Éire and Northern Ireland would meet with no opposition from the Government of the United Kingdom and Mr. de Valera could be assured that in the event of such an agreement being reached he need fear no difficulties of any sort so far as the United Kingdom was concerned.

MR. DE VALERA said that partition was the creation of the Parliament of the United Kingdom and in his view it was not open to the Government of the United Kingdom to wash their hands of any responsibility in the matter. That Government was in fact responsible for the happenings in Northern Ireland. It was quite impossible for the Government of Éire to make contact or any agreement with the Government of Northern Ireland without the support of the Government of the United Kingdom.

Mr. de Valera mentioned factors such as the presence of British troops in Ulster and the various subsidies paid by the Government of the United Kingdom to the Government of Northern Ireland which, in his view, constituted a powerful inducement to Northern Ireland to remain part of the United Kingdom. He also referred to the position in South Down of which he had long been the Representative in the Northern Ireland Parliament and where, in his view, the inhabitants were being deprived of their civil rights and subjected to various kinds of unjust and improper coercion, the consequence of which might well in the long run be highly deplorable. The

Government of Éire considered that the Government of the United Kingdom were responsible for partition and for the injustices and inequalities suffered by a large section of the inhabitants of Northern Ireland. If the Government of the United Kingdom adopted the attitude that the matter was no concern of theirs he felt that no progress towards improving relations between the two countries was possible. There were great dangers inherent in the situation and he much feared the continuance of the present critical state of affairs which might well develop into one of considerable danger. If the problem of partition was not solved it was inevitable that agitation and grave unrest must continue on an increasing scale and that incidents might occur which would be misunderstood by the Government and people of the United Kingdom.

MR. CHAMBERLAIN enquired whether Mr. de Valera did not think that the present state of feeling on both sides of the border was much too unfavourable to offer any prospects of a settlement between the two Irish Governments and accordingly would it not be wiser policy to endeavour to secure an improvement of those conditions as a result of which the people themselves would come to realise the advantages of a united Ireland.

MR. DE VALERA referred to the basis which had been adopted for settling the boundary between Éire and Northern Ireland and contended that in many places including Newry, South Down, South Armagh and Fermanagh the wishes of the inhabitants had in fact been disregarded. This question of partition had caused a deeper and more intense feeling throughout Ireland than any other question. It was this question which had caused him (Mr. de Valera) first to take an active part in politics. In his view the great change which had taken place throughout the country in regard to Mr. Redmond and his policy was mainly due to the action which had been taken in regard to partition. He fully realised the difficulties in the matter of the United Kingdom Government, but he must frankly state that really good relations between the two countries could not be secured unless this question was satisfactorily settled and he must warn the United Kingdom Ministers that he and his colleagues would hold themselves completely free to take such action, in support of their point of view, as they might think fit to do.

MR. CHAMBERLAIN enquired whether Mr. de Valera did not think that agreement on the other outstanding questions would be of great help in improving the relations between the two countries.

MR. DE VALERA replied that throughout Ireland there was very great suspicion of all motives and actions of the United Kingdom. It was not believed that in Northern Ireland the people thought that the Government of the United Kingdom were indifferent as to whether Ireland was united or not. The general view would certainly be that the United Kingdom favoured a disunited Ireland. Undoubtedly the majority in Northern Ireland feared that in some way or other they might lose their majority and become a minority.

MR. CHAMBERLAIN said that the suspicion that the United Kingdom desired the disunity of Ireland was a profound delusion. As he had said, the Government of the United Kingdom had no desire to prevent in any way a free and voluntary agreement between the two Irish Governments on the subject if such an agreement could be reached. He was sure that Mr. de Valera would recognise that in the present circumstances it would be impossible to bring about a united Ireland except by the employment of force against Northern Ireland.

MR. DE VALERA said that if he were in Mr. Chamberlain's position he would bring pressure to bear on Northern Ireland of a moral character.

SIR SAMUEL HOARE said that he entirely agreed with what the Prime Minister had said on this subject. As Mr. de Valera was no doubt aware his views were those of a typical Conservative but he had never opposed the unity of Ireland, and in his view this was a development which in course of time might reasonably be expected to come of itself. He was well aware of the views of Lord Craigavon who was an eminently reasonable statesman and of other reasonable leaders in Northern Ireland, and also of public opinion in the United Kingdom. Any coercion or the mere suggestion of coercion was quite impossible and this was the fully considered view of every United Kingdom statesman who had studied the matter in the last twenty years. While he thought that a united Ireland was the ultimate solution, he was satisfied that it would only be possible to attain that end by greatly improved relations. Mr. de Valera had mentioned certain causes of complaint which he had against Northern Ireland. He would not, he felt sure, mind if he, Sir Samuel, stated that Northern Ireland had certain causes of complaint against Éire, as, for example, in regard to the special discriminatory duties. He was sure that it would never be possible to coerce Northern Ireland and accordingly if Mr. de Valera's objective was to be attained it would be necessary to persuade her. As a result of these discussions it was hoped that better relations between the United Kingdom and Éire would be promoted, and it might well result as a consequence that relations between Éire and Northern Ireland would, in turn, greatly improve.

MR. DE VALERA enquired what Sir Samuel Hoare meant by special discriminatory duties in the case of Northern Ireland. So far as he was aware Northern Ireland was affected by the discriminatory duties in precisely the same way as the rest of the United Kingdom and not to any greater extent. Whilst he was bound to admit that, in his view, the coercion of Northern Ireland would, in all the circumstances, be justifiable, he would not himself favour a policy of coercion as he was certain that this would merely create greater difficulties than it would solve. When United Kingdom Ministers spoke of coercion they should always remember that the majority in Northern Ireland were continuously coercing the minority.

SIR SAMUEL HOARE observed that Northern Ireland would probably retort by pointing to the hardships suffered by the minority in Éire.

MR. DE VALERA said that there was no real comparison in the two cases. The minority in Éire was insignificant in numbers and in other respects and was in any case in no position to cause the Government of Éire the least anxiety, but in Northern Ireland one-third of the total population constituted the minority and that large fraction ardently desired to transfer themselves to Éire. It was idle to talk of coercion when it was generally recognised that one-third of the population of Northern Ireland were, in fact, being coerced.

MR. CHAMBERLAIN pointed out that if one-third of the population of Northern Ireland were transferred to Éire, Northern Ireland would be left with the remaining two-thirds and that the problem would then be as difficult if not more difficult of solution.

MR. DE VALERA agreed but said that he had never favoured, nor would he ever agree to, a solution of this character. When he had discussed the question with Mr. Lloyd George in 1920 he had advocated arrangements for the transference of Powers and guarantees for those who might be deprived of their civil rights. He repeated that in his opinion the United Kingdom Government were in a position to point out to Northern Ireland the great advantages that would accrue to Northern Ireland from unification and to exercise moral persuasion on Northern Ireland to accept that solution.

SIR SAMUEL HOARE said it was very difficult to consider this suggestion when there were so many responsible persons in Northern Ireland and elsewhere who took the view that, as a result of recent constitutional changes and policies, Éire was breaking the connection between the two countries and drifting out of the British Commonwealth. The people of Northern Ireland attached enormous importance to their connection with the United Kingdom and greatly valued their membership of the Empire.

MR. DE VALERA expressed surprise that the hard-headed inhabitants of Northern Ireland were influenced by any sentimental considerations.

SIR SAMUEL HOARE assured Mr. de Valera that in this respect Northern Ireland was every bit as sentimental as Éire.

MR. DE VALERA maintained that the people of Éire would not have accepted any proposals on constitutional lines short of those which had now been embodied in the new Constitution. As a result of the adoption of the Constitution a position of relative stability had now been attained so far as Éire was concerned.

MR. CHAMBERLAIN doubted whether Northern Ireland would agree that a position of relative stability had been reached in Éire. In their view the Government of Éire were engaged in severing all the cords which bound them to the British Commonwealth. In his view what was really required was a complete restoration of confidence and it was only when confidence had been fully and genuinely restored that Éire could hope to look for some favourable response from Northern Ireland.

MR. DE VALERA said that he felt bound to warn the United Kingdom Ministers of the reaction in Éire which must result from their attitude. In particular, the position would be greatly strengthened of all those who had throughout maintained that there was no half-way house and that, therefore, the best solution would be for Éire to leave the Commonwealth. These persons maintained that their only hope was to see the United Kingdom involved in serious dangers and difficulties. He, on the other hand, favoured the maintenance of the strength of the British Commonwealth, frankly because he saw in such maintenance the best and most effective protection for his country. He hoped that the United Kingdom Ministers realised that there were many people of the Left Wing in Éire who welcomed the adage that 'England's difficulty is Ireland's opportunity' and who would be only too ready to prepare accordingly.

MR. MACDONALD said that he had naturally given much thought to this problem. It was due to Mr. de Valera to say that from the outset he had put this question in the forefront of all the conversations which had taken place between them, and that he had always maintained with complete frankness that unless and until the Partition question could be satisfactorily settled no real good relations between the two countries were possible. His colleagues would agree that he had always faithfully passed on to them Mr. de Valera's views on this subject. Mr. de Valera believed, as did his colleagues and the people of Éire, that the United Kingdom Government were interested in the maintenance of Partition. He had always tried to remove this complete misconception of the position of the United Kingdom Government. It was no doubt true that among private individuals in the United Kingdom and elsewhere the opinion was held that partition should be maintained for its own sake but their view was not that of the Government of the United Kingdom which was that while there should be no coercion of or pressure on Northern Ireland, if Northern Ireland changed her present opinion and favoured unification, there would be no opposition of any sort or kind from the Government of the United Kingdom. Mr. de Valera, however, went somewhat further and said that if we were really sincere in what we said we could take steps to use moral persuasion. He entirely agreed with what Sir Samuel Hoare had said on this subject and he did not believe for a moment that any attempt by us on these lines would serve any useful purpose. Mr. de Valera had spoken of contributions made by the United Kingdom in aid of Northern Ireland. It should be remembered that the contributions made by Northern Ireland to the United Kingdom exceeded in amount those made by the United Kingdom to Northern Ireland. But even if we were to withhold all our contributions, the result in his opinion would be precisely the same, and Northern Ireland would still maintain her objection to any union with Éire. The United Kingdom could do nothing except work for improved relations in all other respects and by so doing improve relations between Éire and Northern Ireland and so bring about perhaps a better realisation in Northern Ireland that Éire had in fact reached the state of relative stability to which Mr. de Valera had referred. These were his views stated with all frankness and sincerity.

MR. DE VALERA said that as a result of the discussion each side was now in possession of the point of view of the other. It seemed to him that one very important part of the mission of himself and his colleagues to London must be left undone. Some patching in regard to other questions might be possible but it must be realised that the conference had failed to get down to bedrock.

MR. CHAMBERLAIN said that United Kingdom Ministers had to face the realities of the situation in precisely the same way as Mr. de Valera and his colleagues had to face them. As had been explained, the United Kingdom could not usefully exert any influence on Northern Ireland to unite with Éire, but he thought that if it was found possible to reach agreement in other respects, better relations would be created and this, in the course of time, might well enable the United Kingdom to act in a mediatory capacity between Éire and Northern Ireland.

MR. DE VALERA replied that in the position in which they found themselves it was almost impossible for the Ministers of Éire to bring about the conditions essential to an improvement of relations between the two countries. It seemed that we had got into a vicious circle. Unless some real effort was going to be made to end partition he was very much afraid that relations would deteriorate. The mere fact that in certain respects his Government had tended to move to the Right had much intensified the strength of the Left Wing in Éire.

MR. CHAMBERLAIN enquired how far the feeling in Éire to which Mr. de Valera had referred was due to the suspicion that the United Kingdom Government was opposed to Irish unification.

MR. DE VALERA said that this view was held universally in Éire. Public opinion would never credit the United Kingdom Government with any different policy.

MR. CHAMBERLAIN enquired whether the position would be changed if the United Kingdom made a public announcement on the subject.

MR. DE VALERA said that his public opinion would want action rather than words. The United Kingdom Government said that there should be no coercion, though in point of fact one-third of the population of Northern Ireland was being coerced. A public statement might help, but much would depend upon its terms.

SIR JOHN SIMON said that he was not sure that he fully appreciated the point about coercion. So far as he knew no-one had suggested that Northern Ireland should be compelled to join Éire. He himself detested coercion in any shape or form and he would have thought that the only possible way to secure unification was by the free and voluntary agreement of all the people concerned.

MR. DE VALERA did not dissent and said that he himself would be disposed to join with Northern Ireland if the United Kingdom attempted to coerce her by force. If he was Prime Minister of the United Kingdom he would say to Northern Ireland 'Cannot you play your part in bringing about greatly improved relations between the whole of Ireland and the United Kingdom'? The trouble was that Governments in the past had failed to seize their opportunities. The United Kingdom might at one time have made a comprehensive settlement with Mr. Redmond. It might well be that in the future regret would have to be expressed that the present Conference had failed to find a solution.

MR. CHAMBERLAIN asked what would be the reply if Northern Ireland said to us that they did not agree that this particular method was a solution of the problem?

MR. DE VALERA said that in those circumstances he would tell Northern Ireland plainly that as they refused to make any contribution they could not look for help from the United Kingdom.

SIR SAMUEL HOARE said that Northern Ireland sincerely and honestly believed in the British Commonwealth, and thought that they would best serve Imperial interests by remaining as they were at present. They would maintain that Éire was drifting away from the Empire, and if they were to be convinced that their view was wrong it would first be necessary to establish confidence and secure much better relations than existed at present.

MR. DE VALERA repeated that in his view the main consideration in Northern Ireland was the fear of the majority that they might become a minority.

SIR SAMUEL HOARE said that the difficulty was rooted in centuries of history. Any suggestion of coercion by the United Kingdom would provoke the maximum possible opposition in Ulster to unification.

MR. MacENTEE thought that an approach by Éire to Northern Ireland would be very difficult. The Treaty had contained a provision for Proportional Representation. This provision had been maintained in the Irish Free State and in Éire throughout because of the desire to be fair to the minority. On the other hand, Northern Ireland had abolished Proportional Representation and had gerrymandered the Constituencies in favour of the majority. The United Kingdom were in the position of a trustee for the minority of Northern Ireland and in the view of the Government of Éire they had failed in their duty as a trustee. Considerations of this kind created intense suspicion and made it very difficult to persuade public opinion in Éire to follow its Government. Secondly, the arrangements in Northern Ireland for the preservation of peace and the maintenance of law and order were open to grave criticism. The supporters of Éire in Northern Ireland were not treated properly. It was very difficult indeed for the Government of Éire to approach Northern Ireland. Would it not be possible for the United Kingdom Government to ask the Government of Northern Ireland to restore Proportional Representation and to secure proper treatment for the minority?

MR. CHAMBERLAIN said that speaking for himself he saw very great difficulty in approaching Northern Ireland by Éire at the present time. When the time came for such an approach the United Kingdom Government might be in a position to facilitate matters, but any approach now would merely be regarded by Northern Ireland as a betrayal by the United Kingdom. If, however, relations could be improved and confidence re-established between Éire and the United Kingdom, the United Kingdom would be in a very much better position to exercise mediatory influence. In his view it was not possible to carry this matter further, and he suggested that note should be taken of the respective points of view of the two countries and that the Meeting should agree at a later time to consider the possibility of the United Kingdom issuing a statement on their attitude towards unification.

MR. DE VALERA emphasised the difficulties of himself and his colleagues in regard to this matter. Public opinion in Éire would certainly regard it as a betrayal if agreement having been reached on other matters, no arrangement of any sort regarding Partition was made. In the absence of such an arrangement it would be very difficult indeed to conclude agreements on a number of matters which he would much like to see settled.

MR. CHAMBERLAIN enquired whether Mr. de Valera meant that he thought that no useful purpose would be served by discussing the other outstanding questions.

MR. DE VALERA replied in the negative, but repeated that in the absence of some arrangement regarding Partition it was out of the question to hope to get greatly improved relations.

SIR SAMUEL HOARE observed that the only sure way of securing progress was to proceed step by step.

MR. DE VALERA said that he wished United Kingdom Ministers to realise that this question of Partition was a vital and fundamental issue to all Irish people, both at home and abroad.

MR. CHAMBERLAIN said that United Kingdom Ministers fully realised the position and difficulties of Mr. de Valera and his colleagues, but they felt themselves bound by the realities of the situation and could not help feeling that the re-establishment of confidence between Éire and Great Britain would pave the way for an improvement of relations between Éire and Northern Ireland. It must be remembered that if United Kingdom Ministers made a settlement which was not acceptable to the House of Commons the position would be much more difficult even than it was at present.

MR. DE VALERA said that the position was even more difficult for himself and his colleagues. A mistake made by Irish negotiators might well result in their country being plunged into turmoil. In England a mistake made by English negotiators would at most result in a change of Government.

MR. CHAMBERLAIN enquired what subject Mr. de Valera would like to discuss next.

MR. DE VALERA suggested that they should discuss the question of the occupation by the United Kingdom of the ports.

The Meeting adjourned in order to secure the attendance of Sir Thomas Inskip, Minister for Co-ordination of Defence.

THE DEFENDED PORTS

MR. DE VALERA said that the claim of Éire to the Defended Ports rested primarily on the doctrine of National Sovereignty. As the Irish people saw it, the presence of British detachments in these ports was nothing less than an act of aggression.

Secondly, the British occupation of the ports constituted a distinct danger. There was always the possibility of an attempt on the part of some section of the Irish population to eject the garrisons. It would be no pleasant duty for any Irish Government to employ force against persons making such an attempt.

The third point in his case related to the use of the ports. What did the United Kingdom Government want them for? He took it that the idea was to secure that no foreign power should make use of them for the purposes of an attack against the United Kingdom.

This object, he suggested, could be secured equally efficiently by different means. If the United Kingdom delegates had met him in a more satisfactory way over the Partition issue, he would have been able to go further. As things were, he was prepared to repeat (what he had already said in public) that the Irish people were prepared to take over the Treaty ports and, having done so, would organise themselves to prevent the ports from being used as bases of attack by any foreign power on the United Kingdom.

It might be objected that Éire did not possess sufficient strength for the purpose. It was true their strength was far smaller than that of this country. Up to the limit of their power, however, they would organise themselves for the task. Was it indeed likely that the people of Éire, having won their independence, would hesitate to take all possible steps to secure it?

Next, to the extent that the strength of Éire was insufficient, he was of the opinion that when the emergency came the Government of the day, in the exercise of its own judgment and responsibility, would take steps to obtain assistance. The natural direction in which to look for such assistance would be from the Government of the United Kingdom. That Government in its turn would be more secure for the purposes of the emergency if the help which they extended to Éire had been freely asked for by the Government of Éire.

His confidence would be complete if it were not for the attitude of the United Kingdom Government towards Partition. That attitude might result in a section of Irish opinion criticising their Government for inviting United Kingdom co-operation, while Irish freedom was still impaired. Those who took this line might point to the freedom obtained by the Succession States in Central Europe. These States had obtained their independence owing to the break-up of the Austrian Empire.

MR. CHAMBERLAIN suggested that this last argument did not rest on very solid foundations. At the present moment some of the Succession States did not feel too happy about their independence.

MR. DE VALERA appreciated the dangers of the European situation. Another analogy which occurred to him was that of the South African Republics. General Smuts had said to him that his (the General's) people were far freer now than in the days of the independent Republics. A war however had had to be waged before he could persuade all his people of the soundness of his opinion.

MR. CHAMBERLAIN did not doubt that the people of Éire, if they obtained the Treaty Ports, would do their best to defend them against all comers. So far as this country was concerned, he did not hesitate to say that (assuming that the ports had become the property of Éire) we should be ready and anxious to help in time of emergency, subject always to our other responsibilities at that time.

His anxiety, however, was not that the ports would not be defended. It was rather that the ports should be made available for the use of the United Kingdom forces. He was assured by the military experts that in the event of a major war (e.g. against Germany) it was most important that we should have their use for the assembly or the protection of convoys.

SIR THOMAS INSKIP said that Berehaven and Lough Swilly would, according to the best military opinion, be of special importance in the circumstances contemplated. As Mr. Chamberlain had said, the object was not so much to deny those ports to the enemy, but to use them for the purpose of protecting the vitally important shipping which brought us our supplies from Ireland itself, from the other Dominions, from the Far East, etc. For reasons of geography these ports were the best places from which anti-submarine operations could be carried out. This was the United Kingdom Government's primary use for the defended ports. A secondary use would be as assembly places for convoys.

Naturally if, for one reason or another, we were unable to use the defended ports, we should have to use United Kingdom ports for both the purposes which he had mentioned. They would, however, be only a second best.

The enemy submarine attack would obviously be directed against Éire as well as against the United Kingdom. It was, therefore, in the common interest for the forces of both countries to be able to use the ports.

The Éire Delegation would appreciate that what was expected from Germany, if that country became our opponent, was an attempt to force a decision by means of a short sharp war which would include an intensive attack against our shipping, food supplies and ports. The risk of actual invasion was not considered very great. So far as we were concerned, the submarine would remain one of Germany's chief weapons.

MR. DE VALERA said that Mr. Chamberlain and Sir Thomas Inskip had raised a new and difficult issue. If they had stopped at a demand that the treaty ports should be denied to the United Kingdom's enemies, he would have had no hesitation in saying that it might safely be left to whatever government was in power in Éire at the time to invite United Kingdom co-operation.

The moment, however, that the United Kingdom asked for the use of the ports by its own forces, as a right, the people of Ireland would suspect an encroachment on their territory. They would feel that it was no longer their own. Frankly, if he were asked to give his assent in advance to such an arrangement, he would have to refuse.

SIR THOMAS INSKIP did not see why there could not be a satisfactory understanding. A land-owner could give the use of his land for a particular purpose, but it remained his own.

MR. DE VALERA said that he personally would not take the responsibility of promising any such arrangement. He said this particularly in view of the fact that there appeared to be no hope of a genuine understanding with the United Kingdom. He was referring to the issue of partition in Northern Ireland.

As things were, he could not bind future governments of Ireland beyond the point which he had already mentioned. Anything further would have to be determined by events.

MR. CHAMBERLAIN asked whether he was right in gathering that Mr. de Valera might have returned a different answer if United Kingdom Ministers had met him over partition.

MR. DE VALERA said that this would have been so. The hatchet would have been buried, and things would have been fundamentally different. The Irish people would have realised that their own defence interests were best served by the United Kingdom and the overseas Dominions maintaining their strength. Éire would have contributed to the common strength of the Commonwealth. Past difficulties would have disappeared, and the people of Éire would have come to realise that our[1] desire to use the ports in time of war was not for the purpose of interference in Irish affairs.

---

[1] The minutes of these meetings were taken by the British, because Britain was the host country, and later checked by the Irish.

MR. CHAMBERLAIN said that it was certainly not our desire in any way to invade the sovereignty of Éire; our desire to use the ports was in the interests of our own existence. The last war had shown us how important they were.

He had to deal with public opinion in the United Kingdom just as Mr. de Valera had to deal with public opinion in Éire. What was he, Mr. Chamberlain, to say to public opinion here if he gave up the ports, the use of which was secured to this country by the 1921 Treaty, and received no assurance in exchange?

MR. DE VALERA said that public opinion appeared to give rise to equally insuperable difficulties on both sides.

MR. CHAMBERLAIN pointed out that there were precedents for what United Kingdom Ministers were proposing, i.e., treaty arrangements with foreign countries, entitling us in certain circumstances to the use of points in their territory.

MR. DE VALERA could only say that he believed that when the time came the Irish people could be ready to co-operate.

SIR THOMAS INSKIP said that it was of considerable military importance to know in advance what facilities one was going to enjoy in war. In our own case we had our preparations to make and we must know whether they were to be preparations suitable for Berehaven or for Pembroke.

MR. DE VALERA realised the force of this. It was the urgent need of military preparation in the difficult conditions of the present time which had led him to propose the Conference.

SIR JOHN SIMON enquired whether Mr. de Valera contemplated the absolute transfer of the ports by this country to Éire, without any kind of assurance from Éire that they would be kept in a proper state of defence.

MR. DE VALERA said that he was prepared to give a public assurance and to implement it, that Éire would deny the defended ports to all other powers.

MR. CHAMBERLAIN enquired whether Éire would agree to consult with this country regarding the nature of the defences required.

MR. DE VALERA said that he would have been able to go further if a real ending to the Anglo-Irish quarrel had been in prospect. In such circumstances it would have been the most natural thing for Éire to consult the United Kingdom.

As things were, Éire started with a strong desire not to become involved in war. She made her plans for resisting aggression from what ever quarter it came. Since, however, the likelihood existed that any enemy of the United Kingdom might consider using Éire as a base against the United Kingdom it followed that Éire's defensive system must be planned as part of a system common to the two countries.

SIR THOMAS INSKIP said that in modern conditions defensive systems had to be planned in advance.

MR. DE VALERA was afraid that the majority of the Irish people would be suspicious of any consultation in the ordinary sense, i.e., staff conversations.

There was, however, a lesser degree of consultation and to this he was prepared to pledge himself in public. The argument would be that the defensive system of Éire was planned to maintain the national independence; that the possibility existed of an enemy wishing to use Éire's ports against the United Kingdom; and that the further possibility existed of the Government of Éire asking for United Kingdom assistance in the defence of those ports. It followed from this that the defences of the ports must be planned to suit circumstances in which there would be co-operation with the United Kingdom.

More generally, the United Kingdom had considerable military experience and Éire had little. Éire must therefore look to the United Kingdom for technical advice. It was very desirable to arrange for interchangeability of equipment and spare parts between Éire and the United Kingdom.

SIR THOMAS INSKIP asked whether Mr. de Valera would agree that co-operation with the United Kingdom would bring important advantages to Éire.

MR. DE VALERA said that he fully realised the facts. Some of these facts, however, were difficult to explain on the other side of the Irish Sea. A very difficult situation would arise if any suggestions were made that the United Kingdom Government were going to have the use of the defended ports, except if the Government of Éire in the exercise of their own judgment asked for this form of co-operation.

MR. CHAMBERLAIN said that he would be glad if Mr. de Valera would give the Meeting his candid opinion as to what would happen on the outbreak of a major war, if the United Kingdom had no rights in the defended ports.

MR. DE VALERA said that he would give his opinion without reference to the question of partition in Northern Ireland. His estimate was that on the outbreak of war some sections of the Irish people would be inclined to hold out against co-operation with the United Kingdom. The Government of Éire would be in a position to draw attention to the considerations which told in favour of co-operation, e.g. the danger of interruption to the food supply, but the whole of the Irish people would not be convinced. The Government of Éire might say to the Government of the United Kingdom, assuming that friendly relations existed between the two Governments, 'our people do not yet realise the position; we shall have to wait before we can ask for your assistance'.

If the probabilities were as he thought, he would advise the United Kingdom Government to lay their plans on the basis that the Irish Defended Ports would not be available to them. They should provide, however, for the possibility of switching over to the use of the Irish Ports at a later stage. It would be the height of unwisdom for the United Kingdom Government to make any more favourable assumption.

SIR SAMUEL HOARE asked whether Mr. de Valera could not go a little farther. Was it not possible to draw a distinction in advance between situations obviously of interest to Éire and situations not of interest to Éire?

MR. DE VALERA thought this quite impossible. It must be left to the Government of Éire of the day to consider where their country's interests lay.

SIR SAMUEL HOARE said that the next war was expected to be entirely different from that of 1914/18. If Germany was involved she was expected to stake everything on bringing the war to an end within a few weeks or months. There would be no question of any preparations being useful which were not in readiness at the outset. He envisaged a great concentrated attack on the means of existence of both the United Kingdom and Éire.

MR. DE VALERA said that if he were persuaded of this view he would say that it was both the interest and the duty of the Government of Éire to start at once preparations in the defended ports (i.e. on the assumption that the ports were theirs). It was possible of course that the burden of preparation might become too great for Éire to carry.

Before the Government of Éire would take these steps they must be convinced that they were necessary in their own interest.

MR. MACDONALD asked how far Mr. de Valera would be prepared to go in such matters as consultation on defence plans and the interchangeability of equipment.

MR. DE VALERA said that he was personally satisfied of the necessity of these measures in the interests of the people of Éire. He would do his best to lead his people in that direction.

If the Government of Éire took over the ports, and if it were left entirely clear that they were free agents in taking their decision, they could probably say frankly for what purpose they were organising their defences in those parts of the country. They might be able to say, without much danger, that the possibility existed that Éire would be used as the base for an attack on the United Kingdom; that plans were being made which included the possibility of asking for assistance from the United Kingdom; and that consultations were taking place with that possibility in view.

MR. CHAMBERLAIN supposed that an Irish ship would have to be torpedoed before the people of Éire would take the situation seriously.

MR. MacENTEE thought that the principal thing necessary was that the Government of the United Kingdom should use their efforts to bring North and South together. If they were successful Irish opinion might develop with remarkable rapidity.

MR. DE VALERA did not altogether agree with his colleague that Irish opinion on defence questions could be expected in any circumstances to develop rapidly. Time would be required.

One fact of the situation was that the Government of Éire had an incomplete knowledge of the dangers of the international situation. They realised that re-armament was most expensive and they did not wish to spend money in the wrong directions.

They had not of course the vast financial resources of the United Kingdom, and they would soon feel the pinch if they spent any considerable sums on armaments. As he had pointed out in the 1932 conversations with the United Kingdom Government, the latter had gone off with all the assets of the former partnership.[1] They ought to be paying money to Ireland.

MR. CHAMBERLAIN suggested that finance might be left until a little later. What else could be done to make the defences of Éire effective? This country was in a position to give Éire much helpful information in such matters as anti-aircraft defence.

---

[1] See DIFP Volume IV, Nos 136, 137, 138 and 140.

SIR SAMUEL HOARE suggested that much could be done without any publicity by talks between experts. After these the Government of Éire would be in a position to place their orders.

MR. DE VALERA saw no objection of principle, provided that it was made clear that co-operation with the United Kingdom was not a fundamental point of Irish defence, but was being undertaken with a view to a particular contingency.

MR. MACDONALD said that there was a similar understanding between this country and the other Dominions.

MR. CHAMBERLAIN enquired whether the Government of Éire contemplated setting up munitions factories. If the United Kingdom Government wanted to purchase some of the products of those factories, would there be any objection?

MR. DE VALERA agreed that it was desirable to set up munitions factories in Éire. He thought that there would be no objection to United Kingdom purchases from them, provided it were clear that the primary object of the factories was to supply the needs of Éire. There was of course the danger that the Government of Éire might be regarded as committing themselves in advance to a situation in which they would co-operate in war with the United Kingdom Government.

MR. CHAMBERLAIN pointed out the enormous range of materials involved in modern armaments. The purchase from the Irish factories might, for example, be not shells, but merely certain components for shells.

He had mentioned the matter because he had thought that the Government of Éire might be glad of orders. So far as the United Kingdom Government were concerned, they could probably provide for their own requirements in this country.

MR. DE VALERA said that he would not rule out the possibility of supplying the United Kingdom Government. The first business of the Irish factories, however, would be the equipment of the forces of Éire.

Turning again to the question of the defended ports, Mr. de Valera said that it had occurred to him that in view of the great development of aircraft these ports might now be of less importance to the United Kingdom.

SIR THOMAS INSKIP said that, on the contrary, the importance of the defended ports had increased. Berehaven and Lough Swilly were now considered to be of the greatest importance for anti-submarine operations. The technique, in a word, was to get as near as possible to the point of assembly of the enemy submarines.

FINANCE AND TRADE

On the invitation of Mr. Chamberlain, MR. DE VALERA opened the discussion on this item. The first point on which he wished to insist related to the Land Annuities. United Kingdom Ministers were familiar with the view taken of this matter in Éire, and it was unnecessary to argue the case again. The Government of Éire felt very strongly the injustice of being called upon to make payments which they did not regard as due.

His second point was the necessity for looking ahead in economic matters.

He wished to see the agricultural industry of Éire built up, with the result that food supplies in time of crises would be insured. The industry's production could be greatly increased. It was possible that it could even be doubled. The great obstacle in the way was the penal tariffs imposed by the United Kingdom.

He did not, however, envisage a purely agricultural economic life for Éire. Without embarking on unnecessary developments he wished to see his country produce as many manufacturing goods as it reasonably could. His Government could not forego their right to build up their industries.

On the other hand, there were certain classes of manufacture in which Éire would be ill-advised to compete, on account of its small population.

Éire had considerable need for capital equipment.

MR. CHAMBERLAIN thanks Mr. de Valera for his opening statement. He was afraid, however, that something more remained to be said. This country had not desired an economic war with Éire. Our special duties had only been imposed in order to recoup ourselves for the monies which we believed to have been unjustly withheld from us.

It was to be hoped that the present Conference would result in new financial and economic arrangements acceptable to both countries.

MR. DE VALERA said that so far as the R.I.C. Pensions were concerned, the people of Éire looked upon that Organisation as an armed force maintained by Britain for Imperial purposes and they would not regard it as reasonable to pay the pensions of members. They also considered Éire's responsibility for a share in the public debt of Gt. Britain as absolved by the 1925 Agreement. Indeed, so far as the merits were concerned, they thought that an examination of both sides of the account would show that payments were not due from Éire to Gt. Britain and that they were taking a generous line if they did not look for some repayment from Gt. Britain.

SIR JOHN SIMON said he thought it would be a good plan for both sides to face the situation as it existed to-day, and to see whether means could not be found for negotiating an improvement in it. Éire wished to increase her exports but, for reasons which were well appreciated, Gt. Britain had imposed certain duties in answer to which Éire had been obliged to introduce export bounties. The position, in fact, approximated to one of economic war and was deplored by both sides. On the assumption, for the moment, that Gt. Britain's claim was sound, they originally expected to receive in round figures £5 million per annum from the Free State, made up of just over £3 million in respect of the land annuities; a further £1^1/2 million in respect of R.I.C. Pensions and Local Loans, and £1/2 million per annum for compensation for damage to property. The latter item, had, in fact, been paid regularly. That arrangement, never mind for what reason, broke down and special measures were instituted by which this country received in round figures some £4 million per annum, plus the £1/2 million in respect of compensation to damaged property. These measures had led to other counter measures and the whole position seemed rather unfortunate. His suggestion would be that the facts of the present situation should be taken as a basis and an endeavour made to see whether, by looking at it from a practical point of view, some suitable adjustment could not be made. The House of Commons would undoubtedly continue to authorise the machinery which brought in £4 million per annum for as long as it was necessary, but he would like to be able to go to Parliament and say that some adjustment had been reached in the interests of a better general understanding all round. It might, for example, be possible to reduce the special duties in the hope that Éire would consider whether there were not some other items of expenditure at present borne by the British Exchequer which they would undertake to meet, for example the pensions of Ex-Service men living in Ireland.

MR. DE VALERA thought that there would be difficulties in the way of meeting the cost of that particular item.

SIR JOHN SIMON observed that the question of financial adjustment and improved trade went hand in hand and the topics should be dealt with as a connected whole. Mr. de Valera was anxious for a bigger outlet for Irish produce in British markets and arrangements to this end should be part of a trade agreement to be included in a general settlement.

MR. DE VALERA said that a reduction only of the special Import Duties was not the best way of approaching the problem. So long as these were continued at all they would give the effect that economic warfare was being continued. He recognised that Great Britain was in a position to extract contributions from Éire. If they had been able to find a way of resisting the extraction they would be adopting it at present. It was difficult to suggest the best method of approach, but he did not think it could be done on the basis that the Irish people would be prepared to enter into an agreement to buy off the duties. If, however, a solution could be found on the basis of making a certain payment, it would have to be made clear that such a payment did not include anything in respect of the land annuity claim. There was no chance of coming to a financial settlement if payments were to be made under that head. If the Import Duties were to continue there would be no point in making a financial agreement. On the other hand, if the financial difficulties could be suitably adjusted, perhaps on agreement of a sum to be paid, negotiations for a trade agreement could go on independently on a purely trade basis. He added, however, that any general agreement would have to take into account the increased burdens on the country that would be imposed by the development of a Defence Programme. All these aspects were interlocked, and it was difficult to know exactly how a start should be made.

MR. CHAMBERLAIN asked whether Mr. de Valera contemplated the payment of a lump sum.

MR. DE VALERA replied that it would depend on the terms of settlement. Such a basis had advantages and disadvantages, but in as much as they desired to lay the foundations of good relations between the two countries the sooner continuing payments ceased to be made the better; so far as they were in respect of items which Irish people were not convinced were due they would always give rise to agitation. Proceeding, he said that there would be difficulty in doing anything to meet the cost of R.I.C. pensions even if restricted to pensioners living in Éire. Apart from the feeling of the country that this force constituted a special type of army organised to preserve

British Imperial power, they were not satisfied that the apportionment of the total cost of pensions was fair to the Free State, based as it was on the geographical distribution of the force.

MR. CHAMBERLAIN suggested that the difficulties might to some extent be mitigated if the payments were made in capitalised form.

SIR JOHN SIMON recognised the force of popular feeling in Éire in the case of the R.I.C. pensions. He asked whether the same feelings would operate against judicial, civil and revenue pensions.

MR. DE VALERA said he thought there would not be the same difficulty.

MR. MacENTEE enquired whether a particular appropriation was really necessary to meet specific items.

SIR JOHN SIMON said that, from his own point of view, he did not think this country could face a financial agreement under which they gave up revenue to the extent of £4 million without something to replace at least part of it. He did not rule out discharge of the special duties as part of an agreement but unless they were covered by some concessions from Éire in another direction the gap of £4 million would still remain unfilled. He did not think that it was necessary to earmark every item that might help to fill the gap so long as their total added up to a reasonable sum. Would it be possible, for example, for their Government to make some contribution towards the Ex-Service pensioners in so far as they lived in Éire?

MR. DE VALERA said that he could not take responsibility for such an undertaking, apart from the fact that he did not accept the view that such a payment was in any way an Éire liability. His Government were prepared to go a certain distance to reach a settlement. He had already told Mr. MacDonald that, though on the general merits he did not think that any payment should be made, in view of the special circumstances, he thought that a compromise was possible on some items, though not on all. He was therefore prepared to examine them in detail to see how far it would be possible to deal with them.

MR. CHAMBERLAIN thought the difficulty was one of presentation. Could they not put it that in return for the cancellation of the payments at present in default Éire was prepared to make a lump sum payment equivalent to the capitalised value of the special duties and to make other adjustments in the form of a Trade Treaty?

MR. DE VALERA said that he would have to explain the basis of the calculation. His Government had stated that they would go out of Office rather than pay the Land Annuities.

MR. CHAMBERLAIN pointed out that the proposal was to wipe out the Land Annuities.

MR. DE VALERA agreed, but observed that they would have to be free to point out, in regard to any settlement that might be made, that they were not paying Land Annuities but only a sum considered suitable in the circumstances to end the economic war. The form of such announcement might not be very satisfactory to this country.

MR. CHAMBERLAIN said that he did not see anything inacceptable in putting it in the way proposed.

MR. DE VALERA thought that a start could be made on that basis, and that a detailed examination of the items should be carried out by officials. The most objectionable feature was the payment in regard to R.I.C. Pensions.

MR. CHAMBERLAIN suggested that the mention of specific items could be avoided.

SIR JOHN SIMON said that the Land Annuities represented some £3,000,000 per annum out of the £5,000,000 per annum which this country originally expected to receive. A proposal to reduce a lump sum payment representing the capitalised value of the Special Duties by the equivalent of the Land Annuities would require very serious consideration.

MR. MacENTEE observed that there was more in the matter than a mere reduction in payments. There was to be a new beginning between the two countries and the differences between them were to be resolved.

MR. MACDONALD pointed out that the terms of any agreement reached would have to be acceptable to the House of Commons.

MR. MacENTEE said that, for their part, they would be unable to carry through any agreement in which they acknowledged responsibility for payment of the Land Annuities.

MR. DE VALERA pointed out that the sum involved was relatively a much more serious matter for Éire than for Great Britain in view of the taxable capacities of the two countries. A million pounds raised by Éire was equivalent to many million pounds raised in Britain.

MR. CHAMBERLAIN observed that on this basis a remission of payments to Great Britain was of relatively greater importance to Éire. He looked at the question from a practical point of view rather than from one of principle. Provided agreement could be reached on a basis which would bring Great Britain a sum which they considered reasonable, their view would not be affected if, under the agreement, they gave up payments to which they might be justly entitled.

MR. DE VALERA said that his Government was in a difficult position. He had been returned to power in spite of the sufferings in Éire caused by the economic war. It would be necessary to have another Government in Éire if responsibility for the Land Annuities was to be recognised.

MR. CHAMBERLAIN said that the British Government were not asking for the payment of Land Annuities or R.I.C. Pensions. They would be prepared to take off the Special Duties in return for a lump sum payment not less than the capitalised value of those Duties, plus some further compensation in the sphere of trade.

MR. DE VALERA recognised that, whatever sum was fixed, there would no doubt be criticism as to its reasonableness. He must be in a position to convince his people that they were not being saddled with a burden which they could not carry, and that he had not got rid of one burden to replace it by another.

So far as the Defence programme was concerned, it must be clear that Éire was providing for its own purposes and defending its own country. If it was thought to be assisting Britain directly or indirectly it would at once be asked why they should pay.

MR. CHAMBERLAIN suggested that the experts should get together to see whether, in the light of their discussion, some basis could be found for a possible financial agreement. Proceeding, he asked what would be the basis for a trade agreement.

MR. DE VALERA said that they would have to proceed on the basis that they could not allow industries which had recently been started in Éire to be destroyed by competition with this country. Some form of protection for them would have to be continued. On the other hand where there was an open market they would be prepared to grant preferences to this country of an amount to be agreed upon.

MR. LEMASS said that exports from Éire were rather less than half the imports and that the adverse trade balance, in spite of invisible exports, had increased since the special duties were imposed. There was not, therefore, much room for any large expansion in imports, but he thought that there was scope for some change in their origin.

MR. CHAMBERLAIN said that he understood that the openings which Éire sought for her exports were mainly agricultural and he thought it would be useful to hear the views of Mr. Morrison.

MR. MORRISON said that he felt sure that Mr. Ryan, as a fellow-sufferer in the world of agricultural difficulties, would appreciate that the prospect of increased imports into Britain of Irish agricultural produce would not be hailed with great enthusiasm by the agricultural population of this country. At the same time if increased openings for such produce would contribute towards a general trade agreement the matter was clearly one for discussion. The market situation in this country was, however, not the same as that existing before the present difficulties with Éire started. In the interval[,] powers had been secured and an organisation built up to prevent unregulated imports of agricultural products which would threaten the stability of markets. Éire herself, for example, was a member of the world Beef Conference. The regulation of imports would clearly have to continue. He mentioned the point because Mr. de Valera, earlier in the meeting, had made use of the expression 'free entry'. No one now had a free entry into the agricultural markets of this country.

MR. DE VALERA observed that special considerations were applicable to Éire. In making preparations against a crisis he thought it would be fundamental for this country to wish to see agricultural development carried out near at hand. The food supply that could be produced in Éire might not constitute a big fraction of the total food requirements of Great Britain, but it might prove extremely valuable to tide over a period of special difficulty. What made Éire different from Canada or Australia was its close proximity to this country.

MR. CHAMBERLAIN agreed that such a supply would be very valuable provided it could be brought over to this country.

MR. DE VALERA said he thought things would be in a very bad way if communications could not be kept open between Britain and Éire.

MR. CHAMBERLAIN observed that it might depend on the extent to which this country was allowed facilities for submarine hunting.

MR. DE VALERA said that the existence of a good market for their supplies would be conducive towards dealing satisfactorily with the common interests of the two countries. As regards the regulation of imports he recognised the necessity for this but he hoped that a bigger proportion would come from Éire than was the case at present.

MR. MACDONALD observed that Mr. de Valera had suggested that it was more important to this country that the agricultural industry in Éire should be in a flourishing condition than that of certain Dominions or oversea countries, and he drew the conclusion that agricultural produce from Éire should be treated possibly better, or at any rate as well as, that from Canada or Australia. It would be difficult to persuade other Dominions that this was a reasonable procedure if those Dominions gave better treatment to imports from this country into their countries that Éire was prepared to do.

MR. STANLEY added that the other Dominions made appreciable contributions in return for the treatment accorded agricultural produce imported into Gt. Britain from them. The tariff concessions granted by them in exchange went beyond the mere giving of preferences over foreign competitors and cut into the systems designed to protect their own industries. It would be difficult to explain the position to them if no corresponding contribution was made in the case of Éire.

MR. LEMASS observed that the cost of transport over the long distances to the overseas Dominions in itself provided some form of protection which did not exist in the case of Éire. The scope for making concessions was further restricted by the comparatively small size of the Éire market.

MR. STANLEY suggested that it might be possible to make a good deal of progress by looking into the position with regard to a number of individual items.

MR. LEMASS said they were quite prepared to do this. It might well be possible to give preferences over other countries in respect of classes of goods of which manufacture in Éire was not practicable.

MR. MORRISON said that agricultural produce covered a large variety of products and the economics of each branch of the industry were different. The arrangements for marketing the produce varied with each product and no general picture could be presented until the questions of pigs and eggs, etc., had each been separately considered. He thought, however, that it was necessary to make clear the general principle that it would not be possible to contemplate excluding Éire produce from the regulations which were applicable to agricultural produce not only from other parts of the world, but also from the Home industry.

Agreements had been reached on the coal-cattle pact in the past and he felt confident that it would be possible to do the same again in the future.[1] The argument that agricultural development in Éire strengthened the position of this country could not be advanced here with the same assurance as Mr. de Valera used since it provoked the retort that the position would be still better if the development took place in Gt. Britain.

---

[1] See DIFP Volume IV, Nos 221, 223, 240, 241, 242, 243, 246, 247, 301 and 317.

MR. DE VALERA said that he thought it would be more difficult for an industrially minded nation, such as Gt. Britain, to carry out agricultural development than for a country such as Éire to do so. In Éire the difficulty at present was to prevent the agricultural population leaving the land.

MR. MORRISON said that the same position existed in this country.

SIR SAMUEL HOARE said that he wanted to draw attention to the case of the United Kingdom trade with Éire proceeding through Northern Ireland. He understood that this was the category of British trade which had suffered most from the duties imposed by Éire, and that it had been specially hit by certain taxes. He did not propose to go into the matter in detail but it was a factor which could not be ignored in the discussions on the trade agreement.

MR. DE VALERA said that they had taken no deliberate steps against Northern Ireland by reason of the imposition of the Special Duties by Great Britain. One of the reasons why he would like to see a Trade agreement was that it might result in the removal of certain fears held by the North in regard to trade barriers. He thought that a settlement between North and South would be of great advantage to the Northern Linen manufacturers. When he was in America he found that a number of supporters of the Irish Independence Movement had organised a deliberate campaign to boycott Belfast linen.

MR. CHAMBERLAIN suggested that the next step was for the experts from Éire to meet the Treasury Officials with a view to reaching a basis for settlement in regard to the Special Duties. This should be explored before proceeding to deal with the problem of a Trade agreement.

CONCLUSIONS

THE CONFERENCE agreed:-

(a) To issue the communiqué to the Press which was drafted by Mr. MacDonald and read to the Conference by Mr. Chamberlain.[1]

(b) That Mr. de Valera and Mr. MacDonald should agree the general lines on which they should reply to Press enquiries.

(c) That experts from Éire should meet Treasury officials on the morning of 18th January with a view to exploring the basis of a settlement in regard to the Special Import Duties.[2]

(e) To resume the discussion at No. 10 Downing Street, at 12 noon on Tuesday, 18th January, 1938.[3]

---

[1] See below No. 123.
[2] Not printed.
[3] See below No. 124.

No. 123 NAI DT S10389 (Annex)

Press communiqué following the conclusion of discussions on 17 January 1938
(Copy)

LONDON, 17 January 1938

PRESS COMMUNIQUÉ

'A meeting was held between representatives of the Government of Éire and representatives of the United Kingdom Government at 10, Downing Street this afternoon, with the Prime Minister in the chair.

A general survey of the outstanding questions affecting the relations between the two countries was begun. The meeting adjourned shortly after 6.30, and will be resumed to-morrow at 12 noon.'

No. 124 NAI DT S10389 (Annex)

Minutes of the conference between representatives of the
United Kingdom and Ireland
(Secret) (I.N. (38) 2nd Meeting) (Copy)

LONDON, 12 noon, 18 January 1938

CONFERENCE
between
REPRESENTATIVES OF THE UNITED KINGDOM AND ÉIRE
Secretary's Notes of the Second Meeting of the Conference
held at 10 Downing Street, on Tuesday, 18th January, 1938,
at 12 Noon

PRESENT:

UNITED KINGDOM	ÉIRE
The Rt. Hon Neville Chamberlain, M.P., Prime Minister.	Mr. Eamon de Valera, Prime Minister and Minister for External Affairs.
The Rt. Hon. Sir John Simon, G.C.S.I., G.C.V.O., O.B.E., K.C., M.P., Chancellor of the Exchequer.	Mr. Sean F. Lemass, Minister for Industry and Commerce.
The Rt. Hon. Sir Samuel Hoare, Bt., G.C.S.I., G.B.E., C.M.G., M.P., Secretary of State for the Home Department.	Mr. Sean MacEntee, Minister for Finance.
The Rt. Hon. Malcolm MacDonald, M.P., Secretary of State for Dominion Affairs.	Dr. James Ryan, Minister for Agriculture.

THE FOLLOWING WERE ALSO PRESENT:

The Rt. Hon. Sir Thomas Inskip, Mr. J. W. Dulanty, C.B., C.B.E.,
C.B.E., K.C., M.P., Minister for High Commissioner for Éire.
Co-ordination of Defence.

Secretary   Mr. W.D. Wilkinson, D.S.O., M.C.

THE DEFENDED PORTS
MR. CHAMBERLAIN said that he and his colleagues of the United Kingdom Delegation had been giving further thought to the question of the defended ports, in the light of yesterday's discussion.[1] If they could, they were anxious to meet Mr. de Valera in this matter; they would take as sympathetic a view as possible. On the other hand, the United Kingdom Delegation were not sure that they had been successful in conveying to Mr. de Valera and his colleagues the extent and the serious nature of their fears regarding the shipping and food supply situation in the next major war. They had attempted yesterday to indicate what a dangerous weapon the submarine was expected to be in the next war; but he doubted whether Mr. de Valera had appreciated how essential it was that the necessary anti-submarine precautions should be ready to start from the moment hostilities broke out. It was no use saying that the Government of Éire of the day must be trusted to take the proper steps, in the exercise of its unfettered judgment. That would probably mean not until a few Irish ships had been sunk. Measures taken at that stage might be altogether too late to save the situation.

He felt bound to bring this important matter to Mr. de Valera's notice once more. Had the latter given it further thought, and was he prepared to go further than he had indicated on the previous day?
MR. DE VALERA said that he had given much thought to this matter, not only since the previous day, but on many occasions in the past. He hoped that he had appreciated the defence considerations to which Mr. Chamberlain had referred. Nevertheless, he (Mr. de Valera) was afraid that he could not take the further step which Mr. Chamberlain suggested. It raised formidable difficulties. On the other hand, if the Conference had made any progress over the partition issue, the atmosphere in Éire would have been very different, and the facts of the situation could have been explained to the people of Éire in a much more convincing way.

As it was, he (Mr. de Valera) could only repeat what he had already said in public, namely, that it was in the interest of the people of Éire to build up their defences; that Éire would not permit any foreign power to make use of the defended ports for the purpose of attacking the United Kingdom; that the two countries stood in common peril of an attack; that plans must be made to meet this common emergency; and that it must be left to the Government of Éire to decide when the time had come to bring those plans into operation.

---

[1] See above No. 122.

He could not contemplate adding to such a statement anything which might be construed as admitting an infringement of the national sovereignty of Éire. If he did, he would be laying up trouble for the future. Indeed, he felt certain that trouble would flare up almost immediately. He was afraid he could go no further on this point – even if it should prove to be the point on which the Conference broke.

MR. CHAMBERLAIN asked Sir Thomas Inskip whether it would be practicable that the United Kingdom defence plans for the emergency contemplated should (a) proceed on the assumption that the defended ports would not be available, but should nevertheless (b) take account of the possibility that they might become available at a later stage.

SIR THOMAS INSKIP said that plans conceived on those lines would not be entirely satisfactory. As had been said on the previous day, they would only be 'a second best'. It would be understood that the submarine hunting plans of the Naval Staff depended largely on the certainty that particular equipment would be present when war came in a particular place.

MR. DE VALERA was afraid that agreement on 'the second best' was all there was any hope of getting now. If his Government went a step further, it would be tantamount to running away from everything for which they had stood in the past.

It was his firm hope, however, that step-by-step relations between the two countries would improve, until the point was reached when the vast majority of Irish people would want to play their part in any common emergency.

SIR SAMUEL HOARE said that, speaking as a former First Lord of the Admiralty, he knew that the essential thing in anti-submarine precautions was to have ready on the spot, before hostilities started, a proper supply of nets, booms, etc. The United Kingdom and Éire were facing a common peril. Would Éire be ready to make the preparations he had mentioned?

MR. DE VALERA thought that the answer would be in the affirmative. The people of Éire, however, would want it clearly demonstrated to them that these precautions were measures of self-defence. If anything was done which went beyond the limits of self-defence, all hope of securing the willing co-operation of Éire would be at an end. If he were to say that he would go beyond that point, his colleagues in Dublin would not support him.

SIR THOMAS INSKIP said that considerable scientific study of anti-submarine tactics had been made in this country since the last War. The question was whether, on the basis suggested by Mr. de Valera, the United Kingdom authorities would be justified in communicating to the authorities of Éire the results of all this research.

MR. DE VALERA was certain that the authorities of Éire had never yet betrayed any confidence which the United Kingdom Government had seen fit to place in them. He was most anxious to employ efficient and up-to-date methods in his defence preparations. The one thing certain was that the United Kingdom and Éire would not be on opposite sides in war. The fact was that they were faced with a common peril. The right course was clearly that their respective staffs should lay their plans for acting together promptly, if their Governments gave the word.

MR. CHAMBERLAIN enquired whether Mr. de Valera contemplated defence plans which should include provision for the use of the defended ports by the United Kingdom authorities, i.e. when the Government of Éire of the day so decided, not automatically on the outbreak of war.

MR. DE VALERA assented, on the clear understanding that it would be for the Government of Éire to determine when the moment had come.

MR. CHAMBERLAIN said that it was the logical consequence of Mr. de Valera's view that staff conversations and joint planning should take place in time of peace. To some extent Mr. de Valera's assent had reduced his anxieties for the future.

SIR THOMAS INSKIP said that mutual confidence was the only possible basis for such consultations. Joint planning would have to be based on the communication of a considerable part of the results of the scientific research to which he had already referred.

MR. CHAMBERLAIN said that, like the Government of Éire, the Government at Westminster had to defend their actions to Parliament and to their public opinion. He was afraid that public opinion in this country would find it very difficult to stomach the handing over of the defended ports without any assurance that United Kingdom forces were to have the use of those ports in war.

Mr. de Valera had said that it was impossible for him to give such an assurance. Let it be assumed for the moment that the United Kingdom Government were prepared to waive their demand for that assurance. The United Kingdom Government could in those circumstances properly ask for another kind of assurance, viz. an assurance as to what Éire was prepared to do to put the defences of the ports into a satisfactory condition of readiness.

MR. DE VALERA said that this was mainly a question of £.s.d. It was clear, for example, that Éire would not be able to afford expenditure on this scale at the present moment, when the economic war was in full swing and the penal duties were unrepealed.

MR. CHAMBERLAIN asked what idea Mr. de Valera had formed regarding the speed at which the defended ports could be modernised.

MR. DE VALERA said that everything again turned on the partition issue, on which he had found the United Kingdom Government to be unhelpful. If they had been able to bury the hatchet, he would have done his utmost to arouse the enthusiasm of the Irish people on the defence question. He would have said to them 'Britain is not now among our possible enemies. The British have left the defended ports. It is our duty to see that their action in leaving is not going to expose them to a foreign attack based on those ports'. He would then have set about a recruiting campaign.

In the present circumstances it was more difficult to answer Mr. Chamberlain's question. He would put things in this way. The two countries were faced with a common peril. One of them was relatively ignorant of war. Would the other advise her in what way she could best utilise her available strength? Assuming that the United Kingdom communicated the relevant part of their plans, the Government of Éire would (a) adopt this part of the British plans as their own plan against the common peril, and would (b) super-impose on it other plans to meet other perils.

The Government of Éire had not reached a decision as to the amount of money they would be able to spend on defence. It was clear that they would have to shoulder a heavy burden. At present their army was a mere skeleton force. It would need expansion and in addition the enrolment of some kind of volunteer force.

Mr. de Valera realised, however, that the United Kingdom advice to him might be to spend the money available on small naval vessels or coast defences, rather than on increasing the army.

He would hope to commend this policy to his people, basing himself on the fundamental plea that they had obtained their freedom and must now be prepared to defend it. He realised that United Kingdom Ministers might find his statement rather vague. The fact was that at the present moment the Government of Éire did not know what direction their planning ought to take.

MR. CHAMBERLAIN asked whether Mr. de Valera wished the defended ports to be handed over to Éire complete with the defences and other works in them.

MR. DE VALERA said that what he hoped for was the denunciation of Articles 6 and 7 of the 1921 Treaty.[1]

MR. CHAMBERLAIN enquired whether, leaving the Treaty aside for the moment, Mr. de Valera contemplated that e.g. the guns in the defended ports were to be handed over. It might be very difficult to defend such handing over to public opinion in this country.

MR. DE VALERA said that he imagined the guns were obsolete and useless.

MR. CHAMBERLAIN thought this was not the case. Although somewhat out of date, they would still be of value. Let it be assumed for the sake of argument that the defended ports, with everything in them, were handed over to Éire. How was the United Kingdom Government to know that the Éire authorities were going to bring the defences of the ports up to a higher standard, instead of merely 'sitting back'? Would Mr. de Valera put his hand to an undertaking to this effect?

MR. DE VALERA said that he would find it easier to make a statement in his Parliament than to give a written assurance. He would be prepared to say in his Parliament 'we shall keep up our defences, including the defended ports, on such and such lines', i.e. the lines which he had mentioned during the present discussion.

Even in making an oral statement of this kind, he would be running a certain danger. He would be exposing himself to the charge that he was keeping up the defended ports for the United Kingdom to occupy.

MR. CHAMBERLAIN agreed that it would be reasonable, assuming that Éire took over the defended ports, for the Government of Éire to determine the standard at which their defences were to be maintained. He would like it to be said, however, that the United Kingdom would be consulted in the matter and would be given the opportunity of making representations.

MR. DE VALERA was very dubious about this last suggestion. It would be

---

[1] For the text of Articles 6 and 7 of the Anglo-Irish Treaty see Appendix 4.

calculated to retard co-operation, not to assist it. It was better to leave matters on the basis he had mentioned, viz: that it was in the interests of Éire to guard against the common peril, and that it must be assumed that she would act in accordance with those interests.

MR. CHAMBERLAIN said that the people of the United Kingdom also had their susceptibilities. As regards the work of bringing the defended ports up to date, it seemed to him that there would have to be a short delay at first, during which Mr. de Valera's Government made their preparations. They would have to decide over what period they intended to spread the process of modernization. The financial difficulty would depend on the length of this period.

Would there not be a transitional stage, during which the Government of Éire might want to be able to count on help from this country?

MR. DE VALERA said that, so far as he was concerned, he would be quick to appeal for United Kingdom assistance if the common peril arose during the transitional stage. There would be no stage, however, in which Éire would leave the ports ungarrisoned.

As he had indicated, he was exposing himself to misrepresentation in his own country by going as far as he had done. Why, it would be said, was he concentrating on the defence of these particular localities? His answer would be that any potential enemy would places as high a value on the defended ports as did the United Kingdom. These, therefore, were the objectives for which that enemy would make.

SIR THOMAS INSKIP suggested that another argument might be to say that the Éire Government's pledge to defend their country against external aggression would have no meaning if the ports were left undefended. Those ports were natural harbours and most attractive to any aggressor.

MR. DE VALERA said that he agreed. Turning to another point, might he ask for Mr. Chamberlain's opinion whether the danger existed that war would break out suddenly during the stage before the ports could be put into order?

MR. CHAMBERLAIN said that he could only give the answer which he was accustomed to return to similar enquiries. The most dangerous time of all was the present moment. The United Kingdom was every month becoming more formidable for an enemy to tackle. The longer one waited to make one's preparations, the greater the danger.

Éire would have to do as this country had done, namely, not to apply the whole of its financial strength to rearmament, but to arrive at a working compromise between the claims of rearmament and those of ordinary peace-time trade. They would have to strike a balance.

MR. MacENTEE imagined that there was no question of Éire's defence expenditure being concentrated in one year. It would have to be spread.

MR. CHAMBERLAIN agreed. There would, in any case, be great difficulty in obtaining the necessary supplies within any one year. Probably it would have to be a two to three year programme.

MR. DE VALERA assented. He would like to remind the Meeting of his warning that he would not be able to concentrate defence on the ports. The people of Éire would be highly suspicious if the ports were modernized in isolation. Parallel with that there would have to be a more general defence programme.

SIR THOMAS INSKIP said that Éire was not the only part of the Commonwealth where there were defended ports with a programme of modernization, an order of priority etc. For example, the Union of South Africa paid for the modernization of their ports, but concerted their programme in consultation with this country.

MR. CHAMBERLAIN enquired whether Mr. de Valera expected a guarantee from this country that we would give assistance to Éire if we were called upon.

MR. DE VALERA said that this was so.

MR. CHAMBERLAIN asked how Mr. de Valera proposed to leave the question of technical assistance, e.g. in equipment, in training and in the establishment of munitions factories. What did the Government of Éire intend to do about purchasing those materials which they would be unable to provide themselves?

MR. DE VALERA said that he could give no answer until he had consulted his Cabinet, which had, as yet, hardly come to grips with these problems. The provision of gas masks was one of the questions which would have to be tackled. On all these matters public opinion in Éire was totally unprepared.

MR. CHAMBERLAIN feared that a rude awakening was in store for it.

MR. MACDONALD suggested that, in practice, the Government of Éire would find it best to purchase in this country what they could not make at home. They would find that there were advantages in the interchangeability of equipment.

MR. DE VALERA said that he personally agreed. In Éire's geographical situation it would be essential for her equipment to be interchangeable with that of the United Kingdom, even if Éire had no connection with the Commonwealth.

MR. CHAMBERLAIN entirely agreed. He would like to emphasize the fact that in war it was not enough to make a good start. It was vitally important to be assured that one could replace one's spare parts. He realised that all this was very delicate ground for Éire.

MR. DE VALERA agreed. It was such delicate ground that he would not have trodden upon it if he had not been absolutely convinced that he ought to do so in the interests of the people of Éire.

MR. CHAMBERLAIN thought that, at this stage of the discussion, it might be profitable to begin putting something on paper. Did Mr. de Valera agree that the material now existed for a first tentative draft?

MR. DE VALERA was much opposed to this. It would be found that the moment the two sides attempted to put decisions on paper their difficulties would revive.

MR. CHAMBERLAIN was afraid that it was nevertheless essential to do so. Failing this the Conference would have produced no concrete results.

MR. DE VALERA said that he also was concerned to obtain the best results. It was with this in view that he wished to avoid putting conclusions on paper.

MR. CHAMBERLAIN indicated that there was great difficulty in having only a 'gentleman's agreement'. All of them would be very closely questioned by the Press, who would be sure in the end to find out that a 'gentleman's agreement' existed. The moment this fact was divulged, both the Parliament in Westminster and the Parliament in Dublin would demand to see the text. The pressure would be irresistible.

MR. DE VALERA thought that it might be enough to inform the public that Articles 6 and 7 of the 1921 Treaty had been abrogated.

SIR JOHN SIMON was afraid that this abrogation was not easy ground for the United Kingdom Government to defend. Article 7 read as follows:-

'The Government of the Irish Free State shall afford to his Majesty's Imperial Forces:-

(a) In time of peace such harbour and other facilities as are indicated in the Annex hereto, or such other facilities as may from time to time be agreed between the British Government and the Government of the Irish Free State; and

(b) In time of war or of strained relations with a Foreign Power such harbour and other facilities as the British Government may require for the purpose of such defence as aforesaid.'

The House of Commons would be certain to ask how the United Kingdom was to know, in the absence of Article 7, that it was not being left in the lurch. How could there be any assurance that the defended ports were being kept in a proper state?

MR. DE VALERA said that the only answer would be to refer to his public statements in which a guarantee was given that Éire would not permit the defended ports to be used as bases for an attack on the United Kingdom, and would take steps to implement her undertaking.

In addition, it ought to be obvious that the interests of Éire itself would make it essential for that country to deny the defended ports to any foreign power.

MR. CHAMBERLAIN was afraid that the House of Commons would not be satisfied with oral statements. They would be certain to demand a White Paper. Was there any valid objection at the present stage of the negotiations to the two sides asking their respective officials to draw up a preliminary draft? The Conference could then examine that draft and alter it as required.

MR. DE VALERA was afraid that the respective positions of the two sides were too far apart. It was beyond the wit of man to draw up a formula which would both hand the ports over to Éire and yet lay it down that the United Kingdom had the right to use them in an emergency.

MR. CHAMBERLAIN said that Mr. de Valera had misunderstood. He (Mr. Chamberlain) had accepted Mr. de Valera's insistence that there could be no question of giving an assurance here and now that the ports would be made available for the use of United Kingdom forces in the event of a major war. He was not pressing Mr. de Valera further on that point.

SIR JOHN SIMON ventured to point out to Mr. de Valera that the concession which had been made to his (Mr. de Valera's) view by Mr. Chamberlain made it absolutely essential that the terms of agreement should be put on paper. It would be impossible to defend an oral agreement on such an important issue.

MR. DE VALERA did not see how the position could be put into writing without depriving the people of Éire of some of their sovereign rights.

MR. CHAMBERLAIN said that he entirely agreed with Sir John Simon's last remark.

Mr. de Valera must not assume that United Kingdom Ministers were going to be difficult. They had entered the Conference with a sincere desire to reach agreement if it were at all possible. They would not insist upon any non-essentials. When the draft had been produced, if Mr. de Valera and his colleagues took exception to any point, United Kingdom Ministers would undertake to consider whether the words objected to were capable of modification.

MR. DE VALERA said that in view of Mr. Chamberlain's appeal the Delegation of Éire would naturally agree to a draft being prepared for examination by the Conference. He must warn them, however, that they would not find drafting easy. Both he himself and his advisers had tried in vain to draft a satisfactory formula dealing with these issues.

MR. CHAMBERLAIN suggested that the Éire authorities had not at that time known how far the United Kingdom was prepared to go in order to meet them.

MR. MACDONALD ventured to refer to the Éire Parliament's well-known dislike of unpublished agreements. It seemed to him that this was another argument which made it quite essential that there should be a published document of some kind.

MR. DE VALERA did not dispute this, provided it was possible to agree on a text. He ought to warn the Conference that if agreement were reached he would not be able to go further than putting his initials to the text, until it had been examined and approved by his Cabinet in Dublin. He proposed to be extremely cautious, particularly because he had not brought his draftsmen or legal advisers with him. It might be that the legal advisers in Dublin would point out insuperable objections to any text agreed upon at the Conference.

MR. CHAMBERLAIN said that the United Kingdom Delegation for their part would have to submit the text for approval by their Cabinet. There was no reason, however, to suppose that the Cabinet as a whole would take a different view from that of the United Kingdom Ministers now present.

MR. DE VALERA said that on the whole he would prefer that the draft should be furnished by the United Kingdom advisers. In agreeing to consider a draft, he wished to place on record his view that defence was not an isolated problem. It was interwoven with all the other issues before the Conference.

MR. CHAMBERLAIN assented.

Sir Thomas Inskip was invited to give instructions, in the light of the preceding discussion, for the preparation of a preliminary draft, for examination by the Conference.

It was agreed to issue the following Press Communiqué:-

A further meeting between representatives of the Government of Éire and representatives of the United Kingdom Government was held at No. 10, Downing Street at 12 noon to-day, with the Prime Minister in the Chair. The discussion, which was begun yesterday, was continued. The meeting adjourned at 1 o'clock and will be resumed this afternoon at 3 o'clock.

The Meeting then adjourned.

No. 125 NAI DT S10389 (Annex)

Minutes of the conference between representatives of the
United Kingdom and Ireland
(Secret) (I.N. (38) 3rd Meeting) (Copy)
LONDON, 3.00 pm, 18 January 1938

CONFERENCE
between
REPRESENTATIVES OF THE UNITED KINGDOM AND ÉIRE
Secretary's Notes of the Third Meeting of the Conference
held at 10 Downing Street, on Tuesday, 18th January, 1938,
at 3.0 p.m.

PRESENT

UNITED KINGDOM
The Rt. Hon Neville Chamberlain, M.P., Prime Minister.

ÉIRE
Mr. Eamon de Valera, Prime Minister and Minister for External Affairs.

The Rt. Hon. Sir John Simon, G.C.S.I., G.C.V.O., O.B.E., K.C., M.P., Chancellor of the Exchequer.

Mr. Sean F. Lemass, Minister for Industry and Commerce.

The Rt. Hon. Sir Samuel Hoare, Bt., G.C.S.I., G.B.E., C.M.G., M.P., Secretary of State for the Home Department.

Mr. Sean MacEntee, Minister for Finance.

The Rt. Hon. Malcolm MacDonald, M.P., Secretary of State for Dominion Affairs.

Dr. James Ryan, Minister for Agriculture.

THE FOLLOWING WERE ALSO PRESENT

The Rt. Hon. Oliver Stanley, M.C., M.P., President of the Board of Trade.

Mr. J.W. Dulanty, C.B., C.B.E., High Commissioner for Éire.

The Rt.Hon. W.S. Morrison, M.C.,
K.C., M.P., Minister of
Agriculture and Fisheries.

Secretaries   Sir R.B. Howorth, K.C.M.G., C.B.
              Mr. C. N. Ryan, D.S.O., M.C.

CONFERENCE BETWEEN REPRESENTATIVES OF THE
UNITED KINGDOM AND ÉIRE
FINANCE

MR. CHAMBERLAIN suggested that the Conference should further examine the question of Finance in regard to which he understood that a meeting of the Treasury Officials of the two countries had been held that morning.[1]

SIR JOHN SIMON said that he would make a very brief report in regard to the meeting in question, as no doubt Mr. de Valera had already heard from his own representative what had taken place. Mr. Chamberlain had, himself, suggested that the most hopeful procedure would be to search for some figure which might form the basis for a financial agreement without the use of any labels. He (Sir John Simon) was sorry to say that up to the present the figures which had been suggested by the representative of Éire were quite inadequate and could not possibly form the basis for a negotiation. The discussion between the officials had proceeded on the basis of the payment by Éire of a capital lump sum, this capital payment to be in final settlement and to close all the old disputes. It would be settled on the assumption that both the special duties and the Éire retaliatory duties would be taken off. The representative of Éire had at the outset offered a lump sum capital payment of £2 million which he had subsequently increased to one of £3 million. The representative of the United Kingdom Treasury had intimated that he was not authorised to accept a smaller capital payment than one of £37 million and this was on condition that the £250,000 a year for Compensation would continue as an annual payment. The United Kingdom official had also intimated that while the offer of a capital sum of £8 million could not be entertained, an offer of £25 million, e.g. in three annual instalments, might be a basis for discussion.

As he (Sir John Simon) had pointed out, at the meeting on the previous day, the existing payments due by Éire to the United Kingdom amounted in round figures to £5 million per annum in respect of which the United Kingdom were at the moment receiving in round figures some £4 million per annum from the special duties, plus the £250,000 per annum in respect of Compensation. It was generally recognised that there was room for some reduction in this figure of £4^1/2 million per annum. He, himself, was convinced that in order to avoid any recurrence of debates and controversy it would be much better to terminate the system of annual payments by Éire to the United Kingdom in favour of a capital sum payment. The difficulty that Éire might be unable to make a single capital payment could be got over by

---

[1] Not printed.

arranging for the payment to be made say in two or three annual instalments. In any case, whether there was a single payment or a payment in instalments, his idea was that the whole question should be finally got rid of. He hoped that by continuing the discussions between the officials of the two countries it might be possible to reach some figure which would be a reasonable and proper compromise. At the moment, it was no use pretending that the representatives of the two Governments were in sight of any agreement.

MR. DE VALERA said that the point of view of himself and his colleagues in regard to this matter might be stated as follows. For the reasons which he had already given it was quite out of the question for the Government of Éire to contemplate the payment of any capital sum which would include either directly or by implication the land annuities. When he had discussed this question with Mr. MacDonald he mentioned the possibility of a compromise; but in referring to this possibility he wished again to emphasise his conviction that none of the payments in question were legally or properly due from Éire to the United Kingdom. He recognised that no useful purpose would, however, be served by a restatement of the very strong arguments on which he relied and he had greatly hoped that on the present occasion it would have been possible to have discovered some compromise figure, the payment of which he could have justified to his own public opinion. The figures which had been mentioned by the United Kingdom Official at the meeting that morning were in his view open to the insuperable objections that they were much greater than Éire could afford to pay, and their size was such that it would be hopeless for him to attempt to justify them to his own people. He fully appreciated the point of view of the United Kingdom in this matter and he sincerely hoped that it might be found possible to reach a settlement on a much smaller figure than those which Sir John Simon had mentioned.

SIR JOHN SIMON enquired what kind of a figure Mr. de Valera had in mind.

MR. DE VALERA said that it was inevitable that Éire would in future have to carry a very heavy financial burden in regard to defence. Having regard to future commitments in regard to defence and other services he thought that it would be very difficult for Éire to make a capital sum payment in excess of £10 million. The most he thought she could offer to pay was £8 or possibly £9 million.

Taking the particular items other than the Land Annuities he (Mr. de Valera) was advised by his Experts that the capital value of the Local Loans annual payment was something over £4 million.

SIR JOHN SIMON said that the United Kingdom Ministers were advised that the capital value of this item was £7.35 millions.

MR. DE VALERA observed that in speaking of these items he must not be taken as finally committing himself and his colleagues in any way. He would always argue, as he had done in the past, that payments in respect of them to the United Kingdom were not legally or properly due, but he would have to explain that in order to reach some settlement he had been obliged to bring them into account. As regards the R.I.C. pensions this, of course, was a decreasing service and he was advised that the present cost of the payment to R.I.C. pensioners resident in Éire amounted to about £750,000 per annum, while the cost of the R.I.C. pensions in the case of persons resident outside Éire amounted to about £240,000 per annum. The suggestion made to him was that Éire should assume financial responsibility for the R.I.C. pensioners resident in Éire in which case the charge would continue to be an annual one, while in respect of the R.I.C. pensioners outside Éire the matter should be disposed of by being brought into account in the lump sum capital payment. In this connection, however, the point had occurred to him that the United Kingdom might in all the circumstances wish to retain control of the expenditure on this particular service, especially in view of the consideration which he had always urged that the R.I.C. were a special responsibility of the United Kingdom and were, in fact, a United Kingdom and not an Irish service.

MR. MacENTEE observed that the Government of Éire were without any information of their own as to the capital equivalent of the present annual expenditure on R.I.C. pensions. He understood that the United Kingdom Experts estimated that in the case of the pensions of R.I.C. resident in Éire the capital equivalent would be about £9.1 millions, the corresponding figure in the case of those resident outside Éire being £3.2 millions.

SIR JOHN SIMON referred to Mr. de Valera's observations on the serious burden which Éire would have to assume in respect of Defence, and enquired whether he was right in understanding that in calculating the lump sum capital payment which Éire could afford to make Mr. de Valera was proceeding on the assumption that Éire would assume complete financial responsibility for the capital cost of the reequipment of the ports to be handed over to her, and for the future maintenance of those ports and of their garrisons.

MR. DE VALERA said that his calculations had been made on this basis. In any new financial settlement that might be reached it was imperative that account should be taken of the fact that Éire would have to find both the capital cost of the re-equipment of the ports and the very serious recurrent annual expenditure of their maintenance.

SIR JOHN SIMON said that he was prepared to agree that this was a consideration which it was possible to take into account.

MR. DE VALERA said that his idea was that the items other than the Land Annuities should be carefully examined with a view to arriving at some lump sum capital payment which could be accepted by both Governments. He would certainly be asked as to the nature and extent of the commitments which he had entered into in regard to Defence. This was a matter on which public opinion in Éire was extremely sensitive. It would be necessary for those concerned in Éire to confer with the Defence Experts of the United Kingdom in regard to Defence generally, and in particular in regard to the re-equipment of the ports. It might well transpire as a result of these discussions that both the capital cost of re-equipment and the annual cost of maintenance would be beyond the capacity of the people of Éire. If he were in the place of United Kingdom Ministers he would reply to any criticism of the financial arrangements by pointing out that the Government of Éire was going to enter into very heavy commitments, both capital and recurrent, in regard to Defence and that this expenditure would indirectly greatly benefit the United

Kingdom by relieving her of the necessity in future of contributing to the defence of Éire.

He repeated that he saw very great difficulty indeed in agreeing to any lump sum capital payment in excess of £10,000,000.

SIR JOHN SIMON agreed that in justifying in the United Kingdom Parliament any arrangements that might be reached it would be right and proper to emphasise that in future the Government of Éire would meet the whole annual cost of the re-equipment of the ports and all future maintenance charges in respect thereof.

MR. MacENTEE said that the Government of Éire had never been in a position to make any estimate of the capital expenditure and annual maintenance charges which would be necessary to meet in regard to the ports now to be taken over. Figures prepared by the United Kingdom authorities had, however, been furnished to them and he confessed that these figures were very alarming.

MR. DE VALERA said that what caused him very great anxiety was not so much the capital cost of re-armament in Éire, great though that would have to be as measured by the financial resources of the country, but the very grave burden which Éire would have to bear in future, by reason of the increased maintenance charges, in regard not merely to the ports to be handed over, but as regards the general defence of the country. Public opinion in Éire argued that their country enjoyed friendship with every other country and that there was no reason whatever why they should ever engage in war, except in some war in which the United Kingdom was a participant. In these circumstances, it was urged that there was no justification for further expenditure on defence in Éire and that the more money that was expended on this service the more likely was it that Éire would sooner or later be plunged into war. Public opinion definitely thought that no more, or, at most, that very little more should be expended on defence in Éire than was being expended at present, namely about £1.5 million per annum.

MR. CHAMBERLAIN said that Sir John Simon had already pointed out that United Kingdom Ministers would have to explain and justify to Parliament a proposal, under which, in effect, the United Kingdom revenues would be reduced by several million pounds. Disregarding for the moment the point of view of public opinion in Éire it must be recognised that public opinion in the United Kingdom would be certain to ask how much the Exchequer of the United Kingdom was being saved, both in regard to the capital cost of re-equipment and future maintenance charges, by the assumption by Éire of responsibility in future for these charges as regards the ports to be transferred. Whatever might be the position in regard to these particular ports, it could not, for a moment, be argued that the United Kingdom was in any way responsible for expenditure on the general defence services of Éire. Indeed, it would be in the highest degree improper and unconstitutional for the United Kingdom to attempt to concern herself or interfere in any way with the defence of Éire, which was the responsibility of the Government of Éire. In these circumstances, he felt that it was imperative to accept the situation as it is at the moment, namely, that the financial responsibility of the United

Kingdom for the defence of Éire is strictly limited to the three defended ports, while the Government of Éire are responsible for the defence of the rest of the country. Under the arrangements now contemplated the three defended ports would pass from the responsibility of the United Kingdom to that of Éire. He fully appreciated that the figures to which reference had been made of the cost of re-equipment and maintenance of the ports must, from the point of view of Éire, appear very substantial.

MR. DE VALERA said that the point which he wished to emphasize was a somewhat different one. The Government of Éire had to carry very heavy burdens in connection with their present defence commitments. Public opinion in Éire was disposed to be very critical of this expenditure and to argue that it would be much better for Éire to have no defence forces at all and for her to rely in future on a policy of neutrality and to follow the example, in this respect, of Denmark and other small Powers. In order, however, to prevent Éire being used by some enemy of the United Kingdom, as a base for attacking the United Kingdom, it had become necessary to contemplate the expenditure of very large sums of money in re-arming the country for a purpose which many people in Éire would argue was much more a United Kingdom interest than an Éire interest.

MR. CHAMBERLAIN said that he must have regard to the point of view of critics in the United Kingdom. It would be urged that at a very dangerous and critical time the United Kingdom Government had decided to hand over the defended ports in Éire and, in so doing, were running very grave risks. More than this, it would be represented that, by making financial settlement with Éire of the kind contemplated by Mr. de Valera, and for the reasons urged by him, the United Kingdom were, in fact, being called upon to pay indirectly for the whole of the defence of Éire.

MR. DE VALERA said that the United Kingdom could always rely on the assurance that, so far as Éire was able to do so, she would deny the use of her country to any foreign power, as a base for an attack on the United Kingdom. But this assurance would be rendered nugatory and impossible to implement if the United Kingdom maintained her demand for such a heavy capital lump sum payment as would make it quite impossible for Éire to find the necessary money to put her defences in order and thereafter to maintain them. In other words, Éire would have to forego her promise to defend herself against a foreign aggressor.

MR. MacENTEE said that he also wished to stress the very important consideration of securing the goodwill of public opinion in Éire. A better understanding was quite impossible so long as the special duties remained. Compared with the United Kingdom, Éire was a very poor country and burdens which could readily be borne by the United Kingdom represented very grave difficulties in Éire. It was no exaggeration to say that, in present circumstances, every beast exported from the country to the United Kingdom was a source of irritation and indignation to the Éire farmers.

MR. DE VALERA observed that the only way in which it was possible for his colleagues and himself to justify the payment of any capital sum, was that it was essential to make such a payment in order to end the economic war. He and his colleagues recognised that the United Kingdom were in a position effectively to put pressure on Éire by means of the special duties, and he could assure United Kingdom Ministers that if the Government of Éire had been able to discover any effective answer to that policy they would not have hesitated for a moment to have adopted it.

THE HOME SECRETARY enquired whether any estimate had been formed of how much the Treaty Ports would cost Éire to re-equip and maintain.

MR. DE VALERA replied that it had not been possible for the Éire authorities to prepare any estimates on the subject, but some figures had been furnished them by the United Kingdom experts.

MR. CHAMBERLAIN said that the United Kingdom figures for the future annual maintenance of the ports was about £230,000 per annum, while the capital cost of re-equipping the ports had been estimated at about £750,000.

MR. DE VALERA said that he would much like to receive expert advice as to the best line on which the Éire re-armament scheme should proceed; for example, would it be better to develop the Air side of their defence forces or spend money on some types of small naval vessels? At present the Government of Éire had no plans, and before making any start it was of course essential that they should have some idea of what the financial commitments would be. He had seen some very hypothetical figures, but felt little confidence in them.

SIR SAMUEL HOARE assumed that the re-equipment of the ports now to be handed over would in any case be properly carried out. This was a very vital consideration from the point of view of the United Kingdom.

MR. DE VALERA and MR. MacENTEE stated emphatically that the ports in question would in any event be properly re-equipped and maintained.

THE SECRETARY OF STATE FOR DOMINION AFFAIRS, replying to a suggestion that the inhabitants of Éire were subject to much heavier taxation than comparable inhabitants in the United Kingdom, pointed out that if some compromise could be reached on the financial question, the result would be the disappearance of the Special Duties, which would mean that the Éire farmer would have more money to spend, while the cessation of the bounties would mean relief to the Éire tax-payer.

MR. MacENTEE agreed that this would have been so, if there had been no necessity for the Éire taxpayer to assume the heavy additional burden of re-armament, which represented in his view the export of so much capital. The capital cost of re-armament in Éire had been put at £10,000,000 to £15,000,000, and this included the provision of reserves of ammunition, equipment, etc. As Mr. de Valera had stated, this expenditure would be generally regarded throughout Éire as having to be made much more in the interests of the United Kingdom than in those of Éire. This constituted a strong argument in favour of the United Kingdom assuming responsibility for the expenditure.

MR. CHAMBERLAIN stated that in the last two or three years the United Kingdom Government had been faced with ever increasing pressure and urgency to expend larger and larger sums on every form of re-armament, protection of the civil population, and kindred services. The commitments and estimates had grown to such vast figures that the United Kingdom

Government had been forced to inform their experts that it was quite impossible to carry out in all respects the advice which was given to them, and which was based on insuring the country against all likely risks and dangers. It had, in fact, been necessary for the United Kingdom Government to reduce their commitments, and in doing so to take certain risks. Considerations of this kind made it very difficult, if not impossible, to entertain suggestions such as that the United Kingdom should contribute towards the cost of the defence of Éire, or should keep up reserves of ammunition and equipment in that country.

MR. DE VALERA observed that inevitably it must be a cause of great anxiety to the Government of the United Kingdom to have so close upon their flank a large island which a hostile power might use as a base for attack upon the United Kingdom. As the result of the assurances which he had given, the United Kingdom was being protected against this serious danger, and it was in his view very important that the United Kingdom should do nothing in regard to finance which would make it impossible for Éire to fulfil the assurances that he had given, that she would defend herself against a hostile aggressor. The present time, with the possibilities of war on the horizon, was, he was convinced, the very worst time to persuade the people of Éire to undertake additional defence burdens. They would certainly say that any new defence commitments were merely the result of some alliance with, or pressure from the United Kingdom. He must repeat that it was impossible for himself and his colleagues to entertain the lump sum capital figures which had been mentioned at the discussion between officials that morning, and had been repeated by Sir John Simon that afternoon.

MR. MacENTEE observed that it was quite impossible for Éire to spend money on re-armament if this meant cutting down social services. It was inevitable that more money would have to be found for social services in Éire from now onwards.

SIR JOHN SIMON thought that it would be advantageous to continue the conversations between the Treasury officials. The result of the discussion that afternoon had shown that there was considerable common ground. For example, it appeared that in calculating the lump sum capital payment regard might be had to items such as R.I.C. Pensions, Local Loans, and Judicial etc. Pensions. There were, in fact, three or four items of a quite substantial character outside the Land Annuities, which could profitably be brought into account. No doubt Mr. Chamberlain would indicate the United Kingdom view of the relationship between the financial and trade issues.

MR. DE VALERA said that a financial agreement would have to be closely linked with a trade agreement. From his point of view a trade agreement was essential. In the absence of such an agreement his people would feel that there was no guarantee for the continuance of the peaceful relations between the two countries.

MR. CHAMBERLAIN said that, as he saw it, the position was that this country was asked to make bigger reductions in the special duties than they felt could be justified to the House of Commons. The question was, therefore, first whether some further adjustment of the financial proposals could not be effected, and secondly, how far it was possible to bring in on the one side defence expenditure in Éire, and on the other side advantages to this country from a trade agreement to which attention could be drawn in the House of Commons. By some such procedure as this they might hope to find a basis for a general agreement. As regards the defence problem he recognised that at present the Government of Éire was in the dark as to the exact requirements and the expenditure that would be needed to meet them. He would be glad to hear the views of the Éire Delegates as to what might be expected to follow the disappearance, or reduction to a great extent, of the special duties. He assumed that the retaliatory duties would also disappear.

MR. DE VALERA agreed.

MR. CHAMBERLAIN then referred to the bounties to the farmers. Would they disappear *pari passu* with the special duties?

MR. RYAN said that so far as live stock was concerned he thought they would, but in the case of other produce, such as butter, bacon and eggs, marketing schemes were in existence under which exports were to some extent subsidised by the home consumers.

MR. MORRISON said he thought that the details might be left for discussion at a later stage. He was concerned that if the special duties disappeared, then insofar as the assistance of bounties was inaugurated to counteract the special duties, those bounties would disappear also.

MR. LEMASS referred to the effect of the Ottawa duties on certain classes of goods. Some bounties were given to offset the effect of those duties.

MR. STANLEY said that he thought that no goods affected by the Ottawa duties were also subject to the special import duties.

MR. MORRISON said that butter was subjected to a 40% duty plus an Ottawa duty of 15s. per cwt. He suggested that it would be a wise move in undertaking the trade agreement discussion to take the line that the special duties were a financial measure imposed to compensate this country for payments to which they thought they were entitled, and which had been withheld, and that any modification in them was in liquidation of the financial dispute. This avoided the difficulty of looking upon the special duties as protective duties, and would make it easier for him to justify any reduction to the farming community in this country. The trade agreement could then be considered in the light of the Ottawa and other duties on the basis of mutual tariff preferences.

MR. STANLEY said that there would be some political difficulty if the bounties did not disappear. If the special duties were removed, but the bounties remained, United Kingdom farmers would say that they had to compete against bounty-fed produce.

MR. MacENTEE suggested that some political advantage might result from the benefit accruing to the urban population. The imports of such produce might help to keep down the cost of living.

MR. MORRISON said that he felt that the section of public opinion which would be most sensitive to the removal of the special duties would be the rural communities.

MR. CHAMBERLAIN asked whether the matter could be carried any further.

MR. DE VALERA said that he quite appreciated the difficulties of the position and the different avenues of approach which the two Governments were obliged to take. At the same time, if the United Kingdom Government maintained their position, the only course open to the Éire Government would be to continue to endure the existence of the special duties as best they might. If there was a chance of agreement it would be worthwhile making one in terms on which they would be able to carry their own people with them.

MR. CHAMBERLAIN agreed that if no settlement could be effected, all that remained was to carry on as at present, but he would not willingly fall back on that state of affairs until he was quite certain there was no chance of some settlement. Sir John Simon was going to look into the question again and see if it was possible to make a more favourable report.

SIR JOHN SIMON enquired what the relation between the financial settlement and the defence problem would be.

MR. CHAMBERLAIN said that the heads of subjects for discussion in regard to the defence problem were being put down on paper and this would be completed later in the day. He suggested that the matter might be further discussed tomorrow.

The question arose whether in any case it would be possible to reach a final all-round settlement at the present series of meetings, and if not, in what way they should be suspended so as to facilitate their resumption later on. Further information and data were required bearing on both the financial and defence problems which could be explored in greater detail if there was an interval in the meetings of the Delegations.

MR. DE VALERA said that he was rather apprehensive of the result of undue delays which provided an opportunity for interested parties to influence public opinion and to spread all kinds of rumours. If they could secure some form of agreement at an early date which they could take back to their colleagues for endorsement, such a course would have many advantages. What would be acceptable to-day might become impossible in three weeks' time.

MR. LEMASS said that all their exporters knew that these negotiations were going on and the fact of their existence created a great deal of uncertainty and difficulty. He hoped that the period of negotiations would be as short as possible.

MR. CHAMBERLAIN agreed that this was most desirable. No final general settlement could, however, be secured until a trade agreement had been completed in detail, which must be a matter of several weeks. Uncertainty was an inevitable factor during the negotiations for any trade treaty and he did not see how this could be avoided. This country had had experience of this uncertainty on several occasions in the past.

MR. DE VALERA said that delay would give chances for persons to create an outcry that, although partition continued, Éire was to be committed to Britain's wars and that, though they might be going to be relieved of one burden, it would only be exchanged for another. He recognised, however, that time was required for consideration of the details of the trade treaty and that his Government would have to face this position.

MR. STANLEY said that by reason of the Coal-Cattle Agreements his officials were already in contact with a great deal of the detail work in relation to trade between the United Kingdom and Éire. The completion of a treaty that would be really worth while must inevitably take some weeks.

MR. DE VALERA said he wondered whether the best course would be to suspend the meetings between the Delegations without referring to any tentative agreements which might be reached to-morrow.

MR. CHAMBERLAIN said that from the British point of view it would be difficult to justify coming to any settlement on the financial dispute in advance of the conclusion of a trade agreement.

SIR JOHN SIMON felt that the result of their meetings should be presented as a whole: it would have some good and bad elements from the point of view of both sides. He would certainly find it very difficult, in advance of a general settlement, to inform the House of Commons that the Special Duties had been given up.

MR. MACDONALD said that in the interval, contact could be maintained throughout in regard to finance and defence questions.

MR. DE VALERA agreed. He had deliberately avoided bringing over representatives of the Department of Defence as he did not wish to excite public opinion in Éire. He thought it would be much better to consider the problem on the basis of seeing what is necessary and preparing a plan in accordance with the requirements. They were anxious to know what Great Britain would do if they remained responsible. When they knew what the requirements were they would be able to estimate their cost. This could be taken into account in any compromise effected on other aspects of the financial dispute but he must make it clear that if that cost, when added to any lump sum that might be agreed upon in settlement of the financial dispute, encroached into the sphere of the land annuities payments, he could not take the responsibility for urging such proposals as a solution of their difficulties.

In answer to a question by Mr. de Valera, MR. MACDONALD suggested that any information given to the Press in regard to the interval in the negotiations should indicate that the Delegations had carried out a preliminary exploration of the questions under consideration, that no agreements had yet been reached and no commitments entered into, but that a stage had been reached at which a detailed examination of the various questions was to be carried out by officials who would report to their Ministers with a view to further meetings between the latter being held later on.

THE CONFERENCE agreed –
(i)   To issue a communiqué to the Press prepared by Mr. MacDonald and read to the Conference by the Prime Minister;
(ii) To meet again at 12 noon at 10, Downing Street on 19th January, for further discussion on the defence problem;
(iii) That a meeting should take place on the morning of Wednesday, 19th January, at the Board of Trade, between the President of the Board of Trade, the Minister for Agriculture and Fisheries and their officials and the corresponding Éire Ministers and their officials, for preliminary

discussion of matters affecting a trade agreement. The time of the meeting to be fixed by mutual arrangement.

No. 126 NAI DT S10389 (Annex)

Press communiqué following conclusion of discussions on 18 January 1938
(Copy)
LONDON, 18 January 1938

PRESS COMMUNIQUÉ

'The discussions were continued at 3 o'clock this afternoon with the Prime Minister in the Chair. Some of the matters which were discussed yesterday came under further review. The meeting adjourned at 4.15 and will be resumed tomorrow at 12 noon. A meeting will be held at the Board of Trade between the Ministers concerned with the questions of trade and agriculture tomorrow morning at 10.'

No. 127 NAI DT S10389 (Annex)

Minutes of the conference between representatives of the
United Kingdom and Ireland
(Secret) (I.N. (38) 4th Meeting) (Copy)
LONDON, 12 noon, 19 January 1938

CONFERENCE
between
REPRESENTATIVES OF THE UNITED KINGDOM AND ÉIRE
Secretary's Notes of the Fourth Meeting of the Conference
held at 10 Downing Street, on Wednesday, 19th January, 1938,
at 12 Noon

PRESENT

UNITED KINGDOM	ÉIRE
The Rt. Hon Neville Chamberlain, M.P., Prime Minister.	Mr. Eamon de Valera, Prime Minister and Minister for External Affairs.
The Rt.Hon. Sir John Simon, G.C.S.I., G.C.V.O., O.B.E., K.C., M.P., Chancellor of the Exchequer.	Mr. Sean F. Lemass, Minister for Industry and Commerce.
The Rt.Hon. Sir Samuel Hoare, Bt., G.C.S.I., G.B.E., C.M.G., M.P., Secretary of State for the Home Department.	Mr. Sean MacEntee, Minister for Finance.

| The Rt.Hon. Malcolm MacDonald, M.P., Secretary of State for Dominion Affairs. | Dr. James Ryan, Minister for Agriculture. |

THE FOLLOWING WERE ALSO PRESENT

| The Rt.Hon. Sir Thomas Inskip, C.B.E., K.C., M.P., Minister for Co-ordination of Defence. | Mr. J. W. Dulanty, C.B., C.B.E., High Commissioner for Éire. |

Secretary   Mr. C.N. Ryan, D.S.O., M.C.

THE CONFERENCE had before them a draft outline for a defence agreement which had been circulated to the members before the Meeting.

A copy of this document as amended at the Meeting is attached as an Annex to these Minutes.

DRAFT DEFENCE AGREEMENT

MR. DE VALERA said that, owing to the pressure of various other engagements, he regretted he had been able to do little more than glance through the document. He had not so far had any opportunity of giving it careful consideration in conjunction with his colleagues. He thought, however, that a fundamental difficulty would arise immediately. The people of Éire would demand to be the arbiters of what should be done in regard to defence, but it would be represented by them that the United Kingdom was really the judge.

CLAUSE 3

MR. CHAMBERLAIN pointed out that in the document the United Kingdom Government had specifically refrained from constituting itself the final arbiter. He agreed the point did arise as to who was to have the last word on the question of the adequacy of the defensive arrangements. Responsibility for this, however, was not placed by the document on the United Kingdom Government, or even on some impartial body. At the beginning of Clause 3 it was placed squarely on the Government of Éire and the only qualification was that later in the paragraph there was an undertaking that the Government of Éire would invite the Government of the United Kingdom to consult with them.

MR. DE VALERA said that the difficulty arose from the fact that the United Kingdom, by reason of its relatively greater strength, would be able to insist on their own interpretation of what was adequate if a difference of opinion should develop between the two Governments.

MR. CHAMBERLAIN said that the United Kingdom Delegation has not the least intention to convey any suggestion of that kind. The criticism which they anticipated from their people would be that a decision on adequacy had been left solely to the Government of Éire, and the answer, which they would have to make would be that this was so, but that that Government could be trusted.

MR. DE VALERA suggested that a further answer could be found in as much as the United Kingdom realised at the back of their mind that, in a situation of vital importance to them, they would be able to take a quick way to ensure that the measures which they desired were carried out.

MR. CHAMBERLAIN said that if that view was held by Éire nothing could prevent the apprehension about United Kingdom intrusion into Éire affairs except the patent unwillingness of the United Kingdom to do so.

MR. DE VALERA said that the absence of anything in the nature of a specific contract would make a great difference in the way in which a defence agreement would be regarded by his people. They would be very suspicious of any form of specific undertaking.

MR. CHAMBERLAIN observed that they had already gone a long way in their negotiations and it was clearly possible to go further. It would be a pity if there was to be a breakdown owing to suspicion. The document prepared by the United Kingdom Government was intended to mean that the Government of Éire should be final judge in the matter of adequacy. All the United Kingdom Government asked was to be allowed to offer advice, and they were then ready to leave the decision whether to take it or not to the Government of Éire.

MR. DE VALERA said that he was anxious to make sure that any document on which they might agree was on the face of it as satisfactory as possible from the point of view of his people. Unless there was something explicit in the document, the people of Éire would ask who was to determine whether the conditions as regards adequacy were satisfied and would hold that Éire had been committed to the United Kingdom. It was of the utmost importance that all possible sources of friction should be eliminated.

MR. CHAMBERLAIN said that he was about to propose an addition in the last sentence. He suggested that after 'the Government of Éire' there should be added – 'shall be the final judge of what is adequate, but before coming to a conclusion'.

MR. DE VALERA said he thought that insertion would go a long way towards avoiding friction. He was disturbed at the prospect that the United Kingdom might want Éire to undertake certain additional measures which the Government of Éire would consider to be beyond their means. He had no very strong objections to the general tone of the document but he would like to see Éire's position safeguarded as far as possible. The document might be represented as placing Éire in an important treaty relationship with the United Kingdom.

CLAUSE 4

Turning to Clause 4 he said that this dealt with the transitional period after the ports were handed over, but before the Government of Éire provided the actual forces to defend them. He thought this period should be as short as possible and deprecated any idea that the process of handing over would be unduly prolonged. He was not personally in a position to judge how long this period should be, but perhaps the Minister for Co-ordination of Defence would have some observations.

SIR THOMAS INSKIP said that the actual exchange presented no very difficult problems. This paragraph, however, referred to personnel not to armament. At present the garrison in the three Treaty Ports consisted of nearly 600 men of the Royal Artillery and Royal Engineers and an additional 50 or 60 would be required to bring the forces up to fighting establishments. Some additional to these numbers would probably be necessary when the defence of the ports was placed on a perfectly satisfactory footing and the provision of some aircraft and small naval craft would also be required.

MR. DE VALERA said that when the Delegation returned to Éire their colleagues would naturally question them in regard to the draft agreement, particularly in reference to the magnitude of their liabilities. He recognised that the United Kingdom was much more experienced in this type of problem and it would be a great help to him if he could be furnished with a statement of the forces and equipment which, in the opinion of the United Kingdom, would be required for the Government of Éire to carry out the terms of the agreement.

SIR THOMAS INSKIP said that this information could be quickly supplied in regard to the Treaty Ports, but the agreement also covered the defence of the whole coast of Éire. This was important in view of the possibilities for submarine refuges afforded by the western seaboard of Éire.

SIR SAMUEL HOARE said that it would be necessary to keep in mind that the problem facing the Government of Éire was somewhat different to that with which the United Kingdom would be faced if they had to carry out the same task. Under modern conditions it was difficult to localise war. If the British Government were faced with the problem of defending the Irish Ports they would do so behind the general protective cover afforded by the Grand Fleet of the British Navy.

MR. DE VALERA said that, in framing the contemplated defence programme for Éire, it was necessary to assume that the relations between the two countries were friendly and that the Government of Éire would naturally wish to effect such economies as were possible from a joint consideration of the problem. He would like to know how far the ground was covered by the United Kingdom forces and to be given an indication of the best way in which Éire could fill the gap. Action would be taken by the two countries separately but in view of certain common potential dangers, it was only prudent to take steps to minimise the possibility of over-lapping measures.

MR. CHAMBERLAIN drew attention to the terms of Article 6 of the 1921 Treaty in which it is provided that until coastal defence is taken over by the Irish Free State the defence by sea of Great Britain and Ireland was to be undertaken by Great Britain. Under the new conditions this undertaking would be abrogated.

MR. DE VALERA said he would like to see Articles 6 and 7 of the Treaty completely wiped out and their place taken by the agreement now under discussion.

He had always read Articles 6 and 7 together but he understood that at some discussion with representatives of the Irish Free State Government some years ago the view had been taken that they were quite independent.

At the time he had considered this ruling to be arbitrary.

MR. CHAMBERLAIN said that he thought the question of facilities at ports must be associated with the question of defence by sea. No navy could defend a coast without using its ports.

MR. DE VALERA reverting to Clause 4 of the draft agreement said that an arrangement which provided for the handing over of the ports on a particular date would be very satisfactory from his point of view, but if this was impracticable he would like to have the various defence functions handed over as and when desired by the Government of Éire. As soon as any agreement was signed he would like to get possession of the fortifications and thereafter the handing over might be done by stages, subject to the proviso that full possession should be taken after as short an interval as possible.

SIR THOMAS INSKIP observed that it was for Mr. de Valera to say when the Government of Éire would be ready to replace, man for man, the present garrisons. On the assumption that they had trained gunners and engineers to man the defences the handing over could be done in a relatively short time.

MR. MacENTEE thought that there need not be much delay in the provision by the Government of Éire of land forces, but he anticipated some difficulty in regard to the naval and air forces.

SIR SAMUEL HOARE said he thought as drafted this Clause did perhaps look more formidable than was really their intention. It was only meant to refer to expedients to be adopted in a purely interim period and had no long-term significance.

MR. CHAMBERLAIN said that he did not see in this Clause any insuperable difficulty which could not be got over. The draft agreement was not to be published forthwith and there would be time to consider necessary and desirable adjustments. As he saw it the procedure to be adopted would be that the Government of Éire would first take over the guns, munitions and material on the spot. They would not, of course, take over the personnel but would replace them by their own personnel as soon as they could do so. In the meantime they would gradually re-equip and supplement the armament of the ports in accordance with any decisions which they might reach. Even if it was impossible to state at once what would constitute the transitional period, it seemed quite clear that it could not, in any event, be a long period.

MR DE VALERA said that there was a reference in the Clause to naval and air forces, and the Clause itself applied not only to the ports but to the whole coast-line of Éire. If Clause 4 could be confined to the forces at the ports then the position would become much easier, but he was definitely anxious at the magnitude of the scheme envisaged in defending the whole of the coast-line.

MR. CHAMBERLAIN suggested that Mr. de Valera's difficulties would be met by confining Clause 4 to the ports, and said that he was prepared to accept this limitation.

SIR THOMAS INSKIP observed that the word 'development' might convey the wrong implication and suggested that 'allocation' might be more suitable.

MR. DE VALERA proposed to substitute for the first three lines of Clause 4 the following:-

'Pending an intimation that the Government of Éire is in a position to undertake the defence of the ports'.

He added, however, that he was more anxious to settle on general principles than on the actual drafting, which could be left to a later stage. In dealing with principles there were two big difficulties which he had to face. First, he must be certain that it was the Government of Éire who would be responsible for interpretation on the question of "adequacy" and he must make sure that in any agreement this was presented in a way which carried conviction to his people. Secondly, he would have to contend with those sections of the people of Éire who would be opposed to any full or close co-operation with the United Kingdom so long as partition continued.

CLAUSE 5

Turning to Clause 5, Mr. de Valera said he would like to end the paragraph at 'defence plans' in the third line.

SIR THOMAS INSKIP observed that, though in form this Clause covered undertakings by the United Kingdom Government, in substance that Government only acted if invited to do so. It gave them no right to say that the Government of Éire were not giving them enough invitations in regard to training or the other matters referred to in the Clause.

MR. CHAMBERLAIN suggested that the last two lines should be replaced by: 'and any other matters connected with defence.'

MR. DE VALERA accepted this suggestion. He added that he understood that in the past some Éire officers had been sent for courses of instruction both to this country and to the United States. He would like it to be understood that the Government of Éire considered that the conclusion of any agreement on the lines of the discussion should not in any way fetter their freedom to send their officers to whatever countries they thought fit. They were anxious to be able to do this without causing friction with the United Kingdom Government. If they continued to send officers to the United States and to France, it would be a demonstration to his people that Éire was still a free agent in such matters.

MR. CHAMBERLAIN said that no objection could possibly be raised to the Government of Éire sending officers to the United States, but he thought the position would be a little different if they sent officers regularly to Germany.

SIR SAMUEL HOARE pointed out that there was a great difference between sending individual officers on specialist courses or for the purpose of making particular enquiries, and sending batches of officers at regular intervals to receive their normal training. A United Kingdom Minister was at present in Germany investigating their air raid precaution arrangements. He thought that the Government of Éire would find it highly convenient, indeed almost necessary, in order to secure satisfactory training, for their personnel to be trained by those providing the equipment and accustomed to its use.

MR. DE VALERA asked the Prime Minister whether he thought it was really necessary for this undertaking by the Government of the United Kingdom to be included.

MR. CHAMBERLAIN said he was looking at the question, as was Mr. de Valera, from the point of view of the appeal which this document would make to the people of his own country. The Éire Delegation, broadly speaking, thought that, from their own point of view, the less reference that there was in the document to co-operation the better. On the other hand, the point of view of the United Kingdom Delegation was exactly the reverse.

MR. DE VALERA said he recognised the existence of these two stand-points and appreciated that there might be some difficulty in reconciling them.

DR. RYAN suggested that Clause 3 might be regarded as covering the purpose of Clause 5.

MR. CHAMBERLAIN said that this was a case in which the desiderata lay in opposite directions. The United Kingdom Delegation had already modified the draft agreement on a number of detailed matters to meet the views of Mr. de Valera and he felt that they must press for the retention of Clause 5 as now amended.

MR. DE VALERA said that the powers of his delegation were limited. There was some difference of opinion inside his own Cabinet. Some of his colleagues held that unless there was to be full co-operation in regard to partition, no commitments should be entered into regarding full co-operation over defence questions. If the defence agreement was couched in the general form of effect being given to it on the initiative of the Government of Éire, he thought he might get agreement with his colleagues. Otherwise he anticipated difficulty in his Cabinet, his Party, and with the Dáil. He had had a long experience of propaganda and he could see that a good deal of useful propaganda from the point of view of the Government of the United Kingdom, could be derived from this document. This fact alone might lead certain sections of the people of Éire to consider the arrangement less attractive for their own country. However, he would like to take back with him an outline of the agreement in a reasonably final form, and his Government would then have an opportunity of examining it.

SIR THOMAS INSKIP said that the attitude referred to by Mr. de Valera depended upon the assumption that the good faith and intentions of the contracting parties were valueless. Clause 5 conveyed at any rate some appreciable advantages to the Government of Éire. By it, for example, they were placed in a position to ask the United Kingdom for information and help regarding all the most up-to-date scientific equipment of value in war and the United Kingdom was not in a position of refuse disclosure. This would enable the development of the defence forces in Éire not only to proceed much more quickly but much more cheaply than would otherwise be the case.

MR. DE VALERA agreed that might be so but one of his difficulties was that the people of Éire might not be appreciative of such a gift at the present time. However, he would undertake to go as far as he possibly could to meet the point of view of the United Kingdom. He would like any agreement which they might reach to cover the ground as far as possible from the publicity point of view, so that additional statements could be avoided which were liable to cause misunderstanding and friction between the two sides.

MR. CHAMBERLAIN observed that whilst he did not go so far as to say that Clause 5 as drafted and amended was vital to any agreement, he was anxious to get as near as he possibly could to its present form.

CLAUSE 6

MR. DE VALERA said he had no strong objection to this clause. The question of including some reference to matters of quality and price had occurred to him, but he did not think it would be appropriate to include such a reference in a document of that character.

MR. MacENTEE suggested that the clause might form part of the Trade Agreement.

MR. CHAMBERLAIN said he thought this would be inappropriate as the questions concerned were quite different.

MR. DE VALERA observed that if the negotiations for a trade agreement went through satisfactorily, then on general trade grounds the Government of Éire could justify making their munitions and equipment purchases in the United Kingdom, except of course in the case of very special types of equipment for which they might have to go elsewhere.

MR. CHAMBERLAIN suggested that the qualification 'so far as possible' gave the Government of Éire sufficient discretion as to the interpretation they could place upon this clause.

MR. DE VALERA then asked the Prime Minister if he would be so good as to amplify the special value which the United Kingdom Government placed upon the inclusion of Clauses 4, 5 and 6 in the draft agreement.

MR. CHAMBERLAIN explained that he felt the problem of defence would prove a difficult, perhaps the most difficult, matter of all the various subjects to be covered by a general settlement on which to conclude mutually satisfactory arrangements. At the present time the people in the United Kingdom were intensely interested in all questions affecting the security of the country. The defence question in relation to Ireland was dealt with fully in the 1921 Treaty, which contained articles giving the United Kingdom specific responsibilities and rights. Any agreement which the United Kingdom Government might reach with the Government of Éire under this heading would be very closely examined by many sections of the community, to see if the Government had given away anything which it was considered essential to maintain. Personally, he felt that if the United Kingdom Delegation were satisfied with the terms of a draft agreement, they would be able to carry their views through the Cabinet and Parliament, but he did not want to have important sections of the community distressed by genuine doubts, anxieties and suspicions. He thought that would be a great pity and would create a most unfortunate atmosphere. Any features of an agreement which would serve to allay those anxieties and to create a spirit of trust and friendship were of great value. The reason why he attached such importance to Clauses 4, 5 and 6 was that they did to some extent effect this purpose.

MR. DE VALERA thanked the Prime Minister for his statement, and said that he fully appreciated it. In considering any drafting alterations they would bear his views in mind.

CLAUSE 2

MR. DE VALERA then referred to the reference in Clause 2 of an attack 'on the communications' of Éire. If this was intended to refer to attacks by submarines on supplies in Irish waters he could accept it, but the term seemed to him to be of rather wide application and might be stretched to cover communications with Japan.

MR. CHAMBERLAIN said that the examples of attack referred to in this Clause were all connected with the purpose of aggression. It was implicit, therefore, that the attack referred to was a local one, whereas cutting communications with Japan could not be regarded as local.

MR. DE VALERA thought it might be necessary to repeat the word 'purpose'. He had no qualms about the drafting so far as it concerned direct attack, but he thought that no form of attack could be more direct than an interruption of vital communications. The people of Éire were prepared to defend their own country and to prevent it being used as a base for an attack on the United Kingdom, but they could not be committed to operations in a distant area. He would prefer to see the phrase in regard to communications omitted.

MR. CHAMBERLAIN said that the phrase had only been put in to indicate that the people of Éire might be subjected to grave aggression, without an actual enemy landing in their country, through attacks on their trade with the United Kingdom, or even with other countries. The whole of their overseas trade might in fact be stopped. He suggested that 'an attack on their trade' should be substituted for 'an attack on the communications of that country'.

MR. DE VALERA approved this amendment.

Discussing the next step, he repeated that he was anxious to get a statement of the action which the United Kingdom would take if they had the responsibility for implementing the draft agreement in so far as Éire was concerned. He was anxious, so far as it would prove possible, to make sure that in an emergency, steps which would have been taken by the United Kingdom, if the responsibility had been theirs, would not be left undone. Consequently, he was anxious to consider what provision should be made of personnel and equipment. He would like to have an indication of the requirements in these respects together with an estimate of their cost.

SIR THOMAS INSKIP said that he would be able to furnish proposals, and to include a broad estimate of the cost. Those in regard to the ports could be available quite soon, but proposals related to the other aspects of defence would take a little longer. He would proceed on the assumption that the British Fleet and Air Force were in being and were fulfilling their normal roles.

MR. MacENTEE observed that the rate at which their defence organisations could be developed would have an important bearing on their budgetary position. He would be very glad to see the estimate of requirements which the Minister for Co-ordination of Defence was going to be good enough to furnish, and he thought that it should be framed on the basis of co-operation against a common attack.

MR. MacDONALD said that fresh copies of the draft outline for the defence agreement would be ready in the afternoon incorporating the amendments made that morning. He suggested that these should be regarded as drafts for further consideration and that both Delegations should take them away for this purpose. Further communications in regard to them could be made though Mr. Dulanty.

[SIR THOMAS INSKIP left the Meeting at this point.]

FINANCIAL AGREEMENT

MR. DE VALERA enquired whether there was anything to report in regard to the financial agreement.

SIR JOHN SIMON said there had not been much further progress up to the present. The gap between the views of the two Delegations was serious and he was bound to say that they could not regard the offer of a lump sum of £8,000,000, which only represented two years purchase of the value of the special duties, as providing a basis for settlement. He thought that contact should be maintained between the two sides, and that the problem should be kept constantly before the Delegations.

MR. MacENTEE said that the reaction of the contemplated defence programme for Éire upon the financial issue must not be overlooked. There were in Éire a large number of people who thought that the country should maintain a strictly neutral position and felt that the best chance of their being able to do so was to remain in a patently helpless position from a military point of view. This was not the view of the Éire Government, which attached great importance to the provision of the necessary defence requirements. But in order to do this some budgetary relief was essential and this could not be made if the lump sum payment in millions of pounds was to run into two figures. He begged that a strict evaluation of the amount brought in by the special duties should not be taken as a basis for a settlement. He thought that some abatement of certain claims, even if they were just, might be made in order to create an atmosphere of goodwill and friendship which had been wanting in the past.

SIR JOHN SIMON said that he was fully seized with the importance of taking a broad view. He thought that the position should be dealt with by a single transaction and not regarded as a series of separate issues. This aspect should be kept steadily in mind. On the financial issue he was personally not convinced that the method of payment by a capital sum was the best, but that was a technical point which could be left to the technical experts. He was not taking a narrow Treasury view of the financial issue and he did not contemplate dealing with it on a strict accounting basis. In any case it was important to keep in view that this issue should not be dealt with in isolation. Other aspects of the negotiations would not be without effect on the financial problem. He thought that they should make as much progress as possible with those negotiations and observe the direction in which they were leading. He hoped that the Secretary of State for Dominion Affairs shared this view.

MR. MacDONALD said he entirely agreed with the Chancellor. He referred to the fact that at present the Government of Éire had not got the information on which to form an estimate of the sum involved by a defence programme. The cost of that programme was bound to be reflected in the view which they would take in regard to the other questions under consideration.

MR. DE VALERA said that before they left Éire his Delegation was given powers to conclude agreements provided that they did not accept any charge in respect of the land annuities, enter into any definite defence commitments or agree to continue the United Kingdom rights in respect of the Treaty Ports. If they were to achieve any useful progress in Éire in the interval before discussions between the Delegations were resumed, it would be a great help to them to be able to take back a rough outline of a scheme of settlement. They had been disappointed in regard to the question of partition, information was not yet available to deal with the question of defence, progress was difficult in the financial discussions, whilst consideration of the details regarding a trade agreement would take some time. In these circumstances it would be difficult for him to achieve much progress in influencing his colleagues in Éire towards a general settlement in the interval elapsing before the Delegations resumed meetings.

SIR JOHN SIMON said that the financial discussions were going on at present between the officials of the two Treasuries. The essence of the position could be explained quite briefly. The annual payments which, rightly or wrongly, were claimed by the United Kingdom amounted to £5 million of which just over £3 million was made up by the land annuities. He quite understood the attitude which Mr. de Valera's Government was bound to take, but after subtracting them from the full amount of the claim there remained an annual sum of £1.9 million in regard to items which they had discussed at the meeting the previous day. Some of these annual payments were for a shorter term than the land annuities, but under no form of calculation could they be capitalised at a sum remotely approximating to £8 million.

MR. MacENTEE stressed again the great importance of the political advantages to be derived from a single payment which would mark the beginning of a new chapter in the relations between the two countries.

MR. CHAMBERLAIN pointed out that the Éire Delegates were urging the United Kingdom to make very large financial concessions in order to bring about a fresh era in the relations between the two countries whilst at the same time saying that the people of Éire would object to the slightest manifestation of such relations in the defence agreement.

MR. DE VALERA said he had hoped that progress would have been made towards the solution of difficulties in regard to matters which would have ended the objections of the people of Éire to full co-operation with the United Kingdom.

MR. CHAMBERLAIN said that certain steps could be taken. A suggestion had already been made for a method of approach to a financial settlement. As a start all labels in respect of specific items should be wiped out and consideration should be given to the possibility of reducing or abolishing the present special duties in return for some payment. The Éire Delegation preferred that the payments should take the form of a lump sum. Up to that point there was no difference in principle between them. The difficulty arose in regard to the size of the sum. So far as the United Kingdom Delegation was concerned, they recognised that if it proved possible to get agreements which would be of mutual advantage in regard to defence, trade, and agricultural questions such agreements could properly be taken into account in assessing the lump sum payment. Even so it might be that the lump sum would still be too large for the Government of Éire to accept. In that event, he thought the next step was to consider whether there were any items covered by the lump sum which the Government of Éire would be prepared to meet by annual payments, thereby reducing the lump sum to manageable proportions. That seemed to him as far as it was possible to go for the present, until further information about the defence programme was available.

MR. DE VALERA said that under existing conditions, the Government of Éire was faced with a difficult internal security problem. The Northern Boundary was undoubtedly a danger point. Some sections of the community in that area were armed and these arms were not under Government control. The same considerations applied to the Treaty Ports. In order to guard against dangers which might arise from these conditions the Éire Government was put to considerable expenditure, and there was a definite limit beyond which their resources could not be stretched. He was aware how much the farmers had suffered in the last four or five years, but he was not averse to placing burdens upon the people of Éire and telling them they must be faced, provided that he was completely satisfied that the burdens were justifiable. So far as a general settlement was concerned he did not want to give his people an opportunity to say that he had merely transferred their burden from one head to another.

SIR JOHN SIMON explained that the kind of financial settlement which the United Kingdom had in mind did not provide for payment in respect of the land annuities. Of the annual sum of £5 million claimed by the United Kingdom £3.1 million represented the land annuities leaving a balance of £1.9 million per annum in regard to other items. In so far as the United Kingdom was collecting £4 million per annum by means of the special duties, it might be argued that they were securing an offset to some extent against the default on the land annuity payments. If, however, the lump sum payment to be made by the Government of Éire was related to the total claim of the United Kingdom less the sum representing the land annuities, the Government of Éire could truthfully say that they were not paying anything 'in meal or malt' in regard to the land annuities. The way in which the various items amounting to £1.9 million per annum should be capitalised was a technical question but it could be worked out and agreed by the experts of both sides. He thought the amount of this capitalised sum should be ascertained. This figure could then be considered without attaching any labels to the various items from which it was built up. He felt that this was the way to approach the problem though he was bound to add that it did not, according to his calculations, lead to the conclusion that a figure of £8 million could be regarded as adequate.

MR. DE VALERA said that Sir John Simon's statement did not quite give the whole story. The United Kingdom Government had taken away a large number of assets whilst expecting the Government of Éire to continue paying charges. Moreover, they had given the Government of Éire no credit for the land annuity payments which had been made in the past.

The Conference adjourned at this point until 3 p.m.

No. 128 NAI DT S10389 (Annex)

Annex draft outline for defence agreement revised after conference meeting
(Copy)

LONDON, 12 noon, 19 January 1938

The Government of the United Kingdom and the Government of Éire agree as follows:-

1. The harbour defences (including buildings, magazines, emplacements, fixed armaments with the ammunition therefor at present on the spot, and instruments) of Berehaven, Queenstown and Lough Swilly now occupied by United Kingdom care and maintenance parties will be handed over to the Government of Éire.

2. The Government of Éire having taken over these harbour defences will defend the whole of their territory against external aggression, whether the purpose of the aggression be a direct attack on the people of Éire, or an attack on their trade, or as a means of securing a base from which to attack the United Kingdom.

3. The Government of Éire will bring the defences of the ports and of the whole coast of Éire up to an adequate standard of equipment and efficiency, and will maintain the defences at that level, providing the personnel and material sufficient for the purpose, including small naval vessels and aircraft. The Government of Éire shall be the final judge of what is adequate but before coming to a conclusion will invite the Government of the United Kingdom to consult with them as to the extent of the defences necessary, and to co-operate with them in any way in which co-operation may be desired by the Government of Éire.

4. Until such time as the Government of Éire can arrange for the allocation of forces adequate for the defence of the ports, the Government of Éire will invite the Government of the United Kingdom to co-operate in their defence by the supply of such forces, and the Government of the United Kingdom will so co-operate on such terms as may be agreed between the two Governments.

5. The Government of the United Kingdom will, when so invited by the Government of Éire, afford technical advice and assistance in the development of defence plans and any other matters connected with defence.

6. The Government of Éire will, where the necessary munitions or equipment cannot be made locally, purchase so far as possible their requirements in the United Kingdom.

No. 129 NAI DT S10389 (Annex)

Minutes of the conference between representatives of the
United Kingdom and Ireland
(Secret) (I.N. (38) 5th Meeting) (Copy)
LONDON, 3.00 pm, 19 January 1938

CONFERENCE
between
REPRESENTATIVES OF THE UNITED KINGDOM AND ÉIRE
Secretary's Notes of the Fifth Meeting of the Conference
held at 10 Downing Street, on Wednesday, 19th January, 1938,
at 3.0 p.m.

PRESENT:-

UNITED KINGDOM	*ÉIRE*
The Rt. Hon Neville Chamberlain, M.P., Prime Minister.	Mr. Eamon de Valera, Prime Minister and Minister for External Affairs.
The Rt. Hon. Sir John Simon, G.C.S.I., G.C.V.O., O.B.E., K.C., M.P., Chancellor of the Exchequer.	Mr. Sean F. Lemass, Minister for Industry and Commerce.
The Rt. Hon. Sir Samuel Hoare, Bt., G.C.S.I., G.B.E., C.M.G., M.P., Secretary of State for the Home Department.	Mr. Sean MacEntee, Minister for Finance.
The Rt. Hon. Malcolm MacDonald, M.P., Secretary of State for Dominion Affairs.	Dr. James Ryan, Minister for Agriculture.

THE FOLLOWING WERE ALSO PRESENT

The Rt. Hon Oliver Stanley, M.C., M.P., President of the Board of Trade.	Mr. J. W. Dulanty, C.B., C.B.E., High Commissioner for Éire.
The Rt. Hon. W.S. Morrison, M.C., K.C., M.P., Minister of Agriculture and Fisheries.	

Secretary   Mr. W.D. Wilkinson, D.S.O., M.C.

FINANCE
SIR JOHN SIMON reminded the Conference that the discussion on finance had not been completed at the morning's Meeting. The suggestion before the

Conference was that Éire should pay this country a compromise figure, in the form of a lump sum settlement. He would suggest that no part of this single capital payment should be 'labelled' as representing any of the existing items due by Éire to this country. The total would in any event be low enough to make it clear that the capital equivalent of the Land Annuities was not included in it.

The two sides were not at the moment agreed as to what the lump sum should be. It did not seem to him (Sir John Simon) necessary that the gap should be bridged that day. The meetings were going to be resumed shortly, and it was the hope of all those present that a global agreement would result. That agreement would cover defence and trade questions as well as finance, and there was no necessity to reach finality on one of the items now. In the interval before the meetings were resumed, the Treasury would keep in touch with the Dublin Ministry of Finance.

MR. DE VALERA said that for his part he would certainly have wished to get nearer to an agreement on finance before the adjournment. He had a fair idea of the financial obligations which he was entering into as a result of his new commitments on defence. He knew of course that a major war was not impossible, and that this would greatly increase those obligations.

He would have liked to be able to give his Cabinet colleagues in Dublin some fairly close indication of the terms of the eventual financial settlement. As it was, he was not clear how Sir John Simon wanted the question left. If Sir John was asking for the capital equivalent of all the former payments, Land Annuities only excepted, he was afraid that was an impossible demand.

SIR JOHN SIMON said that he was suggesting adjourning the discussion on finance because the Éire Delegation were apparently unable to increase their offer. The figures contemplated by the two sides were at present so far apart that an adjournment seemed the best course.

MR. DE VALERA said that he had already indicated that the kind of figure which he had in mind was a single capital payment of some £10,000,000. He did not see how he could improve on this in view of his new defence commitments.

MR. MacENTEE pointed out the objections to a series of annual payments, from the point of view of Éire.

SIR JOHN SIMON enquired whether the Éire Ministers had considered a combined method of payment, i.e. part of the sum due to be met by a single capital payment and part by a series of annual payments.

MR. DE VALERA feared that political considerations would rule out this suggestion. Anything in the nature of annual payments would be the starting point for a new agitation. He wanted to avoid this and to bring the chapter to an end. His remarks must be understood as being subject to the Minister for Finance's judgment on what the credit of Éire would stand. It might be that Mr. MacEntee would have to raise loans for the capital equipment of the defence forces.

MR. MACDONALD suggested that there might not be so much objection to annual payments if they were not being transmitted across the Irish sea.

Could not the pensions payable to citizens of Éire be dealt with on an annual basis as before?

MR. DE VALERA said that it was quite out of the question to keep up an annual series of payments in respect of these pensions. They were paid for services rendered to the United Kingdom, not to Éire.

The line he would propose to take in defending a single capital payment would be somewhat as follows. 'My desire was to bring to an end the economic war, with all the bad feeling which it has caused. I wanted to lay a foundation for good relations between the two countries. There was no way of securing this without making a lump sum payment. For that reason I recommend the payment for approval. I decline to relate it to any particular item among the payments formerly made to the United Kingdom'.

If his supporters took the trouble to make the calculation they would see from the size of the capital payment that it could not include the capital equivalent of the Land Annuities. The question would then become one of what he could ask the people of Éire to pay, not one of principle.

MR. MacENTEE said that Mr. MacDonald's suggestion was open to several objections. For one thing, the Éire citizens who received the pensions might dislike the pensions machinery being handed over to the Dublin Government.

SIR JOHN SIMON said that he was willing to accept the principle of a single capital payment, which might be absolutely without any 'label' and without any explanation – save one on the lines just suggested by Mr. de Valera.

MR. CHAMBERLAIN appealed to the Éire Delegation to consider the proposal seriously. The capital equivalent of the existing payments due by Éire was £104.05 millions. Of this total £78,000,000 was on account of Land Annuities. If the £78,000,000 were wiped out only some £26,000,000 would remain. If that £26,000,000 was the total of Éire's lump sum payment what excuse would there be for anybody ascribing it to the Land Annuities?

It was true that there was a pretty big gap between £26,000,000 and the £10,000,000 which Mr. de Valera had offered.

In reply to a question by Mr. MacEntee, SIR JOHN SIMON explained that the £104.05 millions included a figure of £5.85 millions on account of compensation for damage to property.

MR. MacENTEE said that his Government were prepared to continue paying this compensation on an annual basis. Would not this reduce the United Kingdom Government's claim from £26,000,000 to about £20,000,000?

MR. DE VALERA was afraid that public opinion in his country would not be happy about continuing the compensation payments. He believed the annual £250,000 for this item to be the actuarial equivalent of an original capital sum of about £5,000,000. The ordinary person in Éire was not an actuary and would think that his representatives were paying far more than was due.

MR. MacENTEE said that he was not satisfied with the figures of capital equivalents furnished by the United Kingdom Delegation – i.e. leaving Land Annuities and compensation for damage to property out of account. The figures in question were:-

R.I.C. Pensions in Éire	£9.1	millions
R.I.C. Pensions outside Éire	£3.2	millions
Judicial, etc. Pensions	£ .4	millions
Local Loans	£7.35	millions

He disputed this last item. According to his calculation it should be £3.9 millions.

MR. CHAMBERLAIN again drew attention to the inadequacy from the United Kingdom standpoint of Mr. de Valera's offer of £10,000,000. Mr. de Valera had referred many times to the difficulty of commending this or that proposal to the people of Éire. Did he realise how difficult it would be to justify to the people of this country any further reduction in the payments due to them, beyond a reduction of £78,000,000, i.e. the capital equivalent of the Land Annuities? It could certainly only be considered if compensation were made for it in some other part of the all-round settlement.

MR. DE VALERA quite saw Mr. Chamberlain's argument. From their own point of view United Kingdom Ministers had made a big concession.

The Irish point of view was very different. He did not ask the United Kingdom Delegation to accept his contention, but he was prepared to argue that most of the items in the list rested on a very shaky foundation. For example, R.I.C. Pensions were entirely a matter for the United Kingdom. The Land Annuities were a thoroughly unjustified payment, and the Local Loans item was one which ought to have been extinguished under the agreement of December, 1925. He did not believe that these items would survive examination by a fair-minded arbitrator.

The two sides approached the matter from very different angles. For example, the political separation between the two countries was nothing else but a dissolution of partnership – in which the United Kingdom had gone off with all the assets of the partnership. There was no excuse for sending Éire away empty-handed. Complete bankruptcy on the part of the United Kingdom would have been the only justification.

Whatever the merits of the case, the Éire Delegation as a result of the present discussions had accepted the principle of a single capital payment. It only remained to fix this at an amount which should not bear unfairly on the Irish people.

He wished to remind the Conference once more that he had undertaken to place a new and substantial burden on the shoulders of his tax payers on account of Defence. It was his duty now to see to it that the double burden (Defence plus Capital Payment) was not too crushing.

MR. CHAMBERLAIN suggested that it would not be necessary for Mr. de Valera to paint the picture in such gloomy colours when he got back to Éire. He would be entitled, if he wished, to make a great deal of the fact that the United Kingdom Government had agreed to wipe out the Land Annuities payments. It was true that a considerable unbridged gap remained between the United Kingdom figure of £26,000,000 and the Éire figure of £10,000,000. Neither side, however, had abandoned hope of agreement. It would be very premature to do so. At the present stage of negotiations, however, it seemed impossible to carry the matter further.

It was agreed that the discussion on finance could not be carried further at the present stage of the negotiations.

TRADE
MR. STANLEY reported that a joint Ministerial meeting had been held that morning, and that Éire officials had been in negotiation with United Kingdom officials throughout the day. Negotiations were going ahead without interruption.

ADJOURNMENT OF CONFERENCE AND DATE FOR RESUMPTION
MR. STANLEY went on to say that the negotiations for a trade agreement would take between three and four weeks on the most favourable assumptions. MR. DE VALERA and MR. LEMASS believed that if work was carried on at intense pressure the negotiations ought not to take more than one week.
MR. STANLEY promised that so far as the United Kingdom Departments were concerned the pace of the negotiations would not be allowed to slacken. He suggested, however, that the task of the United Kingdom negotiators was much more complicated than that of the representatives of Éire. The Éire demands would presumably relate to a small number of important agricultural commodities. The United Kingdom demands would relate to a very large number of industrial commodities. Some of these commodities would be quite small, but consultation would nevertheless be required with the industries concerned.
MR. DE VALERA thought that a way out might be found by means of a general formula.
MR. STANLEY said that this possibility had already been explored. It had been found, however, that the exceptions were so numerous that the suggestion was not worth pursuing. He thought Mr. Lemass was in agreement with him on this.
MR. DE VALERA said that he was very anxious that the interval between the two stages of the Conference should not be long. What he would wish to do when he got back to Dublin was to lay the position, as it existed on the adjournment of Ministerial negotiations, before his Cabinet colleagues,[1] and also before one or two selected representatives of his party. Apart from that he would wish to keep silence. In practice it would be extremely difficult to do so. He would be bombarded with questions from every possible angle. In addition, a whole crop of rumours was certain to start.
MR. CHAMBERLAIN appreciated these difficulties. Very similar difficulties would arise in this country.

PRESS COMMUNIQUÉ
The discussion now centred on the Press communiqué to be issued at the close of the Meeting.
On the proposal being made that the communiqué should state that at the meetings during the day further consideration had been given to questions

---

[1] See below No. 132.

of defence, finance, trade and agriculture, MR. DE VALERA said that this list of subjects would be very embarrassing to him. It would indicate clearly that at the actual adjournment of the Conference no attention had been given to the partition issue.

He admitted that in the circumstances it was extremely difficult to decide whether to include a reference to partition or not.

MR. CHAMBERLAIN suggested the substitution of the phrase 'Further consideration was given to matters arising out of questions already discussed'.

This suggestion was adopted.

It was next considered in what form mention should be made of the date for the resumption of the Conference after the interval.

MR. CHAMBERLAIN pointed out that it would be undesirable for the Conference to resume just before the Northern Ireland elections, which were fixed for February 9th.

The discussion then turned upon the inclusion of a phrase at the end of the communiqué indicating that the meetings of Ministers would be resumed either 'about the middle of next month' or 'before the middle of next month'. After some discussion, it was agreed to use neither of these phrases, but to conclude the communiqué with the words 'to be resumed as soon as the necessary data are available for further conversations'.

DR. RYAN pointed out that it would be very difficult at the Press interview to refuse to give some indication of the length of the adjournment contemplated.

It was agreed that it should be indicated informally at the Press interview that the adjournment was for not more than a few weeks.

The Press communiqué was then approved in the form contained in the Appendix to the present Minutes.[1]

MR. DE VALERA said that on behalf of his colleagues and himself he wished to thank [the] United Kingdom Ministers for the friendly spirit they had shown during the three day's discussions. Everything of course had not gone as the representatives of Éire would have wished, but it would not have been possible for matters to be tackled in a better spirit. He was hopeful of a successful issue, resulting in the beginning of an era of better relations between the two countries.

MR. CHAMBERLAIN said that on behalf of [the] United Kingdom Ministers he cordially reciprocated this wish. He looked forward to the resumption of the discussions.

The Meeting then adjourned.+
+ On the adjournment Mr. MacDonald handed to Mr. de Valera copies numbered 1 to 7 of the 'Draft outline for Defence Agreement' as revised after the Fourth Meeting of the Conference held earlier in the day.[2]

---

[1] See below No. 130.
[2] See above No. 127.

No. 130 NAI DT S10389

Press communiqué following the conclusion of discussions on 19 January 1938
LONDON, 19 January 1938

PRESS COMMUNIQUÉ
At meetings held at 10 o'clock this morning, at 12 noon and at 3.0 o'clock this afternoon between representatives of the Government of Éire and representatives of the Government of the United Kingdom further consideration was given to matters arising out of questions already discussed.

While no agreement has yet been reached upon any of these questions, which are closely connected with one another, it was felt that the discussions have proceeded far enough to justify a more detailed examination of a number of points by officials of the respective governments.

This examination will proceed forthwith and pending its completion the meetings of Ministers will be suspended, to be resumed as soon as the necessary data are available for further conversations.

[initialled] MOM[1]

No. 131 UCDA P67/156

Letter from James J. McElligott to Seán MacEntee (Dublin)
LONDON, 20 January 1938

My dear Minister,
1. I saw the Treasury people again today. They had been in touch once more with the Chancellor of the Exchequer and according to their information their claim still stood at a figure of £26,000,000 being the difference between the total estimated value of the sum alleged to be due by us, £104,000,000 less the estimated capital value of the Land Purchase Annuities, £78,000,000. This net figure of £26,000,000 was, they contended, exclusive of the capital value of the Damage to Property Compensation Annuity which they put at £5,850,000. I expressed surprise at this which was quite contrary to the impression conveyed in the course of Ministerial discussions. Without the Compensation Annuity the items claimed could not make up a total of £26,000,000, being as follows:-

R.I.C. (Internal)	9.1	Million Pounds
R.I.C. (External)	3.2	" "
Civil and Judicial Pensions	.4	" "
Local Loans	7.0	" "

19.7

2. They then pursued another tack which was briefly as follows:-
(a) The Chancellor puts aside all labels. He is collecting four and a quarter million pounds in duties and getting £250,000 per annum Compensation Annuity.

---

[1] This press communiqué was initialled by Maurice Moynihan on 9 February 1938.

(b)   The Chancellor would be prepared to reduce the duties so as to yield £2,000,000 a year – period not specified.
(c)   The Chancellor and the Prime Minister are agreed on the advantages from our point of view of the lump sum and would regard £26,000,000 rounded down to £25,000,000 as a basis for discussion, to cover everything except Compensation Annuity.
(d)   This takes account of the fact that if we get back the Ports considerable military expenditure, capital and recurring, will necessarily arise in respect of them as well as in respect of other defence measures.
(e)   Despite the figures produced to them they repeated that the £25,000,000 was in addition to the Compensation Annuity.

3. I said I perfectly understood their own unwillingness to discuss labels in as much as their estimate under each particular label seemed to be grossly exaggerated. In regard to Local Loans the capital value outstanding was now only 3.9 million pounds as compared with their estimate of 7, while the R.I.C. (Internal) should be only about 6.5 million pounds as compared with their 9.1 million pounds. The R.I.C. (External) I completely rejected while the Civil Pensions of .4 million pounds I promised to go into if supplied with figures.

4. They then brought in some actuarial people who supplied me with a number of figures which I will examine tonight and I have arranged for another meeting at the Treasury tomorrow.

5. Leydon is meeting the Board of Trade people tomorrow and will remain in more or less continuous session until he gets finished. Twomey tells me that the Agriculture people informed him today that they might not be ready until Monday, but in the meantime he is having informal discussions with Street with a view to expediting consideration of our proposals.

I hope all the party had a successful journey across and that the weather was more favourable than on our previous trip.

With kindest regards,
Yours sincerely,
[signed] J.J. McELLIGOTT

P.S. We expect to have tomorrow the minutes of meetings, which will clear up the point about the Compensation Annuity.

[initialled] J.J. McE[1]

No. 132 NAI DT S10389

Extract from the minutes of a meeting of the Cabinet
(G.C. 1/4) (Item 3)
DUBLIN, 21 January 1938

CONFERENCE WITH BRITISH GOVERNMENT, 1938
The Taoiseach gave a general report on the matters discussed at the Conference with the representatives of the British Government.

[initialled] POC[2]

---

[1]   The postscript to this document is handwritten by McElligott.
[2]   Padraig Ó Cinnéide, Assistant Secretary to the Cabinet.

No. 133 UCDA P150/2183

Letter from Joseph P. Walshe to Eamon de Valera (Dublin)
(Secret)

LONDON, 22 January 1938

Dear President,

Thanks for your letter of the 21st January.[1] Since your departure I have continued to impress on Harding the necessity of doing something in relation to the Six Counties. I read for him the Washington Cable of the 19th January containing Press comments on the Conference.[2] (As you are I am sure aware the American Press has adopted the attitude which you formulated in the sound film on Wednesday night.) I intend to leave a copy with him immediately so that he may show it to his Secretary of State. Meanwhile I am asking Sean Murphy to send to me all the good Press comments available from the United States. It seems to me that American opinion is playing a very important part in the negotiations.

I think that it would help very much if you would make a concrete suggestion as to the first step which the British should take towards bringing partition to an end. You will remember that Harding told me during our first conversations immediately after Christmas that any concrete suggestion should come from our side. At present I cannot see them going any further than agreeing to the establishment of a common organ which would constitute a means of co-operation between the Belfast Government and ours, and which would at the same time be external evidence that the process of unification has begun. Naturally I shall have to be very careful in my talks with Harding about this matter, and the more evidence of discontent with partition (both in Ireland and in America) I can have the better my case will be.

While I am pressing the matter with Harding the High Commissioner will maintain pressure, as he has been doing, on the Secretary of State.

I hope that, notwithstanding the last paragraph of your letter, you are fundamentally optimistic about the ultimate issue of the negotiations. After the Six Counties elections, when the negotiations resume, the British will have a freer hand in regard to doing something positive and if the responsible American press could be induced to continue the campaign in favour of unity as a factor of world peace I have a very real hope that the British will take some substantial step towards the desired goal.

With great respect and esteem,
I remain,
Dear President,
Yours sincerely,
[signed] J.P. WALSHE

---

[1] Not located.
[2] Not printed.

No. 134 UCDA P67/156

My dear Minister,
I have talked to various people at the Treasury on Saturday and today and have got further figures from them, the effect of which and the various arguments about which are summarised in the following paragraphs. These paragraphs should be read in the light of the letter to me from the Government Actuary's Department of 22nd January 1938 and the Treasury memorandum (undated) which reached me on Saturday.[1] A copy of both these documents is enclosed. The Table referred to in the final paragraph on the second page of the Treasury memorandum has not yet been received.

Local Loans:

(1)	Initial British Claim	£7	million
(2)	Revised British Claim	7.35	"
(3)	Second Revised British Claim	6.92	"

The Local Loans Fund did not get any of the Special Duties until 1936-7 when £350,000 was paid by Exchequer and in 1937-8 (current year) £125,000 is expected to be paid.

These amounts were one-half the balance available after meeting the various payments excluding (i) Local Loans Fund and (ii) Sinking Funds on Land advances. Applying the same system in respect of years 1932-33.....1935-6 (4 years) they credit the Fund with £715,000.

The figure of £6.92 million is arrived at by adding to the present value at $3^1/2\%$ of the remaining payments the accumulated excess of the payments due between 1932 and 1938 over what the British now regard (on an arbitrary basis) as having been available in those years out of the Special Duties. These items are respectively £4.20 million and £2.72 million.

We cannot accept the £2.72 millions on the grounds that it is immaterial to us whether the Fund was actually recouped out of the Duties by the Treasury or whether in fact such Duties yielded the necessary amounts.

We ought accept either of the following:-

(i)   Their own statement that 'The Treasury consider that the only equitable method to calculate the capital equivalent is to discount future annuities at a rate of interest roughly equivalent to that at which the United Kingdom Government could borrow, namely $3^1/2\%$.' On this basis the liability as at 31st March 1938 is £4.195 million, as at present is £4.155 million

      (The only disadvantageous point in this arrangement is that we acquiesce in the rate of interest which is that at which the United Kingdom Government can borrow. If basis of negotiations is mutual equity should not rate at which Irish Government can borrow be taken into account? This is example of British play for safety).

---

[1]   Not printed.

(ii) The liability in (i) is somewhat higher than the capital outstanding according to the Schedule in their own accounts, namely £4.126 million.

The British contend that the Schedule should be ignored because the £600,000 annuity for 20 years was accepted on the basis of an average price of £81.13.3 to liquidate a liability of £10,343,000 and that the present price of Local Loans stock is very greatly in excess of £80. In reply to this I have argued

(a) that the £10,343,000 was a *nominal* liability, i.e. it was the nominal amount of stock outstanding

(b) that the actual liability which the British wrote into their accounts in respect of it was £8,446,000 (which was on the basis of the average price). It might be argued that they should only have written in the amount according to the then current market price which was about 65 (instead of 81) – but this argument should be used with caution because it would involve a repercussion inasmuch as the annuity should, for consistency, be calculated on an equivalent interest basis.

The point under (b) really is that the *actual* liability was much less than the £10,343,000

(c) The present price is not *very greatly* in excess of £81.13.3 (not 80 as they say) – being about 88. In this connection they seem to have overlooked the fact that the price was constantly less than 70 from 1926 to 1931 during which period they must have been able to purchase considerably more stock than the Schedule shows could have been written off on the basis of a price of £81.13.3d.[1]

Apart from Local Loans the following claims arise:-

	Original British Claim	Revised British Claim	Further Revised British Claim
1. R.I.C. (Internal) Pensions	9.1	9.1	?
2. R.I.C. (External) Pensions	3.2	3.2	?
3. Civil and Judicial Pensions	.4	.4	?
4. Administration and Audit Expenses		.15	?
	12.7	12.85	£11.7

The reduction in the British claim by 1.15 million is due to changing the date at which liability is calculated from 31st December 1936 to 31st March 1938. The method adopted for this purpose is a reasonable approximation and the computations are correct on figures submitted, and I doubt whether much, if any, advantage to us would accrue from investigation of precise figures which Harvey[2] says would take 7 to 10 days. In any event they would only relate to 30th September 1937 and would have to be further adjusted.

---

[1] The last sentence on the original document (at this point) is missing, the document appears to have been torn.

[2] Sir Percy Harvey (1887-1946), Deputy Government Actuary (1936-9).

Suggestions for reducing claim of £11.7 million:-
(a) This includes R.I.C. (External) which in 1936 was £3.2 million and on proportionate basis would be £2.9 million in 1938. On grounds that the Externals include a large proportion of older men it is suggested that the proportionate basis is not quite appropriate and 3.0 or 3.05 might be defended.
(b) What about 'Disbandment' and 'Others' allocation? This to some extent cuts across the 'internal' and 'external' division and is inconsistent with it.
(c) The capitalisation of the £10,000 a year at $3^1/2\%$ giving .15 is on basis that this sum is payable for about 22 years. This seems excessive and should be reduced more rapidly. We should knock off the .05 i.e. £50,000.
(d) All calculations are at $3^1/2\%$ interest. There may be a case for higher rate.

I have arranged to supply the British on paper with a number of the foregoing arguments, but do not like to do so until I have seen the official minutes of the Ministerial discussions which are not yet forthcoming. The absence of these is a considerable handicap as all the Treasury officials with whom I have had contact have had access to them or actually have copies of them. Walshe has been expecting to receive them daily for the last three or four days, but up to late this afternoon they had not arrived.

I have arranged an interview with Sir Warren Fisher at the Treasury. While, as you will see from the figures, I have made some impression on the officers lower down, it has not been as much as I had hoped.

Yours sincerely,
[signed] J.J. MCELLIGOTT

No. 135 UCDA P67/156

Letter from James J. McElligott to Seán MacEntee (Dublin)
LONDON, 25 January 1938

My dear Minister,
I enclose herewith draft of a memorandum[1] which I have prepared in criticism of the Treasury memorandum which I forwarded with my letter of yesterday.[2] You will notice that, taking the items separately, the lowest figure to which I am able to get, on the arguments made is, £12 millions. My letter to you of the 21st instant[3] reached a figure of £10 million by viewing the matter from another angle, namely by attempting to beat down the £25 million which I was given to understand included the Compensation Annuity. Apart from the fact that this approach to the problem produced a lower net figure for the British claim than the total (at that time) of the figures under separate heads, and that our figure for Local Loans should have been £4.1 millions

---

[1] See enclosure below.
[2] See above No. 134.
[3] Not printed.

instead of £3.9 millions, subsequent discussions and the correspondence from the Government Actuary's Department make it clear that the estimate in respect of the liability under pensions was arrived at on a quite impartial basis and contained no margin for contingencies to safeguard the Treasury. Accordingly the only reduction which could be effected was in respect of bringing forward the figures by two years, and I am afraid that the £10 millions could hardly be defended now.

2. I can see no ground for further attack with a view to reducing the £12 millions unless we introduce some argument about the 'Disbandment' element of the R.I.C. You will recollect that you were committing to paper certain representations the purpose of which was to refuse liability for pre-Treaty pensions and to accept a 'fair' share of the disbandment pensions. As the point is primarily a political one which may, as I indicated in my letter of yesterday,[1] cut across our attempts to avoid the liability in respect of the external element, I would welcome some guidance from you in the matter. You will no doubt have noticed that the Government Actuary's liability of £12.3 millions for R.I.C. pensions as on 1st April 1936 was divisible into £9.4 for disbandment cases and £2.9 for others.

3. I had a long discussion at the Treasury today with Sir Warren Fisher. Like all other British officials he was courteous and anxious to help. He spoke at length on the desirability of a settlement from the point of view of both countries but seemed disappointed that further progress had not been made in that direction before the Ministers left for Dublin. He hoped that negotiations would be resumed at the earliest possible date and brought to a successful conclusion. His general conversation was all on these familiar lines.

I put it to him that he could contribute to the desired end by inducing a more reasonable approach and more rational methods of calculation in regard to the various financial matters outstanding. His reply was that they had already wiped out exactly three-fourths of their claim, that is £78 millions out of £104 millions (although they could have collected it all if they wished) and that in regard to the remainder they had made substantial reductions in deference to our views but that we had shown no desire to accommodate ourselves to their point of view. From £26 million they had come down to something between £18.2 millions and £18.6 millions and could hardly be expected to go on making further reductions especially as we had not shifted from our original offer of £10 millions. I elaborated our various reasons for differing even with their lowest figure, including the point about defence expenditure. He took the latter very well and said that no Treasury man could dispute the fact that all estimates of defence outlay for any purpose whatever were liable to be grossly understated. He said the views of military and naval men on the cost of modern defences were entirely worthless and that a multiplier should be always used.

I am seeing Warren Fisher again tomorrow and we will continue our discussion.

---

[1] See above No. 134.

Unless you have something further for me to do here I was thinking of returning before the end of the week, on say, Friday.

Yours sincerely,
[signed] J.J. McELLIGOTT

[Enclosure]
1. The Treasury memorandum of the 24th instant indicates that the United Kingdom claim in respect of items in dispute, other than Land Annuities and Compensation for Damage to Property, amounts as at 1st April 1938 to £18,572,000. The Department of Finance is unable to accept this figure for reasons explained in the following paragraphs which deal separately with (1) pensions and (2) local loans, in accordance with the arrangement in the Treasury memorandum.

(1) Pensions
2. The British claim under this heading is £11,653,000, comprising the following items:-
(a)   R.I.C. pensions
(b)   Judicial, Civil and revenue Department pensions (excluding Post Office Pensions)
(c)   Administrative and minor expenditure (including cost of audit and annuities under the Railways (Ireland) Act 1896 and the Marine Works (Ireland) Act, 1902).
The figure of £11,653,000 is arrived at by making an estimate of the liability as at the 1st April 1938 from figures supplied by the Government Actuary in respect of items (a) and (b) as at 1st April 1936 and by treating item (c) in a similar manner.
3. The Department of Finance agrees to accept the figures furnished by the Government Actuary as being a fair estimate at $3^1/2\%$ of the outstanding amounts payable to pensioners and further accepts, as a working arrangement, the approximate method of re-assessing the amounts as at the 1st April 1938. The sum of £11,653,000 cannot, however, be accepted as a liability of the Irish Government for the following reasons:-

(i) The Actuary's estimate of the capital value of R.I.C. pensions as on 1st April 1936 amounts to £12.3 millions. It is understood that this amount is divisible as to £9.1 millions pensions payable in Ireland and £3.2 millions payable outside Ireland. The Department of Finance is unable to assume liability in respect of pensions payable outside Ireland and, according to the figures supplies, this would mean a reduction of £3.2 millions in the total of £12.3 millions. The corresponding reduction (on a proportionate basis) in the liability as on 1st April 1938 would be about £3 millions.

(ii) It is suggested that the amount taken as the capital value of item (c) is excessive. As $3^1/2\%$ is the basis adopted in the calculations, the figure of £150,000 regarded as the capital value of an annual sum of £10,000 presumes a continuance of that payment annually for about 22 years. Having regard to the fact that administration charges will fall not only because of decreasing numbers of pensioners but also arising out of any settlement which may now be reached, it is contended that a sum of £100,000 ought to meet the charges under this heading.

4. On the basis of these considerations, the figure of £11.7 millions should be reduced by £3.05 millions, leaving £8.65 millions.

Local Loans

5. The British claim under this heading is fixed at £6,919,000, which is arrived at by adding together the following two items:-

(a) Excess (accumulated with interest at $3^1/2\%$) of sums not paid by the Irish Government in the years 1932 to 1938 over the amounts paid and amounts purported to have been paid by the Exchequer to the Local Loans Fund in that period; and

(b) The present value at $3^1/2\%$ of the remaining payments falling to be made.

6. The Department of Finance cannot accept any liability under the heading (a). The British Government imposed Special Duties on Irish imports for the purpose of recouping itself in respect of the sums withheld and the Irish Government cannot be held responsible for any British domestic arrangement which did not adequately recoup the Local Loans Fund nor, indeed, for any insufficiency in the total amount of Special Duties actually collected.

7. It is agreed that the basis suggested by the Treasury for calculating the capital sum outstanding in respect of the remaining annuity payments, namely, to discount future annuities at an appropriate rate of interest, is a fair one. It is observed that the rate of interest suggested is $3^1/2\%$, being roughly equivalent to that at which the United Kingdom Government can borrow. It has to be borne in mind that a lump sum payment calculated at such a rate of interest would fully compensate the Treasury but it is suggested that some regard should be had to the higher rate of interest at which the Irish Government can borrow. From this point of view it seems reasonable that the liability should be computed from the Schedule which appeared in the Local Loans Fund account 1926 – which involves a rate of interest of about £3.13.6. The amounts on the two bases are £4,195,000 and £4,126,450 respectively.

8. It is observed that the Treasury do not consider that the calculation should be made with reference to the Schedule mentioned in the previous paragraph having regard particularly to the fact that the present price of Local Loans Stock is very greatly in excess of 80. According to Stock Exchange Reports the current price of this Stock is about 88 and it is thus only about 6 points above the average price of £81.13.3. upon which the initial liability was calculated. This difference in price is much less than that which existed in 1926 when the current market price was between 60 and 65 and the liability in respect of the *nominal* amount of outstanding stock was written into the British Accounts at the price of £81.13.3. It is also pertinent to remark that the price of the stock was much less than 70 during the whole of the period 1926 to 1931. During this period, considerably more purchases and cancellation of stock could have been made and accordingly considerably more written off capital account than the schedule actually provided for.

9. Summarising the position in respect of (1) and (2), the Department of Finance contends that the appropriate amount in respect of pensions should be £8.65 millions and in respect of Local Loans £4.1 millions, making a total of £12.75 millions. After allowing for a slightly higher rate of interest in respect of the pensions calculations and rounding to the nearest million, the sum of £12 is proposed as the total liability.

10. It must not be overlooked that in the event of a settlement considerable outlay on the protection of certain ports and harbours will have to be incurred by the Government of Éire. No precise estimate is available as to the possible cost of the various defence measures to be undertaken but a capital figure of nearly £1 million and an annual figure of between $£^1/_2$ million and £1 million have been mentioned. These very substantial sums must be considered as in some degree offsetting the claims of the British Government even when the latter have been reduced to their lowest level. Savings will also result to the British Exchequer as a result of liabilities taken on by Éire.

No. 136 UCDA P150/2836

Letter from Eamon de Valera to Franklin D. Roosevelt (Washington)
(Copy)
DUBLIN, 25 January 1938

Dear Mr. President,

Another great opportunity for finally ending the quarrel of centuries between Ireland and Britain presents itself. The one remaining obstacle to be overcome is that of the Partition of Ireland. The British Government alone have the power to remove this obstacle. If they really have the will they can bring about a united Ireland in a very short time. I have pressed my views upon them, but it is obvious that they recognise only the difficulties and are not fully alive to the great results that would follow a complete reconciliation between the two peoples. Reconciliation would affect every country where the two races dwell together, knitting their national strength and presenting to the world a great block of democratic peoples interested in the preservation of Peace.

Knowing your own interest in this matter, I am writing to ask you to consider whether you could not use your influence to get the British Government to realize what would be gained by reconciliation and to get them to move whilst there is time. In a short while, if the present negotiations fail, relations will be worsened. I am sending this by the hands of a trusty friend, Mr. Frank Gallagher,[1] who is in a position to give you any information you may desire concerning the facts of Partition and their bearing on the relations between Great Britain and Ireland.

I avail of this occasion, Mr. President, to express to you my sincere regard.
[copy letter unsigned]

---

[1] Frank Gallagher (1893-1962), Editor, *Irish Press* (1931-5), Deputy Director, Radio Éireann (1935-40), Director, Government Information Bureau (1940-54).

No. 137 UCDA P150/2183

Letter from Joseph P. Walshe to Eamon de Valera (Dublin)
LONDON, 25 January 1938

Dear President,

I spent some two hours with Harding yesterday on the necessity of doing something substantial and evident on the partition question. I left him in no doubt that unless an inroad were made on partition at this moment of history it would be impossible for you to come to an agreement in relation to defence matters.

After this conversation I am, if possible, more convinced than before that an agreement which excludes defence would be of no real value to the British. I also feel that in our case such an agreement if it were feasible would be only postponing the evil day. The British are hankering after an agreement because it is essential for them to close the ranks as far as the Commonwealth is concerned, and still more because they want to get the goodwill and if possible the actual co-operation of the United States in the difficulties which are now facing them. Harding listened to all I had to say most carefully. I gave him the actual words of your letter[1] and he can hardly have any illusions left about the possibility of a settlement without some concrete step towards unification.

At the same time I can see in Harding a pretty good representative of the main body of the Unionist party, and he did not hesitate to repeat what he had said to me so frequently before that the one thing the British Government could not do was to sacrifice their internal unity. It is clear that they value this internal unity more than the extra degree of goodwill and friendship which a settlement with us would bring them from America. They have set very definite limits to the concessions which they can make to us in relation to partition, and it is because these limits are somewhat narrow they are ready to give us practically everything in all the other matters in dispute. They still want a concrete suggestion from you. Do you think it wise to make one? If left to themselves I feel that they will hardly go beyond the Council of Ireland, slightly elaborated, and more definite with regard to dates of meetings and functions. In fact I think whether we make a suggestion or not that some such organ, which might be regarded as a symbol that the process of unification has begun, will be the limit of their concessions. With regard to the method they appear to be ready, if the suggestion is made by you or approved by you, to press its acceptance on Craigavon. Their fear of their party seems to be genuine, and Harding urged very strongly with me that we should not ask them to do anything which would make the position of the Prime Minister difficult. The slightest hint of coercion or of any intention to put an early end to partition would destroy the Government's position here and would make it impossible for them to make any settlement at all. I think we should take this as a relatively fair estimate of the difficulties of the British Government. The strongest element in the party seems to be as fanatical as the Belfast Government itself.

---

[1] Possibly a reference to No. 136 above.

I shall continue by every means in my power to persuade Harding of the gravity of the situation and to try and inform you as nearly as I can to what precise point you can push them without running the risk of getting nothing at all on partition or on the other matters being discussed.

I have given to Harding the Press telegrams from America and I shall continue to do so as I receive them. I am of course emphasising especially strongly the position of the Nationalists in the partitioned area. The High Commissioner argued in substantially the same manner with MacDonald. This afternoon we are trying to get Pakenham[1] to write an answer to Craigavon's letter in today's 'Daily Telegraph'.

We shall keep the chief American Press correspondents here inspired in so far as it can be done: material sent from London seems to have more authority than the same material sent from Dublin.

As Sean Murphy has told you I feel that a direct appeal to Cordell Hull through MacWhite to move the British to take some concrete step would be more effective than an appeal going indirectly from the American Minister in Dublin who probably does not cut much ice with the State Department. A word from Cordell Hull to the British Ambassador in Washington would have more weight than all the propaganda we can do put together.

Meanwhile I have a very good hope that we shall secure all we desire in non partition matters and enough in relation to that question to enable us to carry out what the British regard as the essentials for an agreement.

I remain,
Dear President,
With great respect and esteem,
Yours sincerely,
[signed] J.P. WALSHE

No. 138 UCDA P150/2179

Letter from John W. Dulanty to Eamon de Valera
LONDON, 26 January 1938

Dear President,[2]

I enclose herewith four copies – numbered 1, 2, 3, and 4 – of the Notes of the five Meetings with the British Government in London on the 15th, 16th, and 17th of this month.[3]

Mr. Walshe and myself are the only people on our side who have seen the Notes and I arranged with Mr. MacDonald that the British would not circulate them until we had agreed to such circulation.

---

[1] Frank Aungier Pakenham (Seventh Earl of Longford) (1905-2001), British Labour politician, and author (including *Peace by Ordeal* (London, 1935), an account of the 1921 Anglo-Irish Treaty negotiations).

[2] Handwritten.

[3] The dates given by Dulanty are not correct. Meetings with the British government began on the afternoon of 17 January. See above Nos 122, 124, 125, 127, and 129.

In conversations with Mr. MacDonald I have followed closely the line indicated in your note to Mr. Walshe of 21st January.[1]

I reminded Mr. MacDonald how at the first two meetings you had emphasised in terms no one could misunderstand the supreme importance of a United Ireland and I entreated him to try to find some way of doing something substantial and evident on the question of partition.

In reply he said in great confidence and for 'Mr. De Valera's ear only' he had already tried in discussion with Lord Craigavon[2] to find some line which would help us and lead later to a United Ireland. He had unfortunately not been successful. Mr. MacDonald said several times that this was for your ear alone.

If his Prime Minister could go to Lord Craigavon and say that the British had reached an agreement with us and that the agreement was working he thought something might be done, but he was afraid any plans short of an agreement between ourselves and them would be of no avail. The way to begin a solution of the Partition riddle as he saw it was to show Lord Craigavon an agreement working satisfactorily – anything less he thought would not be seriously regarded in the Six Counties.

Mr. MacDonald suggested that February 14th, 15th and 16th, would be convenient dates for the British to resume the conversations.

I remain, Dear President, with great respect and esteem,

Yours sincerely,

[signed] JOHN W. DULANTY[3]

No. 139 NAI DT S10389

*Extract from the minutes of a meeting of the Cabinet
(G.C. 1/7 A) (Item 1)*

DUBLIN, 3 February 1938

NEGOTIATIONS WITH BRITISH GOVERNMENT, 1938

The Minister for Industry and Commerce[4] reported on the progress of the discussions between the Secretary of his Department (Mr. Seán Leydon) and representatives of the British Board of Trade.

It was agreed that further discussions might proceed on the following basis:-

1. The British Government to undertake that free entry will be granted for Irish products into the United Kingdom Market, i.e. that the Ottawa duties shall be abolished over the whole field and that where there is quantitative restriction on agricultural products the quantities fixed for Irish exports will be sufficient to enable this country to export the whole of its surplus production to the United Kingdom Market.

---

[1] Not located.
[2] In this document, Craigavon's name has been inserted by hand by Dulanty on each occasion it occurs.
[3] Handwritten.
[4] Seán Lemass.

2. The Government of Ireland to undertake that a review shall be made as soon as practicable by the Prices Commission of existing protective duties and other import restrictions in accordance with the principle that such duties and restriction shall not exceed such a level as will afford Irish industries adequate protection against imported products having regard to the relative costs of economical and efficient production, provided that in the application of such principle special consideration may be given to the case of industries not fully established.

It was further agreed that if necessary the word 'reasonable' might be substituted for the word 'adequate' in the seventh line of the formula contained in sub-paragraph 2.

It was decided that while the Irish Representative might intimate to the British Representatives that the Minister for Industry and Commerce agreed to the discussions proceeding on the above basis, the Irish Representative should make it clear that the Minister was not in a position to bind the Government in the matter.

[initialled] POC[1]

No. 140 UCDA P150/2183

Handwritten letter from Joseph P. Walshe to Eamon de Valera (Dublin)
LONDON, 8 February 1938

Dear President,

I haven't sent a report for some time. One day is more or less a repetition of another and I am simply keeping up the pressure on Harding and Batterbee.

There are however some things which deserve particular mention. Last Thursday I saw, with Batterbee, three military members of the Committee of Imperial Defence – Cols Hollis,[2] Lunn and Wing Commander Frazer.[3] They were cold and aloof and rather gave the impression that they were doing the task of the moment from a sense of duty exclusively. I don't think I was entirely wrong in my instinctive reaction that this beginning of a surrender of the defences of Ireland to Irishmen was distasteful to them.

Their curiosity was not excessive. They had before them the information given in our estimates for the current year and they were satisfied when I told them that we should prefer an estimate of our real defensive requirement to one based on our existing equipment and personnel. I gathered generally that they think that an extremely mobile force is best suited to the conditions which would have to be should an attack be made upon our coasts. They wanted to fit into – or to superimpose upon – our present cadre the further elements deemed necessary by them, keeping as close as possible to our present expenditure. They hoped to make up for numbers and for quantity of equipment by extreme mobility. I don't believe their original detailed

---

[1] Padraig Ó Cinnéide, Assistant Secretary to the Cabinet.
[2] Colonel Leslie Chasemore Hollis (1887-1963), Admiralty representative on the Committee of Imperial Defence (1936-46).
[3] Wing Commander Hugh Henry MacLeod Fraser (1896-1962).

questions had any other motive. They have easily available in their war stores dept. all the information they desire. I still feel that the military are suspicious of us and if there is an agreement we shall be obliged in our own interest to remove their suspicions as quickly as possible. Otherwise we shall not get any serious military information and there would be a slight risk of their advice being directed to keeping our forces so small that their aid would have to be asked for immediately on the occurrence of an emergency. There are of course, other reasons why they would not desire an extensive development of our forces until they had got rid of their suspicions. I thought it better to remark in confidence to Batterbee that there would have to be an easier atmosphere engendered before our military people and theirs got talking together; that, in fact, the British would have to examine the foundations of their suspicions of us with the same care as we examined the cause of our suspicions of them. There would have to be a freer atmosphere if we were to work together.

He will have conveyed this hint to the members of the C.I. Defence and I am earnestly hoping that when our military colleagues meet these officers they will not have the same cause to freeze up as I had.

This is a relatively trivial matter, and I should not have reported it did I not think it fitted with the background of the atmosphere of hostility which has always existed in military circles here – and to meet which we have to take definite measures. When talking with you on this subject I have occasionally referred to information given to me by a remote relative and friend of mine who was until recently lecturing in the Staff college. He had told me about modifications made in lectures because of the presence of Irish officers – of the very marked hostility in the army here to a settlement which would deprive them of the treaty rights in time of danger. He had suggested that Military Conferences of some kind would diminish the hostility and distrust felt towards us. My last conversation with him was in April 1937 and I had met him off and on since 1925. There had been no change of attitude during all those years.

I hope to have their draft plan and estimate on Saturday.

Partition is of course the main burden of all my talks with Batterbee and Harding (I see the former when Harding is not there). They continue to emphasize the extreme difficulty in which their P.M. will find himself when facing the problem of doing something about Partition. Harding repeats that Chamberlain 'can do nothing fundamental', and enlarges on the influence of the N. Eastern Unionists in England. I point out the injustice of the principle of partition, and emphasize with all the figures and quotations at my disposal the disgraceful position of the minority in the six counties. I think this repetition is beginning to have a serious effect and I regret, more and more, each time I talk to these officials that we did not prepare for the negotiations a year or so ago by sending them a series of despatches on the treatment of the minority.

Your statements to the Press have had good results, though I don't think they were enthusiastic about your German parallel in the message to Havas.

I am keeping in touch every day and endeavouring to sum up the position – seeing whether it is more or less favourable to us.

They still want a settlement. You have seen from Sean Leydon's report that they are ready to go the whole hog in trade – or nearly so – and that they will give us free entry for our agricultural products. Defence is the price and without it we shall get nothing. The millions will go up or down according to the extent to which you modify or accept the existing formula. If it remains as it is or substantially so you will certainly get them down to your ten millions.

Harding told me yesterday that they felt dissatisfied about the defence formula, and would ask for something much more definite if we insisted on introducing changes to suit our point of view. That may, or may not be, bluff but we shall have a hard task to get all the concessions we hope for without a substantially similar defence formula. We have no chance whatever in existing circumstances of getting any form of Parliament for the whole of Ireland. Even a form of council plus a formal renunciation of the principle of partition will be hard enough to get.

The crisis is not sufficiently obvious to their own people to enable them to force the pace on the six-counties question. They continue to argue that the first real step is an understanding on defence matters between London and Dublin. There is some stratum of truth in this and I think we should not forget that cooperation is a dynamic thing depending entirely on our will at any given moment. If we find that they are inclined to forget partition we shall have it in our power to show them by inaction or positive opposition that unity is our constant aim.

If we get the British out of the ports and establish a fairly effective defence force we shall be in a much better position to talk to them on unity. I should be ready to make real sacrifices to get rid of the Treaty. The sacrifice we are asked to make in defence is more apparent than real, because it is the only means of preventing the possible permanent loss of our independence in the almost certain crisis of a Great War.

I hope they will not have got very far with the Italians before the resumption of the negotiations. Some progress towards an agreement with the Italians and a pro-British policy resulting from the changes in Germany – would make the going more difficult for us on the 21st February. However the Germans are not likely to change so quickly in that direction, and the Japanese are getting more aggressive in the Hong Kong area, so I hope the factors will still be in our favour. However if the British agree to the postponement to the 21st we should not suggest a further postponement. The possible gains in relation to the six county issue might be offset by serious losses in the general atmosphere if world conditions became modified in favour of the British.

Although I should like a few days at home, I shall feel happier, on the whole, if I can remain in touch with things here. I think the advantages are on the side of my not leaving until the negotiations are finally over.

I beg to remain, dear President,
with great respect and esteem,
Yours sincerely,
J.P. WALSHE

No. 141 NAI CAB 2/1

Extract from the minutes of a meeting of the Cabinet
(G.C. 1/8) (Item 3)

Dublin, 11 February 1938

RESUMPTION OF DISCUSSIONS WITH THE BRITISH GOVERNMENT

Approval was given for the sending of a Delegation consisting of the Taoiseach, the Minister for Industry and Commerce, the Minister for Finance and the Minister for Agriculture to resume, on Monday, 21st February, 1938, the discussions commenced with the British Government on the 17th January, 1938, on the various outstanding questions at issue between the two countries.

No. 142 UCDA P67/155

Draft letter from Seán MacEntee[1] to Eamon de Valera

Dublin, 17 February 1938

Dear Taoiseach,

In view of the recent Cabinet discussions I feel bound to set out without reserve my personal position for your consideration. The net issue which has now emerged may be stated as follows:-

Provided the British Government is prepared

(1) To abrogate Articles 6 and 7 of the Treaty of 1921, thereby handing over to us the harbour defences of Berehaven, Cobh and Lough Swilly and relinquishing all claim to such other facilities as in time of war or strained relations are reserved to them under these Articles;

(2) To conclude with us a Trade Treaty which would give our products free entry to and preferential treatment in the British Market in return for some lesser concessions from us in regard to their products; and

(3) To settle the financial dispute on the basis of (a) a complete waiver on their part of any claim to the Land Annuities, and (b) an agreement as to what might be paid by us in respect of other items in dispute having regard to (i) the fact that we have contested the validity of the British claims to certain of these items, and (ii) the increased expenditure which we shall be called upon to incur in providing henceforward for the defence of our own territory;

Shall we on our part (a) agree in some such as the following terms, viz. :- The Government of Éire in the exercise of its own sovereignty will defend its territory against all aggressors; or (b) refuse to agree until the British Government shall have taken 'some substantial and effective (or is it 'evident'?) steps to end Partition'.

---

[1] This draft letter of resignation is from MacEntee's personal papers and there is no indication that it was sent to de Valera. The editors have included it because the document shows MacEntee's strong feelings on policy towards Northern Ireland and his perception of the shortcomings of Irish defence policy.

On the net issue which is thus raised I feel strongly that the Government of Éire ought to agree to defend its territory against all aggressors, for the following reasons:-

1. To defend its territory against all aggressors is *in every circumstance*[1] the natural and unavoidable duty of the Government of Éire. *It is not a rational thing, therefore, to refuse to agree to do so.*[2]

2. The proper defence of the twenty-six counties involves agreement, consultation, and co-operation in the defence of the thirty-two, even to the extent in the case of a European War it is almost inevitable that some part of our forces would be posted to the Six Counties. We should therefore be defending all the territory we claim, and to that extent not only should we have prevented the extension of Partition from the political to the strategic plane, but we should have transferred the practicalities of the problem to a milieu in which Great Britain would be as concerned as ourselves to find a solution for them. *I have expressed this view on many occasions in writing and otherwise, e.g. my letter to you dated 20th January, 1937.*[3]

3. The Government through you as its head and Minister for External Affairs *has already stated its policy in this regard*[4] and it is ridiculous to pretend now that when you, who are not only Minister for External Affairs, but Taoiseach (or P.[resident]), leader of the Party, and President of the Organisation, spoke on these matters, you did not speak on behalf of the Government and with the authority of the Government behind you – ~~has already~~ *when you*[5] declared that 'we are not going to allow our territory *under any conditions whatever* to be made use of …. as a base of attack against Britain. We give that *assurance* because we are determined not to be coerced even by Britain herself.' But the assurance given in these terms is of no practical value unless we are prepared to defend our own territory. If we are *in fact*[6] so prepared why cannot we put our hand to a statement to that effect.

4. It is imperative in the interests of the agricultural industry upon which our whole economic life depends that a settlement of the financial dispute with Great Britain should be made upon any terms which we can in honour accept. I regard the terms now in prospect as honourable and favourable terms. *I think it unreasonable for* ~~any~~ *the Government to put the prospective settlement in jeopardy by refusing to agree to do its natural duty by its citizens.*[7]

5. It is likewise imperative that the Government should address itself seriously to the problem of national defence, and take such steps as it can to safeguard the lives and properties of our citizens and to defend our territories against such menace as a European war may bring. I feel that this is a matter which brooks no further delay. Our cities and towns are defenceless against any attack, whether by land, or from the sea or air, by gas or by bomb. The

---

[1]   The words in italic are handwritten by MacEntee.
[2]   This sentence is a handwritten insertion by MacEntee.
[3]   Not located. This sentence is handwritten by MacEntee.
[4]   Handwritten insertion by MacEntee.
[5]   Handwritten insertion by MacEntee.
[6]   Handwritten insertion by MacEntee.
[7]   Handwritten insertion by MacEntee.

Shannon and Pigeon House Power-Stations and the whole electrical system upon which our industrial life depends are in the same condition. But we cannot deal with this expensive and difficult task unless we can secure an immediate relief in the budgetary burden. We are in fact in the relation of present services to present taxation facing a deficit next year of about £950,000. Where on top of this can we find the money for defence, while at the same time we carry on the Economic war.

6. I feel that the Partition problem cannot be solved except with the consent of the majority of the Northern non-Catholic population. It certainly cannot be solved by their coercion. Hitherto we as the Government here have done nothing of ourselves to secure a solution, but on the contrary have done and are doing certain things which have made a solution more difficult. The demand which we make continuously that the British should compel the Craigavonites to come in with us, has only had the effect of stiffening them against us. Our only hope is to cultivate a better feeling in the North towards us, and we shall not do that by refusing to agree to defend ourselves unless Britain exerts either physical or economic compulsion upon Belfast and the contiguous areas. *And if we are sincere in our conviction ~~belief~~ that ~~the problem~~ coercion cannot be used ~~solved by~~ that conviction must be adhered to with rigid consistency. We must resist temptation to invoke coercion directly or indirectly whenever the circumstances appear to us to favour it, as they do now, otherwise we shall only intensify the distrust of the people in the North whose confidence we wish to win.*[1]

7. I believe that the British Government alone cannot end Partition. No member of our Government was under any misapprehension as to this when the negotiations opened. I sent you on or about the tenth of last month a memorandum,[2] which was an attempt in its earlier part to redact the discussions and conclusions – possibly provisional conclusions – at which we arrived before we finally decided to meet the British. *The memorandum supports my view that we*[3] felt then that we could not settle Partition, nor even as has been so often said 'get a budge out of' the British in regard to it. This was our position also on the Friday before we went. We did feel however that we could wipe out Articles 6 and 7 of the 1921 Treaty, end the Economic War, and secure a favourable Trade Agreement, and therefore we went. The three objectives which six weeks ago we thought practicable appear to be within our grasp. The question is whether we shall secure them now, or abandon them because we cannot get immediately what we all, with maybe the exception of yourself, *feel*[4] is at the moment unobtainable.

8. I believe a failure to settle the Economic War will be bad for the country and disastrous for the Government and the Party. Notwithstanding the admonitions of political amateurs, who will always demand that a Government should make bricks without straw and omelettes without eggs, the country is looking for a settlement, expects to get one, and does not regard Partition as more than a theoretical obstacle to a practical agreement.

---

1 Handwritten insertion by MacEntee.
2 Not located.
3 Handwritten insertion by MacEntee.
4 Handwritten insertion by MacEntee.

Indeed the fact which is now known of your several meetings with Mr. Eden and Mr. MacDonald, has led the general public to believe that the whole thing is already cut and dried and that these London discussions are mere theatre. If there is no agreement now because we have chosen to break on Partition the revulsion against us will be overwhelming. That this position would be likely to arise in the case of a break was so clear to me – as it must have been equally clear to whosoever went through the Treaty crises – that I would have opposed to the bitter end any question of negotiations on an issue about which we knew in advance, as we knew about Partition, there was bound to be a disagreement. We should not have been permitted to go, we should not have been sent, if we were compelled to break upon this issue regarding which I have never concealed the fact that I was not prepared to break – at least not in the circumstances in which it has now been raised. I for my part feel that the way in which we have been manoeuvred into this situation by those who *do not* want ~~no~~ a settlement of the Economic War upon the only basis which is practicable, and who are labouring to reverse the policy enunciated in your speech of May 1935, has destroyed the only basis upon [which] a Cabinet can last: that of agreement upon the essentials of policy and a pervading confidence that the policy having been stated it will be accepted by all. It is clear now that your speech of May 1935 has not been accepted by the Minister for Lands[1] nor by the Minister for Posts and Telegraphs[2] as an authoritative statement of Government policy – though how in these circumstances the former could have remained in the Government and the latter have entered it *after the speech* was made passes my comprehension. In any event it is clear that these Ministers hold themselves free to undertake a filibuster against those of their colleagues who propose to think and speak and act upon the principle laid down by you in 1935. Even upon this issue alone I have no desire to remain in the Government, and therefore my resignation as Minister for Finance is at your disposal whenever you deem it advisable to accept it.

In dealing with the eighth reason for not breaking I have digressed into a consideration of a matter which is not strictly 'ad rem', and in any event is of narrow and personal application only. I presume therefore insofar as the main question as to whether we ought to break or not *is concerned*[3] you will ignore it. On the main question I ~~wish to~~ *must*[4] say that for the reasons which I have outlined I am convinced that it would not be in the national interest to break off the negotiations if by agreeing to defend our own territory against aggression we can secure:-

(1) The abrogation of Articles 6 and 7 of the 1921 Treaty and the defensive control of our own ports and harbours and all that territory over which by Article 3 of the Constitution we proposed to exercise immediate jurisdiction; (2) A trade agreement which, in view of the preferential position which it would accord to them in the British market vis-à-vis their Danish and other

---

[1] Gerald Boland (1885-1973), Minister for Lands (1936-9).
[2] Oscar Traynor (1886-1963), Minister for Posts and Telegraphs (1936-9).
[3] Handwritten insertion by MacEntee.
[4] Handwritten insertion by MacEntee.

competitors, our farmers might regard as their charter there; (3) A financial agreement which would wipe out the Land Annuities and by so reducing the payments to be made under other heads would enable us to improve our social services and to make reasonable provision for our own defence. I do not think it would be contrary, however, to the national interest to seek an agreement in regard to trade and finance only, provided that it is clear that our refusal to agree to defend ourselves does not operate to the ~~grievous~~ *serious*[1] detriment of our farmers or our people in the making of these agreements. If therefore you consider it advisable at this stage to maintain the appearance of unanimity in regard to the new course which is now proposed, I am prepared to go to London and while there to do everything I can to help you to secure the new objective. I am prepared *whether* I go to London and remain in the Cabinet or not if the negotiations break down upon it to acquiesce in the new plan and not to express *public* dissent *for so long as honourable silence is possible for a public [representative]*[2] I am willing to follow this equivocal course *in regard to a plan in which I do not believe*[3] because I feel that in the position in which we now find ourselves to manifest open disagreement would be disastrous to whatever chance you have of bringing your plans to a successful issue. But beyond silent acquiescence in the plan I cannot go. I am not prepared to defend it for instance at a General Election and accordingly will not stand again for the Dáil *if it still remains our policy*. In fact I feel no conviction whatever, as to the wisdom of the course upon which we are now embarking, and embarking *in my view* without having any practical idea in our own minds as to what we should do here in Ireland to re-establish some contacts with the representatives of the Six County majority *and* ~~so as~~ to create that atmosphere in which we can begin to talk politics. We are relying on England's big stick and it will fail. In the meantime we are hurrying to disaster should a European War come and catch us defenceless, at variance with Great Britain, and uncertain as to what our policy is to be.

I have written at length because I feel bound in honour to let you know my whole mind on the present situation as it presents itself to me. In the light of all I have said it is for you now to consider whether I should go to London at all or whether I should resign from the Government either now or later. I am at your disposal for whatever course you think will serve the national interest best.

I[4] know you will understand why I had to write this letter. In our relations of more than twenty years there has not so far as I know been any reserve between us when we have been discussing matters affecting the nation. We have had differences of opinion as to the wisdom or unwisdom of a line of policy and I have always been prepared in the last resort to defer to your judgment. But I cannot concede that full deference now, because in regard to Partition we have never had a considered policy. It has always been an affair

---

[1] Handwritten insertion by MacEntee.
[2] Handwritten insertion by MacEntee; word in brackets is not decipherable.
[3] Handwritten insertion by MacEntee.
[4] The remaining paragraph of this document has been handwritten.

of hasty improvisations, a matter of fits and starts. We are giving it first place now in the practical business of Government. When did we do that before in regard to any of those activities by which [---][1] citizens are consolidating and intensifying Partition. Why we would not risk antagonising one Gaelic Leaguer or G.A.A. [---][2] in order to undo Partition – as it could be undone in sport and amusement. And yet we are prepared to subject our farmers and our people as a whole to further and intensified hardship in order to compel Great Britain to force the Northern non-Catholics to associate with us, when with our connivance every bigot and killjoy, ecclesiastical and lay is doing his damnedest here to keep them out. Where is the reason in asking us to pursue two policies so utterly at variance with each other. It is because I believe that some of us are subordinating reason to prejudice, that prejudice which may be blameless in the heart of an individual, but should be banished from the minds of statesmen, in regard to this matter of defence, and are only raising the Partition issue now to coerce their colleagues to defer to their prejudices that I feel the essential unity and confidence of the Cabinet has been destroyed.

No. 143 NAI DT S10389 (Annex)

Minutes of the conference between representatives of the United Kingdom and Ireland
(Secret) (I.N. (38) 6th Meeting) (Copy)
LONDON, 5.00 pm, 23 February 1938

Secretary's Notes of the Sixth Meeting of the Conference held in the Prime Minister's Room, House of Commons, on Wednesday, 23rd February, 1938 at 5.0 p.m.

PRESENT

UNITED KINGDOM	*ÉIRE*
The Rt. Hon Neville Chamberlain, M.P., Prime Minister.	Mr. Eamon de Valera, Prime Minister and Minister for External Affairs.
The Rt. Hon. Sir Samuel Hoare, Bt., G.C.S.I., G.B.E., C.M.G., M.P., Secretary of State for the Home Department.	Mr. Sean F. Lemass, Minister for Industry and Commerce.
The Rt. Hon. Malcolm MacDonald, M.P., Secretary of State for Dominion Affairs.	Mr. Sean MacEntee, Minister for Finance.

---

[1] Word indecipherable.
[2] Word indecipherable.

Dr. James Ryan,
Minister for Agriculture.

THE FOLLOWING WERE ALSO PRESENT

The Rt. Hon Sir Thomas Inskip,   Mr. J. W. Dulanty, C.B., C.B.E.,
C.B.E., K.C., M.P., Minister for   High Commissioner for Éire.
Co-ordination of Defence.

Secretaries   Sir R.B. Howorth, K.C.M.G., C.B.
                 Mr. W.D. Wilkinson, D.S.O., M.C.

*CONFERENCE BETWEEN REPRESENTATIVES OF THE UNITED
KINGDOM AND ÉIRE*

DEFENCE

MR. CHAMBERLAIN invited Mr. de Valera to open the discussion.

MR. DE VALERA, said that when he and his colleagues got back to Dublin a careful re-examination had been made of the possibility of making a Defence Agreement on the lines of the draft which had been prepared as a result of the discussions which had taken place in London in January. They had also considered the whole question of a Defence Agreement between the two countries in the light of what Mr. Chamberlain and other United Kingdom Ministers had said as to the position and attitude of the United Kingdom in regard to the Partition question. As a result of this further and very full re-examination of the position the Government of Éire had decided that they could not assume responsibility for sponsoring a Defence Agreement on the lines contemplated so long as no hope could be held out to them that Partition would be terminated. It seemed, therefore, that a deadlock had been reached and that if there was really no hope of Partition being brought to an end it would be necessary to abandon any idea of making a Defence Agreement on the lines of the draft which had been discussed in January.

Mr. de Valera said that he had already told Mr. Chamberlain and Mr. MacDonald of the attitude of his public opinion on the subject of Partition. There was no question on which the people of Éire felt more deeply or on which they were more united than on the need for the union of the whole of Ireland. In the view of the Éire Government, Partition had been established in an arbitrary fashion and under the legislation of 1920 and 1922 there had, in fact, been separated from the then Irish Free State the largest area in North-Eastern Ireland that would give a permanent and stable Unionist majority to the Government of Northern Ireland. It should be noted that the territory so separated did not comprise the whole of the province of Ulster. What was, in fact, cut off in this arbitrary manner was an area surrounding Belfast. If the four counties of Londonderry, Tyrone, Fermanagh and Armagh were taken as a whole, it would be found that a majority of their inhabitants would be in favour of a united Ireland. It was only if the other two countries, namely, Antrim and Down were added that that majority was converted into a minority. In the city of Belfast there was a Catholic and Nationalist minority of about 22 per cent of the population. In this connection it might be observed that the number of those in favour of a united Ireland exceeded the Catholic population. It could be taken for granted that every Catholic was in favour of the abolition of partition, and that in addition that view was shared by a number of non-Catholics. Adjoining the border of Éire there were substantial majorities in South Down and in South Armagh in favour of the abolition of partition. The Nationalists in these areas had decided to boycott the recent elections in Northern Ireland although had they decided to vote they would, as in the past, have returned Nationalist representatives to the Northern Ireland Parliament by substantial majorities.

It would therefore be seen that along the Northern Ireland side of the border there was a population keenly desirous of joining with Éire but prevented from doing so by arrangements for which there could be no possible justification. This was a very serious and acute question and he (Mr. de Valera) and his colleagues could not return to Dublin without making very strenuous attempts to find a remedy. Under the administration of the Government of Northern Ireland there was a great deal of indefensible discrimination against the Nationalist and Catholic minority. He had received numerous memoranda on the subject, and he understood that similar representations had been made to Mr. Chamberlain. One example of this discrimination was the granting and withholding of employment. The Northern Ireland Government had failed to act in the spirit of the 1920 legislation that there should be no discrimination on the grounds of religious belief.

In the view of the Government of Éire it was impossible for the Government of the United Kingdom to maintain that they had no responsibility in the matter. While it might be argued that that Government had no direct legal responsibility for what happened in Northern Ireland, it was clear that they had a very definite moral responsibility because of considerations such as the reserved powers under the 1920 Act. In view of these and other considerations the people of Éire felt so very strongly on this subject that it would be impossible for the Government of Éire to enter into any agreement on the subject of Defence with the Government of the United Kingdom so long as the Partition question remained unsolved.

MR. CHAMBERLAIN said that he and his colleagues were very sorry indeed to hear of the conclusion to which the Government of Éire had come. That conclusion seemed to make impossible the signing of a Defence Agreement between the two countries on the lines which had been contemplated. He could not too strongly emphasise that the United Kingdom Government possessed no legal powers or authority which would enable them to compel the Government of Northern Ireland to change their alleged attitude towards the minority in Northern Ireland, even if any discrimination was, in fact, shown against that minority. From Mr. de Valera's observations he had gathered that there were really two main difficulties: (1) the alleged discrimination of the Government of Northern Ireland against the Nationalist and Catholic minority in Northern Ireland; and (2) the larger question of the continuance or otherwise of Partition. These questions were, of course, of a very different character. It would be possible to remedy any discrimination against the minority in Northern Ireland without having recourse to the abolition of Partition. For example, one possible way of dealing with the problem might be to transfer to Éire those areas on the border which were predominantly Nationalist and Catholic. It was, however, clear from what Mr. de Valera had said that the real objective of Éire was to get rid of Partition and secure a united Ireland. He (Mr. Chamberlain) must once again point out that not only had the United Kingdom Government no legal power to implement such a policy without the full consent and approval of Northern Ireland, but it would be politically impossible for the Government of the United Kingdom to take any action or to put any pressure upon the Government and people of Northern Ireland to force them to agree against their will to the abolition of Partition. No Government in the United Kingdom could adopt such a policy and survive, and it must be clearly recognised that any such proposal was quite out of the question and could not, in any circumstances, be entertained. Mr. de Valera had said that the Government of Éire could not make a Defence Agreement with the United Kingdom unless they received satisfaction in regard to the question of Partition. Was there any other possible alternative which Mr. de Valera would like to suggest?

MR. DE VALERA said that there appeared to him to be two possible alternative courses which might be taken. The first of these might be that the two Governments should make an agreement covering finance and trade but leaving outstanding the question of the defended ports and all other items of a defence agreement. In effect this would mean that there would be a settlement of the outstanding financial and economic questions at issue but that the outstanding political questions would remain unsolved. He thought that in the circumstances a solution on these lines would probably commend itself better to the majority of the people of Éire than any other solution which did not satisfactorily provide for the termination of partition.

The second possible course was one which he (Mr. de Valera) and the Members of his Government would themselves prefer. If this course were adopted the defended ports would be taken over by the Government of Éire without that Government entering into any Agreement of any sort with the Government of the United Kingdom on the subject of defence. In this event he (Mr. de Valera) would be able to inform his people that the Government of Éire were assuming full military responsibility for the ports in the same way as they were now responsible for the other defences of Éire, and also the responsibility for the very considerable financial consequences which would be involved in the transfer, and the expenditure of large sums of money which could not be regarded as productive. He would have to explain that in assuming these responsibilities the Government of Éire had entered into no commitments or engagements of any sort or kind with the Government of the United Kingdom, and that the military policy of the Government of Éire in the future would be directed to preventing any hostile strangers from entering Éire territory and repelling any aggressor who attempted an invasion. He would, in fact, repeat the assurances which he had already given on the subject in the Dáil that it was the intention of the Éire Government to protect their territory and forbid its use to any foreign hostile

Power. If he was questioned on the subject, and he was not prepared to volunteer the information if he was not questioned, he would take the opportunity in a debate on the defence estimates in the Dáil to outline the general policy of his Government in regard to defence, which would be based on two alternatives. If the Government of Éire could reach an entirely satisfactory settlement of all the outstanding questions with the Government of the United Kingdom, including a satisfactory solution of the partition question, he would be able to go a very long way in the direction of giving the kind of assurances which were contemplated in the draft defence agreement. If, however, it was not found possible to solve the partition difficulty, he would have to say that in the unhappy event of Éire being involved in some conflict she would naturally have to see where, in her own interests, she could best obtain assistance. In this respect regard must be had to the fact that it was most improbable that Éire would ever have any foreign enemies who would wish to attack her, and that if she was attacked by some foreign Power it would only be because that Power wished to use Éire territory in order to facilitate an attack upon the United Kingdom. It would probably be found desirable that the defence plans of Éire, in such an eventuality, should be such as would dovetail in with the defence plans of the United Kingdom. If this were so it would naturally mean that there would have to be meetings between the defence experts of the two countries for consultation and advice. He must make it clear, however, that he could not possibly enter into any formal agreement covering matters of this kind.

He could not too emphatically impress upon United Kingdom Ministers that the establishment of good and close relations between the two countries could not be looked for so long as Ireland remained partitioned. The people of Éire would be prepared to make very great financial and other sacrifices if the question were one of defending the whole of a united Ireland, but if a united Ireland was withheld from them they would see no reason or justification why they should in any way relieve the United Kingdom of any of her anxieties or of the heavy capital and other costs of the defended ports.

MR. CHAMBERLAIN said that he would like to ask certain questions. The draft defence agreement consisted of five clauses of which the first read –

1. The harbour defences (including buildings, magazines, emplacements, fixed armaments with the ammunition therefor at present on the spot, and instruments) of Berehaven, Cobh (Queenstown) and Lough Swilly now occupied by United Kingdom care and maintenance parties will be handed over to the Government of Éire).

As he understood it, under Mr. de Valera's proposal this clause would stand while clauses 2 and 3 would disappear. Clause 4 read as follows:-

4. Until such time as the Government of Éire can arrange for the provision of the forces necessary for the defence of the ports, the Government of Éire will invite the Government of the United Kingdom to co-operate in their defence by the supply of such forces, and the Government of the United Kingdom will so co-operate on such terms as may be agreed between the two Governments.

Was it proposed that this should stand?

MR. DE VALERA said that he would prefer some much simpler arrangement in place of Clause 4. He thought that a date for transfer should be fixed and that until that date such arrangements regarding the ports should be made as might be agreed between the two Governments.

THE SECRETARY OF STATE FOR DOMINION AFFAIRS pointed out that Clause 4, as at present drafted, provided for more than was covered by Mr. de Valera's formula.

MR. CHAMBERLAIN did not think that the transitional arrangements contemplated in clause 4 should give rise to any particular difficulty. He observed, however, that at present the United Kingdom had certain obligations in regard to the Naval defence of the coasts of Éire. Did Mr. de Valera suggest that these obligations should be modified?

MR. DE VALERA said that he recognised, of course, that the security of Éire ultimately depended on the Royal Navy keeping the command of the sea. This was a consideration which must always be in the mind of every Irish Government. In these circumstances he recognised that if the United Kingdom lost the command of the sea, Éire would be unable to effectively defend herself against a strong aggressor. Clearly Éire could not undertake the Naval defence of her own coasts though she might be able to make some contribution by providing and maintaining a certain number of small Naval craft. All that he had said was, of course, much more applicable to the circumstances of a united Ireland than to those of a partitioned Ireland. The whole attitude of the Government of Éire and the people of Éire would be very different indeed if partition could be got rid of and an entirely different spirit would prevail. This would particularly apply to Naval defence matters.

SIR SAMUEL HOARE said that United Kingdom Ministers fully appreciated Mr. de Valera's difficulties *vis-a-vis* his own public opinion. Mr. de Valera must, however, realise that United Kingdom Ministers must have regard to public opinion in the United Kingdom, which was certainly much less embittered than was the case years ago. If however the Government of the United Kingdom were to hand over the defended ports to the Government of Éire on the terms which Mr. de Valera suggested, there would be very severe criticism and dissatisfaction from almost every quarter of the United Kingdom, and this would be all the more difficult to deal with if Mr. de Valera was unable to adopt towards this defence question a less detached and a more sympathetic attitude than he had indicated. Was it not possible for Mr. de Valera to go further than he had done?

MR. DE VALERA said that it was quite out of the question for him to enter into any formal contracts or agreements with the United Kingdom on the subject of defence. He had no idea of the kind of reception the proposals he had envisaged would get in Éire. There would be a criticism from at least two quarters. There would be those who would maintain that in regard to defence the right course was to maintain the *status quo* which was quite satisfactory and under which Éire would in fact be effectively protected in any emergency that might arise. Another section would urge that defence should be made a lever in order to secure a united Ireland and would argue that only in this way could effective pressure be brought to bear on the United

Kingdom to facilitate the abolition of partition. He, Mr. de Valera, could not do or say anything which failed to take account of criticisms of this character.

MR. CHAMBERLAIN observed that the comprehensive agreement covering Defence, Finance and Trade resembled a three-leaved shamrock, and it was necessary for United Kingdom Ministers to consider very carefully how public opinion in the United Kingdom would regard such an agreement. He would be very sorry indeed if, after all, it was found impossible to reach agreement, but even this regrettable outcome would be preferable to a revival of bad feeling between the two countries if it was subsequently found that the Government of the United Kingdom were unable to carry Parliament and public opinion with them and had to denounce the agreement as unfair and unjust. It would, in any case, be very difficult indeed to defend and justify to United Kingdom public opinion the making of Finance and Trade Agreements of the kind now contemplated. It would be necessary to persuade the public opinion of this country to make very large and important financial sacrifices and the Government would be asked why the country was being required to make these sacrifices. Under the trade agreement it was proposed that the United Kingdom should abandon the Special Duties. Public opinion would ask what the United Kingdom was to get in return, and would have to be told that the principal contribution to be made by Éire was the establishment of a Prices Commission to review Éire's protective duties, which might or might not make recommendations satisfactory to the United Kingdom trader. The critics would say that in return for concrete and tangible concessions we were to receive assurances and very little besides, and that, in fact, the United Kingdom were showing much faith and confidence and were getting little, if any, tangible benefits in return for irrevocable, solid and permanent concessions. He had hoped that United Kingdom Ministers would have been able to answer their critics by pointing to certain provisions in the Defence Agreement which would be of material assistance to the United Kingdom and would justify the Government of the United Kingdom in agreeing to other matters in regard to which they might feel considerable doubt and hesitation. This would have been possible if the Defence Agreement could have taken the form of the present draft. He and his colleagues could have said that we had handed over the ports to Éire, that they would be maintained in full efficiency and that there would be co-operation in defence questions generally. Assurances of this kind would have been of very great help in securing approval of the other parts of the general agreement. As it was, the outlook was going to be very bleak and gloomy. The events of the last weekend had not made the position of the United Kingdom Government stronger, but rather weaker.[1] The supporters of the Government were being bombarded with letters from their constituents and the bombardment would be greatly intensified if the United Kingdom Government had to publish an agreement of the kind Mr. de Valera desired. In these

---

[1] Foreign Secretary Anthony Eden resigned over differences of opinion with Chamberlain over British policy towards Italy and because of Chamberlain's increasing contacts with Italian diplomats behind Eden's back.

circumstances the supporters of the Government might not be in a position to resist the pressure of their constituents.

MR. DE VALERA said that he fully agreed and realised well enough the political difficulties with which United Kingdom Ministers would be faced. The real fundamental difficulty was that there was nothing tangible that Éire could give. Her people regarded the defended ports and other items which the United Kingdom were proposing to concede as theirs by right, and that they were only recovering what had been wrongfully taken away from them.

SIR SAMUEL HOARE said that so far as he was concerned it would make a considerable difference if he could feel that there had been some forward movement on the part of Mr. de Valera and his colleagues. Could not Mr. de Valera, with his great influence in Éire, make some substantial advance and so help materially in bringing about a comprehensive agreement fully satisfactory to both sides?

MR. CHAMBERLAIN said that he would like to use his recent conversations with the Italian Ambassador as an illustration.[1] He had pointed out to the Ambassador [that] for a variety of reasons, of which recent events in Spain were probably the most important, the United Kingdom and Italy had not been on the best of terms. He had suggested to the Ambassador that, if things were to be got moving, a gesture of goodwill on the part of Italy would be most desirable. If possible this should take the form of Italy's acceptance of our formula for the withdrawal of troops from Spain.

Count Grandi had pointed out the difficulties which lay in the way of Italy's acceptance, but had agreed, on Mr. Chamberlain's insistence to put the matter to his Government. The result had been satisfactory, for the Italian Government had very quickly notified us that they were willing to make the gesture which we had suggested. They had done so for the sake of getting Anglo-Italian conversations started.

Was it asking too much of the Government of Éire to suggest that they also, for the sake of healing the breach between the two countries, should make a helpful gesture of a kind which would carry conviction to the United Kingdom Parliament and people? Failing some gesture of the kind, opinion here would be only too certain to regard an Anglo-Éire Agreement on the lines now in contemplation as an extremely bad bargain.

The best advance which Éire could make to meet this country would be a gesture of goodwill in the direction of Northern Ireland – for example, some concession in the Trade Agreement which would ease the Northern Irish position.

Mr. Chamberlain added that he knew Éire had already made concessions in the Trade Agreement. Could they not go further?

MR. DE VALERA said that he would have liked to do so if it had been possible. He was certainly animated by no ill-will against Northern Ireland; he wished it every prosperity, if only for the reason that one day, sooner or later, it would be part of a reunited Ireland. The trouble was that Great Britain and Northern Ireland constituted one fiscal system. He could not

---

[1] Count Dino Grandi, Italian ambassador to Britain (1932-9).

make concessions to Northern Ireland without making them to this country also. That meant a small population of 4,000,000 people opening their doors to the mass-produced exports of a great country of 42,000,000 people. It could not be done.

He much regretted that this should be so. Many years ago, when partition first took effect, he had wondered whether something could not be done to retrieve the position by means of a Customs Union of all Ireland. On examination of course, he had found that this was impossible.

SIR THOMAS INSKIP said that it was not only in Éire that the view was held that the partition of Ireland must one day come to an end. Many people in this country also took the same view. Mr. de Valera, of course, was more interested in the present than in the distant future. He wanted to see the unity of Ireland achieved in his own day.

That being so, it was for Mr. de Valera to make a move. The position was not unlike what often happened in a great industrial strike. Each side made it a point of honour not to budge from its position. The task of the peacemaker was to get one side to move first.

The move might come either on the Trade Agreement or on Defence. He (Sir Thomas) had wondered whether, if the Defence Agreement went through, it might create a tendency towards the unification of the measures for the defence of Ireland. After all, Lough Swilly, although not in 'Northern Ireland', was in the extreme North of Ireland.

MR. DE VALERA said that he realised the force of these arguments. It was certainly his intention, if the general Agreement went through, to use it as a jumping-off ground for entering into better relations with Northern Ireland. At first, of course, he would have to do something to steady and to educate his own people. This was why he was unwilling to enter into a Defence Agreement. It would mean losing his own people and not getting into touch with Northern Ireland either.

MR. MACDONALD pointed out that there was another step which lay within Mr. de Valera's power, which would be of the greatest possible assistance in promoting better relations with Northern Ireland. His meaning was that Éire should do something to emphasize that its membership of the British Commonwealth of Nations was a reality. The sooner something was done in this direction the better. People in Ulster believed that Éire was gradually moving out of the Commonwealth, rather than talking its rightful place inside it.

MR. DE VALERA said that this was a matter in which he would have to move very slowly indeed. His people, at the best, regarded association with the British Commonwealth of Nations as a sacrifice which the majority in Éire ought to be prepared to make in order to achieve unity with the minority.

His people, however, were most anxious to get on good terms with Great Britain. They were very willing to think of the future, not of the past.

SIR THOMAS INSKIP said that he was anxious to know how United Kingdom Ministers were to make public reference to whatever understanding existed between Éire Ministers and themselves in the matter of defence. The suggestion now was that this country should hand over the Treaty Ports without securing the rest of the draft Defence Agreement. Nevertheless, Éire Ministers had given utterance during the negotiations to views on defence which would be satisfactory to the people of the United Kingdom, if they were allowed to know of them. Would Mr. de Valera allow it to be stated publicly that during the negotiations he had said that he would take certain steps regarding defence?

[MR. CHAMBERLAIN left at this point to keep another engagement.]

MR. DE VALERA said that Sir Thomas Inskip's request put him into a difficulty. His (Mr. de Valera's) statements during the negotiations on the subject of defence were, of course, an indication of the direction in which he conceived that the interests of the people of Éire lay.

On the other hand, not only was a formal defence agreement politically impossible, but it was equally impossible for him to enter into an understanding. He had not done so and would tell his people that he had not done so.

There was no question of there being any understanding just because he had told United Kingdom Ministers what was the defence policy of the Government of Éire. He was perfectly entitled to do that at any time.

SIR THOMAS INSKIP suggested that the distinction was a subtle one. The practical difficulty, however, remained, viz. that United Kingdom Ministers were being asked to inform the House of Commons that, without securing any defence agreement with Éire, they had handed over the defended ports.

MR. DE VALERA said that United Kingdom Ministers could refer to his (Mr. de Valera's) published statements. They could add that they understood that his policy was unchanged.

It would, of course, be better still if he could make his next statement on defence before the debate in the United Kingdom House of Commons. He did not, however, know whether he could arrange this.

SIR THOMAS INSKIP suggested that United Kingdom Ministers would go on to say that they knew that Mr. de Valera could be relied upon to keep his word. Would not this, for the purposes of the United Kingdom, amount to the same thing as an agreement, although it was not set out in black and white?

MR. DE VALERA said that, if this was the same thing as an agreement, he certainly did not want it. He would like United Kingdom Ministers, after carefully counting the cost, to take the step of handing over the ports on their own responsibility. He was not willing for them to take this action on the basis of trust in him.

There would, however, be no objection to references being made in the Parliament at Westminster to his speeches on defence in the Parliament in Dublin. It could be added that Mr. de Valera, and his Government, were believed to be still of the same mind.

SIR THOMAS INSKIP had no doubt that this would carry conviction with those who knew Mr. de Valera. The ordinary audience in this country, however, would say, 'we have not had the pleasure of meeting him'.

[A House of Commons Division took place at this point. After the Division, MR. CHAMBERLAIN returned to the Meeting.]

MR. MACDONALD said that he had gathered that Mr. de Valera's next public statement on defence in the Dáil would be either: (1) during the

Debate on the present agreements, if they materialised, or (2) a later Defence Debate. It would help United Kingdom Ministers very greatly if it could be (1), and further if the statement could be made before the Debates in the Parliament at Westminster.

He quite understood the importance to Mr. de Valera of not entering into any understanding on defence, whether published or unpublished.

SIR THOMAS INSKIP suggested that use could be made of the natural assumption that Mr. de Valera's Government would take all necessary steps to defend their own country.

MR. DE VALERA did not dissent. He wished it, however, to be made very clear that nothing which was said over the Conference Table by the Éire Delegation was to be taken as the consideration in return for which the United Kingdom were to hand over the treaty ports.

Mr. de Valera went on to refer to the position of Canada, Australia, New Zealand and the Union of South Africa. It was now, he thought, accepted policy that those Dominions were under no obligation to engage in war simultaneously with the United Kingdom. The same was certainly the position of Éire. Under the new Constitution the power to declare war was reserved for the Parliament of Éire.

The line, therefore, which he would take in his statement would be that Éire was not bound to go to war because the United Kingdom was involved in one. The Government of Éire must be the sole judge of whether it would co-operate or not. If he were asked on what lines Éire staff officers would be instructed to prepare their plans he would answer that those plans would have to be made on two alternative hypotheses, (a) that Éire went to war alone and (b) that United Kingdom interests would be involved and that the United Kingdom also would go to war. In that eventuality Éire would be glad of assistance from this country. The staff would make their second set of plans on that hypothesis.

He would say so much, even at the risk of defeat in the Dáil. In actual fact he did not believe that such a statement would offend his public opinion.

He realised that a statement on these lines would not go far to reassure House of Commons opinion at Westminster. United Kingdom Ministers would probably find it more useful to refer to speeches on defence which he, Mr. de Valera, had made in the past. One of those speeches was very categorical and had caused some dissatisfaction in Éire at the time.

SIR THOMAS INSKIP was not sure that Mr. de Valera's statement of the position of the Dominions with regard to participation in war gave a complete picture of the position. The actual fact was that Australia, for example, depended for her safety on the sea power of the United Kingdom; *a fortiori* Éire was similarly dependent on the Royal Navy.

SIR SAMUEL HOARE said that the theory was that the Dominions were responsible for their own local defence but that the United Kingdom had the responsibility for their overseas defence.

MR. DE VALERA took the view that the relationship of Éire to this country was different from that of Australia.

SIR THOMAS INSKIP said that, from the Defence point of view, Éire's relationship with this country was far more intimate than that of Australia. Her interests were as closely linked with those of this country as if the two were separated only by a land boundary.

MR. CHAMBERLAIN thought that the discussion could not profitably be carried further that evening. Before concluding he would like to refer once more to the economic side of the problem. It might conceivably help towards a solution if Éire could give Northern Ireland some different Customs treatment from that which she gave to the United Kingdom. Would the Éire Delegation think over this suggestion before the next meeting?

MR. DE VALERA indicated that this would be considered.

MR. CHAMBERLAIN said that the United Kingdom Delegation also would explore the suggestion. If nothing helpful emerged from it, he hoped that the Éire Delegation would consider seriously whether they could not make some concession on the particular duties which bore hardly on Northern Ireland. These duties were a great stumbling-block in the present negotiations.

He was glad to hear that the separate discussions on the draft Trade Agreement were to be carried further the same evening.

A matter to which United Kingdom Ministers would have to give some anxious consideration was the difficulty of handing over the Treaty Ports without obtaining the remainder of the Defence Agreement.

Mr. Chamberlain enquired how long it would be possible for the Éire Delegation to remain in London. He greatly regretted that the Delegation had been kept waiting in London for some days owing to the crisis in foreign policy.[1] The Éire Delegation were, of course, in no way to blame for the fact that a beginning was only now being made.

MR. DE VALERA said that he and his colleagues had an important engagement in Dublin on Monday, February 28th. It would be awkward if they could not be back by that date. The engagement was connected with the nominations for election to the Senate and was not one which could be postponed.

Turning to Mr. Chamberlain's suggestion that Northern Ireland might conceivably be given differential Customs treatment, Mr. de Valera expressed the strong hope that there would be no question of giving Northern Ireland anything approaching Dominion status.

MR. MacENTEE suggested that Northern Ireland ought to go some way to meet Éire in this matter. There were a number of ways in which Northern Ireland could co-operate with Éire, without detriment to their present status, if only they were willing.

MR. CHAMBERLAIN remarked that Northern Ireland had repeatedly expressed a desire to be left alone. They said they wanted no change.

It was agreed:-
(i)   That no Press communiqué need be issued at the close of the present meeting. Mr. de Valera and Mr. MacDonald were invited to confer together regarding any guidance which the Press might require.
(ii) That the time for the next full meeting between the two Delegations should be left to Mr. MacDonald to settle. It would probably be

---

[1] The resignation of Foreign Secretary Anthony Eden (see above footnote 1, p. 231).

convenient to meet in the afternoon of the following day, Thursday, February 24th.

No. 144 NAI CAB 2/1

Extract from the minutes of a meeting of the Cabinet
(G.C.1/11) (Item 1)
DUBLIN, 28 February 1938

NEGOTIATIONS WITH THE BRITISH GOVERNMENT
The members of the delegation reported generally on the discussions with representatives of the British Government which took place in London during the week ended the 26th February, 1938.

It was agreed that the delegation should return to London with a view to the resumption of the discussions on Thursday, 3rd March, 1938.

No. 145 NAI DT S10389 (Annex)

Minutes of the conference between representatives of the United Kingdom and Ireland
(Secret) (I.N. (38) 7th Meeting) (Copy)
LONDON, 5.00 pm, 3 March 1938

CONFERENCE
between
REPRESENTATIVES OF THE UNITED KINGDOM AND ÉIRE
Secretary's Notes of the Seventh Meeting of the Conference
held in the Prime Minister's Room, House of Commons,
on Thursday, 3rd March, 1938 at 5.0 p.m.

PRESENT:-

UNITED KINGDOM
The Rt. Hon Neville Chamberlain, M.P., Prime Minister.

The Rt. Hon. Sir John Simon, G.C.S.I., G.C.V.O., O.B.E., K.C., M.P., Chancellor of the Exchequer.

The Rt. Hon. Sir Samuel Hoare, Bt., G.C.S.I., G.B.E., C.M.G., M.P., Secretary of State for the Home Department.

The Rt. Hon. Malcolm MacDonald, M.P., Secretary of State for Dominion Affairs.

ÉIRE
Mr. Eamon de Valera, Prime Minister and Minister for External Affairs.

Mr. Sean F. Lemass, Minister for Industry and Commerce.

Mr. Sean MacEntee, Minister for Finance.

Dr. James Ryan, Minister for Agriculture.

THE FOLLOWING WERE ALSO PRESENT

The Rt. Hon Sir Thomas Inskip,
C.B.E., K.C., M.P., Minister for
Co-ordination of Defence.

Mr. J. W. Dulanty, C.B., C.B.E.,
High Commissioner for Éire.

The Rt. Hon. W.S. Morrison, M.C.,
K.C., M.P., Minister of Agriculture
and Fisheries

Secretary   Sir R.B. Howorth, K.C.M.G., C.B.
              Mr. W.D. Wilkinson, D.S.O., M.C.

*CONFERENCE BETWEEN REPRESENTATIVES OF THE UNITED
KINGDOM AND ÉIRE*

THE DRAFT TRADE AGREEMENT
THE DIFFERENTIAL TARIFF PROPOSAL
MR. CHAMBERLAIN thought that it might be useful if some discussion
could take place on a proposal which had been considered at the previous
meeting on February 23rd, namely that some special arrangement in regard to
the tariff treatment of Northern Ireland by Éire might be found practicable.
MR. DE VALERA said that he had understood from Mr. MacDonald that the
proposal was that Éire should grant to Northern Ireland free entry for products and manufactures of Northern Ireland origin. He had replied that it was
quite impossible for the Government of Éire to entertain any such proposal.
Public opinion in Éire would be very strongly opposed to a suggestion of this
kind and would point out that Northern Ireland had failed to respond in any
way to the overtures made by Éire which had had as their object, the
improvement of relations between the two countries. Reference would be
made to the large numbers of persons in Northern Ireland, and particularly
to those of them living on the Northern Ireland side of the border, who were
in effect deprived of their civil rights, and in this connection he could, if necessary, give a long list of localities where, owing to the gerrymandering of the
constituencies, the Unionists were able to secure a much larger number of
representatives on the local Councils than the Nationalists, even in places
where the voting strength of the two sides was approximately equal. If he
was to agree to this particular proposal, his public opinion, which was
bitterly disappointed at the failure to make any progress in regard to
Partition would regard the proposal as an important step towards stabilising
the present position in regard to Partition and as giving to Northern Ireland
the best of both worlds – namely the continuance of Partition and a most
favourable opportunity of expanding her trade in Éire. As the United
Kingdom Ministers were aware, great efforts had been made in Éire to establish industries of various kinds, and the people of Éire had put much money
into these industries. It would be said that by agreeing to this proposal he
was opening the floodgates to most intensive competition on the part of
Northern Ireland in the Éire market, the results of which were bound to be

highly prejudicial, and in some cases, disastrous to Éire's industries. There could, in his considered opinion, be no more unpopular proposition in Éire than that the products and manufactures of Northern Ireland should be given free entry into the Éire market. He was, however, prepared to examine whether there might not be some other way of meeting Northern Ireland as, for example, by Éire and Northern Ireland negotiating system[1] under which each country gave preferences to the goods of the other. Moreover, it might be possible to consider some special arrangements in the case of those manufactures and products of Northern Ireland which were not produced in Éire. Arrangements of the kind he had in mind were, of course, of an entirely different character from an arrangement based on the principle of free entry. Quite frankly the people of Éire were genuinely afraid of the industrial competition of Northern Ireland. They appreciated, of course, that if Ireland could be united the industrial supremacy of Northern Ireland would have to be faced and acquiesced in, but so long as Partition persisted Éire could not compete industrially with Northern Ireland on an 'open door' basis, owing to factors such as the greater experience and longer traditions of industry in Northern Ireland, and the more onerous labour conditions which prevailed in Éire.

MR. LEMASS fully confirmed what Mr. de Valera had said as to the great difficulties which industry in Éire would find if it was faced with the free and unrestricted competition of the industry of Northern Ireland. In particular he referred to the fact that in Éire labour was in a more advantageous position than in Northern Ireland in matters such as hours of work and other working conditions. This, of course, would be a serious handicap to the Éire industrialists if faced with unrestricted competition from Northern Ireland.

MR. DE VALERA said that, for his part, he attached as much importance to arguments based on the greater experience and longer traditions of Northern Ireland industry.

MR. CHAMBERLAIN observed that there could, he assumed, be no question of competition between the two countries in shipbuilding.

MR. LEMASS agreed and thought that the linen industry was also one in which there would be no competition with Northern Ireland. Éire was not only afraid of the existing industries in Northern Ireland, but was apprehensive that undertakings might come to, and establish themselves in Northern Ireland, in order to take advantage of the Éire market, if the principle of free entry was accepted.

MR. CHAMBERLAIN observed that Northern Ireland was, not unnaturally, very apprehensive of any arrangement under which Éire products and manufactures would come into Northern Ireland free, while Northern Irish products and manufactures entering Éire would be subject to duty.

SIR SAMUEL HOARE said that any such arrangement as this would be quite impossible to defend. He was very sorry to hear the conclusions which Mr. de Valera had reached in regard to the proposal for a differential tariff in favour of Northern Ireland, particularly as, at the previous meeting, Mr.

---

[1] As typed.

de Valera had said that the proposal had considerable attractions, and that, while it was essential that the industries of Éire should be adequately protected against the powerful and organised industry of Great Britain, the position was different *vis-à-vis* the industry of Northern Ireland.

MR. DE VALERA said that he had been thinking over the suggestion that the unification of Ireland might be brought nearer if Éire and Northern Ireland had some special tariff arrangements between themselves, but the proposal for a differential tariff in favour of Northern Ireland went very much further than anything he had contemplated. He had recently spoken to a prominent Éire industrialist, who had made it clear to him that, while Éire industry would face up to and acquiesce in the situation which would result from the abolition of partition, the strongest possible objections would be raised to the adoption of the principle of the free entry of Northern Ireland goods, if partition was to be continued. He (Mr. de Valera) was satisfied that public opinion in Éire would take the view, if he accepted the proposal, that he was conferring very great advantages on Northern Ireland to break down the partition barrier. Éire public opinion very strongly resented the whole attitude which the Government of Northern Ireland had taken up towards the ill-treatment of the Nationalist minority in Northern Ireland.

SIR SAMUEL HOARE said that he was ready to discuss this particular matter with Mr. de Valera. He had made very careful investigations, but had been unable to find any justification at all for general charges of ill-treatment and oppression of the minority in Northern Ireland. If Mr. de Valera had in mind any specific cases of ill-treatment, he (Sir Samuel Hoare) would be only too glad to make special efforts to get any genuine grievances remedied, but he must repeat that the careful and impartial investigations which had been made had satisfied him that there was no justification for charges of general ill-usage and oppression of the Northern Ireland minority.

MR. DE VALERA said that he would be very glad to discuss the matter with Sir Samuel Hoare. He could, if necessary, supply a long list of localities in which there could be no question that the minority were being improperly deprived of their civil rights.

As an example the Parliamentary representation of the county of Fermanagh might be quoted. In this county the arrangement of the constituencies were such that, while 32,000 electors returned one Nationalist Member, 25,000 electors returned two Unionist Members.

SIR SAMUEL HOARE pointed out that, in Northern Ireland, there were today, and had always been, eleven seats in the Parliament of Northern Ireland available for Nationalist representatives.

MR. DE VALERA said that, on the basis of proportional representation, the Nationalists in Northern Ireland should have seventeen out of the fifty-four seats in the Northern Ireland Parliament.

He would be very glad to discuss the question with Sir Samuel Hoare at any time.

MR. MACDONALD said that Mr. de Valera had spoken of the barrier between Northern Ireland and Éire and of his intense desire to remove the suspicions and ill-will which were at the root of the whole partition question.

United Kingdom Ministers entirely shared Mr. de Valera's desire that all suspicions and ill-will should pass away, and in their view the best method of securing this objective would be to make a start by inspiring confidence and good feeling in Northern Ireland and by the Government of Éire making some gesture which would prove to Northern Ireland that her suspicions were not well founded.

It was true that the new Éire Constitution contained certain provisions which, in Mr. de Valera's view, were intended to meet the susceptibilities of Northern Ireland, but Northern Ireland had taken an entirely different view of these provisions which had produced in Northern Ireland not a good but a bad effect. United Kingdom Ministers had made very great efforts to find some means to improve goodwill and inaugurate better relations between Éire and Northern Ireland. Their first suggestion had been that a defence agreement should be made between Éire and the United Kingdom, which they firmly believed would, when published, have had a very good effect in Northern Ireland, because, under the defence agreement contemplated by the Éire and United Kingdom representatives in January, it would have been clear that Éire was not, as Northern Ireland feared, moving away from the Commonwealth, but that she was closely cooperating with the United Kingdom in a vital matter of common concern, namely, various defence questions of interest to the two countries. Mr. de Valera had stated that, owing to the strong feelings in regard to partition of public opinion in Éire it was not possible for him to make a defence agreement with the United Kingdom, so long as partition remained, and the United Kingdom representatives recognised that in these circumstances a defence agreement, of the character which they had hoped to make with Éire, could not be entered into. The United Kingdom representatives had then considered this proposal for a differential tariff arrangement between Éire and Northern Ireland, and had welcomed the prospect of an arrangement of this kind, even though they recognised that it must inevitably prejudice to some extent manufacturers and traders of Great Britain. Because, however, they regarded the arrangement as a step towards the removal of suspicions and the creation of goodwill they were prepared to do everything in their power to bring it about. If this proposal was to be rejected there was very little indeed left which the United Kingdom could do to bring about what Mr. de Valera had continually emphasised as most important, namely, the breaking down of that cloud of ill-will and suspicion which went to the very root of the problem.

MR. DE VALERA pointed out that he had made it quite clear in previous discussions that he could in no circumstances agree to the free entry into Éire of the products and manufactures of Great Britain. While the proposal to restrict the free entry to goods of Northern Irish origin was not, from Éire's point of view, open to the same fundamental objections, public opinion in Éire would certainly have nothing to do with it. Moreover, if such a proposal was accepted by him Northern Ireland would laugh at the simplicity and lack of foresight which the Éire Representatives had shown in agreeing to a proposal so detrimental to Éire's true interests and would not regard it as a gesture but as an act of almost incredible stupidity and weakness. He thought that it might be possible to consider some plan for an exchange of preferences. Éire desired nothing better than to persuade Northern Ireland to co-operate with her but the worst possible way of approach would be on the lines of the present suggestion.

MR. CHAMBERLAIN said that what Mr. de Valera appeared to have in mind was an arrangement that the free entry which Éire got into Great Britain's market should not extend to the Northern Ireland Market.

MR. DE VALERA said that as yet he had reached no definite conclusion, the whole matter would have to be very carefully examined.

SIR JOHN SIMON pointed out that a proposal to allow a part of the United Kingdom to have some special preferential arrangement with Éire was open to the gravest difficulties and objections. If Northern Ireland was to have special treatment the way to give it was by means of the differential tariff proposal.

SIR SAMUEL HOARE agreed. The trade of Northern Ireland was part and parcel of the trade of the United Kingdom. Great Britain was proposing to give Éire most valuable benefits in her market and had hoped that in return Éire would compensate Northern Ireland which was suffering much more than Great Britain from the consequences of the trade dispute between the United Kingdom and Éire.

MR. DE VALERA observed that he had always thought that the desire of the industries of Northern Ireland to obtain free access to the valuable Éire market would be an important factor in bringing partition to an end. He could not too strongly emphasise the opposition which would be raised in Éire to the proposal that, in the present circumstances, Northern Ireland should be given free access for her products and manufactures to the Éire market. He could not possibly hope to carry such a proposal in the Dáil as the various parties would certainly unite to defeat it. Northern Ireland was not apparently prepared to make a gesture of any sort or kind to Éire.

MR. CHAMBERLAIN said that Northern Ireland made precisely the same complaint against Éire, and had represented that under the draft trade agreement the protection which Northern Ireland now enjoyed was to be taken away from her, and at the same time Éire refused to make any favourable gesture towards her.

MR. DE VALERA said that if the matter could be put on a 'give and take' basis Éire might say to Northern Ireland that, in future she could send her products and manufactures to Great Britain, but that she should not send them into Éire. Northern Ireland might answer to the same effect and discussions for some arrangement might then take place between Éire and Northern Ireland.

MR. MACDONALD asked whether it was quite impossible for Mr. de Valera to discuss differential tariff arrangements in favour of Northern Ireland.

MR. DE VALERA answered in the affirmative. He was, however, prepared to discuss some arrangement based on giving of preferences by Éire to Northern Ireland and *vice versa*.

MR. MACDONALD pointed out that, while no doubt there were certain matters in the draft Trade Agreement beneficial to Northern Ireland, they were not comparable in importance and value to the very great advantages which Éire would get under the Agreement in the United Kingdom market.

MR. DE VALERA observed that the main advantages, so far as Éire was concerned, were the cessation of the Special Duties which had arisen out of the financial dispute which had been a quarrel between Great Britain and Éire and not between Éire and Northern Ireland.

SIR THOMAS INSKIP pointed out that Northern Ireland was, of course, part of the United Kingdom.

MR. DE VALERA said that he and his colleagues could not assent to this proposition.

SIR THOMAS INSKIP said that, when he reflected on how far the United Kingdom representatives were prepared to go in making concessions in order to establish real friendship and goodwill between the United Kingdom and Éire, he felt very deep regret that Éire was unable to assent to the differential tariff proposal.

MR. CHAMBERLAIN said that, before the present meeting had taken place, he had invited Mr. de Valera to have a private talk with him, and had been bitterly disappointed when Mr. de Valera told him that it was impossible for the Éire Government to entertain the proposal for a differential tariff in favour of Northern Ireland. He (Mr. Chamberlain) was deeply disappointed, because he had hoped that, as a result of the discussion which had taken place between the United Kingdom and the Éire representatives on the 23rd February a way had been found to make a real beginning towards the dissipation of the heavy cloud of suspicion and ill-will which hung over Éire and Northern Ireland. If Mr. de Valera had been able to make this gesture it would have gone a very long way towards enabling the United Kingdom Government to justify making the very important and valuable concessions which were in contemplation, and the making of which would undoubtedly be subjected to very strong and acute criticism from many quarters in the United Kingdom. He (Mr. Chamberlain) had told Mr. de Valera that on the question of defence the United Kingdom Government would have to face powerful criticism and disapproval, which he would have to answer by pointing out that, in return for the handing over to Éire by the United Kingdom of the defended ports, the United Kingdom were going to receive various undertakings and assurances regarding the use of the ports and the co-operation and collaboration of Éire in times of emergency. He (Mr. Chamberlain) had been very disappointed when Mr. de Valera had informed him that it was politically impossible for him to make a defence agreement of the kind which had been contemplated. The conversation had then turned to the present proposal, namely that Éire should give differential tariff treatment favourable to Northern Ireland. The adoption of this proposal would have gone far to justify the United Kingdom Government in concluding the kind of agreement that they had in mind, and, had Mr. de Valera been able to accept it, the United Kingdom Government would have been prepared to hand over to Éire the defended ports without attaching any conditions to the transfer, but relying on what Mr. de Valera had himself said as to what the policy of Éire would be in an emergency. The United Kingdom Government hoped that, by making this gesture towards meeting Nationalist aspirations in Éire, they would be taking the first step towards the establishment of confidence and improved relations between the two countries.

In view of what Mr. de Valera had now said, the situation had, of course, very much altered. While he (Mr. Chamberlain) did not, in any way, blame the Éire representatives, he felt bound to inform them that, in view of the not altogether unfavourable reception which the proposal had had at the meeting on 23rd February, the United Kingdom had approached the Government of Northern Ireland, recognizing that, in so doing, there was some risk that that Government might have resented the proposition being made to the Éire representatives before the Northern Ireland Government had had any opportunity of examining all its implications. In particular the Northern Ireland Government might have thought that the proposal was open, from their point of view, to the grave political objection that it might appear to be the thin end of the wedge so far as partition was concerned. In point of view, the Northern Ireland Government had informed the Government of the United Kingdom that they welcomed the proposal and were fully prepared to see it adopted. It would now be necessary for the United Kingdom Government to notify the Government of Northern Ireland that the proposal must be abandoned, owing to the refusal of the Government of Éire to entertain it. In the circumstances the position was now very much worse than if the proposal had never been formulated at all. If Mr. de Valera still said that the proposal could not be entertained, clearly that concluded the matter, but he (Mr. Chamberlain) hoped that it might still be found possible to have some further discussion of the proposal.

MR. DE VALERA said that he was quite prepared to consider an arrangement for an exchange of preferences between Éire and Northern Ireland and, in his view, the best course would be if the discussions could take place between representatives of Éire and of Northern Ireland meeting by themselves and working out an arrangement mutually satisfactory to Éire and Northern Ireland. The much larger proposal, namely that Éire should grant freedom of entry to the products and manufactures of Northern Ireland origin, was of an entirely different character and was one which, as he had said, the Government of Éire were not prepared to entertain.

MR. CHAMBERLAIN said that it seemed as if the whole situation would have to be discussed *de novo*.

MR. DE VALERA said that the position about the Treaty ports might be defined as follows. The United Kingdom Ministers had spoken of handing them over unconditionally to Éire. It was not at all certain that the people of Éire would welcome the gift. They would probably take the view that they did not want the ports if it meant undertaking a heavy financial burden. In his view the people of Éire would be right if they took that line. The burden would be a grievous one. His inquiries showed that it would be far heavier than was indicated by the document with which the United Kingdom Government had furnished him. The figures in that document only represented a fraction of the total cost of modernising the defence of Éire.

MR. CHAMBERLAIN observed that Mr. de Valera was referring to the cost of putting the whole country into a state of defence, not to the cost of modernising the Treaty ports.

MR. DE VALERA replied that, according to the advice which he had received, the United Kingdom estimate of the cost of modernising those ports also fell far short of the actual figure.

The United Kingdom estimate had been something like the following:-
Capital expenditure .... £1,400,000.
Annual maintenance costs – something
well in excess of .... £500,000.

The United Kingdom Government were mistaken in thinking that Éire could carry out what was necessary more cheaply than would have been possible for them (the United Kingdom). It would not, for example, be practicable for Éire to garrison the defended ports with voluntary personnel. It appeared rather that Éire would have to add some mobile mechanised units to their Army. In addition they would have to provide some small Naval forces – something on a bigger scale than the minesweepers which the United Kingdom authorities had suggested might be purchased at the outbreak of hostilities.

MR. MacENTEE thought that it was extremely doubtful whether it would be possible to purchase vessels suitable for conversion to minesweeping, after the outbreak of war.

SIR THOMAS INSKIP said that he would have thought that the existing regular army in Éire could have undertaken an appreciable part of the new task.

MR. MACDONALD said that it seemed as if Éire Ministers were determined to look on the black side of the picture. It was true that they would need to spend money on the ports, but it was commonly regarded as the privilege of a Sovereign Power to make provision for the defence of its territory. Would not the people of Éire be pleased at the prospect of recovering these ports in their territory which had been withheld, and of seeing their own flag waving over them? Mr. de Valera's own public speeches had pointed to this as the next national objective. He was now in a position to attain it.

MR. DE VALERA said that his people would form their view of the transaction in the light of existing circumstances. They would certainly not feel any enthusiasm over recovering the defended ports. They would see that war was in the offing and that there was a distinct prospect of social services being cut down in order to find money for armaments. They would blame their Government for entering into such commitments.

The estimate which his advisers had made of the capital cost of putting Éire into a state of defence far exceeded the figures he had mentioned a few minutes before. The Éire estimate was something of the order of £7 million. The annual maintenance costs also were larger in proportion. Was it conceivable that the Éire Minister of Defence should lay estimates before the Dáil to the tune of several million pounds?

SIR THOMAS INSKIP said that this was not putting the matter fairly. The estimate which we had given Mr. de Valera of the cost of modernising the treaty ports allowed of that process being spread over nine years.

MR. DE VALERA did not believe that it would be possible to spread the capital cost in this way. It would have to be found immediately if it was to be of any use. It would be nearer the truth to speak of the new equipment depreciating over a period of nine years.

MR. CHAMBERLAIN asked if Mr. de Valera was trying to make it appear that we were thrusting a burden upon Éire in making her take over the defended ports. He was lost in admiration of Mr. de Valera's skill in dialectics.

MR. DE VALERA retorted that the view which he had been expressing was not his own but that of the people of Éire. He might be able to sway his followers if he had anything like a case to put before them. If, for example, there was some prospect of partition being modified, matters would be very different.

As it was, there was the prospect of a war in which the majority of his people would not be sympathetic towards the United Kingdom.

MR. CHAMBERLAIN said that circumstances had now changed. It appeared that Mr. de Valera had no use for the differential tariff proposal. Possibly United Kingdom Ministers might decide to spare Mr. de Valera the embarrassment of having the treaty ports offered to him.

SIR THOMAS INSKIP observed that Éire Ministers had discovered that sovereignty meant financial sacrifice.

MR. DE VALERA said that if Éire stood alone she would have no fear of international complications. The only reason for any prospect there might be of her becoming involved in war was her propinquity to Great Britain.

Could United Kingdom Ministers indicate which aspect of the situation they would wish to discuss the following morning? Would it be desirable for the Trade Agreement to be considered in full conference?

MR. MACDONALD said that trade could have been discussed the same evening if things had gone better. The situation now was altered. It would be necessary to look once more at the general picture before thinking of continuing the trade discussions.

MR. CHAMBERLAIN thought that the United Kingdom Delegation would have to meet separately to discuss the new situation, with a view to seeing what were the prospects of making progress with the various outstanding issues.

MR. DE VALERA said that the Éire Delegation would welcome the opportunity of a private meeting. It was unfortunate that their Departmental advisers were not at hand.

MR. LEMASS said that there was no lack of subjects for discussion. For example, he would like to see a discussion on the Northern Ireland boundary, which appeared to have been drawn without any regard to the exigencies of the transport system. He had also in mind certain other matters affecting Northern Ireland.

The Meeting adjourned at this point.

It was arranged to hold the next Meeting between the two Delegations in the Prime Minister's Room at the House of Commons at 11.0 a.m. the following day, Friday, March 4th.

No. 146 NAI DT S10389 (Annex)

Minutes of the conference between representatives of the United Kingdom and Ireland (Secret) (I.N. (38) 8th Meeting) (Copy)
LONDON, 11.00 am, 4 March 1938

CONFERENCE
between
REPRESENTATIVES OF THE UNITED KINGDOM AND ÉIRE
Secretary's Notes of the Eighth Meeting of the Conference
held in the Prime Minister's Room, House of Commons,
on Friday, 4th March, 1938 at 11.0 a.m.

PRESENT

UNITED KINGDOM	*ÉIRE*
The Rt. Hon Neville Chamberlain, M.P., Prime Minister.	Mr. Eamon de Valera, Prime Minister and Minister for External Affairs.
The Rt. Hon. Sir John Simon, G.C.S.I., G.C.V.O., O.B.E., K.C., M.P., Chancellor of the Exchequer.	Mr. Sean F. Lemass, Minister for Industry and Commerce.
The Rt. Hon. Sir Samuel Hoare. Bt., G.C.S.I., C.B.E., C.M.G., M.P., Secretary of State for the Home Department.	Mr. Sean MacEntee, Minister for Finance.
The Rt. Hon. Malcolm MacDonald, M.P., Secretary of State for Dominion Affairs.	Dr. James Ryan, Minister for Agriculture.

THE FOLLOWING WERE ALSO PRESENT

The Rt. Hon Sir Thomas Inskip, C.B.E., K.C., M.P., Minister for Co-ordination of Defence.	Mr. J. W. Dulanty, C.B., C.B.E., High Commissioner for Éire.
The Rt. Hon. W. S. Morrison, M.C., K.C., M.P., Minister of Agriculture and Fisheries.	

Secretary   Sir R.B. Howorth, K.C.M.G., C.B.

CONFERENCE BETWEEN REPRESENTATIVES OF THE UNITED KINGDOM AND ÉIRE

The Draft Trade Agreement and the Position of Northern Ireland
MR. CHAMBERLAIN said that after the conclusion of the Meeting between United Kingdom and Éire Representatives on the previous evening,[1] he and his colleagues had discussed the new situation which had arisen and the best way of meeting it. He was sure that Mr. de Valera would fully understand that he (Mr. Chamberlain) was making no complaint but he felt that it was only right that Mr. de Valera and his colleagues should know how very disappointed all the United Kingdom Representatives had been with the conclusions which had been communicated to them on the previous evening by Mr. de Valera in regard to the attitude of Éire on the question of Defence and on the proposal for differential tariff treatment for Northern Ireland. He and his colleagues were all the more disappointed as it had appeared to them that the conversations had been going on fairly smoothly, and that it looked as if there was a good prospect of the ship being brought safely into port. However, it was no use crying over spilt milk, but he feared that he must ask Mr. de Valera once more whether what he had said on the subject of possible differential tariff treatment for Northern Ireland was his final word.

MR. DE VALERA said that the Éire Representatives had also discussed the position among themselves, and Mr. Lemass would indicate the economic difficulties and reactions which were felt to the proposal. He regretted that Mr. Chamberlain should have used the word 'complain' or even that there should have been any idea whatever that he (Mr. de Valera) had given the United Kingdom Representatives any reason to think of that word.

MR. CHAMBERLAIN pointed out that he had expressly disclaimed any intention of making any complaint. No such idea had ever entered his mind.

MR. DE VALERA, continuing, observed that at an earlier stage in the discussions he had stated that he had been turning over in his mind the possibility of a customs union for the whole of Ireland, but all the roads of approach seemed to him to be blocked by the Partition barrier. Moreover, it had been represented to him that there were great, if not insuperable, legal and administrative difficulties in the way of a customs union. In reply Mr. Chamberlain had said that he would be prepared to investigate the possibility of some tariff arrangement between Éire and Northern Ireland which would be beneficial to the latter. He (Mr. de Valera) had then pointed out that the consideration of such a proposal would involve discussions on points of detail and would necessarily take a very long time. He certainly had never accepted the proposal in principle and had never had any idea of any arrangement at the moment other than an exchange of preferences between Éire and Northern Ireland. He did not think that anything that he had said could justify any other conclusion.

MR. CHAMBERLAIN said that the United Kingdom Representatives accepted Mr. de Valera's statement without the least qualification. There had been a

---

[1] See above No. 145.

genuine misunderstanding. He and his colleagues had somehow obtained the impression that the free entry into Éire of products and manufactures of Northern Ireland origin was not unattractive to the Éire Representatives. Mr. de Valera on the other hand, had intended to convey that what he was prepared to discuss was some arrangement for an exchange of preferences between Éire and Northern Ireland.

MR. LEMASS said that up to the present he had had no opportunity of examining in detail with his officials the proposal that the products and manufactures of Northern Ireland should be given free entry into Éire, but he assumed that in any case such an arrangement would not apply to goods subject to the revenue duties, or to goods and products subject to quantitative regulation schemes.

MR. MACDONALD thought that what was contemplated was duty free entry into Éire from Northern Ireland of goods other than those subject to revenue duties. The quantitative restriction arrangements would operate separately.

MR. LEMASS, continuing, said that he would like to summarise certain economic objections which appeared to arise. Firstly, a number of Northern firms, some 20-25, had established factories in Éire in order to escape the Éire import tariff. He was advised that these firms would inevitably have to close down if the proposal was accepted.

MR. CHAMBERLAIN asked whether Mr. Lemass could give any estimate of the amount of employment provided by the factories in question.

MR. LEMASS said that the employment was considerable. Among the industries concerned was that engaged in the manufacture of shirts and collars.

MR. CHAMBERLAIN observed that if the amount of employment given in the factories was considerable this meant that much capital must have been invested in them, and that it was therefore very improbable that the owners would readily face the loss of their capital which closure of the factories would mean.

MR. LEMASS did not agree, and thought that the owners would be forced to close the factories because of the impossibility of successful competition with the comparable industries in Northern Ireland if tariff protection disappeared.

MR. CHAMBERLAIN pointed out that the same result would follow a union of Éire and Northern Ireland.

MR. DE VALERA said that in this event Éire would be prepared to make sacrifices and might indeed have to contemplate payment of compensation to those firms in Éire which would have to close down.

MR. LEMASS said that the second important reaction would be extensive undercutting by the flour and bread industries of Northern Ireland of the similar industries which had been established in Éire in pursuance of the Éire Government's policy of self-sufficiency in such matters. In fact that policy, to which the Éire Government attached very great importance, would probably have to be abandoned. Thirdly, the Éire Government had been compelled to impose restrictions on firms outside Éire opening branch factories within Éire. Legislation had been passed on the subject which made it necessary for an external firm to obtain a licence from the Éire Government before it could open a factory in Éire. That legislation would have to be repealed. Fourthly, there were a number of trades and industries other than those which he had already mentioned which would be very detrimentally affected by the proposal, for example, industries engaged in manufacturing ropes, twine, and paper, and the distributive trades. If the Éire Government accepted the proposal they would at once be faced with very considerable agitation on the part of the many interests which would be affected, and it would be particularly embarrassing to have to meet a situation in which the economic grievances were closely associated with political criticisms.

There were some directions in which it might be possible for Éire to make economic concessions to Northern Ireland without injury to Éire's own industries, but these would need very careful consideration and examination. The fact that hours of work and other labour conditions were more favourable to labour in Éire than in Northern Ireland would strengthen the tendency for industry to migrate from Éire to Northern Ireland. Speaking generally, industry had in the past developed mainly in the North-East corner of Ireland where the people had perhaps a greater aptitude for industrial pursuits than had the people in other parts of Ireland. The establishment in Éire of industry had been handicapped by the difficulty of securing suitable labour, much of which had had to come from off the land and had had to be specially trained.

The Government of Éire would be prepared to go a long way in the direction of the proposal if Partition could be ended, or even if some step could be taken which would mean the end of Partition within a measurable time, but from the purely economic point of view he himself was satisfied that for Éire to agree that the manufactures and products of Northern Ireland should be given free entry into Éire would give rise to well nigh insuperable difficulties.
SIR SAMUEL HOARE said that Mr. Lemass had suggested that, if given time, he might be able to indicate certain special privileges of an economic character which Éire might be able to offer to Northern Ireland and inquired what kind of privileges Mr. Lemass had in mind.
MR. LEMASS said that it would be very difficult for him to give any indication without making further inquiries. If the Éire Government saw some prospect of the ending of Partition they would, of course, bear this situation in mind and would refrain from encouraging the establishment of industries in Éire which would be likely to give rise to difficulty after Partition had disappeared. This was a matter which might very well form the subject of discussion between representatives of Éire and Northern Ireland, with a view to reaching some accommodation.
MR. CHAMBERLAIN said that the impression left on his mind by what Mr. Lemass had said was that if the only objections in the way of acceptance of the differential tariff proposal were of an economic character, there should be no insuperable difficulty in surmounting them, and that the ways and means of so doing could probably best be discussed between the representatives of Northern Ireland and Éire. If, however, in addition to the economic objections there also remained political difficulties of an insuperable character,

then he recognised that the position was different and, while it was perhaps not for him to make representations to the Éire representatives on what was their special responsibility, he felt that it was his duty to point out that he had put forward this proposal for differential tariff treatment for Northern Ireland because he was satisfied that the present was a very good time for breaking down the barrier of suspicion and ill will between Éire and Northern Ireland. He could not too strongly emphasise that if Mr. de Valera and his colleagues desired the union of all Ireland they could only hope to bring this about, not by the use of force or by the exercise of economic or other forms of pressure, but by cultivating the goodwill of the people of Northern Ireland, and in particular by demonstrating to them that their suspicions of the good faith and fair dealing of the Government and people of Éire were unfounded. He had greatly hoped that this proposal would have been a first and very important step towards the realisation of a better state of things. He recognised that, if Éire could have accepted it, it would have involved her in some sacrifices, which in themselves would have constituted a fine gesture to the people of Northern Ireland. It was not, however, only public opinion in Northern Ireland which had to be considered. A gesture of this kind would also have had a very striking effect on public opinion in Great Britain, and Mr. de Valera and his colleagues should reflect that possibly their most hopeful way of influencing public opinion in Northern Ireland would be through the influence of public opinion in Great Britain. The people of Great Britain had naturally not the same strong prejudices as existed on both sides of the border in Ireland. Moreover, the views of British public opinion on the whole Irish question were much less emphatic than they had been in the past. While, as he had stated on several occasions during the conversations, Great Britain would never tolerate any form of pressure on Northern Ireland to unite against her will with Éire, regard must be had to the fact that if public opinion in Great Britain came to the conclusion that on the whole Northern Ireland was adopting an unreasonable and indefensible attitude towards Éire, the fact that British public opinion took this view must have very important repercussions on public opinion in Northern Ireland.

SIR JOHN SIMON said that if the differential tariff proposal could have been adopted, the result would have been to establish a very special relationship between the two separate parts of Ireland. He had tried, to the best of his ability, to understand the intense and sincere feelings in Éire against the Northern Ireland contention that Ulster was an integral part of the United Kingdom, and was not a part of a United Ireland. If it was possible to accept a plan such as this, which made a start on the road towards a better understanding, it would not be difficult to bring home to public opinion in Great Britain the fact that Éire and Northern Ireland were not only geographically united but had many other common bonds and interests. Public opinion in Great Britain would, he felt sure, appreciate considerations of this kind, notwithstanding that they were based on sentiment rather than logic or material interests.

MR. DE VALERA said that it was exactly from the point of view which Mr. Chamberlain and Sir John Simon had expressed that he had endeavoured, though up to the present without success, to secure improved relations and better feeling between Éire and Northern Ireland. It was extremely difficult to establish any satisfactory contacts with Northern Ireland and it was due to this that Éire had been forced to undertake her industrial development programmes without previous consultation with Northern Ireland. It was most difficult for the Government of Éire to mention the question of free entry when Northern Ireland had made no kind of gesture. If he did so, he would be accused by his own supporters of running after Northern Ireland and trying to win them, and he would be mocked by the people of Northern Ireland for having made most valuable concessions without receiving anything in return.

MR. LEMASS said that there were a number of problems including unemployment insurance, transport, etc., in regard to which it would be very advantageous if Éire could get into close touch with Northern Ireland. At present there was no official contact between the two Governments. As an example of the disadvantages of the present lack of contact, he mentioned the strike on the Great Northern Railway, part of which was in Northern Ireland and the other part in Éire. The Éire Government made efforts to settle the strike in Dublin and the Northern Ireland Government made entirely separate efforts to settle the strike in Belfast, without any consultation or co-operation of any kind.

SIR SAMUEL HOARE said that failure to make contact was not the fault only of Northern Ireland. Neither side during the last 15 years had shown any disposition to make contact with the other.

MR. CHAMBERLAIN said that as a result of the discussion he did not propose to press Mr. de Valera and his colleagues any further on the proposal that there should be a differential tariff treatment for Northern Ireland. That proposal must accordingly be treated as withdrawn. It was also clear that there could be no agreement on the subject of defence, whether bilateral or unilateral. The last thing the United Kingdom Ministers wished to do would be to thrust upon the Éire Government a burden which that Government thought that it could not bear and which accordingly it might have to repudiate at some later time. All hope of an agreement on defence must therefore be abandoned.

There remained the question of the trade agreement, and the possibility of further consideration being given as to ways and means of assisting Northern Ireland which, in the events which had happened, had been placed in a difficult position. The United Kingdom Government now proposed to invite Mr. Andrews[1] to come to London accompanied by his experts and to examine the draft trade agreement in detail in order to ascertain whether any provisions were likely to be seriously injurious to Northern Ireland, and also whether there were any further concessions which would make the agreement tolerable and acceptable to Northern Ireland. He did not anticipate that

---

[1] John Miller Andrews (1871-1956), Unionist politician, Northern Ireland Minister of Labour (1931-7), Northern Ireland Minister of Finance (1937-40), Prime Minister of Northern Ireland (1940-3).

Mr. Andrews would adopt an unreasonable attitude and United Kingdom Ministers would certainly not encourage him to be unreasonable. It was imperative that the Government of Northern Ireland should now be consulted in the matter as clearly no useful purpose would be served by the United Kingdom making a trade agreement with Éire if that agreement was at once denounced in Northern Ireland. After seeing Mr. Andrews, the United Kingdom Ministers proposed to confer again with Mr. de Valera and his colleagues and endeavour to reach a settlement on the trade agreement.

MR. DE VALERA enquired how long the discussions with Mr. Andrews were likely to take.

SIR SAMUEL HOARE said that it was hoped that Mr. Andrews would arrive in London tomorrow morning, Saturday, March 5th, and that the discussions with him would occupy the whole day.

MR. DE VALERA pointed out that the meeting of the Éire Cabinet had been fixed for Wednesday next, March 9th, and could not be postponed.

MR. CHAMBERLAIN thought that the United Kingdom Ministers would know the reactions and requirements of Northern Ireland by Tuesday, March 8th, and that meetings with Mr. de Valera and his colleagues could be resumed on that day.

MR. MACDONALD said that the interval might be profitably devoted to further discussions on certain outstanding points on the draft trade agreement which did not directly concern Northern Ireland. While therefore reserving the position of Northern Ireland, perhaps Mr. Lemass would look into the possibility of making concessions to Northern Ireland by way of the special privileges, etc., to which he had referred. A meeting of the United Kingdom and Éire representatives concerned with the trade discussions might take place that afternoon to continue the examination of the other outstanding questions on the draft trade agreement.

MR. LEMASS said that he was not quite sure what Mr. MacDonald had in mind. The extent to which the Éire representatives could go in making a trade agreement or in giving special privileges to Northern Ireland must depend on whether partition was or was not to be terminated.

MR. MACDONALD said that his proposal was to continue the exploration of those other outstanding questions on the trade agreement which had already been examined, but in regard to which no conclusion had yet been reached, such as the position of eggs and poultry, and fish.

MR. CHAMBERLAIN observed that in publicly defending any trade agreement that might be arrived at, each side would naturally have to take the line which suited it best with its own public opinion. There was of course no question of both sides agreeing to take exactly the same line.

MR. LEMASS pointed out that there were certain economic questions at issue between Northern Ireland and Éire, agreement on which would involve legislation. So far as Northern Ireland was concerned that legislation would have to be passed by the Parliament of Northern Ireland and not by the Parliament of the United Kingdom.

SIR SAMUEL HOARE said that he would be very grateful if Mr. Lemass would let him have, entirely without prejudice, a list of the subjects on which it might be possible for Éire to make concessions to Northern Ireland. Such a list would be of very great assistance to him in his discussions with Mr. Andrews. He fully realised that it would not be possible for Mr. Lemass to supply a list mentioning every conceivable item, but he might be able to supply a list giving a number of subjects by way of illustration.

MR. LEMASS said that he was quite willing to supply such a list to Sir Samuel Hoare, without prejudice and on the clear understanding, of course, that the Government of Éire would be in no way committed to making concessions in regard to any matters mentioned on the list.

MR. CHAMBERLAIN said that it seemed to him that the important thing was to try and reach some agreement in principle on any special concessions to be made to Northern Ireland. There was no need to go into details at the moment and these could be worked out afterwards at leisure.

MR. DE VALERA enquired when it was proposed to hold the next meeting of the Conference.

MR. CHAMBERLAIN suggested that the next meeting should be held on the morning of Tuesday, March 8th.

MR. DE VALERA observed that if in the interval substantial progress was made a meeting on Tuesday morning left very little time for an agreement to be concluded. If after the discussions with Mr. Andrews and the further discussions on trade between United Kingdom and Éire representatives, it seemed possible that a basis of agreement was in sight, perhaps the heads of such an agreement could be drawn up for acceptance at the full meeting of the Conference on Tuesday morning.

MR. CHAMBERLAIN said that it might be possible to arrange for a meeting of the Conference on the evening of Monday, March 7th, but he was satisfied that no useful purpose would be served by trying to arrange such a meeting before Monday evening. Steps would be taken to notify Mr. de Valera and his colleagues on Monday morning, March 7th, if there seemed any prospect of a meeting being held on the evening of that day, say at about 6 p.m. at the House of Commons. If for any reason this was found impossible then the next meeting would have to take place on Tuesday morning, March 8th, at No. 10, Downing Street, and Mr. de Valera and his colleagues would be notified as early as possible of the time proposed for this meeting.

MR. MACDONALD suggested that the resumed discussions on trade should take place at a meeting to be held at the Dominions Office that same afternoon at 4 p.m.

The proceedings then terminated.

No. 147 UCDA P67/179

Extracts from a handwritten letter from Seán MacEntee to Margaret MacEntee (Dublin)

LONDON, 5 March 1938

Friday afternoon
My dearest Margaret,
I was delighted to get your note this morning. It was the one bright element in an otherwise disagreeable forenoon. We did not settle things this morning and in my view are now far from a satisfactory conclusion to the whole proceedings. I think definitely – and this is for your own ear and no others – that we shall not get the ports and that if we do ~~get~~ reach agreement about trade finance that it will be much less satisfactory than it would have been if we had been prepared to deal with obvious facts and not to go window-dressing now about Partition. A lot however will depend upon what transpires over the week-end, as the British have asked Andrews of Northern Ireland to come over to discuss some aspects of the proposed trade agreement with them. We are remaining over to continue the departmental discussions this afternoon and to-morrow and in the expectation of having a plenary meeting with the British on Monday evening.
[matter omitted]
I am dining with McElligott and Sir Warren Fisher, the head of the British Treasury here this evening. Rory M-O'F[1] and B.A.[2] were pressing me to dine with them but I had to make this other engagement instead. I don't know yet what we are going to do over the week-end. It is a miserable prospect to look forward to but is unavoidable. I simply loathe here in these circumstances, but there seems to be no remedy. I wish you were here – it is so hard meeting only outsiders all day and not being able to speak freely to them.
[matter omitted]

Yours SEÁN

No. 148 UCDA P67/179

Extracts from a handwritten letter from Seán MacEntee to Margaret MacEntee (Dublin)

LONDON, 10 March 1938

Thursday
My dearest Margaret,
[matter omitted]
De. V's conference with MacDonald did not finish until after 12.30 last night and the upshot of it is that now it is extremely unlikely that we shall be home for the week-end. I understand that the British are meeting Andrews today and are then meeting late to-night and that afterwards it is probable that the

[1] Possibly a reference to the businessman Rory More-O'Farrell.
[2] Not identified.

Trade Ministers may have a meeting some time after 10.00 pm. If the Trade portion of the agreement is settled or is on the way of settlement we may discuss Finance and other questions tomorrow and possibly again on Saturday in detail in the hope of being able to arrive at an agreement by Monday. A great deal at the moment depends on what happens tonight. Everybody here is terribly fed-up with the hanging [on] over the weekend. But it has been difficult to avoid the breakdown, which seemed so imminent last weekend, and to return home now would mean losing a lot of hard-fought ground. Jim Ryan and I went out for lunch to Simpson's in the Strand. It was very good and I think he enjoyed it. We had steak, kidney, mushroom and oyster pudding and I was just saying to him that it contained nearly everything you liked except chicken.
[matter omitted]

Yours
SEÁN

No. 149 UCDA P150/2501

Handwritten note by Eamon de Valera shown to Malcolm MacDonald
LONDON, 12 March 1938

Shown to Mr. McD as the type of statement that would be useful. I kept this copy.

Saturday, March 12, 1938?
The Gov. of the U.K. declare that it is no part of the policy or intention of the Gov. of the U.K. to oppose any arrangement which may be freely and voluntarily entered into between the Gov. of Éire and the Gov. of N.I. The Gov. of the U.K. recognise that such an arrangement would be a valuable contribution to the friendly relations between G.B. and I. and to world appeasement. The Gov. of the U.K. will accordingly welcome every improvement in the mutual relations of Éire and N.I. and far from raising any difficulties will on the contrary be ready to take any practicable steps that may be necessary to facilitate any arrangement desired of the two ~~parties~~ Governments for the development of closer relations between them or for the establishment of a united Ireland.

No. 150 NAI DFA 227/7

Confidential report from Francis T. Cremins to Joseph P. Walshe (Dublin)
(S. 7/36) (Confidential)
GENEVA, 12 March 1938

With reference to the developments in Austria, I have to state, for the information of the Minister, that I enquired at the Secretariat whether any action by the Council had been invoked by any Member, and was informed by Mr. Lester that so far, this morning, nobody had made any move in the matter. You will remember that when in 1931 the question of the Anschluss arose, the matter came before the Council at the instance of the British Government, as both the French and British Governments questioned the legitimacy of the proposed Customs Union which seemed likely to affect Austrian independence, and brought into question, *inter alia*, the Protocol of October 4th, 1922. The international situation is however now very different from what it was seven years ago. For one thing Germany is rearmed, and the axe – not to mention the triangle – exists, which alone will make the Western Powers pause before taking any dangerous steps. Secondly, the League is known to be too weak to bring into play on behalf of Austria the system of collective security. And Italy's interest in the independence of Austria is overshadowed at the moment by her greater interests elsewhere. I find that so far there is little disposition amongst my colleagues to believe that war for the protection of Austria is likely. The situation is admittedly dangerous, and the time may come soon when the Western Powers may seriously question Germany's proceedings in Central Europe, but that time does not seem to have yet arrived.

There is at Geneva much sympathy for M. Schuschnigg[1] and for Austria in the present situation, but it is a question if the Chancellor was not a little too provocative after the arrangement come to at Berchtesgaden. His attitude would have been more comprehensible if he had broken at once with Herr Hitler, but, as an Italian said to me here, he seemed to have only recognised when he had returned home the full implications of the arrangement imposed upon him, and then he found it necessary to endeavour to retrace his steps somewhat. In view of Herr Schuschnigg's statement and attitude, and of the proposal for a plebiscite, the subsequent drastic action by Germany has hardly been a surprise, however reprehensible it may be. Germany, like Japan, has a facility for choosing the psychological moment – with France without a Government, Italy immersed in other difficulties, and Russia shocking the world by her political trials.

I learned last night from one of my colleagues that when Herr Schuschnigg received the ultimatum from Germany he asked Rome whether he could rely on Italian aid but that he received no reply.

[signed] F.T. CREMINS
Permanent Delegate

No. 151 NAI CAB 2/1

Extract from the minutes of a meeting of the Cabinet
(G.C. 1/14) (Item 1)

DUBLIN, 13 March 1938

NEGOTIATIONS WITH THE BRITISH GOVERNMENT
The Taoiseach and the other Ministers who had been in London reported on the stage which had been reached in the negotiations with representatives of the British Government.

---

[1] Kurt Schuschnigg (1897-1977), Chancellor of Austria (1934-March 1938).

No. 152 NAI DT S10389

> *Press communiqué following the return of the Irish Delegation from London*
> DUBLIN, 13 March 1938

PRESS COMMUNIQUÉ

Following the return of the Irish delegation from London this morning, a meeting of the Government was held in Merrion Street at 11.30 a.m., all the members being present.[1] The Taoiseach and the other Ministers who had been in London reported on the stage which has now been reached in the negotiations with representatives of the British Government. The discussion which followed lasted until 2.15 p.m. The Government will meet again tomorrow (Monday) at 11 a.m.

[initialled] MOM[2]

No. 153 NAI DT S10389A

> *Press communiqué following a meeting of the Government*
> DUBLIN, 14 March 1938

PRESS COMMUNIQUÉ

The matters arising at the present stage of the negotiations with the representatives of the British Government were further considered at a meeting of the Government from 11 a.m. to 1.30 p.m., and at a resumed meeting from 4 p.m. to 6.30 p.m. to-day. The discussion will be continued at a meeting on Wednesday, the 16th instant, at 11 a.m.

No. 154 UCDA P150/2179

> *Handwritten letter from John W. Dulanty to Eamon de Valera enclosing a confidential report (No. 9) (Secret)*
> LONDON, 14 March 1938

Dear Taoiseach,

I am venturing to send the enclosed Secret Report Direct to you since at this stage you might think that preferable.

The British hope to send the complete statement in our pouch tomorrow (Tuesday) evening.

I am with great respect and esteem,

Yours sincerely,
JOHN W. DULANTY

---

[1] See above No. 151.
[2] Handwritten footnote by Maurice Moynihan: 'Telephoned above communiqué to Mr. Shán O Cuiv at 2.40 p.m. for issue to the Press 13/3/38'. Shán O Cuiv was Director of the Government Information Bureau (1934-40).

[Enclosure]
(No. 9) (Secret)

In accordance with An Taoiseach's instructions on the telephone this afternoon I went to the House of Commons and told Mr. Malcolm MacDonald informally that it was almost certain that my Government would not be able to accept the proposals of the British Government made at the close of the conversations last week.

The provisions put forward late in the negotiations about our making big concessions to the North had made the proposals completely impossible for the Government of Éire.

It might well be that our people could have accepted the other items even though nothing had been done on the question of partition, but so long as the minority in the Six Counties is treated as it is today any concession to the Six Counties would be a sheer impossibility.

The statement on partition containing as it did nothing of a positive character was altogether inadequate.

I said that An Taoiseach was anxious to have as quickly as possible a letter enclosing a formal statement of the complete proposals, which statement he could circulate to the members of his Executive Council. At present he felt that even he had only received the proposals in a fragmentary form. He would like to have such a formal document before him when he would in reply convey a definite formal decision. An Taoiseach would arrange to try and agree on the form which the public statement by both Governments should take. He did not wish to add to the difficulties of the situation but, as he had stated at the plenary meeting, he was bound to reserve to himself complete freedom of action in regard to Partition. If no final decision was reached by St. Patrick's Day he would certainly in his usual annual messages on that day have to refer to Partition and the Northern question.

Mr. MacDonald expressed his great disappointment at what I said. He would begin immediately to draw up the proposals in such a form as would enable An Taoiseach to circulate them and reach a formal decision. He repeated his regret that the trade proposals about the North and the suggested statement on Partition were unacceptable. In regard to the former, he was afraid there was no possibility of their getting the proposed Agreement, as it now stood, through the House of Commons without that provision. On the proposed statement by the British Government on Partition, he emphasised that their position was very similar to that of An Taoiseach on the question of the ports in that the less they said publicly the more they could do if and when an Agreement were ratified. It was no expression of a merely pious hope but it was their firm purpose to take definite action with the Northern people if they could secure acceptance of the Agreement. I turned once more to the question of An Taoiseach's reference to Partition on St. Patrick's Day. Mr. MacDonald rejoined that that was of course clearly understood and the President was perfectly free to refer to Partition. In view, however, of the importance of trying to keep the right kind of atmosphere he sincerely hoped that care would be taken in any speeches or articles in the newspapers to refrain from expressions which might be embarrassing.

As an example of the need for care in what was said, especially by An Taoiseach's colleagues, he told me that Sir Thomas Inskip had met Mr. Pakenham in the street on Saturday last when the latter said that as usual the Northern people had 'busted the show'. The discussions, said Mr. Pakenham, were proceeding fairly satisfactorily and it looked as though an agreement might be reached when the North came in and dictated terms which made an agreement impossible. Sir Thomas Inskip said to Mr. MacDonald that he felt very upset. He thought after the battles they had had with the North and in which he had taken part it was very hard to be told that the North had dictated the terms, and he thought that Mr. Pakenham had been speaking with someone with inside knowledge. I said that I knew that Mr. Pakenham had consulted An Taoiseach about a lecture he was intending to deliver but I felt sure that An Taoiseach had said no more about the course of the negotiations than he had said to Press men in giving them general backgrounds. Mr. MacDonald said doubtless Mr. Pakenham put his own interpretation on what was said but he wished to do no more than cite it as an example of the need for care. Sir Thomas Inskip had been friendly all through and he was naturally anxious not to lose his support, as seemed probable when Sir Thomas Inskip spoke to him.

[signed] J.W. DULANTY
High Commissioner

No. 155 UCDA P150/2171

Confidential report from John W. Dulanty to Joseph P. Walshe (Dublin)
(No. 10) (Secret)
LONDON, 15 March 1938

On the day of his arrival in London I left a card on Mr. Kennedy,[1] the recently appointed American Ambassador, informing his Secretary that I would make a call later when he had settled in to his new duties. Accordingly an appointment was arranged for today when I called at the American Embassy.

Mr. Kennedy began by speaking of his close and sustained interest in Ireland and the Irish. He did not wish to ask questions about the progress of the negotiations between the Irish and the British Governments but he would like to be allowed to say how much he hoped that they might reach fruition.

Speaking in the strictest confidence he said that President Roosevelt's opinion was that a settlement between the Irish and British Governments was a matter of importance in regard to the question of Anglo-American relations. Whilst that was the President's opinion it could not be regarded as the opinion of the American Government since the subject had not been through or fully considered by the State Department. Nevertheless he had himself spoken to Mr. Chamberlain – a good friend of Éire, the Ambassador thought

---

[1] Joseph 'Joe' Patrick Kennedy Sr (1888-1969), Irish-American businessman and Democratic Party supporter, United States Ambassador to Britain (1938-40) and father of John Fitzgerald Kennedy, President of the United States (1960-3).

– acquainting him with President Roosevelt's opinion. He emphasised the very secret character of what he was saying and entreated me to communicate his remarks to no one but An Taoiseach himself.

[signed] J.W. DULANTY
High Commissioner

No. 156 UCDA P150/2179

Confidential report from John W. Dulanty to Joseph P. Walshe (Dublin)
(No. 11) (Secret)

LONDON, 15 March 1938

In a letter of even date the Secretary of the Department has informed An Taoiseach that in a conversation this morning Mr. MacDonald told me that he would hold up, for the present, the despatch of the formal communications of his Government on the recent London discussions.

At the close of the conversation on that point, however, Mr. MacDonald adverted to An Taoiseach's intention to refer to Partition in his St. Patrick's Day messages. Repeating his observation of yesterday he said it was absolutely clear that An Taoiseach was perfectly free to say whatever he pleased on that subject. On that there could be no question or doubt.

Having said that Mr. MacDonald respectfully suggested it would be a great help to him if on St. Patrick's Day An Taoiseach could keep in mind the very real difficulties the British have in their party in regard to Northern Ireland.

[signed] J.W. DULANTY
High Commissioner

No. 157 UCDA P150/2183

Letter from Joseph P. Walshe to Eamon de Valera (Dublin)
(Secret)

LONDON, 15 March 1938

My dear President,
I saw both Harding and Batterbee this morning, and the High Commissioner saw MacDonald for the purpose of conveying informally your instructions of yesterday evening.

The complete elimination of 'Northern Ireland' and the trade concessions intended therefor would be quite impossible. They must have a Maia to carry the Mercury and concessions of advantage to Northern Ireland form now the only element left to fill that role.[1]

---

[1] 'Maia' and 'Mercury' were the names given to the two components of an experimental system of piggy-back transatlantic flight (the 'Mayo Composite', after its designer Robert Mayo) whereby a modified C-Class Shorts Sunderland flying boat 'Maia' would lift the smaller 'Mercury', a Shorts S-20 floatplane, on its back to a cruising altitude. The 'Mercury', having saved its fuel in the assisted take-off, would then separate from the

From the reactions of Harding and Batterbee I should say that we have a chance of succeeding in your purpose by conceding the list to the United Kingdom as such. They would understand that in the new conditions certain exceptions would have to be made. The inclusion of an Article on contingent concessions to Northern Ireland would not be necessary nor do I think it could be accepted by the British without putting themselves in the position of putting on record a view – at least by implication – that Northern Ireland were here and now persecuting the minority.

I think that your talks with the Prime Minister and MacDonald have convinced them that the discrimination is real, and I believe that they will take measures very soon to put an end to it. Sean Murphy will have told you that the British are sending their formal document through the High Commissioner this evening and they expect you to make your objection and/or proposals in a formal document in return. Meanwhile I think it would be a good thing if Sean Leydon and Jenkins[1] would explore the list with a view to excluding from it the items which you wish to omit.

Harding and Batterbee are becoming somewhat pessimistic about an agreement being reached. I am making due allowance for the element of bluff in this attitude, but I fear that they really apprehend serious difficulties if the European situation becomes more and more the all absorbing occupation of Ministers here.

As I already mentioned to you I am somewhat anxious about the future of the Prime Minister. Should a real war situation develop – as it will if Hitler threatens Czecho-Slovakia – the Prime Minister may have to give way to a younger man before the clamour of the 'pinks' of all parties who think a preventive war now would be the best way to stop Hitler in his headlong career.

The dangerous element in the occupation of Austria is not the occupation itself but the fact that the Germans have used 200,000 men for a task which could easily have been accomplished by 10,000. A further advance from Austria within a short time seems indicated.

You heard from the High Commissioner on the phone on Sunday that the Duce told Colonel Beck[2] that Czecho-Slovakia was to be the next victim and would have her turn within a few weeks. I don't know how much importance should be attached to Secret Service reports of this kind but the facts are ominous enough.

A postponement of the Agreement – if there is going to be one – would in the circumstances be giving hostages to fortune.

(contd. from previous page) 'Maia' and continue on its transatlantic flight. Test flights took place in 1937 and the 'Mercury' was successfully launched in mid-air from the 'Maia' over Foynes, County Limerick, on 21 July 1938. The scheme never saw commercial operation, being superseded by improved C-Class and G-Class flying boats and superior American Boeing flying boats. In Greek mythology the nymph Maia was the eldest of the Pleiades, the seven daughters of Atlas and Pleione. She was the mother of Hermes, the Messenger of Zeus (Hermes' father) and the Herald of the Olympian gods. Hermes' counterpart in Roman mythology is Mercury. Mercury is also god of travellers, commerce and speed.

[1] T. Gilmour Jenkins, Head of the Commercial Treaty Department, Board of Trade, London.
[2] Colonel Józef Beck (1894-1944), Polish Foreign Minister (1932-39).

The phantom of the reunification by force of these countries is never wholly out of my mind, and as we come nearer to the unknown and incalculable factors involved in a war situation I can't help feeling that the phantom might become very real.

It may be an idle fear but you will not take it amiss if I express it once more to you at this very critical hour of our history.

However much time it may take from our duties at home I believe we should go on now to the final discussion without interruption. Perhaps enough progress can be made within a few days to send you a final and acceptable document. You could then come over and sign.

I remain, My dear President,
With great respect and esteem
Yours very sincerely,
[signed] J.P. WALSHE

P.S. When coming to the end of this note I got your instruction about the document. I immediately phoned to Harding and have since seen him. The High Commissioner has also seen MacDonald. The document has been held up and the Board of Trade are expecting Mr. Leydon to discuss the list with them. Their political difficulties according to Harding will be greatly increased by the suggestion to omit Northern Ireland but we hope to win them round to your point of view.

No. 158 NAI DFA 227/7

Extract from a confidential report from Francis T. Cremins to Joseph P. Walshe
(Dublin)
(S. 7/36) (Confidential)

GENEVA, 15 March 1938

[matter omitted]

With regard to the international situation there seems to be some increase in pessimism here, and less hope of a peaceful solution. It is being whispered with regard to Lord Halifax's talks with Hitler that the latter's aims proved to be so outlandish in regard to expansion, etc. that consideration by the other Powers is hardly to be thought of. No details are of course given, but those who always opposed concessions to Germany on the ground that the German people could never be satisfied, and that there was therefore no use in endeavouring to satisfy them, continue to argue that the sole way in which German aims can be damped down is to push on with the present dangerous armaments policy and to hope for the best from America.

No. 159 NAI CAB 2/1

Extract from the minutes of a meeting of the Cabinet
(G.C. 1/17) (Item 3)

DUBLIN, 22 March 1938

NEGOTIATIONS WITH THE BRITISH GOVERNMENT, 1938

The Taoiseach adverted to a Question to be addressed to him in the Dáil on Wednesday, 23rd March, 1938, by Deputy Cosgrave,[1] asking whether he was yet in a position to make a statement to the Dáil on the negotiations with the British Government. He stated that he proposed to reply on the following lines:-

'I regret that I am not in a position to make a statement at present. We are endeavouring to bring the negotiations to a conclusion as quickly as possible, and I can assure the Deputy that I will take the earliest opportunity to make a statement to the Dáil.'

The proposed reply was approved.

[initialled] POC[2]

No. 160 UCDA P150/2179

Confidential report from John W. Dulanty to Joseph P. Walshe (Dublin)
(No. 13) (Secret)

LONDON, 22 March 1938

I told Mr. Malcolm MacDonald that An Taoiseach would be replying to a question in the Dáil tomorrow (Wednesday) asking whether he was in a position to make a statement about the negotiations between the Irish and British Governments, and that An Taoiseach intended to reply that he regretted he was not in a position to make a statement at present but would suggest that a similar question might be put down in a week's time.

Mr. MacDonald thanked me for the information but said he was gravely doubtful whether they would be through with their discussions with the Six County people by tomorrow week. They, the British, had been set a difficult task and it might be better not to raise the hope that in a week's time a definite statement would be possible.

Mr. Jenkins, who is in charge of the Commercial Treaty Department of the British Board of Trade, has all through the negotiations been helpful. He told me today that the Six County people had asked for a much longer time in which to carry out their investigations but that he had refused and had insisted upon the Northern Ireland officials meeting him without delay. He had been speaking to Belfast this morning he told me and it was expected that the Northern Ireland officials would be over here on Friday of this week. It was

---

[1] William T. Cosgrave (1880-1965), first President of the Executive Council (1922-32), leader of the Cumann na nGaedheal party (1923-33), Leader of the Opposition (1932-44), leader of the Fine Gael party (1933-44).

[2] Padraig Ó Cinnéide, Assistant Secretary to the Cabinet.

almost certain that, after the officials had conferred, reference back to the Six County Ministers would be necessary, involving a journey back to Belfast and then back to London. Mr. Jenkins felt confident that it would be at least a fortnight from today before they were in a position to make a definite statement on the Northern questions.

Although I think his personal views and his official attitude have been much more in support of our case than that of the Six County proposals he did say to me today that he thought the Six County people were in a real difficulty, apart entirely from any political considerations. They form at present one of the most depressed of the depressed areas of the United Kingdom and even a slight reduction in their export trade would be a serious matter for them. He hoped they would be able either by depressed area assistance i.e. financial help or some other way to buy off the Northern opposition but he made the point that before they could reach the stage even of making proposals of this character a good deal of prior investigation and discussion was unavoidable.

[signed] J.W. DULANTY
High Commissioner

No. 161 UCDA P150/2179

Confidential report from John W. Dulanty to Joseph P. Walshe (Dublin)
(No. 14) (Secret)

LONDON, 23 March 1938

Mr. Malcolm MacDonald called a meeting at five this evening in his room at the Dominions Office of the High Commissioners. In addition to Mr. MacDonald there was Mr. R.A. Butler, Parliamentary Secretary for Foreign Affairs. All the High Commissioners attended except Mr. Massey,[1] who was out of town.

We were handed a copy of a telegram – nine foolscap pages in length – which was being despatched to-night informing the several Commonwealth Governments of the main lines of Mr. Chamberlain's speech on foreign affairs to-morrow, Thursday, afternoon in the British House of Commons.

We read fairly quickly through the telegram without being able to study carefully the full significance of its numerous paragraphs.

Before the discussion began I called Mr. MacDonald's attention to the fact that the 'Daily Telegraph' last week had stated that the British Prime Minister was considering the opinions of the other Commonwealth Governments. I also referred to a reference by the Parliamentary Correspondent (generally well-informed from Whitehall) of the London Times in its issue of to-day to messages which had passed between the Government of the United Kingdom and the Governments of the Dominions, and also to a question which is to be put to Mr. MacDonald to-night in the House of Commons as

---

[1] (Charles) Vincent Massey (1887-1967), Canadian High Commissioner in London (1935-46), Governor General of Canada (1952-9).

to whether the Dominions were consulted with regard to the situation which was created by Mr. Eden's resignation from the Government. There seemed to me to be a risk that the conclusion might be drawn that Éire had been consulted by the British Government on this question of foreign affairs and I wished to make it clear beyond any doubt that I was attending the meeting solely for the purpose of receiving any information which the British Cabinet wished to have transmitted to my Government. In no sense was I there for the purpose of consultation.

Mr. MacDonald agreed entirely and said that both his office and the Prime Minister's office had tried to get the press to give the correct view. The British telegrams were despatched to the Commonwealth Governments and the meetings of High Commissioners, including the present one, were called *simply to acquaint the partner*[1] Governments of the position and intentions of the British Government. It was true that whilst some Dominion Governments had, on receipt of these telegrams and reports from their High Commissioners, instructed the latter to inform the British Government of the views of the Governments they represent, other Commonwealth Governments did no more than receive the information. It was therefore quite clear to him that the meetings – such as the one then in progress – were for information only.

Some desultory discussion then took place on the draft of the final form of the telegram which the Department will doubtless receive this evening.

[signed] J.W. DULANTY
High Commissioner

No. 162 NAI DFA 119/45

Extracts from the New York Consulate annual report from Leo McCauley to Robert Brennan (Washington)

NEW YORK, 31 March 1938

[matter omitted]

Deportations, Desertions, Etc.

Seventy-one deportation cases were dealt with of which thirty were concluded.

Enquiries were received from 40 persons in Ireland seeking to find missing relatives and the Consulate General was successful in finding 9 of these persons and putting them in touch with their relatives.

Ten cases of desertion were dealt with during the period and financial contributions for the deserted spouse in Ireland were obtained in 4 of these cases. Twenty-two distress cases were brought to the notice of the Consulate General.

[matter omitted]

---

[1] Underlined by reader.

New York World's Fair, 1939

Preliminary enquiries, discussions and reports concerning Irish participation in the Fair made increasing demands on the time of the officers of the Consulate General as the year advanced. Numerous visits had to be made to the Fair Corporation's offices at the Empire State Building and also to the Fair site at Flushing, Long Island. Additional work arose from the necessity for dealing with letters and visits from engineers, designers, architects, publicity firms and other persons offering their services in connection with the Irish exhibit. The activities connected with the Fair made very heavy demands on the time of the Consul General towards the end of the period under review. In his capacity as Commissioner General for Ireland, he signed the contract reserving space on the 31st March, 1938.
[matter omitted]

Pan American Airways

As in previous years, the Consulate General was in touch with Pan American Airways in connection with the proposed Transatlantic Air Service.
[matter omitted]

Repayment Office for Dáil Éireann External Loans

The work of repayment was terminated during the year and the Repayment Office closed on the 31st October, 1937. A certain amount of correspondence has been carried on by the Consulate General with Bondholders since that date, but every effort has been made to restrict this correspondence as much as possible.
[matter omitted]

No. 163 NAI DFA Madrid Embassy 10/11

Confidential report from Leopold H. Kerney to Joseph P. Walshe (Dublin (S.J. 10/1) (Copy)

St Jean de Luz, 13 April 1938

Frank RYAN

Further to my minute of 4th inst.,[1] relating to the capture of Frank RYAN by Franco's forces in Spain, I give you hereunder a summary of information obtained by me last night from Carney, the correspondent of the 'New York Times' in Franco's territory. I would, however, remind you of an opinion expressed by me on more than one occasion to the effect that Carney's outlook is prejudiced by his partisan feelings which make it impossible for him to take a detached and purely objective view of matters relating to the civil war in Spain.

Frank RYAN was captured with his battalion on the road between Alcaniz and Gandesa on the day on which Gandesa was occupied by Franco's forces, either Friday 1st or Saturday 2nd April. Ryan is a Captain in the Major Attlee Battalion of the 15th International Brigade and Carney believes that he is actually Commander of that Battalion. He was captured with about 350 others of

---

[1] Not printed.

British, American and other nationalities, having been taken by surprise by
Italian troops. Carney says that if these men had been captured by other than
Italian troops they would have been shot out of hand; he says that the Italians
are anxious to avoid reprisals on Italian prisoners in the hands of their
enemies and saw to it that these men were loaded up in lorries for removal to
Zaragoza. He states that other 'guarantees', without specifying the nature of
these, were taken by the Italians for the safety of their prisoners. It is apparently quite a normal thing for prisoners to be put to death on the roadside by
their captors whilst being escorted from the front to the rear. Carney says that
the Tercio (Foreign Legion) and the International Brigade are particularly
ferocious towards each other and that it is definitely established practice not
to take any prisoners alive when these forces meet in battle.

Reuter's agent did not see Frank Ryan when he sent his report of latter's
capture; he obtained this information from Spanish journalists who had noted
the names of several of these prisoners; a photograph of Ryan was taken either
by these journalists or by the authorities but no copy is available. Carney saw
Frank Ryan at the prison in Zaragoza on Monday 4th April being accompanied
by Colonel Jusset, Franco's military juridical assessor; he was the only foreign
newspaper correspondent allowed to see him. Colonel Jusset, who was with
Carney during the evening and till a late hour at night, told Carney that there
had been some intervention on behalf of Frank Ryan and that Franco 'was very
annoyed' that there should be any intervention on behalf of such a man. For
this reason it was desired that there should be no publicity at all given to
Ryan's case and instructions had been given accordingly to the different journalists, although too late to prevent Reuter's message.

I would here mention that my telegram from San Sebastian on Monday 4th
April[1] would have reached Burgos probably at about 3 p.m. and, if the intervention referred to by Colonel Jusset was mine, news of it must have been
transmitted to him by telephone from Burgos to Zaragoza the same afternoon.

Carney states that Arnold Lunn, an American author and occasional newspaper correspondent who is now in Spain and who is very much pro-Franco,
has been interesting himself on behalf of Frank Ryan but Carney was not very
communicative on this point and did not know Lunn's present whereabouts.
He states that no other Irish volunteers from Ireland were arrested with Ryan;
he had not heard anything about a man named Byrne from Dublin mentioned
in Reuter's message. Carney could hardly find words emphatic enough to
express the bad opinion he had formed of Ryan, who, it appeared, had glow-
ered at and insulted his visitor and who 'looked like a gorilla'. Ryan accused
Carney of doing fascist propaganda in the 'New York Times' and of being in
the pay of the fascists; when Carney remarked in the course of conversation
that the I.R.A. had been dissolved he was told that he knew as little about
Spain as he did about Ireland and this insult rankles very much in Carney's
mind; he accuses Ryan of being an atheist and anti-religious, of wanting to
have nothing to do with the Church or the priests who are on the side of fascism. He states that the man's whole attitude is such as to turn everybody

---

[1] Not printed.

against him and make his case even worse and that he declares himself to be a separatist republican just like the Basques and the Catalans.

Colonel Jusset told Carney that Ryan was fighting with the Republicans when Brunete was taken from Franco in July 1937 and that he had found on Ryan certain documents, apparently of a compromising nature, and also some jewellery which had been the property of one of Franco's officers who had been taken prisoner and killed on that occasion. Colonel Jusset said that Ryan would be tried juridically and given a fair trial. Carney was told by some American prisoners that Ryan was 'a tough guy' and that anybody might not be very safe in his company and that he frequently killed prisoners. It appears that Ryan has a certain military reputation both on his own side and with Franco's people. One of the men captured with him was a Scot who, after a previous capture about a year ago, had been released by Franco with about 50 others to each of whom a sum of Frs.500 had been given when they had been put across the frontier.

Ryan and the other prisoners were removed from Zaragoza to a concentration camp on Wednesday 6th or Thursday 7th April. Carney does not know to what camp Ryan may have been sent but he states that there are four such camps – 1 at Miranda de Ebro, 1 in the vicinity of Burgos, 1 at Deus, near Santona, and 1 at Santona (near Santander) which is in reality a prison.

I asked Carney whether trials of prisoners were always public; his reply was that many such trials were public.

I took the opportunity of point out to Carney, who is persona grata with the Franco authorities, that if Ryan were to be executed this might and probably would tend to alienate some of the sympathy which exists for Franco in Ireland, where public opinion might jump to the conclusion that any charges of murder and looting made against Ryan were not justified in fact, and that the life of this man would mean very little to Franco but possibly very much to Franco's cause in Ireland. Carney says that when prisoners are executed information on the subject is not usually allowed to transpire for a considerable time afterwards.

As your appeal for clemency has been received in Burgos and as Ryan was still alive at the time this appeal was received, and, as the Viscount de Mamblas will in all probability have reminded General Jordana[1] of your interest in this case, it does not appear as if there were any further effective steps which could be taken at the present moment. I do not think that even any visit of mine to Burgos for this express and unique purpose would be likely to carry any weight. It might, however, be worth while considering whether the British Agent in Salamanca should not be instructed at some early date – in the event of no news reaching us from other sources – to enquire at the Ministry for External Affairs in Burgos as to Ryan's fate.[2]

[copy letter unsigned]
Aire Lán-Chómhachtach

---

[1] General Count Gómez Jordana y Sousa (1876-1944), Spanish Foreign Minister (Jan. 1938-Aug. 1939).

[2] This final sentence has been highlighted by two lines drawn in the left-hand margin.

No. 164 NAI DFA Madrid Embassy 10/11

Code telegram from the Department of External Affairs to Leopold H. Kerney
(St Jean de Luz)
(No. 5) (Copy)
DUBLIN, 12.10 pm, 14 April 1938

Your telegram 3[1] very disturbed to learn Ryan is likely to be tried on serious charges. You should endeavour to obtain official information and if report confirmed represent that Irish government would greatly appreciate a lenient attitude towards Ryan's case. Public opinion here would be greatly incensed if punishment involved Ryan's life.

No. 165 NAI DFA Madrid Embassy 10/11

Confidential report from Leopold H. Kerney to Joseph P. Walshe (Dublin
(S.J. 10/11) (Copy)
ST JEAN DE LUZ, 16 April 1938

Frank Ryan
Further to my telegram and minute of 13th inst.,[2] and with reference to your telegram No. 5 of 14th received here at 1.30 pm.,[3] I saw the Viscount de Mamblas in Biarritz late on Thursday 14th. He had kept his promise by reminding General Jordana in Burgos of our appeal on Ryan's behalf but did not give me any indication of the Minister's attitude in this particular matter. He told me, however, that Sir Robert Hodgson[4] had been furnished with information regarding the prisoners captured at the same time as Ryan and who might be deemed to be British and that Hodgson had made some classification of these according to their records and antecedents. He had spoken to Hodgson about Ryan; Hodgson considered Ryan's to be 'a bad case' or 'a very bad case'; de Mamblas gathered from Hodgson that Ryan had indulged in 'profiteering' (i.e. looting); in reply to my enquiry as to the possibility of any graver charge, de Mamblas gave me to understand but did not definitely assert that there might be some more serious accusation than that of looting.

De Mamblas was unable to say whether Burgos would advise us of the sentence that might be imposed on Ryan, or whether our appeal for clemency would prevent any death sentence from being executed. I informed him of the terms of the importance, from Franco's point of view, of not estranging public opinion in Ireland. I induced him to agree with me that it would be at least advisable, in the interests of all concerned, that I should be able to notify you of the charges that were being made against Ryan; I pointed out to him that there would be all the greater reason for disclosing these charges if they were of a serious nature because, however hopeless it might be to

---

[1] Not printed.
[2] Not printed.
[3] See above No. 164.
[4] Sir Robert Hodgson (1874-1956), British Agent to Nationalist Spain (1937-9).

attempt to convince public opinion in Ireland of the justice of any death sentence, it would be of very great importance to leave the Irish Government in no doubt as to any such sentence being fully warranted. Consequently, de Mamblas undertook to wire Burgos from Irun on Good Friday morning on these lines, but he could of course not make any promise as to when a reply would be received.

To my question as to whether, in the event of my desiring or being instructed to do so, I would be permitted to visit Ryan in his concentration camp, de Mamblas replied that such permission would certainly be refused; such permission was given, however, to foreign agents accredited to Burgos.

He commented on the fact that extreme action had not already been taken against Ryan and said this was all to the good.

[copy letter unsigned]
Aire Lán-Chómhachtach

No. 166 NAI CAB 2/1

Extract from the minutes of a meeting of the Cabinet
(G.C. 1/21) (Item 1)
DUBLIN, 19 April 1938

NEGOTIATIONS WITH BRITISH GOVERNMENT, 1938
The members of the Delegation were authorised to return to London with a view to the signature of Agreements with the Government of the United Kingdom on Monday, 25th April, 1938.

No. 167 UCDA P150/2506

Memorandum on the draft trade agreement with Britain by John J. Hearne to
Eamon de Valera (Dublin) with handwritten cover note by Seán Murphy
DUBLIN, 19 April 1938

Taoiseach
I attach copy of Mr. Hearne's memorandum on the Trade Agreement.
Seán Murphy

POINTS ON FORM OF TEXT OF DRAFT TRADE AGREEMENT[1]
1. It is decided to retain the word 'Éire' in the draft Agreement?
2. The expression 'any country not within the British Commonwealth of Nations' occurs throughout the draft Agreement conveying the implication that Éire is a country within the British Commonwealth. The text does not actually mean that Éire is a member of the British Commonwealth; it merely implies it. It is difficult to get any way out of the expression referred to. The British alternative would be 'foreign country' as in the Ottawa Agreements and that would be more objectionable from our stand-point. We could, of

---

[1] Annotation by de Valera: 'This was duly considered by S.[eán] L.[eydon] and Mr. Hearne'.

course, suggest a Schedule of countries following our own Aliens (Exemption) Order 1935. But this would not really remove the implication. In addition, a device suitable to our own law might not be suitable to an international agreement and presumably would not be acceptable to the other party to this particular Agreement.

It is suggested that in the last paragraph of the Letter on the subject of Zinc there is a more definite implication that Éire is a member of the British Commonwealth of Nations than elsewhere throughout the text. This could be remedied by deleting the word 'other' in that paragraph.

3. Article 2 provides for a preferential rate of duty in respect of goods (of Irish origin or consignment) mentioned in Schedule 1 of the draft Agreement. These goods are amongst those covered by the general right of free entry into the British market conferred by Article 1. It would seem at first sight, therefore, that the effect of Article 3 might be to limit, as regards the goods covered by Article 2, the right of free entry secured for those goods, amongst others, by Article 1. This, however, is not the intention.[1] The intention, it is understood, is, that the rate of duty on the goods mentioned in Schedule 1 shall always be nil. It is suggested, therefore, that this intention would be made clearer if Article 2 were so worded as to leave no room for doubt on the form of the text that the rate of the duties of customs chargeable on the goods mentioned in Schedule 1 produced or manufactured in and consigned from Éire on importation into the United Kingdom will be nil.

4. The formal emphasis on the powers of the United Kingdom Government in Articles 3 and 4 is, no doubt, the result of a desire on the part of the United Kingdom Government to reassure British agricultural interests (as a matter of policy) against the possibility of the dumping by Irish producers. Presumably no restriction of Irish trade with the United Kingdom, arising out of the said powers of the United Kingdom Government, is likely to take place. It is not worth while therefore seeking any change in the form of the Articles, or the deletion of any provision of one or the other at this stage.

5. With a view to reducing the number of times in which the expression 'the Government of Éire undertake' appears, would it be desirable to delete Articles 12 and 13 and insert them as additional paragraphs in Article 8 to which they relate?

No. 168 NAI DFA 119/45

> *Annual report from Robert Brennan to Joseph P. Walshe (Dublin)*[2]
> *(108/11/38)*
>
> WASHINGTON, 21 April 1938

As will be seen from the summaries enclosed,[3] the work of the Legation and of the various Consulates continues to increase from year to year. The total fees received for the year ending the 31st of March 1938 were $34,340.00 as

---

[1] Annotation by de Valera: 'Has this been fixed?'.
[2] This document is annotated as having been seen by Joseph P. Walshe.
[3] Not printed.

against $90,877.00 for the preceding year, but this is entirely due to the reduction of the visa fee from $10.00 to $2.00. Actually the total number of visas issued shows an increase of 1328 on the previous year, the number being 8736. There were 2361 passports issued and 1071 renewals; documents legalized totalled 1228, and there were 1716 registrations under the Nationality and Citizenship Act. A considerable number of estate cases were handled by the Consulates and as will be seen from the various reports, considerable sums of money – which might otherwise have been lost to the heirs – were through the instrumentality of the Consulates transmitted to heirs in Ireland either through the Department or through local Solicitors.

During the past year there have been more demands than ever on the Legation for information regarding developments in Ireland. This was in a measure due to the coming into effect of the new Constitution and the change of name, but the queries covered all sorts of subjects bearing on the political, economic, social and cultural developments in the country. In this connection we very badly need a Year Book, something on the lines of the Saorstát Hand Book of 1932.[1] The information we supply on various subjects including the Irish language, Irish literature, plays, family names, vital statistics, etc., though it entails a great deal of work, could not of course replace the information that would be given in such a publication. From the cultural point of view, the reissue of this book up-to-date would create a very good impression. Everyone who has seen it has expressed appreciation of its beauty and stated that it outranks any Year Book issued by any other country.

We were able to supply a great deal of tourist literature and to answer more fully questions on tourism thanks to the more abundant supplies and better informed literature furnished by the Irish Tourist Association and the Travel Companies. There is more and more interest being taken here in Ireland as a tourist resort, and this is shown not merely by the increased number of tourists (about 14,000 for the year) but also by the increased number of queries we receive. There is no doubt but that increased publicity here would produce good results in this respect, but from a remark made by Mr. O'Brien[2] of the Irish Tourist Association when he was here recently I gathered that they are not quite ready yet for a big influx of American visitors.

The Legation supplied a great deal of material for St. Patrick's Day addresses in various parts of the country and also for articles and speeches on other subjects. When the partition issue suddenly appeared on the horizon, we were able from the material in our files to supply to the Consulates and various bodies interested, a fairly complete statement of the case for the unity of Ireland and a great deal of favourable publicity resulted.

Annexed are the reports from the various Consulates.[3]

[signed] ROBERT BRENNAN
Chargé d'Affaires a.i.

---

[1] *Saorstát Éireann: Irish Free State Official Handbook* (Dublin, Talbot Press, 1932).
[2] J.P. 'Jack' O'Brien, Secretary of the Irish Tourist Association.
[3] Not printed, but see above No. 162 for excerpts from the annual report of the Irish Consulate in New York.

No. 169 NAI DT S10389A

Statement to be issued on conclusion of negotiations with the British Government

LONDON, 22 April 1938

Statement to be given out in London this Evening (22nd April) at 7 p.m. for Publication the following morning

The discussions between representatives of the United Kingdom Government and the Government of Éire have now been concluded and agreement has been reached. Mr. de Valera and his colleagues will come to London to meet the Prime Minister and his colleagues for the purpose of signature next Monday afternoon, the 25th April.

No. 170 UCDA P150/2836

Letter from Eamon de Valera to Franklin D. Roosevelt (Washington) (Copy) (Confidential)

DUBLIN, 22 April 1938

Dear Mr. President:

I received your very kind letter of February 22nd, and have been informed by Mr. Cudahy of the steps, following your instructions, taken by Mr. Kennedy on his arrival in London.

The knowledge of the fact that you were interested came most opportunely at a critical moment in the progress of the negotiations. Were it not for Mr. Chamberlain personally the negotiations would have broken down at that time, and I am sure that the knowledge of your interest in the success of the negotiations had its due weight in determining his attitude.

I am now happy to state that an agreement between the two Governments has been reached. The terms will have been already published before this reaches you.

So far as the matters covered are concerned, the agreement will, I believe, give satisfaction to both countries. Unfortunately, however, the matter which most affects national sentiment – the ending of the partition of our country – finds no place in the agreement. A complete reconciliation, to the importance of which I referred in my previous letter, remains still for the future. All we can hope is that the present agreement will be a step towards it.

I want to express to you my thanks for your kind interest, and for your assistance. I know of the many difficult problems of your own country which are engaging your attention, and I am deeply grateful that you could find time to give a thought to ours.

With renewed regards,
Sincerely yours,
[copy letter unsigned]

No. 171 UCDA P150/2511

On board Holyhead to Dún Laoghaire Mailboat
Everything that makes for a better understanding between people is to be welcomed – particularly in the world conditions of today.

The Agreement which has just been signed between the representatives of the Irish and British peoples will I believe be universally received in that spirit. It removes the existing, and the more dangerous potential causes of quarrel between the two countries – all except one. Unfortunately that one outstanding, the partition of our national territory, is that on which the I. people feel most keenly. I confess that it is somewhat of a heartbreak that it has not been possible to include this question also and wipe the whole slate clean. However the agreement that has been reached can hardly fail to be a step even towards the solution of partition. I am confident that the work which has been done today will not be allowed to remain marred by this omission and now that partition has been isolated as the one remaining obstacle to a final reconciliation between the two nations the efforts of all people of good will will be directed towards removing it.

I repeat what I have been saying for nearly a quarter of a century. Gt. Britain has nothing to fear – nothing to lose but everything to gain from having as her neighbour a completely free independent Ireland and that the wisest Br. Statesmanship will make that conviction the basis of its policy. It is a matter of great satisfaction to me that the Br. Gov. of Today are acting on that view so far as the present agreement. My anxiety is that they should not stop short of what is necessary to make the policy effective.
[matter omitted][1]
I am aware that the friendly interest of the American nation in seeing an ending of the age-old [blank][2] has been an important factor in making this agreement possible. I may perhaps express the hope that that interest will remain active until the full solution is reached – and a completely free united Ireland.

I believe that the agreement will prove to be advantageous to both countries and I think I can confidently recommend its acceptance to ours.

Prepared on boat from Holyhead to Dún Laoghaire and said to Press on board at Dún Laoghaire.

No. 172 NAI DT S10634

AGREEMENT WITH UNITED KINGDOM (CAPITAL SUM) BILL, 1938
Authority was granted for the drafting of a Bill relating to the payment of a capital sum to Great Britain.

---

[1] The omitted matter is a repetition in rough draft form of the text reproduced in the paragraph above.
[2] De Valera left out a word or words at this point.

No. 173 UCDA P150/2345

Handwritten notes by John J. Hearne on the External Relations Act
DUBLIN, 23 April 1938

An Taoiseach,
It occurred to me, Sir, that the attached propositions might be useful.

JOHN J. HEARNE
23rd April

The Executive Authority (External Relations) Act, 1936, was passed before the Constitution was approved.

So clearly and completely is the National Constitution a Republican Constitution that, if no provision had been made in it validating the Executive Authority (External Relations) Act, 1936, in relation to the National Constitution, that statute would have lapsed, and legislation, even in the tenuous terms of that statute, would have been impossible. I hold that, so long as any prospect remains, of securing national unity on the basis of the Executive Authority (External Relations) Act, 1936, it would have been wrong to invalidate it altogether and thus deprive any Government which might be in office of that method of approach to the solution of the problem of national unity. The Constitution was designed to promote national unity not to prevent it.

No. 174 NAI DT S10638A

Handwritten notes by Maurice Moynihan on the Taoiseach's decisions of 22 April 1938
DUBLIN, 23 April 1938

Taoiseach's decisions on 22/4/38
(1) We may proceed with the arrangements for the printing of the text of the Agreements if instructions to the contrary have not been received by 3.30 p.m. on Monday 25th April.
(2) The British Command Paper may be used as printer's copy with such necessary amendments as the changing of the order of reference to the two Governments, where appropriate, the amendment of 'the Govt. of Éire' to read 'the Govt. of Ireland' on the title-page and the transposition of the Irish and British signatures.
(3) The text of the Agreements is to be presented to both Houses of the Oireachtas.
(4) The resolution of approval is to be tabled in Dáil Éireann only and is to be put down in the Taoiseach's name.
(5) The drafting of the Prices Commission Bill, the Lump Sum Bill and the Finance Bill may be formally authorised.

[initialled] MOM
23/4/38

Further points to be attended to early

(1) Speak Mr. Little[1] re para 1 of notes of conference of Ministers on 20/4/38.

(2) Speak Prof. Whelehan[2] re rushed printing on Monday, 25th April.

(3) Speak Colm O'Murchadha[3] re parliamentary procedure.

(4) Speak Seán Murphy re questions of broadcasting announcement on Friday night, 22nd April and news re provisions of agreements on Monday night, 25th April.

(5) Remind Taoiseach re settlement of terms of communiqué on Friday night, 22nd April.

1) Spoke Mr. Little in accordance with para.1 and informed him of time-table for communication to Mr. Doyle.

[initialled] MOM
21/4/38

2) and 3) The Taoiseach has instructed me to defer these steps until Friday evening, 22nd April.

[initialled] MOM
21/4/38

4) Spoke Mr. Murphy. The B.B.C. will not broadcast news in this connection on Friday 22nd or Monday 25th April. It follows that our service should not broadcast.

[initialled] MOM
21/4/38

5) Done. Mr. Murphy has received text of proposed British communiqué.

[initialled] MOM
21/4/38

(2) and (3) above done on Friday, 22nd April.

[initialled] MOM
23/4/38

---

[1] Patrick J. Little (1884-1963), Parliamentary Secretary to the President and the Minister for External Affairs (1933-9).

[2] Professor J.B. Whelehan, Tariff Commission, formerly of the Department of Industry and Commerce.

[3] Clerk of Dáil Éireann.

No. 175 NAI DT S10389A

British-Irish tripartite agreement on Trade, Finance and Defence
(P. No. 3104)

LONDON, 25 April 1938

ÉIRE

AGREEMENTS BETWEEN THE GOVERNMENT OF IRELAND
AND THE GOVERNMENT OF THE UNITED KINGDOM

Signed at London, 25th April, 1938

PRESENTED TO BOTH HOUSES OF THE OIREACHTAS
BY
THE MINISTER FOR EXTERNAL AFFAIRS

The Government of Éire and the Government of the United Kingdom, being desirous of promoting relations of friendship and good understanding between the two countries, of reaching a final settlement of all outstanding financial claims of either of the two Governments against the other, and of facilitating trade and commerce between the two countries, have, subject to Parliamentary confirmation, entered into the Agreements hereinafter set forth:-

AN AGREEMENT REGARDING ARTICLES 6 AND 7 OF THE ARTICLES OF
AGREEMENT OF DECEMBER 6, 1921

The Government of Éire and the Government of the United Kingdom have agreed as follows:-

1. The provisions of Articles 6 and 7 of the Articles of Agreement for a Treaty between Great Britain and Ireland signed on the 6th day of December, 1921, and of the Annex thereto shall cease to have effect.

2. Thereafter the Government of the United Kingdom will transfer to the Government of Éire the Admiralty property and rights at Berehaven, and the harbour defences at Berehaven, Cobh (Queenstown) and Lough Swilly now occupied by care and maintenance parties furnished by the United Kingdom, together with buildings, magazines, emplacements, instruments and fixed armaments with ammunition therefor at present at the said ports.

3. The transfer will take place not later than the 31st December, 1938. In the meantime the detailed arrangements for the transfer will be the subject of discussion between the two Governments.

Done in duplicate at London, this 25th day of April, 1938.

Signed on behalf of the Government of Éire:	Signed on behalf of the Government of the United Kingdom:
EAMON DE VALERA	NEVILLE CHAMBERLAIN
SEAN F. LEMASS	JOHN SIMON
SEAN MacENTEE	SAMUEL HOARE
SEAMAS O'RIAIN	MALCOLM MacDONALD
	T.W.H. INSKIP

A FINANCIAL AGREEMENT

The Government of Éire and the Government of the United Kingdom have agreed as follows:-

1. The Government of Éire agree to pay to the Government of the United Kingdom on or before the 30th November, 1938, the sum of £10,000,000 sterling.

2. Subject to the provisions of Article 3 of the Agreement, payment of the sum specified in Article 1 shall constitute a final settlement of all financial claims of either of the two Governments against the other arising out of matters occurring before the date of this Agreement.

3. The provisions of Article 2 of this Agreement shall not affect:-

(i) payments made or liabilities incurred by one Government to the other in respect of agency services or ordinary inter-governmental transactions, whether for goods supplied, services rendered, disbursements made, or otherwise;

(ii) the payment of £250,000 a year by the Government of Éire to the Government of the United Kingdom in respect of damage to property under the Agreement of the 3rd December, 1925;[1]

(iii) any payments made or to be made in pursuance of arrangements which have been or may hereafter be reached between the two Governments in respect of the following matters:-

    (a) Unredeemed Bank notes;

    (b) Withdrawal of United Kingdom silver coin from Éire;

    (c) Trustee Savings Banks;

    (d) Double Taxation.

4. The Government of the United Kingdom undertake to abolish, as from the date on which the accompanying Trade Agreement between the United Kingdom and Éire comes into force pursuant to Article 19 thereof, the duties of customs chargeable under the Irish Free State (Special Duties) Act, 1932, on articles imported from Éire into the United Kingdom, or exported from Éire to any other country and thence brought into the United Kingdom.

5. The Government of Éire undertake to abolish as from the date on which the accompanying Trade Agreement between the United Kingdom and Éire comes into force pursuant to Article 19 thereof, the duties of Customs known as Customs (Emergency) Duties (Tariff list Reference Nos. 280, 281 and 288) chargeable on goods produced or manufactured in the United Kingdom and imported into Éire.

    Done in duplicate at London, this 25th day of April, 1938

Signed on behalf of the Government of Éire:	Signed on behalf of the Government of the United Kingdom:
EAMON DE VALERA	NEVILLE CHAMBERLAIN
SEAN F. LEMASS	JOHN SIMON
SEAN MacENTEE	SAMUEL HOARE
SEAMAS O'RIAIN	MALCOLM MacDONALD

---

[1] See DIFP Volume II, No. 368.

A TRADE AGREEMENT

The Government of Éire and the Government of the United Kingdom have agreed as follows:-

ARTICLE 1

(1) The Government of the United Kingdom undertake that goods grown, produced or manufactured in, and consigned from, Éire, which, on the day on which this Agreement comes into force are liable to duty under the Import Duties Act, 1932, or under Section 1 of the Ottawa Agreements Act, 1932, and also such goods which are on that day free of duty, shall enjoy entry free of customs duty into the United Kingdom. This paragraph does not apply to goods which, on the day on which this Agreement comes into force, are liable to duty both under the Import Duties Act, 1932, or the Ottawa Agreements Act, 1932, and under some other enactment.

(2) Provided that as regards eggs, poultry, butter, cheese and other milk products, the undertaking contained in the first paragraph of this Article shall operate only until the 20th August, 1940.

ARTICLE 2

(1) The Government of the United Kingdom undertake in respect of the goods enumerated in Schedule 1 to this Agreement that the difference between the rate of the duties of customs chargeable on such goods produced or manufactured in and consigned from Éire on importation into the United Kingdom and the rate chargeable on similar goods the produce or manufacture of any country not within the British Commonwealth of Nations shall not be less than that set out in that Schedule.

(2) Provided that, except as regards dead guinea fowl and game birds, the undertaking contained in the first paragraph of this Article shall operate only until the 20th August, 1940.

ARTICLE 3

(1) The Government of Éire, recognising that it is the policy of the Government of the United Kingdom to promote the orderly marketing of agricultural products, declare their readiness to co-operate in any arrangements made or approved by that Government for this purpose, and the Government of the United Kingdom, for their part, will not seek to regulate the quantity of any such goods produced in Éire and imported into the United Kingdom unless it appears to them that the orderly marketing of such goods cannot otherwise be secured.

(2) Before any such regulation is put into force, there shall be consultation between the two Governments, and the Government of the United Kingdom undertake that, in determining the quantity of percentage share to be allotted to Éire, regard shall be had so far as practicable to the past position of Éire in the trade and to any special conditions which may have affected, or be affecting, the volume of Éire exports to the United Kingdom.

(3) The Government of Éire, when so requested by the Government of the United Kingdom, will furnish estimates of the quantities of any agricultural product likely to be exported from Éire to the United Kingdom in any period.

(4) This Article shall apply to fish and fishery products as it applies to agricultural products.

ARTICLE 4

(1) The Government of Éire undertake to consult from time to time with the Government of the United Kingdom as to the quantities of eggs and poultry to be exported from Éire to the United Kingdom, and to exercise such control of exports as may be necessary to make effective any agreement so reached.

(2) Should consultation between the two Governments fail to lead to a satisfactory arrangement, and should imports from Éire so increase as, in the opinion of the Government of the United Kingdom, to endanger the stability of the market for eggs or poultry in the United Kingdom, then the Government of the United Kingdom shall be entitled to regulate quantitatively those imports to such extent as may be necessary for securing the stability of the market. In such cases the quantities to be admitted from time to time shall be the subject of consultation between the two Governments and shall be fixed in accordance with the general principles of this Agreement.

(3) Should, however, the two Governments agree that the purpose in view can be more conveniently effected by means of duties than by quantitative regulation, then, notwithstanding anything to the contrary in Article 1 of this Agreement, the Government of the United Kingdom may impose such duties as may be necessary for securing the stability of the market. In that case the rate of duty shall be decided after consultation between the two Governments.

ARTICLE 5

(1) The Government of Éire undertake that goods produced or manufactured in the United Kingdom of the classes or kinds enumerated in Part 1 of Schedule II, which are not now liable to customs duty (other than duties of customs known as Customs (Emergency) Duties (Tariff List reference Nos. 280, 281 and 288)) or quantitative regulation, shall continue to enjoy entry into Éire free of customs duty (other than Package Duty) and quantitative regulation.

(2) The Government of Éire undertake to admit free of customs duty and quantitative regulation goods of the classes or kinds specified in Part II of Schedule II produced in the United Kingdom.

ARTICLE 6

(1) The Government of Éire undertake in respect of consignments or parcels of imported goods of United Kingdom origin, to reduce from two shillings and sixpence to one shilling the Minimum Charge of Customs Duty at present applicable to consignments or parcels of all imported goods.

(2) The Government of Éire undertake, in respect of customs entries for imported goods of United Kingdom origin which are not charged with customs duty, to repeal the Stamp Duty which is at present charged in respect of customs entries for all imported goods.

(3) The Government of Éire undertake, in respect of parcels of goods of United Kingdom origin not liable to duty, imported through the post, to abolish the Post Office delivery charge of sixpence per parcel levied in respect of all parcels of goods not liable to customs duty.

(4) The Government of Éire undertake that the duty of customs known as Package Duty shall not be charged upon goods produced or manufactured in

the United Kingdom at rates exceeding one penny per pound (or part of a pound) or one penny per pint (or part of a pint).

(5) The Government of Éire undertake that Package Duty shall not be charged upon goods of United Kingdom origin in respect of:-

(a) packages containing goods imported for the personal use of the importer and brought in by such importer or his servant or a member of his family;

(b) packages containing goods which are gifts for the use or enjoyment of the consignee and are imported through the post;

(c) packages imported through the post which are not made up of internal packages or which, if made up of internal packages, do not contain more than six such internal packages.

ARTICLE 7

The Government of Éire undertake that, where licences are issued for the admission of dutiable goods into Éire either free of duty or at a rate of duty less than that ordinarily charged on such goods, any goods covered by such licences which are produced or manufactured in the United Kingdom shall be admitted free of duty, and similar goods covered by such licences, produced or manufactured in any country not within the British Commonwealth of Nations, shall be subject to a duty of not less than 10 per cent. *ad valorem* (or an appropriate rate of specific duty) unless they are of a class or kind of which supplies of goods produced or manufactured in the United Kingdom are not for the time being available.

ARTICLE 8

(1) The Government of Éire undertake that a review shall be made as soon as practicable by the Prices Commission of existing protective duties and other import restrictions in accordance with the principle that such duties and restrictions upon goods produced or manufactured in the United Kingdom shall be replaced by duties which shall not exceed such a level as will give United Kingdom producers and manufacturers full opportunity of reasonable competition, while affording to Éire industries adequate protection having regard to the relative cost of economical and efficient production, provided that in the application of this principle special consideration may be given to the case of industries not fully established. The tariff on goods produced or manufactured in the United Kingdom will be adjusted where necessary, to give effect to the recommendations of the Prices Commission.

(2) In regard to any protective duties or restrictions which may be imposed by the Government of Éire after the date of this Agreement, a similar procedure shall be followed at the request of the Government of the United Kingdom.

(3) It is understood that quantitative restrictions may be imposed in accordance with the provisions of Article 10 (2) and may, subject to and in accordance with the recommendations of the Prices Commission, be maintained in respect of any of the goods specified in Schedule III.

ARTICLE 9

(1) The Government of Éire undertake to admit free of customs duty, except as provided in the fourth paragraph of this Article, goods of the classes or kinds specified in Schedule IV produced in the United Kingdom.

(2) The Government of the United Kingdom recognise that it may be necessary for the Government of Éire, in pursuance of their agricultural policy, to regulate the imports of certain agricultural products, including those enumerated in Schedule IV.

(3) In such cases the quantities of United Kingdom products to be admitted from time to time shall be the subject of consultation between the two Governments and shall be fixed in accordance with the general principles of this Agreement.

(4) Duties may be imposed by the Government of Éire in agreement with the Government of the United Kingdom in cases where it appears to them that the purpose in view can be more conveniently effected by this means. In such cases the rate of duty, and the margin of preference to be accorded to United Kingdom goods shall be decided after consultation between the two Governments.

(5) This Article shall apply to fish and fishery products as it applies to agricultural products.

ARTICLE 10

(1) The Government of Éire undertake that the duties of customs charged upon the importation into Éire of goods produced or manufactured in the United Kingdom of the classes or kinds enumerated in Parts I and II at Schedule V to this Agreement shall not exceed the rates shown in those parts of that Schedule. Provided that, on the abolition of control by quantitative regulation, higher rates of duty may be charged on the goods enumerated in Part II of that Schedule subject to the recommendation of the Prices Commission.

(2) If the imports into Éire of any class or kind of goods enumerated in Parts I and II of Schedule V should increase to such an extent as to endanger the prospects of success of the producers or manufactures of such goods in Éire, and if it should appear that such increase in imports is due to the reduction of customs duties in pursuance of this Article, then the Government of Éire shall be entitled to apply quantitative regulation to imports of such goods. In that event the quantities of such goods produced or manufactured in the United Kingdom to be admitted into Éire shall be fixed after consultation with the Government of the United Kingdom.

ARTICLE 11

(1) The Government of Éire undertake that goods produced or manufactured in the United Kingdom shall be entitled to admission into Éire at the preferential rate of duty wherever such a rate exists and that existing margins between the full and the preferential rates shall not be reduced.

(2) The Government of Éire undertake that the rates of customs duty charged on goods of the classes or kinds specified in Schedule VI, the produce or

manufacture of any country not within the British Commonwealth of Nations shall be not less than those specified in that Schedule, and that the margins of preferences thereby accorded to goods of United Kingdom origin of those classes or kinds shall be maintained.

(3) Whenever new duties are imposed or the existing rates of duty charged on any goods on importation into Éire are adjusted in accordance with the provision of Article 5 (2), Article 8 or Article 9, the difference between the rate of customs duty charged on such goods the produce or manufacture of the United Kingdom and the rate charged on similar goods produced or manufactured in any country not within the British Commonwealth of Nations shall be not less than one-third of the latter rate, or 10 per cent. *ad valorem* or under (or the equivalent), whatever is the greater.

ARTICLE 12

The review provided for in Article 8 shall be held first upon the classes of goods for which the Government of the United Kingdom request early consideration.

ARTICLE 13

The Government of Éire undertake that United Kingdom producers and manufacturers shall be entitled in full rights of audience before the Prices Commission when it has under consideration matters arising under Article 8 of this Agreement.

ARTICLE 14

If the Government of either country are satisfied after enquiry that goods the produce or manufacture of the other country are being imported and sold in the former country at less than their comparable price in the home market, due allowance being made for transport and other charges, they shall be at liberty, after consultation with the Government of the other country, to impose special duties or other import restrictions on such goods.

ARTICLE 15

Except to the extent that may be necessary to maintain production in Éire on an economic basis or to secure the effective operation of schemes for the orderly marketing of agricultural products, the Government of Éire undertake to withdraw the export bounties or subsidies that have been paid in respect of goods exported from Éire to the United Kingdom. In particular they undertake to withdraw export bounties and subsidies in so far as the intention of such payments has been to counteract the effect of duties of customs on such goods on importation into the United Kingdom, in all cases where such duties have been abolished.

ARTICLE 16

It being the intention of the Government of Éire that coal, coke and manufactured fuel of United Kingdom origin shall continue to be imported into Éire in not less than the proportions which such coal, coke and manufactured fuel formed of total imports of those products into Éire in the year 1937, they undertake to abolish the present control by licence of the importation of coal and to admit into Éire coal, coke and manufactured fuel of United Kingdom origin free of duty and to charge a duty of not less than 3s per ton on coal, coke and manufactured fuel of other origin.

ARTICLE 17

(1) The Government of Éire undertake that complete or substantially complete aggregates of parts for complete or substantially complete motor vehicles, motor vehicle bodies, or motor vehicle chassis, manufactured in the United Kingdom shall not on importation into Éire be subject to quantitative restriction (with the exception of the goods specified in Schedule III and, pending review by the Prices Commission in accordance with Article 8, laminated springs and leaves), and shall not , for the purpose of admission at the rates of duty known as Compounded Duties where such rates are at present applicable, be subjected to more onerous conditions as regards degree of assembly at the time of importation than those at present in operation.

(2) It is however, understood that on the removal of quantitative restrictions from electric filament lamps in accordance with paragraph (1) of this Article, such lamps may be subjected to rates of duty higher than the rates of duty known as Compounded Duties.

(3) The Government of Éire undertake that completely assembled private motor vehicles of a c.i.f. value of £750 or more, manufactured in the United Kingdom, shall enjoy entry into Éire free of quantitative restriction, and that the rate of Customs duty to be charged on such vehicles shall not exceed $22^2/9$ per cent.

ARTICLE 18

Should either Government come to the conclusion that the objects of this Agreement are not being attained say in any particular respect or that a change of circumstances necessitates a variation in its terms, the other Government, upon receiving a notification to that effect, will enter immediately into consultation with the first Government and both Governments will use every endeavour to find an equitable solution to the matter.

ARTICLE 19

This Agreement shall come into force on a date to be mutually agreed between the two Governments. It shall remain in force for a period of three years from the date of its coming into force and, unless notice of termination shall have been given by either Government to the other six months before the expiry of that period, it shall remain in force until the expiry of six months from the date on which notice of termination is given.

Done in duplicate at London, this 25th day of April, 1938.

Signed on behalf of the Government of Éire:	Signed on behalf of the Government of the United Kingdom:
EAMON DE VALERA	NEVILLE CHAMBERLAIN

SEAN F. LEMASS	JOHN SIMON
SEAN MacENTEE	SAMUEL HOARE
SEAMAS O'RIAIN	MALCOLM MacDONALD
	W.S. MORRISON

No. 176 NAI DT S10634

Letter from Padraig O'Cinnéide to P.S. Ó Muireadhaigh[1]

DUBLIN, 25 April 1938

A Chara,
1. I am to inform you that the Government, on the 19th instant, decided that any legislative proposals arising out of the proposed agreements with the British Government should be referred to a Committee of the Cabinet consisting of the Taoiseach, the Minister for Industry and Commerce, the Minister for Finance and the Minister for Agriculture for consideration and settlement at all stages up to and including the approval of the text and the authorisation of circulation to deputies.[2]
2. In pursuance of this decision, the Committee on the 23rd instant, authorised the drafting of a Bill relating to the payment of a capital sum to Great Britain and a Bill relating to trade and finance. (S.10635)
3. The texts of these Bills, when ready, should be submitted to this Department for approval by the Committee.

Mise, le meas,
(Sgd.) P. O'CINNÉIDE
Rúnaí

No. 177 NAI DT S10634

Extract from the minutes of a special committee of the Cabinet
(Item 4)

DUBLIN, 27 April 1938

AGREEMENT WITH UNITED KINGDOM (CAPITAL SUM) BILL, 1938
The text of the above Bill was approved and authority given for its introduction in the Dáil and for its circulation to Deputies.

No. 178 UCDA P150/2179

Confidential report from John W. Dulanty to Joseph P. Walshe (Dublin)
(No. 18) (Secret) (Copy)

LONDON, 2 May 1938

In accordance with An Taoiseach's instructions I saw the King's Private Secretary, Sir Alexander Hardinge, at Buckingham Palace on Thursday last,

---

[1] Private Secretary to the Minister, Department of Finance.
[2] Handwritten annotation: 'This decision is on file S10631'.

an earlier appointment not being possible owing to his being out of London.

I told him that I brought a personal message from An Taoiseach for transmission to the King. It was a personal satisfaction to An Taoiseach that a settlement had been brought about. Whilst that settlement was only partial, inasmuch as the question of Partition had not yet been reached, it did mark a step forward towards the attainment of that full friendship and complete goodwill between the Irish and the British peoples which An Taoiseach had publicly declared to be one of his principal political aims.

An Taoiseach would have liked, I explained, when in London at the close of the negotiations to have called upon the King. Such an action at this stage was, however, not possible. Instead of still further improving the relations between us it would have an exactly opposite effect. But he was not without hope that the day would come when he could visit the King who would, he felt sure, understand that there was no personal element in his not calling at present.

Sir Alexander Hardinge said he would convey An Taoiseach's message to the King immediately.

(Signed) J.W. DULANTY
High Commissioner

No. 179 UCDA P150/2179

Confidential report from John W. Dulanty to Joseph P. Walshe (Dublin)
(No. 19) (Secret) (Copy)

LONDON, 2 May 1938

At Buckingham Palace this morning Sir Alexander Hardinge asked me to convey to Mr. de Valera the following personal message from the King.

The King wished to say how gratified he was on receiving Mr. de Valera's personal message which I had transmitted a few days ago.

His Majesty joined with Mr. de Valera in the sincere feeling of satisfaction that so real an improvement in the relations between the two peoples had been achieved by this recent settlement of certain outstanding questions.

It was his hope that this new era might soon lead to conditions under which it would be possible for Mr. de Valera to visit him without compromise or embarrassment. Subject only to his wish to avoid any difficulty to Mr. de Valera the King, for his part, would be glad to see him anytime.

In conveying the King's thanks I was to assure Mr. de Valera that His Majesty fully understood that no personal consideration had entered into his decision not to pay a visit at present.

(Signed) J.W. DULANTY
High Commissioner

No. 180 NAI DFA 119/48

Extracts from the annual report from Leopold H. Kerney to Joseph P. Walshe
(S.J. 19/5)

St Jean de Luz, 2 May 1938

ORGANISATION and ACTIVITIES of the IRISH LEGATION in SPAIN (temporary headquarters St. Jean de Luz) for the year ended 31st MARCH 1938

INTRODUCTORY STATEMENT
My last similar report from Madrid related to the period ended 31st March 1936.[1] Perhaps, therefore, it may be desirable to record briefly the following events.

On 17th April 1936[2] I sent a report from Madrid on disturbances in Spain in which I stated that the use of violence was creating an atmosphere of civil war and that the existence of a spirit of civil war was very manifest.

On 18th May 1936 I fell seriously ill. On 8th July I left Madrid on sick leave and Miss Donnelly[3] was entrusted with the charge of the Legation during my absence. The Spanish civil war broke out on 17th July. On 13th August, acting on imperative instructions, Miss Donnelly closed down the Legation and left Spain. I was convalescent until the end of 1936. It was decided that I should not return to Madrid but establish temporary headquarters in St. Jean de Luz, about 8 miles from the French side of the Spanish frontier, whither most of the Diplomatic Corps have moved from San Sebastian on the outbreak of the civil war. I reached St. Jean de Luz on 8th February 1937. I re-established contact with the heads of other diplomatic missions accredited to President Azaña in Madrid but stationed temporarily in France. Henceforth my activities were chiefly concerned with the observation from outside of political events in Spain and reporting on their development.

In March 1937 I proceeded, on instructions,[4] to Salamanca for the purpose of securing material for a full report to enable the Government to come to a decision with regard to the eventual recognition of the authorities there.

On 13th March I reported the result of my investigations, pointing out, however, that we should neither anticipate the capture of Madrid in the early future nor a war of short duration.

LEGATION PREMISES in ST. JEAN DE LUZ
The temporary official address of the Legation since 8th February 1937 is the Golf Hotel, St. Jean de Luz, (B.P.), France.

---

[1] See DIFP Volume IV, No. 329.
[2] See DIFP Volume IV, No. 332.
[3] Mary Elizabeth 'Maisie' Donnelly, born Wexford, 1910, resident in Barcelona with members of her family since 1928. Clerk, typist and stenographer at the Irish Legation in Madrid. Donnelly was let go after closing down the Legation in Madrid and later re-employed when the Legation opened at St Jean de Luz.
[4] See above, No. 34.

RELATIONS between the LEGATION in ST. JEAN DE LUZ and SPANISH AUTHORITIES

My first direct contact with the insurgent or nationalist authorities was established by my visit to Salamanca; subsequent channels of communication were the Viscount de Mamblas (an agent of General Franco with headquarters in Biarritz), Sr. Sangroniz, at one time head of Franco's Diplomatic Cabinet and now Introducer of Ambassadors in Burgos, and, more recently, Franco's Minister for External Affairs in Burgos.

The Spanish Government (with headquarters in Madrid till May 1937, subsequently in Valencia till November 1937, and since then in Barcelona) has no liaison agent in this part of France; consequently, there is no effective contact between the Legation and the Spanish Government, which has never sent any written communication to me here; it must be mentioned, however, that the Spanish Government recently addressed to the Irish Legation in Madrid a Verbal Note acknowledging receipt of a Note sent by the Legation in St. Jean de Luz in relation to the murder of an Irish national in Spain. [matter omitted]

OFFICE FURNITURE

The following requisites were obtained locally or supplied from home:
(1) Typewriter,
(2) Despatch Cases for storing the Madrid archives which were delivered to the Legation in St. Jean de Luz on 17th February 1938.
It was deemed unnecessary to purchase Filing Cabinets for the Legation files, which are kept in a cupboard.

LIBRARY

The following books were supplied from home:
1 Spanish Dictionary,
1 English-Irish do.,
1 Irish-English do.,
Thom's Directory.

STAFF

I have here as assistant Miss Donnelly, whose services as clerk-stenographer-typist were dispensed with after the temporary closing down of the Legation in Madrid and who was re-employed in a similar capacity when it was decided to open temporary Legation premises in St. Jean de Luz.

TRADE and COMMERCE

I have not been called upon to discuss any matters affecting trade between Ireland and Spain. Under existing circumstances no trade between the two countries would be possible otherwise than on a basis of barter or by means of a clearing agreement; payment for Irish exports to Spain could not be assured otherwise.

The question of Irish accounts outstanding in Spain for goods exported to that country before and after the outbreak of the civil war was the subject of correspondence with the Department (reference numbers 107/40, 107/98 and 115/288). The total amount claimed is relatively unimportant but, even in those cases in which the importing firms make no difficulty as regards payment in Spanish currency in Spain, official restrictions render it impossible for the debtors to acquire the necessary foreign currency for the payment of these accounts in Ireland. No solution for this difficulty is likely to be found until such time as trade negotiations with Spanish authorities may be renewed.

PROTECTION
Steps were taken by me for the protection of a number of Irish nationals in Spain.

I made representations to the authorities in Salamanca for the withdrawal from the danger zone and eventual repatriation of various minors serving as volunteers under General O'Duffy, and was assured at an early stage that latter agreed to the withdrawal from the danger zone of those whose names had then been put forward but did not approve of their being sent home; I was subsequently informed that in the majority of the cases submitted by me the persons concerned were opposed to their removal from the front; their return to Ireland did not take place until the main body of the volunteers returned with General O'Duffy.[1]

Repeated efforts have since been made to secure the liberation of one minor who remained behind as a volunteer in the Spanish Foreign Legion, but who has not yet himself made the necessary application to the military authorities to be released from the engagement voluntarily subscribed by him.

During the period under review, representations were made by me to the Spanish Government with a view to the repatriation of a minor serving, as a volunteer with the Government forces, under Frank Ryan, but these representations met with no response.

In May 1937 the authorities in Salamanca, in reply to a request made by me on behalf of any Irishmen who might have been made prisoners at the same time as a batch of British prisoners, gave me the names of two such Irishmen who had been given their liberty.

A question of the liberation from custody by the Spanish nationalist authorities in Irun and the eventual repatriation of a certain Miss Cronin[2] was the subject of considerable correspondence but, in the absence of any request from this person for repatriation, and in view of the fact that information supplied by her as to the date of her birth was found to be incorrect, her repatriation has not taken place, nor has it been possible for the Spanish authorities to give effect to the expulsion order issued against her seeing that she holds no passport and is, consequently, refused admission into France.

The assassination on the 16th June 1937 of Miss Bridget BOLAND, an Irishwoman who held a British passport, was the subject of investigations

---

[1] O'Duffy's volunteers returned from Spain in June 1937.
[2] See below No. 315.

which I made in Bilbao on 1st July and which eventuated in the presentation of claims for reparation on 15th February 1938.

Efforts to secure the release of Miss Muriel INGRAM, an Irishwoman holding a British passport, who was arrested by the Franco authorities in Bilbao after the capture of that city, occupied the attention of the Legation, more especially when it was learned that she objected to any British intervention on her behalf; she was released in November 1937.

Successful efforts were made on behalf of John G. de PRENDERGAST, an Irishman who had been fighting on behalf of the Basques and who was subsequently arrested on returning to Spain from France in August 1937; there was reason to fear that a death sentence might be passed on this Irishman if it became known that he had held the rank of officer in the Basque forces. He was released and crossed the French frontier on 23rd December.

The question of the repatriation from Bilbao of a Miss Mary T. BUCKLEY arose for consideration but this person subsequently withdrew her application.

The attempted torpedoing of the S.S. 'CLONLARA' on 19th January 1938[1] was the subject of a note of protest addressed to the Spanish Nationalist authorities and acknowledged by them in a Verbal Note from Burgos on 11th February.

At the request of one of her relatives in Ireland, I offered the assistance of this Legation to a Miss GUINEY, employed as a governess in Segovia, who was alleged to be destitute and without means of returning home; as a result of my intervention Miss Guiney's employers undertook to pay her some salary and to pay her fare home at some later date.

At the request of a Miss GREALLY, who was anxious to get in touch with a Spanish family whose whereabouts were unknown to her, latter's address was ascertained, this Spanish family being desirous at the same time of discovering the whereabouts of Miss Greally who was thus able to enter their employment as a governess in San Sebastian.

NATIONALITY AND REGISTRATION of IRISH CITIZENS
No application for registration of Irish nationality was received, nor is it to be expected that any such application will be addressed to me until such time as the Legation may be re-opened on Spanish soil.

PASSPORTS AND VISAS
No passports were issued by this Legation during the past year. The passport of a Miss GUINEY was made valid for a journey to Spain by the Irish Legation in Paris, on the suggestion and at the request of this Legation and on instructions from the Department. The passport of a Miss MANNIX was similarly endorsed by me, on instructions from the Department. The passport of a Miss ROONEY was also so endorsed by me.

---

[1] The *Clonlara* (1,203 tons), of the Limerick Steamship Company, was commissioned in 1926 and intended for cattle trade between the west of Ireland and Liverpool. Following the attempted torpedoing, the vessel suffered slight damage in July 1938 when docked at Valencia during an air raid. On 22 August 1941 the *Clonlara* was torpedoed and sunk with the loss of eleven of her twelve crew when en-route from Cardiff to Lisbon during an attack by U-564 on Gibraltar-bound convoy OG-71.

NOTARIAL WORK
No occasion presented itself for the discharging of work of this description. Advice was, however, given to an Irishwoman in Bilbao with regard to the execution of a Power of Attorney in the presence of the British sub-agent in that city and, through the instrumentality of this Legation, the signature of the British agent was subsequently legalised by the British and American Consular authorities in Barcelona, the document being required for the American courts.

POLITICAL REPORTS
I enclose herewith a list of 75 reports on the political position in Spain submitted by me during the year.[1]

CORRESPONDENCE
389 letters were received and 454 despatched by the Legation.

[signed] L.H. KERNEY
Aire Lán-Chómhachtach

No. 181 NAI DT S10634

Extract from the minutes of a meeting of the Government
(G. 1/32) (Item 1)

DUBLIN, 6 May 1938

AGREEMENTS WITH BRITISH GOVERNMENT: Consequential Legislation
It was agreed that a resolution should be introduced in the Seanad asking the concurrence of that House, in accordance with the provisions of subsection 2 of section 2 of Article 25 of the Constitution, in a request by the Government to the Presidential Commission to sign each of the under-mentioned Bills as soon as may be after it shall have been presented for signature.

It was also agreed that in the event of the concurrence of the Seanad being secured, the Presidential Commission should be asked to sign each of the Bills in question as soon as may be after it shall have been presented for signature.

TITLES OF BILLS
1. Finance (Agreement with United Kingdom) Bill, 1936.
2. Agreement with United Kingdom (Capital Sum) Bill, 1938.
3. Prices Commission (Extension of Functions) Bill, 1938.
4. Diseases of Animals Bill, 1938.
5. Agricultural Products (Regulation of Import) Bill, 1938.
6. Agricultural Produce (Cereals) Bill, 1938.

---

[1] Not printed.

No. 182 UCDA P150/2183

Handwritten letter from Joseph P. Walshe to Eamon de Valera (Dublin)
KHARTOUM, 13 May 1938

My dear Sir,
I came down here by flying boat just a week ago, and have done quite a lot of exploring in spite of a shade temperature of 105 degrees during the day and 95 degrees at night. On Wednesday I went to Barakat 120 miles from here. It is the centre and the administrative headquarters of the great cotton growing area between the Blue and White Niles. We did the journey in an old Ford car following a desert track along the line of the Blue Nile. Were it not for the intense heat we should have given into temptation to continue for another two hundred miles to the Abyssinian border. The people, who get blacker and blacker, as you go further south are invariably very courteous and you are not in the least disturbed at not meeting any white people.

I called on the Governor General Sir Stewart Symes[1] – a very decent fellow, a close friend of the Nuncio's. He invited me twice to dine to meet the principal Govt. officials and generally was most anxious to give me every facility to see and understand how British rule operates here. He is an idealist as is his wife – who is a R. Catholic – and his very long experience in the Near East Africa has not made him the narrow minded imperialist one expects to find in a post such as his. He can go where he likes here with a few unarmed policemen. The Festival of the Birthday of the Prophet is on at the moment and although there are tens of thousands of Arabs in the two adjoining cities of Khartoum and Omdurman there isn't a trace of disorder. The aim Symes has in view is to get into a position in which he and his successors will be advisers to the Sheiks. He is making no effort to anglicise the people. English is not taught in the schools though no doubt it will be when a Sunday school system has been established. He makes all the officials learn and speak Arabic and the local dialects. No doubt the British could stay here for centuries if they had always men of Symes' type to do the Governing for them, but with the growing power – especially cultural – of Arabia which is only just across the Red Sea and is their Religious homeland, one wonders whether any white nation can hold out in these regions for more than another fifty years. While the people move slowly they are accustomed to sudden and profound changes. We have only to remember that this whole area was Christian long before St. Patrick came to Ireland, and there isn't a trace left except a few recently discovered ruins of Churches of the 4th century.

Of course, I found Omdurman very interesting. I met some old warriors there who had fought against the British (under Kitchener)[2] in 1898. The Sons

---

[1] Sir Stewart Symes (1882-1962), Governor General of Sudan (1934-40).
[2] Horatio Kitchener (1850-1916), born near Ballylongford, County Kerry. Entered the Royal Engineers (1871) and served in Palestine (1874-8), Cyprus (1878-82) and the Sudan (1883-5). In 1898 Kitchener became a national hero when he successfully led the British Army in the Sudan. As a result of his victory at Omdurman he was granted the title Lord Kitchener. Kitchener was later Commander-in-Chief in India (1902-9) and Military Governor in Egypt (1911-14) and served as Secretary for War (1914-16).

of the Mahdi and of the Khalif who succeeded him are local potentates (no doubt enjoying fat salaries from the British) and close friends of the GG.

I have met a great many people with Irish blood among the officials – who all expressed unfeigned delight at the Anglo-Irish rapprochement. One result is that they tell you of their Irish blood after about two minutes. Before they waited about four days. Cairo has some Irish amongst its leading citizens – the two brothers Delaney being the principal. Arthur Delaney was present as an officer of the Dublin Fusiliers at the Easter week surrenders and he is most anxious to be received by you. As he is coming to Dublin in August I told him I felt sure you would be glad to see him. These two men have always proclaimed their Irish nationality in Egypt and have had no small trouble with the Freemason crowd. Naturally they are very proud of the results achieved by you in the Agreement with the British. This sentiment is very general even amongst British officials with Irish blood, and I find a new and very real desire to know all about the language and culture of the country. 'Éire' notwithstanding certain drawbacks is proving a god send in a lot of ways. It connotes a different language, a different people. It brings pride to these representatives of our people scattered in British spheres throughout the world.

I am going back to Cairo tomorrow morning. It is only six hours by air from here (four days and four nights by surface travel). I will write from there when I have talked with Lampson[1] and some of the officials. I had only exchanged courtesy calls before leaving Cairo as I had to go to Alexandria for a few days.

Will you give a little thought to the question of a colony when you have leisure. It would be a splendid training ground for our people, and colonial budgets can be made to balance without subsidies from the home Government.

It was very consoling to read that you got the Agreement through without serious difficulty. I hope you are thinking of taking a holiday of some kind before long. This last year has been a time of very trying tasks for you.

I remain, my dear Sir, with great respect and esteem,

Yours very sincerely,

J.P. WALSHE

No. 183 UCDA P150/2517

Letter from Malcolm MacDonald to Eamon de Valera (Dublin)
(Personal)

LONDON, 17 May 1938

Dear Mr. de Valera,

I am sending this note just to say that our legislation will be through both Houses of Parliament in time for the King's Assent to be given to it tonight.

---

[1] Miles Lampson, 1st Baron Killearn (1880-1964), British High Commissioner to Egypt (1934-6), Ambassador to Egypt (1936-46).

I should like to add, in no mere formal way, an expression of my pleasure at the final accomplishment of what we have been patiently endeavouring to do over so many months. I do congratulate you and our Prime Minister on what you have done in the cause of friendship between our two peoples, and I shall always feel proud that I was privileged to play some part in the negotiations. I cherish especially the memory of our friendly and fruitful talks together. If the personal relations which we established are a symbol of the friendship which will gradually grow between the peoples of the two Islands, then indeed is the future bright.

With kindest regards[1]
Yours very sincerely
[signed] MALCOLM MACDONALD

No. 184 NAI DFA Secretary's Files S77

Letter from Peadar MacMahon to Joseph P. Walshe (Dublin)
(2/54281)

DUBLIN, 18 May 1938

I am directed by the Minister for Defence to refer to the Agreement regarding Articles 6 and 7 of the Articles of Agreement of December 6, 1921, recently signed between the Governments of Ireland and the United Kingdom and to state that, with the concurrence of the Government, it is proposed that the transfer of the harbour defences at Cobh should take place at the earliest possible date.

It is contemplated, in this connection, that the British authorities should be requested to make available at Cobh instructors for the training of the non-commissioned officers and men who will be attached to the Coastal Defence arm and that when the latter are adequately trained, arrangements should be made for the transfer of the remaining harbour defences and properties. It is further proposed that the officers whom it is intended to appoint to the Coastal Defence arm – approximately twelve – should be sent to England to undergo a course in coastal defence duties.

As a preliminary step, it is considered desirable that a mission should travel to London for the purpose of consultation with the appropriate British authorities as to the essential requirements in regard to personnel, supply, accountancy and any other relevant matters. It is proposed that the mission should consist of Major P. Maher, Director of Artillery, Commandant J.F. Kinneen, Acting Director of Military Engineering and Mr. J.B. O'Connell, Finance Officer, Department of Defence.

The Minister would be glad, accordingly, if the views of the British authorities on the proposed consultation could be ascertained and if they could also be requested to indicate, in the event of their concurrence in the proposal, the earliest suitable date for the visit of the mission to London.

[signed] PEADAR MACMAHON
Rúnaidhe

---

[1] These closing lines are handwritten.

No. 185 NAI DFA Secretary's Files S78

> *Letter from Seán Murphy to John W. Dulanty (London)*
> *(Secret) (Copy)*
>
> DUBLIN, 19 May 1938

Dear Dulanty,

You will probably have seen in the press that Dr. Douglas Hyde and the Taoiseach have been invited by the Saul Memorial Diocesan Committee to attend the consecration of the National Memorial to St. Patrick at Saul, Co. Down, on the 12th June.

Several years ago when the Taoiseach proposed to attend some function in the Six County area we got in touch with the Northern Government by telephone to inquire if any objection would be raised. We were informed in reply that the expulsion order against Mr. de Valera of some years back was still in force. No further action was taken on that occasion.

The Taoiseach is very anxious to attend the ceremony on the 12th June and I should accordingly be glad if you would ascertain from the British Home Office what the present position is. It seems absurd that in present circumstances an order of that sort should be in force against the Head of the Government here. You should inform the Home Office that if any difficulty is raised on this occasion by the Six County Government the Taoiseach will feel bound to make public the reason why he is unable to attend the ceremony at Saul.

We should be glad to know the position as soon as possible as the Taoiseach wishes to reply to the invitation.

Yours sincerely,
(Sgd) SEAN MURPHY

No. 186 NAI DFA Secretary's Files S77

> *Confidential report from John W. Dulanty to Joseph P. Walshe (Dublin)*
> *(No. 17) (Secret)*
>
> LONDON, 21 May 1938

Further to my telephone conversation I saw Brigadier R.B. Pargiter and Captain Jones at this Office yesterday to make arrangements for a preliminary discussion on the subject of the transfer of the ports.

Brigadier Pargiter handed me a typed note setting out the 'Questions which Representatives of the War Office would like to discuss with Military Representatives of Ireland'. This note I sent in the pouch to the Department last evening.

After the British representatives had read the note in question I explained to them that my Government would like, to begin with, to take over the port of Cobh if possible by the 29th June. We thought that we had a certain amount of experienced personnel who could take over this port but we were not sure that we had sufficient personnel for this purpose and it would be desirable if the British could see their way to provide Instructors who could train such further personnel as was necessary.

Brigadier Pargiter said that our ideas and theirs seemed in the main to follow the same line. He felt sure there would be no difficulty in the provision of Instructors. He also expressed the opinion that they would be able to hand over Cobh by the 29th June but for certain personnel difficulties and they would be glad if we could give them a little more time. He referred to paragraph 7 of their note and said that the British would like to see the War Department civilian employees, e.g. District Gunners, the Irish Ratings in the War Department Fleet, civilian employees on the R.A.S.C. &c., fixed up in some other employment. It was, he said, clearly a responsibility of theirs and they would do their best to provide for these people. It appeared from the conversation that apart from this work of getting alternative employment they would be perfectly willing to arrange the transfer as from the 29th June.

It was arranged that the first meeting would be held in this Office at 3 o'clock on the afternoon on Wednesday, the 25th May.

Brigadier Pargiter informed me that the defences in our ports were exactly the same as the defences which the British themselves have in this country.

I formed the impression that Brigadier Pargiter – who is a General Staff Officer, first grade, under the Director of Military Operations and Intelligence, and is in charge at the War Office of Air Defence matters – is anxious to make the transfer as quickly as possible and would be ready to help in any way he can towards that end.

J.W. DULANTY
High Commissioner

No. 187 NAI DFA 127/116

Confidential report from Francis T. Cremins to Joseph P. Walshe (Dublin)
(S. 7/27) (Confidential)
GENEVA, 24 May 1938[1]

With reference to the German-Czechoslovakian situation, I have to update, for the information of the Minister, that the situation is viewed here with anxiety, but, in international circles, I do not find undue alarm as if the outbreak of war were immediately in prospect. On Saturday night, when the anxiety was at its height, and when I found a very gloomy view indeed taken in certain Swiss circles, M. Soubotitch (Yugoslavia) expressed to me his view that the position was 'serious but not dangerous'. That I think is really the general view here – nobody expects that Germany will at once go to war with Czechoslovakia because of isolated frontier incidents, while practically everybody takes the view that any extensive troubles in Czechoslovakia in which Germans are victims must almost inevitably result in armed intervention by the Reich which would be resisted by Czechoslovakia thereby bring-

---

[1] Marginal annotations: 'Dr Rynne', 'Seen M.R., 30/5/38, Registry please P.[ut] A.[way] on file'.

ing in France and possibly Great Britain. At the same time, many here express the view that, unless action is dictated by the general European situation, and by Germany's ultimate aims, France will not move to the help of Czechoslovakia, that is, that the mobilisation of France will depend on the extent of German designs in Czechoslovakia, and on the estimated results of such an aggrandisement on the balance of power in Europe. Satisfaction is expressed at the reported efforts of Great Britain to have the Sudeten question settled quickly and peacefully, by almost unlimited concessions by the Czech Government.

I had a conversation on the matter today with the Polish Delegate (M. Komarnicki). He does not expect immediate war, and he thinks that a peaceful settlement is still possible, but he warns against too much optimism. As regards the attitude of Poland, he says that if Germany interferes in Czechoslovakia, Poland cannot remain indifferent and must interfere too. That does not, he adds, mean, as some newspapers pretend, that Poland will support the Czechs. I take it that what it really means is that Poland would take the opportunity of German intervention to settle to her satisfaction her own territorial problem with Czechoslovakia. The Czechs have been unwise all along to incur the enmity of Poland by retaining a comparatively unimportant piece of territory on the Polish border, 90% of the population of which (about 100,000) are claimed to be Polish. At the same time M. Komarnicki says that Poland could not permit Germany to take over the whole of Czechoslovakia. It struck me, when speaking to him, that there is room for a 'deal' between the Czechs' two great neighbours, if there is any armed intervention. He expressed the view that the central European problems will be settled this year – he hoped without war – that the summer will be a time of great anxiety, and that, if war can be avoided, a period of five years' comparative tranquillity can be looked forward to!

I asked M. Komarnicki if he thought that Henlein[1] would press for the breaking of the Czech-Russian alliance, and he expressed the view that such a condition would be regarded as indispensable. It is part of Polish policy also. We cannot afford to be surrounded, he said, and added that Czechoslovakia is now suffering for the faith which she always placed in Russia. He ridiculed the idea that the U.S.S.R. would be able to traverse any part of Poland in order to aid Czechoslovakia militarily.

I enquired of M. Komarnicki what he thought of the calling up of reserves by the Czech Government, and he said that in his view such a measure was essential for the maintenance of order, and the Government finds it almost impossible to keep the internal situation in hand. He states that this situation is serious, and that the Slovaks and other minorities, apart from the Germans, are determined to secure a measure of autonomy. He expressed the view that the Czech Government is beginning to suffer from nerves, and that while it is hardly probable, an internal collapse can be visualised.

---

[1] Konrad Henlein (1898-1945), founder of the Sudetendeutsch Partie (1935), Reich Commissar for the Sudeten Deutsch territories (1938-45), captured by United States forces, 9 May 1945, committed suicide 10 May 1945.

I attach for your information some propaganda maps which have been circulated here today, apparently from German sources.

[signed] F.T. Cremins
Permanent Delegate

No. 188 NAI DFA Secretary's Files S77

Memorandum by Sheila Murphy of a phone message from Seán Murphy (London) with replies from John Hearne

Dublin, 26 May 1938

Phone message from Mr. Murphy 26.5.38 (Replies as indicated given to him by Mr. Hearne on 27.5.38)

1. Generally speaking, the meeting yesterday was quite satisfactory. The other side are quite ready to give us all the information which we asked for. There will be another meeting on Friday for the purpose of communicating to our representatives the information they desire to have.

2. The British Authorities are anxious to know whether when the handing over takes place we would wish for an exchange of ceremonial salutes. It was gathered that unless we wanted such a ceremony the British do not mind one way or the other. If there is to be no ceremony they will probably begin sending the maintenance parties away before the actual transfer takes place, and about one-half to three-quarters would be gone before the date of the transfer. If there is to be a ceremony, the whole garrison would remain.[1]

3. They said that if the date was fixed for the end of June they felt the interval between now and then would scarcely be sufficient to enable them to get their people out. If we were keen on that particular date they would fit in with our views and arrange accordingly, but they wondered if we could agree to an extension of the time. Mr. Murphy said that he did not think our people would have any great objection to an extension of the time, for, say, one week. They said that that would help them, but that if we were still keen on the end of June it would be all right.[2]

4. It became quite clear in the course of the discussions yesterday that there is a lot of stuff in the forts which our people may wish to take over – barrack equipment, armaments, etc. Our people are not sure whether they would wish to take these things over until they see what is actually there. It is suggested therefore that an administrative conference should take place at Cobh itself between the 7th and the 10th June. It is the only way of seeing whether we could take over the material referred to, and it is also the only way of making any estimate of its value at all. The proposal is that when this conference is over on Monday or Tuesday of next week some of our officers should go down informally to walk round and examine things for themselves. That could be arranged by the Department of Defence by a telephone message to Colonel Love.[3]

---

[1] Reply by Hearne: 'Can and yes'. Hearne's brief replies are written in the margin of the document in Sheila Murphy's hand.
[2] Reply by Hearne: '11th July'.
[3] Reply by Hearne: 'Agree'.

5. Between now and the 30th June the British feel that a number of War Office people might go to and from Cobh for the purpose of making inventories, etc. They consider that train journeys would be a waste of time. Apparently Cobh is under the direction of the Western Command Headquarters, which is situated at Chester. They suggest that the War Office people should come and go by seaplane. They would like a general permission during the period referred to for their people to come and go as they thought fit without an actual permission for each individual visit. They could not say how often they would come, and frequently it might be a last-minute decision.[1]

6. The Taoiseach will recall that in the note from the High Commissioner Mr. Dulanty referred to a request from the other side as to what we could do for the civilian employees.[2] They are mostly people from the district, ex-Army and ex-Naval men, but they perform civilian duties exclusively – e.g. attending to the electric light, operating motor launches, carpentry and plumbing. Many of them are there for a long time, and the British Government feels a certain responsibility for them. There are at Berehaven and Cobh 95 civilians, at Spike (Cobh) 70-78. They would be anxious that something could be done for them. They are experienced people, and it might be possible for us to retain them. The British attitude on the matter is: if we can retain them they will be glad, but if we cannot they will not very much mind.[3]

7. Owing to the shortness of the time they feel that they will not be able to take away from the ports whatever we do not want before the actual transfer. They desire to know whether there would be any objection on our part to their leaving them to take away as and when they can.[4]

8. They would like to know whether we have any views on the subject as to how the actual evacuation should take place. The most convenient thing for them would be to take the men from Cobh to Cork and embark them there for Fishguard. They would take the men away in batches. That is alternative A. Alternative B would be to get a special boat to come to Cobh Harbour and embark the men there. That would be a laborious proceeding, they think, but they would be prepared to do it if we had any objection to Alternative A. The difficulty about Alternative A might be anything in the nature of a demonstration at Cork.[5]

---

[1] Reply by Hearne: 'Agree'.
[2] See above No. 186.
[3] Reply by Hearne: 'No responsibility of any kind we will see how far we could utilise their services'.
[4] Reply by Hearne: 'Alright acquisitive'.
[5] Reply by Hearne: 'To avoid fuss or incident it would be safer to go [word indecipherable] although we recognise inconvenience'.

No. 189 UCDA P150/2517

Letter from Eamon de Valera to Malcolm MacDonald (London)
(Personal) (Copy)
DUBLIN, 30 May 1938

Dear Mr. MacDonald,

I am very glad to have your letter expressing your pleasure at the outcome of the negotiations.[1]

I feel that were it not for the happy combination on your side, of yourself and the Prime Minister, the negotiations could not have been successful, or begun.

I have no doubt the happy ending of the disputes in question has begotten a new attitude of mind on the part of our people, and if we could only now succeed in solving the problem created by partition, a happy future of mutual understanding and fruitful co-operation in matters of common concern lies ahead before our two peoples.

It has been such a pleasure to have one so understanding as you to deal with in the difficult matters of the relations between the two countries, that I regret your departure from the Dominions * Office.[2] I hope most sincerely that in the equally difficult task you have undertaken, your knowledge and zeal will serve you equally well.

Sincerely yours,
[copy letter unsigned]

*By the way, this inappropriate title should now be changed

E. de V.

No. 190 NAI DFA Madrid Embassy 10/11

Letter from Seán Murphy to Leopold H. Kerney (St Jean de Luz)
(144/35)
DUBLIN, 30 May 1938

I am directed by the Minister to refer to your minute (No. S.J. 10/11) of the 24th May[3] containing further information on the prospects of Mr. Frank Ryan's release. The Minister wishes to express his appreciation of the care which you are continuing to devote to this case. You are aware of the great interest taken by him and by the Government in the safety of all the Irish prisoners in Spain and their anxiety for the success of the efforts being made in their behalf.

[signed] Sean MURPHY
Rúnaí

---

[1] See above No. 183.
[2] MacDonald had returned to the Colonial Office and was succeeded at the Dominions Office by Lord Stanley on 16 May 1938.
[3] Not printed.

No. 191 NAI DFA Secretary's Files S77

Confidential report from John W. Dulanty to Joseph P. Walshe (Dublin)
(No. 24) (Secret)

LONDON, 1 June 1938

Adverting to the secret note which the Assistant Secretary of the Department addressed to me on the 19th ultimo[1] on the proposed visit of the Taoiseach and Dr. Douglas Hyde to Saul, County Down, I have had several conversations with the British Secretary of State for the Dominions and officers of that Department.

I referred to the experience of several years ago, referred to in the second paragraph of the note under reply, and explained that the Taoiseach was anxious to attend the ceremony at Saul. Naturally, he could not accept any conditions and if any difficulty were raised by the Six County Government the Taoiseach would be compelled on this occasion to state in public the reason why he could not enter the Northern area.

The Ceremony, I understood, would be of a religious character. There might afterwards be some social occasion, such as a luncheon, at which the Taoiseach would make a short speech and whilst he could not, as I had already stated, accept any conditions he would not take any action which might lead to friction or embarrassment either for his Government or that of the Six County.

The Dominions Office inform me to-day that the Northern Ireland Government will raise no objection to the visit to Saul of Dr. Douglas Hyde and the Taoiseach. In reply to my enquiry as to the expulsion order on the former occasion, I was informed that any expulsion action rested not on any particular document but upon Statutory Orders which would not be invoked against Mr. de Valera.

J.W. DULANTY
High Commissioner

No. 192 NAI DFA Secretary's Files S77

Letter from John W. Dulanty to Joseph P. Walshe (Dublin) with copies of the
minutes of the British-Irish meetings regarding the transfer of Treaty Ports
(Confidential)

LONDON, 1 June 1938

I have to-day received from the British War Office and send herewith twenty copies of the Minutes of Meetings held on the 25th, 27th and 28th May at this office, regarding the transfer of the Ports. In a note transmitting these copies Captain Jones, who compiled the Minutes, states that he and his colleagues are actively engaged in trying to get a clear definition from the War Office point of view of what vessels, training guns etc. form part of the fixed

---

[1] See above No. 185.

defences and also the British responsibility for making good deficiencies in stores etc.

[signed] J.W. DULANTY
High Commissioner

[Enclosure]

Minutes of Meetings held on May 25th, 27th and 28th 1938 at the Office of the High Commissioner for Éire between representatives of the Government of Éire and the Government of the United Kingdom to discuss details regarding the transfer of the harbour defences of Lough Swilly, Cobh and Berehaven to Éire.

PRESENT

Mr. J.W. Dulanty   High Commissioner for Éire
(in the Chair)

Representing the Government of Éire

Mr. Sean Murphy	Assistant Secretary, Department of External Affairs.
Major P. Maher	Director of Artillery.
Commandant Kinneen	Acting Director of Military Engineering.
Mr. J.B. O'Connell	Finance Officer.
Mr. C.J. O'Donovan	Secretary to the Office of the High Commissioner.

Representing the Government of the United Kingdom

Brigadier R.B. Pargiter	Representing Director of Military Operations and Intelligence, War Office.
Brigadier J.S. Wilkinson	Representing Director of Movements and Quartering, War Office.
Captain C.I.V. Jones	General Staff, War Office.
Mr. F. Whittle	Assistant Secretary, War Office.
Colonel F.G. Drew	General Staff, Western Command
Lieutenant-Colonel R.H.A.D. Love	Commanding South Irish Coast Defences.
Mr. J.E. Stephenson	Assistant Secretary, Dominions Office

1. *Date of evacuation*

It was originally proposed that Cobh should be evacuated by June 29th. The War Office representatives, however, pointed out that there were considerable difficulties in disposing of personnel by that date and after discussion it was finally agreed that the date of evacuation of Cobh should be July 11th.

2. *Stores left behind by War Office and Admiralty*

The War Office representatives pointed out that in the short time available little more than personal and unit equipment could be shipped to England and that it would be necessary to leave behind many tons of other stores.

It was agreed that the War Office and Admiralty should reserve the right to withdraw these stores after the date of the evacuation but that meanwhile they should be stored as far as possible in buildings to be selected by representatives of the War Office and the Department of Defence and that they should be taken care of by personnel employed by the War Office.

3. *Fixed armament*

It was agreed that the fixed armament at the Ports which should be transferred under the terms of the Agreement included the following:-

Cobh

Fort Templebreedy	two 9.2" guns
Fort Westmoreland	two 6" guns
Fort Carlisle	two 6" guns
Mounted in reserve	one 9.2" gun
	one 6" gun

Bere Haven

Two 6" guns
Two 12 pdr. guns

Lough Swilly

Two 9.2" guns
Two 6" guns

The War Office representatives pointed out that at Fort Templebreedy one 9.2" gun has a cracked 'A' tube and that they had been trying to replace this gun for a long time and that the other 9.2" gun had steel choke.

They explained that it was impossible to exchange the former by the date of evacuation but that they would replace it by a fully serviceable 9.2" gun before December 31st 1938. They would endeavour to lap out the other gun by July 11th 1938 but if that were not possible, before December 31st 1938.

In both cases the cost would be borne by the Government of the United Kingdom. The War Office representatives explained that in view of Article 2 of the Agreement which provided for the transfer of armament etc., 'at present at the said ports' they would be unable to accept a similar obligation in the case of any other deficiencies, though they did not believe that any such deficiencies existed. The Irish representatives were unable to accept the view expressed in the last sentence because their interpretation of Article 2 was that the transfer of the harbour defences necessarily meant the transfer of effective services and complete equipment. In their view the War Office interpretation implied that the Irish Department of Defence might be called upon to make good deficiencies which were not apparent at the date of transfer.

The War Office would hand over with the fixed armament the stores equipment and shops at present at the ports necessary for fighting and servicing the fixed armament and for essential training including the engineering equipment shown in the list handed to the military representatives of Éire on the 27th May 1938.

The representatives of Éire claimed that all 12 pdr. equipments in the Ports not shown above were part of the fixed defences and therefore should be transferred free. The War Office representatives reserved their opinion on this question.

4. *War Department Fleet*

The War Department Fleet on the South Irish Defences at present included the following vessels:-

1. 'John Adams'	--	Diesel Engine Barge – shallow draught – sea-going.
2. 'Wyndham'	--	Target Towing with winding gear.
3. 'General McHardy'		do
4. 'Haldane'	--	do
5. 'Swift'	--	Speed Launch
6. 'Rover'	--	Patrol Picquet Boat
7. 'Raven'	--	do
8. 'Jackdaw'	--	do.) one condemned
9. 'Magpie'	--	do.)

The representatives of Éire claimed that the War Department vessels should be regarded as part of the fixed defences and therefore transferred free. The War Office pointed out that two vessels the 'Haldane' and the 'Swift' were only attached and not based permanently at Cobh or Berehaven; that while the target towing vessels might perhaps be regarded as part of the fixed defences, the remainder could not be so regarded. The representatives of Éire still contended that all the vessels except perhaps the 'Haldane' and the 'Swift' must be regarded as part of the fixed defences and the War Office agreed to reconsider the matter.

The War Office undertook to ascertain whether there were any War Department vessels based on Lough Swilly.

5. *Movable armament*

The representatives of Éire agreed that they did not want to take over the 18 pdr. guns, Vickers guns and Lewis guns at any of the Ports and they had no objection to their removal as soon as convenient. They wished, however, to consider taking over on payment the 4.5" Howitzers at Berehaven and Lough Swilly and it was agreed that these should not be withdrawn, at present.

6. *Courses*

The War Office representatives said that it would be possible to take 12 officers on a Coast Artillery Course beginning on June 19th and lasting three weeks. Two or three of these officers could remain a further two weeks or could remain if they wished until the end of September. The two weeks which the majority of the officers would miss would deal only with counter-bombardment work (9.2") and the fortress system of rangefinding.

They also said that the vacancy now allotted to Éire on the Gunnery Staff Course would be allotted for the Field Artillery branch but that it was possible to allot Éire a further vacancy on the Coast Artillery and Anti-aircraft branch at the Gunnery Staff Course beginning in October.

Attendance of the officers on these courses would be on the usual financial terms applying to Dominions officers.

7. *Detail of personnel*

Details of artillery, engineer and civilian personnel now employed in Cobh were handed by the War Office to the Éire representatives together with full details of the electric light, pumping etc. plant installed in Cobh.

8. *Training cadre*

It was agreed that the War Office should leave behind after July 11th a training cadre consisting of:-

R.A. personnel

Officers	2
N.C.Os.	9
Master Gunners	3

R.E. personnel

Officers	1
Mechanists	1
Foreman of Works	1
N.C.Os.	3

Royal Corps of Signals personnel

Sergeants	1
Other ranks	6

The loan of personnel would be on the usual financial terms for the loan of personnel to the Dominions.

The War Office emphasised that personnel could not be ordered to remain in Cobh or any other Port after evacuation had taken place, that these men must be volunteers and that Éire would have to offer some financial inducement to them. The question of what this inducement should be would be taken up by the War Office. These men would remain in Cobh for a minimum of four months and Éire should have the option to extend their stay up to a further two months.

9. *Lands*

It was agreed that the War Department would collect rents and discharge outgoings up to June 24th 1938, that Éire would collect rents and any arrears of rent after that date and that arrears of rent so collected would accrue to Éire.

The War Office agreed that Éire would be given the original title deeds etc. of lands as early as possible.

It might be necessary to ask the Government of Éire for an indemnity against possible action by lessors in the case of leases under which the Secretary of State for War has covenanted to hand back the property of the lessors when no longer required by him.

10. *Ceremonial*

It was agreed that some ceremonial was desirable at the final handover in the nature of an exchange of salutes between two guards and the lowering of one flag and the hoisting of the other. It was agreed that details of this ceremonial should be settled locally and should be discussed at an administrative conference which was to be held on June 8th.

11. *Evacuation of Lough Swilly and Berehaven*
The War Office asked that they should be given at least three months notice of the taking over of Lough Swilly and Berehaven[1] and it was finally agreed that although no definite time could be given, Éire would give the War Office as much notice as possible.

12. *Visits to the Ports*
It was agreed that an early visit by the Éire representatives to the Ports was desirable and that to start with details for a visit to Cobh should be arranged direct between the Defence Department in Dublin and the Officer Commanding South Irish Coast Defences.

13. *Stores*
It was agreed that the War Office should supply the Department of Defence as soon as possible with a schedule showing the types and quantities of stores held at the various Ports. The Department of Defence would then indicate the amount of serviceable stores (*if any*) which they might consider purchasing. Any stores so indicated would after inspection and approval be valued by the War Office and would be taken over at the evacuation provided that agreement as to price had been reached by the two Departments.

14. *Embarkation*
It was agreed that Cobh and not Cork should be used for the embarkation of British troops on evacuation.

15. *Movable armament ammunition*
It was agreed that at present all 18 pdr. and 4.5 howitzer ammunition should be left at the Ports until Éire had decided if they wished to take any of it over on the terms indicated at paragraph 13 above.

16. *Small arms ammunition*
It was agreed that Éire did not wish to take over any small arms ammunition and that this could be removed by the War Office as convenient.

17 *Sea planes*
It was agreed that the Government of the United Kingdom could land sea-planes as required in Cobh harbour without special permission being sought until the evacuation was complete.

18. *Civilian employees*
It was agreed that Éire could accept no responsibility for these but their representatives agreed to consider and to notify the War Office before the date of evacuation how far the services of such civilian employees could be retained.

19. *Evacuation of stores not required*
It was agreed that the War Office could begin the removal forthwith of any stores which the representatives of Éire have indicated they do not wish to take over or which are definitely personal or unit stores.

20. *Private and regimental property*
It was agreed that Éire would consider the question of taking over at evaluation, private and regimental property such as squash courts etc. as soon as the War Office has indicated the expenditure on such property out of private and regimental funds.

---

[1] Berehaven and Lough Swilly were transferred to Irish control respectively on 29 September 1938 and 3 October 1938.

21. *Administrative conference*
It was agreed that an administrative conference should be held in Cobh on June 8th attended by representatives of Éire, Western Command and a representative from Northern Ireland District in order that experience could be obtained for the handing over of Lough Swilly.

22. *Defence schemes*
The representatives of Éire indicated that they wished to have the defence schemes and other relevant plans and documents of the Ports and the War Office promised to make these available.

23. *Press notice*
It was agreed that it was desirable to issue a notice to the Press which should be issued simultaneously in the United Kingdom and in Éire giving the date on which Cobh was to be evacuated.

A draft notice was approved (copy attached).

DRAFT PRESS NOTICE
The meetings at the Irish High Commissioner's Office between officials of Éire and the United Kingdom were concluded on Saturday morning. As a result of the discussions arrangements have been agreed upon for the formal transfer of the defences of Cork Harbour on the 11th July 1938. An Administrative Conference will be held in Cobh on the 8th June at which discussions will take place to consider the disposal of certain stores and private or regimental properties not forming part of the Port defences proper.

The fixing of the date of the transfer of the Harbour defences at Berehaven and Lough Swilly which under the terms of Article 3 of the Agreement of the 25th April 1938 are to be handed over not later than the 31st December 1938 was deferred for later decision.

No. 193 UCDA P150/2183

Handwritten letter from Joseph P. Walshe to Eamon de Valera (Dublin)
CAIRO, 2 June 1938

My Dear Sir,
Seán wired me that you had dissolved the Dáil and I felt very glad indeed that you took the inevitable decision without further delay. We all want you to be in a position of sitting back without extrinsic worries and building up the country according to the ideals you have inspired us with. For that you had to be free from anxieties regarding your majority in the Dáil, and I earnestly hope you will achieve your purpose. The omens are all favourable.

I shall be back in Dublin on Wednesday next. I arrive by flying boat in England on Monday but I am going to remain over Tuesday in order to pay a few visits of courtesy to officials who kindly secured me facilities in the Near East.

I had a very long chat with Miles Lampson. He told me, in the frankest manner about his difficulties here, and gave me all the information available about Palestine. His conclusions about the latter country indicate that a proposal for a ten year truce is in the air. The Arabs and Jews will thus have time to come to some understanding. No doubt G.B. will consolidate her position in the meantime with both sides. The policy of divide and conquer is to be abandoned being over worked and too crude to achieve any lasting results. Egypt is taking an increasing interest in Palestine and so far the declarations of the Government have been moderate and wise. The Jewish people are influential amongst all classes here – and they have identified themselves more than any other foreign element with the aspirations of the Egyptian people.

Lampson assumed during his whole talk with me that I had been sent – this year and last – by the Government on a voyage of exploration. He emphasized how enormously important it was for any country interested in world peace to keep in touch with this region of the world. I told him that you encouraged me to travel and keep you informed of conditions wherever I went, that you realized, in particular, the importance of Egypt as one of the chief sensitive areas in the world and were fully conscious of the difficulty of the problems involved in the renaissance of the Jewish and Arab peoples. He spoke very highly of your work at Geneva.

In a quiet way I got confirmation from officials and others of Lampson's statements. Sharara Pasha the permanent head of the Department of Foreign Affairs was very friendly.

He is strongly convinced, as I am, that, in the course of the next few years, there ought to be an exchange of legations between the two countries. There is and there will continue to be a certain similarity of relationship vis a vis G.B. There is an instinctive sympathy for Ireland and Irishmen. Some of them – one a brother of the Minister for the Interior – suggested that we should lend them 200 officers to train their army. Arthur Delaney is the Head of the Broadcasting Stations, and the Egyptians would not have an Englishman in such a key position. I find all concerned favour the idea of concluding a treaty of friendship with us in particular, but also with the other countries associated in varying degrees with the Commonwealth.

They see the advantage of linking up with the individual associated States rather than with G.B. alone. Egypt could form the first unit of the new group which would change the Commonwealth's character and give us an opportunity of sliding quietly out of the King's orbit. I found Lampson so communicative that I mentioned the possibility of Egypt coming into a group more broadly based than the present Commonwealth group. To my surprise he had given the subject a good deal of thought. As he seems to find the Foreign Office as impervious to new ideas as we have found the Dominions Office. He agreed instantly that no red tape or precedent should be allowed to make serious difficulties about the adhesion of separate monarchies or republics to a new Commonwealth.

I feel that an Irish legation here would quickly obtain the good will and confidence of the Egyptian Governt. and I should not be surprised if our influence with them became greater than that of the British Embassy. If that position were realized – and a zealous worker should reach it fairly soon – our prestige and influence here would react favourably on our more immediate position vis-à-vis the British at home. Indeed I cannot keep feeling that there is still a certain 'colonialessness' and absence of personality about our Legations abroad – which make them almost useless as instruments in our fight for recognition of our national distinctiveness, or as factors in our relations with G.B. What is at the root of the evil! Would a six years truce to acquire a complete knowledge of Irish not be a very good tonic for all of them as well as for the service at home. Egypt has unfortunately one great weakness which makes her a C3 state in her relations with G.B. She has no really patriotic leaders and the Service as well as the Cabinet is venal to the last degree. This is recognised by all good Egyptians and they look forward to the time when they will have a Leader who will be simpleminded and ruthless with corruption. Most of the higher civil servants have interests in commercial concerns which they favour at every opportunity to the detriment of the general welfare of the State. They accept either direct bribes, or indirect in the shape of motor cars at reduced prices – houses at a nominal rent etc. In fact they are all – with a few splendid exceptions – very much on the make and their work for the State is neither zealous nor efficient. This appalling defect leaves them completely at the mercy of foreign or private interests and nothing but an extremely strong national movement will afford a remedy. T.G. that movement can be seen in Germ already.

I explored the southern Sinai area with my friend. We drove through desert tracts and river beds to the Holy Mountain some three hundred miles from here. The way lay through Suez, across the Canal and down the Red Sea to Abu Zeneeman.[1] The scenery through the mountains of Sinai was a fitting setting for the greatest drama of our race. I felt here more impressed on the mountain of the Ten Comdts. than in Palestine. We stayed two nights in the Greek Monastery at the foot of the mountain and discussed age old problems including the procession of the Holy Ghost (on which they were not very enlightening).

The Monastery is 1400 years old. They seem to live outside time, but still not so much as not to know about our new constitution, and the appt. of Dr. Hyde as President. All the hundreds of papers in Egypt in various languages gave this appointment great publicity. In fact the interest displayed in Ireland by everybody one meets here is a constant cause of surprise.

I went to see the Luxor monuments last week and the heat was terrific but with such marvellous beauty on every side one forgets personal discomfort.

With all good wishes for success I remain, my dear Sir, with great respect and esteem.

Yours very sincerely,

J.P. WALSHE

---

[1] Abu Zenima.

No. 194 NAI DFA Secretary's Files S77

Letter from Michael Beary to Joseph P. Walshe (Dublin)
(2/54437)

Dublin, 3 June 1938

In confirmation of telephonic discussion with Mr. Murphy of your Department this morning, I am directed by the Minister for Defence to state that during the recent discussions held in the office of the High Commissioner in London with regard to the impending transfer of the harbour defences at Berehaven, Cobh and Lough Swilly, the United Kingdom representatives were requested to arrange for twelve officers of the Defence Forces, whom it is proposed to appoint to the Coastal Defence Army, to undergo a course in England in Coastal Defence duties.

The British War Office has agreed to reserve (a) twelve vacancies for Artillery Officers on the first part of Course No. 338 (Coast Artillery – regular) which will commence at Shoeburyness, Essex, on the 19th June, 1938, and terminate on the 9th July, 1938, and (b) three vacancies on the second part of this course (Counter Bombardment and Fortress System of Range Finding) which will last for a period of two weeks. The War Office further agreed that the officers who attend the second part of the course should remain on until the completion of a Gunnery Staff course which is at present in progress at the Military College of Science, Woolwich, and which will terminate on the 30th September, 1938. Verbal sanction has been received from the Department of Finance.

The following Officers have been detailed to attend the first part of Course No. 338:-

Captain	D.J. Collins
"	C. Trodden
"	M.P. MacCarthy
"	D.J. Farrell
2/Lieut.	A. Dalton
"	W. Donagh
"	P.J. Hally
"	J. Murray
"	C. Shortall
"	J.H. Byrne
"	W. Rea
"	P.J. O'Callaghan

Of these, Captains Trodden, Farrell and MacCarthy will undergo the second part of the Course and Captains Trodden and Farrell will remain on for the Gunnery Staff Course terminating on the 30th September next.

I am, accordingly, to request that you will be good enough to inform the British War Office without delay of the acceptance of the vacancies and to intimate that it would be appreciated if an early indication could be given of the fees chargeable; the time and date on which the Officers should report and whether public quarters will be available on a repayment basis.

[signed] M.J. Beary
Leas Rúnaidhe

No. 195 NAI DFA Secretary's Files S94/39

*Memorandum on co-operation with Northern Ireland from John Leydon
to Seán Lemass (Dublin)*

DUBLIN, 10 June 1938

MEMORANDUM

In the course of a discussion yesterday with Mr. Jenkins (Board of Trade), Mr. Braddock (U.K. Trade Commissioner), and Messrs. Scott and Parr (Secretary and Assistant Secretary respectively to the Ministry of Commerce, Belfast), I referred to the question of co-operation between the Government here and the Government in Northern Ireland on matters of common concern. I mentioned in particular the question of a link between the existing electricity system here and the system in the North which would be mutually advantageous; the present position on this matter is that the Electricity Supply Board and the Electricity Board in the North have agreed, with our knowledge and approval, to have it examined generally by their Technical Advisers. Mr. Scott agreed that this was a matter which offered a prospect of useful co-operation which would be mutually beneficial to North and South and said that he personally would welcome an arrangement which would provide a link between the two systems.

I then went on to refer to the hydro electric possibilities of the River Erne; while making it clear that I was not speaking with Governmental authority, I suggested that it also was a matter on which there might usefully be co-operation between the two Governments. The catchment area is in Northern Ireland and the Falls are at Ballyshannon, so that the Power Station must be located on this side of the Border if the River is to be used for the generation of power. I suggested that as the two Governments are concerned in any question regarding a hydro electric scheme for the Erne and as both could use the power which could be generated there the scheme is one which offers the possibility of co-operation and is therefore suitable for joint examination and investigation. Mr. Scott said that he also was in favour of co-operation in connection with such a scheme and he promised to look into it immediately on his return to Belfast.[1]

I then mentioned the question of Unemployment Insurance on which it has not hitherto been found possible to secure anything in the nature of a reciprocal arrangement. I suggested to Mr. Scott that this also might form a basis of discussion between the Departments concerned on both sides. He promised to make this suggestion to the appropriate Minister in Belfast.

Mr. Scott enquired whether it would be possible to make any concession for bricks manufactured at two small brick factories (which he thought are located in Dungannon and Enniskillen); these factories could probably do a small trade across the Border if they got some tariff concession and they would be unlikely to do serious injury to any Irish industry. I told him that we have a large number of brick manufacturers here and that some of them are at present having a very lean time, but I said that if he would give me

---

[1] The construction of the Erne hydro-electric scheme was approved in Dublin in 1943 and in Belfast in 1946; construction began in 1952 and the scheme was completed in 1957.

fuller particulars regarding his proposal I would have it examined and would let him know whether anything could be done.

No. 196 NAI DFA Secretary's Files S94/39

*Memorandum on co-operation with Northern Ireland from
John Leydon to Seán Lemass (Dublin)
(Secret)*

Dublin, 15 June 1938

Minister

I have already given you a verbal report of the discussions which took place last week when Mr. Jenkins of the Board of Trade and the Secretary[1] and the Assistant Secretary of the Ministry of Commerce,[2] Belfast, came here for the purpose of discussing certain points arising out of the Trade Agreement.

2: The attached notes indicate the various matters which came under consideration. So far as the Board of Trade is concerned, there is really nothing of any importance to talk about and there is no doubt that Mr. Jenkins' real object in arranging for the discussions is shown at the passage I have marked 'A' in his letter to me of 30th May.[3]

3: The atmosphere was extremely friendly throughout the discussions; the officers of the Northern Ireland Government said they were very anxious to promote closer co-operation between the two governments and to meet at fairly frequent intervals for the discussion of matters of common concern; they suggested that the next meeting should take place in Belfast at an early date. They expressed the hope that it might also be possible at a comparatively early stage to arrange for a meeting of Ministers of the two Governments even if those meetings should only be of a rather informal character. This, in my opinion, would be all to the good, and Mr. Scott thought that it might be possible to arrange that his Minister, who sometimes comes to Dublin, should call to see you.

4: I venture to suggest that in present circumstances co-operation between officers of the various Departments concerned in Dublin and Belfast will afford a useful method of improving relations between the two Governments. Apart from matters in which this Department is interested, there are also, I think, a number of matters which concern the Department of Agriculture; flax is one of them and I should think that it offers considerable possibilities in this particular direction.

5: Mr. Scott seemed to be quite keen on the scheme for hydro-electric development on the Erne. If this scheme should offer any reasonable possibilities from the commercial point of view it has occurred to me that it might be possible to establish some kind of a Joint Operating Company which it has been agreed to establish in connection with Transatlantic Air Services; I did not, however, mention this suggestion to Mr. Scott.

---

[1] Sir William D. Scott, Secretary, Ministry of Commerce, Belfast.
[2] G.H.E. Parr, Assistant Secretary, Ministry of Commerce, Belfast.
[3] Not printed.

No. 197 UCDA P150/2179

Confidential report from John W. Dulanty to Joseph P. Walshe (Dublin)
(No. 26) (Secret)

LONDON, 16 June 1938

Mr. J.H. Thomas, whom I had not seen since his resignation,[1] lunched with me on Friday last.

He spoke of his real pleasure in the recent Agreements though he would be less than human if he didn't express his deep regrets that the British Cabinet had, long ago, turned down his own proposals for a not essentially different settlement. His terms were much the same as those agreed upon except that his annuity figure was £20 millions. More than any other Cabinet Minister Lord Hailsham[2] was responsible for the rejection of this plan. Several months later he lost much of his influence in the Cabinet through his holding on so long to the Lord Chancellorship when it was unmistakeably clear to the least observant that he was physically unfit to do the work of that office.

He told me that one of the people most pleased with the Agreements was the present King. The latter, and a different person altogether, Mr. J.L. Garvin,[3] had both said to him within the past few days that they would like to meet An Taoiseach.

Lord Baldwin and Lady Baldwin recently stayed for a week-end with Mr. and Mrs. Thomas at their house in Sussex. 'I welcomed him' Mr. Thomas told me, 'by saying to him – "here is the luckiest politician alive coming to stay with the unluckiest".' 'I did not have to come all this way to learn that, Jim' was Lord Baldwin's answer.

After a eulogy of Lord Baldwin – 'one of the most honourable and fair-minded men God ever made' – there followed some remarks about other former colleagues. Mr. Chamberlain and Mr. Thomas it appears throughout their membership of the British Cabinet sat side by side in the Cabinet meetings. Frequently Mr. Chamberlain in undertones would make remarks in the Cabinet to Mr. Thomas about Mr. Baldwin which no colleague should have made about another. Mr. Thomas said he was the intermediary between Mr. Baldwin and Mr. Chamberlain on the subject of the latter's succession to the Prime Ministership. He mentioned this as showing the close and friendly character of his relations which Mr. Chamberlain. Yet he feared he must describe him as a pure opportunist with no grasp of principle. (As the conversation went on Mr. Thomas showed great bitterness about the fact that although Lord Baldwin had been to stay with him, Mr. Chamberlain had left him completely alone since his resignation – a circumstance to be borne in mind when considering Mr. Thomas's criticisms.)

Sir John Simon was an enigma. Some of his colleagues doubted even his

---

[1] Thomas was forced to resign in May 1936 after he leaked information regarding the upcoming budget to stock exchange speculators.

[2] Douglas Hogg (Lord Hailsham) (1872-1950), British Conservative politician, Lord Chancellor (1935-8).

[3] James Louis Garvin (1868-1947), editor of the *Observer* (1908-42).

veracity. Despite his great ability he would never win the trust even of his small party much less the House of Commons. Lord Hailsham was slowly dying and counted for little nowadays. Of the younger men in the Cabinet he thought Mr. Walter Elliot the most promising. Lord Stanley was as decent and as straight a man as you would meet but most certainly not a man of brains.

It was a pity he was sent to the Dominions Office where the senior staff were not really big or progressive-minded as was the case in a number of other Departments such as the Treasury, the Admiralty, and the Board of Trade. When he went to the Dominions Office he did not get the support he expected and which he had received elsewhere. 'Didn't you know that I sacked Harding? Only for Warren Fisher and Baldwin I would have succeeded. He was so reactionary and unsympathetic to my ideas not only on Ireland but on other matters that I felt my position almost impossible. Batterbee, being his brother-in-law, was merely an echo of Harding. The papers sent to the Cabinet often revealed a difference of opinion between senior people in the same Department and these different points of view were of great help to Ministers. Though they became less reactionary and we got on moderately well, Harding and Batterbee continued to hold the same view on practically every question.'

About his political downfall he said few men had ever known such bitterness of spirit as had been his. All he said to Sir Alfred Butt[1] was a kind of 'leg pull'. Sir Alfred Butt had asked no question. He is a very rich man and Mr. Thomas said he had told Sir Alfred Butt, in a tone of banter, that he and other big capitalists like him who thought they could get armaments piled up without paying for them would be disillusioned. 'I am, and always will be, a gambler' Mr. Thomas said, 'So is Butt. On that jesting remark Butt goes straightaway and insures against a Budget rise and right enough makes a bit of money as lots of others did'. Would not the general public conclude, I asked, that Sir Alfred Butt had special information whereas the others insured on their own interpretation of the Budget position. 'The answer to that' Mr. Thomas said, 'is a letter I hold from a leading firm of Lloyds saying that Butt had regularly taken Budget insurances with Lloyds for over twenty years and had usually been on the right side!' I record the immediately foregoing only for its relation to what followed.

'We all know' Mr. Thomas said, 'there isn't any gratitude in public life. I accept that. But what makes me feel suicidal is that I have been publicly disgraced for giving away a secret I never gave away – I who probably hold more secrets locked up in my direct personal experience than half the members of the Cabinet put together. When Lady Astor's[2] son was in trouble for

---

[1] Sir Alfred Butt, Conservative politician, MP for Wandsworth, Balham and Tooting, Chairman of the Theatre Royal, Drury Lane.

[2] This word is handwritten into a blank space left by the typist. Nancy Witcher Astor, Viscountess Astor (1879-1964), American socialite who married into the prominent Astor family, the first woman to serve as a member of the House of Commons. Her son from her first marriage, Robert Gould Shaw III (1898-1970), was infamously arrested under the British Criminal Law Amendment Act (1885) in 1931.

homosexuality[1] who got that put right with complete secrecy? Jim Thomas. When the Prince of Wales was outraged because his nomination of Mr. Simpson[2] to a Masonic Lodge had been turned down because the Lodge said Mrs. Simpson was the Prince's mistress and this was a "blind" for the Prince, who brought the Prince before the three blackballers of His Royal Highness's own nomination, and got an emphatic denial from the Prince about his relation with Mrs. Simpson and consequently secured Mr. Simpson's election, thus saving a most embarrassing situation for the country? The answer again is Jim Thomas. Who was called in when the Duke of Kent[3] was terribly and, as it seemed to his mother, inextricably involved with a notorious Society prostitute – a scandal that would have altered history had it been revealed? Who got the incriminating letters and photographs at a fourth of the price the prostitute demanded when she was in a position to demand almost any figure? Jim Thomas is again the answer. Isn't it the irony of ironies that I who hold and have never given away any of these real secrets am damned for ever because they say I gave away a supposed Budget secret which I never did.'

Queen Mary, the King, and Lord Baldwin had shown consistent sympathy and solace to Mrs. Thomas and himself in their great distress.

[signed] J.W. DULANTY
High Commissioner

No. 198 NAI DFA Madrid Embassy 10/11A

Memorandum from Leopold H. Kerney to Joseph P. Walshe (Dublin)
(S.J. 10/11)

ST JEAN DE LUZ, 29 June 1938

Frank RYAN (Your 144/35)[4]

Further to my minute of 20th inst.,[5] you will have seen the item of news in the 'Times' of 24th June according to which Hodgson was reputed to be making progress with arrangements for 100 British prisoners to be exchanged for 100 Italians and that the selected 100 British prisoners had been removed from San Pedro de Cardena and were under an Italian guard at Palencia, but that the approval by the Republican Government of the proposed exchange was awaited; you will have also seen that in the British House of Commons on 27th June a similar statement was made and that further progress had

---

[1] This word is handwritten into a blank space left by the typist.
[2] Ernest Aldrich Simpson (1895-1958), the second husband of Wallis Simpson (who later married Edward, Duke of Windsor, the former Edward VIII). Ernest and Wallis remained close friends after their divorce in October 1936.
[3] 'Duke of Kent' handwritten by Dulanty into a blank space left by the typist. George, Duke of Kent (1902-1942), was the fourth son of King George V. He is known to have had many affairs with men and women before and during his marriage to Princess Marina of Greece (m. 1934). He was killed in a plane crash whilst on active service on 25 August 1942.
[4] See above No. 190.
[5] Not printed.

been made in the matter, but that the views of the Spanish Government were still awaited.

The Count de Pourtalés is going to Burgos in 1 or 2 days' time to obtain official confirmation as to the present whereabouts of Frank Ryan and the 99 other prisoners who were removed from San Pedro on 13th June and to endeavour to get in touch with these men; it is hoped that it will be possible to send them in due course correspondence forms.

Meanwhile, Mr. Muntadas says that they have no official news with regard to these prisoners but that he had learned from a private source that they were in *PLASENCIA*, which is in the province of Caceres, and not at Palencia, which is between Burgos and Valladolid.

I am of opinion that Frank Ryan's Italian gaolers will be careful that nothing should happen to him as he is almost certainly the most important in rank of the 100 prisoners to be exchanged by Burgos. The supposed intention to court-martial Frank Ryan has apparently been definitely abandoned.

Aire Lán-Chómhachtach

No. 199 UCDA P194/550

Handwritten letter from Joseph Walshe to Michael MacWhite (Rome)
Dublin, 3 July 1938

My dear Michael,

I hope Rome is treating you and Paula[1] kindly in the matter of Climate. I passed through the air in the neighbourhood and spent a $^1/_2$ hour at Bracciano on the morning of the 6th June, but did not feel justified in asking you to come to see me for so short a time.

The immediate object of this note is to tell you that our Sheila Murphy whom you know well is going to Rome for a short holiday and is arriving there about 9.30 p.m. on Thursday 8th July. No doubt Devlin with whom she has been in touch has told you of her project.

As Sheila is a valuable and v. amiable member of our Service, the Minister and all the brethren here will be grateful if you help to make her stay in Rome pleasant.

I should like to have a personal note from you telling me your reactions to things Roman and your hopes of doing work there.[2]

I was sorry to have missed you during your stay in Ireland. I hope my wanderings are over for some time.

All good wishes to you both,
Yours sincerely,
J.P. Walshe

---

[1] MacWhite's wife Paula (nee Gruttner Hillerod), a well-known Danish painter. They had married in 1921.
[2] It is not clear from the documents extant if MacWhite wrote a specific report in reply to this point. However he did deal with Walshe's request in a number of despatches to Dublin. See for example below Nos 205, 213 and 216.

No. 200 NAI DFA 243/67

Statement by Francis T. Cremins to the fourth (public) meeting of the Evian-les-Bains Refugee Conference

EVIAN-LES-BAINS, FRANCE, 11 July 1938

The Irish Government are deeply grateful to the Governments of the United States and France for the opportunity which this meeting affords of expressing their sincere sympathy with the objects for which the Committee has been convened, and their hope that substantial results will follow from consideration of the problems before the delegates. They have been happy to accept the invitation extended to them in order to demonstrate their sympathy, even though, for reasons which I shall briefly set out, they are not, to their great regret, in a position to make any substantial contribution to the solution.

Ireland is a small country with jurisdiction over a population of something less than three million people. Notwithstanding the steady progress which has been made in recent years in regard to the creation of new industries, by far the greater part of our people still derive, and will continue to derive, their living from the land. I need not attempt to explain the land problems which have arisen in Ireland; it is sufficient to say that there is not enough land available to satisfy the needs of our own people.

Although every effort is being made by the Government to expedite industrialisation in a country which had been greatly under-industrialised, the new industries are not yet capable of absorbing the regular increase in our population, so that each year numbers of young people are forced by circumstances to emigrate. While such emigration remains imposed upon our national economy, it is obvious that we can make no real contribution to the resettlement of refugees.

So much for the agricultural and the industrial sides. On the professional side, it will suffice to say that, in our medical schools, there qualify every year more doctors than are required to care for the health of our people. And similar conditions of over-crowding apply to the other professions. It is for these various reasons that we are not in a position to contribute in any appreciable degree to the solution of this urgent problem, and we are naturally anxious not to promise more than we could hope to perform.

It has, I think, emerged from the speeches already made that there is little likelihood that the fully settled countries will be able to provide homes for more than a fraction of the unhappy persons with whom we are concerned.

The only alternative solution which has been suggested is the opening-up of new or underdeveloped territory. The Irish Government have no such territory under their control, and they are accordingly reluctant to urge the taking by other Governments of measures in which they themselves could not participate. The Irish delegation, however, ventures to express the earnest hope that, notwithstanding the difficulties, the mass of human suffering involved in the refugee problem may, by some such means, be substantially alleviated.

No. 201 NAI DT S9377

*Memorandum to the Government by the Department of Industry and Commerce
on continued Irish membership of the Imperial Economic Committee and the
Imperial Shipping Committee*

DUBLIN, 12 July 1938

QUESTION OF CONTINUED MEMBERSHIP OF THE IMPERIAL ECO-
NOMIC COMMITTEE AND OF THE IMPERIAL SHIPPING COMMITTEE

1. In November, 1933, the Oireachtas approved the recommendations contained in the Report of the Imperial Committee on Economic Consultation
and Co-operation, 1933. This involved liability on the part of this country for
an annual contribution at the rate of 4% of £24,000, viz., £960, for a period of
three years, commencing on the 1st October, 1933, and ending on the 30th
September, 1936. Of this amount, £888 was borne on the Vote for Industry
and Commerce in respect of :-

(a)	Imperial Economic Committee	£808
(b)	Imperial Shipping Committee	80
	Total	£888

The balance of £72 was in respect of the Executive Council of the Imperial
Agricultural Bureaux and was accordingly borne on the Vote for Agriculture,
thus increasing the annual provision in that Vote for these Bureaux to £872.
An outline of the constitution and functions of the two Committees is contained in an Annex to this memorandum.[1]

2. The Government, on the 24th November, 1936, decided that, pending an
anticipated review of the work of the Imperial Economic Committee and the
Imperial Shipping Committee by the Commonwealth Conference to be held
in 1937, Ireland should continue a member of the Committees at the existing
rates of contribution.

3. The Government, on the 12th March, 1937, approved of the payment of
annual contributions totalling £1,125 per annum for the five years from the
1st April, 1937 to the 31st March, 1942, to organisations under the control of
the Imperial Agricultural Bureaux. In those contributions, which will be
borne on the Vote for Agriculture, is merged the sum of £72, referred to in
Paragraph 1, and previously paid by that Department. The Government have
also sanctioned the payment of an annual contribution of £93.15.0 for the first
five years to a proposed Imperial Forestry Bureau under the control of the
Imperial Agricultural Bureaux. This latter contribution will be borne on the
Vote for Lands.

4. Contributions due by Ireland to the Imperial Economic Committee and the
Imperial Shipping Committee have been paid to the 31st March, 1938.

5. The work of the two Committees mentioned was examined by the
Commonwealth Conference held in May, 1937, which approved of the
continuance of the Committees as then constituted, with the modification
that the annual fund of the Imperial Economic Committee in respect of the

---

[1] Not printed.

five-year period from the 1st April, 1938 to the 31st March, 1943 should be increased from £20,200 to £22,000, making a total annual contribution to both Committees for the period £24,000, as compared with £22,200 previously. The Conference also approved of the continuance of the scales of contributions laid down in 1933. The annual contribution which would be due by Ireland to the Committees in question during the period from the 1st April, 1938 to the 31st March, 1943, in the event of the Government agreeing to continued membership, would, therefore, be at the rate of 4% of £24,000, viz., £960, divided as follows:-

(a)	Imperial Economic Committee	£880
(b)	Imperial Shipping Committee	80
	Total	£960

This amount would be borne on the Vote for Industry and Commerce.

6. The decision taken by the Government on the 24th November, 1936, covers Ireland's membership of the Committee referred to for the period up to the 31st March, 1938. The decision of the Government is now sought as to whether this country is to continue a member of the Committees after that date.

7. In so far as the Department of Industry and Commerce is concerned, the direct and positive advantage derived from the contribution to the Imperial Economic Committee and the Imperial Shipping Committee has not been strong, though the Minister for Industry and Commerce recognises that the work of these Committees probably has a beneficial effect on the development of our export trade and may have some importance from the point of view of the development of aviation here. He considers, however, that the question of continued membership should be decided rather from the viewpoints of the Ministers for Agriculture[1] and External Affairs.[2]

8. The Minister for Agriculture considers that, from the point of view of his Department, an adequate return is obtained for the expenditure involved by membership of the Imperial Economic Committee, and he has recommended that this country should continue to be a member of the Committee and should undertake to pay thereto, in respect of the five years from the 1st April, 1938 to the 31st March, 1943, an annual contribution based on the total annual contribution recommended by the Commonwealth Conference, 1937.

9. The High Commissioner for Ireland in London has pointed out that, by reason of this country's membership of the Imperial Economic Committee, State Departments, Chambers of Commerce, and Universities in Ireland receive, apart from occasional publications by the Committee, free issues of weekly, monthly, and annual publications to the value of about £250 a year, while, in addition, about 60 creameries save a total of about £210 a year on their subscriptions to the weekly Dairy Produce Notes. He has also pointed out that frequent and helpful references are made by his Office to the material issued by the Committee, as well as applications for information on special subjects.

---

[1] Dr James Ryan.
[2] Eamon de Valera.

10. The Minister for External Affairs has intimated that, as the Minister for Agriculture and the representative of this country on the Imperial Economic Committee are satisfied that an adequate return is received for the payment of our contribution, he concurs in the reconsideration of the Minister for Agriculture in regard to continued membership of the Committee.

11. The Minister for Finance[1] has no objection to this country's continuing to be a member of the Imperial Economic Committee and of the Imperial Shipping Committee after the 31st March, 1938, and to its undertaking to pay, in respect of the five-year period commencing on the 1st April, 1938 and ending on the 31st March, 1943, an annual contribution based on the total contribution recommended by the Commonwealth Conference, 1937, viz., £960.

12. The Minister for Industry and Commerce agrees with the proposal that membership of the Imperial Economic Committee and of the Imperial Shipping Committee should be continued after the 31st March, 1938, and the formal sanction of the Government for the proposal is now sought.

No. 202 NAI DFA 105/82

> *Letter from Joseph P. Walshe to Peadar MacMahon (Dublin)*
> *(105/82) (Secret)*
>
> DUBLIN, 16 July 1938

I enclose copy of a Memorandum[2] received from the Dominions Office, through the High Commissioner, setting out the desire of the British Air Council to establish a range for bombing and firing from the air on the North Eastern shore of Lough Foyle.

Sir Harry Batterbee called on the High Commissioner yesterday and communicated the contents of the Memorandum, unofficially, to him. 'The British Government,' he said, 'would not have chosen this site in normal circumstances and they had only selected the Lough Foyle site on account of the rapid expansion of the Air Force and the difficulty of finding sites for practice grounds.' Sir Harry Batterbee approached the High Commissioner, informally, because on this matter the British Government were most anxious to avoid doing anything near our Border which might embarrass our Government. The High Commissioner told Sir Harry Batterbee that it would be unfortunate if there appeared to be any further consolidation of British Forces in the Six-County area and he felt that the proposal would not be agreeable to our Government. Sir Harry Batterbee declared that the matter was urgent and added that it would be a matter of serious disappointment to the Air Council if they could not proceed with this proposal.

I am directed by the Minister for External Affairs to enquire whether there are any circumstances from the military point of view which might constitute a factor, one way or the other, in coming to a decision as to what reply should be given to the British communication. Owing to the urgency of the matter,

---

[1] Seán MacEntee.
[2] Not printed.

the Minister for External Affairs would be glad to hear the views of the Minister for Defence as early as possible.

[stamped](Signed J.P. WALSHE)
Rúnaí

No. 203 NAI DFA 105/82

Letter from Peadar MacMahon to Joseph P. Walshe (Dublin)
(S. 46) (Secret)

DUBLIN, 20 July 1938

I am directed by the Minister for Defence[1] to refer to your letter of the 16th instant[2] with enclosure, relative to the desire of the British Air Council to establish a range for bombing and firing from the air on the North Eastern shore of Lough Foyle, and to state that, from the military point of view, there is no objection to the proposal which can adequately be advanced. At the same time, the Minister feels strongly that on general principles, the establishment of the range is undesirable and that the Air Council should be discouraged to the greatest possible extent against putting the proposal into effect.

[signed] PEADAR MACMAHON
RÚNAIDHE

No. 204 NAI DFA 105/82

Letter from Joseph P. Walshe to John W. Dulanty (London)
(105/82) (Secret)

DUBLIN, 22 July 1938

Your minute No. 31 of the 15th July,[3] concerning the desire of the British Air Council to establish a range for bombing and firing from the air practice on the North Eastern shore of Lough Foyle.

The Minister would be very glad indeed if you could prevail on the Dominions Office to prevent this project being put into execution. From every point of view it is objectionable. The area selected is just across the Foyle opposite Moville, and, apart from the disagreeable political aspects, the townspeople and the farmers of the district would be sure to raise violent objections to the disturbance caused by the explosions and the noise of the engines.

You should remind the Dominions Office that protests have been made successfully in many places in Great Britain during the past year against similar invasions. The political objection, which is the major one here, was not present in Great Britain.

In all the circumstances, the Dominions Office should not have any very serious difficulty in persuading the Air Council to forego their intentions

---

[1] Frank Aiken
[2] See above No. 202.
[3] Not printed.

with regard to the Lough Foyle area. The better alternative, from the political point of view, would be to select some spot in Great Britain, though we are hardly in a position to raise more than a mild objection to the establishment of a practice area in parts of the Six Counties remote from the Border.

[stamped] (Signed J.P. WALSHE)
Rúnaí

No. 205 UCDA P194/550

Letter from Joseph P. Walshe to Michael MacWhite (Rome)
(Secret)

DUBLIN, 26 July 1938

My dear Michael,

I was very glad to receive your letter, dated 19th July,[1] this morning. I hope you will be able to write often in future just in this personal way. The more closely we keep in touch the better. We are very anxious to hear all about Italy. As you know, the Taoiseach – now that he is free from the ordinary internal political worries – wishes to get down to a programme of planned reconstruction. A great deal has indeed been done over the past several years, but he realises that it is only by planning on a large scale, somewhat after the Italian model, that big results can be achieved. Your own knowledge of this country will be a sufficient guide to you as to the particular form of activity coming under your notice which might be worth while imitating here. Apart from gaining the goodwill of the Italian Government and people for Ireland – a role in which by universal acknowledgment you were so successful in the United States – I quite understand that in the strictly diplomatic line there is not very much to do in Rome. At the moment, however, the dread of war is weighing heavily upon us all, and you are at a very important outpost from which you can keep us informed from day to day how the situation appears from the Rome angle.

Do you not think, for instance, that, if England and Germany go to war – whether about the Czechoslovak question, or, more directly to determine finally which of the two is going to control the destines of Europe – Italy will in the last resort abandon Germany and throw in her lot with England? One has an instinctive feeling that the Italians do not trust the Germans, and that they feel that a German victory would be eventually followed by the loss of Trieste and all that that implies in the diminution of Italian prestige in the Mediterranean.

These are difficult questions to put to anybody in a position to reply in a Dictator State, but, from the attitude of your Italian friends who are close to the powers that be, you may be able to give us something.

As you know, we have the right to neutrality in any war in which England may be involved, but everybody here recognises that Germany would not hesitate for a moment to attack this country if by doing so she

---

[1] Not printed.

could hope to achieve her purpose of defeating England. So that the feeling of the country in the present war atmosphere is somewhat pessimistic, and we seem to be likely to be involved whether we wish it or no. We are, therefore, interested in providing ourselves with a system of defence proportionate to our means but adequate for the purpose of warding off an invasion for a sufficiently long period to allow the British to come to our aid. That is a humiliating outlook after our long struggle with the British, but the rise of racialism and ideologies involving religious persecution in Europe has made the people think of immediately threatening disasters, and has somewhat blunted their feelings of antagonism against the British.

Your own military experience and your observation of what Italy is accomplishing in military matters will help you to note any ideas which might be useful in the arming of this country. Here we may not speak of re-arming, because in truth we are hardly armed at all, and at the present moment we should be unable to repel even a serious landing of troops from the air.

I wonder do you intend to come to Ireland this year? I have already taken my holiday, and so shall be here without interruption until Christmas.

I hope you and Paula and Owen[1] will like Rome. Of all places I have visited, none has impressed me so much, and I am always looking forward to my next visit there. It seems to grip one more than any other city in the world.

With all good wishes,
Ever yours sincerely
J.P. WALSHE

Sheila M.[urphy] wrote to me about your kindness to her.

J.W.[2]

No. 206 NAI DFA 126/73

Extract from a memorandum on the Nineteenth Assembly of the League of Nations from Francis T. Cremins to Joseph P. Walshe (Dublin)
(Ass./19)

GENEVA, 26 July 1938[3]

[matter omitted]

As regards the question of the Minister heading the Delegation, I have already stated my views fully in previous years, and my views on this question are unchanged. To my mind, the recent settlement of all but one of the serious matters in dispute with the British Government and the increased prestige which the Taoiseach has acquired from his handling of the negotiations and from the results, is an added reason why he should come to the

---

[1] Eoin MacWhite, MacWhite's son. See p. 43 footnote 1.
[2] Handwritten postscript by Walshe.
[3] Marginal annotation: 'Dr Rynne. File with you'.

1938 Assembly. The situation in Spain and in Europe is at the moment such that it is not possible to say yet whether any questions concerning it will come before the Assembly.[1]

No. 207 NAI DFA Secretary's Files S77

Letter from Seán Nunan (for John W. Dulanty) to Joseph P. Walshe (Dublin)
LONDON, 2 August 1938

With reference to your minute of the 21st ultimo (No. S.77)[2] regarding the proposed dates for the transfer of the harbour defences at Berehaven and Lough Swilly, I have now been informed, semi-officially, by the Dominions Office that the proposed dates, viz. the first and the third week in October respectively will be acceptable to the authorities concerned, subject to confirmation.

It is felt, however, that the dates proposed for the preliminary visits (viz. 9th and 16th August) give rise to a little difficulty, since the authorities concerned wish to make sure that the lists of equipment, stores, etc. are fully considered here before the administrative conference takes place, and they are not satisfied that sufficient time would be available for this purpose unless the preliminary visits are postponed until (say) the 23rd August and 6th September respectively. If these dates are adopted, the administrative conferences could take place 14 days thereafter and there would still be a month available before the final transfer, in which to clear up outstanding points.

The Dominions Office have promised to write again as soon as it is possible to make a definite proposal for the dates of the various meetings, and these suggestions are made so that you may have preliminary notice of what the authorities here have in mind.

[signed] SEÁN NUNAN
For High Commissioner

No. 208 NAI CAB 2/2

Extract from the minutes of a meeting of the Cabinet
(G.C. 2/7) (Item 1) (S10732)
DUBLIN, 4 August 1938

EMIGRATION OF CATHOLIC CHILDREN TO AUSTRALIA:
Proposed State Assistance

Consideration was given to a memorandum, dated 22nd July, 1938,[3] submitted by the Department of the Taoiseach, regarding a proposal by the Reverend Brother P.A. Conlon, Principal of the Christian Brothers Agricultural School, Tandon, Western Australia, for State aided migration of Catholic children to Australia.

It was decided that the Government could not support the scheme.

---

[1] This extract has been highlighted in the original document by a double line in pen down the left hand side of the page.
[2] Not printed.
[3] Not printed.

No. 209 NAI DFA 207/10

Letter from Seán Murphy (for Joseph P. Walshe) to Charles Bewley (Berlin)
(107/220) (Copy)

DUBLIN, 11 August 1938

I have been directed by the Minister to state that consideration has been given to the position of Irish trade to Austria consequent upon the incorporation of the latter country in the German Reich, particularly as to whether goods described as of Austrian origin are in future to be regarded as of German origin for the purposes of the German-Irish Trade Agreement and whether the regulations relating to the production of Certificates of Origin for German goods are to be applied in the case of Austrian goods.

As regards the commercial relations between this country and Austria, the position was that Ireland had no commercial relations with Austria. Irish goods upon importation into Austria were, however, accorded most favoured nation treatment by reason of Clause 24 of the United Kingdom-Austrian Treaty of the 22nd May 1924, which provided that goods produced or manufactured in India or in any of the self-governing Dominions, Colonies, Possessions or Protectorates shall enjoy complete and unconditional most-favoured-nation treatment so long as goods produced or manufactured in Austria, are accorded in India or in any of the self-governing Dominions, Colonies, Possession or Protectorate treatment as favourable as that accorded to goods produced or manufactured in any foreign country.

The German Legation in Dublin formally notified the Minister in a note dated the 15th March last of the absorption of Austria in the Reich. The note was formally acknowledged.

The Minister has since addressed notes to the German Legation regarding the reimposition of the visa requirement for holders of German and Austrian passports, and it is thought that the Notes referred to could be interpreted by the German Government as constituting an act of recognition by the Irish Government of the incorporation of Austria into the German Reich.

In the circumstances represented, the Minister is of opinion that the existing Commercial Agreement between this country and Germany may now be held to cover Austria, and that the statistics of imports into Ireland to be submitted in future to the German authorities for the purposes of calculating the amount to be made available for the payment of imports into Germany from this country should include the figures of Irish imports from Austria.

The minister would be glad if you would make representations on these lines to the German Government and report the result thereof in due course. It is desirable that the Revenue Commissioners should be in a position at an early date to impose the requirement of duplicate Certificates of Origin for Austrian goods imported into this country. No doubt the German authorities will notify Austrian exporters of the requirement also

[stamped] (Signed) SEÁN MURPHY

No. 210 NAI DT S10795

*Minute by Padraig Ó Cinnéide on a proposed radio broadcast by President
Douglas Hyde to the New York World Fair*
DUBLIN, 18 August 1938

NEW YORK WORLD FAIR: Broadcasting Programme
Following the receipt of my letter of the 16th instant,[1] Mr. McDunphy spoke
to me and said that he had some doubt as to whether the occasion was of sufficient importance to justify a broadcast in which the President would take
part but he asked me to have a further word with the Taoiseach about the
matter. I spoke to the Taoiseach again today and he said that while he did not
wish to press the point at all he felt that on the whole the balance was in
favour of the President participating in the broadcast. He thought, however,
that the President's contribution should be very short and should be confined to something in the nature of a greeting.
I communicated these views to Mr. McDunphy verbally today.
[initialled] P O'C

No. 211 NAI DT S11007A

Letter from Stephen A. Roche to Denis J. Coffey[2] *(Dublin)*
(69/3070)
DUBLIN, 20 August 1938

A Dhuine Uasail,
I am directed by the Minister for Justice[3] to acknowledge the receipt of your
letter of the 16th instant regarding the offer which University College,
Dublin, has decided to make of free attendance at lectures to a limited number of Austrian students,[4] [and to state that, as you are doubtless aware, the
question of the assistance which could be afforded to German and Austrian
refugees[5] was the subject of an inter-Governmental Conference held at Evian
in July last.[6] Ireland was represented at the Conference and the attitude of
this country was made clear. It was explained that the Irish Government
were in full sympathy with the objects for which the Conference was
convened but that while Ireland remained a country of emigration it was
obvious that we could make no real contribution to the resettlement of
refugees, and that particularly on the professional side there was an existing
problem of overcrowding.][7]
The main difficulty in the way of accepting temporarily for purposes of
study or otherwise, persons who desire to leave Germany and Austria is that

1 Not printed.
2 President of UCD (1908-40).
3 P.J. Ruttledge.
4 Anonymous handwritten marginal note: 'Are the proposed students "refugees"?'.
5 Underlined in pencil.
6 See above No. 200.
7 The brackets are handwritten in the original text.

once such persons emigrate, it is almost certain that their passports will be cancelled and their previous nationality withdrawn. When this happens it is impossible to secure their return to Germany or Austria and they may be unable to obtain permission to enter any other country. It follows that the admission of such persons for the purposes of study may involve their permanent residence in this country and once they have settled here permanently a strong case can be made against preventing them from practising in the professions for which they have qualified.

This must result in diminished opportunities for our own nationals – as the professions are already overcrowded (?)[1]

The Minister would not raise any objection to the admission of such persons for the purposes of study, [*provided*][2] adequate guarantees ~~were given~~ that on the conclusion of their studies they would be allowed to settle elsewhere. ~~In practice, however,~~ It is unlikely that any such undertaking ~~will~~ would be forthcoming or that if given it could be enforced.

~~In all the circumstances,~~ The Minister regrets *therefore*[3] that he cannot see his way to authorise the granting of visas to such students and he would prefer that no publicity should be given to the decision of the Governing Body to make the offer mentioned in your letter.

Mise, le meas,
[unsigned]
Rúnaidhe

No. 212 NAI DFA Secretary's Files S92

Letter from Joseph P. Walshe to William J.B. Macaulay (Rome)
(Most Secret)

DUBLIN, 20 August 1938

I am directed to inform you that it has been suggested to the Taoiseach by a responsible and well-informed quarter that the Irish Government might take the initiative in endeavouring to bring about a cessation of hostilities in Spain. The proposal was discussed by the Taoiseach with the Nuncio[4] who, it is understood, has sent a telegram to the Cardinal Secretary of State in the following sense:

The Barcelona Government were apparently still holding out because of their fear of executions and general reprisals after a capitulation. Could the Secretariat[5] ~~Department~~ of State discover whether General Franco would make a statement foregoing reprisals of every kind and formulating reasonable conditions of surrender.

There is not much hope that this démarche will produce the desired result, but the Minister could not let the opportunity pass without making soundings

---

[1] The clause following the dash has been added in by hand.
[2] Handwritten marginal insertion in the text: 'if it were possible to excuse'.
[3] Handwritten insertion in the text.
[4] Monsignor Paschal Robinson.
[5] Handwritten insertion.

through what seems to be the best channel of approach to General Franco. We shall keep you informed of any further developments.

[stamped] [Signed J.P. WALSHE]

Rúnaí

No. 213 UCDA P194/536

Extract from a letter from Michael MacWhite to Joseph P. Walshe (Dublin)
(Personal)

ROME, 29 August 1938

My Dear Joe,

During the Summer months little or no work is done in official circles here. A Coupon which I sent to the Foreign Office three weeks ago for the release of some gasoline has not yet been attended to. This is nothing unusual. It took me over a fortnight to get my car released despite personal representations to the U.[nder] S.[ecretary] for Foreign Affairs and to the Director of Customs. In the United States these things would have taken about forty eight hours.

Nearly all the diplomatic people have been absent since early July and are not expected back before the middle of September or the beginning of October. The corridors of the Chigi Palace[1] are therefore deserted. There, it would be considered an act of discourtesy to raise any important issue until the effect of the Summer heat has faded away and the Autumn breezes have cooled the atmosphere a little.

The Italians take their holidays seriously and in accordance with ancient tradition. Titled people, and here everybody seems to bear one, are obliged to visit the same resorts year after year unless they are very wealthy when they can afford to ignore the tyranny of custom. The only people here who seem to have money to spend are the middle classes and the small shop-keepers and industrialists. Many of these have autos to take them from place to place but the Dukes, Counts and Barons travel by Bus or on foot. They may own fine houses and beautiful paintings but, as a rule, these are designated as National monuments which nobody wants as they cannot be taken out of the country. No Italian is wealthy enough to buy them and no foreigner can acquire them. They cannot even raise money on them in a pawnshop.

The political situation in Europe is still somewhat cloudy though Simon's[2] speech of a couple of days ago introduced some clarifying elements. As regards British Italian relations it seems as if the recent agreement has gone into cold storage much to the chagrin of Lord Perth and Count Ciano, as neither of them can have forgotten the embarrassing lesson of the gentleman's agreement of a couple of years ago. The Duce is not inclined at the moment to withdraw any of his troops from Spain. Nor can it be expected that he will be able to do so until Franco's victory is assured, which may, yet,

---

[1]   The headquarters of the Ministry of Colonies and the Ministry of Foreign Affairs.
[2]   Sir John Simon, Chancellor of the Exchequer.

be many months in the offing. Rightly or wrongly, he is convinced that this has been retarded by the cupidity of France in facilitating over her territory the transport of men and war munitions to the Red Government of Barcelona and Valencia, despite her apparent adhesion to the Non-intervention agreement. The Italo-British deadlock is indirectly due to the French attitude and so, also, is the apparent consolidation of the Rome-Berlin axis. This latter, in my opinion cannot last very long after Franco's [...][1] has been established over all of Spain as the Italian people seem altogether opposed to it. They dislike the Germans for the same reason that the Germans dislike and despise them. It is the fear of isolation that forces the Duce into a position which is considered by some of his immediate associates to be repugnant to his innermost sentiments. Nevertheless, in case of a general conflagration, before the Spanish question is solved in accordance with his desires, he would most assuredly march shoulder to shoulder with Germany. But I am equally convinced that after a Nationalist victory in Spain, and the causes of friction with France are disposed of, the Duce would welcome the opportunity to gracefully retire from a situation which is causing him many a heartache.

The Italian General Staff knows very well that, in case of war, it would be subordinated to that of Germany, a fact that would, in all probability, break the morale of the Italian troops and, at the same time, endanger the Fascist Regime which, amongst other things, has raised Italy to the level of a first class Power. Whatever people may say of Mussolini he is a brilliant statesman who has made very few mistakes. His past shows that he does not hesitate to shift his position should circumstances demand it. There is a widespread feeling in Italy to-day that between Ethiopia and Spain the people have had enough of war to last them for some time to come more especially as the material advantages appear so insignificant. Italian industrialists and bankers who have not yet recouped their losses from recent Fascist adventures are consequently opposed to any further gambles. Another Ethiopia would bankrupt Italy and another levy on capital would so weaken the industrial and financial structure as to leave grave doubts as to whether her economic system could survive the shock.

For want of something more sensational the Fascists, a month or so ago, started a race campaign directed mainly against the Jews which appears to serve no special purpose as there is only one of the tribe of Israel to every thousand inhabitants some of whom can count on eight or ten generations of Italian ancestry. The stand taken by the Pope in their defence, especially where he pointed out that the Duce was only attempting to copy the policy of the Fuehrer, so angered the Fascist Party as to induce them to make threats against Catholic Action but they soon realised, as His Holiness emphasised, that 'he who eats the Pope dies'. It may be taken for granted that the Party will take no irrevocable step against the Church as they know that it is stronger in Italy to-day than when the march on Rome took place sixteen years ago. Clerical observers assure me of this fact. Under the parliamentary regime reli-

---

[1] Word missing in the original.

gious instruction was forbidden in the schools, whereas under Fascism it is compulsory. In the last century anti-clericalism amongst the workers and Freemasonry amongst the middle classes were encouraged. Political advancement was not possible otherwise. How different things are to-day. Instances were pointed out to me where some local Fascist leaders were expelled from the organisation for discourtesy towards the clergy in their districts. Before the war it was snobbish to be Anti-clerical; now, it is a decided breach of good taste, detrimental to the promotion of those in office as well as to their standing in the community. One must read foreign newspapers in order to get conversant with the controversy between Campodoglio[1] and Castel Gandolfo[2] as the native press gave only two or three lines to it. So far as Fascism is concerned, it was only meant for foreign consumption.

There are some phases of Fascism which I am endeavouring to get a firm grasp of about which I will write you at a later date. At the moment my knowledge of them is rather superficial and subject to verification as one cannot always rely on official publications some of which are only propaganda.

It will be a great relief to Paula and myself […][3] we can lease the Flat now under consideration but difficulties arising out of local regulations, too long to write about, are standing in the way. The question of a deposit equivalent to three months rent which would stand without interest for the duration of the tenancy is the main one. The owner would dispense with this clause but her Counsel says she cannot as it would be an infringement of the Law. I hope we will be able to get over it somehow as the Flat would suit our purpose excellently and is more impressive than the Holy See Legation. [matter omitted]

No. 214 NAI DFA 126/73

Memorandum on the Nineteenth Assembly of the League of Nations from
Francis T. Cremins to Joseph P. Walshe (Dublin)
(Ass./19)

GENEVA, 29 August 1938

With reference to my minute of the 27th August, 1938 (Ass./19)[4] regarding Item No. 27 of the Assembly Agenda – Protection of the Civilian Non-Combatant Population against Air Bombing in case of War – I venture to suggest that if the Minister has any intention of intervening in the general debate this year he might consider the question of dealing *inter alia* with the item which has been placed on the Agenda by the Barcelona Government, and of adding an appeal that this vital question should be lifted out of the sphere of possible propaganda and dealt with seriously by the Assembly on a purely objective plane.

---

[1] Mussolini's headquarters were located in the Palazzo Venezia at Campodoglio (The Capital) in the centre of Rome.
[2] The summer residence of the papacy.
[3] Word missing in the original.
[4] Not printed.

It is of course more than doubtful that any definite results can be obtained in existing circumstances, but nevertheless something might be possible, and in any case the effort should be made. It is clear that no side will have the monopoly of such bombing and that the slaughter of civilians can contribute comparatively little to the winning of war.

Another subject which could be considered is the serious situation in Central Europe. This could be dealt with from different angles. From the German angle, the possibility that any conflict on a large scale in Central Europe might degenerate into a world war, with the obvious danger that a State which immediately provoked such a conflict might by its rash decision lose all that it had hitherto gained – a gambler's throw. And from the Czechoslovakian angle, that it is incumbent on any State, the continuance of whose existence in case of serious conflict is dependent on other States, to make all necessary sacrifices for the removal of sources of trouble in order that those other States concerned should not be needlessly involved in a conflict. Even if it could be argued that the extension of the conflict to other States would follow not for the sake of protecting a State victim of aggression, but from the general consideration that the preservation of that particular State might be regarded as essential to the preservation of the balance in Europe and therefore of the security of the other States involved, the necessity would remain for the smaller State to go to the utmost limits to remove all reasonable causes of serious dispute with its neighbours. It must be recognised that the States which might ultimately be involved and which would have so much to lose, should from the circumstances have the right to impress this consideration on the State in question. The existence of Article 19 in the Covenant gives the right to any Member of the League to refer to the question of revision of treaties in case such treaties become a menace to world peace, and, so far as Germany is concerned, the Minister is in a better position than most to speak plainly of the dangers which rash decisions might involve, seeing that he has previously expressed himself in a manner friendly to the consideration of German claims. In this connection, a tribute could be paid to certain revisions of treaties that have been brought about by peaceful means, for example, that of the treaty dealing with the Dardanelles, the removal of Capitulations in Egypt, the recent agreement with Bulgaria by the members of the Balkan Entente, the removal of the penal clauses against Hungary and the sincere attempts which are apparently being made by States of the Little Entente to arrive at an agreement with that country in regard to minorities. And a reference to the settlement of all but one of the serious matters in dispute between Ireland and Great Britain could also if desired be added. Settlements like these count more than armaments for the preservation of peace and for the improvement of relations between nations.

It could be pointed out that complaint is often made that many important questions are being dealt with outside the League. It would of course have been all to the good if they could have been settled long ago within the League, but what does it matter now how they are settled, if they are settled? The state of affairs which needs settlement in Central Europe today was not brought about by the League or within the League. The League was saddled from the beginning with these problems, and it is the Peace Treaties rather than the League which have not worked. Moreover, but for the unhealthy situation which has existed in Central Europe, the efficacy of the League might not have been challenged in other quarters.

Points might also be obtained from the recent statements of President Roosevelt and Mr. Cordell Hull. These statements referred to the necessity of providing methods of peaceful settlement, as well as to the dangers of resort to force. There is no doubt that many States developed on democratic lines which were by no means antagonistic to reasonable claims by Germany are becoming increasingly anxious for their security in face of the doubts which exist as to the limits of the ambitions of the dictatorial Powers. And granted that those European States which always urge peaceful settlement had shown themselves too long unwilling to settle anything, at the same time it is a factor which cannot be ignored that even if the madness of an animal is due to intemperate treatment, measures of control have to be employed if the animal becomes a serious menace.

Another point that suggests itself is the anti-religious attitude in Germany and the dangers even to Germany itself which might eventually result from the building up of what might turn out to be a purely materialistic State. An appeal might perhaps be made that the leaders of the Reich should consider from all its angles a question which is causing grave doubts and concern to many who have always had the greatest admiration for Germany and its people.

If the Minister thought well of it, a reference could also be made from the humanitarian point of view to the vital necessity which exists of rescuing the children of Spain from the physical, mental and moral dangers to which they are exposed. These children will be the men and women of tomorrow, and everything possible should be done to lessen their sufferings and to prevent them from becoming a future menace in their own country and thereby a possible menace to other nations. I am aware that any such reference might be regarded as a suggestion that the League should provide some funds. This aspect will no doubt be given due weight, as China will probably be looking for funds again this year for the relief of the sufferings of the Chinese civilian population, including children, and for the prevention of epidemics. It is, however, a big humanitarian question and is of interest internationally.

The foregoing are merely a few rough ideas on which a statement might perhaps be based in case the Minister may be considering the question of intervening in the debate. If he speaks at all in the general discussion, I would suggest that he should do so *very early* – this, I think, would be desirable as other statements may be on somewhat similar lines – and, in that case, perhaps, if you agree, a rough draft on strong but objective lines could be prepared in the Department and discussed with the Minister before the Delegation leaves. There is as you are aware always little time in the Delegation for the preparation of a speech here before the general discussion opens. There is a possibility of course that events may happen in Europe which might necessitate a revision of any draft that may now be prepared, but to my mind the existing situation provides an occasion for a statesmanlike speech, which would be all the more valuable coming from a Minister who has always been objective in his interventions. In the existing circumstances, this meeting of the Assembly should not in my view be allowed to pass without some such intervention.

The necessity from the Spanish as well as from the European standpoint for the continuance of the policy of non-intervention in Spain, even though there has been obvious intervention on both sides, is another matter which could be referred to if the Minister thought well of such a reference.

[signed] F.T. Cremins
Permanent Delegate

No. 215 NAI DT S10823

Extract from the minutes of a meeting of the Cabinet
(G.C. 2/11) (Item 5)

Dublin, 7 September 1938

MEASURES TO BE TAKEN IN THE EVENT OF EUROPEAN WAR:
Committee of Heads of Departments.
It was decided that a Committee of Heads of Departments responsible to the Government, under the Chairmanship of the Taoiseach, should be established to act as a general planning, co-ordinating and supervising body, and to consider the measures which it is necessary to take in preparation for the eventuality of a European war; the Committee to consist of the Secretaries of the following Departments:-

Agriculture;[1]
Defence;[2]
External Affairs;[3]
Finance;[4]
Industry & Commerce;[5]
Justice;[6]
Taoiseach.[7]

It was also decided that a legislation Committee should be set up to consider and draft, subject to the approval of the Government, whatever legislative measures may be necessary to deal with a war situation; this Committee to consist of representatives of the Attorney General's Department, the Department of External Affairs and the Department of Justice.

---

[1] Daniel Twomey.
[2] Peadar MacMahon.
[3] Joseph P. Walshe.
[4] James J. McElligott.
[5] John Leydon.
[6] Stephen A. Roche.
[7] Maurice Moynihan.

No. 216 UCDA P194/536

Letter from Michael MacWhite to Joseph P. Walshe (Dublin)
(Personal)

ROME, 9 September 1938

Dear Joe,

The Anti-Semitic campaign here is causing a lot of under surface comment. The average man does not know quite what to think of it or what it may lead to, but many of the working class are under the illusion that it will open up to them a number of posts. The places of the five or six hundred University and High School Teachers who have been dismissed is nothing more than a drop of water among an ocean of aspirants, and the number of Jews who support themselves by manual labour is infinitesimal.

What is coming next, nobody knows. There are a few who are of the opinion that after a lapse of five or six months those Hebrews who have not left Italy will be given the option of either going to Ethiopia or having their property confiscated. This possession did not figure in the list of those from which the Jews are debarred.

But the real cause of the Race campaign is a mystery to *all but*[1] those who do not enjoy the confidence of the Fascist Grand Council and they are very few indeed. While some believe it is due to the pressure from Hitler others attribute it to the aspirations of the Duce to become the accepted protector of the world of Islam. The strife in Palestine has roused Moslem feeling to a state of exaltation unprecedented in our time. Italy's restrictions on the Jews must consequently make a favourable impression on them, giving them comfort and relief while England's attitude only provokes their resentment and illwill. If this is the case, as it would seem, the Duce has found another means of propaganda among the Arabs to replace the Radio appeals that were suspended in accordance with the recent Anglo-Italian Agreement.

The antagonism of the Pope to the Racist programme is said to have so provoked the Fascist leaders that many of them are for tearing up the Lateran Agreements. The less hot-headed, however, realise the danger of such a step. Behind the scenes they are by no means a happy family. The Duce alone stands above their rivalries and squabbles. Even on international matters they are said to be sorely divided. The leadership of a pro-German group is attributed to Ciano, and of another group, seeking a better understanding with England and France to Ambassador Grandi. Other members of the Grand Council are lined up behind these either through conviction or interest or both. The differences that divide them are said by foreign newspapermen with inside contacts to be so acute that there is danger of the faction who eventually gets the upper hand making a short shrift of its opponents. The Duce is aware of all that is going on but his policy is one of non-interference. He commands the loyalty and obedience of all of them and evidently does not wish to diminish his authority and prestige by taking sides.

[1] These words have been inserted by hand, probably in MacWhite's writing.

While it was believed by many that the Italian Govt. was neutral in the Czecho-German dispute an official note issued yesterday (annexed)[1] indicates the contrary to be the case. It states that Italy has not mobilised in reply to France as her internal mechanism permits her to face any situation at a moments notice. Nevertheless, the Polish Ambassador who was in here yesterday told me that several Aviation and Artillery units were moved up closer to the French frontier.

More anon, Sincerely
[unsigned]

No. 217 NAI DFA Madrid Embassy SJ 52/2

Letter from Joseph P. Walshe to Leopold H. Kerney (St Jean de Luz)
(Secret)

DUBLIN, 9 September 1938

I have your minute of 6th September,[2] concerning the instructions regarding a special mission which was to be confided to you. Unfortunately, the preliminary steps, which do not depend on our Government, have not yet been completed, and it is still impossible to give you the instructions. It did seem possible, and it is still possible, that this country may be accepted as a mediator between the contending forces in Spain, and, so long as that possibility remains, it is better that you should not leave your post.

Moreover, the Minister feels that, so long as the Frank Ryan case remains unliquidated, there is always danger of a fresh crisis in his regard. Your absence from your post at such a moment would be seriously criticised here.

You have, no doubt, been following as closely as it can be done at St. Jean de Luz the international situation. It is exceedingly grave, and at the moment we are afraid that a general European war is very near. At least, in the general interest of the State, we are taking it for granted that preparations must be made for an immediate war. If our fears are realised, it will be essential for our officers abroad to be at their posts. In your own sphere, the situation is bound to become still more complicated if a major war ensues.

The Minister regrets very much that you should have to dispense with a holiday for the time being, but the facts of the situation impose this decision upon him.

[signed] J.P. WALSHE
Rúnaí

---

[1] Not located.
[2] Not printed.

No. 218 UCDA P150/2808

> *Three versions of a handwritten letter from Eamon de Valera to Neville*
> *Chamberlain (London)*
> *(Purely Personal)*
>
> DUBLIN, 15 September 1938

[1]

Mr. Chamberlain
Prime Minister
London
Do not let the irresponsibility or rashness of others halt or deflect you in your effort to secure peace. The tens of millions of innocent people on both sides who have no cause against each other, but ~~who are in the pursuit of~~ are in danger of being hurled against each other with no alternative but mutual slaughter, ~~depending on~~ are looking to you to find ~~some~~ a way of saving them from this ~~awful~~ terrible doom.

      Question   (1)   Should I send it
                     (2)   Publication (here or London)

[2]

Dear Prime Minister,
You will have succeeded or failed when you receive this. I merely want to tell you that one person at least is ~~how~~ *completely* ~~I am satisfied~~ satisfied that you are doing the right thing no matter what the result.
    ~~I hope and pray you will be successful.~~ I believe you will be successful. Should you not be so, you will be blamed ~~I have no doubt~~ for having gone at all. To stop half way – to stop short at any action which held out the slightest hope of success in view of what is involved would be wrong.
    Should you fail you need have no qualms. What a business man wd. do ~~with far less reason~~ – you who have at this moment the fate of millions ~~in his hands~~ who cannot help themselves depending on you are certainly entitled to do and should do.

> May God bless your efforts,
> Sincerely Yrs.
> E. de V.

[3][1]

You will have succeeded or failed when you receive this. I merely want[2] to tell you that one person at least is *completely*[3] satisfied that you are doing the right thing – no matter what the result.

---

[1] This version of the letter was published, with slight alterations (which are indicated below in footnotes), by Keith Feiling in his *The life of Neville Chamberlain* (London, 1946) (p. 364); Sir Keith Feiling (1884-1977), biographer of Neville Chamberlain and Lecturer in English history at Christ Church College, Oxford.
[2] In the version of the letter published by Feiling 'want' is reproduced as 'write'.
[3] In the version of the letter published by Feiling 'completely' is reproduced without underlining (underlining reproduced as italics in DIFP).

I believe you will be successful. Should you not be so, you will be blamed for having gone at all. To stop half way[1] – to stop short (at any)[2] of taking any action which held out even[3] the slightest chance (hope)[4] of success, in view of what is involved, would be wrong.

Should you fail[5] you need[6] have no qualms. What a business man would do, you, who have at this moment the fate of millions[7] who cannot help themselves[8] depending on you, are certainly entitled to do and should do.

May God bless your efforts.

This is the copy sent by Mr. Feiling. It is not an exact copy of the Taoiseach's *draft copy* written from Geneva but he may have altered the letter which he forwarded and did not make the alterations in the draft (copy).[9]

No. 219 NAI DFA Secretary's Files A20

> *Memorandum by Joseph P. Walshe on Leopold Kerney's actions to gain*
> *the release of Frank Ryan*
> DUBLIN, 16 September 1938

Mr. Kerney[10] suggests that the Taoiseach might take advantage of the presence in Geneva of Senor del Vayo, Minister of State, Barcelona, to confirm our desire to secure the exchange of Frank Ryan for a prisoner in the hands of the Barcelona Government.

The suggestion is that Ryan should be exchanged (1) for José Lopez Pinto, son of a General in Franco's Army, or (2) for an Italian aviator of the rank of captain *or* (3) for a number of Italian private soldiers.

Mr. Kerney has ascertained that Franco would agree to the first proposal. The Italian Ambassador at San Sebastian suggested the other alternatives, as there is no Italian prisoner of the rank of Major (Ryan's rank in International Brigade).

Mr. Kerney telegraphed the three alternative proposals to the Ministry of State, Barcelona, on the 3rd September but has had no reply. The Barcelona Government had previously offered to exchange an Italian sergeant for Ryan. This proposal was, of course, worthless as Ryan's rank is that of Major.

A full record of Mr. Kerney's correspondence with Barcelona is attached.

[unsigned]

---

[1] In the version of the letter published by Feiling a comma has been inserted at this point.
[2] Handwritten insertion.
[3] This word has been circled in pen.
[4] This word has been written above 'chance'.
[5] In the version of the letter published by Feiling a comma has been inserted at this point.
[6] 'You need' has been circled in pen.
[7] In the version of the letter published by Feiling a comma has been inserted at this point.
[8] In the version of the letter published by Feiling a comma has been inserted at this point.
[9] Handwritten insertion
[10] Handwritten insertion by Sheila Murphy, 'Copy sent to Taoiseach 16.9.38'.

[Attached]

SUMMARY

22nd July, 1938   Mr. Kerney telegraphed the Ministry of State, Barcelona, requesting them to examine possibility of exchanging an Italian officer for Frank Ryan.

24th July, 1938   Acknowledgment by telegram from Barcelona saying that question was being examined.

9th August, 1938   Further telegram from Barcelona saying that 'exchange of Frank Ryan, Major, International Brigade, has been proposed against Alfonso Tanner, station sergeant.'

Mr. Kerney ascertained from Italian Ambassador, San Sebastian (through Red Cross) that there are no captive Italian majors. The Ambassador suggested the exchange of some specialised aviator of the rank of Captain or alternatively a number of private soldiers.

10th August (a.m.)   Mr. Kerney telegraphed Italian Ambassador's suggestion to Barcelona.

Later on the same day Mr. Kerney heard from Mr. Meade, an American journalist in close touch with Franco Authorities, that it might be possible to arrange release of Ryan in exchange for José Lopez Pinto, son of a Spanish General serving under Franco.

10th August (p.m.)   Mr. Kerney telegraphed Barcelona suggesting exchange of Pinto.

Mr. Meade later confirmed that Franco would accept this exchange, and on

3rd September   Mr. Kerney again telegraphed Barcelona requesting urgent and favourable reply.

No. 220 UCDA P194/536

Confidential report from Michael MacWhite to Joseph P. Walshe (Dublin)
(It/110/38) (Copy)

ROME, 16 September 1938

Despite the tension in the rest of Europe during the last couple of days, things seem to be comparatively calm here – on the surface at least. Outside of the two notes in the 'Informazione Diplomatica' and the open letter to Runciman[1] – that appeared in the 'Popolo d'Italia' – all of which are said to come from the Duce's own hand – Italian newspapers look objectively at the international situation. Naturally they publish large accounts of diplomatic activities in London, Paris and elsewhere, but they do not act as if the country was on the brink of war.

Many diplomats here interpreted the second note as a definite moral commitment from Italy to support the Fuehrer and the first clear indication that Italy would back German demands in Czechoslovakia. My friend, the American Ambassador,[2] holds, however, that in case of war, the Duce would

---

[1] Walter Runciman, later Viscount Runciman (1870-1949), President of the Board of Trade (1931-7). In July 1938 Chamberlain sent Runciman on an unsuccessful mission to mediate between the Czech government and the Sudeten Germans.

[2] William Phillips (1878-1958), United States Ambassador to Italy (1936-41).

stand out unless force of circumstances should drag him in and public opinion, whatever it may be worth, is definitely against further military adventures.

In diplomatic circles here the Duce's solution of the Czechoslovak problem as outlined in the letter to Runciman is regarded as thoroughly sound: that is a plebiscite in the frontier districts and a kind of cantonal system in the more inland parts where foreign elements are in large numbers. If Beneš[1] does not accept a solution of this nature the danger of war will, like the sword of Damocles, continue to hang over his head even if temporarily averted now.

Chamberlain's visit to the Fuehrer is regarded as a master stroke of diplomacy, and if, as is likely, the outcome will be a roundtable conference of Britain, Germany, Italy and France, the results may be far-reaching and provide for the settlement of other matters that now darken the international horizon.

The United States Ambassador told me on Monday that he was sailing yesterday for America as he did not think there was any danger of war. By Wednesday things, however, had got so bad that he was obliged to postpone his departure.

[unsigned]

No. 221 UCDA P150/2809

Three sections of handwritten notes by Eamon de Valera in preparation for a speech to the Nineteenth Assembly of the League of Nations (Geneva)[2]

GENEVA, September 1938

1. We should [...] League
2. Faults – should [...] how although to maintain frontier is against will of inhabitants
3. Self Determination - Wilson examine.
4. People will not go to war for other peoples.
5. Wars in China, Spain, wars in China, Abyssinia.
6. Right cla[3]

* * *

[page missing?] That the, will of men seems powerless to avert a benumbing fatalism. It has required no small exercise of restraint to remain here. The members of the several Delegations are either men who are members of governments or high officers carrying heavy responsibility in their own country. Were a war to break out every one of them would have important duties to perform. Behind whatever attention is paid to other items on the

---

[1] Eduard Beneš (1884-1948), President of Czechoslovakia (1935-8, 1945-8).
[2] The first two sections of draft notes are very early drafts of a speech which was ultimately delivered as a radio address from Geneva to the United States on 25 September 1938; the last section is an early version of material used in de Valera's closing address as President to the League Assembly on 30 September 1938.
[3] This point is unfinished.

agenda is the ever insistent question – How will our people be affected by a war. What are the greatest dangers to be apprehended – and finally they come back to the old old question: Is it inevitable that there should be wars like the last war so awful in the sufferings it caused during its duration – so terrible in its aftermath – so futile as a means of solving in any lasting fashion the econ. soc. or political problems in which it originates. And the minds of everyone reverts to twenty years ago.

Those phrases that caught the imagination of the people the plain people – as Mr. Wilson called them are still ringing in our ears: the self determination of peoples, the rights of the small nations as well as those of great – the iniquity of handing our people against their will from Governments to Governments as if they were chattels: we ask ourselves were these merely clever propaganda to inspire propaganda of what again analyse the meaning of these phrases and after twenty years experience ask ourselves whether the solutions they were intended to suggest is practicable in this actual world of ours with clashing wills with evil every arranged and [word indecipherable] against the good. We know that the League of Nations for the foundation of which he was responsible – had within a decade and a half from its inception proved itself incapable of fulfilling the functions for which above all other its was created – the preservation of peace.

It was intended as a joint security for all its members. It has failed to secure peace to its members in Asia it has failed to secure its members in Africa – It failed to secure its members in America.

And despite all its evident failure it is the only ideal to which all desire peace, obedience to law and ordered society revert. There are only two ways in which order and law can be secured. One is by one unified State getting so powerful that it can impose its will on all the other States that they will accept the law it imposes – a Roman peace: the other that there should be a coming together of the States each because of the advantage of peace submitting itself voluntary[1] to a rule of law and sacrificing its selfish desires when they [clash?] with the rule of law.

We would need an international parliament to declare the law. An international judiciary to interpret it and an international authority with police force to see that the law be kept. There are whose who would use their power and force to take possession of what belongs to another and wars that arise [word order unclear] clash of opposing rights against the aggressor pure and simple it is easy to mobilise opinion – all decent minded people reach to an appeal to assist against the robber bully. His own people will not in the [word order unclear] task again and if he is beaten there is an end to all. But when either side can show a rightful claim – when neither side sees why it should surrender its right to the others claim. Then each side is assured of the support of its own people, outside opinion is divided and takes opposite say a long struggle can ensue and a victory by force can only settle the question temporarily. The vanquished today sets his will with renewed energy to become the conqueror of tomorrow. That there can be such wars is evident

---

[1] 'Voluntarily'

and if we could only organise ourselves in the first instance so that these could be ~~avoided~~ obviated then the first great step to avoid all wars would have been taken negotiation arbitration, judicial determination are the ways that are open – it is vital that the will to avail of these methods of solution should be cultivated: the people must be taught to accept the sacrifice which what is essentially a compromise entails: the most noble of these methods is the method of negotiation – but the danger of the method is that each tries to have the ultimate result to force as a bargaining factor in order that he may have the best of the compromise – if their side is strong and the other weak – the only defence of the weak is the determination to sacrifice everything rather than submit to unfair treatment. Were there machinery by which the stronger would have to submit to the judgment of our honest arbitrator .

* * *

I am sure that there can hardly have been a single member of the 40 delegations from the 40 States represented here [that] have not felt as I have felt – that we were merely fiddling. We have had our committees and our plenary sessions – the delegates have done their formal work recorded the Committees giving their Governments attitudes on the various subjects on the agenda. But at the focus of every mind was the supreme question. Was Europe to be dragged into another great conflict and if so how each particular delegates own country would fare – were their people as well prepared for it as they should be – were their defences as well organised as they should be.

Frankly and at a time like this with peace and war hanging in the balance to speak frankly what one felt was to risk doing harm with little corresponding hope that anything one might say could do good.

The delegations from the states that are meeting here at Geneva are all men and women who have a very clear conception of what another world war would mean for their respective countries and for Europe – and I would certainly not represent them if I were not fully alive to the importance of saying nothing which might even in the slightest degree make a dangerous situation more dangerous or hamper ever so little those who had undertaken the delicate task of trying to get a solution.

It is a significant indication of the present position of the League.

If only this Assembly were really where the Law of Nations. The first thought [word indecipherable] is of President Wilson – his work his success and his failure. One cannot help thinking what a monument this great building and institution would be to his memory if the League were really able to perform the functions [that the average person interested] plain people as he called them expected of it.

In the mind of the average person the chief function of the League should be to secure the maintenance of peace. The war a little while ago in Abyssinia, the war in China [~~is proof that~~], the threatened war in Europe which the League is helpless to stop are all proof that whatever else the League may be able to do it cannot maintain peace between the nations.

No. 222 NAI DFA 126/50

Mr. President,

I desire to state as briefly as I can the views and policy of the Irish Government on the question before us, namely, the status of Article 16 of the Covenant in the relations between the members of the League.

The Government of Ireland desire to place on record their considered opinion that the provisions of the Article now impose no legal or moral obligation upon any member of the League to apply the system of sanctions therein referred to in any circumstances. They are satisfied that in the interest of the maintenance of the Covenant itself, the preservation of the League, and the acceptance of League principles by an increasing number of States in the future, the right of each of the member-States to decide for itself whether sanctions should or should not be applied by it ought to be placed beyond doubt. The policy of the Government of Ireland in the matter of its relations with all other States, as well members of the League as non-members, will be based upon the existence and recognition of that right. The Committee will appreciate that, in these circumstances, the Government of Ireland are unable to accept the view that the juridical effect of the Covenant in this regard remains unaltered. They would have preferred to see the whole question of military, economic and other sanctions reconsidered at the present juncture with a view to the conclusion of an agreement on the matter appropriate to the actual situation now existing. I am sure that a number of other delegations also would have considered such a course more satisfactory. The method of approach to the problem which the Committee have adopted is perhaps unavoidable but the result may give rise to misunderstanding hereafter. In any event, the Irish delegation desire that the position of Ireland in this matter should be placed beyond doubt. The effect of the present declaration will be that so far as that country is concerned, the obligatory character of the provisions of Article 16 is removed.

There is another and equally important aspect of this question on which the Irish delegation desire to make a further declaration. A number of definitions of aggression and of the aggressor have been formulated from time to time in certain instruments and in various memoranda and resolutions prepared and considered during the last eighteen years. The definition, however, which is relevant in the present connection is that contemplated by the terms of Article 16 itself. The legal notion of aggression for the purpose of Article 16 consisted in a resort to war by a Member of the League in disregard of its covenants under Articles 12, 13 or 15. My delegation do not feel called upon to enter into any discussion here on the relations between these various Articles and Article 16 itself or of the procedure heretofore followed or hereafter to be adopted for the determination of the aggressor. But they desire to place on record their view that, whatever the procedure, the determination of the aggressor by the appropriate organ of the League will not affect the exclusive right of the Government of Ireland to determine that question for themselves and will accordingly not involve that Government in any commitment or obligation either to consult or to take common action with the other members of the League on the basis only of the League's decision. This, of course, they regard as a principle which any other member of the League may apply in its own regard. I must, however, add that, while that principle will form an essential part of Irish national policy in this connection until a general system of collective security satisfactory to them is established, the Government of Ireland will not fail should occasion arise to consider their attitude to any State which they have determined to be an aggressor, in the light of their conception of the duty in all the circumstances of the case of an honourable member of international society.

The Irish delegation desire to have this statement placed on record with the other declarations made in the Committee and forwarded to the Assembly.

No. 223 UCDA P150/2183

> *Letter from Joseph P. Walshe to Eamon de Valera (Geneva)*
> Dublin, 24 September 1938

My dear Sir,
I am writing this note at half past six in the evening after a day of considerable pessimism in the press and on the wireless both here and in Great Britain. I have not shared this pessimism because I could not imagine the British Government going back at this stage on the principle of self-determination merely because they don't like the methods by which Hitler means to realise it. I have urged on the High Commissioner whenever he sees MacDonald these days with the other High Commissioners to emphasise the extreme folly of having a general war on what is in all the circumstances a mere matter of punctilio. As far as I can see the situation from the confusion of telegrams received today Hitler has told Chamberlain that the Czech army must retreat behind the fifty per cent line, the German army must then advance to that line. Hitler does not object to a plebiscite under an international commission in part of the German occupied area and he avers himself as being ready to withdraw from any areas in which an adverse vote is given. Whether the area in which a plebiscite is to be taken extends beyond the fifty per cent line is not yet clear as we have not yet decoded the memorandum which he handed to Chamberlain before the latter's departure for London. Chamberlain on his side wanted Hitler to accept the suggestion that the Sudeten Germans should themselves police the area in question and that there should be no advance of German troops into Czechoslovakia. Hitler refused to have anything to do with this proposal and Chamberlain left him promising to put Hitler's proposal to the Czech Government but apparently without accepting responsibility for it. The last telegraph we have received takes us back to late last night when the British Ambassador[1] in

---

[1] Sir Eric Phipps (1875-1945), British Ambassador to France (1937-39).

Paris informed his Government that ~~Beneš~~ Bonnet[1] seemed to hope that arrangements could be made whereby German troops would occupy gradually and with consent of Czech Government the Sudeten areas because he held that German troops would be more likely to be able to maintain order than the Czech police who would in any case have to leave eventually. While the British Ambassador and Bonnet were talking the news came in of the Czech mobilisation and Bonnet remarked that this would have very grave consequences and might cause Hitler to attack. This statement appears to be at cross purposes with the fact revealed in another telegram that the British and French Ministers in Paris were instructed to tell Beneš yesterday that their Governments could no longer take the responsibility of advising him *not* to mobilise. The British Cabinet are meeting at the present moment but we have no information as to the reply sent by the Czech Government to Hitler's demand forwarded to them by the British Government this morning. One has a definite impression that the British Government are getting a little funky of the opposition which is growing in Great Britain against yielding to Hitler's demands. Otherwise I feel certain that Chamberlain would insist ~~with~~ on the Czech Government ~~on~~ accepting some compromise which allowed a partial occupation by the German troops. The Poles and the Hungarians are getting away with good propaganda in the United States as I learned on the radio this morning from that country, and I have a definite feeling that the linking up of the demands of the three minorities is going to weaken very much Czechoslovakia's position in the eyes of the world and to lessen considerably the danger of a general war. Moreover British Statesmen must be becoming daily more conscious of the potential evils of joining with Russia to destroy the only barrier, undesirable though it may be, between Western Europe and Bolshevism.

We are looking forward to your early return. The events of the next twenty-four hours will no doubt determine whether you will put an end to the Assembly[2] at the beginning of the week or allow it to run its normal course. If anything really serious occurs I shall get on to you on the telephone.

I beg to remain, my dear Sir,
With great respect and esteem,
Yours very sincerely,
[signed] J.P. WALSHE

[1] Georges Bonnet (1889-1973), French politician, Minister for Foreign Affairs (1938-9), Minister of Justice (1939-40).
[2] De Valera was President of the 1938 Assembly of the League of Nations.

No. 224 NAI DT S8083

Memorandum taken over the phone from Geneva by Seán Murphy of Eamon de Valera's views on reform of Article 16 of the Covenant of the League of Nations, with covering note from Murphy to Maurice Moynihan

DUBLIN, 24 September 1938

Mr. Moynihan

I send you herewith a copy of the statement I took on the phone from Geneva giving the President's views on the position if Article 16 of the Covenant is invoked. I am having 15 copies made and will send them to you in the course of the day.

[initialled] SM

(1) On any allegation of resort to war by a member of the League in violation of Articles 12, 13 or 15 of the Covenant, providing for the Pacific Settlement of Disputes, the Council will meet at once at the request of any Member of the League to consider the situation. Representatives of all the neighbouring States, of all States with close economic relations with the State alleged to have violated the Covenant and of all States whose direct co-operation in any action to be taken by the League would be required, will be invited to attend the meeting.

(2) The first business of the Council once it had been convened would be to express its opinion as to whether or not the Covenant had in fact been violated. If the Council arrived at an affirmative conclusion on this question a copy of the Council's opinion would be sent to all the Members of the League, who would be asked to shape their action accordingly. No Member of the League would be justified in rejecting the Council's opinion unless it were manifestly contrary to what the Government of that Member considered right and just.

(3) The next stage would be the setting up by the Council of a technical committee to elaborate the measures of an economic, financial, and commercial character to be taken by the Members of the League of Nations collectively in execution of paragraph (1) of Article 16 of the Covenant against the State alleged to have violated the Covenant. This Technical Committee will include representatives of the States directly concerned in the execution of the contemplated measures. The Committee would report to the Council which would thereupon recommend to the several Members of the League the measures which each of them should take in pursuance of the common plan, and the date upon which the measures in question should be brought into operation. Although no Member of the League can refuse to participate in a common plan of action under paragraph (1) of Article 16 without violating its obligations under the Covenant, nevertheless, technically speaking, the particular recommendations made by the Council in this connection do not impose legal obligations on the States concerned. The measures which the Council might recommend at this stage would vary with the circumstances of the case, but it is understood that such measures might include a

prohibition of imports from, and an embargo on the export of arms and of all essential raw materials to the State alleged to have violated the Covenant, as well as the withholding of credits and the interruption of shipping and other communications. In recommending the measures to be taken by each State in execution of the common plan of action, the Council must take into account the particular circumstances of each State, and may vary its recommendations with a view to minimising national loss and inconvenience.

(4) The next stage would be the breaking off of diplomatic relations. The consular and humanitarian relations with the State alleged to have violated the Covenant could be maintained.

(5) If the measures adopted in the first instance are not successful the Council may recommend more rigorous measures of the same character. If these more rigorous measures fail the League may revert to a blockade of the sea-board of the State alleged to have violated the Covenant. It is expressly contemplated that the conduct of the blockade operations would be entrust-ed to a limited number of Members of the League, that is, those in a position to take the necessary naval measures. In the case of this, as in the case of other measures of collective action which the League might take, special efforts would be made to secure the cooperation or acquiescence of non-member States.

(6) As the task of the League is to maintain peace the application of military measures will only take place in extreme cases in which the other measures taken have failed in their object. In this event it would be for the Council to draw up a plan of collective action and to recommend to each State the effective contribution which it should make to the collective forces of the League. The Council's recommendations in this connection do not impose legal obligations on the Members of the League to which they are addressed. But provided that the collective character of the proposed action is maintained, and provided that the Council's recommendation is made with due regard to the geographical circumstances and to the state of the armed forces of the Member of the League concerned, it would be contrary to the spirit of the Covenant for the member concerned to refuse to take part in the collective military action to be taken by the League, if asked to do so by the Council.

This is the President's view of what the position is under Article 16. This is meant to convey what we would have to do in the most extreme circum-stances.

No. 225 NAI DFA Secretary's Files S77

Memorandum from Joseph P. Walshe to Seán T. O Ceallaigh on the return of the Treaty ports

Dublin, 27 September 1938

The Tánaiste.
Colonel Eadie of the War Office called at the High Commissioner's Office yesterday evening, and requested that every effort should be made to

expedite as quickly as possible the transfer of the harbour defences at Berehaven and Lough Swilly. Colonel Eadie stated that the matters in dispute regarding a 12-pounder gun at Berehaven and one or two minor matters seem to be the only things holding up the transfer. The War Office are ready to waive their point of view in order to obtain an early evacuation. Colonel Eadie asked to be informed immediately of the earliest possible date on which the transfer could take place.

I shall be very grateful if you will find an opportunity of discussing this matter with the Minister for Defence[1] and letting me know what reply I am to send.[2]

No. 226 UCDA P150/2183

> *Letter from Joseph P. Walshe to Eamon de Valera (Geneva)*
> DUBLIN, 28 September 1938

My dear Sir,

You will have read the full report of Chamberlain's speech and of his wonderful triumph in the House of Commons. Dulanty told me that the only fly in the ointment was when Churchill came up to Chamberlain before he left the House and said 'You have had wonderful luck'. It appears that Churchill and Lloyd George had prepared very venomous attacks on the Prime Minister and his policy. I have no doubt at all that your message published in the press this morning played its own part in securing goodwill for Mr. Chamberlain.

The latest information we have from the British shows that Chamberlain has fully guaranteed that Czech promises shall be carried out, and he has expressed his confidence that agreement can be reached within a week. You will have learned from the High Commissioner of the plan suggested by Chamberlain to Hitler in his message sent from London at 6.45 last evening. It seems to be the type of plan which Hitler could accept and save his face before his people. No doubt it will be a basis for the discussions on the British side beginning in Munich to-morrow, though the absence of any mention of it in Chamberlain's speech this afternoon may indicate that the British have dropped it. I am, however, enclosing a copy.[3] There are certain verbal mistakes in it, due to cipher difficulties as well as certain obscurities which I shall try to have cleared up. You may some day wish to use it as a model. The announcement of the meeting at Munich seems to have had an electric effect on British opinion, and Chamberlain may at last have the opportunity of bringing about with the full support of his own public opinion the European settlement which he so earnestly desires. It is unnecessary to tell you of the immense relief felt by the Tánaiste, all the

---

[1] Frank Aiken.

[2] Handwritten marginal note by Sheila Murphy: 'Minister/Defence informed Secy. that he wd. be ready to take over both ports on Thursday 29th Sept. Secy. has informed H/C on phone. SGM 29/7/38'.

[3] Not printed.

Ministers and the Civil Service at what must be at least the beginning of the end of the crisis.

I beg to remain, my dear Sir,
with great respect and esteem,
Yours very sincerely,
[signed] J.P. WALSHE

No. 227 UCDA P194/536

Confidential Report from Michael MacWhite to Joseph P. Walshe (Dublin)
(It/123/38) (Copy)

ROME, 1 October 1938

After the historic meeting at Munich Signor Mussolini returned to Rome last night amid the tumultuous enthusiasm of his people who regard him as the saviour of world peace. Diplomats who have spent many years here say this spontaneous demonstration of delight and affection surpassed anything the city has seen since the war.

As his car rolled slowly along the main streets from the station to the Palazzo Venezia, with the Duce standing alone in the back, the crowd broke through the police cordons and surged after him. About twenty thousand persons crowded the Piazza Venezia of which I had a commanding view. As he arrived there the cheers were deafening. Bands played and Fascist hymns were sung. Soon after entering the building he appeared on the balcony to return the people's salute. He looked on a different crowd, perhaps, to that which he was accustomed – a crowd despite its enthusiasm, somewhat sub-dued, and showing signs of relief and averted calamity. The Italian people wanted peace and were happy that through the Duce's intervention it had been assured them.

In response to the enthusiasm of the calls the Duce came on the balcony fifteen times. Everybody expected a long speech from him, but he was strangely taciturn. He expressed himself in twenty four words as follows:-

Comrades, You have lived through memorable hours. At Munich we laboured for peace with justice. Is not that the ideal of the Italian people?' A thunderous 'yes' answered him. Then he raised his right hand in salute, turned abruptly and entered the Palace. Some believe the pacific response was not pleasing to him as it was perhaps deeper and more sincere than any of his more militant appeals brought forth.

The huge crowd on the Piazza was the most orderly I have ever set eyes on. Despite its density there was not a single case for first aid although women and children were numerous.

After the Duce's last appearance on the balcony the cheering and singing continued for nearly half an hour, after which the different groups with their banners formed into line and as if by magic the way was opened up for them. In about twenty minutes that immense throng had disappeared in all direc-tions contented and happy. There was no shouting, no disorder, no playacting as these peace loving, sober and industrious citizens returned to their homes.

There can be no doubt that the position of the Duce has been strengthened by his work as a peacemaker at Munich, whereas heretofore his militant appeals seemed to bring the best response.

[unsigned]

No. 228 NAI DFA 227/87

Memorandum on events in Spain, with covering letter, from Francis T. Cremins to Joseph P. Walshe (Dublin)
(S. 9/12) (Confidential)

GENEVA, 5 October 1938

I have to forward,[1] for the information of the Minister, a memorandum regarding a conversation which I had on the 19th September, 1938, with Señor D. de las Bárcenas, Minister Plenipotentiary, Representative of the National Government of Spain. Señor de las Bárcenas was formerly Under Secretary of State at the Spanish Ministry of Foreign Affairs. He resigned his post at the fall of the Monarchy.

[signed] F.T. CREMINS
Permanent Delegate

Confidential
MEMO

Señor D. de las Bárcenas, Minister Plenipotentiary, Representative of the National Government of Spain, called to see me on Monday, 19th September, 1938, the object of his visit being to ask that the Irish Delegation should do what it could to ensure that the question inserted on the Agenda of the Assembly by the Barcelona Government, namely, the protection of civilian populations against air bombardment in case of war, should be treated objectively, in the Report of the Third Committee, and that no censure of the Nationalist Government or forces should appear. He said that if the question were treated objectively, everyone could agree regarding it, but he feared that the Spanish Delegation would endeavour to use the Committee's report for propaganda purposes and he was anxious that that should be prevented. He added that as a matter of fact 44 out of the 46 reports made to the British Government by the Commission which investigated the bombing of towns in Spain were favourable to the Nationalists. I told him that I would do what I could in the Third Committee to ensure that there would be no censure of anybody, and that I shared his view that in the interests of a solution of the problem it was essential that the question should be treated objectively.

In the course of conversation, Señor de las Bárcenas remarked on the fact that the Irish Government had not yet established any representation at Burgos. He said that the Government of Ireland had not 'followed the example of Great Britain'.

On instructions from the Taoiseach, I took advantage of the conversation with the Burgos representative to suggest on behalf of the Taoiseach that it

---

[1] Marginal note: 'Secy [marked as seen by Walshe], P.[ut] A.[way]'.

might help to bring about a cessation of hostilities if General Franco could reassure those on the Barcelona side that their lives would be safe in case of Nationalist victory. Information which had reached the Irish delegation was to the effect that the Barcelona forces were now engaged in a war of desperation; that they believed that there would be wholesale shootings in the event of surrender, and that they were therefore convinced that they might as well continue fighting. Senor de las Bárcenas said that General Franco had promised that no one would be executed merely for taking part in the war on the side of Barcelona, but that of course there would have to be justice. He, for example, knew the man who had murdered his sister, and he added that 100,000 persons had been murdered by the Reds in Madrid alone. I asked if that meant that all persons who were known to have committed serious crimes would be dealt with: in view of the number, it might be difficult to bring about surrender on such terms. I urged that notwithstanding the personal feelings of the relatives and friends of those who had been murdered, something more than justice – and I suggested amnesty – was necessary if the war was to be ended speedily, and if further huge losses to Nationalist Spain were to be avoided. There was the further consideration that a general outbreak of war in Europe might have serious repercussions on the fortunes of the Nationalist side, as France might intervene directly for Barcelona. He appeared to be impressed and remarked that certainly there would be dangers from a European conflict. He said that he would report the conversation at once to Burgos, and would direct special attention to the matter when in the near future he returned to Spain. He asked me to express to the Taoiseach his gratitude and appreciation for the interest which he was taking in the matter.

[signed] F.T. CREMINS

I have already reported this conversation verbally to the Taoiseach.[1]

[initialled] FTC

No. 229 NAI DFA 119/49

*Extracts from the annual report on the Irish Legation in Paris by Art O'Brien
to Joseph P. Walshe (Dublin)
(P. 19/34)*

PARIS, 7 October 1938[2]

[matter omitted]
On St. Patrick's Day I gave a reception for Irish persons in Paris which brought together some 350 people many of them belonging to our Paris colony in this city and including all the prominent persons in it, others normally resident elsewhere in France and some only temporarily in Paris. This Legation function, which has now become a regular yearly event, apart from

---

[1] Handwritten note by Cremins.
[2] Marginal annotation by Sheila Murphy: 'Secy.' [marked as seen by Walshe]; 'A/Secy., To See! SGM'.

its primary purpose of enabling our nationals to feel at home on the National Feastday, serves the further object of giving them some sense of solidarity. As things at present are there are no facilities for Irish persons in Paris to meet each other regularly as, in the complete absence of anything in the nature of society or club rooms there is no place to which an individual national can resort, during the free intervals from what in the great majority of cases is a long day of work, in the certainty of meeting compatriots. Some members of the colony have tried from time to time to establish some sort of a club but all efforts in that direction have so far quite failed as it is a matter in which money or at the least much free time is necessary and our nationals living here have in general got neither. So far the most that the colony has regularly achieved is to hold a dinner and dance on St. Patrick's Day. As in previous years I presided at this dinner and in my speech dealt with the lines which I consider it important that Irish persons resident abroad should follow. Earlier in the day, as guest of honour at the monthly luncheon of the American club which was attended by many prominent people, I spoke on Ireland, its present condition, its inherent unity and its international position. The speech was very warmly received and reported in some detail in the main page of the next day's Paris edition of the New-York Herald.

The International Exhibition, held from the 21st May to the 26th November, occasioned a very largely increased influx of Irish visitors to Paris and a corresponding increase in visitors to and enquiries at the Legation. During that period the Legation had the benefit of the services of an extra male clerk who helped to meet the increased demands made upon it. The Exhibition, too brought with it a number of international Congresses at some of which the Government was represented by headquarters delegates who were facilitated by the Legation as far as possible and at others of which (such as that of the Air Navigation Commission, the Congress relating to Open Air Holidays, the Semaine Internationale de Droit, Congress on Deaf Mutes, the Annual Conference of the Union des Femmes pour la Paix) representation was effected by the Legation. In all these instances as also in the case of other Congresses or manifestation at which the Government was not directly represented but where the material dealt with was of interest to home departments (e.g. Sécurité dans la Vie Moderne, Congrés International de Sauvetage) reports and documents were obtained and transmitted by the Legation.

The calls upon my own time were exceedingly heavy on account of 1) the excessive number of official ceremonies, 2) diplomatic receptions in connection with the Exhibition pavilions and visits of foreign statesmen, etc. and 3) the very considerable number of visitors from Ireland, many of them friends or acquaintances of my own, others officially introduced, and others bearing introductions from friends or acquaintances in Ireland. In 90% of these cases entertainment of one kind or another was necessary or advisable. I calculated that in the 3 months June, July and August, Miss O'Briain and I had not sat down to a meal (lunch or dinner) alone more than about a dozen times. The season was extremely exhausting and trying. All my diplomatic colleagues shared this same feeling and we are all very glad that the exhibition was not continued for another year.

[matter omitted]

The number of callers, national and other, to the Chancery during the year was about 550. Interviews covered a wide variety of subject ranging from requests for information as to the means of getting to Ireland to enquiries as to the best living Irish and Anglo-Irish authors, the present state of the Irish language and bibliographies for theses.

[matter omitted]

It is to be noted that, whilst the work of the Legation has greatly increased since 1935, I have now less staff than was at the Legation in that year. I have brought this position of affairs to the notice of the Department on several occasions. Unfortunately the Department has not been able to meet my request for extra staff. The work of the Legation cannot to my mind be adequately and effectively dealt with unless the staff is increased. Under present conditions much of the less important work must accumulate and many desirable activities cannot be initiated.

A few of the matters dealt with by the Legation deserve more particular mention.

The passing by Dáil Éireann and the entry into force of the constitution imposed certain exceptional duties on the Legation. During and immediately after its passage through Parliament the Legation received a large number of requests for information in regard to the Constitution in general and some particular provisions. The commemoration of the entry into force of the Constitution involved the distribution to the French and Belgian Press of a circular concerning the Constitution Postage Stamp and the subsequent change in the name of the State, the issue of some 140 circulars to the French and Belgian Diplomatic Corps and to the Press. Frequently too it has been proved necessary to recall the change of name to the attention of the Press and of other bodies and even some Departments of the French Government.

A large quantity of occasional literature was distributed as in previous years, on behalf of the Irish Tourist Association apart from 'Irish Travel' of which a certain number of copies is distributed each month. As in previous years also literature was distributed in connection with the Royal Dublin Society to some 50 selected destinations. The Irish Trade Journal has also been regularly distributed.

The question of necessitous nationals which is a permanent problem became relatively serious on several specific occasions during the year but the difficulty in each case was more or less satisfactorily solved. In such matters the Legation secures very great assistance from the Reverend Father O'Grady of St. Joseph's Church in Avenue Hoche. Father O'Grady is, as you are aware from my reports on this subject, on the Committee of the British Charitable Fund and in close relation with the Hertford British Hospital, the two main British benevolent bodies in Paris. He is always most willing to help Irish persons in every way he can and has never failed to bring to bear to that end all the influence which his position in regard to these bodies gives him. He has, however, found a marked unwillingness on the part of the other members of the Committee of the Fund to incur expenditure on behalf of persons who, they consider, only acknowledge the existence of these bodies when their needs make it imperative to do so. Of this attitude Father O'Grady has informed me in the many interviews we have had on the subject, as I have on a few occasions reported to you. To show the reasons for the attitude of the Committee he has also furnished me with statistics of the numbers of Irish persons treated or supported by the Hospital or the Fund – the number supported by the Fund in August last was, as reported in my minute of the 2nd September 1937,[1] 19. Unfortunately, however, our nationals must in present circumstances when in need depend on the resources of both these bodies and the Legation has frequently, as an alternative to seeing nationals remain penniless here, had to refer them there indirectly. The whole position as it has existed hitherto is in my opinion both unsatisfactory from a national view point and undignified from that of the Legation and I sincerely hope that the consideration which you are at present devoting to the subject will lead to some solution.

Consular assistance was also given to a number of nationals who found themselves badly treated by their employers. In one instance it proved possible, by an intensive correspondence and considerable investigation to recover the full amount of the claim made by the employee (see minute of 15th January 1938, Dept. Ref. A.45)[2] and in others relative satisfaction was secured for our nationals. In one particularly long-lived case full satisfaction was eventually secured for a national but only after the Legation had issued a total of 64 letters of which 25 fell within the year. Visits were paid by a member of the Legation staff to a national who was mentally unwell and wished to return to Ireland. Some support was also rendered by the Legation in a few cases where nationals were, rather unjustly, refused workers' identity cards by the authorities. Various enquiries were also dealt with on behalf of girls intending to come 'au pair' to France, or to families or to Universities and teaching institutions.

A satisfactory arrangement was reached for the publication and production of an Irish translation of a well-known French play. For another Irish author the Legation provided information in regard to a French newspaper of 40 years ago. Some French writers of books and articles were, on the other hand, given information by the Legation both on a number of particular points and on Ireland and Irish history and life in general; and in a few cases the means of study were placed at their disposal at the Legation.

A long correspondence was carried on with some publishers and authors in regard to incorrect information or particulars likely to create a wrong impression furnished in regard to Ireland and after many representations it was found possible to secure the correction of an article reflecting unfavourably on Irish education. This matter was also dealt with to some extent with newspapers.
[matter omitted]

---

[1] Not printed.
[2] Not located.

TRADE

In spite of the fact that considerable attention was devoted to trade work during the year the situation in respect of both France and Belgium, though for different reasons, leaves much to be desired.

In the case of Belgium our trade throughout the year continued to be regulated by an agreement reached in the last months of 1936. This agreement secured to Ireland a minimum quantity of imports into Belgium in certain commodities (mainly cattle and woollens) and a minimum share of the total quantity of other products (mainly butter and tinned meat) allowed into Belgium.
[matter omitted]

The balance of trade with Belgium continues strongly against us – it reached relatively a new low level in 1937 when imports from Belgium stood at £1,243,000 and exports at £204,500 and the January and February figures for 1938 show a further fall (of about 33%) over those for 1937. The deterioration observed had, however, little to do with the inherent difficulties of the Belgian market but was rather due to general unfavourable conditions or deficiencies in our supply. The bulk of our exports has, for several years past, been constituted by cattle, horses, butter, with latterly pelts hides and skins taking a prominent place. During the eleven months ending February 1938, there was a very marked decline in the market value of our exports of cattle (over 65%) and horses (over 35%), while pelts hides and skins showed no great change. The decline in cattle exports to Belgium is to some extent due to an improvement in conditions elsewhere and a fall in prices ruling on the Belgian market. While the value of our exports of butter increased (by about 30%) we were not, however, able to take full advantage of the possibilities in that line. Belgian prices for the greater part of the season were exceptionally favourable both absolutely and because of the reduced licence tax.
[matter omitted]

We were, however, unable to meet our full quotas largely owing to the difficulties encountered from home producers, at the time when storage should have taken place, owing to the very high prices temporarily ruling in Great Britain. As regards tinned meat which is covered by our agreement, it has proved impossible to supply any since the early part of the year.

Because of the existence of an agreement in the matter and the fact that there are two reliable agents for cattle and butter in Belgium, the main portion of the Legation's work during the year in regard to Belgian trade was more in the nature of replies to individual enquiries from Belgian firms and the provision of information for individual Irish firms. A general report was, however, furnished in connection with the possibility of new negotiations and several minor reports were sent home in regard to the butter trade in particular. The agreement of 1936 was also renewed for a further period of one year.

In the case of trade with France our greatest difficulty as in previous recent years, arose from the elaborate quota system which covers most of the products in whose export in any quantity we are interested. As things are at present we receive comparatively very small quotas and, what is more serious, in a very irregular manner.

[matter omitted]

While failure to grant a quota in successive quarters for a product which we have been used to export to France is not common it does, however, happen and is the source of an important aspect of the Legation's work in regard to our trade with France as well as being very prejudicial to that trade.

During the calendar year our imports to France fell from £49,393 to £30,854 in value; for all 11 months April to February inclusive exports were £27,857 as against £43,477 for 1936-37. However, imports in the first two months of the present year have been slightly better than in 1937 though it is noticeable that a quota for cheese in the first quarter, obtained exceptionally and with some difficulty, had not so far been taken up. Two special factors may have contributed to the decline in our trade with France in the year under review: French currency further depreciated over the period by about 40% and French business circles were almost continuously pessimistic.

[matter omitted]

During the greater portion of the year under review the rather rigid attitude of the French authorities towards demands on our side was unchanged. More recently, however, they have shown a tendency to meet us to some extent. This tendency is undoubtedly due in a large measure to the unsatisfactory position of the French commercial balance. In that balance Ireland occupies a unique position in that the ratio of trade is at least 6:1 in favour of France (only 9 other countries had a passive balance with France in 1937). While our trade is relatively of very small dimensions in the total of French foreign trade it is not quite negligible and has a very important character from one point of view in that we are one of a declining number of countries with a free currency. I feel it is a pity that when the position of our trade here is going from bad to worse each year we do not take advantage of the hints given to us in the matter and send out a trade delegation even if our hopes are not high.

[matter omitted]

No. 230 NAI DFA Secretary's Files S94/39

*Memorandum from Joseph P. Walshe to Eamon de Valera
on relations with Northern Ireland*

DUBLIN, 8 October 1938

TAOISEACH

RELATIONS WITH THE NORTH

It has appeared from our discussions with the British leading to a parallelism of organisation for a time of emergency that the collaboration with the British imposed by our national interests will be seriously hampered unless we establish a closer collaboration with the Six County Government. Transport, food control, petrol storage, rationing, control of aliens (and no doubt to some extent censorship and counter-espionage) are of immediate importance. If you so direct me, I can obtain a full list from Mr. Leydon and Mr. Twomey of the matters requiring very early discussion. Mr. Scott, Secretary of the Belfast Department of Commerce, was in Dublin in June for the purpose of discussing with Mr. Leydon and Mr. Jenkins (British Board of Trade) certain matters relating to our Agreement with the British.[1] Relations between our two Department of Agriculture are cordial. There seems therefore to be no reason why these discussions should not begin at once. It will probably be realised by the Government of Northern Ireland after these discussions that the community of interests between us is sufficiently great to warrant discussions of a wider scope.

No. 231 NAI DFA Secretary's Files A20

Letter from Leopold H. Kerney to Joseph P. Walshe (Dublin)
(S.J. 10/11)

St Jean de Luz, 10 October 1938

Frank RYAN. Your 144/35[2]

Further[3] to my minute of 8th October,[4] the Viscount de Mamblas informed me by telephone late on Saturday night 8th October that, in reply to an enquiry made by him urgently in Burgos at my request, he had received an advice dated 7th October stating that Ryan was alive; he went on to say that about six weeks or so ago there had been a critical moment when it was just touch and go whether he would be 'popped off', that he believed the danger to be past and that 'there are three or four influential people, of whom you are the first, interested in him'.

I thanked de Mamblas for the official assurance that Ryan was alive; I begged him to intervene – and he promised to do so – with a view to obtaining permission for Ryan to communicate with his family; he also agreed to ascertain in Burgos whether the authorities there would accept the principle of an exchange in this particular case, in which event I stated I would gladly endeavour to induce Barcelona to agree to the liberation, in exchange for Ryan, of any particular prisoner of corresponding rank or importance whom Burgos might wish to rescue; he was of the same opinion as myself as regards the certainty of any exchange negotiations being spread over a long period; it is clear, however, that, once Burgos admits the principle of an exchange and gives me the name of a nationalist prisoner in Republican Spain, this will almost constitute a guarantee for Ryan's safety, providing of course that nothing untoward should subsequently befall the nationalist prisoner in question.

Perhaps I should add that, when commenting on the fact that Ryan had so narrowly escaped execution, de Mamblas explained that Ryan had of course 'a very bad background' – presumably in Ireland rather than in Spain; it may be that a bad background justifies a death sentence where Franco holds sway.

[signed] L.H. Kerney
Aire Lán-Chómhachtach

---

[1] See above Nos 195 and 196.
[2] See above No. 190.
[3] Marginal note: 'Secy. File with you'.
[4] Not printed.

No. 232 NAI DFA Madrid Embassy 17/4

Extract from a letter from Leopold H. Kerney to Joseph P. Walshe (Dublin)
(S.J. 17/1) (Confidential)

St Jean de Luz, 11 October 1938

I understand from Mrs. Kerney that you have informed her that the Minister is now willing that I should proceed to Ireland for the purpose of spending a limited period of leave there if, in my opinion, there is no likelihood of anything serious happening to Frank RYAN during my absence.

I am satisfied that everything possible has been done to assure Ryan's safety and that his life is now no longer in danger; as you know, steps have been taken with a view to obtaining his liberation by way of exchange, but, whatever the developments may be in this direction, any rapid arrangement is out of the question.

As regards O'TOOLE,[1] nothing more can be done at the moment, and I have faith in the assurance given to me that, in any event, this boy's life is not in danger.

There is nothing else, as far as I can judge, to make my absence at this moment undesirable, and I consider that the two matters above referred to will not be prejudiced in any way by my absence.
[matter omitted]

No. 233 NAI DFA 119/17

Extract from a letter from Leopold H. Kerney to Joseph P. Walshe (Dublin)
(S.J. 19/1) (Copy)

St Jean de Luz, 12 October 1938

CONVERSATION WITH MR. de CAUX
[matter omitted]
Mr. de Caux tells me that the Irish flag is no longer floating outside the Irish Legation premises in Madrid but that the reason for this was that the Government some time ago ordered the removal of all flags on the plea that they might have a provocative effect.
[matter omitted]

No. 234 NAI DT S9215A

Memorandum on Irish cultural interests in the United States of America from
Maurice Moynihan to Joseph P. Walshe (Dublin)
(S9215) (Copy)

Dublin, 13 October 1938

I have to state, for your information, that the question of the promotion of Irish Cultural interests abroad, particularly in the United States of America,

---

[1] Andrew O'Toole was a minor who volunteered to fight with General O'Duffy's Irish Brigade. His father petitioned for O'Toole's return throughout his time in Spain. He returned home in July 1939. See below Nos 281, 295 and 315.

has been under consideration in this Department. A proposal has recently been received from Dr. Eoin McNeill[1] the purpose of which is to bring people of Irish connections or affections abroad to a knowledge of all matters pertaining to Irish National Culture, past and present. Dr. McNeill's proposal aims at securing the institution of a special Irish Cultural Section in Public Libraries and in the libraries of Schools, Colleges and Universities. Towards this end he had suggested that a special agent should be sent to America to make a tour of certain cities, Universities, etc., equipped with a specimen collection of publications which are regarded as a suitable foundation for such a Library Section.

It has been tentatively agreed that Miss Roisin Walsh, Chief Librarian of the City of Dublin Public Libraries, should visit the United States of America for the purpose, subject to the concurrence of the City Manager. It is contemplated that she will leave Ireland in the Spring of next year and remain in the United States for two or three months for the purpose of a preliminary exploration of the ground. Her itinerary will be confined mainly to the Eastern States and it will probably include the following cities:- New York, Boston, Springfield, Montreal, Ottawa, Toronto, Buffalo, Cleveland, Detroit, Michigan, Pittsburgh, Chicago, St. Louis, Cincinnati, Baltimore, Philadelphia, Washington, Chapel Hill, N. Carolina, Providence.

Miss Walsh will visit the New York World Fair at which, it is learned, an Irish Cultural Exhibition will form part of the Irish Section. It is thought that Miss Walsh will be afforded an opportunity to deliver one or more talks on Irish Culture there. In general, it is anticipated that she will endeavour to stimulate interest in Irish literature, publications, the language revival movement, the promotion of Irish scholarship, folklore and archaeology. Dr. McNeill and Dr. Best[2] of the National Library will supply illustrative material for her lectures in the form of a small representative collection of books, manuscripts, facsimiles etc. relating to Ireland.

Miss Walsh has had discussions with Dr. McNeill, and with officials of this Department and the Department of Industry and Commerce regarding her proposed visit to America. She is acquainted with Librarians, University Professors and other persons likely to be interested in the scheme in a number of cities which she proposes to visit. It is assumed that your Department will be in a position, through our representatives in the United States, to obtain further facilities for her in the course of her visit.

[signed] (Sgd.) M. Ó MUIMHNEACHÁIN
Rúnaí

---

[1] Eoin MacNeill (1867-1945) Minister for Finance (Jan.-Apr. 1919); Minister for Industries (Apr.-Aug. 1921); Ceann Comhairle of the Dáil during the Treaty debates; supported the Treaty; Minister without Portfolio in the Provisional Government (Jan.-Aug. 1922); Minister for Education (Aug.-Dec. 1922); Free State representative on Boundary Commission (1923-25); Professor of Early and Medieval Irish History at University College Dublin (1909-41); brother of James McNeill.

[2] Dr Richard Irvine Best, Director of the National Library of Ireland, Dublin.

No. 235 NAI DFA Secretary's Files S94/39

*Memorandum, with covering letter from John Leydon to William D. Scott
(Belfast), on co-operation with Northern Ireland
(Confidential)*

Dublin, 17 October 1938

My dear Scott,
When yourself and Parr[1] were here with Jenkins in June[2] last you will recall
that we visualised the possibility of a further meeting at a later stage.

I now send you herewith a list of items which I think could usefully form
the basis of discussion between representatives of the two Governments. If
you agree perhaps we might arrange a meeting. Next week or preferably the
following week would suit me.

I should be very glad to see you in Dublin again if you could manage to
come down. If not I could go to Belfast on whatever day we fix as mutually
convenient.

What I have in mind is that we might have a general discussion over the
whole field and that if necessary we could thereafter arrange for further discussions under such heads as may be necessary by men who are more familiar with the details.

I am sending a copy of this letter to Jenkins.

Yours sincerely,
[unsigned]

[Enclosure]
Matters for discussion with the GOVERNMENT OF NORTHERN IRE-
LAND
1. Co-operation in the preparation of measures to be taken in the event of a
major emergency:-
    rationing schemes for petrol, food, etc.;
    regulation of exports of agricultural products;
    desirability of uniformity on both sides of the Border.
2. The linking up of the electricity system in the two areas. The existing systems could be linked by a high tension line between Belfast and Dundalk.[3] A
new source of supply could be provided by a hydro electric scheme from the
development of the Erne; the catchment area is in Northern Ireland and the
fall is on this side of the Border so that the generating station would be located in our area. Both sides could take advantage of the available supply of
electricity from the scheme.
3. Drainage of the River Erne; this has been the subject of desultory discussion
for many years between the Office of Works in Dublin and the appropriate

---

[1] G.H.E. Parr, Assistant Secretary, Ministry of Commerce, Belfast.
[2] See above Nos 195 and 196.
[3] The proposed link was established in 1942, following the German bombing of Belfast in
    April and May 1940; it was intended for emergency use should the Belfast power station
    be put out of action in an air raid.

authorities in Belfast. It has some bearing on the question of a hydro electric scheme.

4. Transport problems. The difficulties confronting road and rail transport are at present in a large measure common to both areas.

5. Tourist development.

6. Reciprocity in Unemployment Insurance.

7. Reciprocity in the matter of Widows and Orphans Pensions.

8. Supply of fresh Milk from Donegal to Derry.

9. Piers and Slips on the Donegal side of Lough Foyle.

10. Appointment of Medical Officers in Northern Ireland; requirement as to parentage and residence qualification.

11. Pensions of certain officers dismissed on political grounds by the Belfast Corporation from the Fermanagh County Council: but it is somewhat doubtful whether this point should be raised until progress has been made on the others.

12. Irish Lights.[1]

No. 236 UCDA P194/536

Letter from Michael MacWhite to Joseph P. Walshe (Dublin)
(Confidential) (Copy)

ROME, 20 October 1938

Dear Joe,

The political situation viewed from Rome seems more disturbed now than before the Munich gathering. War was no doubt averted by that, but only on the condition that Hitler had his own way.

The Duce, although he was justly acclaimed for his efforts in the cause of peace is, nevertheless, dissatisfied with his German colleague and this dissatisfaction is finding expression in the support he is giving the 'just revendications' of Poland and Hungary.

The Czechs are resisting the common frontier idea but it is apparent that in doing so they have German backing. Italian support of Poland and Hungary at this juncture will give the Duce good cards to play later and create perhaps another axis in East Europe that would still function when the Rome-Berlin one gets too hot. A very high Polish official told me that despite officials' denials they can count on Italian support for their claims.

A new French Ambassador is coming in a few days. It is common property that Daladier[2] made this move, recognising the Empire out of spite because the Chamberlain-Hitler agreement was negotiated without his being aware of it. The result is, of course, that British-Italian relations have not been bettered and political pressure at home has obliged Chamberlain to ask for the withdrawal of more than double the number of Italian troops from Spain than would have satisfied him two months ago. It seems that Perth has had

---

[1] Handwritten insertion.
[2] Edouard Daladier (1884-1970), French Prime Minister and Minister for National Defence (1938-40).

several conversations with Ciano during the past fortnight without being able to make much progress. The French recognition of the Empire should facilitate the British rather than serve as a fresh barrier.

Because of many difficulties in the line of furnishing, I have not yet been able to get in the new premises, but I hope to get possession on Saturday. I will cable the Department immediately on doing so.

With kind regards,
[unsigned]

No. 237 NAI DT S10760

Statement issued by the Government Information Bureau on the conclusion of a trade agreement with Germany

DUBLIN, 3 November 1938

The following statement was issued today by the Government Information Bureau.

Following negotiations in Dublin between representatives of the Irish and German Governments, the Trade Agreement with Germany signed in January, 1935, and extended by further agreements signed in April, 1936, and December, 1936, has been prolonged for a further period of 12 months as from the 1st January, 1939, by Notes exchanged today between the Minister for External Affairs and the German Minister in Dublin.

Arrangements have been made for the export to Germany in 1939 of cattle, eggs, meat products, and herrings in prescribed proportions. The German Government are free to purchase other Irish products, including butter and horses, in such quantities as they may require from time to time. The new Agreement provides that as from the 1st January next agricultural products will be purchased by Germany in the open market here, thus obviating the necessity for special price arrangements between the Governments and eliminating any risk of loss to the Irish Government.

As from the 1st January, 1939, the agreed ratio will apply to the trade exchanges between Éire and the German Reich, including the former Federal State of Austria and the territories ceded to Germany by Czechoslovakia. The existing arrangement under which German goods imported into Éire must be accompanied by a Certificate of Origin in the prescribed form made out in the duplicate will apply as from the 1st January 1939 to all goods originating in the German Reich including the territories referred to.

The following tables indicate the exchange of trade between Éire and the territories concerned in recent years, according to Irish official statistics:-

	Imports from Germany £	Exports to Germany £
1931	1,225,792	107,602
1932	1,302,527	69,910
1933	1,749,819	183,720
1934	2,314,242	163,828
1935	1,414,598	493,982

1936	1,378,856	640,102
1937	1,431,389	840,492
1938	1,132,165	705,409
(nine months)		

	Imports from Austria	Exports to Austria
1931	11,387	789
1932	6,487	869
1933	10,156	933
1934	9,552	1,299
1935	29,073	1,081
1936	61,893	2,059
1937	46,401	2,025

	Imports from Czechoslovakia	Exports to Czechoslovakia
1931	220,905	350
1932	261,099	288
1933	450,270	248
1934	181,724	236
1935	215,433	14,559
1936	298,816	27,941
1937	253,115	23,565

It is impossible to make any reliable estimate as to what proportion of Czechoslovakian external trade is attributable to the ceded territory.

No. 238 UCDA P194/536

Confidential report from Michael MacWhite to Joseph P. Walshe (Dublin)
(It/149/38) (Copy)

ROME, 4 November 1938

I had a long conversation lasting over an hour with the Acting Minister for Foreign Affairs, Signor Bastianini,[1] yesterday. Much of it was devoted to recent political developments, particularly from the Munich meeting when France and England yielded the sceptre of European supremacy to Italy and Germany and where Mussolini played the outstanding role as pacificator instead of that of rabid trouble-maker such as he has been labelled in the so-called Democratic countries.

During the conversation the name of England was not mentioned nor was any reference made to the steps now being taken by the British Premier

---

[1] Giuseppe Bastianini (1899-1961), Italian Ambassador to Poland (1932-6); Under-Secretary for Foreign Affairs (1936-9); Italian Ambassador to Britain (1939-40); Governor of Dalmatia (1941-3); Under-Secretary for Foreign Affairs (1943-4); voted against Mussolini in July 1943 when the Italian leader was dismissed and served under Marshal Badoglio; condemned to death on Mussolini's return to power but escaped to Switzerland (1944).

towards bringing the Italo-British accord of last April into operation. The recognition of the Empire, however, by England will in all probability have a profound effect in Italy. It is likely in the first place, to heal the sore created by the Sanctions' policy initiated by Eden at Geneva and in the second place it will have a modifying effect on Italian policy in Mohammedan countries which are in a state of ferment because of the Palestine revolt. From the European angle it may even be more far reaching as observers here are of the opinion that the Duce is anxious to find some good excuse for neglecting the Rome-Berlin axis.

In the recent negotiations at Vienna where Count Ciano and von Ribbentrop[1] have been determining the Czechoslovak-Hungarian frontier, Italy's friends did not get anything like what they wished for. The idea of a common frontier between Poland and Hungary which had the support of the Italian press was rejected by Hitler as it would raise another barrier on the road of his Drang nach Osten. On the other hand, a common frontier, according to the views of the countries concerned, would strengthen the forces that stand against Bolshevik penetration from the East. Italy has another interest in cultivating the friendship of Poland and Hungary. At the opportune moment they may be used as a check on German ambitions and an embarrassment to Hitler.

Signor Bastianini said Italy took a particular pleasure in the recent move to the right in French politics. Premier Daladier is regarded sympathetically here but the Fascists, judging by past experience, ask how long he will be able to remain in office, or his majority going to last. They seem to think the French are incorrigibly shifty and unreliable politically. The refusal of the French Government to allow the train of wounded members of the Barcelona Foreign Volunteers to enter France was regarded as a step in the right direction. Had the French authorities been so energetic and closed the Spanish frontier twelve months ago the Civil war would have been ended by now.

In regard to the newly appointed Italian Minister to Dublin, Signor Berardis, the Acting Secretary said he was an exceptionally good man whom he could warmly recommend. He is cultured, serious and painstaking and was for three years secretary of the Italian Legation at Athens when Signor Bastianini was Minister to Greece.

Some time ago I called the attention of the Foreign Office to the fact that Irish shareholders of Italian companies could not enter into possession of the dividends allotted to them and invited an indication as to how they could get satisfaction. So far I had no reply. My colleagues here tell me not to expect any answer to an embarrassing question. I brought the matter to the attention of the Acting Minister, who appeared sympathetic. He asked me to send him an aide memoire covering all the questions at issue. He suggested also that under the present conditions the easiest way out would be by the negotiation of a trade agreement. I pointed out that for the first six months of 1938 Ireland had purchased about 9,000,000 lire worth of Italian goods while

---

[1] Joachim von Ribbentrop (1893-1946), German Ambassador to London (1936-8), German Foreign Minister (1938-45), executed 1946.

Italy's purchases from us were less than 10,000 lire. He considered the situation to be absurd and justly so. He thought, as we were the sufferers, that the initiative in a trade agreement rested with us. I pointed out that a draft agreement had been submitted a few years ago to his Government but we were unaware that it has ever been considered. He replied that consideration of any draft submitted before the currency control became effective would be only a waste of time, as the situation has completely changed.

It is my opinion that the time is now ripe to renew trade negotiations with Italy and to that effect I should like to be furnished in due course with a memorandum on the subject that would form the basis of discussion with the Italian Government.

[unsigned]

No. 239 NAUK DO 35/893/6

Letter from Eamon de Valera to Malcolm MacDonald (London)
DUBLIN, 5 November 1938

Dear Mr. MacDonald,
I was very glad to learn that you had gone back to your old Department.[1] Having done so much already to improve relations between the two countries, I hope you will be able to see the task completed by the removal of the chief remaining obstacle – the partition of Ireland. This is bound to assume more and more importance and become increasingly urgent as the months pass. I am sure you realize that the solution will not be made easier by delay and that time is very important in the matter.

With all good wishes,
Yours very sincerely,
[signed] EAMON DE VALERA

No. 240 NAI DFA Secretary's Files S94/39

Letter from John Leydon to Joseph P. Walshe (Dublin), enclosing a memorandum of a conversation with G.C. Duggan and a note from W.D. Scott, on co-operation with Northern Ireland
(Secret)
DUBLIN, 12 November 1938

Dear Walshe,
I send you herewith a copy of a note of a telephone conversation I had today with Scott (Secretary to the Northern Ireland Ministry of Commerce). I enclose also a copy of a note I made of a conversation I had with Mr. G.C. Duggan on the 2nd November and copies of Scott's letter of yesterday's date and of a letter dated 10th October which I received from Jenkins.[2]

Yours sincerely,
[signed] JOHN LEYDON

---

[1] MacDonald returned to the Dominions Office on 31 October 1938.
[2] The letters are not printed.

[Enclosure]

Mr. G.C. Duggan, Ministry of Finance, Belfast, called to see me today. He said that Mr. Scott had asked him to explain to me the position in connection with my letter of the 17th October. The matter had been under consideration by Ministers in Northern Ireland and he had not yet got a decision as to whether he could arrange for discussions. He was disposed to think that the Items no. 6, 7, and 11 on the list attached to my letter of the 17th October[1] might be regarded as controversial in Northern Ireland and therefore unsuitable for discussion at this stage.

I told Mr. Duggan that if the Northern Ireland Authorities were not prepared to discuss certain of the Items we could at least usefully discuss the others. As regards No. 6, he said that it would probably be considered essential from their point of view to have representatives of the Ministry of Labour in London present at any detailed discussion; I said that I thought this would be a distinct advantage. As regards No. 11, he thought that difficulty would arise in connection with Lough Foyle because of controversy as to where the boundary should be drawn. I told him that I had not contemplated that any such difficulty would arise as I had been hoping that we could devise a scheme which would obviate any necessity for dividing the lights as between Northern and Southern Ireland.

(Initd) J.L.
2 November 1938

[Enclosure]

After discussion with the Minister, following receipt of Mr. Scott's letter of yesterday's date, I telephoned Mr. Scott this morning. I said that it was not clear to me whether his intention was that we should discuss *only* the question of licences or whether he was in a position to discuss the other items (or some of them) if we agreed to the inclusion of the licensing system on the Agenda.

Mr. Scott said that the atmosphere is not at present favourable for discussion on any of the items on the list which accompanied my letter of the 17th October and that he did not think we could really make any progress at the present stage having regard to the revival in a somewhat acute form of the Partition controversy.[2] He hoped, however, that by some easement of the trade situation it might be possible to secure a somewhat better atmosphere.

I told Mr. Scott that I did not think it would be possible from our point of view to have discussions relating to trade alone because in matters of trade any concessions to be given would be entirely one-sided. I said that we are quite prepared to discus the licensing system in so far as it affects Northern Ireland provided that the other items which I mentioned to him can be discussed as well. I urged that there are only a few items on the list that could give rise to political issues.

---

[1] See above No. 235.

[2] On 17 October 1938 in an interview with the London *Evening Standard* newspaper de Valera had outlined a possible federal solution to the partition of Ireland. The interview was not well received by the government of Northern Ireland.

Mr. Scott said he could only repeat that he could see little prospect of any useful discussions at the present stage and that he thought it would be better to postpone any further steps for the moment. He expressed the hope that when the Prices Commission has issued a few reports it might be possible, in the light of the indications thereby given as to the working of the Trade Agreement, to reconsider the matter and possibly to open discussions; and he hopes that in the meantime the general atmosphere will have improved.

JL
12th November, 1938

No. 241 UCDA P194/536

Confidential report from Michael MacWhite to Joseph P. Walshe (Dublin)
(Copy)
ROME, 16 November 1938

I took advantage of the opportunity offered by the invitation from the Royal Dublin Society to the Italian Government to call on the Minister of Foreign Affairs, Count Ciano, yesterday evening. After complimenting him on all the Duce and he had recently accomplished in the cause of world peace and the appeasement of peoples (at which he seemed to be very pleased) I told him that the Irish people were deeply interested in the rectification of the Czecho-Slovak frontier for we, too, had a boundary problem which had international repercussions, due to the fact that an integral part of the Irish nation consisting of six of its thirty-two counties were cut off politically from the rest of the country by an Act of the British Parliament for which no Irish member, either from the North or the South, voted.

The Minister did not let me proceed further but sitting up in his chair he spoke as follows:- Well, another great step in the appeasement of peoples will be consummated to-morrow when the Anglo-Italian Agreement will be signed. The effect of this act will, in all probability, have far reaching consequences and benefit not only the countries directly concerned but other disturbed centres in Europe, Asia and Africa. The Spanish question was rapidly approaching a satisfactory solution and France had already commenced to repair the errors made by the Popular Front. He continued in this vein for a couple of minutes. Then, turning to the table he took the envelope I handed to him on my arrival and after glancing at it said he would pass it on to the Minister of War and let me have the reply in as brief a delay as possible.

The Minister ignored my remarks on the Boundary altogether but judging by the serious expression that came over his face as I spoke of it they did not make any particular appeal to him. His reference immediately afterwards to the Anglo-Italian Agreement showed what was uppermost in his mind.

No. 242 NAI DFA 249/9

> *Letter from Charles Bewley to Joseph P. Walshe (Dublin)*
> *(32/33)*
>
> BERLIN, 18 November 1938

A Dr. Gradenwitz called today at the Legation and stated that a Commission had been formed in England for the purpose of forming a Jewish colony in Ireland and that the Commission had selected a district for settlement of Jews in Ireland.

The idea seems ridiculous on the face of it; but I shall be glad of formal instructions so that it shall be denied in the case of any further Jewish inquirers here.

[signed] C. BEWLEY

No. 243 NAI DFA Secretary's Files A20

> *Letter from Joseph P. Walshe to Charlotte Haldane[1] (London)*
> *(Copy)*
>
> DUBLIN, 25 November 1938

Dear Madam,

I have been asked by the Taoiseach, Minister for External Affairs to acknowledge the receipt of your letter and enclosure of the 16th November concerning Mr. Frank Ryan. The Taoiseach desires me to inform you that he is aware of Mr. Ryan's imprisonment in Spain. On learning in April last that he had been captured and that his life was in danger, the Taoiseach on behalf of the Irish Government made an urgent appeal to General Franco's Authorities. Since that date this appeal has been constantly renewed through Mr. Kerney, our Minister to Spain, who is in close touch with General Franco's representative in Biarritz. Mr. Kerney is also in touch with the International Red Cross Committee in St. Jean de Luz through which he has been able to send some money, clothes and books to Mr. Ryan on behalf of his family. The latest information received by Mr. Kerney was an assurance from General Franco's representative in Biarritz on the 8th October that Mr. Ryan was alive and was still detained in the Central Prison at Burgos.

For some months past we have been endeavouring to negotiate the exchange of Mr. Ryan for a prisoner in the hands of the Barcelona Government. Although these efforts have not so far met with success they are being continued.

Yours faithfully,
(Signed) J.P. WALSHE

---

[1] Honorary Secretary of the International Brigade Dependents and Wounded Aid Committee.

No. 244 NAI DFA Secretary's Files S77

Confidential Report from John W. Dulanty to Joseph P. Walshe (Dublin)
(No. 68) (Secret)

LONDON, 2 December 1938

With reference to your Minute S.77 of yesterday,[1] we have today received the following reply to our enquiry regarding the three old 'trophy' guns at Cobh.

'Efforts have been made by the authorities concerned to ascertain the history of these guns, but without result. It is believed that they have no historical value and are simply samples of antiquated British ordnance, but only a detailed examination of the guns can really determine their history. It might be possible to arrange for such an examination to be carried out by one of the armourers still at Cobh on loan to the Éire forces. Would you let me know whether the Éire authorities would like this done?'

[signed] J.W. DULANTY
High Commissioner

No. 245 NAI DFA Secretary's Files S94/39

Memorandum by John Leydon on co-operation with Northern Ireland
(Secret)

DUBLIN, 2 December 1938

Mr. Jenkins telephoned me today about his letter of the 22nd November.[2] I told him that I was examining the matters referred to on the second page and that I had intended to send him a reply when I had investigated the figures relating to trade.

Mr. Jenkins then asked me what I thought of the position and I said that there did not seem to be much prospect of making any progress at the moment. I told him that I thought there would be no difficulty about my going to London for a discussion such as he suggested provided that it was understood that such a discussion was not merely limited to demands by Northern Ireland for concessions by us; I said that, of course, such requests could be considered but that it would be necessary also to consider the questions (or at least some of the questions) which we had put forward. I pointed out that most of the items which I had suggested for discussion do not in fact involve any concession from either side and seemed therefore to be peculiarly suitable for discussion.

Mr. Jenkins said that in present circumstances, having regard particularly to the political atmosphere, there seemed to be no prospect of Mr. Scott's[3] Ministers[4] giving him authority even to discuss with us questions of co-operation. Moreover, the Northern Government are now taking the line that any matter for discussion arising out of the Trade Agreement is a matter purely

---

[1] Not printed.
[2] Not printed.
[3] Sir William D. Scott, Secretary, Ministry of Commerce, Belfast.
[4] Sir Basil Brooke.

between the United Kingdom and this country. Mr. Jenkins was therefore disposed to think that perhaps it might help if he would arrange for a further discussion of trade matters between himself and myself; and he might be able to arrange that Mr. Scott could come along as his adviser. I said that I would, of course, be prepared to discuss any points that he might wish to raise on the Trade Agreement as between the United Kingdom and Éire and I expressed the view that such a discussion could appropriately take place in Dublin; it was at any rate clear that it could not take place in Belfast. Mr. Jenkins agreed and said that when we reached the point of discussion it might be possible to get Mr. Scott to talk informally about some of the matters which we had proposed for discussion.

Mr. Jenkins referred to the general situation arising from the anti-Partition campaign and said that while it did not give rise to uneasiness on the part of those who understood the situation in London it did certainly create a certain amount of irritation up and down the country, particularly in so far as public speeches on this side adopted the line of placing the blame for Partition on the British Government. He said that Mr. Malcolm MacDonald had been contemplating speaking to the High Commissioner about the adverse effects of the campaign, but that he (Mr. Jenkins) had felt that any such representations would do no good and might be misunderstood in Dublin and that Mr. MacDonald had accordingly abandoned the idea of doing anything about it. This information was, of course, communicated to me on a strictly personal and confidential basis.

Mr. Jenkins will discuss with Mr. Scott at a convenient opportunity the possibility of arranging a meeting in Dublin.

[initialled] J.L.

No. 246 NAI DFA 127/119

Confidential report from John W. Dulanty to Joseph P. Walshe (Dublin)[1]
(No. 69) (Secret)

LONDON, 5 December 1938

Adverting to your minute of 18th November[2] about ex Chancellor Schuschnigg, I give below Mr. MacDonald's confidential reply, dated 1st December, to my inquiry:-

'You wrote to me on the 19th November[3] about the position of ex-Chancellor Schuschnigg.

I have made enquiries and I find that the latest information in the Foreign Office is that, at an interview which took place at the end of October between Herr Hitler and Herr von Schuschnigg, the latter insisted that he should be tried before a Special Court which was shortly to be constructed in Vienna, although Herr Hitler was ready to waive a trial on

---

[1] Marginal annotation by Sheila Murphy: 'Seen by Secy'.
[2] Not located.
[3] Not located.

certain conditions (the nature of which is not known to us). It is also reported that the charges against Herr von Schuschnigg will not be pressed with any great vigour and that it is probable that he will eventually be sent to some private house in the country in North Germany where he will be able to live quietly and freely. The persons against whom charges are most likely to be pressed are Herr Schmitz, the former Mayor of Vienna and Herr Hornbostel.

As regards the question of representations to the German Government, Sir Nevile Henderson[1] took up the case of Herr von Schuschnigg and other Austrian political prisoners with Field-Marshal Goering early this summer, and a little later Lord Halifax also raised the matter with the German Ambassador in London.[2] Shortly before the crisis, it was suggested to Sir Nevile Henderson that he should make a further appeal on behalf of these persons, but he considered the moment inopportune, and it was decided to do nothing for the time being. After the Munich settlement the question of an appeal was again considered here, but, before any action could be taken, there occurred the new Jewish persecutions and the German Press campaign against this country which have destroyed the favourable atmosphere that is an essential prerequisite to any such action. Indeed the feeling in the Foreign Office is that, the official German attitude towards this country being what it is at present, any intervention on the part of the United Kingdom Government on behalf of Herr von Schuschnigg or other Austrian prisoners would be likely to do them more harm than good.'

[signed] J.W. DULANTY
High Commissioner

No. 247 UCDA P194/536

Confidential report from Michael MacWhite to Joseph P. Walshe (Dublin)
(Confidential) (Copy)

ROME, 6 December 1938

From the report of the interview I had with Count Ciano when I referred to the question of Partition and from the other reports I have forwarded to you since then it should not be difficult to conclude that it would be an illusion to count on Fascist Italy taking any particular interest in Irish affairs.

From time to time, though not so much recently, the Italian press has played up Ireland just as it has played up Palestine, and may do so again, not because of any particular sympathy for us but rather as a convenient weapon with which to belabour John Bull. Since the adoption of Sanctions by the League of Nations Ireland has figured on the map of countries blackened over that voted for the 'economic stranglehold' of Italy. This map still hangs

---

[1] Nevile Henderson (1882-1942), British Ambassador to Berlin (1937-9).
[2] Herbert von Dirksen (1882-1955), German Ambassador to Japan (1933-8), German Ambassador to Britain (May 1938-Sept. 1939).

in the Foreign Minister's office. Ireland is also regarded as one of the props of the League of Nations which institution is loathed as much by Fascism as is Soviet Russia.

There is little doubt that the Fascists think also of Ireland as a satellite in Britain's orbit. Ambassador Buti, Head of the European Division of the Foreign Office at the Pirow[1] luncheon a week ago said to me 'Your country like South Africa differs sometimes in your foreign policy with that of Great Britain but the logic of facts impose on you all a system of common defense'. I told him of the Taoiseach's remarks on the subject five or six weeks before and also reminded him of Pirow's statement on the same subject a few days previously. He made no reply beyond a facetious smile.

The question of Partition in Ireland has no significance for Fascists. It is vague and far away, and when one speaks of it they appear bored and indifferent, and that says much for a people who, as a rule, present a courteous exterior. They will not listen. Besides, the bludgeoning of Nationalists or the gerrymandering of Electoral districts in the North is amateurish when compared with their methods where the people vote when and as they are told, and where freedom of speech and of the press are non-existent.

To attempt to convince Continental peoples of the objectivity of our views in a case where England is concerned is a rather difficult task for they have always regarded the Irish question as something that is, in itself, anti-British. For the moment the policy of Fascism is one of closer friendship with England and there is no newspaper in Italy would publish a line that might be considered even vaguely as retarding this much desired objective. Italian newspaper men avoid meeting diplomats if they wish to hold their Fascist cards which mean their jobs and diplomats have no opportunity of establishing contacts with them without the aid of bona fide press attaches.

During my time here I have not, as you may well understand, had occasion to meet many persons outside of the Diplomatic Corps. I arrived here with very light diplomatic baggage ignorant of the language and conditions and no previously planned lines to follow. Much time was wasted in looking for Legation premises and until I get a working acquaintanceship with the language progress will not be very rapid. A list of the officials who have lunched or dined with us is annexed hereto[2] but to say that I have close contact with any of them would be an exaggeration.

[unsigned]

---

[1] Oswald Pirow (1890-1959), South African Minister for Railways, Harbours and National Defence. A supporter and admirer of European fascism who founded and led the fascist 'New Order' movement in South Africa.

[2] Not printed.

No. 248 NAI DFA Secretary's Files A20

Letter from Joseph P. Walshe to Eilís Ryan[1] (London)
(144/35) (Copy)

DUBLIN, 8 December 1938

Dear Miss Ryan,[2]

With reference to our telephone message of 2nd December, we have now received from our Legation to Spain confirmation of the result of the enquiries about Mr. Ryan made by the Viscount de Mamblas, General Franco's representative in Biarritz, during his visit to Burgos. The Viscount de Mamblas, on his return from Burgos, assured Mr. Kerney that your brother was 'alive and kicking', and added that he was 'still being troublesome'. He said that the question of his exchange for a prisoner in the hands of the Barcelona Government has been put before the newly-formed Committee in San Sebastian which is carrying on negotiations for the exchange of prisoners of all nationalities. He will be advised as soon as a decision has been reached, and will inform Mr. Kerney immediately.

I have today received a letter addressed to Mr. de Valera by your father,[3] with reference to the attached cutting from the 'Sunday Chronicle'. Your father asked for permission to inform this paper of the action taken on your brother's behalf by the Minister for External Affairs. I should be glad if you would be good enough to inform him that the Minister is quite satisfied that your family are aware of his efforts to obtain the release of Mr. Ryan, and that he feels no useful purpose would be served by entering into a Press controversy.

Yours sincerely,
[stamped] J.P. WALSHE

No. 249 NAI DFA 202/63

Report from Charles Bewley to Joseph P. Walshe (Dublin)
(43/33)

BERLIN, 9 December 1938

In[4] response to your request for a report on the anti-semitic movement in Germany, I desire to point out in the first place that it would be impossible to give anything like a complete analysis of a question on which more has been written and spoken than on perhaps any other question in modern politics. The most which it is possible for me to do is to summarise as well as I can the following three matters:

---

[1] Sister of Frank Ryan.
[2] Marginal note: 'PSS. File with Secy'.
[3] Vere Ryan.
[4] Marginal notes: 'Secy. 12/12/38'. 'Copies in reports file 119/1'. This file (119/1) contained confidential reports from Berlin and ran from January 1937 to December 1938. It was destroyed on de Valera's orders in May 1940 when it was feared that a German invasion of Ireland was imminent.

1. The reasons which have induced the Governments of Germany, Italy, the three parts of the Czecho-Slovak Republic, Hungary, and Poland to adopt discriminatory measures in respect of the Jews:
2. The measures which have been taken in the various countries mentioned to carry out such policy of discrimination:
3. The manner in which the measures taken by the Governments of, and the events occurring in, these countries have been treated in the Irish press.

1. The Governments of the countries mentioned have been led by their experience to the conviction that Jews, even when settled in a particular country for centuries, do not become assimilated to the people of that country, but, when the interests of the country of their birth come into conflict with their own personal or racial interests, invariably sacrifice the interests of the country of their birth to Jewish interests. It is thus claimed that during the War German Jews in the vast majority acted against the interests of Germany, and that, as soon as England had definitely espoused the cause of Zionism, they worked for Germany's defeat in the War. The same conviction is held in Hungary. The Italian Government has stated that, when relations were strained between Italy and England in 1935, the whole body of Italian Jews (who should have been assimilated if assimilation was possible, owing to the fact that their ancestors had in many cases been over a thousand years in Italy) openly declared themselves Zionists, or in secret conspired against Italian interests.

It is also claimed in all the countries mentioned that the chief supporters and organizers of Communism are almost invariably Jews. That the Bolshevist movement in Russia was almost entirely led by Jews is a fact so well known as to need no emphasis: I would however refer to a pamphlet entitled 'The Rulers of Russia' by the Rev. Denis Fahey, C.S.Sp.,[1] also the fact alleged for many years in Germany, and now officially confirmed in the evidence recently given before the Commission at present sitting in the United States of America for the purpose of studying un-American movements in the U.S.A., and in 1917 the Bolshevist movement was financed by American-Jewish banking houses, as Kuhn, Loeb & Co. When Communist Governments were set up after the War in Hungary and Bavaria, the majority of the leaders in each case were Jews, – Bela Kun, Szamuely and many more at Budapest, Eisner, Toller, Axelrod, Leviné and Levien at Munich. In recent years the governments of all the mid-European states have formally prohibited the Communist party, and have effected very numerous arrests for illegal communist activities: the vast majority of the guilty persons in each country have been Jews: this is not merely a statement made by the German press, but is proved by a perusal of the reports of trials of Communists in any country in Central Europe.

In the second place, it is claimed that in Germany and the other countries mentioned the Jews had acquired so dominating a position in the financial

---

[1] Denis Fahey C.S.Sp. (1883-1954), Holy Ghost priest, Professor of Theology at the Holy Ghost Seminary, Kimmage, Dublin, a prolific writer who held strongly anti-Semitic beliefs which are reflected in his works.

world that they were in a position to control public policy, and up to a certain point public opinion, that they monopolized the learned professions and held important positions in the universities out of all proportion to their numbers, and in fact had become a force in face of which the lawfully elected government was in many cases powerless.

Anyone who knew Germany before 1933, whatever be his political opinions, must admit the truth of this particular claim. The whole press, theatre, cinema, stock-exchange, the banks were completely under Jewish control. In Berlin and the other chief towns the medical and legal professions were composed of roughly 70% Jews and 30% Germans; even the hospital nurses were in many nominally non-Jewish hospitals exclusively Jewish. Jewish professors held important positions in the universities: their influence was frequently anti-Christian, anti-patriotic and Communistic, as in the case of Professor Gumpel of Heidelberg best known for his statement in a lecture that the Germans who had fallen in the War had fallen 'on the field of dishonour'. This situation of course no longer exists in Germany; it exists at the present day in Warsaw, Budapest and Prague, although measures are being adopted to alter it in those countries also.

Another cause of the special measures taken against the Jewish community is the fact that almost in no cases do Jews work in the sense of being manual workers, labourers, farmers or artisans. This is, of course, obvious whether in Germany, America or Ireland. The Jew in Germany mainly devoted himself to finance or 'business' in the large towns: the result was a series of grave financial scandals (Barmat, Sklarek, Kutisker, etc., etc.), by which the German State was robbed of milliards of marks. Similar scandals have occurred in Austria, Poland, Hungary, Romania, etc.; almost always the fraudulent financiers have been Jews. Stavisky, the fraudulent financier who swindled the French state to an enormous extent was also a Jew.

Apart from the large financiers, the small Jew either opened a shop or acted as middleman. In each capacity his commercial activities are claimed to have been marked by a want of scruple which enabled him to enrich himself at the expense of his non-Jewish neighbours. In all the countries mentioned the governments have felt themselves compelled to intervene in the interests of the native community against the usury and fraud of Jewish money-lenders, employers, and middlemen.

Even in the countries to which Jews have been allowed to emigrate in the last couple of years for the purpose of working productively, the same difficulty has arisen: I am informed by various diplomats in Berlin that the Jews whom they have admitted do not remain on the land, but very soon desert it for the purpose of exploiting the inhabitants of the country. They have thus produced strong antisemitic feeling in a number of states where it was formerly unknown owing to the absence of Jews.

In connection with the occupations adopted by members of the Jewish race it is also important to remark that the figures of the persons belonging to the different religious denominations who fell in the War have recently been published, not only for Germany but for Italy and France, and in each case it is found that the proportion of Jews was minimal in comparison with that of the Germany, Frenchmen or Italians, whether Protestant or Catholic: hence the inference is drawn, not only in Germany, that the Jew endeavours with success to avoid doing his duty in defending the state in which he resides. Anyone who witnessed the immigration into Ireland of English Jews after the introduction of conscription in England will feel inclined to adopt the German view. When it was found in Germany, as in many other countries, that the Jew had not only succeeded in avoiding military service but also in enriching himself during the agony of the country, it is comprehensible that popular feeling has tended to become anti-semitic.

A further reason given in Germany and all the other countries of Central Europe for introducing discriminating legislation against the Jews is their demoralizing influence on the communities among which they live. It is a notorious fact that the international white slave traffic is controlled by Jews. No one who has even a superficial knowledge of Germany can be ignorant that the appalling moral degradation before 1933 was, if not caused, at least exploited by Jews. The German stage was the most indecent in Europe; it was a Jewish monopoly. German papers appeared of a purely pornographic nature: the proprietor and editor were invariably Jews. Jewish members of the Reichstag were responsible for the introduction of a number of measures abolishing legal penalties for abortion and a number of other practices which are visited by the most severe punishments in every Christian country. Jewish emigrants in the countries which they have been permitted to enter have created and are creating grave moral scandals and are a source of corruption of the populations among which they dwell.

The German police have recently published statistics showing the far higher proportion of Jewish criminals to those of German race: if any doubt should be felt about the authenticity of the statistics, it might be well to peruse the English Black List (an unimpeachable authority), from which it will appear that the undesirables of Jewish race outweigh those of other races in an overwhelming degree.

Furthermore, it is right to mention the fact which determined the last and most severe measures of the German Government against the Jews, – the murder of vom Rath in Paris. It is claimed that this is one of a series of murders committed by Jews against persons who they considered enemies of their race; and lists are given including the murders of the Austrian Minister President Sturck in 1916, the German Minister to the Ukraine Count Mirbach in 1918, the former President of the Ukraine Petljura in 1926, and Gustloff in 1936: in each case the assassin was a Jew, and in each case the murder was committed where there was no death penalty, or where it was a moral certainty that the jury would not convict, or by a young Jew like Grynszpan who could not be executed on account of his age.

To the suggestion that these cases are exceptions, and that the whole Jewish community should not be held responsible for the crimes of particular Jews, the answer is given that, when a non-Jew commits a non-political crime, the whole of his country does not rally in his defence, but that international Jewry at once rallies in the support of a Jew, whatever be the crime of which he is accused. Anyone familiar with the criminal courts even in

Ireland must be aware that every Jew convicted of a crime can count with confidence on the Chief Rabbi testifying on oath that he knows the man intimately and is convinced that he could not possibly be guilty of the crime of which he has been found guilty by an Irish jury.

Finally, the German authorities have frequently pointed out that the concern expressed by Jews for the fate of the Catholic Church in Germany is not to be reconciled with the treatment of the Church in states where Jews have had the control. In Russia, to take the most obvious instance, not only have the Catholic clergy been practically exterminated, but Christian morals have so far as possible been wiped out. When a Jewish Communist Government came into power in Hungary, the clergy were massacred, religious teaching was naturally abolished, and 'sexual instruction' of a revolting type was introduced by the Jewish Minister of Education.

There are of course very many other reasons adduced for the elimination of the Jewish element from the public life of Germany: I cannot for obvious reasons enter into them all. I desire however to point out that the facts here stated are well known to everyone who has lived in Central Europe, or who has taken the trouble to make enquiries from non-Jewish sources into the situation as it really is.

2. In consequence of the various facts as set out above, the German Government, as well as the other governments of Central Europe, has felt itself obliged to eliminate the Jews from the public life of the state. It has done this by stages and in different ways, but the result is that Jews are now for practical purposes completely isolated from Germans. They are not entitled to vote or be elected to Parliament, or to hold any public office. They are not entitled to practice as doctors or lawyers, except for the purpose of healing or legally representing other Jews. They cannot be journalists except in purely Jewish publications, or appear on the stage or take any part in theatres or cinematographs except Jewish ones. They cannot of course take any part in the education of Germans, and young Jews cannot enter any schools or universities except Jewish ones. They have been eliminated from the Banks.

Since the murder of vom Rath by a Jew with a Polish passport who had passed all his life in Germany, the measures have become considerably more severe. Only a limited number of Jewish shops will be allowed, which will cater only for Jewish customers. Jews will not be allowed to enter theatres, cinemas, museums, etc.; they have their own cinemas and theatres, and it is considered that this should be sufficient. They are forbidden to own or drive motor cars or motor cycles, or to enter particular streets in Berlin. It will be required of them in the future to reside in particular districts. And, immediately after the murder of vom Rath, there was an obviously organized movement to smash the windows and in some cases the fittings of all the Jewish shops in the cities of Germany; and in addition a fine of a milliard marks has been placed on the Jewish community, which also has to repair the damage done without receiving any compensation from the insurance companies.

In addition, Jewish households are not allowed, on moral grounds, to have non-Jewish female servants under the age of 45, and all marriages and other relations between Jews and non-Jews are forbidden under heavy penalties.

These are the chief measures introduced by the German Government in regard to the Jews in Germany: there are no doubt others which do not occur to me at the moment. The measures in other countries have been similar, though not yet so drastic. Hungary, for instance, has prohibited Jews from entering in a proportion of over 20% into the professions or commerce: the present proportion is about 80%, and the 60% in excess are eliminated without compensation. The government of Slovakia under Monsignor Tiso and that of Carpatho-Russia under Monsignor Woloschin have introduced much more stringent measures, eliminating Jews completely from the professions and universities, and allowing Jewish shops only to trade with Jews. In these countries, as in Germany, a number of synagogues have been burned. In Italy the policy is very similar to that of Germany, it has become much more drastic than originally intended in consequence of the anti-Italian attitude taken up by the Italian Jews in the recent crisis and the numerous cases of fraud on the revenue carried out by Jewish organisations. In Poland the Jewish societies, like the Masonic organization and the Communist party, have been dissolved; a numerus clausus has been introduced for universities, professions, etc., and Jewish students are not allowed to sit with Poles. It is certain that the anti-Jewish legislation will become very much more stringent in the near future. In Bohemia, and particularly in Prague, it will be increasingly strict, and the number of Jews applying for baptism (for strictly business reasons) is said by members of the Czech Legation to be enormous.

Up to the present the method of the 'Western democracies' in dealing with the Jewish problem has been to deny that the problem exists, and to consider the matter settled by calling those who think otherwise 'anti-semites'. Since the government of Mr. Léon Blum it would appear that the French public, like that of such states as Holland and Belgium, realizes that a problem exists. What are the best methods of dealing with it are presumably matters for the individual governments to determine. For members of a foreign country like various English politicians to make solemn pronouncements in complete and often wilful ignorance of the circumstances would appear neither helpful to the cause of international peace nor of assistance in finding a solution of the problem.

It is perhaps well to refer to the fact that very few, if any, of the measures introduced in Germany in relation to the Jewish problem cannot be paralleled in the measures introduced by the Popes in relation to the Jews of Rome. Under various Papal decrees Jews were forbidden to have Christian servants. Christians who had recourse to Jewish doctors were excommunicated. Jews lived in special parts of the city and carried a distinctive mark (a wheel or circle) on their clothing, marriages between Jews and Christians were not admitted.

Obviously the fact that, not only in Germany but in every state where they exist in any quantity, the Jews are regarded as an alien body (this is the case even in Persia and Iraq) makes an attitude of assumed moral superiority towards Germany somewhat out of place. If every state which has experience of Jews, including those with Catholic clergymen at their head, finds it necessary to introduce similar special measures restricting their activities, it is impossible to take up with any degree of reason the attitude that they should be treated like ordinary citizens of the country. It is of course necessary to be aware of the particular circumstances prevailing in each country before it is possible to judge whether the measures adopted are necessary or not. Naturally this would not apply to cases of deliberate cruelty on the part of the Government, but I am not aware of any such towards Jews on the part of the German Government.[1] There has been no episode in connection with Jews in Germany which could even remotely be compared with the atrocities of the Communists in Spain or Russia or the English in Palestine.

3. The newspapers published in Ireland, like the rest of the English press, take their information from English press agencies which are in fact in Jewish hands, – Reuter, Exchange Telegraph, etc. They do not apparently wish to have any news from any other source, and refuse to publish it if sent them. All measures taken against Jews are consequently printed on their front news page in a form most likely to capture the imagination of their readers. They give favourable publicity to statements by members of the Jewish community. On the other hand, they frequently suppress reports of criminal cases where the accused person is a Jew. I understand that this phenomenon results from the knowledge that, if they do not do so, they will lose their Jewish advertisements. They do not of course even suggest to the Irish public that there may be any reason for the Governments of Germany and the other mid-European countries to take the steps which they have taken in recent years, – still less that the Governments in question believe themselves to be acting in necessary defence of the people entrusted to their charge.

So long as this is so, it is of course impossible to expect that the Irish public will have any opinion on international affairs other than that which is suggested to them by Anglo-Jewish telegraph agencies, and by the articles written in the same sense by editors who apparently, like the public, swallow without investigation the versions given them by the Anglo-Jewish agencies to which they subscribe. This of course means that, in the long run, public opinion on foreign affairs and public policy in international relations are formed, not by the Government of Ireland but by anonymous agencies acting on the dictation and in pursuance of the policy of persons who are neither Irish nor Catholic but bitterly opposed both to Irish Nationalism and to the Catholic Church.

Even more misleading to the Irish public is the fact that, while, as I have pointed out, reports of 'persecutions' of Jews are invariably 'featured' in the newspapers published in Ireland, the crimes of anti-Fascists are systematically suppressed. Recently a priest in Poland was shot during Mass by a man who stated that he did so in the name of international Communism: though the event and subsequently the trial filled the pages of the press all through Central Europe, it was not allowed to come to the knowledge of the Irish reader. Every time aeroplanes belonging to National Spain bombard Madrid or Valencia, detailed accounts of the damage to civilians, particularly women and children, is given by the English telegraph agencies in the Irish press (the

---

[1] This sentence and the next have been highlighted in pen in the margin by a reader.

military damage is less often mentioned): on the other hand the number of civilians massacred by Spanish Communists, while sometimes formally mentioned, is never given in such a form as to strike the imagination of the readers, nor do the leading articles show the same moral indignation over the burning alive of Catholic clergy as for the breaking of Jewish shop windows. No one would dream, after a perusal of the Irish Times, Irish Press and Irish Daily Independent that atrocities are at present every day being committed by British troops in Palestine, compared to which the atrocities of the 'Black-and-Tans' in Ireland were a trifling matter. The fact that Jewish interests are involved is sufficient to prevent the international telegraph agencies from referring to British crimes: the Arab Nationalists are referred to as 'terrorists', just as Irish Nationalists were eighteen years ago, and the Irish people is not even allowed to know the facts.

It may be suggested that matters occurring in other countries do no affect, in one direction or the other, the question of the treatment of Jews in Germany. It is however clear that if the Irish press and public opinion indulge in parox-ysms of moral indignation at the treatment of Jews but remain blind and deaf to atrocities committed on Christians in other parts of the world, they lay themselves open to a charge of ignorance or hypocrisy, and scarcely con-tribute to an amelioration of the general international situation.

I know of course nothing of the methods which could be employed by the Government in altering such a state of affairs, and would not dream of expressing an opinion on the subject. I have no doubt, however, that the Minister will be glad of an exposé of the situation as it is, of the very incom-plete view of the Jewish problem which under present circumstances is per-mitted to the Irish public, and of the complete want of proportion in the importance ascribed to events in Germany.

As I stated in the beginning of this report, it is impossible to give even a summary of the Jewish problem except in very insufficient form. The German official view is set out fairly fully in an official publication of some 400 pages. If the Minister so desires, I can forward it to the Department. If there are any further points to which I have not referred, I should be very glad to discuss them with the Minister during my approaching visit to Dublin.

[signed] C. BEWLEY

No. 250 UCDA P150/2550

Memorandum on passports from Joseph P. Walshe to Eamon de Valera
DUBLIN, 12 December 1938

TAOISEACH, MINISTER FOR EXTERNAL AFFAIRS
I must admit I do not feel entirely happy about our instruction to the High Commissioner.[1]

Let us take, first of all, the hypothesis that the British acquiesce, however reluctantly, and do not take any fresh measures to render our passport less

---

[1] These instructions have not been located.

effective for its purpose. The only external evidence of our association with the States of the Commonwealth disappears. This would be followed by the general assumption that we do not belong to the association at all. A lessening of interests on the part of Canada and South Africa in our constitutional welfare must then be expected. They will say that, if we do not want to make public mention of our association with them, they are under no corporate obligation to influence the British Government in our regard. And in this connection we must admit that in the whole course of our evolution towards our present status we have had the powerful moral support of Canada and South Africa and, to some extent, also, of Australia. Up to now so long as we gave tangible external evidence of belonging to the group they felt that their own vital interests were involved in any attack made on our interests, especially our constitutional and political interests, by the British Government. The feeling of solidarity is still a very real one. So long as the principal Members of the Commonwealth other than Great Britain stand by us, we can maintain our independence even in the extremely difficult circumstances of the world war which seems to be rushing upon us. If we isolate ourselves – and the British can make this new step appear to be a definite move away from the Commonwealth – it seems to me that we are, to some degree at any rate, leaving ourselves at the mercy of any party in Great Britain who wishes to restore the unity of these islands. No one can foretell whether such a movement may not occur at the very beginning of the world war, and if Great Britain only just escapes defeat – as is the most likely hypotheses – the movement for unity is bound to come at the end of the war. Our re-absorption in the United Kingdom is a continuing danger so long as the world crisis persists, and I believe that solidarity with the Members of the British Commonwealth is a much greater protection against that happening than the goodwill of the United States.

As far as the use of the King's name is concerned, the arguments in its favour are not ~~very~~ so strong, but its omission can have an almost similar effect on the minds of the principal associated States in so far as their influence on our future destiny is concerned. It also can be questioned whether the omission of the King's name from the passport is not going to make our task in the restoration of the unity of Ireland much more difficult.

We cannot forget that so far in these politico-constitutional matters the British have exercised a restraint far greater than their normal usage should lead us to expect. Can we be sure that this restraint will continue to be exercised? If they so desired, they could make use of the new modifications to wage such a subtle campaign against us as would leave us very little of the strong support which we now have in Great Britain itself and in the Dominions.

The more likely hypothesis is that the British Government will react violently to the new suggestions, refusing to grant us the good offices of their representatives if we make the changes. Are we prepared in that case to persevere nevertheless and to suffer the consequences?

On the whole, I respectfully suggest that you should not take this step without a preliminary personal conversation with Mr. MacDonald, in the course of which you would be able to gauge the likely reactions. Otherwise, trivial though the matter appears on the surface, we may be letting ourselves in for endless trouble altogether out of proportion to the immediate gain. It is quite conceivable that unless we proceed with the greatest caution at this vital moment all the astounding advances of the last six years may be brought to naught. The[1] basis of the concessions in the Trade Agreements is Imperial preference i.e. in making it we admitted membership of the Commonwealth. For the British, I have no doubt the passport, is *the* badge of Ireland. The King can cease to exist elsewhere in our Constitutional system by inanition i.e. if the Government cease to advise him to do anything. Over that the British can exercise no control. They could make our passport useless.

[initialled] J.P.W.

No. 251 UCDA P194/536

Confidential report from Michael MacWhite to Joseph P. Walshe (Dublin)
(Confidential) (Copy)

ROME, 17 December 1938

The shyness of Italian diplomats whom I have met here after previously experiencing their cordiality and friendship in Europe and America has been a source of some surprise to me since my arrival in Rome. It is only with difficulty one can get them to accept an invitation and even at table they appear ill at ease.

Recently, however, I have learnt that only a very small number among the higher officials of the Italian Foreign Office are permitted to frequent Embassies or Legations or to accept the hospitality of foreign diplomats. Those not included in this restricted group who cultivate the friendship of diplomats have a special mission to fulfil the successful outcome of which must be of particular interest to the Italian Government. Any other officials who associate with foreigners would soon find themselves facing a Courtmartial and consequent punishment.

Every Embassy and Legation in Rome has a special guard of at least two gendarmes either in full uniform or in plain clothes. The Soviet Embassy has two at each of its four corners and the French Embassy is, at the moment guarded by only about fifty men. The object of this guard is ostensibly to protect diplomats from molestation but it has also to note and describe callers. After my arrival here a couple of plain clothes men were always in the hotel corridor outside the door of the apartment. The Belgian Ambassador who occupied a suite on the same floor had also his guard. I am convinced that in our absence these men entered our rooms either in the guise of valets or waiters because on one occasion the Dial of a small radio we brought from America was unscrewed and replaced the wrong side up. This happened while we were at dinner. They thought probably it had a secret transmitter.

---

[1] From this point on the document is handwritten.

After this, we always kept the Messenger in the Office while at meals – even on Sundays.

After moving into this Flat our guard moved with us. One of them rarely goes more than fifty or sixty yards from the main entrance. If anything escapes him the Concierge who is always on hand will be able to keep him posted, for no Concierge of an Apartment house can hold the job unless he is a member of the Fascist Party and he is sworn to give information to the police about the inhabitants, their movements, habits, visitors and guests. Every person who spends a night in any house in this country must produce an identity card or Passport for registration either with the Porter or the head of the Household both of whom are liable to fine and imprisonment for neglect of duty in this respect. It would not therefore be possible for a person in Italy native or foreign who sleeps in a habitation to escape the surveillance of the authorities for much more than twenty four hours.

I have been assured by some of my colleagues that Diplomatic pouches, out and inward bound, have from time to time been tampered with. The British, French and some of the more important Missions have their own Couriers travelling to and from Rome with their dispatches. The others, like ourselves, use the ordinary postal channels. It would not be a difficult task for an expert to make duplicate keys and seals, but it is much easier to rip the side of the Pouch and have it restitched with the same kind of thread. A high church dignitary told me that dispatches from the Papal Nuncio at Berlin were secured on this side of the Austrian border and copies conveyed to the German authorities. By this means, it is believed, the Nazis obtained immediate and first hand information of the plans of the hierarchy for Catholic defense in Germany.

A retired newspaper man who had relations with the Italian police assured me that the special Post Office branch had photostatic copies of most of the private correspondence which Ambassadors and Ministers confide to the mails. Letters from Italians to one another are also investigated as a result of which indiscreet writers find themselves frequently in trouble. Practically all letters going abroad are suspected to contain notes or cheques and are therefore subject to examination. This system of espionage has been known in Italy for generations but to-day it has been reduced to a fine art.

No. 252 UCDA P194/550

Handwritten letter from Joseph Walshe to Michael MacWhite (Rome)
Dublin,[1] 18 December 1938

My dear Michael,
A line to wish you Paula and Eoin a very happy Christmas and New Year. Judging from your reports you are finding Rome just as interesting as Washington. In some ways it must be more so. Mussolini has much more to say to the reshaping of Europe than Roosevelt, though Hitler's star must soon take all the shine out of his.

---

[1] This letter was written by Walshe from his home address, 37 Pembroke Park. Dublin.

Do you feel that war can be avoided? I can't see it myself unless England makes up their mind to take second place. Six months ought to decide things one way or the other. By that time Germany will have become too strong and she can go on her way undisturbed. At least that is how it looks from here. With Romania coming under her wing she should soon be in a position to dictate to Poland and Russia can hardly make a fight against the liberation of the Ukraine.

Every happiness
Yours ever
[signed] JOE

No. 253 UCDA P194/536

Confidential report from Michael MacWhite to Joseph P. Walshe (Dublin)
(Confidential) (Copy)

ROME, 19 December 1938

The political situation in Europe appears to grow more complicated from day to day. The friendly gestures exchanged between Italy and Poland immediately after Munich seem to have been affected by a premature blight, for the proposed visit of Count Ciano to Warsaw which was announced to take place has been called off. The Poles are of the opinion that after having first received a pat on the back and a friendly hint to go ahead, Mussolini at Hitler's behest suddenly grew indifferent to their aspirations for a common frontier with Hungary. This desire was, ostensibly, based on the creation of a stronger rampart against the inroads of Bolshevism from the East, but it would also have the effect of erecting four frontiers instead of two in the path of the Germans in their drang nach Osten.

Now, it would seem that the eastern part of Czechoslovakia on which Poland had set her eyes is to form the kernel of a great Ukrainian state under the aegis of Germany. Agitation to this effect was set in motion amongst the Ukrainians some time ago the outcome of which may be that, instead of having her frontiers extended as she ambitioned, Poland may be forced to cede some of her territory to this new State now in the making. Some of my colleagues from the Baltic States assure me that Germany is behind this propaganda – a school for the promotion of which she had established in Danzig some time ago.

The recent visit of Ribbentrop to Paris may not be foreign to preparations for a German move towards the East as by it the inviolability of their western frontier is assured. If they succeeded in annexing Austria and in reducing Czechoslovakia to a state of vassalage in the face of opposition from the great Powers why should they hesitate about taking Ukraine where they have only the disorganised army of Soviet Russia to contend with.

If it is true, as reported, that Ribbentrop gave an undertaking to Bonnet that Germany was disinterested in the Mediterranean area, one can understand better the efforts of the Italian press to convince the people of the solidity of the Rome-Berlin axis. Some months ago the belief was general here that as soon as the Duce had implemented the Accord with Great Britain and clar-ified his situation in Spain he would gradually pull away from Hitler. Now, however, the shoe appears to be on the other foot. Somewhere in his mem-oirs Bismarck wrote that Germany did not want an Ally but a horse. As soon as that animal had rendered the desired service he could be abandoned with-out regret.

For months the Italian people have been assured by their leaders that France is incapable of giving good government to those of her colonies that fall within the orbit of Italian aspirations, and as these are indispensable to the future of the new Italian Empire they should be acquired by force unless they are gracefully surrendered. As I have mentioned in a previous report there is danger in the bluff he may attempt in the realisation of his ambitions and in the justification of his actions before his own followers. He cannot afford to retreat with empty hands, and as he is now in a situation that appears to observers here to be more difficult than any with which he has previously been confronted, time alone will tell if he will be able to extricate himself without damage to his prestige. Increased representation on the Board of the Suez Canal will hardly be considered as a satisfactory price, and he may not even get that.

It has come to my knowledge from a reliable source that the Italian Fleet, in full war strength, is assembled in Sardinian waters. It is regarded as of special significance that Engineer specialists who are always released from service with the approach of Winter have been maintained with the colours. In case of war this Fleet would naturally attempt to cut off Continental France from her African Departments and Possessions by a line, about three hundred miles long, from Sardinia to the island of Majorca. On the other hand, a large part of the French Fleet is concentrated in the lake of Bizerta at the further end of which is the naval arsenal of Sidi Abdalla. The French forces, if temporarily cut off from France could get almost all their necessary supplies from Algeria without much danger as the roads and railways of that province were built by the army and form part of the scheme of National defence.

[Unsigned]

No. 254 NAI DFA Secretary's Files S94/39

Memorandum by John Leydon on co-operation with Northern Ireland
(Secret)

DUBLIN, 21 December 1938

Mr. Jenkins telephoned me last evening about the question of discussions with Mr. Scott. He said that as there had been delay in making any progress with the matter he had that morning telephoned to Mr. Scott who said he had just got his Minister's permission to come to *London* for discussions; and Mr. Jenkins suggested that I should come to London for a discussion with him-self and Mr. Scott about matters of trade arising out of the Agreement, and he further suggested that the week beginning the 9th January would be a convenient time. He added that Mr. Scott had now undertaken to prepare a Memorandum setting out the points he wished to have discussed.

I told Mr. Jenkins that I thought there would be no difficulty about my going to London if it was understood that the discussion is not to be confined to the points to be raised by Mr. Scott; I thought it would be regarded as essential from the point of view of the Irish Government that we should also be in a position to discuss the other matters on the list which I had already furnished to him or at any rate some of them. Mr. Jenkins said that he himself is extremely anxious to have the discussions started over the widest possible field, but that the difficulty is to get Northern Ministers to agree to have them discussed; they are not now apparently prepared even to allow Mr. Scott to come to Dublin. Mr. Jenkins is himself quite prepared to come to Dublin, though it is not very clear how that would advance matters; he felt that if once we could arrange to meet there might be some possibility of getting the discussions with the North extended to the item in which we are interested. I pointed out that there could be no inducement for the Irish Government to give any sort of concession to the North if the Northern attitude is going to be an absolute refusal even to discuss matters of common concern.

I promised Mr. Jenkins that I would think the matter over and let him know my views in the course of the next few days.

[initialled] J.L.

No. 255 UCDA P150/2530

Memorandum from Joseph P. Walshe to Eamon de Valera
DUBLIN, 24 December 1938

Passports
Perhaps the following would be a suitable reply:-[1]
'The first passports of the Irish Free State were issued by the Governor General in the name of King George V, following the model of the passports issued in Canada, South Africa, Australia and New Zealand. A struggle, however, immediately arose on the question of the description of the bearer's nationality.[2] The British Government took up the attitude that, unless the Irish Government used the description "British Subject" on the passport, they would instruct their agents all over the world to refuse facilities to bearers of Irish passports. The Irish Government refused to apply that description to Irish Citizens, and a position of serious inconvenience for these latter was created.

In 1929, a compromise was reached. The passport, instead of being issued by the Governor General, was issued by the Minister for External

---

[1] The reply was to be given to the Secretary of State for Dominion Affairs, Malcolm MacDonald.
[2] This is a recurring theme in DIFP volumes and is covered through Volumes I to IV of the series, but see in particular DIFP Volume II, Nos 179, 182-4, 204, 317 and 330 and Volume III, Nos 5, 18, 113, 133 and 252.

Affairs (as is done in Great Britain), but still in the name of King George V, and "Citizen of the Irish Free State" was accepted. As you are aware, "Citizen of Ireland" is the present description.

It is hoped, in the course of the process of adapting our forms to the new Constitution and the Executive Authority (External Relations) Act, 1936, to eliminate the use of the King's name from the passport.

I am sending you herewith a cancelled passport so that you may have a precise idea of its present form.

Your information about Irish citizens being described as "British citizens" has no foundation in fact.'

You said, in reply to a question of General McEoin's[1] on 30th November, that the general question of the form of all documents of an international character which are at present signed on advice is now receiving attention in the light of the new Constitutional position and the Government's policy. The passport is, however, not one of these documents. It is not signed by the King. The entire active element in the passport is the Minister for External Affairs, and I doubt very much whether the words 'continues to act' in section 3 of the Executive Authority (External Relations) Act, 1936, can be related in any way to the form on the request page of the passport.

It will be noted that, in the appointment of diplomatic and consular representatives and the conclusion of international agreements, the King definitely signs something, and is to that extent an active agent. The form of the request must be regarded as belonging to the sphere of politico-Constitutional relations depending on custom and mutual agreement.

[initialled] J.P.W.

---

[1] General Seán McEoin (1894-1973), revolutionary and politician (Cumann na nGaedheal and Fine Gael), TD for Sligo (1929-65), Minister for Justice (1948-51), Minister for Defence (1951, 1954-7).

1939

No. 256 NAI DFA 119/48

*Memorandum by Leopold H. Kerney to Joseph P. Walshe (Dublin)[1] on
General Franco's relations with the Church in Spain
(S.J. 19/1) (Private)*

St Jean de Luz, 3 January 1939

THE CHURCH AND FRANCO

I had a conversation on Sunday afternoon, 1st January, with Mr. de Caux, who was preparing to return to Barcelona the following day. He told me of an interesting conversation which he had had with Francisco Herrera. You will recollect latter as having paid a visit to Dublin in 1935; he was then pro-prietor of 'El Debate', the Catholic newspaper founded in 1916 by his brother Angel Herrera, who, is now studying for the priesthood and is a seminarist somewhere in Germany; Francisco Herrera had and no doubt still has close relations with the Jesuits and was the principal promoter and supporter of Gil Robles;[2] I heard from a Spanish Nationalist friend here some time ago that Herrera and Robles were no longer on friendly terms, and this friend also assured me that, prior to the civil war, Herrera had placed his faith in the late General Mola and had helped the latter in making preparation for the rising, but I have never obtained confirmation of this rumour elsewhere. Francisco Herrera's name is familiar throughout Spain, and he himself is of outstanding importance because of his identification with Catholic Action there. I do not know what are his special activities at the moment, apart from the fact that he owns three or four newspapers in Nationalist Spain and that he crosses back and forwards across the French frontier from time to time.

What de Caux told me was that Herrera, about three months ago, had approached him and sought to induce him to start a campaign in the 'Times' in favour of a restoration of the monarchy (but not of Alfonso) in Spain, but that he had had to reply that this could not be done, or at least that he could not do anything in the matter. Herrera's argument was that it was 'absolutely essential' to get rid of Franco and to put a stop to the encroachment of Nazi influences in Spain, and that it would be to England's advantage to throw her weight in the scale in favour of a restoration of the monarchy, as she had

---

[1] Marginal note: 'Seen Secy', 'Seen M.R. 11/1/39'.
[2] José Maria Gil Robles (1898-1980) founder of Acción Populaire (political party) and a leading figure in the Confederación Española de Derechas Autónomas (CEDA), Minister for War (1935), appointed Franco Chief of the General Staff but refused to side with Franco; expelled from France, Gil Robles went to Portugal where he became advisor to King Don Juan, the father of King Carlos of Spain.

done in Greece. De Caux said that Herrera's moral character was such that he was scarcely the right man to lead Catholic opinion in Spain, and he made some allusion to his being seen at times in the company of women. De Mamblas had expressed the opinion to de Caux that Herrera was 'imprudent'. And now, within the past few days, Francisco Herrera had been refused permission, at the Spanish side of the International Bridge at Irun, to re-enter Spain.

I had not much time to discuss this question with de Caux, as it was close on 4.30 p.m. and he had given an appointment at that hour to Herrera, who was shown into the room as we were talking. The purpose of their interview is unknown to me, but perhaps de Caux will again take me into his confidence when he returns from Barcelona at Easter. His opinion is that serious trouble and perhaps further civil war must take place in Spain if there should be a victory either for Burgos or for Barcelona; it is because I share this belief that I deem it possible that, sooner or later, influential Spaniards will come to realise that the most effective if not the only way to remove the danger likely to result from radical tendencies on the left and on the right is to find a means of bridging the gulf between less extreme opinion on either side and forming a strong central administration, whether republican or monarchist in form.

My report of 19th December last on Cardinal Goma[1] is of additional interest now that we know the attitude of Francisco Herrera, which also seems to justify to some extent the views expressed on page 6 of my report of 4th August 1938[2] on Nationalist Dissensions.

Herrera's attitude leads me to believe that Franco has identified himself definitely with the Falange Española philosophy and programme, and I presume that extreme opinion in that organisation no longer distrusts him; I think you know that Falange Española has always very much resented that imputation that they were in any degree anti-catholic; I have noticed of late a certain amount of publicity given to Franco's devout observance of his religious duties. However, Catholic distrust, anxiety and hostility seem to be exemplified in the attitude of Herrera, and the exclusion, even if only temporarily, of Herrera from Catholic Spain is a clear indication of strained relations between Franco and Catholic Spain.

There is, then, good reason for hesitating to take any step which might associate us more closely with Franco at a time when he is beginning to be looked upon with distrust by the leaders of Spanish Catholic thought. It may yet be found that, by refraining from taking any positive step which might be interpreted as a departure from neutrality, we shall find ourselves in due course in a position to cooperate in peaceful efforts which may some day be made to reconcile conflicting opinions in Spain.

[signed] L.H. KERNEY
Aire Lán-Chómhachtach

---

[1] Not printed.
[2] Not located.

No. 257 UCDA P194/537

Confidential report from Michael MacWhite to Joseph P. Walshe (Dublin)
(Confidential) (Copy)

ROME, 4 January 1939

It would take a prophet to say when the war which everybody regards as inevitable will eventually break out. The inflammable material is daily piling higher but the war lords hesitate to apply the torch. At the moment, however, sparks are flying about and one of them may accidentally cause a premature explosion. Herein lies the immediate danger. Italy could not fight a long war and Germany is probably in the same situation. There are observers who are convinced that both these countries would be in the throes of a revolution within ninety days after the outbreak of hostilities. There are some grounds no doubt for their convictions and it is in the nature of things that disintegration in totalitarian states would proceed at a rapidity unknown to democratic countries.

The determined steps taken by France during the last fortnight have given the dictators food for reflection. For despite their internal bickerings and the seemingly erratic play of their party politics the French have the only army in Europe that is ready for war. They have a strong reserve of material and munitions and their naval and air forces will be able to give a good account of themselves should the occasion arise. This has been privately admitted by one of the highest military authorities in this country.

On the other hand Italy is not ready for another war. For years she had been building ships and airplanes for the conquest of Ethiopia. The efforts she put into that work were considerable and the success that attended them gave place to a period of physical and material exhaustion from which she has not yet recovered. Besides, the reward of victory for those who contributed to it was disappointing. The fertile land promised to the volunteers has not materialised and the hundreds of thousands of Italians who expected to emigrate to this new country are vegetating in every town and hamlet of Italy nursing their grievances and their disappointment. Of the many who answered the call, few, in verity, were chosen.

War equipment deteriorates rapidly. It is said on good authority that not more than one fourth of Italian armaments are in first class condition. The remainder is being replaced rather slowly. The raw material for this purpose comes mainly from Germany and delivery is said to be very slow because of the particular requirements of that country for her own immediate use.

A rumour has been going the round of diplomatic circles here which is probably true, to the effect that Hitler, in answer to the Duce's request for military assistance in case of a conflict with France, offered him only 200,000 men. As military experts know this force would not in itself be sufficient to turn the tide of battle. It may, on the other hand become an embarrassment unless its effectives are always kept up to full strength, of which there was said to be no assurance. Such a force could not be considered as anything more than a gesture.

I learned from one of the French Embassy staff yesterday that his government were agreeably surprised at the political and diplomatic reaction provoked everywhere by their determined resistance to what he described as the fantastic demands of the Duce. Their blunt warning to Chamberlain to refrain from discussing French interests during his visit to Rome has shown that Daladier has to some extent taken the wind out of his sails. He cannot now gain new prestige in 'giving away other people's property' as the French Ambassador recently said. His talks here with the Duce may therefore cover only matters of minor importance such as the possibility of extending credits to Italy and the rectification of British-Italian colonial frontiers. It is difficult to see how the Spanish question can be discussed excepting in so far as Italy's part in implementing the Easter agreement remains unfulfilled. One of the Fascist newspapers asserted a couple of days ago that no more Italian troops will be withdrawn until 10,000 of the foreigners fighting on the Loyalist side have been disbanded.

A big amusement programme is being arranged here for Chamberlain and Halifax. On the evening of their arrival they will have a conference with the Duce who that night will give a dinner and reception in their honour at the Palazzo Venezia. On Thursday morning they will visit the Royal Palace and sign the Book after which they will lay wreaths on the tombs of the Unknown Soldier and the Fascist Martyrs. Then they will lunch with the King. Later in the afternoon they will have a conference with Count Ciano who will have them to Dinner and the Opera. On Friday, they will visit the Pope after which they will lunch with the British Minister to the Vatican. On Friday afternoon there will be a concert in their honour at the Fascist Headquarters. Later they will witness gymnastic displays by Fascist youth at the Foro Mussolini and at night will assist at the Dinner and Reception with which Lord Perth will honour them. At noon on Saturday they will take their departure. In between these functions it will of course be possible to arrange for some talks but that will depend on the circumstances.

As a result of the despatch of French troops to Djibouti Italy has called up the volunteers who had already served through the Ethiopian war, very likely to serve in Africa again. The mobilisation note came as a New Year surprise. Secrecy is being maintained in relation to this move just as it was about the mobilisation of the Alpine divisions last September. Its significance cannot very well be ignored.

No. 258 NAI DT S10795

Memorandum on the programme of a broadcast to the United States of America
DUBLIN, 7 January 1939

RADIO ÉIREANN to U.S.A./Salute of National Programme
Sunday 8th January, 1939/6.30 to 7 p.m. Irish Time 1.30 to 2 p.m. New York Time

6.30	-	Announcement/Irish National Anthem
6.32	-	'St. Patrick's Day' – excerpt from 'Irish Rhapsody' by Victor Herbert, played by the Irish Radio Orchestra
6.36	-	A medley of Hornpipes and Reels played by Dublin Metropolitan Garda Ceilidhe Band under direction of Supt. C. O'Donnell, Mus.B. (National University of Ireland)
6.42	-	'Eibhlin a Rúin' sung by Máire Ní Scolaidhe 'My Land' sung by Michael O'Higgins 'Lúibín Ó Lú' – Máire Ní Scolaidhe. 'The Lark in the Clear Air' – Ml. O'Higgins.
6.48	-	Taoiseach – Eamon de Valera.
6.58	-	National Anthem/6.59 - Close.

The National Anthem of Ireland will be played by the Irish Radio Orchestra, conducted by Dr. Vincent O'Brien, Radio Éireann, Director of Music.

No. 259 NAI DFA Secretary's Files S94/39

Memorandum by John Leydon on co-operation with Northern Ireland
(Secret)
DUBLIN, 23 January 1939

Mr. Jenkins telephoned to me today about the question of arranging a meeting to discuss matters arising out of the Trade Agreement with particular reference to the question of co-operation between the Government here and the Government of Northern Ireland. I told him that since we had previously discussed this matter the position could scarcely be said to have improved from the point of view of the atmosphere which would be necessary in order to promote co-operation on the part of the Northern Government. I told him that I did not myself feel that there is anything to be gained by my going to London at the present stage.

He then went on to say that, while he recognises the difficulties from the point of view of the Belfast Government, he thought it would at any rate be worthwhile to keep on trying and he asked me whether there would be any use in his coming to Dublin. I told him that, of course, we should be very glad to see him if he came here but that the important thing was to see co-operation from the Northern Government. He said he fully recognised this and he then suggested that he should go to Belfast in the first instance and endeavour to see some of the Northern Ministers and if possible bring Mr. Scott to Dublin with him. I agreed that it might be worth trying and that in any case it did not seem to be likely that such a course would do any harm. Mr. Jenkins said that he would in that event arrange to go to Belfast about the

beginning of next week and come to Dublin on the 31st January. I told him
that I would arrange to hold myself at his disposal if he comes.

[initialled] J.L.

No. 260 NAI DFA 243/9

Report from Charles Bewley to Joseph P. Walshe (Dublin)[1]
(32/33D)

BERLIN, 25 January 1939

I desire to refer to the minute of 8th December, 143/112,[2] in which it is stated
by the Department that 90 non-Aryan Christians are to be 'temporarily'
admitted into Ireland, fifty for the purpose of receiving training in agricultural work, twenty adults whose maintenance will be guaranteed by well-to-
do families, and twenty children whose maintenance and education will be
guaranteed by well-to-do families. A notice in the Irish Press of 26th
November states that 'it is expected that this first group will be able to emigrate to some other country at an early date.'

I had supposed that further details would be sent me with regard to the
measures to be taken in order to secure that the persons admitted should not
be of an undesirable type and that only such persons should be admitted as
would be able to leave Ireland after their 'temporary' sojourn and could be
deported in the event of their refusing to leave voluntarily. As no such details
or instructions have been sent, it is my duty to make the following comments.
1. It is a notorious fact that in the last few months thousands of Jews have
been baptized for the purpose of avoiding certain inconveniences to which
they were exposed by membership of the Jewish religion (see my minute of
20th January, 32/33D).[3] No statement is made by the Coordinating
Committee or the 'non-Aryan Christian refugees' themselves at what date
their baptism took place. There is therefore, so far as I have been informed,
no safeguard that the 'non-Aryan Christians' admitted into Ireland are
not Jews who have applied for Christian baptism merely for the material
benefits which they hoped to derive from such a step.
2. None of the persons so far admitted under the schemes referred to has, so far
as I have been informed, been given any guarantee by any other government
that they will be admitted to such other country after the expiration of their
'temporary' sojourn in Ireland. It is clear from the statement issued by the
Coordinating Committee that its members have not the slightest idea to what
country it will be possible for the refugees to emigrate. It is doubtful where a
territory can be found for the numerous Jews, whether belonging to the

---

[1]   Marginal note by Sheila Murphy: 'Seen by Secy., SGM.'.
[2]   In 1939 this minute and other material on file 143/112 was transferred to file 243/9
    'Forming of an Irish Co-ordinating Committee for Refugees'. File 243/9 can be consulted
    at the National Archives, Dublin.
[3]   Not located. The Irish Legation in Berlin was destroyed by a heavy air raid on the night
    of 22 November 1943. The archives were lost, with the exception of a telegram register
    (dating to July 1942) and the codebook. It is not clear from the document where this
    minute was filed in the Department of External Affairs in Dublin.

Christian religion or not, who are desirous of leaving Germany, Poland, Hungary and other European countries, or whether such territory can be found at all. Even if such territory is found, it will scarcely be sufficient for all the Jews from Central Europe. In any event, the last persons to be considered for it will be those who have been voluntarily admitted by such states as Ireland.

3. Even if territory were found for the settlement of Jews from Europe, and permission were given to the Jews admitted into Ireland to obtain citizenship of it, there is no guarantee whatever that the Jews in question would wish to leave Ireland for, say, Guyana or Madagascar, and in this event it would not be possible to deport them. There would therefore be no possibility of getting rid of these persons for the rest of their lives, while their children would presumably be Irish citizens.

4. This Legation has been informed that no enquiries are to be made about various persons who, it is presumed, are recommended by the Coordinating Committee (see minute of 29th Nov. No. 102/302B).[1] It is not known what enquiries, if any, have been made by the Committee or the persons with whom it has correspondence in Vienna and other parts of Germany. There is therefore, so far as I have been informed, no guarantee whatever as to the character of the persons admitted.

5. In the case of persons called Karrach the Department decided that visas should not be given (see minute of 12th October 1938, 102/453);[2] apparently their decision is overridden by a minute of 16th November 1938,[3] no reference number, in which it is stated that the persons in question are to be granted visas immediately, and that no enquiries are to be made. This would apparently indicate that the Committee, working in cooperation with such bodies as the Society of Friends or the Swedish Mission, is entitled to overrule previous decisions of the Department.

6. It has been the experience of numerous other countries that the Jews admitted for the purpose of agriculture abandon their agricultural work at the first opportunity and go to live in the cities. In Ireland it would in any event be impossible for them to obtain holdings of land. It is therefore safe to say that the fifty persons admitted for training in agricultural work will abandon the country for the cities, where they will live at the expense of the Irish community.

7. The well-to-do families who have guaranteed to maintain 'temporarily' twenty adults and twenty children have obviously no idea of the impossibility of getting rid of these people after the expiration of the temporary period. It cannot be expected that they will continue to maintain them for the rest of their lives. Therefore the persons in question will either be supported directly by the Irish taxpayer, or will obtain employment and thereby increase the number of Irish unemployed.

---

[1] File 102/302B 'Applications for Visas from German and Austrian Nationals', on which this minute was placed, was confidentially destroyed on the orders of Eamon de Valera on 25 May 1940. The register of files in the Department of Foreign Affairs Archives shows that the file ran from 16 June 1938 to 11 February 1939.

[2] Not printed. The minute can be found on file 102/453 at the National Archives, Dublin.

[3] Not located.

8. The twenty children will presumably enter one of the already overcrowded professions, thereby increasing the difficulty of making a living for the Irish students who have received the same education at the expense of their families. These objections to the admission into Ireland of young persons were recognized by the Minister in the case of Buchholz (see minute of 13th October 1938, 102/427).[1]

I have put forward these considerations in some detail in the hope that they will be of assistance to the Minister for Justice in connection with the carrying out of the scheme of the Coordinating Committee and because they have to my knowledge been submitted by various Ministers accredited in Berlin to their respective governments in connection with similar schemes. I shall be glad to have full instructions as to what steps should be taken in order to avoid the various difficulties which I have outlined above.

I should like to add in conclusion that I should much regret if it were thought that I was in any way lacking in sympathy towards Jews desirous of leaving Central Europe. I cannot however help feeling that when their interests are for the reasons above set out in obvious conflict with the interests of the people of Ireland, it is my duty, as it is that of all persons concerned, to subordinate all feelings of personal sympathy to the protection of Irish interests.

[signed] C. BEWLEY

No. 261 NAI DFA 219/4

Letter from Joseph P. Walshe to Charles Bewley (Berlin)
(Confidential) (Copy)
DUBLIN, 26 January 1939

The Minister will be glad to receive from you urgently a comprehensive report on the European situation so far as Germany is concerned and on what you consider to be the prospects of peace or war in the near future. The Minster is disappointed that no report on the international situation has been received from you since July 1938,[2] notwithstanding the gravity of the September crisis and the predominant part which is being taken by the German Government in a situation which might at any moment bring our government face to face with issues of vital importance to the Irish people.

[stamped] (Signed J.P. WALSHE)
Rúnaí

---

[1] File 102/427 'Permission for German Student Son of Frau Elsa Bucholz to attend Newtown School Waterford', was confidentially destroyed on the orders of Eamon de Valera on 25 May 1940. The register of files in the Department of Foreign Affairs Archives shows that the file ran from August to October 1938.

[2] A reference to a confidential report that Bewley sent to Dublin on 29 July 1938 entitled 'Position of the Sudeten Germans' (Berlin reference: 43/33). This document was put on file 119/1. File 119/1,'Confidential Reports from Berlin', was confidentially destroyed on de Valera's orders on 25 May 1940 when it was feared that a German invasion of Ireland was imminent. The file ran from 14 January 1937 to 7 December 1938.

No. 262 NAI DFA 227/4

Confidential report from Leopold H. Kerney to Joseph P. Walshe (Dublin)
(S.J. 19/1) (Confidential)
ST JEAN DE LUZ, 30 January 1939

The moment is perhaps opportune for examining afresh the question of our relations with Spain.

When direct diplomatic relations between Ireland and Spain were re-established in 1935, I was sent to Madrid as Minister Plenipotentiary and accredited to the President of the Spanish Republic who was at that time the uncontested head of the Spanish State. Subsequently, civil war was let loose, with the result that, in the place of the one Spain to which I was accredited, there were now two Spains – one under Republican control recognising President Azaña (the successor of President Alcala Zamora to whom I had presented my letters of credence) as head of the State, and the other under the control of Spaniards recognising General Franco as head of the State.

Our attitude has been that it is a matter for Spaniards themselves to decide as to who shall be head of the Spanish State and that, when their choice is beyond doubt, it is to the head of the State accepted by all Spain that an Irish Minister should be accredited, but that, pending the conclusion of the struggle between the two rival candidates, no positive step should be taken which might imply intervention by the Irish Government in a war in which the combatants on each side are Spaniards.

It seemed that the temporary closing of the Legation in Madrid, the temporary transfer of the Legation to non-Spanish territory, the consequent slackening of the ties between the Irish Legation and the Republican Ministry for Foreign Affairs, the continuation of relationship by correspondence with the Republican Government and the entering into relationship by correspondence with the Government of General Franco to the extent to which Irish interests had to be protected, were a clear indication of our impartial attitude in what was a family dispute, and that this attitude was in the true interests of both Ireland and Spain although certain to be criticised and possibly misjudged by the contending parties.

Certain countries sided definitely, and more or less openly, with one or other of the opposing regimes in Spain, although such countries subscribed to a non-intervention agreement. Others found it convenient, as time went on, to have official agents accredited to General Franco's Government, whilst continuing their diplomatic relations with Republican Spain; England set the lead in this respect, and those countries which followed her example were actuated largely by commercial, economic or financial considerations but also by the desire to follow closely the development of a situation in Spain which might have important international repercussions; in certain cases the agents appointed to Burgos were men of high military rank.

Ireland had no particular commercial, economic, financial or political interests necessitating the presence of an official Irish agent in the Spain that was under General Franco's control; it seemed that any questions which might arise concerning, for instance, the Irish College in Salamanca or the fate of Irish nationals in that part of Spain could be dealt with otherwise.

Prior to the establishment by various countries of official relations, on the English model, with insurgent or nationalist Spain, some of these countries would undoubtedly have recognised the Franco regime, at least de facto, if General Franco had succeeded in capturing Madrid, the seat of Government in Spain for centuries past.

The position which has now arisen is that Barcelona (the only city in Spain, other than Madrid, to have more than a million inhabitants) has fallen to Franco; it seems inevitable that republican resistance in the rest of Catalonia must soon be overwhelmed; the republican Government has temporary headquarters in Catalonia, but President Azaña is reported to be in Madrid; the odds are now so heavy against the republicans that an early general collapse, followed by the surrender of Madrid, is a possibility which has to be taken into consideration.

Would it not be advisable at this stage to go into the question with a view to our being ready to take action without loss of time in the event of the Spanish capital passing under General Franco's control in the immediate future? Can it be admitted that the fate of Madrid will be justification sufficient for the taking of a decisive step on our part? And, in this case, would it not be advisable that I should be instructed now to notify the Viscount de Mamblas, verbally if necessary but in any case without delay, that it is our desire to accord full diplomatic recognition (merely de facto recognition would be out of the question) to General Franco as soon as he is master of Madrid. It would, in my opinion, be a mistake to wait for that event to occur before moving in the matter; it may be taken as certain that most of these States that already have agents in Burgos will hasten to accord de jure recognition of the new regime immediately after the fall of Madrid. If we wait, we may find that the Irish Legation may be one of the last to be re-opened in Madrid. Any preliminary steps which may now be decided on should shorten the delay in my return to Madrid after the conclusion of hostilities, and it would of course be useful to make sure in advance that I would be persona grata to General Franco, although I have no reason to doubt that this would be the case.

I would recommend that this question should be given urgent consideration.

As mentioned in my report of 19/12/38,[1] nationalist Spain is recognised juridically by the Holy See and by two of the greater European Powers (Italy and Germany), by three other independent European States (Portugal, Hungary and Albania), by Japan and her protégé Manchukuo, and by three of the minor South American Republics (Guatemala, Salvador, Nicaragua).

Czechoslovakia is now said to have decided to grant de jure recognition to Franco, apparently as a result of the capture of Barcelona.

Therefore, as regards the smaller European States, there are four countries (Portugal, Hungary, Albania and Czechoslovakia) ahead of us, even if we were to give diplomatic recognition to Franco right away; this is of course not

---

[1] Not printed.

intended as an argument in favour of recognition but merely to recall to your mind the precise position as it is to-day.

[signed] L.H. KERNEY
Aire Lán-Chómhachtach

No. 263 NAI DFA 227/4

Memorandum from Joseph P. Walshe to Eamon de Valera on the recognition of General Franco's government in Spain
(Urgent)

DUBLIN, 4 February 1939

Recognition of General Franco's Government
Our position vis-à-vis Franco's Government would be described as de facto recognition. We have been in communication with that Government through his appointed agent at St. Jean de Luz for nearly two years.[1] In fact, our Spanish relations have been almost exclusively with Burgos. The British inform us this morning that the resistance in Catalonia is futile and cannot last long. Some of the leaders are already in France, and others in Valencia are seeking to ensure their safety in case of sudden collapse. The British have been informed by the French Minister for Foreign Affairs that a total Franco victory is imminent and that he is appointing an agent to Franco. In your speech in the Dáil of the 27th November 1936 you said:- 'If you recognise a new Government you should recognise it when there is some clear indication of stability, some clear indication that the Government will continue to be able to speak on behalf of the nation of which it is the Government. Everybody knows that if General Franco does become the head of a de facto Government in Spain he must immediately receive de facto recognition from those who have interests in Spain and who have therefore in regard to these interests to deal with some authority in Spain. … as a prudent rule recognition is not given before there is a fair hope of stability.'

We were informed by our Minister at St. Jean de Luz, and his information is confirmed by Press telegrams, that Ireland, Belgium, France, Russia, Lithuania and Latvia were the only countries not represented in Nationalist Spain. Since that report Franco's position has been considerably strengthened, and France and Belgium are sending diplomatic agents to Burgos immediately. We now find ourselves more or less isolated in the company of Russia, Lithuania and Latvia.

Full de jure recognition has been given to Franco only by the following 12 States:-

Holy See, Italy, Germany, Portugal, Hungary, Albania, Guatemala, Salvador, Nicaragua, Japan, Manchukuo, Czechoslovakia.

The question for us to decide is whether we shall give de jure recognition now or after the fall of Madrid. I fear that, if we wait for the fall of Madrid, we shall appear to be following the lead of France and Great Britain and their

---

[1] Viscount de Mamblas.

satellites, who no doubt will give de jure recognition in the near future for the purpose of winning Franco's favour and weaning him away from the Berlin-Rome axis. It might be better for us to get in before them and to recognise Franco immediately. In that way we shall be more likely to secure whatever special kudos or credit is to be got from advanced recognition. The fall of Madrid may be a long way off. It is now clear that Franco's army has refrained from making a really serious artillery attack upon it. As in the case of Barcelona, he does not want to destroy the city or to turn the people against him. He may therefore be content to force surrender by exhaustion. If we say now that we shall give recognition as soon as Madrid falls, we shall put ourselves into the position of having to wait until that event occurs, and we may find ourselves last in the race.

We have informed the British that we intend recognising Franco after the fall of Madrid. No reaction on their part has yet become apparent.

In all the circumstances, an early decision seems to be called for.

No. 264 NAI DFA 219/4

> *Letter from Charles Bewley to Joseph P. Walshe (Dublin)*
> *(43/33) (Copy)*
>
> BERLIN, 4 February 1939

I beg to acknowledge your minute of the 26th January 1939.[1] I much regret that the Minister should be disappointed at not having received a report on the international situation, and hope to send one when possible.[2]

[stamped] C. BEWLEY

No. 265 UCDA P194/550

> *Letter from Joseph P. Walshe to Michael MacWhite (Rome)*
> *(Confidential)*
>
> DUBLIN, 6 February 1939

Dear Michael,

I am very glad to see from your letter of the 2nd February[3] that you are feeling more optimistic about the European situation than you had been in previous letters. That feeling is reflected here. Some ten days ago we were all in the dumps, as all our information, especially the Press despatches in the 'Times' and the 'Telegraph', seemed to point to an early onslaught by Hitler in the West. It was difficult to accept that thesis completely, as one could not help realising the enormity of the catastrophe which was likely to follow a defeat, and the ultimate defeat of Germany seemed a certainty. We hear, as no doubt you do, that the material element in the German railway traffic system and in their factories is deteriorating. The financial and economic

---

[1] See above No. 261.
[2] See below No. 268.
[3] Not printed.

situation seems to be at least unfavourable for a warlike adventure, and if Hitler strikes now he will only do so because his internal situation has become so intolerable that only the external distraction of war can provide a remedy. Mussolini looked as if he might provide us with a sensation over the week-end, but fortunately, judging by the Press at any rate, he made no threats during the meeting of the Grand Fascist Council.

Of course, while Great Britain and Germany are arming at such a rate against each other the temptation must exist on both sides to finish the business once for all, and the danger and tension will continue to exist until some agreement is reached.

With all good wishes,
[signed] JOE

No. 266 NAI DFA Madrid Embassy 50/19

Letter from Joseph P. Walshe to Leopold H. Kerney (St Jean de Luz)
(Secret)
DUBLIN, 6 February 1939

Dear Mr. Kerney,
I have put your suggestion concerning the recognition of the Franco Government to our Minister (Your letter S.J.19/4 of 30th January).[1] He will require some little further time to consider it. If you were to inform the Count de Mamblas now that we should recognise his Government after the fall of Madrid, we might be putting ourselves in the position of being last in the race. The other countries concerned may decide to give recognition long before Madrid has actually fallen. However, if the Minister has to reply to a question in the Dáil on the matter within the next ten days, he will reply that the change in the situation in Spain naturally brings the issue of recognition to a head and that it is being considered by the Government. Having followed a non-interventionist attitude so far, the Minister does not want to give any impression of haste. I shall instruct you when a decision has been reached. You may take it that it will not be a long delay, and you could certainly begin to think of making remote preparations for your return to Madrid so soon as conditions allow you to do so.

There is a general feeling of relief here regarding the international situation, and the impression is gaining ground that the danger of war has at least become more remote. Ten days ago the feeling was one of extreme pessimism.

Yours sincerely,
[signed] J.P. WALSHE

---

[1] See above No. 262.

No. 267 NAI DFA 219/6

Confidential report from Michael MacWhite to Joseph P. Walshe (Dublin)[1]
(Confidential)

ROME, 8 February 1939

With the fall of Catalonia to the Nationalist forces one of the main danger spots in Europe seems to have been eliminated. The civil war in Spain is nearing its end and the granting of belligerent rights to Franco cannot be much longer delayed, after which the Republican forces may not count on further supplies from the outside world. This will not, however, mean the withdrawal of the Italian forces as was promised Chamberlain during his recent visit to Rome. The Duce now insists on a political as well as a military victory.

With the internment of some 200,000 of the Republican army in France the political situation has changed. In any future Franco-Italian negotiations these forces may play an important role. Unless they are returned to their native soil, they can always be held, like the sword of Damocles, over Franco's head, so it is necessary that their destiny be decided before the Italian Legion returns. This is how one awkward situation leads to another. It is also an indication that the Duce has not been satisfied by the results obtained from Chamberlain's visit. Something of a practical nature was expected that evidently has not materialised.

The internal situation in Italy is a cause of some concern at the moment. The factories in the big industrial centres of Milan and Turin are said to be working at little more than one-third capacity and the munition factories are barely marking time due mainly to the lack of raw materials. The workers are said by visitors from Northern Italy to be giving expression to their grievance more openly than has been the case since the march on Rome. The popularity of the Duce is, however, much higher than that of the Fascist Administrators.

I learned from a usually well informed source yesterday that during discussions preliminary to the renewal of Italian contracts for petrol with American, British and Dutch concerns, the Minister for Exchanges and Currency said he would only give his consent and signature for the purpose, on condition that the companies concerned placed credits for five million pounds sterling at his disposal immediately. Italy could get all her petrol requirements from Mexico and Venezuela in exchange for machinery and manufactured articles, but for these raw material is necessary and that has to be paid for in cash.

It was generally expected that at the meeting of the Fascist Grand Council on Saturday night the Duce would make a pronouncement on International questions, but to everybody's surprise he maintained silence. A diplomatic colleague assures me that earlier in the day he had a telephone conversation with the Fuhrer who advised prudence especially in regard to France. Roosevelt's supposed reference to the American frontier being on the Rhine

---

[1] Marginal annotation: 'Seen by Secy., SGM', 'Asst. Secy.' Marked seen by Frederick Boland.

has impressed the German leaders more than they would care to admit. They appeared to be convinced that American intervention in European affairs was absolutely impossible and were suddenly brought to a sense of the reality of the situation by the secret meeting of the Military Committee of the United States Senate.

Germany is coming closer to Russia in the hope, perhaps, that she could obtain some territorial concessions by negotiation, and it is noticeable that the Italian papers today say an Italo-Russian trade agreement is to be signed one of these days. This has been hanging fire for the last two years. On the other hand Russia knows that sooner or later she will have to fight Japan and when that time comes she wants her Western frontier free from embarrassments.

It is well within the scheme of things that Rumania will be the next victim of German drang nach Osten. The Iron Guard,[1] which is subsidised by German funds, is not dead notwithstanding the official killing of its leaders a few weeks ago. Its operations at the moment are said to be beneath the surface and therefore, all the more dangerous. Poland has got an assurance from Ribbentrop that her borders and the city of Danzig are safe for some time to come, at all events, and Ciano is to carry further consolation to Warsaw where he is expected towards the end of the month. His visit to Belgrade a few weeks ago was not very happy as it resulted in the overthrow of the Conservative Premier, Stoyadinovitch, and his replacement by another with Leftist tendencies. The former had come to some tentative agreements with Count Ciano which evidently displeased public opinion and provoked his downfall. It would seem the only East European country that has been avoided by the Rome-Berlin diplomats is Rumania. A part of Ukraine by a friendly arrangement with Russia and a part of Bessarabia by friendly or forceful methods, as the case may be, would make an excellent State, bounded by the Dneiper and the Danube, under German tutelage, and then there is the possibility that no shot need be fired in bringing it into existence. The danger of war is not so imminent as appeared some weeks ago.

[signed] M. MacWhite

No. 268 NAI DFA 219/4

Confidential report from Charles Bewley to Joseph P. Walshe (Dublin)[2]
(43/33)

BERLIN, 8 February 1939

It is at all times difficult to form a general view of the future of the international situation, which obviously depends not on the events taking place in one country or the attitude adopted by one government, but on the mutual interaction of events and policies in a number of different countries. In other

---

[1] The Legion of the Archangel Michael, also known as the Iron Guard, was the main fascist movement in Romania.

[2] This report was sent in response to No. 261 and No. 264 above. Marginal annotations: 'Secy'; 'Seen by Secy'; 'F.H.B'.

states, so far as I am aware without exception, it is the aim of the Ministry of Foreign Affairs to secure that its Ministers abroad shall be as well informed as possible; and for this purpose they are furnished at frequent intervals with the reports sent to their government from Legations in other countries. They are thus enabled to form an objective opinion of current events by comparing the reports so furnished them with the impressions which they receive in the country of their accreditation and by checking their impressions in the light of material thus made available to them. In the absence of such information their impressions must of necessity be incomplete; and it is only by virtue of a highly developed critical sense and a determination not to be unduly influenced by environment that I am able to attain that objectivity of which your minutes of 6th May 1937, 119/1,[1] and 23rd September 1937, 105/45,[2] you so rightly indicate the value.

Since the German Chancellor's speech in the Reichstag on 30th January the general opinion (in which I join) is that there is little danger of a war being brought about through Germany's action. His statement, 'I believe in a long peace', is further confirmed by the fact that the claim of the return of the German colonies, which he placed in the forefront of his demands, does not assume the form of an ultimatum, and obviously contemplated negotiations rather than a coup de main, as evidenced by the chain of argument on which it is based. Of course this does not exclude the possibility of a crisis on the colonial question in the future if England and France insist on the retention of 'mandated' territory on the same grounds which were advanced in 1919; but at the moment Germany obviously hopes to reach a settlement on a more or less friendly basis.

The only other suggestion of danger lies in the words referring to Germany's friendship with Italy, – 'a war started without reason from whatever motive against the Italy of to-day will summon Germany to the side of her friend' (the expression vom Zaun gebrochen cannot be literally translated, but undoubtedly implies an element of unreasonableness or wantonness). Here the actual words are in my opinion very far from promising help to Italy in every war in which the latter might choose to engage and have so been generally understood: moreover Germans, even in official positions, declare openly that they have not the slightest intention of entering a war in order to recover Tunis or Corsica for Italy. Even the juxtaposition in the speech of Germany's services to Italy in the Abyssinian War and Italy's return of Germany's friendship in 1938 would appear to be intended to imply that neither now owes anything to the other.

The only danger of war in the immediate future would thus appear to be a war of ideologies, – i.e., a war in which the authoritarian states would be on one side and the democratic states including Soviet Russia on the other. That such a war would be started by Germany is out of the question:

---

[1] This minute, along with the other documents on file 119/1 'Confidential Reports from Berlin', was confidentially destroyed on de Valera's orders on 25 May 1940 when it was feared that a German invasion of Ireland was imminent. The file ran from 14 January 1937 to 7 December 1938.

[2] This minute, along with the other documents on file 105/45 (later renumbered 214/8) 'Articles in the Irish Press uncomplimentary to Germany', was confidentially destroyed on an unknown date.

National Socialism, like Fascism, is essentially national and depends on race, and it would be a contradiction in terms for it to fight in order to convert other states to the doctrines of German nationalism, which according to those very doctrines they are incapable of appreciating. On the other hand, liberalism like communism is in its essence international, and, as has become increasingly evident in the last years, is intolerant of systems of government which do not pay at least lip-service to 'democratic' theories. This attitude does not appear to constitute a threat to the peace of the world.

Of course it would be ridiculous to suggest that the average Englishman or Frenchman desired a war for the purpose of establishing a democratic Government in Germany against the will of the German people. The panic in London in September 1938 and the hysterical relief at the Munich agreement far outweigh the warlike sentiments now being uttered in England in the comfortable knowledge that they will have no practical effect.

At the same time it should not be forgotten that in England and France, and even more in the United States of America, there exists a class of persons, many in influential positions, who desire war for an ideological pretext: German opinion divides them into persons with a commercial or financial interest in war, persons desiring a war for imperialistic reasons, persons desirous of avenging the special treatment of Jews in Germany, and persons who wish to see the triumph of Communism. The majority of the various categories referred to would in all probability not themselves take any share in the actual fighting.

As an example of the various motives mentioned above the German press adduces President Roosevelt and his advisers. It is pointed out that his friends Morgenthau[1] and Baruch[2] are both directly or indirectly connected with the munitions industry, that Jews hold many of the prominent positions in America today and that the Government and its advisers are without exception members or partisans of the Jewish race, that various ministers in America have done much to encourage Communism, and that President Roosevelt was, apart from the Communist President Azaña, the only head of a nominally Christian state who sent a telegram of congratulations to Stalin on the occasion of the twentieth anniversary of the Bolshevist Government.

It is also pointed out (in the French press as well as in the German) that on numerous occasions the same elements have done their utmost to bring about international crisis by the spreading of false rumours (landing of Germans in Morocco, fortification of positions overlooking Gibraltar, despatch of Italian regiments to Spain, etc., etc. (see my minute of 2nd June 1938, 43/33)),[3] by the garbling and mistranslation of speeches on the radio

---

[1] Henry Morgenthau Jr (1891-1967), United States Treasury Secretary (1934-45).

[2] Bernard Baruch (1870-1965), American financier and adviser to Presidents Wilson and Roosevelt.

[3] Possibly a reference to a confidential report that Bewley sent to Dublin on 2 June 1938 that was entitled 'German-Czechoslovakia situation' (Berlin reference: 43/33). The register of documents for this file shows no reference to a specific report on the situation in Spain, to which Bewley here refers. This document was put on file 119/1. File 119/1'Confidential Reports from Berlin', was confidentially destroyed on de Valera's orders on 25 May 1940 when it was feared that a German invasion of Ireland was imminent. The file ran from 14 January 1937 to 7 December 1938.

(omission of the moderate portions of Hitler's speeches in September in England and France, omission of the conciliatory portions of Chamberlain's speeches at the same time in France and in the German translation given by the B.B.C.), by the deliberate attempt to provoke a war psychosis (Roosevelt's suggestion that Germany, Italy or Japan were likely to attempt the invasion of America).

All these matters do not mean the immediate outbreak of war, but they undoubtedly maintain a state of international tension, as they are intended to do, and prevent the world from attaining a durable peace. Moreover, if the saner counsels of Chamberlain and Daladier were to be overruled, and a more or less official boycott of the authoritarian states were to be adopted, together with a blank refusal to discuss the return of the German colonies, it is not impossible that a war might result, in which Germany and Italy might be the nominal aggressors but the persons really responsible would be those who in the name of democracy denied them the means to live. This is in my opinion undoubtedly a danger, and would become a grave one if governments presided over by, say, Messrs. Blum and Eden were to come into power in France and England.

To sum up as shortly as possible: Germany, as stated by the Chancellor in his recent speech, is devoid of many raw materials and food stuffs. To obtain these, either (1) she must have colonies, or (2) she must import – which implies corresponding exportation. If she is refused colonies and deprived of the power of exporting, she cannot live; and obviously the danger of war would be a very imminent one. If on the other hand the question of colonies and raw materials is regulated in accordance with the principle of justice, I can see no reason why the world should be in any imminent danger of war.

[signed] CHARLES BEWLEY

No. 269 NAI DFA 227/4

Code telegram from the Department of External Affairs to Leopold H. Kerney
(St Jean de Luz) (No. 3) (Secret) (Copy)
DUBLIN, 10 February 1939

Please inform Burgos Government immediately that Government of Ireland recognize them de jure as from receipt of that communication. Arrange for simultaneous publication here and in Burgos of fact of recognition and inform us by wire. Inquire to whom your Credentials should be addressed and exact style of addressee and wire full information.

ESTERO

No. 270 NAI DFA Madrid Embassy 50/1

Code telegram from Leopold H. Kerney to the Department of
External Affairs (Dublin)
(No. 21) (Copy)

St Jean de Luz, 11 February 1939

Your telegram No. 3[1] I have handed to Mamblas this morning note addressed to Jordana informing latter of decision to give immediate de jure recognition and requesting early simultaneous publication of decision in each country. In covering letter I have requested Mamblas to telephone contents of note to Burgos so that recognition may take effect from today's date and with view agreeing to publication in Monday's Irish and Spanish newspapers. I have requested Mamblas to give full style of Franco as head of state and also to ascertain whether I am persona grata. Owing to difficulties of communication definite reply may not reach me till tomorrow Sunday but Mamblas considers we may take agreement approved as regards publication Monday.

No. 271 NAI DFA Secretary's Files 103/39

Letter from Joseph P. Walshe to John W. Dulanty (London)
(Copy)

Dublin, 14 February 1939

The Minister wishes you to make an early appointment with Sir Thomas Inskip[2] for the purpose of informing him that as a matter of courtesy the Minister for External Affairs wishes to let him know that he is considering a change in the existing form of the Irish passport. The request page would read as follows:-

'I, the undersigned, Minister for External Affairs of Ireland, hereby request all whom it may concern to permit safely and freely to pass, and in case of need to give all lawful aid and protection to .... a citizen of Ireland.

Given under my Hand and Seal at Dublin.'

The first page of the passport would carry simply the description of the bearer with the heading 'Passport', and underneath 'Ireland'.

The model being followed generally is the United States passport, a copy of which is attached.

Sir Thomas Inskip will agree that the association of the States of the Commonwealth is bound as time goes on to depend less and less on the use of forms and symbols and more and more on the real advantages, social and economic, which the individual States may derive from it. These forms and symbols have very little binding force in themselves. They may even have the opposite effect, and in the case of Ireland they do definitely create antagonisms and discontent which tend to make isolation from the Commonwealth

---

[1] See above No. 269.
[2] Inskip was Secretary of State for Dominion Affairs from January to September 1939.

group a desirable aim of all Nationalists. Ireland is the only member of the association in which the form of the Request Page of the passport is opposed to the will of the majority of the people, and the people do not understand why they should have to accept such a humiliating position. It is not necessary to recall that the King in Ireland is ineradicably associated in the minds of our generation with domination and ascendancy. The proclamations and the laws (down to the year 1921) intended to suppress the aspirations of the Irish people were issued in his name, and the continued use of it in the passport can have no other result than to perpetuate bitter memories between the two countries. The Irish Government, in proposing to eliminate it from the Request Page of the passport, feel sure they are taking a step which is not only in accordance with the will of the Irish people, but which will also remove another obstacle in the way of friendly relations with England.

In relation to the whole position of the passport, you should have in mind that originally the request was issued by the Governor-General in the name of the King and that the description 'British Commonwealth of Nations' did not appear. We had refused to describe our citizens as British subjects, and the Dominions Office thereupon succeeded in getting instructions issued to all British consular and diplomatic posts refusing their services to holders of Irish passports. Such persons, however, could be granted facilities if they surrendered their Irish passport and accepted instead a British passport on which they were described as British subjects. In 1929 we adopted the British form for the Request Page, and we are still the only member of the association except Great Britain in which the request is made by the Minister for External Affairs. We inserted the description 'British Commonwealth of Nations' on the first page and used 'Citizen of the Irish Free State' to describe our nationals. The British, on their side, cancelled the instruction. You will note that the chief point in relation to the new form of the passport is that the name of the King is being omitted from the Request Page and the description 'British Commonwealth of Nations' from the first page. The adoption of the new form follows the Government's general policy of removing from the relations between the two countries anything which might constitute an obstacle to co-operation and friendship.

You will remember that when the Duke of Devonshire was passing through Dublin on Tuesday, 31st January, the Minister spoke to him at length about this matter. Perhaps you should begin by asking him whether he has communicated the Minister's intentions to Sir Thomas Inskip.

[copy letter unsigned]
Rúnaí

No. 272 NAI DFA Secretary's Files S103/39

Letter from John W. Dulanty to Sir Thomas Inskip (London)
LONDON, 16 February 1939

Dear Secretary of State,
Further to our conversation on the 7th February when I handed you a note on the question of Police information raised in your note on the 31st January,

your Police authorities at Scotland Yard have since made inquiries of our Chief Commissioner in Dublin[1] about the identity of certain persons (whose photographs were forwarded) held in custody in England on suspicion of having participated in the recent bomb incidents. My Government feel that the position of our Guards – whose effectiveness must depend not a little on popular support – would be seriously undermined if persons already detained in England on suspicion of having participated in what they and their friends would describe as acts of political violence were sentenced to terms of imprisonment in England on information supplied from Ireland. The Irish Police Authorities will certainly do their best to keep the British Police informed of anything which might be necessary to prevent the commission of acts of violence in Great Britain. If, however, our police had to make enquiries relating to the antecedents or associations or movements in Ireland of Irish persons arrested in England in the circumstances under consideration, the sympathy of the ordinary country people which is so necessary for them in the detection of ordinary crime would be alienated.

There is moreover, the risk of serious ill-feeling being engendered against the Irish Police which might have grave consequences.

Yours sincerely,
[signed] J.W. DULANTY

No. 273 NAI DFA Secretary's Files S103/39

Confidential report from John W. Dulanty to Joseph P. Walshe (Dublin)
(No. 9) (Secret)

LONDON, 16 February 1939

Last evening I informed Sir Thomas Inskip that the Minister had instructed me to inform him, as a matter of courtesy, that a change would shortly be made in the existing form of our passport. The details of and the reasons for this change, as set out in the minute which I received from you yesterday,[2] I explained to Sir Thomas Inskip.

He said that whilst he agreed that the less the association of the States called the British Commonwealth depended on forms the better, he gravely doubted whether we were right in thinking that changes of this character would help forward a friendly relationship in England. He feared it would have the opposite effect. It was a step in the wrong direction, more particularly so far as the removal of Partition was concerned, since it would increase the difficulties of the British in trying to get the Six County people into a state of mind which would make some solution possible.

His own hope was that after the Agreement of last year a new chapter might have been opened in which we might have seen the King in his true position today as a monarch acting only on advice. He thought it was the politicians rather than the Kings who are to be blamed for the happenings of the past. The Commonwealth group represented a system of freedom which

---

[1] Michael Kinnane, Garda Commissioner (1938-52).
[2] See above No. 271.

he thought would fall to pieces if it were not for its common centre, not of Authority but rather of sentiment.

I suggested that whilst there was doubtless a case for the people who sincerely felt the sentiment of English Kingship there was nothing to be said for a people like ourselves proclaiming a sentiment which we did not feel. Sir Thomas Inskip agreed and said that it was not so much regretting our leaving the King out of the passport, which was as we had contended only a form, but the fact that we had not the feeling of respect for the King of which the form was but the expression.

What he feared was that even people in his own party who were well disposed towards our Government and were ready to recognise the realities of the situation would ask him where this process was going to stop.

The impression which I formed from this conversation was that Sir Thomas Inskip did not feel that the change presented any great difficulty but that he would have to endure over it a certain amount of embarrassment from the Diehards in the Six Counties and also in this country.

[signed] J.W. DULANTY
High Commissioner

No. 274 NAI DFA Paris Embassy P5/5

Telegram from Joseph P. Walshe to the Irish Legation in Paris
DUBLIN, 17 February 1939

Unnumbered for your information following statement is being given by the Minister to associated press tonight.

Begins: 'The desire of the Irish people and the desire of the Irish government is to keep our nation out of war. The aim of the government policy is to maintain and preserve our neutrality in the event of war. The best way to and the only way to secure our aim, is to put ourselves in the best position possible to defend ourselves, so that no one can hope to attack us, or violate our territory with impunity. We know, of course, that should an attack come from a power other than Great Britain, Great Britain, in her own interests must help us to repel it. Mr. de Valera said that the Irish government had not entered into any commitments with Great Britain. His government was free to follow any course that Irish interests might dictate. Statement will be circulated in the press'.

No. 275 UCDA P150/2183

Memorandum from Joseph P. Walshe to Eamon de Valera
(Secret)
DUBLIN, 22 February 1939

The British note handed to the High Commissioner by Sir Edward Harding of the Dominions Office on the 31st January was accompanied by a memorandum containing a summary of information regarding the recent acts of violence committed in Great Britain. The following is the exact text of the note:-

'The attached memorandum[1] contains a summary of information regarding the recent outrages committed in this country. It will be seen that the grounds are given for supposing that these outrages are the result of activities organised by the Irish Republican Army in Dublin.

It is hoped that, in the light of the information now supplied, the Government of Éire will be prepared *to take such steps as may be practicable and necessary to prevent the organisation in Dublin of further criminal activities in the United Kingdom,*[2] and in particular, to authorise the Police authorities in Éire to communicate immediately to the Police authorities in the United Kingdom *any information which may from time to time be available to them with the object of assisting the prevention of further outrages.'*[3]

The note takes it for granted that the acts in question were organised in Dublin, and, in asking us to take such steps as may be practicable and necessary to prevent the organisation in Dublin of such activities in the United Kingdom and to authorise our police authorities to communicate to the British police authorities any information available with the object of assisting the prevention, the British Government have not departed from normal practice. Indeed, in all the circumstances, the note is very mild.

On the 3rd February, we instructed the High Commissioner as follows:-
'With reference to the Dominions Office memorandum enclosed with your note of the 1st February, the Minister wishes you to inform the British Government as follows:-

"With a view to helping to prevent the commission of acts of violence in the United Kingdom by persons living within their jurisdiction, the Irish Government have given instructions to their police authorities to communicate to the United Kingdom police authorities any information coming to their knowledge which might be useful for that purpose."'

Perhaps a general statement on the question could be made on the following lines:-

'We were informed by the British that they had grounds for supposing that certain recent acts of violence were the result of activities organised by the Irish Republican Army in Dublin, and we were asked to take such steps as might be practicable and necessary to prevent the further organisation here of such activities in Great Britain. We were requested, moreover, to authorise our police authorities to communicate to the British police authorities any information available to them which would assist in the prevention of the activities mentioned.

We informed the British Government that we had instructed our police authorities to communicate to the United Kingdom police authorities any information which would help prevent the commission of acts of violence in Great Britain by persons living within the jurisdiction of the Irish

---

[1] Marginal addition by Walshe to the text at this point in pen: 'In the Dept. of Justice is a summary of charges against persons brought before court'.
[2] These words have been underlined in pen.
[3] These words have been underlined in pen.

Government. In so doing, we were following the principle of international law in virtue of which it is the duty of every State to refrain from any act designed to encourage terrorist activities directed against another State, and to prevent the acts in which such activities take shape.'

[initialled] J.P.W.

No. 276 UCDA P150/2183

Memorandum from Joseph P. Walshe to Eamon de Valera
(Secret)

DUBLIN, 22 February 1939

Protest by German Chargé d'Affaires

The German Chargé d'Affaires, Herr Thomsen, came to see me by appointment this morning (Wednesday, 22nd February). He began by remarking that, although he liked the nice Spring weather, he found the people not so congenial as the Norwegian people amongst whom he had just been living. The reason for that was that the Norwegians were a Protestant people, and the Irish were almost exclusively Catholic, and, for that reason, dominated by the Clergy.

After this somewhat surprising and impudent beginning, he showed me a newspaper report of the Pastoral of Dr. Browne, Bishop of Galway[1] with a sentence marked in which the latter accuses Germany of violence, lying, murder and the condemning of other races and people. He proceeded to say that Dr. Brown had no right to discuss Germany's affairs. Moreover, it should be remembered that any measures taken against the Catholic Clergy in Germany were very largely due to the immorality of the priests. Germany's aim was to confine the Church to its own sphere, and to prevent the Clergy interfering in matters affecting the State exclusively.

The Chargé d'Affaires then produced a copy of the 'Irish Press' of Tuesday, 21st February, containing a leader attacking the anti-Christian element in German State doctrine and practice. As this paper was controlled by the Government Party, the Government would have to accept some responsibility for these attacks on Germany. The Government should remember that there were a great many things in Ireland which could be criticised by Germany, e.g., the extreme poverty of large numbers of the people, and the absence of any organised effort to remedy it.

I gave all the usual replies, and a little more, to this outburst, but I was careful to let him run his full length before replying, as it seemed to my mind important to get to know the type we have to deal with in Herr Thomsen. He is a complete contrast to Dr. Hempel, the German Minister, who – although sometimes lacking in a sense of humour – never allows you to forget that he is a cultured gentleman. Herr Thomsen is insolent, bombastic, and apparently devoid of any sense of the real values of life. He is the first German I have met who seems to combine in himself all the worst ideas behind the Nazi regime.

---

[1]   Michael John Browne (1895-1980), Bishop of Galway (1937-76).

At the end of our conversation, I suggested to him, as I have frequently done to his Minister and his Minister's predecessor, that the ~~setting up~~[1] existence of a Nazi organisation in Dublin, no doubt representing the views he had expressed to me in the course of our interview and having as its chief member and organiser an employee of our State, was not calculated to improve relations between our two Governments. I could hardly imagine his Government tolerating a similar organisation in Germany. He answered, not quite in so many words, that the Nazi organisation in Dublin was really none of our business.

In my previous talks with the German representatives during the last three years, I endeavoured to convince them in the most friendly fashion that, as the measures against the Catholic Clergy in Germany increased in severity, antagonism was bound to develop here. In time our Catholic people and Clergy would begin to make public protests and the Government would be placed in a very awkward situation when the position of Dr. Mahr,[2] Director of the National Museum, as head of the Nazi Cell in Dublin, became a matter of public controversy. Dr. Hempel told me, in July, 1938, that Dr. Mahr was resigning from his leadership of the Cell, and I understand that Dr. Mahr so informed the Minister for Education[3] about the same time. However, so recently as December last, Dr. Hempel told me that Dr. Mahr had not yet resigned his position in the organisation owing to unforeseen difficulties, but was about to do so immediately, and that he was to be replaced in that position by Herr Mecking,[4] who is an employee of the State (at least indirectly) under the Turf Board.

After Dr. Brown's Pastoral, we may expect an increase in anti-Nazi feeling and protests, and Dr. Mahr's position cannot fail to be brought into question at an early date. No ordinary Civil Servant is allowed to be a member of a political organisation, and it could not be regarded as an injustice if Dr. Mahr were ordered to cease his membership of the Nazi Cell.

[signed] J.P. WALSHE

No. 277 UCDA P194/537

Confidential report from Michael MacWhite to Joseph P. Walshe (Dublin)[5]
(Confidential)

ROME, 22 February 1939

More Italian reservists have been called to the colour this month for training purposes. At the same time the Italian troops in Libya, whose effectives were

---

[1] This word has been crossed out by Walshe.
[2] Dr Adolf Mahr (born 1887), Keeper, Irish Antiquities Division, National Museum (1927-34), Director, National Museum (1934-39), head of the Dublin Branch of the Nazi Party's Auslandsorganisation (1934-38).
[3] Thomas Derrig (1897-1956), Minister for Education (1932-Sept. 1939), Minister for Posts and Telegraphs (Sept. 1939); Minister for Lands (Sept. 1939-43).
[4] Heinz Mecking (died 1945), Expert Adviser to the Turf Development Board (1936-39). Mecking had joined the NDSAP in 1931; he was head of the Nazi organisation in Dublin from June to September 1939. He later joined the German army and served on the Eastern front.
[5] Marginal annotations: 'File with ~~A/Secy~~ Dr Rynne.', 'Seen by Secy.', 'A/Secy.', 'Dr Rynne' 'M.R. 1/3/39'. Document marked as seen by Joseph P. Walshe and Frederick H. Boland.

reduced to about half strength in accordance with the promise given the British Ambassador on the occasion of the signature of the Italo-British accord, have now been increased to 70,000 and may be increased still more. The French are said to have 100,000 men occupying the Daladier line on the Tunis-Tripoli frontier.

Anti-British feeling in the Italian press is gradually growing. Chamberlain's umbrella has now become a blunderbuss, a sword and a stiletto and British diplomacy would no doubt be described as Machiavellian if it were permissible to associate an Italian name with such dubious methods. America is, however, coming in for most of the hard knocks and Roosevelt is referred to as a war monger.

Until a few weeks ago the Totalitarian States were convinced that the United States had definitely turned her back on Europe and that nothing would tempt her again to intervene in affairs on this side of the Atlantic. It came as a great shock to them to discover that, on the contrary, Roosevelt was giving moral and material aid to France and Britain in such a way as could leave no further room for doubt. As their eyes are being opened, their cries are becoming less strident.

One of the spokesmen of the Foreign Office in a recent article said it was immaterial whether Roosevelt spoke about the Rhine frontier or not as the essential thing was the state of mind revealed by the resulting discussion. Further he said 'the mechanism which leads to a "war for democracy" is beginning to go into action and American spiritual rearmament is more serious than her enormous material rearmament'. This fear of American intervention is another factor in the preservation of Peace in Europe.

[signed] M. MacWhite

No. 278 NAI DFA Madrid Embassy 50/19

Extract from a letter from Leopold H. Kerney to Joseph P. Walshe (Dublin)
(S.J. 50/12) (Copy)
St Jean de Luz, 24 February 1939

With reference to our recognition of General Franco and to your telegram No. 6 of 23rd inst.[1] advising me that my credentials would be forwarded within a few days, I have requested the Viscount de Mamblas to make the necessary arrangements for instructions to be given to the Spanish officials at the frontier at Irún so that not only myself but also Mrs. Kerney and Miss Donnelly may be allowed to pass into and out of Spain without any question.

I propose to pay a visit to San Sebastian on Monday 27th inst. and to call at the Ministerio de Jornada there and discuss matters with Mr. Castillo, who is a sort of Agent de liaison between the Government and the Diplomatic Corps. Subsequently, on receipt of my credentials, I will again see Mr. Castillo and request him to ascertain the precise date on which I may present

---

[1] Not printed.

my credentials in Burgos. It will no doubt be necessary on the occasion of my visit to Burgos to take Miss Donnelly with me so that she may assist me in arranging certain protocollary visits etc.; I am not certain at the moment whether Mrs. Kerney's presence will be necessary.

The headquarters of the Legation will have to be established in San Sebastian and, from enquiries which I have made, I am satisfied that the most suitable address will be the Hotel Maria Cristina, where I trust it may be possible for me to secure accommodation.

[matter omitted]

No. 279 UCDA P194/550

> *Letter from Joseph P. Walshe to Michael MacWhite (Rome)*
> *(Confidential)*
>
> DUBLIN, 25 February 1939

The Minister, accompanied by myself and Captain Brennan,[1] will leave Dublin on Tuesday, the 7th March, for Rome. He will spend Wednesday night in Paris, and will leave there by the evening train on Thursday, arriving in Rome on Friday evening. We are presuming that the crowning will take place on Sunday, the 12th March.

It is the Minister's intention to remain in Rome for two or three days for the purpose of seeing the new Pope.

During the Minister's stay in Rome, he would like to have an opportunity of a chat with Lord Perth, for whom, as you know, he has a very high esteem. I have written to the Minister to the Vatican[2] on this question, and have suggested that he get in touch with you to consult as to the best way of arranging the meeting.

The question will also arise of a visit by the Taoiseach to Signor Mussolini. Would you please also consult with the Minister to the Vatican on this matter and make the arrangements accordingly.

The Minister intends going to Zurich from Rome in order to see Dr. Vogt, and he will probably spend a day or two there.

If there are any points you wish to know, or suggestions to make, please write or telegraph.

[signed] J.P. WALSHE
Rúnaí

---

[1] De Valera's Aide de Camp.
[2] William J. B. Macaulay.

No. 280 UCDA P194/537

Confidential report from Michael MacWhite to Joseph P. Walshe (Dublin)
(Confidential) (Copy)

ROME, 28 February 1939

In reference to your cable No. 8 of yesterday's date[1] and to your confidential minute of the 25th instant[2] relative to the visit of the Taoiseach to Rome next week for the Coronation of the Pope, I forwarded you the following telegram today:

'Must visit to Duce be after audience with Pope as colleague insists. If so advisable take no steps about it before arrival here as question of protocol in that respect is highly delicate'.

I discussed the matter at some length with Mr. Macaulay who says that as Taoiseach is coming here specially for the Coronation it would be deeply resented at the Vatican if he called on the Duce before the principal functions connected with his mission have been completed. These include an audience with the new Pope which may not be accorded for two or three days after the Coronation.

On the other hand, it is well known that the Duce does not appreciate visitors who subordinate their calls to the convenience of the Vatican. When he was Minister for Foreign Affairs he is said to have tolerated a few of that nature, but now that he has relinquished that office he is more difficult of access. As nobody knows his mind, it might not be prudent to say anything too far in advance of the Taoiseach's desire to visit him as the day before or the day after the Coronation might be suggested which would, of course, be most embarrassing.

[unsigned]

No. 281 NAI DFA Secretary's Files A20/1

Letter from Frederick H. Boland (for Joseph P. Walshe) to Leopold H. Kerney
(St Jean de Luz)
(144/35A)

DUBLIN, 11 March 1939

The Minister wishes you to take the opportunity of your forthcoming visit to Burgos to make personal representations to General Jordana about the case of Mr. Frank Ryan. You might say that, on the inauguration of formal diplomatic relations with the new Spanish State, the Irish Government desire to make a strong and urgent appeal to General Franco for Mr. Ryan's release. Such a gesture at this time would be highly appreciated not only by the Irish Government but by the Irish people generally.

Perhaps you would also find it possible, while in Burgos, to make enquiries about the fate of Andrew O'Toole.[3] O'Toole's father informs us that

---

[1] Not printed.
[2] See above No. 279.
[3] See also Nos 232, 295 and 315.

he wrote recently to the Duke of Alba and received a reply saying that his son was not amongst the 'prisoners of war' in General Franco's hands. Mr. O'Toole appreciates that the boy, if arrested on a desertion charge, would not be treated as a prisoner of war, but he is very uneasy about the lack of official confirmation of your information about the boy's arrest.

[signed] F.H. BOLAND
Rúnaí

No. 282 NAI DFA 219/4

Confidential report from Charles Bewley to Joseph P. Walshe (Dublin)[1]
(43/33)

BERLIN, 15 March 1939

Recent events in Czechoslovakia have succeeded one another with a so bewildering rapidity that it is difficult to keep track of the episodes which have led up to the present crisis. However, the broad principles are clear and worth recording.

I had long ago reported on the origin of the dispute between Czechs and Slovaks (see report of 3rd May 1938, 43/33).[2] Up to the crisis of September 1938, in consequence of the refusal of the Czechs to fulfil their promise that Slovakia should enjoy full autonomy under the Pittsburgh Agreement,[3] relations had become strained almost to breaking point. The Catholic population of Slovakia resented more and more the anti-Catholic policy of the Czech Government (see report of 9th July 1938, 43/33)[4] and in particular the freedom given to Masonic and Bolshevist propagandists. Both the German and Polish Governments looked with sympathy on the Slovak claims; Poland especially owing to the fact that Slovakia was being used as a base for Communist propaganda in Poland (see report of 1st June 1938, 43/33).[5] A

---

[1] Marginal annotations: 'Secy'; 'FHB 20/3'; 'Seen M.R. 21.3.39'.
[2] A reference to a confidential report that Bewley sent to Dublin on 3 May 1938 that was entitled 'German-Czechoslovakia situation' (Berlin reference: 43/33). This document was put on file 119/1. File 119/1'Confidential Reports from Berlin', was confidentially destroyed on de Valera's orders on 25 May 1940 when it was feared that a German invasion of Ireland was imminent. The file ran from 14 January 1937 to 7 December 1938.
[3] In 1918 Czech statesman Thomas Masaryk had signed an agreement at Pittsburgh, USA, with American Slovaks promising Slovaks autonomy in a Czechoslovak state. Ultimately a centralised government ran Czechoslovakia and the Slovaks did not gain their autonomy.
[4] A reference to a confidential report that Bewley sent to Dublin on 9 July 1938 that was entitled 'German minority in Czechoslovakia' (Berlin reference: 43/33). This document was put on file 119/1. File 119/1'Confidential Reports from Berlin', was confidentially destroyed on de Valera's orders on 25 May 1940 when it was feared that a German invasion of Ireland was imminent. The file ran from 14 January 1937 to 7 December 1938.
[5] A reference to a confidential report that Bewley sent to Dublin on 1 June 1938 that was entitled 'German – Czechoslovakia situation' (Berlin reference: 43/33). This document was put on file 119/1. File 119/1'Confidential Reports from Berlin', was confidentially destroyed on de Valera's orders on 25 May 1940 when it was feared that a German invasion of Ireland was imminent. The file ran from 14 January 1937 to 7 December 1938.

delegation of Slovaks in America came to Slovakia to press their claims on the Prague Government. The Slovak National Party of Father Hlinke demanded an independent state.

Under the compulsion of events, and with the knowledge that England and France did not propose to abide by their promises of support, the Czech Government offered to abide by the Pittsburgh Agreement, which it had disregarded for 20 years. Slovak opinion was divided between the party who stood for an independent Slovak republic and those who were satisfied to remain in association with the other members of the Czecho-Slovak group of nations, – the Czechs and the Carpatho-Ukrainians. The usual arguments against independence were employed by the moderate party, – that the economic life of Slovakia was so closely connected with that of the Czechs that separation would be economic suicide, that Slovakia was too poor to stand alone and that without Czech help it would infallibly fall a prey to some other state, that Czechs and Slovaks, though not identical, had become in the course of time very similar and were united by ties of language, intermarriage and association, that certain Slovaks, as the Minister Hodža,[1] had advanced to high positions in the Czecho-Slovak state, and that the Czechs, whatever their oppression might have been in the past, had experienced a change of heart in 1938 and would doubtless treat the Slovaks as equals. The National party did not believe in these arguments, but it considered it tactically prudent to give a trial to the system of association in a group of 'independent nations.'

Events had proved the justice of the attitude of the National party. As it had anticipated, association between a state so large, wealthy and economically developed as the Czech state and one so small and poor as Slovakia, and still more the Carpathian Ukraine, developed rapidly into a relation in which the Czechs claimed to be able to veto measures of which they did not approve in the other states, and an attempt was made to abolish the governments of both Slovakia and the Carpathian Ukraine and substitute for them ministers more amenable to the influence of Prague.

From the purely military point of view, Slovakia and the Carpathian Ukraine alone could not have resisted the Czech army for a week. Monsignor Tiso,[2] however, the successor of Father Hlinka as Slovak national leader and Minister-President of Slovakia in the Czechoslovak state, appealed for help to the German Chancellor, and, so far as I can ascertain, to the Polish Government. Together with the leading supporter Dr Durcanski he arrived in Berlin, where he presumably received promises of support, for on his return to Pressburg he convoked the Slovak parliament, which unanimously declared Slovakia an independent republic. In his declaration Monsignor Tiso has emphasised the Catholic character of his government, and announced the introduction of new legislation dealing with the Jewish

---

[1] Milan Hodža (1878-1944), Slovak politician and journalist, Prime Minister of Czechoslovakia (1935-8).
[2] Jozef Tiso (1887-1947), Catholic priest, leader of the Slovak People's Party, later President of the pro-Nazi Slovak Republic of 1939-45.

problem on German lines. In the meantime Hungarian forces have entered the Carpathian Ukraine, which they will presumably completely occupy and annex. The population of this territory consists of only about one half million, and is among the poorest and most backward in Europe. It possesses no towns, and the capital Chust is a village. By race it is Slav, but with little resemblance to the Czechs, from whom it differs further in being strongly Catholic and anti-Communist. In any event, after the liberation of Slovakia it would be impossible for the Czechs to remain politically united with a district physically separated from their territory, so that incorporation in Hungary would appear to be the best solution to the problem, and is, so far as can be ascertained, probably in accordance with the wishes of the population, which is obviously for economic and cultural reasons incapable of forming an independent state.

As regards the Czech provinces of Bohemia and Moravia, their future has been settled by the action of the Czech president Dr Hacha in 'placing the fate of the Czech people and land confidently in the hands of the leader of the German Reich'. The Fuehrer in accepting the declaration of the Czech president has undertaken to guarantee to the Czech people an autonomous development of its national life. How this will work out in the future is a matter on which prophecy would be difficult.

Apart from the fate of the former Czechoslovak republic, the most significant feature of the whole series of events is the complete disregard by all parties of the western democracies. That the prestige of England and France had fallen in September 1938 was clear; it could have been in part restored by a demonstration that their Munich policy had been dictated by a genuine and disinterested desire for peace and not by mere military weakness, but by the subsequent conduct of the English and French Governments, influenced in each country by the official opposition and the fear of popular opinion has convinced not only Germany but the other states of Central Europe that they were willing to wound but afraid to strike, and the estimation in which they are held at present is the inevitable consequence of their failure in every international crisis to abide by their pledges when the fulfilment of such pledges might involve them in danger. The events of the last few days will go far to convince the remaining countries of middle and eastern Europe that democracy as a political system can only lead to weakness and eventually disaster.

[signed] CHARLES BEWLEY

No. 283 NAI DFA 219/7

> *Extracts from a confidential report from Francis T. Cremins*
> *to Joseph P. Walshe (Dublin)*
> *(Copy) (Confidential)*
>
> GENEVA, 20 March 1939

With regard to the present international situation, I have to report that following the events in Czechoslovakia, a state amounting to alarm prevails amongst the population here, and in Switzerland generally, which has hardly been assuaged by the terms of the statement on the situation which was broadcasted on Saturday, 16th March, by M. Etter,[1] President of the Confederation. I attach a copy of the statement.

[matter omitted]

The reactions of the democratic Powers are, I think, welcomed here, but they bring home to the people the diminishing possibility of a peaceful settlement, and therefore the increasing danger in which the small Western States would find themselves in the event of war.

[matter omitted]

The question on everyone's lips here is what will be Germany's next move. Some think that the question of Memel will flare up. Others, that the ball will be passed to Mussolini. It is said that in Italy amongst the population the *axe* is not at all too popular and that the Italian people will not appreciate being dragged to the verge of war for gains which all seem to go to Germany. Italy therefore may be tempted to take a risk in order to have something to show for her membership of the *axe*. Signor Mussolini's speech on the 26th March is looked forward to as an indication of possible developments in the Mediterranean.

[matter omitted]

No. 284 NAI DFA Paris Embassy 19/34

Confidential report from Seán Murphy to Joseph P. Walshe (Dublin)
(P. 19/34) (Copy) (Confidential)

PARIS, 20 March 1939

You will be aware that the reaction in France in regard to the events of last week has been very strong. In its note of protest to the German Government, the French Government has stated that it cannot recognise the legitimacy of the occupation of Moravia, Ruthenia and Slovakia and that it cannot accept that 'the state of fact recorded in the agreement of the 15th March between the German and Czech statesmen is given a foundation of right by this agreement'. The Government after the first day of uncertainty immediately asked for special powers to enable it to take by decree up to the 30th November next, the 'measures necessary for the defence of the country'. Although hotly debated by the Socialists and Communists in the Chamber, these powers were eventually granted by 321 against 264. In the Senate, as was anticipated, they were passed without delay by an overwhelming majority. M. Daladier has indicated that among the measures which he intends to take on the basis of these powers, a general modification of the 40 hour week so as to enable the defence industries to work at full pressure will figure prominently. He rejected a demand for a Government of National Union because the Socialists made it a condition of such a Government that he should leave.

Public opinion is mainly preoccupied with the direction in which Germany will move next. It is felt that unless she consents to arrest her advance towards the East, she must inevitably subordinate both Rumania

---

[1] Philip Etter (1891-1977), President of the Swiss Confederation (1939, 1942, 1947 and 1953).

and Hungary. Hungary is regarded as an extremely doubtful quantity and if anything as favourable to Germany in spite of the recent change in the Government there. The Nazi party is considered to be extremely powerful and likely to become more so and German consent to the occupation of Ruthenia by Hungary might bring her completely on the German side. On the other hand, in so far as the common Hungaro-Polish frontier is to be taken as meaning cooperation between these two countries rather than as representing the recovery by Hungary of a frontier which she regards as particularly hers some resistance to Germany will be expected. A further factor in regard to Hungary is the position of Italy which is thought to be particularly interested in Hungarian independence. Rumania will it is felt sure, resist if French and British support are forthcoming. The future position of Rumania, therefore, depends primarily on the consultations being undertaken by the British Prime Minister. In this connection it was commonly reported yesterday that there is a division of opinion in the British cabinet as to the line on which a definite stand should be taken up. It was suggested that one section of the Cabinet favours putting that line on Russia, the Dardanelles and Egypt and that the other and larger section which includes Lord Halifax, is in favour of making a stand on a line West of Rumania and taking in the Balkan countries. If she is not sure beforehand of the full backing of France and England there is little doubt that Rumania will give way in one form or another. At the same time it is confidently believed that during the visit of Mr. Gafencu,[1] the Rumanian Foreign Minister, to Warsaw last month an understanding was come to envisaging the constitution of a block of countries including Bulgaria which would oppose German expansion, it being agreed that if necessary for Bulgar support, Rumania would consent to transfer to Bulgaria part of Transylvania. Poland is regarded as favourable to France and England and to resistance in Germany. Russia, because of the recent British attitude of friendliness towards her is again counted upon as a major element in the present conjuncture. Italy's position is regarded as uncertain and there is a definite tendency to believe that if it should come to a general war, she would not back Germany fully or for long. The argument used is that Italy has gained very little from the existence of the axis and that German hegemony over Rumania and Hungary would considerably worsen Italy's situation. It has been suggested in the 'Journal' that if France were quickly to make an offer to Italy to constitute Djibouti as a free port, to give her further shares in the Djibouti railway, some seats on the Suez Canal Council and a more equal regime for the Italians in Tunis, she might bring Italy completely around to her side. It is felt, however, that the Italian standpoint will not be fully known until Mussolini speaks on the 26th March when it is expected he will deal, at least in principle, with Italian claims against France. The American reaction is finally regarded as of the greatest importance and the coincidence of the imposition by the U.S.A. of increased tariffs on German imports is thrown into high relief.

[stamped] (Signed) SEAN MURPHY

---

[1] Grigore Gafencu (1892-1957), Foreign Minister of Romania (1938-40).

No. 285 NAI DFA Secretary's Files 103/39

Confidential report from John W. Dulanty to Joseph P. Walshe (Dublin)
(No. 11) (Secret)

LONDON, 22 March 1939

Sir Thomas Inskip today handed to me the enclosed note dated 22nd March on the subject of our proposed amended form of passport. He said that although I had stated in my conversation with his on the 16th February that I thought the change had been decided upon, the letter which I handed to him[1] said that Mr. de Valera 'is considering a change in the existing form of Irish passport". The note he was now handing me was based on the hope that the question might be further considered. I think he regarded such a hope as rather remote.

He said that, as the Irish Government must be aware, a certain amount of ill-feeling had arisen about the large numbers of young Irishmen who were coming to England to secure employment. Sir Thomas Inskip feared that if and when the alteration in the form of the passport became known this feeling would be aggravated. The critics of his Government would contend that so far the British had treated these young men as coming from a country which was a member of the Commonwealth, but if the Irish Government proceeded with their proposal to omit the King's name from the form of the passport, the present state of public feeling to which he had referred would certainly grow stronger.

He thought that the proposed change would be bound to accentuate the difference between the Government of Éire and that of Northern Ireland.

I reminded Sir Thomas Inskip that at our meeting on the 16th February I informed him that I was making this intimation about the proposed change in the form of the passport as a matter of courtesy, since my Government regarded this matter as one for them to decide. I would make sure whether the change was actually in process and in any event I would of course acquaint the Taoiseach with Sir Thomas Inskip's views.

As an evidence of his genuine desire to avoid difficulties both for us and for them he mentioned that he had arranged to suspend the proposal of the British Air Ministry to set up an experimental firing range on the North East shores of Lough Foyle. He was, however, under the impression that when he discussed the matter with the Taoiseach in September last, the latter had said he would communicate further with him. I told Sir Thomas Inskip that I was present at the breakfast when this subject was discussed and all that the Taoiseach had said was that there might be a further discussion on his return from Geneva. It would be remembered that it had not been possible to arrange a further meeting on Mr. de Valera's homeward journey.

In the conversations of yesterday and the 16th February Sir Thomas Inskip had never even adumbrated the possibility of the British refusing the assistance of their Consular and diplomatic organisation to holders of the

[1] See above No. 273.

amended passports. My impression is that the disturbing incidents in the European situation in the last few weeks have relegated this passport question to the grade of minor importance. Sir Thomas Inskip hinted somewhat on these lines in apologising for the delay in replying to my note of the 16th February.

[signed] J.W. DULANTY
High Commissioner

No. 286 NAI DFA 219/6

Extract from a confidential report from Michael MacWhite to Joseph P. Walshe (Dublin)
(Confidential)

ROME, 23 March 1939

Notwithstanding the seriousness of the international situation provoked by the annexation of Bohemia and Moravia to the Reich[1] the Italian public, outwardly, show little emotion. Under the surface, however, the majority of them give expression to anti-German sentiment. In northern Italy, this is particularly pronounced.

Despite pretence to the contrary it is believed in well-informed circles here that the Duce had only post factum information on Hitler's designs on Czechoslovakia. Because of this apparent lack of candour he sent no message of congratulations to Berlin such as he forwarded to Budapest, nevertheless, on Wednesday morning, the Fascist Grand Council reaffirmed the solidarity of the partners in the Rome-Berlin axis. On Monday all Italian reservists between the ages of 32 and 39 were called to the colours. Heretofore, on occasions of alert, only the unemployed were drafted, but a more serious view was evidently taken of the present crisis. It has been asserted on good authority that the bulk of these troops were diverted towards Trentino rather than towards Piedmont as one might be inclined to conclude. If true, this is significant.
[matter omitted]

No. 287 NAI DFA 219/7

Letter from Frederick H. Boland (for Joseph P. Walshe) to Francis T. Cremins
(Copy)

DUBLIN, 27 March 1939

I am directed by the Minister to thank you for your report of the 20th instant on the international situation, which he has read with much interest.[2]

I am sending you, in accordance with your request, typed copies of the report for your files.

[stamped] (Signed) F.H. BOLAND

---

[1] The Czechoslovak provinces of Bohemia and Moravia were occupied by the Wehrmacht on 15 March 1939.
[2] See above No. 283.

No. 288 NAI DFA Madrid Embassy 50/15

Letter from Leopold H. Kerney to Joseph P. Walshe (Dublin)
(E.S. 50/15)

SAN SEBASTIAN, 7 March 1939

I would like to call your attention to the possibility which may present itself very shortly for me to visit Madrid for the purpose of inspecting the Legation premises there, of re-hoisting the Irish flag as a measure of protection and reporting on the condition in which I find State property left there when the Legation was temporarily closed down on 13th August 1936.

Certain foreign journalists expect to be allowed to enter Madrid immediately after the fall of the city, and some of these journalists have already provided themselves, in France, with food supplies likely to suffice for a fortnight or longer. It may be supposed that Ambassadors and Ministers accredited to Burgos will be given facilities for visiting the capital as soon as military requirements permit.

I feel that it may be your desire that I should take the first available opportunity of visiting Madrid, and, in this case, I would suggest that I should be so instructed immediately.

Any visit to Madrid should be of the shortest possible duration, living and sanitary conditions there being abnormal; I would have to take food and water supplies with me; I would have to billet myself in the Legation flat which cannot be in a very habitable condition; Madrid is a day's journey by road from San Sebastian; the checking of the Legation linen, china, glassware and other property would make it necessary for me to have the assistance of Miss Donnelly and desirable, for the sake of greater speed in checking and for the purpose of attending to our food requirements, that I should also be accompanied by Mrs. Kerney. I am of opinion that a minimum period of absence from San Sebastian would be 4 days, and it is clear that or stay in Madrid under present circumstances should not be one moment longer than is absolutely necessary.

If some time elapses between the fall of Madrid and my inspection of the Legation premises there, any violation of latter can be imputed to those who now hold Madrid in opposition to General Franco. I would therefore recommend that we should decide as to our attitude as soon as possible and in advance of events which may develop rapidly.

[unsigned]
Aire Lán-Chómhachtach

No. 289 NAI DFA 219/22

*Annual report on the work of the Irish Legation in Berlin for 1938-39
from Charles Bewley to Joseph P. Walshe (Dublin)[1]
(49/31)*

BERLIN, 28 March 1939

In reply to your minute of 18th March 1939, 219/22,[2] I beg to furnish the following report.

The Department is already aware that the promotion of trade between Ireland and Germany can only be effected by increased purchase of German goods in Ireland, and that, until the appropriate steps are taken for such increased purchase, this Legation can do nothing to increase German purchases of Irish goods, which are automatically regulated by the Irish purchases in Germany. For the convenience of the Department I enclose copy of my report (A) of 4th April 1938, 25/32,[3] in which the facts of the situation are fully set out and the possibilities of increasing trade with Germany are indicated. The situation has scarcely altered since last year; the ratio for 1938 of imports from other countries than Great Britain and Northern Ireland to exports to such other countries is 11.3:1; if imports to and exports from Germany are not counted it is 21.6:1. The various Departments concerned have no doubt considered whether all possible steps are being taken to secure alternative or additional markets to the British market.

It is worth while adding that I recently had a conversation with one of the Irish industrialists who habitually take part in the Leipzig Fair. He informed me that his business acquaintances in this country had on his recent visit to Leipzig informed him that they saw no reason why Germany should agree to take goods from Ireland in the proportion of 2 to 3 when Ireland made no effort to buy German goods and apparently was just as willing to buy from other countries such as Sweden which took nothing in return.

In addition, it should be remembered that under the new treaties with Slovakia, Lithuania and Roumania Germany will have more sources than she had in the past for the purposes of agricultural products, and that she will not be in the slightest dependent on Irish cattle, butter or eggs.

As regards matters other than trade, the request was made in a minute of 23rd September 1937 that I should send 'constructive suggestions as to what really should be my work in order to promote our interests in other than purely commercial circles.'[4] I replied by a minute dated 9th October 1937, 43/33,[5] pointing out what work was habitually done by other Ministers in Berlin and

---

[1] This document is marked as having been seen by Joseph P. Walshe.
[2] Not printed.
[3] Not located.
[4] See above No. 89.
[5] This minute, along with a later minute on the same subject sent by Bewley on 28 October 1937, is recorded as having been received in the Department of External Affairs and placed on file 105/45 (the file later being renumbered 214/8). This was confidentially destroyed on an unknown date.

elsewhere. I have not had any indication whether the Minister agrees or disagrees with the suggestions which I then made at the request of the Department, or what in the opinion of the Department should 'really be my work in order to promote our interests in other than purely commercial circles.' I enclose for your convenience a copy of the minute of 9th October 1937, 43/33. (B).[1]

I have been anxious to carry out the suggestion contained in a minute dated 9th November 1938[2] that the German Press should be approached with a view to securing publicity for the campaign against the partition of Ireland. In a minute of 14th November 1938, 2/38,[3] I pointed out that in the present state of German public opinion towards England it should be perfectly possible to obtain the publicity required, and indicated the officials whom it would be advisable to approach for such a purpose. I also pointed out that various German officials had mentioned to me their very great regret at the anti-German attitude of the press in Ireland, and suggested that it could scarcely be expected that the German press should help an Irish campaign for reunion while the Irish press considered itself at liberty to indulge in abuse of the German state and its rulers. The Department however indicated in minute of 2nd December 1938[4] that it did not propose either to sanction my approaching the officials who would be in a position to open the German press to anti-partition propaganda or to take any step to restrain the Irish newspapers from commenting as they desired on the policy of the German Government. It has accordingly been impossible to obtain that publicity for the campaign against partition of Ireland which could in all probability otherwise have been secured. I enclose for your assistance copy of the minute in question (C).[5]

As regards the general promotion of good relations between Ireland and Germany (which is usually considered one of the most important, if not the most important, parts of a Minister's duty), I can conscientiously say that I have left nothing undone in order to bring about a friendly feeling towards Ireland on the part of Germans – both in official and unofficial circles. For a long time, from 1933 to 1935 or 1936, the chief obstacle to such friendly relations was the desire prevalent in Germany, and in particular in the National Socialist party, to do nothing which might possibly offend England and the consequent reluctance to show any degree of amity towards Ireland. At present the situation has changed in a most gratifying manner, and the German press publishes articles on atrocities in India, South Africa and Ireland: recently various German papers reprinted in full the chapter in Ernie O'Malley's book 'Another man's wound'[6] in which the author described his

---

[1] This enclosure was not found with the copy printed here from file 219/22. It appears to have been sent to Joseph P. Walshe and filed elsewhere. Its whereabouts are unknown.

[2] Not located.

[3] Not located.

[4] See above No. 108.

[5] The enclosure was not filed with the memorandum.

[6] Ernie O'Malley (1897-1957), IRA activist and writer, fought in the Anglo-Irish War, did not support the 1921 Treaty, fought in the Civil War (Commander of Anti-Treaty forces in Ulster and Leinster), Sinn Féin TD for North Dublin (1923-7), fund raiser for the *Irish Press*. O'Malley wrote a number of volumes of memoirs including *On another man's wound* (Dublin and London, 1936).

tortures at the hands of British officers. The chief obstacle at present is not on the German, but on the Irish, side, notably the attacks on Germany in the Irish papers and particularly in the Irish Press, which the authorities have regard as expressing the views of the Irish Government.

As I have very frequently referred to the subject before, I do not propose to give any instances beyond one which appeared lately and which seems to me to call for comment. In the Irish Press of March 20th under the heading 'Astonishing Maps' appear a series of maps of Europe in which every year Germany is seen to have annexed another country, until in 1948 all Europe has become a German colony. They are stated to have been reproduced by the News Chronicle 'from a leaflet which, it is alleged, was discovered in a raid on the offices of Herr Henlein in Prague during the September crisis'. Of course the maps are so puerile that they could only impress the very simple who accept all British propaganda, – a fact which is apparently recognized by the editor of the Irish Press, who adds: 'There is, of course, nothing to indicate that the leaflet had any official authority or that the extraordinary scheme outlined in it had been endorsed by the German Government.' One can only wonder why, in this case, the Irish Press should have featured the maps, whose sole effect must be that of contributing to the prejudice of ill-informed persons, injuring the good relations which might exist between the two countries, and assisting English propaganda. It is unnecessary for me to point out that it is impossible for cordial relations to exist when the organ which is regarded as that of the Irish governmental party indulges in malignant propaganda of this kind.

A great deal of time and labour has been involved by the introduction of a visa for Germans travelling to Ireland. In the course of the year 1938-9 over 400 visas have been issued; this however represents only a very small proportion of the applicants who numbered at least 3000, and many of whom called here on more than one occasion. In the case of Jews, since the unfortunate episode of the admission of a convicted criminal I have insisted on thorough enquiries being made before any visa is issued; this has necessitated a large amount of work, as there is a tendency on the part of the German authorities to give as favourable a character as possible to Jewish would-be migrants in the hope that they will leave Germany. As neither the Swedish Mission nor the Society of Friends in Vienna have indicated what enquiries they make about the persons whom they recommend I have of course not accepted the recommendations of these bodies as sufficient. The necessity of such an attitude has been confirmed by the admission of the Society of Friends that one of the 'workers' to whom cases are handed over has not even a rudimentary knowledge of the German language, and by the fact that the same worker handed over a passport with visa for Ireland to an applicant even though she had previously been informed by wire that the Irish Government desired that the visa should not be given. I should like to mention in passing that the greatest gratitude is to Mrs. Kamberg and Miss Walsh for their patience in dealing with applicants for visas, and that I know of no other Legation or Consulate where they obtain as sympathetic a hearing.

Considerable time has been given to the assistance of Irish nationals who are in financial or other difficulties. A number of Irish women married to German husbands require advice as to their status, and also as to their best course in time of international crises.

The fact that for the last nine months no study or room of any kind has been available for the Minister has of course rendered the work of the Legation much more difficult than it need otherwise have been. This has already been pointed out in minutes of 30th May 1938,[1] 22nd June 1938,[2] 23rd July 1938[3] and 6th February 1939.[4]

[stamped] C. BEWLEY

No. 290 NAI DFA 219/22B

Extract from the annual report on the work of the Irish Legation in Rome for 1938-39 from Michael MacWhite to Joseph P. Walshe (Dublin)
ROME, 28 March 1939

[matter omitted]
The trade relations between Ireland and Italy are altogether one sided. It seems that in 1938 while we purchased nearly £200,000 worth of Italian merchandise, we sold nothing to Italy in return. The exchange control laws of Italy forbid the export of currency excepting through State agencies for payment of services. The Legation has attempted without success to get dividends due to Irish stockholders transferred to them. They are, however, free to spend such monies for tourist purposes or for re-investment in Italy. Efforts have also been made to collect debts due from Italian sources to Irish business firms and individuals.

During the visit of the Taoiseach to Rome this month, we gave a large reception in his honour which was attended by all the members of the Diplomatic Corps, many high officials of State and members of the Roman Aristocracy. Another reception was given in January on the occasion of the departure of Monsignor Curran[5] for Ireland, at which the Irish clergy resident in Rome and the leading members of Canadian and American Colleges assisted.
[matter omitted]

No. 291 NAI DFA 219/22

Annual report on the work of the Irish Legation in Paris for 1938-39 from Seán Murphy to Joseph P. Walshe (Dublin)
(P. 19/33)
PARIS, 31 March 1939

Following on the changes in the political situation in Central Europe, the number of visa applications increased very considerably over previous years

---

[1] Not located.
[2] Not located.
[3] Not located.
[4] Not located.
[5] Michael Curran (1880-1960), Rector, Irish College, Rome (1930-8).

when the main bulk of such applications came from holders of American passports. This increase was accompanied by a greater complication in examining each application owing to uncertainty as to the validity of the passports submitted. The unsettled political situation also entrained more numerous requests for information and advice on the part of Irish persons residing in France and more frequent enquiries on the part of foreigners as to the conditions governing the acquisition of Irish nationality, settlement for permanent residence in Ireland and the establishment of industries and businesses of various kinds. Enquiries of a purely tourist nature continued to be frequent and there was distributed a large amount of literature published by the Irish Tourist Association. A certain amount of literature relating to the Abbey Theatre Festival, held in August 1938, was also distributed.

The position of Irish nationals in France, particularly in respect of the regulations governing the employment of foreigners was treated by the Legation at various times during the year. Decree-laws made by the Government since April last have considerably stiffened the relevant regulations and for that reason the number of cases in which the advice and intervention of the Legation was requested became relatively much greater. In a few cases, the Legation intervened successfully with the French authorities in favour of nationals whose position was not quite regular but who seemed to have acted in good faith. A certain amount of assistance was also given to students and teachers wishing to obtain tutorial positions in France. The Legation also gave assistance in connection with some estates in which Irish nationals were interested and in one case transmitted an estate of a national dying in France to the relatives in Ireland. The drowning off the coast of Brittany of an Irishman involved certain action on the part of the Legation, both in regard to his death and the salvage of his yacht. There was a number of repatriations, the examination of some cases involving a considerable amount of correspondence and investigation.

The Legation ensured representation at three international conferences: the annual meeting of the International Commission for Air Navigation, the Fédération Equestre Internationale and the Conference held for drawing up an International Act on Intellectual Cooperation.

Apart from general political reports which are being furnished regularly a number of reports on particular matters were also furnished including the ceremony of inauguration of the President of the Republic, the French decree-laws on financial and other matters, the status of foreigners employed in France, the admission to hospitals of insane persons, French marriage regulations, the measures taken by the French Government to develop tourist industry, French efforts in regard to North Atlantic flights, the treatment of the problem of rail and road transport, succession duties in France, the regulations governing the grant of patents and registration of trademarks, the display of foreign national flags in French territory, the Collége de France. Reports were also furnished from time to time in regard to the major events in Belgium.

A particular attention was devoted to the treatment of Irish problems in the French press and especially the problem of Partition. The desirability of informing French public opinion of the facts of this problem was continuously kept in mind although at no time during the year under review were the general circumstances of such a nature as to permit of much progress in this direction being made. On the whole the events in Europe throughout the past year concentrated French opinion on the continent where her interests seemed more directly involved to the exclusion of what was happening elsewhere including Ireland. On one occasion, a long summary of an important statement by the Government on the question of Partition was distributed to the majority of the Paris newspapers.

The Legation collaborated actively with the Irish Colony of Paris in their endeavours to found an Irish Club and it is satisfactory to relate that a club which has some prospects of endurance has now been established. On St. Patrick's Day a reception to which all members of the colony were invited was held at the Legation (Legation minute P.35/1 of 23rd March).[1]

On the trade side the activities of the Legation were not extensive during the past year owing partially to the unsettled conditions which prevailed over most of the period and, in respect of France, to the considerable devaluation of the franc which made competition on the French market difficult for our goods. On the other hand, the more favourable conditions secured under the April agreements for the entry of Irish goods to Great Britain diverted to that market products which might otherwise have sought a market in France or Belgium. The inherent difficulties, however, of both the French and the Belgian markets for the type of products, largely agricultural, which we could hope to sell there continued to prevail and, in normal circumstances, are likely to persist because it is necessary for the Governments of both countries to pay attention to the needs and wishes of their large agricultural populations. A number of particular enquiries on behalf of Irish firms were dealt with and the Legation also at length succeeded in getting a more satisfactory regime instituted for the sale of woollen goods in France which represent one of our most staple exports here. Efforts were also made, in one case with some success, to recover debts owed by French firms to Irish houses.

A tabular statement relating to the passport and general consular service side of the activities of the Legation is attached.[2]

[signed] SEAN MURPHY

No. 292 NAI DFA 219/7

Confidential report from Francis T. Cremins to Joseph P. Walshe (Dublin)
(S. Gen 1/1) (Copy) (Confidential)[3]

GENEVA, 1 April 1939

With further reference to the general international situation, I have to state, for the information of the Minister, that, from conversations with my colleagues here, it is clear that the general impression amongst them is one of

---

[1] Not printed.
[2] Not printed.
[3] Marginal notes: 'Seen by Secy.', 'Dr Rynne', 'M.R., 3/4/39'.

the greatest relief that Great Britain has broken away from tradition by giving, with France, the guarantee to Poland which the British Prime Minister announced yesterday. Official circles in Berne also, M. Holsti[1] informs me, feel now more happy than for a long time at the determination of Britain and France to come to the help of Switzerland in case of a German attack on this country, even though, in case a general war actually broke out from any other cause, this country would of course be immediately in danger. The Swiss feel that the menace of German aggression for the sole reason of acquiring territory which is alleged to be inhabited by 'Germans' is for the present removed.

As regards the Balkans, it is clear here that Yugoslavia, Greece, Romania and Turkey which have been alarmed at the German action in Czechoslovakia view with relief the new attitude of Britain and France towards Poland, but they will expect some definite guarantees in their own cases if they are to resist militarily a German thrust South-eastwards. My Balkan colleagues here with whom I discussed the matter considered that a simple joint declaration for consultation would be of little use. They look for definite engagements for military assistance, or there is a danger, as they say, that such small states may be forced to come to an understanding with the Reich. Even in Bulgaria, I am informed, public opinion is very much against Germany, not because the Bulgarians love the Czechs, or for that matter any members of the late Little Entente, but because they fear for their own independence. Seventy-five per cent of Bulgarian trade is now with the Reich (50% Germany, and 25% with Czechoslovakia).

A question which is much discussed here today is whether the guarantee announced by Mr. Chamberlain regarding matters involving the independence and vital interest of Poland, would cover the case, for example, in which Danzig might decide to join up with the Reich. There is however clearly a loophole left for negotiations between Poland and Germany in regard to problems such as those of Danzig and the Corridor, although it seems to be left to Poland to decide when her 'vital interest' would necessitate armed resistance. There is no doubt that Poland attaches the greatest importance to her interests in Danzig and to a clear and unmenaced outlet to the sea, and the fact that her port of Gdynia is situated to the west of the Free City does not render easy any waiving of her rights, or any accommodation in regard to a west to east passage for Germany to Danzig and East Prussia. In view however of the fact that there is a majority of Germans in Danzig (though the majority in the corridor is Polish) it is difficult to see how peace can be maintained unless there is some serious attempt at settlement of the Danzig problem. Poland will no doubt make serious efforts to avoid a military clash, in consultation with her new allies. Naturally, Great Britain and France would not be seriously perturbed regarding Danzig or the corridor were it not for the possible effect on the general situation and balance.

I had also a talk last night with my Danish colleague. Denmark remains

---

[1] Rudolf Holsti (1881-1945), Finnish Permanent Delegate to the League of Nations and Envoy and Minister Plenipotentiary to Switzerland (1928-40).

very much disturbed at the prospects, although the more definite stand now being taken by the Western Powers bring relief even there. He states however that in case of an attack by Germany, Denmark can do nothing, and he does not expect guarantees or help from any quarter, unless perhaps in the case of a general war. The Danes seem to fear that Germany may seize their country for the food produced there – just as the Swedes fear a German attack for the purpose of securing control of the vast Swedish resources of raw materials of military value. In 1914-18, when the Germans forbade the Danes to export food to Great Britain, the Danes were able to point out that there would be no cattle available for Germany if the British stopped the importation by Denmark of oil cake for feeding. In the same way, when the Allies tried to prevent the exportation from Denmark of food and cattle to Germany, the Danes pointed out that, in case of refusal to export, the Germans might attack them, and then there would be nothing to send to Great Britain. Accordingly, an arrangement was agreed to that Denmark could supply a greater proportion of foodstuffs to the Allies, and the rest to the Germans. My colleague doubts if any such arrangement would be possible in case of another war. He is pessimistic regarding the position of his country, although he shares the present degree of optimism which the firmer attitude of Britain and France has brought about.

I mentioned in a previous report that M. de Velics (Hungary) had told me on the17th March that Hungary had no intention of leaving the League. M. Borberg (Denmark) states that he has it on high authority that the Prime Minister of Hungary[1] stated recently that Hungary was finding it increasingly difficult to remain in the League owing to her German affiliations. The guarantee to Poland may however have the effect of stiffening her attitude, and preventing any hasty action.

I mentioned to you at Zurich my conversation recently with the German Consul-General in which I mentioned to him in friendly fashion the dangers of the existing situation and the alarm which everywhere existed amongst the small States on the Continent following the events in Czechoslovakia. He pooh-poohed any idea of the danger of a European war, and said that he thought that I exaggerated, and that all the 'fuss' was being caused by Britain and France owing to the internal situation in those countries. I said that I greatly doubted that the matter was so simple as that and I referred to the disaster that European war would be for all countries – everybody would be down, but somebody would be under. He emphasised that there was no danger whatever that Germany would make war on anyone, and he expressed his optimism regarding the ultimate outcome of the situation. He knows that the Irish Delegation had always expressed themselves in favour at Geneva of a fair settlement by peaceful means for Germany and for the other 'vanquished States'.

As regards Italy, for some reason or another, the position in the Mediterranean is regarded here now as not being immediately dangerous. Vague stories are going the rounds about growing dissatisfaction in Italy

---

[1] Count Pál Teleki (1879-1941), Prime Minister of Hungary (1939-41).

with the policy of the *axe*, and with Mussolini, and it is said that amongst the ordinary population there is general abhorrence at any idea of war with Great Britain.

On the whole, I would say that the general situation is regarded here today as having improved, although of course all the main problems remain unsettled. I should add however that on Thursday Mr. Jacklin, the Treasurer of the League told me that he found international financial circles pessimistic, and he said that in London the view which formerly was 'war possible, but appeasement probable' was now reversed 'appeasement possible and war probable'.

[signed] FRANCIS T. CREMINS
Permanent Delegate

No. 293 NAI DFA 219/6

Confidential report from Michael MacWhite to Joseph P. Walshe (Dublin)[1]
(Confidential) (Copy)

ROME, 4 April 1939

The feeling throughout Italy was not nearly so tense during the Sudeten troubles in September as it has been during the last fortnight. Everybody here seems obsessed by a foreboding of danger without having any very precise idea of the form it may take. Six classes of reservists and a number of aviation and artillery experts – about 800,000 men – have been called to the colours and it is a well established fact that most of them have been sent to Yugoslav and former Austrian frontiers, as if the danger was anticipated from that direction. The schools along the Italian side of the German border have been closed and two large monasteries were evacuated by the monks to make way for the troops. In the north eastern districts of Italy there is intense military activity which would seem to confirm the oft repeated rumour that the Dictators have little confidence in one another.

Another significant fact about the Italian mobilisation is that many of the reservists who have been called up are still at the local barracks sleeping practically in the open while waiting for uniforms and equipment. From this it would appear that Italy is not ready for war. Notwithstanding the daily affirmations in regard to the solidarity of the Rome-Berlin axis I have come to the conclusion that in case of a European war Italy will avoid fighting. She may play a make believe game up to the last minute before asserting her neutrality. In fighting a battle for right and justice any country has a powerful unseen auxiliary. On the other hand, fighting a war of aggression in which one has but little faith is to court defeat and disaster. Nobody knows better than the Duce that if Hitler goes down Fascism is likewise doomed.

During his visit to Calabria last week, the Duce for the first time asked his audience if it was true, as reported in the Foreign press, that they were

---

[1] The marginal annotations on this document show that it was read by Joseph P. Walshe, Frederick H. Boland and Michael Rynne.

growing indifferent to Fascism and the things it stood for. The answer was naturally a deafening 'no'. An appeal of this kind is begging the question and goes to show that his self confidence is on the wane. He is wearing a troubled look these days. Fascism is likely to last as long as he does but it is aging fast and scepticism increases with old age.

[signed] M. MacWhite

No. 294 NAI DFA Paris Embassy 19/34

Confidential report from Seán Murphy to Joseph P. Walshe (Dublin)[1]
(P. 19/34) (Copy)

Paris, 11 April 1939

The developments in Albania[2] took French public opinion completely by surprise to the extent that it was not expected, especially after the Italian assurances referred to by M. Chamberlain in his statement on the 6th inst. in the Commons, that Italy would move either so quickly or so thoroughly. On the other hand, I think it probable that the Quai d'Orsay had decided beforehand that France would not move on the Albanian issue.

The first reaction of the Press here was one of indignation coupled, in many cases, (as matters developed and it was being reported from London that the British Government did not intend to move pending the receipt of more reliable information) with bitterness at British inaction; for the first judgement here of a large portion of the press was that the Italian action represented a definite menace to British interests in the Mediterranean and almost a direct challenge. This attitude has now entirely disappeared and many organs have given reasons why England should accept the Italian assurances as to the continued validity of the Mediterranean agreement of last year, one of the main reasons being so as to avoid at all costs seeming to provoke a conflict.

It is also pointed out in some quarters that for the Chamberlain Government to accept that the Agreement is at an end would be tantamount to admitting that the whole policy of the Government since Eden left has failed. The general opinion in France is that the motives of the Italian action were of two kinds, the one kind, concerned with prestige to enable the Government to show some 'return' to Italy from the axis policy and the second being to ensure Italian control of the Adriatic, neutralise Yugoslavia and provide the axis powers with a jumping-off ground in the Balkans from which the effort at 'encirclement' can be opposed and a further positive advance in penetration of Southern and South-Eastern Europe can be made. It is thought here that the neutralisation of Yugoslavia is now an accomplished fact and also that Bulgaria has been more or less finally, because of her grievance against both Greece and Rumania, won over to the axis side. The immediate advantages to Italy from the changed status of Albania are

---

[1] This document bears the typist's mark 'CCC/LM', indicating that it was dictated by Con Cremin.
[2] Italian forces invaded Albania on 7 April 1939.

not regarded as great, the ordinary opinion being that she has not got any greater control over the resources of the country than she had previously. However, it is generally held that the situation in South-Eastern Europe has changed radically both because of the success of the Italian coup and because of the possibilities for threatening the other Balkans powers which are inherent in the new position.

On the other hand, it is thought that the whole Moslem world has been antagonised by the attack on Albania and that the attitude of Turkey in particular may now be definitely favourable to the democracies. As a proof of this result, the French press points to the absence, in spite of Italian provocation, of all demonstration in Tunis on the 9th inst., anniversary of some repressive measures taken by the French authorities in 1938.

It has been stated here that the Yugoslav Minister informed Mr. Bonnet on Friday that Yugoslavia would definitely refuse to move in regard to Albania. The Government is remaining in the closest touch with London. The Defence Council met on Sunday and there is to be a Cabinet meeting this evening followed by a Council of Ministers to-morrow.

Of the Pope's speech on Sunday, the section which received by far the most attention here was that relating to confidence in treaties and the given word being essential to stability. This passage is interpreted as directed against the practice of the totalitarian states.

(Signed) Sean Murphy

No. 295 NAI DFA Secretary's Files A20/1

Letter from Leopold H. Kerney to Joseph P. Walshe (Dublin)[1]
(S.S. 10/11)

San Sebastian, 11 April 1939

FRANK RYAN. Your 144/35a

I paid my first official visit as Minister to General Jordana, Minister of Foreign Affairs, in Burgos on Easter Monday 10th April; I called at the Ministry at 12.45 p.m. and was received by him at 2.15 p.m. The Brazilian chargé d'affaires had been given an appointment at 12.30 p.m. but I was given precedence.

I appealed to General Jordana to liberate Frank Ryan. I told him that we definitely sought a favour in this and in another case (O'Toole), and that I did not expect to have to put forward any further similar requests. He replied that Ryan had been condemned to death, that this sentence had been commuted into one of penal servitude for 30 years and that it would be very difficult to comply with our request at this moment. I explained that, quite apart from any interest in Ryan's fate displayed by people with advanced liberal tendencies, there were widespread sympathy in Ireland for him and his family, that he had taken an active part in the fight for Ireland's independence, as well as in the Irish language and cultural movement, and that

---

[1] Marginal annotation: 'Secy. File with you'.

Irish opinion was keenly interested in his fate. I pointed out that it could only benefit the friendly relations between Ireland and Spain if his release were to take place following the presentation of my credentials as Minister to Spain and that such a friendly gesture would be accepted with gratitude by the Irish Government and by Irish public opinion generally. I told him that I knew that Ryan's name had been placed on a list of prisoners whose release was expected shortly by the British and that a reply to a question in the British House of Commons indicated that the British hoped to be able to secure his release as a result of their intervention; I warned him that it would be a fatal blunder to hand him over to the British rather than to myself. He promised to look into the matter and to communicate with me in due course; his attitude was more hopeful in regard to the possibility of a visit to Ryan by his sister, and I suggested that I might accompany latter on that occasion.

I left with General Jordana the aide-mémoire of which I sent you an advance copy of 22nd March.[1]

[signed] L.H. KERNEY[2]
Aire Lán-Chómhachtach

No. 296 NAI DFA 219/4

Confidential report from Charles Bewley to Joseph P. Walshe (Dublin)[3]
(43/33)
BERLIN, 11 April 1939

The last weeks have brought events which in the opinion of many of those most competent to judge created a definite military superiority on the side of the authoritarian states in the eventuality of a war. It will be well to take these events in order so that their importance may be appreciated.

1. The establishment of a German protectorate over Bohemia and Moravia. As is obvious to anyone who has looked at the map of Europe, the former state of Czechoslovakia was a threat in 1918 to the allied states of Germany and Austria; in 1939 it was equally menacing to the Greater German Reich. That it was intended by its creators to constitute such a threat is known to anyone who has read any of the standard works on the Peace Conference of 1919; that it was so considered to the last is clear from, inter alia, a speech of Mr. Cot,[4] French Minister for Aviation, who pointed out that Germany's most important industrial districts could be bombed from Czechoslovakia in a 20 minutes' flight.

That the Czechs of the Masaryk-Beneš regime would have been not only able but willing to carry out the policy so devised for them by the Allied Powers was ensured by the completely Masonic character of the

---

[1] Not printed.
[2] Handwritten marginal note by Sheila Murphy: 'Informed Miss Ryan on phone of Mr. K's report. S.G.M. 18/4/39'.
[3] Marginal annotations: 'Secy'; 'A/Secy; 'File with Mr. Belton'.
[4] Pierre Cot (1895-1977), Minister of Aviation (1933, 1936-8).

Czechoslovak regime, which did not at any time since 1919 seriously attempt to find a modus vivendi with Germany. It was the general opinion in Germany – which was strikingly confirmed by the course taken by subsequent events – that the object of the clique governing Czechoslovakia was not the interests of the Czech peoples but the carrying out of a Franco-British anti-German policy.

Under the circumstances it was scarcely to be expected that Germany could continue to tolerate a perpetual menace to her frontiers. It had been hoped that, when in September 1938 the German, Polish and Hungarian minorities had regained the freedom to join their respective countries, the new government would see its way to pursue a different policy. Unfortunately this was far from being the case; Mr. Chvalovsky committed errors similar to those committed by Beneš the Czechs continued to adopt an attitude of hostility towards the Germans and to deny to the Slovaks the independence which they had promised them in 1918 and again in 1938.

Only one outcome was possible, – the establishment of a German Protectorate over Bohemia and Moravia, and the complete independence of Slovakia, which had experienced a persecution for 20 years from the anti-Catholic Czech Government, and now had formed a Catholic Government under Monsignor Tiso under the protection of the German State.

To Germany the events of March have brought the advantages of an immensely shortened frontier, the acquisition of highly developed armament factories, and the elimination of an enemy on her eastern front.

2. The commercial treaty between Germany and Roumania.
This agreement has been an effective response to the boasts made by English Ministers that English gold was bound to win any war in the long run and to the reference to a blockade of Germany in the English and French Press. Two of Germany's main needs in the event of a war would be wheat and oil; both of these are secured in a very large measure by the treaty. Its importance may best be judged of by the frantic efforts made by England to prevent its coming into operation, – the rumours launched by English agencies on the authority of English officials in Bucharest that it had been brought about by a German ultimatum (which was immediately denied by the Roumanian Government), the newspaper statement that it would not be ratified by Roumania, etc., etc. It is probable that the German view that the treaty makes Germany immune against any attempted blockade by England and France is reasonably accurate.

3. The occupation of Albania by an Italian army.
The existence of a hostile Albania would have presented a grave danger to Italy in the event of a European war. The late King of Albania,[1] who had reached his position by Italian help, had, so far as can be ascertained, lent himself to English intrigues against Italy: inducements offered him by his

[1] King Zog I Skanderbeg III (known as King Zog) (1895-1961), King of Albania (1928-39 and 1943-6).

new friends are alleged to have been of a pecuniary nature. The situation was obviously one which Italy could not tolerate, and accordingly, with the knowledge of Yugoslavia, the Italian army has brought to an end a possible source of danger to Italy.

4. The adhesion of Spain to the anti-Comintern pact.
It was obviously inevitable that Franco would tend to support those countries which had supported Catholic Spain against Communism; and the speeches by Spanish ministers, the special honours conferred by General Franco on General Fieldmarshal Goering, the messages sent to Hitler and Mussolini by the Spanish chief never left any doubt as to the future policy of Spain. It was apparently expected by England and France that, after doing everything possible to support the Communist and Masonic forces in Spain and retarding Franco's victory for at least a year, they could buy the support of the victors. This expectation has been disappointed, and with it the hope that the Catholic Spain of the future would sell its honour for an English loan and support the Western democracies and Soviet Russia in a war against the central powers.

These four events are in themselves, as I have pointed out, of enormous importance in strengthening the position of Germany and Italy in a military and economic sense. From the point of view of prestige they are of almost equal importance, in that they are the best proof to the states of middle and eastern Europe of the impotence of England and France. There was a possibility that the accounts so assiduously propagated by the Anglo-Jewish news agencies of the progress of English rearmament and the obvious efforts of the British Government to form an anti-German front would have a certain success. I do not think that this possibility any longer exists: the fact that Bohemia, Memel and Albania have successively been placed under a protectorate or annexed and that England after protesting has not ventured to lift a finger has in the opinion of those Ministers for East- and North-Eastern states with whom I have talked destroyed English and French prestige completely.

English policy may best be judged by its attitude towards the Memel question. On being interrogated by the Lithuanian Government the British Government declared it the duty of Lithuania to fight in defence of its territory: on being asked what assistance it would give, it stated that England was not in a position to offer any assistance of a military nature. The Lithuanians not unnaturally preferred to come to an agreement with Germany rather than swell the ranks of those countries which had fought at England's request and been deserted in the hour of defeat.

The opinion of the German Chancellor, as I know from a conversation recently held by him with the Minister of a foreign state, is that England and France are completely powerless against Germany, and that both the danger of direct military defeat and that of defeat by a hunger blockade may be regarded as eliminated. If this view is correct, as would appear very probable, and if its correctness is realized by England and France, the danger of a war would appear to have very much receded, as the democratic countries would scarcely engage in hostilities in which they would not have at least a great probability of success.

So far as it is possible to judge, the situation has been realised by the more responsible elements in both England and France. In England, in particular, as the German press frequently points out, the first step necessary towards fighting would be to introduce conscription, but England refuses to do so. Therefore, it must be assumed that England will not venture to make a war, as she cannot in 1939 find other countries willing to be slaughtered in English interests as she did in 1914, and the French are not likely to sacrifice some millions of their youth before England is prepared to send a serious expeditionary force to the continent.

The German press, and indeed most Germans, are indignant at the attempts of the British Government to encircle Germany by a system of alliances directed against the 'Axis', but I do not think that there is any serious alarm. It is perfectly realized that, whatever be Polish hostility to Germany at the moment, no Polish Government could possibly enter into an alliance with the Soviet Government; it is not thought that Roumania would abandon the prospect of good relations with Germany for the usually fatal gift of English friendship; and it is obvious that Yugoslavia knows that her interests be with the authoritarian states.

[signed] CHARLES BEWLEY

No. 297 UDCA P150/2548

Handwritten letter from Eamon de Valera to Neville Chamberlain (London)
(Personal and Confidential)

DUBLIN, 12 April 1939

Dear Prime Minister,
I cannot refrain from writing to you. You and I have worked to bring about conditions which would make it possible to lay the foundations of good neighbourly relations between the British and Irish peoples. The agreement, a year ago was a notable advance in that direction; but the failure to deal with Partition has largely offset what was then accomplished. A free United Ireland would have every interest in wishing Britain to be strong, but when Britain's strength appears to be used to maintain the division of our island no such consideration can have any force. A large section of our people, particularly the young are led to see hope only in Britain's weakness. Can something not be done and without delay?

The consequences of failure in the past to act in time are clear to see and should be a warning. Will the generation that succeeds us have again to deplore the unwisdom of those who did not act when action would have meant success. I know your difficulties and your present pre-occupations with events farther afield and deeply sympathise with you. But the intensification of feeling here and amongst our people in the United States makes it imperative to act quickly lest it be too late to save the situation.

I remain dear Prime Minister
Yours Very Sincerely
EAMON DE VALERA

May I express the hope that you will remain firm in your efforts for Peace notwithstanding the pressure that will be ~~placed~~ brought upon you. Once this war is begun no man can see the end.

[initialled] E. de V.

No. 298 NAI DFA 219/2

Memorandum from Leopold H. Kerney to Joseph P. Walshe (Dublin)[1]
(S.S. 19/1)

SAN SEBASTIAN, 15 April 1939

SPAIN'S FOREIGN POLICY

On Tuesday, 11th April, the Spanish Government, Franco presiding, held a Cabinet meeting in Burgos from 6.30 p.m. till 1 a.m. The official communiqué published the following morning mentioned the various matters which had been discussed; there was no reference at all to matters affecting foreign policy – to my mind the clearest possible evidence that questions of great importance relating to Spain's foreign policy were under consideration at the meeting. On an earlier occasion, quite recently, a cabinet meeting was held; the communiqué gave great prominence to decisions regarding internal policy and dismissed foreign policy in one brief line; the next day Spain joined Italy, Germany, Japan and Hungary in the anti-comintern pact.

On this present occasion, it will be remembered that the Minister for Foreign Affairs was busy with Franco on Sunday night 9th April, and that this prevented him from receiving a visit from me, and also that, for the same reason, he had to keep me waiting $1^1/2$ hours on Monday 10th April, whilst the Brazilian chargé d'affaires, who had arranged an appointment for 12.30 p.m. before leaving San Sebastian, had to wait for over 2 hours, and was somewhat wrath that such a thing should happen to him for the first time in his career of 25 years. It is natural to conclude that foreign policy was very much in the foreground before the Cabinet meeting of 11th April.

The British Ambassador ('Peterson' in one official diplomatic list, 'Petterson' in another) presented his credentials on 11th April – and, by the way, he, a non-military official, gave a military salute, a sort of compromise solution I suppose, when the national anthems were played – and saw the Minister for Foreign Affairs the same afternoon, before the beginning of the cabinet meeting; he may have been interested in Spain's foreign policy.

Prior to the signing of the anti-comintern pact, the French Ambassador, Marshal Pétain, went specially to Burgos to see Jordana, and shortly afterwards returned to France, and he has been seeing Bonnet, Daladier and others in Paris.

It is reasonable to suppose that France and England must be much concerned as to Spain's attitude in the event of war; the strategic importance of Spain is such that France and England may be seeking very definite

---

[1] The marginal annotations on this document show that it was read by Joseph P. Walshe and Michael Rynne.

assurances; Spain's anti-comintern ties will make it very difficult – even omitting the probability of secret commitments entered into with Italy as the price of Italian support – for her to preserve any other 'neutrality' than such as may be useful to Italy and Germany. Two questions present themselves to my mind – Are France and England taking a strong attitude and demanding guarantees of friendly Spanish neutrality? Is Spain free and willing to give assurances without which presumably pro-Italian neutrality may not be respected?

It has to be borne in mind that the new Spain is pretentious and ambitious; one of her ambitions is to figure as a great Power, as in the days of yore; Spain intends to play her part in the Mediterranean and will be encouraged by Italy to do so; the new Spain will choose some propitious moment for raising the question of Gibraltar; the original pre-war Falange Española agitated in a small way for the return of Gibraltar, but in those days the aims and methods of that small organisation were looked upon as fantastic by most people; the day after Madrid capitulated bodies of young men paraded before the British Embassy in Madrid shouting – 'Gibraltar, Gibraltar!'; and level-headed Spaniards, not quite so young, do not need much inducement to speak with indignation of how England robbed them of Gibraltar in peace time; the question is never referred to in the press, which is of course controlled. It is easy to imagine a Spanish 'natural aspiration' for Gibraltar, and mighty consequences arising therefrom.

[signed] L.H. KERNEY
Aire Lán-Chómhachtach

No. 299 UCDA P150/2183

*Note from Joseph P. Walshe to Eamon de Valera (Dublin) enclosing a note
from John Dulanty (London) regarding IRA activities in Britain
(Secret) (Copy)*

DUBLIN, 15 April 1939

I enclose a note received by Dulanty from the Dominions Office yesterday concerning the arrival in England of certain I.R.A. organisers, and requesting us to give them any information which would help the British to prevent these men from engaging in illegal activities. I shall be very grateful if you will tell me on the phone whether you wish me to transmit the note to the Department of Justice and what action you desire to be taken on it.

[signed] J.P. WALSHE

[Enclosure]
SECRET

The Metropolitan Police have received information which they believe to be reliable that some of the organisers of the I.R.A. have recently arrived in this country, and that others will shortly be coming here, to concert plans for further outrages with members of the organisation in this country. The information given to the Metropolitan Police does not include the names or descriptions of the persons concerned, or the precise dates and ports of arrival. Without these particulars it is difficult to make any arrangements for keeping a watch on them on their arrival and so preventing them from engaging in any illegal activities in this country.

It would be most helpful if the Éire police could obtain any information which would be of assistance to the Metropolitan Police in this direction and arrange for it to be communicated at once to Sir Norman Kendal[1] at New Scotland Yard. It is understood that Sir Norman Kendal has already written to the Commissioner of Police, Dublin, on the subject.

No. 300 NAI DFA 219/7

> *Extracts from a confidential report from Francis T. Cremins to*
> *Joseph P. Walshe[2] (Dublin)*
> *(S. Gen. 1/1) (Confidential)*
>
> GENEVA, 18 April 1939

With further reference to the international situation, I have to state that the general feeling here in international circles remains pessimistic as to the outcome, and, so far as I can judge, little of a practical nature is expected from the letters of President Roosevelt. From conversations which I had in Scandinavian circles last week, I gathered that those circles, and the Danes in particular, were extremely pessimistic, fearing that an attack might be made on Demark and/or Sweden in the immediate future – Denmark to ensure supplies and naval bases, and Sweden for raw materials of military value and strategic considerations. Such an attack was expected even before an attack on Danzig and the corridor. I met the German Consul-General also and I asked him as before in a friendly way what was going to happen next. He spoke furiously against France and Britain, repeating that all the excitement was due to those two countries. I asked him whether he retained his optimism, and, on his replying yes, I enquired whether he really felt that nothing which would result in war was likely to happen in the near future. He said 'Something will come, but not now'. I thought that he had lost a good deal of the sang-froid which he had displayed on a previous occasion.
[matter omitted]
With regard to President Roosevelt's letters, the opinion held here in various circles is that they can hardly lead to practical results. First of all, the President had identified himself closely with one side, with the result that he is regarded as an enemy by both Hitler and Mussolini, especially the former. Secondly he as an intermediary on main questions is not in a position to deliver the goods. The proposals also followed rather too quickly his declaration to the Board of the Pan-American Union. The atmosphere for a peace move of the kind was hardly therefore too favourable. The démarche could

---

[1]   Sir Normal Kendal (1880-1966), Assistant Commissioner of the Criminal Investigation Department, New Scotland Yard, London.
[2]   The marginal annotations on this document show that it was read by Joseph P. Walshe and Frederick H. Boland.

however have the effect of putting the dictatorial regimes more completely in the wrong before the American peoples, and might encourage the more moderate elements in Italy and even in Germany to become less enthusiastic than ever for war.

The great gap which I see in the President's proposals is that they do not suggest more directly political discussions. Such discussions are, no doubt inevitably left by the President to the initiative of the Governments which are directly interested, if those Governments deem them necessary or desirable. Presumably he has in mind such questions as Danzig and the corridor between Germany and Poland; colonies between Germany and Britain, France, etc; Tunis, Djibouti, Suez between Italy and France, etc. etc.. Notwithstanding the questions which have already been settled by force, it is principally political problems, and German ambitions in Eastern Europe, which stand in the way of appeasement. To propose that an arrangement regarding armaments should be discussed at the same time as an arrangement in the economic field, with no certainty of even an attempt at fruitful discussions in the political field, does not seem to me to be a really practical proposition, as it has all along been recognised that no serious advance could be made on economic lines – raw materials, etc. – whilst the political problems remained unsolved. And it is hardly likely that Germany and Italy would agree to a limitation or a fixation of armaments until their political claims had been in some way dealt with. I have no illusions that any attempt to settle German or Italian claims would be an easy matter, but, with a world war as the alternative, it seems not unreasonable to expect that discussions of all questions outstanding, no matter what they are, should definitely be tried, and that no question of prestige should stand in the way. It is certainly absurd, for example, that *apparently* for reasons in which questions of prestige play a great part, neither M. Daladier nor M. Mussolini are prepared to get down to discussions regarding the matters in dispute between them.

Bearing in mind, therefore, that the British Premier has more than once stated that in his view there was no question which could not reasonably be regulated by peaceful discussion, and that M. Mussolini at least has stated that his country needs an era of peace, it occurs to me that it might be a good follow-up of President Roosevelt's proposals if both Mr. Chamberlain and M. Daladier took an early opportunity of sending letters to Hitler and Mussolini, setting out frankly the French and the British points of view and indicating that they were ready at any time to discuss peacefully in Conference not only the questions of an effective limitation and fixation of armaments and the opening up of international trade as proposed by the President of the United States, but also any problem that was on the political horizon. Perhaps the Minister, who is also still President of the League Assembly, might be prepared as in September last to give consideration to the question of sounding the persons chiefly concerned (British and French)[1] as to whether such direct action on their part would be a possibility. Both Premiers have of course more than once stated their willingness to discuss any and every question. It is one

---

[1] This paragraph has been highlighted by a line in the left-hand margin to this point.

thing however to express such readiness in general speeches, but it would to my mind be more effective from the points of view of enlightening public opinion, and clarifying the position generally, if proposals were made by letters addressed direct to the principals. Moreover, proposals made in this way reach more certainly the people of the various countries and gain time. It is serious to my mind that on the eve perhaps of hostilities, there is no direct contact between the persons who have or ought to have the power to take decisions. And I still do not believe that in any quarter there exists a hankering for a European war.

[signed] F.T. Cremins

No. 301 NAI DFA 219/7

Confidential report from Francis T. Cremins to Joseph P. Walshe (Dublin) (S. Gen. 1/1) (Confidential)[1]

Geneva, 20 April 1939

With reference to previous reports on the international situation, I have to state for the information of the Minister that I had a brief conversation yesterday with M. Komarnicki (Minister for Poland at Berne) who is here for the meeting of the Governing Body of the International Labour Organisation. I asked him if the reports which appeared in the morning papers of an agreement between Poland and Germany regarding Danzig were true. He replied that the reports had been denied. There was not only no agreement, but no negotiations even were going on. I asked if Poland would fight if Danzig attached itself to the Reich. He replied 'certainly', adding that the Germans might take Danzig, but it would not be a town they would have but the ashes of a town. Poland could destroy Danzig, he said, with her heavy coastal artillery.

I asked for his views on the general situation, and he said that the Germans have placed themselves in such a position that they will find it difficult to draw back. He does not think however that war will break out in the north. He expressed the view that the Germans would leave the starting of a war to Italy, and he gave as his reason that Germany would then be sure to have Italy at her side, whereas if it were a German-started war, the Italians might not join.

Thus, the Yugoslavs express the view that the threat in the north is greatest, whereas the Poles seem to think that the more immediate danger lies in the south. It is hardly worth recording such diverse views, but I record them simply as coming from persons who, one would expect, are in touch with opinion in the different areas.

At present, the general feeling of attente is apparent here. It is regarded I think as being due to the fact that Germany and Italy have to stand back and take stock of the new situation brought about by the Anglo-French guarantees, and to the fact that a date has been fixed for the German reply to

---

[1] The marginal annotations on this document show that it was read by Joseph P. Walshe, Frederick H. Boland and Michael Rynne.

President Roosevelt's letter, before which it is hoped that nothing serious will happen.

[signed] F.T. CREMINS
Permanent Delegate

No. 302 NAI DFA 219/7

Handwritten notes passed between Frederick Boland and Michael Rynne regarding Francis Cremins' confidential report to Joseph Walshe of 18 April 1939

DUBLIN, 21 April 1939

Dr. Rynne,[1]
I doubt whether the course suggested by Mr. Cremins is really politic. What do you think?

[initialled] F.H.B.

Assistant Secretary
While Mr. Cremins' sentiments are no doubt, admirable, it is hard to see what benefit this country would derive out of a démarche by the Minister such as he suggests. Unless we could be sure that such a démarche would result to our international prestige (and not the contrary) it had better not be tried at present

[initialled] M.R. 1.5.39

No. 303 UCDA P150/2571

Memorandum from Joseph P. Walshe to Eamon de Valera (Dublin) regarding President Franklin D. Roosevelt's message of 15 April to Adolf Hitler

DUBLIN, 22 April 1939

Mr. MacVeagh, American Chargé d'Affaires, called yesterday forenoon for the purpose of informing me that he had been instructed to leave 'informally' a copy of the President's message of the 15th April to Chancellor Hitler, and to suggest that a message or statement to the general effect that the message was welcomed by us as a constructive move in the promotion of world peace would be a help in building up public opinion against aggression and war. Mr. MacVeagh was further instructed to inform us that all the Governments on the American Continent had sent messages of approval and that others were now being received from Europe and the Near East. I told Mr. MacVeagh that I would immediately instruct Mr. Brennan[2] to find out from the State Department which European States had replied and what was the general tenor of the replies. I should then be able to convey the desire of the State Department to my Minister with the relevant information. This morning I received a reply from Mr. Brennan saying that 'very few' European countries had yet sent replies, but that the general tenor of those replies was that 'President's message was a constructive move towards peace'. The State

---

[1] See No. 300 above.
[2] Robert Brennan (1881-1964), Irish Minister to Washington (1938-47).

Department, while giving this information to Mr. Brennan, informed him that they would be pleased to have us on record in similar terms.

There are rumours, which have so far received no official confirmation, that the German representatives have been instructed to enquire from the States named in President Roosevelt's message whether in effect they felt themselves menaced by Germany. If the question were put to us, we should be obliged to answer in the negative, and the request of the State Department to give formal approval to President Roosevelt's message puts us in something of a quandary. If we give unqualified approval, we should seem to be accepting the Roosevelt thesis that the Germans had aggressive intentions in our regard. We should also take into account that the State Department's method of correcting their description 'Great Britain and Ireland' was ungenerous, and it leaves still in doubt whether they regarded us as an *independent* State or not. Moreover, as the statement of Mr. Hull[1] has not appeared anywhere in the British Press, we may take it that the State Department made no effort to secure publicity for the correction in Great Britain. For these reasons one feels very reluctant to come to their aid in order to restore life to the President's damp squib. In any case, there would be no harm in waiting to see what response the appeal for replies is going to meet with in Europe. I am asking Mr. Brennan to send us definite information as to the European countries which will have replied by Tuesday. Perhaps you could find a moment to tell me on the 'phone what your wishes are in the matter.

J.P. WALSHE

I attach a possible line of reply

Possible Reply to Mr. Roosevelt
I most earnestly hope that your efforts and those of all statesmen upon whose shoulders rest the responsibility and the duty to prevent the supreme catastrophe of war will lead to fruitful results.

Great sacrifices are required from the rulers of all nations to avert the danger of a new holocaust of the Youth of the world. I urge upon you to make a new appeal to the great Powers calling upon them to make the sacrifices necessary to build a new order based upon justice and upon respect for the freedom and integrity of all small nations.

No. 304 NAI DFA Secretary's Files S.70

Memorandum by Joseph P. Walshe of instructions received from Eamon de Valera (Dublin) for transmission to John W. Dulanty (London)
DUBLIN, 26 April 1939

On the Taoiseach's instructions, I gave the following message to the High Commissioner on the phone at 7 p.m. this evening:-

He was to go to see Mr. Chamberlain, tonight if Mr. Chamberlain could receive him, or, if not, as early as possible tomorrow morning. He was to

---

[1] Cordell Hull (1871-1955), United States Secretary of State (1933-44).

speak to Mr. Chamberlain in the following words, and to leave a copy of his statement with Mr. Chamberlain in writing:

'Mr. de Valera is very perturbed indeed by Mr. Chamberlain's announcement in regard to conscription. He is anxious to have an assurance that there is no intention of applying conscription to the people of the Six Counties. At least a third of the population there are cut off from Ireland against their will. Any attempt to conscript them would be resented as an outrage.

In union with our fellow countrymen in the Six Counties, we are prepared to undertake the defence of the whole of Ireland against any enemy seeking to get a foothold here. That is the constructive line to take and the line that would serve the true interests of Britain, whereas the introduction of conscription in the Six Counties by the British Government for the British Army can only be regarded as an act of war against our nation and will provoke the bitterest hostility to England wherever there are Irishmen throughout the world.'

[signed] J.P. WALSHE

No. 305 NAI DFA Secretary's Files S70

Letter from John W. Dulanty to Neville Chamberlain (London)
(Copy)

LONDON, 26 April 1939[1]

Dear Mr. Chamberlain,

As Sir Thomas Inskip has doubtless informed you, I expressed to him this morning the gravest concern of the Irish Government at the possibility of any form of Conscription being applied in the Six Counties of Northern Ireland.[2]

Mr. De Valera on being informed of the terms of your statement this afternoon instructed me to let you know immediately that he is very perturbed indeed by your announcement.

He is anxious to have an assurance that there is no intention of applying Conscription to the people of the Six Counties. At least one-third of the population there are cut off from Ireland against their will. Any attempt to conscript them would be resented as an outrage.

In union with our fellow-countrymen in the Six Counties we are prepared to undertake the defence of the whole of Ireland against anyone seeking to get a foothold there. That, Mr. de Valera suggests, is the constructive line to take and the line that would serve the true interest of Great Britain, whereas the introduction of Conscription in the Six Counties by the British Government for the British Army can only be regarded as an act of war against our nation, and will provoke the bitterest hostility to England wherever there are Irishmen throughout the world.[3]

Yours sincerely,
(Sd.) JOHN W. DULANTY
High Commissioner

---

[1] Marginal annotation: 'Recd E.A. 29/4/39'.
[2] See above No. 304.
[3] This sentence has been highlighted by a reader with a pencil stroke in the left-hand margin.

No. 306 NAI DFA Secretary's Files S70

Confidential report from John W. Dulanty to Joseph P. Walshe (Dublin)
(No. 27) (Secret)

LONDON, 27 April 1939[1]

I saw Mr. Chamberlain at No. 10 Downing Street this morning. I told him that I had understood from Sir Thomas Inskip that the Conscription proposal of the British Government announced yesterday afternoon would apply to the Six Counties of Northern Ireland. I had informed Mr. De Valera accordingly and he had instructed me to represent to Mr. Chamberlain immediately the gravest concern with which the Irish Government regarded such a proposal.[2]

Mr. Chamberlain asked me in a rather sharp tone why Mr. de Valera should be so concerned.

I said that was a surprising question. Yesterday morning, when my Government had no information beyond rumours in the newspapers of the proposal to introduce Conscription, I had seen Sir Thomas Inskip on Mr. De Valera's instructions for the express purpose of saying how extremely serious the situation would be in Ireland if any form of Conscription were introduced into the Six Counties. Sir Thomas Inskip told me that he had sent a verbal note of my remarks to Mr. Chamberlain and also to Sir Samuel Hoare.

I then handed to Mr. Chamberlain the letter, a copy of which is attached hereto.[3]

After reading this he said he was dismayed by the harsh fate which seemed to dog his steps in regard to Ireland. Following upon his recent conversation with me when I delivered a personal letter to him from Mr. De Valera he gave careful consideration to the Northern Ireland problem and had drafted a letter to Lord Craigavon asking him to come to London to discuss the question with a view to seeing whether something could not be done and done quickly to solve the problem. 'I did not send the letter' Mr. Chamberlain continued 'because Mr. de Valera made a speech which immediately brought forth sharp retorts from the Northern Unionists. I am afraid also his subsequent utterances will put the Northern people still more on edge'.

The Irish aspect of this momentous proposal, I suggested, had not been fully considered. One would have thought a matter of such far-reaching consequences would have been mentioned to the Irish Government if for no other purpose than that of obtaining their view. His own Opposition in Parliament he would remember had made a similar point that they had no prior intimation.

Mr. Chamberlain said that he had regarded this as a domestic question and he had not therefore informed any Dominion.

My rejoinder was that there could clearly be no kind of comparison between Canada, South Africa, Australia, or New Zealand, and ourselves. Apart from our fundamentally different attitude towards the

---

[1] Marginal note: 'Received EA 29.4.39'.
[2] See above No. 304 and 305.
[3] See above No. 305.

Commonwealth conception none of these had part of their territory occupied in the way our six Northern counties were occupied. In that part of our country – I emphasised the words 'our country' – nearly half a million of our people had maintained unbrokenly the position that they were in a state of bondage to a Government they detested, had not the rights of free men, and were coerced into separation from their fellow-countrymen in the rest of Ireland. Mr. de Valera, as Mr. Chamberlain was well aware, had declared his wish for and had worked towards 'good neighbour' relations between the two countries. The introduction of Conscription into the Six Counties would not only completely destroy any progress which might have been made in that direction but would lead for many a year to a state of strife and bitter struggle – an appalling prospect to anyone who knew Ireland.

The speed with which events had travelled within recent weeks, Mr. Chamberlain said, had compelled the British to move in this matter with the utmost despatch. Whether their action would modify Hitler's speech this week or not he was not sure but it was of supreme importance that the announcement he had made yesterday should precede instead of follow Hitler's speech. From every point of view it would have been dead wrong for their Conscription proposal to appear as a retort to Hitler when in fact it was meant to have the influence of restraint.

He would, however, try to see Sir Thomas Inskip and Sir Samuel Hoare. The position was beset with very real difficulties for them. The supporters of the Northern Ireland Government were most eager and anxious for the Conscription Bill to include the Six Counties. 'Rightly or wrongly they regard themselves as part of us' Mr. Chamberlain said, 'and if we leave them out we will be in serious difficulties'. I said the difficulties for the British arising out of exclusion of the Six Counties were as nothing compared to the difficulties for us, and later for the British, by their inclusion. Mr. de Valera felt that no situation fraught with such extreme dangers had arisen since he took office over seven years ago.

Mr. Chamberlain was in the middle of the preparation of his speech introducing the Conscription motion this afternoon in their Parliament but he said in view of these representations he would certainly try his best to find time today to see what could be done.

My impression was that the British Government did not realise the consequences their proposal would have if the Six Counties were included and I am afraid I got the further impression that Mr. Chamberlain this morning was not encouraging about the exclusion of those Counties.

[signed] JOHN W. DULANTY
High Commissioner

No. 307 NAI DFA Secretary's Files S70

Confidential report from John W. Dulanty to Joseph P. Walshe (Dublin)
(No. 28) (Secret)

LONDON, 28 April 1939

In confirmation of my telephone conversations, I have made strong representations as to the extreme danger of any introduction of Conscription into the Six Counties to the undermentioned members of the British Cabinet:-

Mr. Malcolm MacDonald
Sir Thomas Inskip
Lord Halifax
Mr. Walter Elliot
Sir Kingsley Wood[1]
Mr. Hore-Belisha[2]
Mr. Leslie Burgin[3]

the last three named being directly concerned with Defence and the provision of man-power.

I spoke to back-benchers on the Government side of the House including Mr. Harold Nicolson.[4]

On the Opposition side I saw Mr. Greenwood[5] the Deputy leader of the Labour Party who has charge for them of the Conscription question and Sir Archibald Sinclair the Liberal Leader.[6]

I made personal contact with the Editors of the following newspapers

The Manchester Guardian[7]
The Times[8]
The Daily Telegraph[9]
The News Chronicle[10]

and I spoke to Lord Beaverbrook for the Daily Express series of newspapers, and to Lord Harmsworth for the same series of the Daily Mail.

Others approached were
Cardinal Hinsley[11]
The American Ambassador[12]

---

[1] Sir Howard Kingsley Wood (1891-1943), British Conservative politician, Secretary of State for Air (1938-40).

[2] Isaac Leslie Hore-Belisha, First Baron Hore-Belisha (1893-1957), British Liberal National politician, Minister for Transport (1934-7), Secretary of State for War (1937-40).

[3] Leslie Burgin (1887-1945), British Liberal National politician, Minister for Transport (1937-9), Minister of Supply (1939-40).

[4] Harold Nicolson (1886-1968), British diplomat, author and politician (New Party and Labour).

[5] Arthur Greenwood (1880-1954).

[6] Sir Archibald Sinclair (1890-1970), Leader of the Liberal Party (1935-45), Secretary of State for Air (1940-45).

[7] William Percival Crozier (1879-1944), Editor of *The Guardian* (1932-44).

[8] George Geoffrey Dawson (1874-1944), Editor of *The Times* (1912-19, 1923-41).

[9] William Berry, Viscount Camrose.

[10] Sir Gerald Reid Barry (1898-1968), Managing Editor of the *News Chronicle* (1936-47).

[11] Arthur Cardinal Hinsley (1865-1943), Catholic Archbishop of Westminster (1935-43), Primate of the Catholic Church in England.

[12] Joseph 'Joe' Kennedy, Sr.

Sir Warren Fisher
Sir Horace Wilson

To most of these people (Lord Halifax and Mr. MacDonald and Sir Thomas Inskip were exceptions) the problem at first mention seemed to be new or only dimly apprehended. Only a short exposition however was needed for most of them to admit the seriousness of the situation.

The Second Reading debate it is expected will take place on Tuesday next.

I am now waiting to hear from Sir Thomas Inskip who has promised to let me know this evening whether he has any statement to give me.

JOHN W. DULANTY
High Commissioner

No. 308 UCDA P150/2183

Memorandum from Joseph P. Walshe for Eamon de Valera (Dublin)
(Secret)

DUBLIN, 29 April 1939

I have just had a further conversation with the High Commissioner on the phone. His summing up of his conversations with the British Ministers, especially with Inskip, is that the British Government intend to go through with the application in principle of Conscription to the Six County area. They are, however, seeking some method by which the Nationalists can be excluded, and at the moment at any rate it is their intention to try to put a clause into their Bill for that purpose. The Cabinet is meeting on Monday morning at 10 o'clock, and Inskip has promised to give the clause or its purport to the High Commissioner at mid-day on Monday. Whatever they may do about exempting the Nationalists, it is clearly their desire to establish their right to impose Conscription on the Six Counties.

The High Commissioner has found the editors of the principal London papers sympathetic. All of them this morning carry pretty accurate accounts of your attitude. So far as I have learned, the 'Manchester Guardian' is the only paper which has a leader advocating the non-application of the Bill to the Six Counties on the grounds of expediency while emphasising the right of the British Parliament to do so if they desired. I enclose the High Commissioner's two written reports of his interviews, received this morning.[1] The High Commissioner added on the phone this morning that Beaverbrook was wholeheartedly with us and was working might and main to prevent what he regards as a very dangerous step being taken.

[initialled] J.P.W.[2]

---

[1] See above Nos 306 and 307.
[2] Handwritten marginal annotation by Walshe: 'Read for Minister'.

No. 309 NAI DFA Secretary's Files S70

Code telegram from Joseph P. Walshe to Robert Brennan (Washington)
(No. 142) (Copy)
DUBLIN, 29 April 1939

Your 97.[1] Tell Delegates Chief will go to America at earliest possible date, perhaps next month. Ask them to expect suggestion early next week for possible postponement of Congress for short period. Inform them situation extremely grave here owing to possibility of imposition of conscription on Six Counties. Emphasise real danger of bloodshed as people here and in Six Counties will resist to death imposition of conscription on Irish Nation by external power. It is vital to secure public support of our people in America in this matter with all possible speed.

ESTERO

No. 310 NAI DFA Secretary's Files S70

Code telegram from Joseph P. Walshe to Robert Brennan (Washington)
(No. 143) (Copy)
DUBLIN, 29 April 1939

Tell them go ahead and explain full gravity as in my 142.[2] Also tell them emphasise in strongest fashion occupation by British forces of six counties of Ireland is against will of more than three fourths of the Irish people at home and the vast majority of our race everywhere. We regard this occupation as a continuing act of aggression. Britain has of course no more right to conscript our people in the six counties than France or Germany.

ESTERO

No. 311 UCDA P150/2183

Memorandum from Joseph P. Walshe to Eamon de Valera regarding the
proposed introduction of conscription in Northern Ireland
(Secret)
DUBLIN, 29 April 1939

Note for Minister[3]

I have made it clear to the British Government that any attempt to impose compulsory military service in Northern Ireland would constitute an act of war against the Irish Nation.

I have taken that course because I hold that the right of the people of Ireland to govern the whole of this island is sovereign and indefeasible.

I hold that, in contemplation of the law of nations and of the Constitution

---

[1] Not printed.
[2] See above No. 309.
[3] Title handwritten by Walshe.

of Ireland, the national territory is indivisible and the unity of the Irish Nation perpetual.

I hold that no power on earth has the legal or the moral right to conscript Irishmen inhabiting the national territory of Ireland for service in a foreign army.

No. 312 NAI DFA 219/4

Confidential report from Charles Bewley to Joseph P. Walshe (Dublin)[1]
(43/33) (Copy)

BERLIN, 29 April 1939

The German Chancellor's speech of 28th April has no doubt been fully reproduced in the Dublin press, and it would be unnecessary to give any analysis of its contents. The general opinion here (not only in German circles but among the neutral members of the Diplomatic Corps) is that the Chancellor has been very successful in exposing the amateurishness of President Roosevelt's diplomatic offensive. His reference to Ireland and Palestine in particular were received with considerable amusement.

The general effect of the speech seems to be on the whole regarded as conciliatory. The denunciation of the Naval Agreement with England and the German-Polish Pact had been regarded as highly probable, if not inevitable: the fact that in each case the Chancellor has declared himself ready to enter into new negotiations prevents such a step from being regarded as purely aggressive, while putting the onus of continued friendly relations on the other party. It is in my opinion evidence of the desire not to embitter the international situation that no reference was made to the introduction of compulsory service in England, and that in particular there was no allusion to the entirely inadequate nature of the measure or the obvious reluctance of the population of England to submit itself to military training.

The references in the speech to Ireland have no doubt been reproduced in the Irish newspapers. I think it however well to give the translations.

In speaking of the German solution of the Czechoslovak problem, the Führer goes on to say:

'No more than English measures, let us say in Ireland, whether they are good or bad, are subject to German control or criticism, is this the case with these old German principalities.'

And later, in answering President Roosevelt's request that Germany should pledge itself not to attack Ireland, he adds:

'I have just read a speech of the Irish Prime Minister De Valera, in which – strange as it may seem – unlike Mr. Roosevelt he does not accuse Germany of oppressing Ireland, but makes the charge against England that Ireland has to suffer under her continuous aggression. However great Roosevelt's comprehension of the needs and difficulties of other states, it must still be assumed that the Irish President knows the dangers

---

[1] Marginal annotations: 'MR 3.5.39'; 'Original detached for file on Roosevelt message, S.G.M.'.

which threaten his country better than the President of the American Union.'

It will be seen from these extracts that the German attitude towards Ireland is exactly the same as it was before 1914, – that just as Alsace-Lorraine in 1914 was, and Bohemia in 1939 is no concern of England's, so Germany is not prepared to interest herself practically in Ireland, as being in the English sphere of influence. The efforts of Sir Roger Casement,[1] Joseph Plunkett[2] and others to induce Germany to declare the freedom of Ireland as one of her war aims were not successful, mainly because the German Government feared that the opposing powers would draw an analogy between Ireland and Alsace-Lorraine. The same analogy would now exist, whether it be a correct one or not, between Ireland and Bohemia, and of course no German Government would (except possibly in a war) make a direct claim for the liberty and independence of Ireland.

On the other hand, Ireland is at present the object of great sympathy in Germany, – partly from sentimental reasons, partly as being a useful method of propaganda against England. I have not the slightest doubt that, if Ireland wished to increase its trade with Germany, it could do so very largely, – on even better conditions than the present Agreement. I have also little doubt that the officials in charge of the German press would welcome any assistance given then by the Irish Government in regard to propaganda on the general questions of Ireland's position, including the Partition question. Of course any such campaign would be inaugurated by the Press Department of the Foreign Office and the Ministry for Propaganda, – with which, as you indicate in your minutes of 30th June 1937 (114/13) and 21st March 1938, and telegram of 9th July 1939, it is not desired that I should enter into relations.[3] If at any time the Minister should wish me to approach the officials in question, I shall of course be delighted to do so.

[stamped] C. BEWLEY

---

[1] Sir Roger Casement (1864-1916), Irish nationalist, former British consular official who highlighted human rights abuses of indigenous peoples in the Congo and in the Putumayo region of the Amazon basin by colonial authorities and business interests. Retired from the Foreign Office and joined the Irish Volunteers (1913) and became a member of the Provisional Committee, raised money for the purchase of arms, sought arms in Germany, sailed to Ireland and was captured at Banna Strand, Kerry, on 20 April 1916. Charged with high treason and executed in London on 3 August 1916, his remains re-interred in Dublin (1965).

[2] Joseph Mary Plunkett (1887-1916), Irish nationalist, member of the Gaelic League and the IRB. Member of the Military Committee of the IRB that planned the 1916 Rising (largely based on a plan devised by Plunkett). Leader of the 1916 Rising and signatory of the 1916 Proclamation. Executed in Dublin on 4 May 1916. Plunkett's father, Count George Noble Plunkett was Irish Minister for Foreign Affairs (1919-20) and Associate Minister for Foreign Affairs (1920-1).

[3] These documents have not been printed.

No. 313 NAI DFA 219/6

Confidential report from Michael MacWhite to Joseph P. Walshe (Dublin)[1]
(Confidential)

ROME, 29 April 1939

In diplomatic circles here opinion is about evenly divided as to whether the conclusions to be drawn from Hitler's speech in the Reichstag this afternoon leant more towards the side of war or of peace. So far none of my colleagues have seen the text and only a few of them know German sufficiently well to be able to make an intelligent estimate of what was said. Poland was, however, pointed out as one of the unreasonable countries much like Czechoslovakia was last September though on that occasion Beneš, personally was the main subject of attack. It is believed the status of Danzig would already have been changed if Great Britain had not clarified her attitude in regard to Poland. The Polish Ambassador to whom I have just spoken, fears for the worst, although he thinks it possible no aggressive move may be made during the Summer months. The references to Ireland in Hitler's speech were the subject of much comment. One diplomat said 'He put his finger on Britain's only weak spot and then stuck it in Roosevelt's eye'.

During the visit of Goering to Rome a fortnight ago the Duce is said to have asked him to warn the Fuehrer against any aggressive steps for the time being, at least, and to inform him, at the same time, that he could not count on any support from Italy in case of an attack on Poland. Although there was a great fanfare of trumpets on his arrival, his departure passed almost unnoticed. Since then, it would appear that the axis is not so rigid as before. The attacks in the Italian press on France have ceased and while the efforts of the democracies in their policy of encirclement of the totalitarian States occupy much space the undertone is less aggressive. Perhaps the taking over of Albania by Italy forestalled a more important move on the part of Germany.

The French Ambassador called on the Italian Foreign Minister a couple of days ago to straighten out some trade tangle. In the course of the negotiations M. Poncet[2] asked Count Ciano, bluntly, what French concessions would satisfy Italian national aspirations and the reply was – as told me by a person very close to the French Ambassador – 'A free port at Djibouti, participation in the Direction of the Suez Canal and a modification of the status of Italians in Tunisia'. These are concessions which France could make at any time without loss of prestige or dignity if it were not made to appear that they were wrenched from her under threat of war.

The military tension here of the past months has been eased considerably during the last couple of days. The reservists called to the colours have not been disbanded but officers are free to return to civil life as they prefer. They are no longer obliged to sleep in Barracks. This relief is particularly noticeable

---

[1] The marginal annotations on this document show that it was read by Joseph P. Walshe, Frederick H. Boland and Michael Rynne.

[2] André François-Poncet (1887-1978), French Ambassador to Germany (1931-38), Ambassador to Italy (1938-40).

among the civil population. The war clouds that enveloped the horizon a couple of weeks ago seem to have evaporated so far as the Italian people are concerned.

[signed] M. MacWhite

No. 314 NAI DFA Secretary's Files S70

Confidential report from John W. Dulanty to Joseph P. Walshe (Dublin)
(No. 29) (Secret)[1]

LONDON, 1 May 1939

Sir Thomas Inskip told me this afternoon that a Committee was sitting under the Chairmanship of Lord Maugham,[2] their Chancellor, and he thought it likely that they would find in connection with the forthcoming Conscription Bill that Irishmen formally resident in this country would, under that measure, be liable to be called up for the military service. He though Mr. de Valera would not think that unreasonable. I made no comment.

He then said that the Cabinet had had a long discussion this morning when the Prime Minister had informed them of the grave anxiety which Mr. de Valera and his Government felt at the possibility of any form of Conscription being applied to Northern Ireland.

I enquired whether any reference to Northern Ireland would appear in the Bill which would be printed this evening. He replied by reading out the following:-

CLAUSE 15. His Majesty may by Order in Council direct that the Act shall extend to Northern Ireland and to the Isle of Man, subject to such modifications and adaptations as may be specified in the Order.

It appeared that the United Kingdom Minister for the purpose of this contingent provision for Northern Ireland was the British Minister of Labour and a certain amount of time would elapse before anything could be done, assuming that the Act were to apply to Northern Ireland. At my request he wrote the following note:-

'Before the Bill can be brought into operation in Northern Ireland certain administrative arrangements and modifications would have to be made. These will take time and there will therefore be full opportunity for discussion between the interested Governments'.

I pointed out that the last sentence assumed that Mr. de Valera would be willing to discuss a proposal to apply Conscription to the Six Counties. I made it clear that I had no authority to accept such an assumption nor did I think there was the least likelihood of Mr. de Valera entering upon such a discussion. Sir Thomas Inskip said that it would make their task almost impossible if we did not agree to discuss the matter.

They were, he assured me, fully alive to the difficulties of the situation and the very last thing in their minds was to provoke or even to appear to

---

[1] Marginal note: 'Recd. E.A. 4/6/39.'
[2] Frederick Herbert Maugham, First Viscount Maugham (1866-1958), British Lord Chancellor (1938-9).

provoke any trouble in Ireland itself or as between Ireland and England.

At the Cabinet that morning they had discussed various courses. One was to have Conscription in Northern Ireland but to so frame the Order in the Council as to enable a Nationalist to 'opt out' if he so wished. A second course was to provide exemption much on the same lines as conscientious objectors secured exemption in this country. A third plan was to allow a Nationalist exemption provided that he joined the Volunteer force in Éire.

I said the Irish Government would be profoundly dismayed at what Sir Thomas Inskip had told me. After my conversation with Mr. Chamberlain and a number of his colleagues it did seem that – albeit at a late stage – the extreme gravity of the situation was now realised. The British must surely know now that it was the merest statement of fact to say that the extension of any form of Conscription to one, let alone six, of our Irish Counties would involve the ending of our relations with Britain. Yet the proposed Clause 15 and the expedients he had told me of showed no recognition of this inevitable consequence but suggested that they still contemplated compulsion in the North. Mr. de Valera would clearly want to know whether that was the position.

Sir Thomas Inskip said that in all honesty and straightforwardness he could assure me that he did not know what would be done. He did not know whether Conscription would be applied to the Six Counties nor did the Cabinet know. He was saying this to me privately so that Mr. de Valera might know exactly where he, Sir Thomas Inskip, and his colleagues stood at this moment. He would ask that this statement of his should not be used in public debate because it might only tend to deterioration of the present position. He would deplore at this moment any assertion that there would be Conscription and equally deplore any assertion that there would not be. This fits in with Mr. Chamberlain's reply to the Press that the question was under consideration, and I got the impression from Sir Thomas Inskip that he was telling the truth and was not employing a diplomatic reservation.

The British, Sir Thomas Inskip said, were between the devil and the deep blue sea because there was just as much explosive material on the Unionist side in the Six Counties as there was Nationalist. They had incurred bitter discontent from the Unionists in the North by the settlement which they had made with the Irish Government last year. He was not saying that the settlement was not the right one to make; he merely wished to make clear how awkward the position of the British Government was. I said he could not object to my saying in the settlement which they made in returning the Ports they were only giving back what was obviously ours, and expressing a purely personal opinion I thought the British got off far too lightly in the financial settlement.

He made at some length an appeal for help. It would be remembered that the Germans were encouraged in 1914 by the threat of civil war in Ireland. If there was any repetition of this Herr Hitler might be influenced in what were already dangerous designs so that a tremendous responsibility rested upon all to be statesmen instead of politicians. Could not Mr. de Valera do something to assist in this most difficult situation?

I referred him to the letter I handed to Mr. Chamberlain[1] in which Mr. de Valera had said:

'In union with our fellow-countrymen in the Six Counties we are prepared to undertake the defence of the whole of Ireland against any enemy seeking to get a foothold there'.

Sir Thomas Inskip responded very readily indeed to this suggestion saying that it might well prove to yield a solution.

[signed] JOHN W. DULANTY
High Commissioner

No. 315 NAI DFA 219/22

Extracts from the annual report for 1938 to 1939 on Irish relations with Spain from Leopold H. Kerney to Joseph P. Walshe (Dublin)
(S.S. 19/7)

SAN SEBASTIAN, 1 May 1939

[matter omitted]
PROTECTION
Steps were taken by me for the protection of a number of Irish nationals in Spain.

The case of Frank RYAN, a prisoner of war in General Franco's hands, in whose fate the Irish Government and Irish public bodies took a keen interest, engaged the constant attention of the Legation throughout the year; appeals for clemency met with no response and did not prevent a death sentence being passed; Captain Meade, a Spaniard of Irish decent, assured me more than once that my efforts had undoubtedly prevented the carrying out of the sentence, and this may possibly be the case. With the help of the International Red Cross Committee, it was found possible to arrange for Ryan to receive remittances and clothes and to exchange correspondence with his family, but there have been long periods of silence leading to occasional disquieting rumours. Every effort was made, but without success, to secure the exchange of Ryan for some prisoner in the hands of the Spanish Republican forces; these efforts ceased when the Republican Government abandoned Barcelona and when the Spanish Nationalist authorities informed me that Ryan was not a prisoner of war but a criminal guilty of the worst possible crimes. However, Frank Ryan still lives and persistent efforts are being made to secure his release.

Efforts to secure the liberation of Andrew O'TOOLE,[2] a minor who did not return to Ireland with General O'Duffy's battalion but remained behind as a volunteer in the Spanish Foreign Legion, were finally successful, and orders were given on 7th July 1938 for his liberation with a view to repatriation; I was subsequently advised that the boy deserted on 17th July; from an unofficial but trustworthy source I ascertained that he was arrested as a deserter, and from the same source I learn that he is still alive; efforts to

---

[1] See above No. 305.
[2] See above Nos 232, 281 and 295.

obtain official confirmation have not yet met with success, but it is expected that they will do so shortly.

Efforts were made to obtain confirmation of the reported death of a minor (Thomas WOOD),[1] a volunteer on the Republican side, for whose repatriation steps had previously been taken, but the Republican Government left my written enquiries unanswered, and no definite information was obtainable.

Steps were taken with a view to the repatriation of a certain Miss CRONIN,[2] whom the Spanish police authorities had dumped across the French frontier and who was imprisoned by the French police; this person, however, had no genuine desire to be repatriated and, whilst under police supervision, outwitted the authorities and swam back to Spain; the Spanish police, who had previously expelled her as a person of undesirable moral character, allowed her to go free; she secured employment in an English family in Bilbao; she holds no Irish passport, and presumably no British one. [matter omitted]

No. 316 NAI DFA Paris Embassy P19/34

Confidential report from Seán Murphy to Joseph P. Walshe (Dublin)
(P. 19/34) (Copy)

PARIS, 1 May 1939

The more considered French opinion in regard to Hitler's speech seems to be that while in some respects it is a speech 'd'attente', it contains a very definite threat to Poland if she is not prepared to concede the German demands. Practically all agree that the denunciation of the Anglo-German agreement is more a gesture than a threat and some see in it only a proof of the French view which prevailed at the time that the agreement was signed that it was only an effort on the part of Germany to detach England from the side of France in the opposition to the introduction of German conscription and later the occupation of the Rhineland. On the whole, it is felt that such hope as the speech carries for an improvement of the international situation depends on the actions of Germany rather than on what her spokesman may say. In so far as the speech contains a threat against Poland, the situation is believed to be somewhat serious to the extent that most French organs are agreed that Poland will not meet the German demands in regard to Danzig and corridor. A number of this morning's newspapers reproduce statements by Polish statesmen to the effect that the country will resist the German demands even at the risk of war and it is thought that Colonel Beck will officially define the Government attitude somewhat on the same lines in his speech either on the 2nd or on the 5th of this month.

There is no general feeling that Hitler's references to his desire for English friendship will lead to a weakening in Franco-British entente. It is reported that Sir Eric Phipps, when he saw Mr. Bonnet yesterday, assured him of the continued complete identity of view in the policy of the two governments.

---

[1] See above No. 18.
[2] See above No. 180.

Apart from Hitler's speech, the main attention of the press is concentrated on the developments of the Rumanian negotiations in so far as they affect the position of Poland and Rumania, on the development of the Rumanian position and, to a lesser extent, on the visit of General Brauchitsch[1] to Rome. A common suggestion in regard to the latter's visit is that it has to do with the question of the establishment of a single command for the German and Italian armies in case of war. The visit of the Rumanian Foreign Minister to Paris terminated yesterday when he left for Rome. Various statements and declarations made, emphasise the agreement of the two governments. Some papers suggest that the main subject matter of the conversations between M. Gafencu and the Italian statesmen will arise from the desire of Italy to assure herself of supplies of petrol from Rumania and also to include Rumania in a pro-Italian bloc consisting of Hungary, Yugoslavia and Bulgaria. The real situation of Rumania will, however, it is suggested depend to a large extent of the results of the negotiations with the U.S.S.R. as, unless some satisfactory arrangements for assistance to Rumania can be arrived at in these negotiations, the hostility of Bulgaria and Hungary and pressure from Germany may win the day. It is thought, however that progress is being made in the Russian negotiations and that Russia has now promised to undertake to give the kind of aid to Poland and Rumania which they will accept in the event of war and further to give a promise of being actively with both France and Great Britain should they be involved in a war because of their defence of Holland, Belgium or Switzerland, provided that France and Great Britain undertake to guarantee the Balkan states. Polish opposition to accepting assistance from Russia is still regarded as one of the most important factors in the outcome of the negotiations, but some suggest that now that Germany has denounced the treaty with Poland, she will herself feel free to adopt a more friendly attitude towards Russia.

[stamped] (Signed) SEAN MURPHY

No. 317 NAI DFA Secretary's Files S70

> *Confidential report from John W. Dulanty to Joseph P. Walshe (Dublin)*
> *(No. 31) (Secret)[2]*
>
> LONDON, 3 May 1939

Mr. Chamberlain asked me to see him in his room at the House of Commons at five o'clock this evening on the proposed Clause 15 of the Military Training Bill.[3]

In view of my conjecture after a telephone talk last night with his Principal Private Secretary[4] that Mr. Chamberlain would today announce some decision, I thought it better to elicit his statement first.

---

[1] Walther Brauchitsch (1881-1948), Commander in Chief of the Wehrmacht (1938-41).
[2] Marginal note by Walshe: 'HC must send a covering note carrying the day's date with his report as an enclosure J.W. 9/5/39'.
[3] See above No. 314.
[4] Sir Arthur Nevile Rucker (1895-1991).

He began by referring to the statement which Lord Craigavon had that day published saying that the Six County Government, whilst offering the whole of their resources to the British Government, had decided to leave to the latter the decision as to how those resources could best be used.

After careful consideration of this obviously difficult question the British Government, Mr. Chamberlain said, had decided not to extend Conscription to the Six Counties.

He explained that he had put me off from an interview on the preceding evening because he though it better to make this announcement to me *after* the meeting of the Cabinet which was held that morning and at which their decision was reached. He did not want it to appear that the British Government had yielded to 'a last moment pressure from Mr. de Valera'.

They had of course borne carefully in mind the representation which I had made both to him, and, he added, to certain other people – referring presumably to my conversations with members of their Cabinet and others in London during the past few days. They were not to be understood as admitting that as yet Mr. de Valera had any jurisdiction in the Six Counties. The British Government had reached this decision because it had been made clear to them the very serious difficulties in which the proposal would involve both Mr. de Valera and themselves. It was their earnest wish to develop the most harmonious relations with the Irish Government and further it would be a pity to allow differences which really had no connection with the question of British defence to add to the grave problems at the moment confronting the British Government.

Mr. de Valera, Mr. Chamberlain continued, had won his case but he felt sure that he would treat the decision with tact. 'We shall of course be much abused for this decision' but he thought with proper handling on all sides the turn events had taken should lead, as he prayed they might lead, to a better understanding between the peoples of the two countries.

I formed the impression that this question had been a source of considerable anxiety to Mr. Chamberlain and that he was much relieved, not to say happy, at the decision not to apply Conscription. It seemed neither necessary nor desirable at the moment to ask the obvious question as to why they had ever entertained such a proposal.

I therefore limited my remarks to saying that I assumed that Clause 15 of the Military Training Bill would be dropped forthwith. 'Yes' replied Mr. Chamberlain, 'We have decided to drop it because it would, if left in, be a continuing difficulty for Mr. de Valera.'

Walking with me to the door Mr. Chamberlain repeated his hope for a better understanding between Ireland and England. In striking contrast to my interview with him less than a week ago,[1] when his tone was rather sharp and aggressive, his attitude this evening was unmistakably friendly.

[signed] JOHN W. DULANTY
High Commissioner

---

[1] See above No. 306.

No. 318 NAI DFA Secretary's Files S70

Telegram from the Department of External Affairs to Robert Brennan
(Washington)

DUBLIN, 7.00pm 4 May 1939

Your 102.[1] Proposal completely dropped following protests.

No. 319 NAI DFA 219/7

Confidential report from Francis T. Cremins to Joseph P. Walshe (Dublin)
(S. Gen. 1/1) (Confidential)

GENEVA, 4 May 1939[2]

With reference to the international situation, I have to state that I had a further brief conversation with Mr. Soubbotitch, Permanent Delegate of
Yugoslavia, at a farewell dinner offered to him last night by his colleagues.
M. Soubbotitch stated that he had as yet no details of the conversations
which had taken place at Venice and Berlin between Yugoslavia and Italy. He
would learn these only when he returned to Belgrade in a day or so. He could
say however that Yugoslavia was satisfied with the results, and confident
that Yugoslavian interests in Albania would be safeguarded. I reminded him
of his hopes that an agreement regarding fortifications would be reached. He
did not know if any such specific agreement had matured but, as he understood the matter, this would be included in the general agreement regarding
the safeguarding of interests. He could say also that neither Germany or Italy
had invited Yugoslavia to adhere to the *axe* or to join the anti-commintern
pact. Yugoslavia's policy was explained as one of neutrality. There was no
intention, either, on the part of Yugoslavia to leave the League.

As regards the Croatian question, M. Soubbotitch mentioned that an
agreement had been reached, but at the last moment a hitch occurred which
would require new negotiations. The difficulty related to a portion of Bosnia,
occupied by Croats, which the Croatian leaders required to be included in the
'autonomous' area.

I think that the general impression here following Hitler's speech remains
that the speech left the general situation practically as it was, with, however,
a concentration of the danger in regard to Danzig. On the question of Danzig,
I find Polish circles peculiarly confident. The Poles seem to think that the best
solution would be the allotment of East Prussia to Poland instead of the allotment of Danzig and a portion of the corridor to Germany! The Polish Consul-
General here states that Poland is willing to discuss any changes which
would preserve Polish political and economic rights in Danzig, but that the
Polish Government hardly dare give way on any point at the present
moment, owing to the state of opinion in the country.

I had a word with the Italian Consul-General also last week. He seemed

---

[1] Not printed, but see No. 310 above.
[2] Marginal Note by Frederick H. Boland: 'Dr Rynne, see final parag.'.

to be somewhat anxious about the situation, but he thought that war could be avoided 'if Germany did not attack Poland on the question of Danzig'. He seemed to realise that that would mean war. It is the generally expressed opinion here that a German provoked war for Danzig would be anything but popular amongst the masses in Italy. There is also a story which is being whispered about that Balbo,[1] Grandi, and Badoglio[2] had recently addressed a letter to Mussolini pointing out the dangers to Italy of the present Italian foreign policy, and it is also stated that Balbo had made a protest at a meeting of the Fascist Grand Conseil. It is impossible to weigh up what importance if any is to be attached to these stories.

I raised the question in a recent minute as to how I should dispose of code books, etc. if a situation ever arose under which there might be danger that these books, etc. would pass out of my personal control. Mr. Andrews (South Africa) told me a few days ago that he had received confidential instructions to be acted upon in certain eventualities. He did not mention what the instructions were, but he said that he was to destroy codes and cyphers, and to find if possible a neutral legation which would be prepared to safeguard his office files, records, etc. So far as Geneva is concerned, he does not seem to think that the latter is a practical one. Probably he has received a copy of a circular addressed to Legations in other countries which would only have a limited application here. It seems probable that all the Delegations, neutral and others, except those accredited also to the Swiss Government, would leave Geneva in the event of a general war, even if Switzerland were not involved. Of course, Ireland's policy is to remain neutral, in any conflict, but it might happen that events might at some time render it impossible for me to guarantee the safety of the codes, etc. and that was why I asked for instructions in order to be ready for any eventuality

[signed] F.T. CREMINS
Permanent Delegate

No. 320 NAI DFA 219/4

Confidential report from Charles Bewley to Joseph P. Walshe (Dublin)[3]
(43/33)

BERLIN, 4 May 1939

There has been considerable interest here in the Irish question since the Chancellor's references in his Reichstag speech,[4] and the Partition question has naturally been referred to in connection with the conscription issue.

The reference in the Chancellor's speech, as reported not only in the Irish press but also in the English, French and Italian, was to the effect that England has no more right to interfere with German proceedings in Bohemia and Moravia than Germany would have to interfere with English measures

---

[1] Italo Balbo (1896-1940), Italian soldier and aviator.
[2] Pietro Badoglio (1871-1956), Italian soldier, diplomat and politician, Prime Minister of Italy (1943-4), Foreign Minister (1944).
[3] Marginal annotations: 'MR 3.5.39'; 'Secy'; 'Copy on 214/8'.
[4] See above No. 312.

in Northern Ireland. In fact, the word used by the Chancellor was 'Ireland', not 'Northern Ireland', and it so appeared in the whole German press. I do not personally see any motive for the alteration, nor can I conjecture by whom it was made. If the Chancellor had intended to refer to Northern Ireland and said Ireland by inadvertence, the words Northern Ireland would have appeared in the German press, which received typed copies of the speech; on the other hand it is hard to see why the German authorities should have issued another version to the foreign press to that appearing in the German newspapers, and equally hard to understand why the foreign press should with unanimity have changed the wording of the speech.

Members of the Press Department of the Foreign Office have informed me that they are pleased with the reception of the speech in Ireland, and stated that they notice in the last weeks a modification of the hostile attitude of the Irish Press, which they attribute to pressure from the Irish Government, and which they wish to reciprocate by a friendly attitude towards Ireland.

An official of the Foreign Office also mentioned that they did not expect any change in the attitude of the Irish Times, as they knew that it had to take its orders from certain English and international organisations, but that they regretted particularly that the only editor in Dublin with any knowledge whatever of Germany should be so hostile.[1] He also added that they regarded public opinion in Ireland as less unfriendly than official circles. Finally, in referring to the episode of the Lord Mayor of Cork[2] who refused to greet the German training ship,[3] he said that they had not wished to make too much of the discourtesy of an individual especially as they knew that, although he stated in public that his action was dictated by his Catholic sentiments, he had stated to his friends that his real objection to Germany was the suppression of Social Democratic trade unions.

[signed] CHARLES BEWLEY

No. 321 NAI DFA 219/6

Extract from a confidential report from Michael MacWhite
to Joseph P. Walshe (Dublin)
(Confidential)

ROME, 6 May 1939[4]

The political situation in Europe has eased considerably during the past week. Even the fear of a German Polish clash over Danzig and the corridor

---

[1] Robert Maire 'Bertie' Smyllie (1894-1954), editor of the *Irish Times* (1934-54), also wrote under the pen-name 'Nichevo'. Whilst visiting Europe as the tutor of an American student in the summer of 1914 Smyllie had been interned in Germany and spent the duration of the First World War in captivity.

[2] James 'Jim' Hickey, Labour Party politician, TD (Cork Borough, 1937, 1938-43, 1948-54), Lord Mayor of Cork (1937-40).

[3] The German battleship *Schlesien* called at Cobh from 25 February to 3 March 1939 in the course of a training cruise to Central America.

[4] The marginal annotations on this document show that it was read by Joseph P. Walshe, Frederick H. Boland and Michael Rynne.

has almost vanished. It is believed in Diplomatic circles here that Italy declined assistance to Germany in case of an attack on Poland and Count Ciano, who is to meet Ribbentrop in Milan today, is said to carry a message from the Duce to the effect that the settlement of the German Polish differences should be deferred to the arbitration of some neutral country.

Anti German sentiment in Italy is said to be growing. The principal Roman morning paper stated yesterday that rumours circulated abroad to the effect that anti German demonstrations took place in Milan a few days ago were absolutely unfounded. Here it would seem that the more truth there is in a story, the more vehement is the denial.

The Italian papers are giving more space to Irish news than heretofore. The pronouncements of the Taoiseach in regard to the proposal to apply conscription to Northern Ireland were well featured. The explosions in England, which have been attributed to the I.R.A. are always published in a prominent place but without comment.
[matter omitted]

No. 322 NAI DFA 219/4

Confidential report from Charles Bewley to Joseph P. Walshe (Dublin)[1]
(43/33)

BERLIN, 9 May 1939

The press and public opinion are very largely occupied with the Polish question, but so far as I can judge there is not expectation of an immediate war, although the gravity of the situation is realized: if the account of persons who have recently visited London and Paris can be believed, there is far more confidence here than in those capitals. It is assumed that Poland cannot adhere indefinitely to her present attitude, and that as time passes England and France will become even less desirous of fighting for a Polish Danzig. The introduction of conscription in England is treated as ineffective and rather ridiculous, and the rush of young men into the territorial force for the purpose of avoiding military training receives its due share of attention.

This view is shared by the new Roumanian Minister[2] here, who predicts that Poland will be forced to come to terms, because she cannot permanently keep a million men under arms, and because the Entente powers would find it, on moral as well as on national grounds, as hard to fight for Danzig as they did not Czechoslovakia. Anticipations of Germany's possible action must necessarily remain mere conjecture, but his view coincides with my own, namely that the German Government will probably take no step for some months in the belief that time will work more effectively on the morale of their opponents, – although he gave it as his opinion that, even if Germany occupied Danzig tomorrow, England and France would not move.

German opinion is much encouraged by the removal of Litvinoff, with the probability of a change in Russian policy in the direction of isolation. To

---

[1] Marginal annotations: 'A/Secy.'; 'Dr Rynne'; 'MR 27.5.39'.
[2] Radu T. Djuvara, Romanian Minster at Berlin (1938-9).

judge by the denunciations by the Moscow wireless of the attempts of the Western democracies to involve Russia in a war with Germany in English and French interests, such a change does not seem improbable. The treaties of non-aggression recently concluded with Estonia and Latvia and a little earlier with Lithuania are also regarded as very favourable to Germany's position, as is the withdrawal of Spain from the League of Nations. Finally the alliance between Germany and Italy is regarded as a guarantee of unity and rapidity of action against an obviously indecisive and disunited opposition.

There has been much conjecture on the Nuncio's recent visit to the Chancellor at Berchtesgaden, but it is not definitely known whether the three hours' discussion was concerned with the tension between Germany and Poland or the position of the Catholic Church in Germany or both. In any event, it is a striking proof of the new policy in regard to Germany inaugurated by his Holiness Pope Pius XII, and is of good augury for a future settlement of the religious question

[signed] CHARLES BEWLEY

No. 323 NAI DFA 219/6

Extract from a confidential report from Michael MacWhite
to Joseph P. Walshe (Dublin)
(Confidential)

ROME, 13 May 1939

Diplomats in Rome are at a loss to explain the decision of the Axis powers to enter into a formal military pact. The term alliance has been purposely eschewed. On the Italian side it is denied that this step means anything more than elaborating on paper a condition that has for some time existed in a looser form. The public are given to understand that it means nothing new. If such is the case, it seems strange that there should be so much propaganda made out of it by the totalitarian States. It would seem, however, to favour Germany more than Italy as it opens the way to an accentuation of German influence in this country.

The Italian press described the Pact as non-offensive, but points out at the same time that it will have a powerful influence for peace, as though through it the Axis powers will be able to supplant democratic hegemony in Europe with their own. It is not easy to reconcile these statements with one another, nevertheless, one may reasonably conclude that the pact was meant in some way to offset the so-called encirclement policy of Britain.
[matter omitted]

No. 324 NAI CAB 2/2

Extract from the minutes of a meeting of the Cabinet
(G.C. 2/70) (Item 1)

DUBLIN, 17 May 1939

OFFER BY THE EARL OF IVEAGH OF NO. 80, ST. STEPHEN'S GREEN
It was decided to accept the offer made in the Earl of Iveagh's letter of the 4th May, 1939, of his property at No. 80, St. Stephen's Green, subject to the existing head rents and to the firm condition that the open space should be left as such except in so far as the frontage on Hatch Street may be required for the enlargement of the National University.

No. 325 NAI DFA 226/34

Letter from Michael Rynne (for Joseph P. Walshe) to Francis T. Cremins
(Geneva)
(Copy) (226/34)

DUBLIN, 27 May 1939

I am directed by the Minister to forward you herewith, for your information, copies of two telegrams dated the 20th and the 27th May respectively[1] which have been exchanged with the Union of South Africa regarding that country's forthcoming candidature for the League of Nations Council.

The Minister personally considered the South African request and directed that it should be replied to by an assurance of complete approval and support.

[stamped] (Signed) M. RYNNE

No. 326 NAI DFA 219/6

Memorandum on the Italo-German Pact from Michael MacWhite to Joseph
P. Walshe (Dublin) (It/376/39)

ROME, 3 June 1939[2]

Enclosed herewith is a Memorandum dealing with the recent Italo-German pact, its origin and possible consequences.

[signed] M. MACWHITE

[Enclosure]

THE ITALO-GERMAN TREATY
ITS ORIGIN AND CONSEQUENCES
The signature of the Italo-German Treaty at Berlin a fortnight ago, committing each country to give the fullest diplomatic help to the other in peace and

---

[1]   Not printed.
[2]   This document is marked as having been seen by Frederick H. Boland and Michael Rynne.

the support of all its military forces in war, does not seem to introduce any new factor in European politics as the Axis has been from the beginning an Alliance for the purpose of revising certain provisions of the Treaty of Versailles, by force if necessary.

The fact that it was found necessary to put its conditions into documentary form possibly resulted from the successful negotiation of a British Pact with Turkey which affects Italy's position in the Aegean Sea. Be this as it may, the step exemplifies the dangerous point which the policy of revision has now reached. It is more difficult to explain why the Reich, in order to obtain Italy's signature, has curtailed its individual freedom of action through the obligation to consult its ally on all questions affecting common interests as well as the general European situation.

On the other hand, Italy cannot now adopt the attitude of neutrality she had been able to follow in 1914 within the framework of the Triple Alliance, for, under the present Treaty the possibility of unilateral action by one or other of the signatories appears to be excluded, such as was the case in regard to Czechoslovakia and Albania. These changes, if such they be, are meant no doubt to impress public opinion, both at home as well as abroad, and above all, an effort to intimidate Britain and France into making the oft demanded sacrifices to meet Italo-German aspirations.

The fact that this treaty does not rigidly correspond to Italian national sentiment, in so far as the mass of the people show little enthusiasm for collaboration with Germany, will make little difference in its working as the Fascist Party is in absolute control throughout the Kingdom and public opinion is, for many reasons, incapable of making itself felt. Impartial observers, everywhere, admit the conclusion of the pact to be the logical outcome of the Sanctions policy initiated at Geneva in 1935.

In order to understand its full bearing it is necessary to retrace some of the steps in the relations between the two dictators since Hitler took control of the destinies of the Reich. At the outset there was no spontaneous sympathy between the two revolutions although in their origin there were many points of similarity. Italy wanted Austria as a buffer state and the Stresa agreements[1] constituted a serious barrier to the Anschluss. When Hitler made his first move in this direction in 1934, several Italian divisions were sent to the Austrian frontier.

In 1935, however, the Reich took advantage of the Ethiopian war and the Sanctions policy of the League to cultivate the good graces of Italy. The moral effect of that policy which the Italian people felt much more deeply than the material effect shook the confidence which they had until then in the Western democracies. It is from this time one can trace the first sign of an Italo-German understanding. In 1936, gratitude to Germany was such that Italy facilitated the conclusion of the Austro-German agreement which she had

---

[1] The 'Stresa agreement' or 'Stresa Front' was signed at Stresa, Italy, in April 1935 between France, Britain and Italy in an attempt to counter the growth of German power in Europe by reaffirming the 1925 Locarno Treaties, to uphold Austrian independence and resist German attempts to revise the terms of the 1919 Treaty of Versailles.

previously opposed. There was a further manifestation of a new development in Italy's foreign policy when, in the same year, she declined representation at the Brussels Conference for the revision of the Locarno Pact. The policy of the Popular Front in France and the delay in sending a French Ambassador to Rome compromised the advantages that might be derived from the Mussolini-Laval agreement, the intent of which was to stabilise the relations between the two countries.

Rome now turned deliberately towards Berlin and Count Ciano paid his first visit to Hitler in October 1936 when the foundation of what has since come to be know as the Rome-Berlin axis was laid. In May 1937 the German Foreign Minister, von Neurath, visited Rome and was followed a few weeks later by Marshal Blomberg, Minister for War, which gave rise to the supposition of a wider and more general understanding between the two regimes. The visit of the Duce to Berlin in 1937 was the consequent result of this policy which culminated in the signature of the Rome-Berlin Treaty of the 22nd of May. It would, therefore, be a mistake to minimise the effect of this act which had been concluded under the pressure of necessity to realise their policy of revision on which depends, in their opinion, the solution of their difficulties.

According to Signor Gayda, the spokesman of the Duce, the pact constitutes the last invitation to the democratic powers to extend the necessary collaboration so as to assure to all people the just conditions of existence. This means equality of rights and an equal distribution of wealth and of raw materials according to the needs of each people and its capacity for development. In order to attribute to themselves the moral advantage and to gain favourable world opinion the totalitarian states endeavour to make the democracies responsible for the actual situation and accuse them of having violated international justice and the rightful aspiration of a young and prolific people. The policy initiated by England at the time of the Sanctions to defend her hegemony against what Italy claimed to be her own legitimate interests, was, therefore, the origin of the reaction of the Dictators. Encircled and menaced by what has been regarded as Franco-British imperialism, they were forced to create that policy which has kept Europe in a state of suspense ever since.

If, therefore, the Italo-German alliance in its latest phase is the direct reply to the Turco-British pact which has unbalanced the status quo in the Eastern Mediterranean to the detriment of Italy, one may be fairly certain that the conclusion of a Franco-Anglo-Soviet entente which is detested by the Axis Powers will provoke another striking reaction culminating, perhaps, in the denunciation of the Italo-British agreement of last year. In addition, they will, in all probability bring all their pressure to bear on the States of the Balkan peninsula to attach them to their policy, while the situation of Spain does not exclude the possibility of its collaboration with them in the Mediterranean.

[initialled] M.M.

No. 327 NAI DFA 219/2

Memorandum from Leopold H. Kerney to Joseph P. Walshe (Dublin)
(S.S. 50/19)[1]

SAN SEBASTIAN, 7 June 1939

I received at very short notice an official invitation, addressed on behalf of General Franco, to assist at the ceremony of inauguration of the monument to General Mola at Alcocer, 211 km. distant from San Sebastian, on Saturday 3rd June at noon. I regret that I found it impossible to communicate with you telegraphically beforehand, but I trust that you will approve of my decision to accept the invitation.

I left San Sebastian at 8 a.m., taking the Egyptian Minister with me in my car; we reached Alcocer at 11.30 a.m. The ceremony concluded at 1 p.m. We were back in San Sebastian at 6 p.m., after lunching at Vitoria at 2.30 p.m.

The mileage allowance for travelling by car – the only method of travelling available – would be £4. 1. 6.; would you please inform me whether it will be in order for me to submit an account accordingly; I await your confirmation before doing so.

Perhaps I should mention that there is a simmering discontent amongst the heads of Missions in San Sebastian because of the somewhat casual manner in which they are treated by the Spanish Government and the lack of regard shown to them; the Nuncio was present at this inauguration; there was only one Ambassador, the Portuguese; the Japanese, Irish and Columbian Ministers were there, although latter is one of the many who have not yet presented their credentials; there were also the Chargés d'Affaires of U.S.A., Estonia, Egypt, Finland, and also some Counsellors and Secretaries representing their Ambassadors; there were many absentees.

When the ceremony ended, we were all made to wait, standing, the Nuncio with the rest of us, whilst members of the Government got into their motor cars, one after the other; then it was the turn of officials, such as Barcenas and the Introducer of Ambassadors and latter's assistant; I suppose about 15 minutes passed in this way and then we saw a large group of turbaned Moors descending the steps towards the road, whereupon even the mild-mannered Nuncio could not help ejaculating – 'Hasta los Moros!' ('Even the Moors!'); that seemed to him to be about the last straw. The Japanese Minister's car then came along and he drove away; then my car came and I had no choice but to get in, after saying good-bye to the Nuncio and the Portuguese Ambassador; latter went looking for his car; I do not know whether the Nuncio was the last to leave.

[signed] L.H. KERNEY
Aire Lán-Chómhachtach

---

[1] Marginal note by Sheila Murphy: 'Seen by Secy'.

No. 328 NAI DFA Secretary's Files A20/2

Extract from a semi-official letter from Leopold H. Kerney to Joseph P. Walshe (Dublin) (S.S. 50/19)

SAN SEBASTIAN, 17 June 1939

Extract from semi-official letter received from Mr. Kerney

'Ryan has been branded as a Communist; the same perverse thinking will try to link up with Communism any persons or bodies pleading his case publicly, and Ryan's enemies *in Ireland* will gladly avail of any publicity on his behalf to write quietly and privately to their friends in Spain to encourage latter not to let Ryan out of their grasp. What I have felt all along is that if we act quietly, we may be able to steal a march on those bitter Irishmen and Irishwomen who want Ryan to die. Have his friends in Ireland and elsewhere ever stopped to consider how publicity could secure his freedom; Spain is not a democratic country; public opinion does not count; a tearing, raging press campaign in other countries would be simply laughed at by the authorities here, and those who may think otherwise know nothing of present-day Spain. We have been trying to catch Ryan's enemies napping. If others want to spoil that chance, the only chance in my opinion, well I think we can conscientiously say we did our best – short of declaring war on Franco – before they came along and sealed Ryan's fate. I distrust some at least of Ryan's friends, for whom Ryan's death as a martyr would be glorious propaganda. Having given our honest opinion and advice, I would leave it at that; I would not press his friends unduly to abandon their opinion, if they think otherwise, because they would only suspect us of some fell design in keeping things dark.'

No. 329 NAI DFA Secretary's Files A20/2

Memorandum from Leopold H. Kerney to Joseph P. Walshe (Dublin) (S.S. 10/11)

SAN SEBASTIAN, 17 June 1939

Visit to Frank RYAN, 16th June 1939
Your 244/8A[1]
Further to my minute of 7th inst.,[2] your telegram No. 28[3] sent at 2.55 p.m. on 12th was delivered here at 6 p.m. on 13th; I wrote on the 13th to the Inspector of Prison Camps in Burgos in order to fix a date for my visit to Frank Ryan; I telephoned to his office on 14th but he was out; I telephoned again on 15th only to be told that the Inspector only dealt with the Concentration Camps, and I was referred to the General commanding the Sixth Region, i.e. General Lopez Pinto. I could not get in touch with him, so I decided to call up the Director of the Prison, who was quite agreeable to my calling there the next day at noon.

---

[1] Not printed.
[2] See above No. 327.
[3] Not printed.

I left San Sebastian by car at 8 a.m. I reached Burgos at 11.30 a.m. with the intention of calling first on General Lopez Pinto – now our main hope; unfortunately, he had left the same morning for Bilbao, where he will remain till 23rd June; Meade (with whom I am trying to keep in touch by telephone) is also in Bilbao and will certainly see him there; I am leaving it to him to decide as to the most opportune moment for him to plead Ryan's cause, or to suggest a meeting with myself with that end in view.

The Central Prison is a palatial-looking building, built about 8 years ago, about 3 miles on the far side of Burgos. The chief warder was at the main gate; he shook hands with me, perhaps mistaking me for some other friend; the Director (Antonio Crejo) was awaiting me in his office; I arrived punctually at noon; I formed a very favourable opinion of him; we talked for about 20 minutes and he gave me much useful information.

The Prison usually holds 1000 or at the outside 1500 condemned prisoners; at present there are 4500; there is no rule of silence; the prisoners spend all day, from 6.30 or 7 a.m. till 8.30 or 9 p.m., in the open court-yard, where their meals are served and where they mix freely with one another until bedtime arrives; they sleep in large dormitories, in each of which there is accommodation for from 100 to 300 men.

The Director accepted from me for Frank Ryan the parcel of clothes that accompanied your minute (244/8A) of June 5th,[1] 300 cigarettes (which are not usually allowed to reach prisoners), some insecticide powder which I thought might be welcome and a sum of Ptas.150. He agreed that much time would be saved if I were to send future remittances direct to him rather than through the Red Cross. Parcels of any kind are always examined, but the Director told me that on this occasion this would not be done. He said there would be no objection to letting me know the charges against Frank Ryan, if these were in his file, but that, owing to pressure of work, it often happened that the sentence alone was communicated to him and not the reasons for the sentence; he showed me the file of another prisoner setting forth many pages of charges; he called for Ryan's file (expediente) and found that it did not even mention any judgment against him; he explained that this meant that officially, so far as the Director was advised, he was just under preventive arrest, after trial; the document stated that he had been tried on 15th June 1938 under a 'sumarisimo de urgencia 1695 de 1938' by the 'Juzqado Militar No. 4'; the Director allowed me to take a note of this, as being a most important reference in connection with any efforts to secure Ryan's liberation; I had already got on well enough to be able to confide to him my intention to appeal direct to General Lopez Pinto for his liberty; he told me that the Auditoria de Guerra, Burgos, would be the body to deal with the matter, and that the Auditor was Coronel Don José Casado, who would of course be in close touch with the General; the General commanding each military region has a similar body to assist and advise him.

The Director authorised me to visit the prison and Ryan whenever I wished to do so; there would be no objection to Miss Ryan paying him a visit,

---

[1] Not printed.

accompanied by me; conversations must always take place in Spanish, in the presence of a warder, but he would accept my guarantee that no prohibited subjects of conversation would be broached, and, exceptionally in this case, the conversation could take place in English. No reference should be made to the accusations made against him, as this would lead to a questioning of the justice of the sentence.

The chief warder was then summoned and told to accompany me to his office and to bring Ryan to see me there; this was a special privilege as the Director did not want to make me mix with others in the prison parlour, where, I understand, prisoners are separated from visitors by a grill.

Frank Ryan came into the warder's office when I was there, and we shook hands with each other; the good-hearted warder allowed us to speak in English, and even left the room once or twice during our conversation, which lasted at least an hour, and of course I did not take any notes. He told me the prison doctor had already advised him of my visit.

I enquired first about his health, and he said this was excellent, except for his heart; he did not want his family to know about this as it might alarm them needlessly; 4 or 5 years ago he discovered that he had an enlarged heart, but never paid any attention to it until he was in Spain; before the fighting on the Ebro, he was advised by a doctor not to subject it to strain and he had been taking care of himself; recently he had had palpitations, and had been in and out of the infirmary several times, but they were so busy there that he never had his temperature taken, and as soon as his pulse was beating all right out he had to go to make room for others; the assistant doctors were very good, however, and now he was allowed to have longer spells in the infirmary; this meant better food and also less strain, as otherwise he would have to be standing to attention for hours at a time; he thought perhaps I might be able to get some cheese, sausages, &c. sent to him from time to time. He said that a fellow-prisoner, a doctor, had examined him and assured him that the valvular trouble of his heart was not dangerous and could be cured with rest and good food; he said he also had high blood pressure, but remarked laughingly that it was not the prison diet that would make that worse.

His first question to me, however, was to know whether his father and mother were in good health; I at once assured him that they were, and I hope I told him the truth. He thought it would be better not to be visited by his sister, and asked me to so advise her, that the journey would be a costly one and that he was really feeling very fit and in good form in spite of everything; he said I could indeed see that myself, even though he was perhaps a trifle thinner than he used to be. The Director subsequently informed me that it would be beyond his power to allow any women to have a private conversation with a prisoner, such as I had, and remarked that it might be somewhat painful for Miss Ryan to see her brother in the regulation manner.

He had had a couple of teeth out the previous day and the dentist had offered to fit him out with 16 new teeth for 563 pesetas; he asked me to explain this to his family, saying that he could not do better elsewhere and that he never might have so much time and leisure at his disposal again; I told him to accept the dentist's offer and to ask latter to send me the bill, which I would pay and recover directly from his family subsequently.

Prisoners are not allowed to receive newspaper, novels or other reading matter, although they get a prison newspaper; Ryan told me he sometimes gleaned information from latter by reading between the lines; he asked me to get permission to send him an advanced Spanish Grammar. I subsequently got this permission from the Director.

He wants photographs of his family and even of his friends; the Director says that regulations forbid any other photos than those of father, mother, sisters and brothers.

He asked for the latest news from Ireland and enquired for the name of the President; when I told him Dr. Hyde was President, he remarked that they used to be good friends. He asked particularly for news of the Mulcahys of Sligo, which I was glad to be able to give him. He said he was well-treated, that the chief-warder was a decent fellow, and spoke well of the Director who, he said, was a recent arrival. They respected him (Ryan) in the prison, and he had never been punished, although he had at times intervened between subordinate warders and prisoners whom they were maltreating – much to the astonishment of the warders.

He was certain that my visit would have a very good effect on the attitude of the officials towards himself. I expressed the hope that I might be able to see him again soon, perhaps early in July.

He had learned only a few days ago that when he was first made prisoner he had been condemned to death by a drum-head court-martial and was to have been shot the following morning, but that two Italian officers came and took charge of him, saying that he would have to be exchanged against an Italian officer. I am not sure whether it was then, or a day or two later in Zaragoza, that a correspondent of the Catholic Universe, London, tried to intervene in his favour; he does not know the name of the correspondent, but is very grateful to him. He told me that he had been let down in some way by a higher officer prior to his capture, that he had been slightly wounded in the leg and so could not escape, but that he would certainly have been captured a few days later anyway.

No charges were made against him when he was tried on 15th June 1938, but a long letter was read out to him as evidence of character; he says the letter came from Ireland and he believes it was written by Miss Aileen O'Brien or by a Miss Godden, and that O'Duffy knew him too well to be the author of the many inaccuracies in detail; he thinks the letter was based largely on Hogan's[1] 'Could Communism come to Ireland?' He says the letter accused him of practically everything that had happened in Ireland since the civil war or earlier and affirmed that he was the assassin of O'Higgins,[2] Somerville[3]

---

[1] James Hogan (1898-1963), historian and political scientist, Professor of History at University College, Cork. The correct title of the book is *Could Ireland become Communist?: The facts of the case* (Cork, c. 1935).
[2] Kevin O'Higgins (1892-1927), Minister for Home Affairs (1922-7), Vice President of the Executive Council (1924-7), Minister for External Affairs (1927), assassinated, 10 July 1927.
[3] Vice-Admiral Henry Boyle Somerville (1863-1936), Royal Navy, shot dead by the IRA at his home in Castletownshend, County Cork, on 24 March 1936.

and others; he also remarked that Somerville was the brother-in-law of Sir Robert Hodgson,[1] who was supposed by some to be pleading in favour of Ryan; latter mentioned that some newspaper cuttings had been produced at his trial, but he did not know what was in them. He realised that his case was hopeless and that he was going to be condemned to death; his counsel spoke in his defence and pleaded for mercy, saying that Ryan had three sisters who were nuns; he was greatly puzzled as to how his counsel could have got that information. Asked if he had anything to say, he assured the court that, in going to Spain as a recruit for the Republican forces, he had gone to assist a Government recognised by the Irish Government and that he had broken no international law; he asked whether he was being tried for alleged offences in Ireland or in Spain, and stated that, if it was a crime to have fought in the republican ranks then he admitted the crime and had nothing more to say and they could do as they pleased; but first he explained that his chief reason for going to Spain was that O'Duffy was misrepresenting Ireland, describing him more or less as a British agent. Ryan says that, as he left the court, he was saluted respectfully by civil guards and others present. When he was taken to the Central Prison he was kept handcuffed there for 9 hours.

He told me there were three Poles in the prison who were anxious to get a visit from a Polish Consul or from the Minister, and that there was a Welshman there named Jones who was getting in touch with the British.

He enquired whether there was any likelihood of his recovering his liberty perhaps in say 7 or 8 months' time; all I could reply was to urge him to have patience and courage, though this advice was no doubt unnecessary, and to remember that he was not forgotten and would not be, and that a new effort was about to be made.

A fellow-prisoner with whom he has struck up friendship, and who seems to be somewhat privileged, is Sanchez Guerra, former Governor of some island off the coast of Africa, who was condemned to 12 years' imprisonment on setting foot unsuspectingly in nationalist Spain; Sanchez Guerra was Secretary to the President of the Republic and received me in that capacity when I presented my credentials in Madrid in 1935.

After bidding goodbye to Ryan, I again saw the Director, and learned from him that all letters from and to prisoners were first sent to the Jefatura del Servicio Nacional de Prisiones, Ministerio de Justicia, Madrid (this branch of the Department of Justice having now been transferred from Vitoria to Madrid), and that it was entirely a matter for its discretion as to whether such letters should go forward. I am not at all sure that permission can be obtained there for Ryan to communicate freely with his family.

I left the prison at 2 p.m., having thanked the Director for his kind reception, having assured him that I was much more favourably impressed in every way than I had ventured to anticipate would be the case, and having announced my intention of paying him other visits; he accompanied me to the gate, and I was saluted by the men on duty there.

I was nearly forgetting to mention that the Director informed me that

---

[1] Sir Robert Hodgson (1874-1956), British Agent to Nationalist Spain (1937-9).

prisoners could not receive food parcels unless they were completely fed from outside; this was a very strict rule recently imposed because of certain abuses; that was why I saw so many women outside the prison on their daily errand; but he would speak to the doctor and see what could be done for Ryan in the infirmary, where milk and other special food were available.

I arrived back in San Sebastian at 6.30 p.m.

To sum up:

1. The visit was a satisfactory and useful one.
2. The knowledge acquired that there were no definite charges and that the main justification for Ryan's detention is the 'evidence of character' contained in a letter from Ireland clears the way for the approach which I hope to make to General Lopez Pinto – although I have to be careful how I use that knowledge.
3. The reason why the British agent used any influence he had against Ryan can perhaps be explained by me to General Lopez Pinto.
4. In the circumstances, there does not seem to be any insuperable difficulty in the path of the desired measure of clemency, for which the goodwill of General Lopez Pinto must first be secured.

My account for travelling expenses will follow.

[signed] L.H. KERNEY
Aire Lán-Chómhachtach

No. 330 NAI DFA 227/42

Report from Robert Brennan to Joseph P. Walshe
(105/2/39) (Confidential)

WASHINGTON, 30 June 1939

Further[1] to my cable No. 125 of yesterday,[2] I wish to report that Sir Ronald Lindsay, the British Ambassador, called on me yesterday. I had thought that the visit was a farewell one as he was booked to sail on the fifth of July. He told me, however, that he had got a cable postponing his departure to late in August.

He began by discussing the Royal visit, the trouble he had had with the Senators, my trip to the west coast and how I had enjoyed it, etc.

Then in transpired that what he had come to talk about was the Bloom Neutrality Bill, the effect of which in its original form would have been to give power to the President to sell war supplies to England and France in time of war, and withhold them from Germany and Italy. I had known that this Bill was the one desired by the British because Sir Ronald, himself, had discussed it with me, and I had told him four months ago that there would be no difficulty in getting it through. I believed that at the time. Matters underwent a serious change shortly after the Bill was introduced. Firstly, the isolationists came out against it, though they seemed very few; secondly,

---

[1] Marginal note by Frederick H. Boland: 'I read this to T.[aoiseach] today. No actions. F.B. 2/8'.
[2] Not printed.

some of the Senators who had got last-minute invitations to the Royal Garden Party were accused of kowtowing to the British, and in their anxiety to put themselves right with their constituents they decided against the measure; thirdly, M. Bonnet's speech practically telling America it was her duty to decide in advance to throw in her lot with France and Britain had a very bad effect; fourthly, Father Coughlin[1] and individual Irish societies and newspapers were inveighing against the measure, stating that it was drafted in the interests of England. The result was that the Bill was assailed from all sides and its sponsors had already agreed to amendments which emasculated it.

At the time Sir Ronald Lindsay called, the Bill was actually under discussion and a final vote is being taken today.

Shortly before Sir Ronald called I had a talk with Mr. Martin Conboy[2] who was visiting Washington, and I told him I intended delicately hinting to the Ambassador that it was Irish opposition which was responsible for the result because of the continuance of partition. To my surprise Sir Ronald, himself, said what I had been going to hint at.

'The atmosphere was getting sour before Bonnet spoke. I think that it is a disaster to the cause of peace, and that your Irish in America are responsible'.

I said I thought that was so and that I was not surprised because everywhere I had gone on my recent tour I heard the partition of Ireland discussed and England was held to blame.

Sir Ronald asked 'What can we do about it?'

'Show your goodwill in the matter by withdrawing your troops and your subsidies'.

'These Northerners are a tough lot. I don't think that would work'.

'They have seemed a tough lot because they were relying on your big stick to support them.'

I told him that the English were foolish to leave unsolved such a vital question for them. It was having and would continue to have repercussions all over the world. Chamberlain had the solution in his hands by doing what I said, and pointing out to Craigavon that continued partition of Ireland was a menace to the Empire. If Craigavon was as patriotically British as he pretended to be, he would make the necessary sacrifice.

'Can you contemplate with equanimity' asked Sir Ronald 'the downfall of the British Empire'.

'I am afraid' I replied 'that Ireland will consider that an academic question as long as partition continues".

'Do you think' asked Sir Ronald 'that the Irish in America would be satisfied without having the Republic for the 32 counties?'

My answer was 'the vast majority of the Irish in America will be satisfied with whatever satisfies the Irish Government. If the North comes in and they

---

[1] Father Charles Coughlin (1891-1979). A Canadian born priest of Irish parents, Coughlin was one of the first exponents of using radio to preach. A former supporter of Roosevelt's 'New Deal', Coughlin turned against Roosevelt by the late 1930s. He became increasingly anti-Semitic and pro-Nazi in his outlook and his opposition to moves designed to end United States neutrality eventually led to Coughlin being forced off the air in October 1939.

[2] Martin Conboy, District Attorney for the Southern District of New York (1932-5).

get the assistance of the conservative elements in the South it might transpire that you would have a 32 county Ireland with a status similar to the present status of the 26 counties. But even if that did not happen, and an Irish Republic was declared, what have you to fear from a friendly independent Irish Republic'. There was a long pause and Sir Ronald then said 'By Jove perhaps you're right'.

There was much more to the conversation but I have only given the highlights here. The Ambassador was very gloomy when he came and only a little less so when he left. Only when he had gone did it occur to me that his object in calling was to ascertain if I had any direct hand in the present position and, if so, to ask me to use any influence I might have in bringing about a change in the picture. If that was his intention he never got down to it, and I do think I got my message across.

[signed] ROBT. BRENNAN

No. 331 NAI DFA 219/6

Confidential report from Michael MacWhite to Joseph P. Walshe (Dublin)
(Confidential)[1]

ROME, 4 July 1939

The rumour that Mussolini and Hitler met in secret near the Italo-German frontier on June 28th has at last been denied. This denial is said to be due to the deductions drawn to the effect that the former insisted on the latter taking no rash action in connection with Danzig. However that may be, newspaper men here are convinced the meeting took place.

Since Lord Halifax issued his warning to the Totalitarian States last week the Italian papers have raised the unanimous cry that the Democracies are preparing to make war on them because they have asked for justice or as the Germans say 'lebensraum'. Inconsistently enough they are accused both of aggression and inefficiency at the same time. Several newspapers expatiate on race suicide in France while the 'Popolo d'Italia' declares that since the Ethiopian war the flag of Great Britain has been the white flag. She showed it then to Italy as she does today to Japan.

The policy of the Democracies is described as a desperate attempt to arrest the course of events hurling threats and mobilising spirits for war. The 'Messaggero' today quotes German papers to the effect that Britain and France made similar threats twelve months ago in regard to Sudetenland, as they do today about Danzig and that the result would be the same. An organ of the Foreign Office carried the threat that 'to defend Danzig is to make the guns speak and with the guns Italian demands will be satisfied at the same time'.

Notwithstanding all this high talk, it would appear that the recent speeches of both the French Premier and the British Foreign Secretary have

---

[1] The marginal annotations on this document show that it was read by Joseph P. Walshe, Frederick H. Boland and Michael Rynne.

had a very salutary effect on Fascist leaders. They seem convinced now that France and England mean what they say, but, even if the guns refrain from talking, the tension is likely to continue. It becomes more and more difficult to envisage any solution of the actual international situation by peaceful methods.

[signed] M. MacWhite

No. 332 NAI DFA Paris Embassy P19/34

Confidential report from Seán Murphy to Joseph P. Walshe (Dublin)
(P. 19/34) (Copy)

Paris, 4 July 1939

The most common opinion here is that Lord Halifax's speech, followed by M. Bonnet's message on Saturday afternoon to the German Ambassador prevented any decisive step being taken by Germany in regard to Danzig over the week-end. A Council of Ministers had met on Saturday morning and had heard M. Daladier describe the situation as still 'very grave'. That evening M. Bonnet who had already seen the British representatives summoned the German Ambassador to the Quai d'Orsay and informed him, apparently on the basis of the mutual consultation provision of the Franco-German declaration of December last and on the ground that France regarded the events at Danzig as being of a nature 'to lead to international difficulties' that France intended fully to observe her undertaking to Poland if the latter should move in resistance to a threat to her independence. It is not believed however that Germany has given up her design on Danzig but that she will continue to play a game consisting of alternate periods of lull and pressure especially concentrated around the last week of August when the visit of the Koenigsberg to Danzig takes place. French opinion is, therefore, being counselled to be prepared for a recurrence of the atmosphere of last week-end.

There have been some reports here that Herr Hitler may send a message to France – on the basis of the Franco-German declaration of December and in reply to the message delivered to his Ambassador on Saturday. There are also suggestions that Germany is endeavouring to detach France from Great Britain in the matter of the Danzig question, reference being made in this regard to the advice given to France in a speech on Sunday by Herr Buerkel[1] to beware of England which would be sure to betray her. This advice has been rejected specifically in some organs.

Considerable disappointment is felt here at the refusal of the U.S. Congress to modify the neutrality law. This step is regarded as a definite set-back for the Franco-British cause as it was at least hoped here that while possibly preserving the 'cash and carry' provision in the event of war the U.S. Government would have permitted the export of all classes of material and thus directly favour the western powers who would control the Atlantic.

---

[1] Josef Buerkel (1895-1944), Reich commissioner for the reunion of Austria with the German Reich (1938-40), Gauleiter of Vienna and Reichsstatthalter of Austria (1939-40).

Public opinion is now warned that it does not do to take the statement of the President and the administration as quite accurately representing U.S. feeling. Many commentators now admit that the majority of Americans would object strongly to being involved in a European war. Some hope is, however, entertained that the President who is regarded as wholeheartedly on the side of the democracies may succeed in getting matters altered although it is admitted that if the House of Representatives has refused to modify the law it is now unlikely that the Senate will consent to do so.

Today's report that the Russian reply to the Franco-British proposals still contains certain objections and in particular insists that full publicity should be given to the list of states guaranteed and also that it is anomalous to have countries like Holland and Switzerland who have not yet recognised the Soviet Union included in that list. There has been a rumour that Mr. von Papen has been sent to Russia on a secret mission in the hope of preventing the signature of a tripartite agreement.

[stamped] (Signed) SEÁN MURPHY

No. 333 NAI DFA 217/28

Letter from Frederick H. Boland, for Joseph P. Walshe, to William Warnock (Berlin) enclosing a draft memorandum on the change of Irish Minister at Berlin (Copy)

DUBLIN, 1 August 1939

I should be glad if you would address immediately to the German Foreign Office a note in the terms of the attached draft concerning Mr. Bewley's recall and the nomination of his successor.

There should of course be no publicity about the appointment pending the conclusion of the usual formalities.

[stamped] Signed F.H. BOLAND
Rúnaí

[Enclosure]
DRAFT
I have the honour to inform you that my Government have decided to appoint Mr. Charles Bewley to a post in the Department of External Affairs in Dublin and that they propose to appoint as his successor Dr T.J. Kiernan, M.A., Ph.D., formerly Secretary to the High Commissioner's Office in London and now Acting Director of Broadcasting.

A biographical note of Dr Kiernan is attached.[1]

I have the honour to inquire whether Dr Kiernan's appointment as Envoy Extraordinary and Minister Plenipotentiary of Ireland to Germany is acceptable to the German Government.

---

[1] Not printed.

No. 334 NAI DFA 219/4

Confidential report from Charles Bewley to Joseph P. Walshe (Dublin) with covering letter to Eamon de Valera[1]
(Copy)

BERLIN, 2 August 1939

Dear Mr. De Valera,
I enclose copy of report on the general situation, which I trust you will do me the honour of reading.

Yours faithfully,
[signed] CHARLES BEWLEY

I think it well to send a report on the present relations of Germany and Ireland at the end of my six years' occupation of the post of Minister in Berlin. While I am aware that reports made by a Minister are never communicated to Ministers accredited in other countries and are frequently not submitted to the Minister for External Affairs, I desire to put on record a short and objective statement of the facts, in order that no suggestion may be made that I myself have any responsibility for the present state of affairs.

It would be wasted time to set out in detail the arguments in favour of particular measures which are contained in very many of my earlier minutes. I therefore propose to give in as concise form as possible the conclusions at which I have arrived.

1. Ireland, at the end of ten years' separate representation at Berlin, is regarded by the German Government, as by the other Governments where it has representation, as a British dependency, with autonomy but no real independence either political or spiritual. Hitler in his latest Reichstag speech expressly refers to England's treatment of Ireland as a domestic matter in which he would not be entitled to interfere.[2] President Roosevelt in his open letter to Hitler refers to 'Great Britain and Éire' as one of the countries which should be guaranteed.

2. The causes of this impression are numerous. In the first place, foreign spectators naturally pay less attention to phrases like 'Commonwealth of Nations' or 'External Association' than to the reality of the situation, i.e. that Ireland, or the 26 counties, remains a member of the British Empire.

3. This inherent difficulty in the position of Ireland could at least in part be overcome by a manifestation of her will to follow a policy in international affairs independent of English policy. No such policy has been adopted.

4. Instances in the lack of independence from England in deciding on Irish policy are:
A: The continuous following in England's steps in the League of Nations, e.g., the introduction of sanctions against Italy, the insistence on 'neutrality' between the Catholic and the Communist forces in Spain, etc.,

---

[1] Marginal annotations: 'MR 3.5.39'; 'Original detached for file on Roosevelt message, S.G.M.'.
[2] See above No. 312.

etc. The explanation given in minutes of the Department to the effect that English and Irish policy merely happen to coincide is not likely to carry conviction.

B: The apparent approbation by the Irish Government of the refusal of the Irish press and in particular of the Government organ to publish any foreign news except that supplied by British propagandist agencies. Phrases such as 'freedom of the press' are not considered a satisfactory explanation.

C: Acts of submission to the King of England, as for instance the instructions sent to the Irish Chargé d'Affaires in Paris to take part in ceremonies held in honour of His Majesty and attended by the members of the British Empire. Full details appeared in the continental, though of course not in the Irish, press.

D: The complete indifference of the Irish government and officials to the development of trade with countries other than Great Britain and Northern Ireland.

E: The failure to inform the German Government, or any other Government to which an Irish Minister is accredited, of the attitude of the Irish Government on any question of international politics. The silence on the part of the Irish Government is regarded as a proof that it has no policy except to follow that of the British Government.

F: The prohibition of the supply of news to, or even of direct communication with, the responsible officials in the German Foreign Office and Propaganda Ministry on the ground that the relations of the German Government and the Catholic Church are strained. The net result of such prohibition is that Ireland loses such publicity against partition, whereas the German Government does not even know that it is being punished for its misdeeds by the officials of the Irish Department of External Affairs.

G: The preference of the Irish Government to be represented by English consular officials, instead of following the example of independent states in appointing its own consuls. I have been furnished by the Department with a long defence of its practices: as however it was concerned exclusively with the alleged state of affairs in the United States of America, I fear that the world in general would experience the same difficulty as myself in seeing its relevance.

5. As I have pointed out a number of matters obviously requiring reform, I feel that the Minister has a right to ask for my opinion on their cause. I propose accordingly to set out my view with all possible conciseness.

6. The first and most obvious cause of the failure to adopt an independent policy in foreign affairs is what I can only describe by the colloquial term 'inferiority complex'. So long as British institutions (from the system of government down to details of household management) are regarded as the only possible model for Irish Government Departments, so long will it be impossible to expect an objective or independent view on international affairs. Lest it should be thought that I am exaggerating, I desire to refer to a recent correspondence on the payments to be made to the Legation porter during illness: the solution

which appeared natural to the officials of the Irish Department of External Affairs was to inquire as to the practice of the British Embassy.

7. This instance is of course a trivial one though significant: it could be reinforced by very many others. The effect produced on the outside world was summed up by a foreign diplomat no longer in Ireland in the observation 'Your people from the Minister downwards don't really believe that any other country exists except England.'

8. The secondary cause of the failure of the Irish Department of External Affairs to function in the manner in which Ministers of Foreign Affairs in other states function is its lack of experience and apparent reluctance or incapacity to learn. In other states one of the first duties of the Ministry of Foreign Affairs is considered to be the instruction of their Ministers abroad as to the policy of their government, and in particular as to the answers to be given to particular inquiries about that policy. The officials of the Irish Department of External Affairs obviously do not consider such instruction as any part of their duties, and indeed, resent any suggestion that their present practice could be improved in any respect, with the natural result that Irish Ministers abroad are never in a position to explain the attitude of the Irish Government on any subject to the Government to which they are accredited, and that the Government to which they are accredited assumes that the Irish Government has no policy except that of Great Britain. It is not for me to conjecture whether this outward self-satisfaction conceals an inner feeling of inadequacy or not.

9. If in fact the Irish Government has no such policy, the officials of the Department cannot be blamed for not communicating it. If on the other hand an independent policy exists, it is difficult to see why it should be kept as a secret not only from foreign governments but from the representatives of the Irish Government itself.

10. It is of course for the Minister for External Affairs to decide whether his Department shall carry out the duties to which I have alluded. I desire however to suggest the possibility that the practice of all other countries during their centuries of independent national life is not less important than the views held by officials, whose experience began in the year 1922 and has since then for practical purposes been confined to Dublin.

11. I have no doubt that the Minister is already aware of all the facts enumerated by me in this minute. I am confident however that their presentation in tabulated form will be of assistance to him should he in the future contemplate the transformation of the Department into an effectively functioning instrument for the carrying out of a definite policy in international affairs.

No. 335 NAI DF E86/2/34

Letter from Frederick H. Boland to James J. McElligott (Dublin)
(E86/8/39) (Copy)

Dublin, 9 August 1939

With reference to our verbal discussions on the subject of the proposed change of personnel in the post of Minister Plenipotentiary at Berlin, I am directed by the Minister for External Affairs to state, for the information of the Minister for Finance, that he considers it desirable in the interests of the Service that Mr. Bewley, the present occupant of the post, should be recalled for a period of service in Dublin.

2. Mr. Bewley has completed a period of over ten years' service abroad. He has been Minister in Berlin for over six years. It is the practice of many other countries not to leave their representatives abroad too long in any one place. While for some time to come the circumstances of our Service may not allow of a universal application of the principle, the Minister considers that it is a sound one, and he is anxious to apply it so far as may be practicable. Apart from the question of length of residence in a particular place there is the question of length of absence from the home country. The effect of prolonged absence will vary in individual cases with the temperament and outlook of the particular officers concerned. There is always a danger, however, that in particular cases it may reach such a point as to render an officer, on the one hand, wholly unsuitable to represent the country abroad, and, on the other, constitutionally incapable of re-adapting himself to the conditions of service in a Home Department. The Minister considers it very important in the interests of the Service no less than that of the officers concerned that, before this point is reached in any individual case, the officer concerned should be recalled home and enabled by means of residence and official service in Dublin to renew his acquaintance with the local environment. After a recent review of the work of the Berlin Legation the Minister has reached the conclusion, on the strength of the foregoing considerations, that Mr. Bewley should return for a period of service in Dublin.

3. Accordingly the Minister proposes to recall Bewley to a post on the Headquarters staff of this Department. There is at present no post vacant on this Department's establishment carrying a scale of salary equivalent to that which Mr. Bewley at present enjoys. As the Minister for Finance is aware, however, the voted establishment of this Department includes a post of Principal Officer on the scale £700-20-£800 which is at present vacant and was retained in the Estimates for the current year without prejudice pending a decision on the proposals made in this Department's minute A. 247 of the 27th January 1939. Subject to the approval of the Minister for Finance, the Minister proposes that on his return to Dublin Mr. Bewley should 'block' this vacant post of Principal Officer, retaining his present salary scale of £800-25-£1,000, to which will be added, of course, the appropriate home cost-of-living bonus. It is intended that Mr. Bewley's period of service as Minister in Berlin should be terminated as from the 31st July, and that his transfer to Dublin should date as from the lst August. Mr. Bewley has been instructed accordingly.

4. I am now to seek the formal sanction of the Minister for Finance for Mr. Bewley's recall and for his assignment to the vacant post of Principal Officer in this Department on the conditions indicated above. I am to express regret that, following the verbal discussions on the matter between the two Departments, the formal sanction of the Minister for Finance for these proposals was not sought in writing before now.

[stamped] (Sd.) F.H. BOLAND

No. 336 NAI DFA 219/4

> *Confidential report from William Warnock to Joseph P. Walshe (Dublin)*[1]
> *(43/33)*
>
> BERLIN, 12 August 1939

As was to be expected, the speech of Gauleiter Forster[2] in Danzig on Thursday evening received great publicity in the German press. It was not a great oratorical effort, as it consisted for the most part of quotations from statements by British or French writers or politicians, nor did it contain anything really new, but Herr Forster clearly gave his hearers to understand that a reunion of Danzig with Germany is to be expected in the near future.

The newspaper campaign against Poland resembles in every detail that carried on precisely twelve months ago against Czechoslovakia. Each day several columns are given over to reports concerning the brutal ill-treatment of the German minority in Poland. We are told that German families are subject to a constant terror, and that even old age is not respected. German clergy are being turned out of the churches and expelled from the country.

The next thing we may expect, judging from what happened last year, is the establishment of refugee camps.

There is no indication of any weakening in the German attitude towards the Danzig question; rather the reverse. The general public expects the 'Anschluss' to take place very shortly. It is difficult to see how the leaders can draw back at this stage, and it is in any case unlikely they should wish to do so.

None of those with whom I come into contact believe that Great Britain will not intervene in a military way when Germany takes over Danzig (they are quite certain it will be taken over soon). They are firmly of opinion that the British will let Poland down in the same way as they treated Abyssinia, Czechoslovakia, and Republican Spain.

People are interested in our position in the event of war. Many of them feel that we would at least remain neutral, while some of the newspapers have suggested from time to time that we would immediately rise and attack Britain in the rear. The attitude to us in official circles is friendly.

The newspapers are pointing out that though the immediate annoyance is coming from Poland, the real enemy is Great Britain, who is urging the Poles on.

The transfer of the German population from the South Tyrol is passed over without mention. There is undoubtedly strong feeling against it, based on sentimental grounds. The Nationalist-Socialist theory of 'Blood and Land' is being conveniently forgotten. Apologists declare, however, that it is better to solve this problem once and for all. They add that the Poles have had

---

[1] Marginal annotations: 'Secy – File with you'; 'A/Secy'; 'Dr Rynne'; MR 16.8.39'; 'Registry P.A.'.

[2] Albert Förster (1902-52), Nazi Gauleiter of Danzig (1930-9), Gauleiter and Reichstatthalter of Danzig-West Prussia (1939-45), convicted of crimes against humanity by a Polish court and hanged in 1952.

numerous opportunities to settle difficulties amicably, and that matters could have been arranged had not the British interfered.

[signed] W. WARNOCK

No. 337 NAI DFA Paris Embassy P19/34

Confidential report from Con Cremin to Joseph P. Walshe (Dublin)
(P. 19/34) (Copy)

PARIS, 16 August 1939

The general feeling here at the moment could probably be summed up by saying that Germany is now engaged in a campaign in which she intends to use all sorts of means, short of war, to lead to the return of Danzig to the Reich and that it is up to France (and Great Britain) not to yield in their support of Poland in the attitude she has taken up. The German concentration on a settlement of the Danzig problem is not taken to mean that this constitutes her only claim. On the contrary, the opinion, which is general, that the main object of the Salzburg conversations with Count Ciano and those which have taken place and are reported to be about to be renewed, with Count Csaky[1] was to get Hungary completely subordinate to Germany (and to receive the consent of Italy, regarded as having been Hungary's friend, to this idea) implies that German designs even in the near future go further; and this is the general belief which has been nurtured by claims against Poland as a whole advanced in German newspapers over the week-end. It is considered as probable, though not certain, that Italy has agreed in regard to Hungary and, therefore, as not unlikely that Hungary will collaborate with Germany – although reports of opposition in Hungary to such a policy have been reproduced, Italian influence would, it is more than ever believed here, be in favour of moderation and a pacific settlement of all matters but French opinion is becoming more and more openly sceptical of Italy's ability to adopt any foreign policy independently of Germany. The statement in the 'Times' as to a request to Poland from Italy for an aide-mémoire in regard to the Danzig problem and the Polish attitude was made independently here in a few newspapers.

In regard to the immediate problem it is claimed that Germany would like to find a 'Lord Runciman' in the person of M. Burckhardt; but it is also claimed that neither France nor England will accept another Munich. The reports from London that England has no intention of exercising pressure on Poland seem to be welcomed here.

At the week-end there was a certain amount of feeling, especially because of the prolongation of the Salsburg talks that things were rapidly reaching a final crisis. Opinion is, however, being repeatedly warned by the Press to beware of such reported 'crises'. The opinion today, based to some extent on reports of feeling in Berlin, is that the tension is less.

[stamped] (signed) C.C. CREMIN

---

[1] Count István Csaky (1894-1941), Foreign Minister of Hungary (1938-41).

No. 338 NAI DFA 226/31

Minute from Michael Rynne to Joseph P. Walshe
DUBLIN, 18 August 1939

Re Agenda Twentieth League Assembly
The attached Agenda for the Assembly[1] which opens on the 11th September next, was circulated last May. There is a second edition of the Agenda due in some weeks but it will probably not be very different from the attached.

Not one of the twenty-three items on this year's Agenda has any but a technical importance. There are no live political questions listed. As compared, even with last year's agenda, the programme before the Twentieth Assembly lacks interest. Nearly all the items listed have appeared before and many of them (such as item 3, Disarmament) are simply included on principle.

Probably the most interesting subject up for discussion will be that relating to the Rural Life Conference (Item 17) in which we hope to participate next October. The Assembly will, however, scarcely do more than refer that question to its Second Commission where no action will be taken, as none is called for.

[signed] MICHAEL RYNNE

No. 339 NAI DFA 235/65

Report from William Warnock to Joseph P. Walshe (Dublin)[2]
(1/3311)
BERLIN, 19 August 1939

I have received through the Foreign Office an invitation from the Führer and Chancellor to attend the annual National-Socialist Party Congress (Reichsparteitag), which will be held in Nuremberg from the 2nd to the 11th September. I have further received an invitation to an official luncheon given by the Führer's Deputy, Reichsminister Hess,[3] on Friday, 8th September.

As the invitation is issued by the Führer expressly in his capacity as Head of the State, it is expected that his invitation to attend the Congress will be accepted.

I suggest that I be authorised to attend the Congress. It would be impracticable for me to spend the whole nine days in Nuremberg, but I could arrange to arrive on Thursday the 7th September or thereabouts, and remain till Sunday or Monday. I think that the Foreign Office would be satisfied as long as I put in an appearance.

All Missions are regularly represented. Those present last year included even the Czecho-Slovakian Minister.

The Foreign Office has asked for a reply by the 25th inst., and I should

---

[1] Not printed.
[2] Marked as seen by Joseph P. Walshe.
[3] Rudolf Hess (1894-1987).

accordingly be very grateful if you would be good enough to let me have a reply by return.

[signed] W. WARNOCK

Nuremberg Congress cancelled SGM.[1]

No. 340 NAI DFA 219/6

Confidential report from Michael MacWhite to Joseph P. Walshe (Dublin)
(Confidential)

ROME, 19 August 1939[2]

Diplomatic activity over the past week has gone on unabated and it would appear as if some kind of a decision regarding the fate of Danzig is in the offing. It is believed that about ten days ago Hitler's impatience had reached the limit, but that the wiser and more pacific advice of the Duce prevailed.

Ciano's mission to Berchesgaden last week, about which nothing official has transpired, is said to be mainly to persuade Hitler against the employment of force. The Italians are not enthusiastic about a war that would secure Danzig for Germany and the idea of fighting against Poland with which there has been secular ties is repugnant to their spirit and sentiment.

The Duce realises perhaps that despite the threats of Chamberlain and Halifax, England is prepared to abandon Poland to her fate, just as Czechoslovakia was abandoned. The activities of the League High Commissioner for Danzig,[3] which are probably inspired by the British Foreign Office, have for object to try to persuade Poland to come to a pacific agreement with Germany in regard to their mutual problems, but, by all accounts Poland will fight to maintain the status quo in which case England and France might be forced to participate in the conflict.

The Hungarian Foreign Minister, who has been visiting his German colleague jumped into a German plane yesterday morning and flew to Rome without any previous warning. Before starting out he said his visit to Germany was purely personal and had nothing to do with politics, but important new items appeared to the effect that Germany was bringing pressure to bear on Hungary either to join the Axis or to take some measures either against Roumania or Poland. Diplomats here are of the opinion that Count Csaky has come here to appeal to the Duce for protection or to ask him to use his influence with Hitler to modify his demands.

Count Ciano is going on a visit to Albania today which is causing a certain commotion in Greek and Yugoslavian circles.

[signed] M. MACWHITE

---

[1] Marginal note by Sheila Murphy.
[2] The marginal annotations on this document show that it was read by Joseph P. Walshe, Frederick H. Boland and Michael Rynne.
[3] Carl Burckhardt (1891-1974), League of Nations High Commissioner for Danzig (1937-39).

No. 341 NAI DFA 226/31

Confidential report from Francis T. Cremins to Joseph P. Walshe (Dublin)
(Ass./20) (Confidential)

GENEVA, 19 August 1939

With reference to your minute of the 14th August, 1939,[1] regarding the Agenda on the forthcoming session of the Assembly, I have to forward, for the information of the Minister, the enclosed notes containing all the information, regarding some of the items, which is at present available.

As regards the general situation in Europe and the Far East, opinion in Geneva continues to be calm, if not too optimistic regarding the future. I think it is generally considered that Europe will go through a critical and anxious period in the near future, and that very soon it will have become clear whether or not there is to be war in 1939. In League circles, other danger spots in Europe than Danzig have been spoken of, for example, Hungary, where Nazi pressure was regarded as a possibility, and Yugoslavia. I discussed the position with Mr. Walters, Deputy Secretary-General of the League. He seems to be not at all satisfied that the rulers of Germany are convinced, notwithstanding all the statements by Mr. Chamberlain and others, that Great Britain is serious in regard to her obligations to Poland on a question such as Danzig. There is therefore the danger in his view that Hitler will not refrain from taking risks. Mr. Walters stated that he had heard nothing regarding the nature of the recent discussions between the League High Commissioner for Danzig and Hitler. He regarded as satisfactory, so far as it went, the fact that this interview was due altogether to the initiative of the Führer, but he expected little from it and thought that it was a fact that nothing new had been proposed. He doubted the statement of the 'Times' that Hitler did all the talking, as Mr. Burckhardt talks not only exceedingly well but he talks a lot, and his mother tongue is German.

[signed] F.T. CREMINS
Permanent Delegate

No. 342 NAI DFA Paris Embassy P19/34A

Extract from a confidential report from Con Cremin to Joseph P. Walshe
(Dublin)
(P. 19/34) (Copy)

PARIS, 22 August 1939

1. The announcement of the signature of a Non-Aggression Pact between Germany and Russia has taken French public opinion completely by surprise. The impression had become deeply rooted that Germany and Italy were playing a game of intimidation and that France and Great Britain had only to show themselves sufficiently resolved to resist to make the axis

---

[1] Not printed.

Powers mitigate their demands. For James DONNADIEU of the *Epoque* (Nationalist but very anti-'Munich'), writing before the announcement from Berlin and Moscow was known 'the situation at the present moment is the following: either Italy and Germany, conscious of the impossibility of weakening the Peace Front, will retire before a general conflict where they would have everything to lose; or else they will throw themselves into the adventure; a prey to an incomprehensible madness'.

For Romier writing in the same circumstances in the *FIGARO* (Right, Catholic and anti-Axis absolutely convinced of Italian subordination to Germany, distrustful of Russia) 'the term of the "War of Nerves" has come. We arrive at an impasse ... the masters of the Reich either wish still to conceal that an impasse has been reached or else hope still to succeed by the same method as succeeded last year ... the known facts as to the armaments and forces in opposition cannot encourage even the most presumptuous (i.e. Germany) to risk the adventure'. For *'Ere Nouvelle'* (Radical-Socialist opinion but not of great importance) it is now (i.e. yesterday) a question of 'reaffirming both in the matter of military readiness and diplomatic action what has already been done and happily done'. For Leon Blum in the *Populaire* (Socialist, anti-Fascist, rather pro-Russian in sympathy) 'the situation does not vary fundamentally and one can only repeat daily the same reflections and the same advice ... It is probable that the Italo German press campaign is only the newest kind of threat. But let us not waste our time in trying to discover if it betrays a final hesitation of the Dictators or if it presages resolutions already reached. For in both hypothesis the French attitude should be the same – calm, vigilance, firmness'.

2. The above views were, without doubt, those of the average Frenchman yesterday. It was indeed seriously rumoured here last evening (press-men stated that they had been so informed by M. Bonnet on Sunday evening) that the French Ambassador at Berlin[1] had advised that general mobilisation should be decreed this week so as to show Germany that France is in earnest in the attitude she has taken up. Practically all this morning's newspapers also refer to the possibility of the British cabinet deciding today on another declaration of British policy for the same purpose.
[matter omitted]

No. 343 NAI DFA 219/4

> *Confidential report from William Warnock to Joseph P. Walshe (Dublin)*[2]
> *(43/33)*
>
> Berlin, 23 August 1939

As you may well imagine, the news that Germany and the Soviet Union intend to sign a non-aggression pact caused foreign circles in Berlin a great

---

[1] Robert Coulondre, French Ambassador to Berlin (1938-9).
[2] Marginal annotations: 'Secy'; 'File with Mr. McDonald'. The reference is to Denis R. McDonald (1910-83), Third Secretary, Department of External Affairs.

surprise, though rumours have been in circulation for some weeks that Herr von Papen was negotiating such a pact in Moscow.

The English journalists are thinking of leaving the country. Some have gone already. The Daily Express correspondent said to me yesterday in a moment of rather grim humour that the only thing for Great Britain to do was to send an ultimatum to Poland, insisting on the fulfilment of the German demands.

As was to be expected, the newspapers are full this morning of articles pointing out the traditional friendship between Germany and Russia, the great Bismarck being quoted as the most brilliant exponent of the possibilities of co-operation between the two countries. There is general sneering at the collapse of the manoeuvres of the 'encirclers'.

Poland is now left high and dry. There is a feeling that the Poles will fight, but it is not thought that they can offer any effective resistance. The return of Danzig is expected almost at once.

I have as yet no idea of the actual terms of the pact. I think, however, that it will be confined to a simple expression that neither country desires to attack the other. The long drawn-out Russian-British-French searches for formulae and saving clauses have become a standing joke.

It will be interesting to see what happens to the Anti-Komintern Pact. The Spaniards are reported to be displeased, and the Japanese are said to be watching the situation carefully.

The Entente (as Britain and France are often called here) appears to be forced with the alternative of either war or an immense loss of prestige. Germany seems about to become the undoubted leader of Europe.

Various wild rumours are in circulation as to the future of Poland. The most believed is that Germany and Russia will once more divide it between them, and restore the pre-war frontier as nearly as possible.

By the time you receive this the position may be clearer. At present there seems to be a great danger of war, unless either Stalin takes pity on humanity and attempts to avert it, or the British and French climb down completely. At all events I think it would be well to consult with the Department of Posts and Telegraphs as to how communication may be ensured with the Legation should hostilities break out between Great Britain and Germany. I earnestly hope that there will be no need of such precautions, but it is much better for us to be on the safe side.

[signed] W. WARNOCK

No. 344 NAI DFA 217/29[1]

Code telegram from William Warnock to Joseph P. Walshe (Dublin)
(No. 23) (Copy)

BERLIN, 23 August 1939

Your despatch August 1st appointment Dr Kiernan acceptable to German Government.[2]

No. 345 NAI DFA 219/6

Confidential report from Michael MacWhite to Joseph P. Walshe (Dublin)
(Confidential)[3]

ROME, 24 August 1939

Diplomatic colleagues here regard the international situation as extremely serious today. The signature of the German pact of non aggression with Russia is displayed by the Italian press in large headlines, but there is no comment. The 'Messaggero' in a leading article entitled 'It is therefore war' says the Italian people are proud to have at their head at the moment a Man of Providence to watch over their destinies. It does not even insinuate that Italy would be involved in this war, but it appeals to France and England to realise the consequences of their action in support of Poland before the fatal hour has struck.

During the night the Italian Government has called up the special reservists of the Air and Naval forces and last week a number of classes were mobilised, but so far the order for general mobilisation has not gone out.

Outwardly everything is quiet here, but it would seem as if the staff of the British embassy have packed up. They are apparently only awaiting the signal from London to burn the code books and archives. The French are also ready to leave at a moment's notice.

[signed] M. MACWHITE

---

1 Formerly this file was numbered 'S117' in the Secretary's File Series, but was renumbered and reduced in security classification by the Department of External Affairs as 217/29.

2 Due to the outbreak of the Second World War Kiernan did not take up his appointment in Berlin. A 1953 investigation in the Department of External Affairs into the question of Kiernan's appointment found that the Department's papers on the subject did not disclose 'what actually happened subsequent to the receipt of the Berlin Legation's cable and minute of 23rd August 1939' (NAI DFA 217/29, minute, Gallagher to Lennon, 4 July 1953). It seems that because of the outbreak of war Dublin decided not to pursue the question of Kiernan's credentials with London. Under the terms of the External Relations Act (1936) Kiernan's credentials had to be signed by the British Monarch. Michael Rynne, the Legal Adviser at External Affairs, concluded: 'I am satisfied that we never approached the King on this matter at all' (NAI DFA 217/29, minute Rynne to O'Riordan, 14 July 1953). Frederick Boland had earlier written to John Dulanty: 'There was, of course, the question of the Letter of Credence but the difficulty was on our side, not on Hitler's! The German Government of the time would probably have been glad to receive an Irish Minister with any kind of Letter of Credence at all' (NAI DFA 217/29, letter Boland to Dulanty, 4 June 1948).

3 The marginal annotations on this document show that it was read by Joseph P. Walshe, Frederick H. Boland and Michael Rynne.

No. 346 NAI DFA Paris Embassy P19/34A

Telegram from the Irish Legation in Paris to the Department of External Affairs (Dublin)
(No. 16)

PARIS, 24 August 1939

Dar leis anseo tá crot an-olc ar fad ar an sgeal. Seasomhaidh Frainnc is Sasana an fod ní irraidh said ar Pholainn gheilleadh agus mara gheilleann an Pholainn agus go leannann an Ghearmain ar aghaidh gur deallramhach go mbeidh cogadh ann roimh an Domhnach.

No. 347 NAI DFA Paris Embassy P19/34A

Confidential report from Con Cremin to Joseph P. Walshe (Dublin)
(P19/34) (Copy)

PARIS, 24 August 1939

1. I have the honour to confirm the despatch this afternoon of a telegram in Irish[1] to the effect that 'it is thought here that the situation is most critical. France and England will stand firm and will not ask Poland to yield and if Poland does not yield and Germany continues on her course it is (believed) likely that there will be war before Sunday'.

2. Official circles (represented in particular by an Officer in the Cabinet of the Minister of Foreign Affairs with whom I was speaking) seemed to think that the situation today is very much more critical than at any time during the September crisis for the reason that the attitudes of the two sides in opposition and in particular the attitude of the 'Peace front' are very much more definitely taken up than in September last. The issue as represented to me is, as at present, that if Poland should decide to move as a result of the action which has been taken today in Danzig or as a result of any other action which should be taken on the German side there is no doubt whatever that war will result; and I was informed that there is no question of France (or Great Britain) urging Poland not to adopt any course of action which she should consider called for. Mr. Herlihy of Reuters has also told me that the information at his disposal both as to the official French attitude and from other quarters in Europe leaves no doubt that the situation is most critical.

3. No public measure of any importance has been announced after the Council of Ministers today. A third échelon of the Reserve has now been called up (échelon 2 which covers the reservists of the frontier regions). The calling up of this échelon following up on the calling up of the 3rd and 4th échelons last night probably means that at least about 2/5ths of the French man-power has now been mobilised. The right of requisition was declared 'open' in Paris as from mid-night last night.

4. Public opinion in general seems to consider that the situation is rapidly deteriorating. The semi-official Petit Parisien this morning thought that the

---

[1] See above No. 346.

situation was extremely acute and considered it impossible to forecast what the issue might be while mentioning that there is a wide divergence between the ideas of Great Britain and France and the 'irreducible position maintained by Germany', this latter in particular being demonstrated by the curt reply made to the demarche of the British Ambassador in Berlin[1] to Herr Hitler.

5. Of the afternoon papers so far available Paris-Soir thinks that the only hope of a peaceful solution lies in the possibility of success of the appeal made yesterday by King Leopold of Belgium, the appeal which the Pope is announced to be making this evening or a possible intervention of President Roosevelt. This paper still suggests however that French firmness may still make Germany recoil.

[stamped] (signed C.C. CREMIN)

No. 348 NAI DFA Secretary's Files S75

Letter to Irish Legations in Paris, Rome, Berlin and Madrid and to the Permanent Delegate to the League of Nations in Geneva from Michael Rynne (Secret) (Copy)

DUBLIN, 24 August 1939

I am directed by the Minister to state that it has been decided to obtain from our representatives abroad, namely at Paris, Rome, San Sebastian, Berlin and Geneva daily telegrams, starting from the date of their receipt of this minute, concerning the international situation. The purpose of the arrangement will be to place the Government, every day shortly before 1 p.m. Irish time, in possession of a general appreciation of the European situation as seen from the five above-named posts respectively.

In order to save expense and time and to ensure a certain desirable measure of secrecy, your messages may be coded by a single group as shown on the attached sheet.[2]

Although the Irish words which are being used as groups to represent twenty-four different messages, contain only four letters each, your wire will consist of a single five letter group. In your case the letter P.R.M.B.G.[3] should always be added to the beginning of the four-letter Irish word which, when decoded, will provide the best possible description of the day-to-day situation as it appears to you.

Your wires will not require to be numbered and ought to be sent daily, in time to reach Dublin before lunch-hour, without interruption until you receive the telegraphed instruction 'STAD'[4] from the Department. In the event of none of the twenty-four messages providing an adequate vehicle for a particular report, you should, of course, resort to the ordinary code, either alone or in conjunction with one group of the 'situation' code. Suggestions

---

[1] Sir Nevile Henderson (1882-1942), British Ambassador to Berlin (1937-9).
[2] Not printed.
[3] To indicate Paris, Rome, Madrid, Berlin, Geneva.
[4] The Irish language word for 'Stop'.

for further appropriate 'messages' which might be usefully added to the attached list will be appreciated.

[stamped] (Signed) M. RYNNE

No. 349 NAI DFA 219/6

Confidential report from Michael MacWhite to Joseph P. Walshe (Dublin)[1]
(Confidential)

ROME, 25 August 1939

While the tension in the international situation seems to have grown more accentuated over night, things are comparatively quiet here. Outside of the calling up of some Air and Naval specialists yesterday, it does not appear, on the surface at least, that any warlike measures are being taken. The leading articles in the newspapers are moderate in tone, but, while they state that Italy will march at the side of Germany, there is no warlike incitation.

It is incontestable that the Italian people have no enthusiasm for participation in a war that would bring Danzig into the German family, but the Milan pact of last May definitely states that 'if one of the contracting parties is involved in hostilities with another Power or Powers the other contracting party will come immediately to its side as ally and support it with all its military forces on land, sea and in the air'. In view of Italy's present attitude, one might feel inclined to ask if it means what it says or if there is not a loophole somewhere. Or, on the other hand, would not Germany's Southern frontier be better preserved by Italian neutrality?

It is now generally accepted here that Ciano's interview with Ribbentrop at Salzburg ten days ago was far from satisfactory to the latter. As a result he was requested to proceed immediately to Berchesgaden to see Hitler with whom he is said to have spent three uncomfortable hours, as Italy was not prepared to go as far as the Fuehrer desired. The latter wanted further clarifications which the Duce alone could give, with the result that on Monday last the Italian Ambassador at Berlin[2] flew to Berchesgaden with the answer which was again believed to be unsatisfactory. From there he flew direct to Rome. If this is true, and the best informed diplomats here believe it to be so, it may account for the moderation of the Italian press and the calm attitude of the Italian public.

I have just learned that at luncheon yesterday at which one of his sons assisted, the Duce was in exceptional good humour and repeated several times that he held the trump card in his hands and was master of the situation.

[signed] M. MACWHITE

---

[1] Marginal annotation by Sheila Murphy: 'Seen by Secy.'.
[2] Bernardo Attolico (1880-1942), Italian Ambassador to Germany (1935-40).

No. 350 UCDA P150/2571

Memorandum by Joseph P. Walshe on Irish neutrality for Eamon de Valera
(Secret)

DUBLIN, 25 August 1939

NOTE FOR A CONVERSATION WITH THE REPRESENTATIVE OF GERMANY CONCERNING IRELAND'S NEUTRALITY

1. Our position vis-à-vis the European conflict is that of a neutral State.

2. Our neutrality, however, cannot have all the characters of those neutral States which have had a long existence as separate States.

3. We are still linked with the British Commonwealth of Nations, and especially with Great Britain herself, by many ties which the inevitable slowness of our evolution has not allowed us to break. Our State life is only of seventeen years' duration, and it is only within the last decade that our position as an independent sovereign State has been emphasised to the world.

4. Our economic life, and this includes particularly matters relating to finance, currency and shipping, has not yet been fully separated from that of Great Britain.

5. Our geographical position imposes upon us in time of war relations of a peculiarly delicate character with Great Britain. We are of very special importance from the strategic point of view, and we are in constant danger during a war between Great Britain and a Continental Power of being used by that Continental Power as a base of operations against Great Britain. This description holds equally of activities such a propaganda and espionage and of naval, military and air operations in the very widest sense. Any such activities directed against our powerful neighbour would ipso facto constitute a menace to our existence as a separate State. In order to maintain our independence we should be obliged to use every effort to prevent any form of activity which might even remotely affect the interests of Great Britain. An attack on our trade with Great Britain would seriously menace the life of our people, and we should regard it as a violation of our neutrality.

6. We do not intend to participate in any active form in the war against Germany, and we hope that the continuance of the normal relations with Great Britain imposed upon us by historical and geographical considerations will not be regarded as a breach of neutrality on our part.

7. It is of the first importance for this Government in its relations with Great Britain that the German Legation should not allow itself to be used in any way as part of the machinery for the prosecution of the war.

8. Should it not be possible, in the view of the German Minister, to maintain such an attitude, it might on the whole be wiser in the interests of the good relations between Germany and Ireland if both parties withdrew their Legations at the beginning of hostilities between Great Britain and Germany.

9. It would also be an advantage to both sides if we mutually ordered the return of our nationals.

10. Ireland desires to remain on peaceful and friendly relations with all countries in the world. She wishes to remain outside the quarrels of the great

ruling countries of the world and to rebuild her own civilisation undisturbed by world rivalries. The Irish Government earnestly hope that war between Great Britain and Germany may still at this last hour be averted, and Germany and Great Britain may be able to settle their conflicting interests by peaceful means.

[initialled] J.P.W.

No. 351 NAI DFA 219/7

Confidential report from Francis T. Cremins to Joseph P. Walshe (Dublin)
(Confidential)

GENEVA, 26 August 1939[1]

With reference to previous minutes regarding the general situation, I have to state, for the information of the Minister, that in the present crisis public opinion in Geneva remains remarkably calm. Practically everyone clings to the hope that, despite the measures which are being taken in Germany against Poland, and the counter-measures in other countries, the actual out-break of war may even yet be avoided. There is general commendation of the fresh appeal made by the Pope and of those made to Italy, Germany and Poland by President Roosevelt, and also of the statement broadcasted on behalf of the Oslo Powers by King Leopold. Meanwhile people are simply waiting on events and hoping that it will not be necessary for the Western Powers actually to go to war to convince M. Hitler and M. Mussolini that they are in earnest. With the signature of the Anglo-Polish agreement there should hardly be any doubt now upon that point.

The German-Soviet Pact was a surprise to everyone, though there had been vague rumours in the English and other papers of the possibility of some change in attitude between the two countries following the trade agreement. The feeling of surprise was greatly accentuated by the terms of the pact itself which departed so widely from those of other non-aggression pacts into which Russia had entered, omitting as it does the clause under which aggression by one of the parties against a third would enable the other party to free itself from the obligations of the instrument.

My Estonian colleague tells me that he thinks that such a clause was inserted in the U.S.S.R.-Estonian pact of non-aggression at the suggestion of Estonia, as Russia was not at the time a member of the League. It was intended to enable Estonia to obtain its freedom from the obligations, if the other party committed any act of aggression against a third State.

The whole circumstances of the German-Soviet Pact appear to be regarded in nearly all circles here as a cynical performance, and a serious let-down for Britain and France and their allies on the one hand, and for Japan on the other, the balance being against the Western Powers. There appears however to be a slump in its effect, a fact which it is alleged here is beginning to be appreciated by the two Powers of the Axis. I have heard the pact condemned also in Spanish circles favourable to General Franco.

---

[1] Initialled by Michael Rynne as read by him on 30 August 1939.

No doubt Russia felt it highly desirable in her weakened situation to relieve her western front in case of possible trouble in the Far East. She would now, if the pact lasts, be free to concentrate her strength against Japan while also in a position at will to threaten her immediate western neighbours – Poland, Romania and the Baltic States especially Finland. Further, the opinion is freely expressed here that the traditional Soviet policy has found at last a possible opportunity of coming into play: a war between the democratic States and the totalitarian States which would leave both sides exhausted would admirably suit the policy of Russia, which might hope at an opportune moment to find the circumstances favourable for dictating a Soviet peace. Japan may however prove to be a brake on any such ambitions. In Swiss circles, the policy of non-recognition of Russia adopted by Switzerland, which it was decided a day or so ago to continue, is certainly more than ever approved.

From many quarters, I hear that in Italy, up to yesterday at any rate, the general feeling was that there would be no war – and war is certainly not wanted there, especially on the question of Danzig – but Italians of course regard the whole question from their own angle – they consider that the so-called policy of encircling Germany has failed, and that, in consequence, the democratic powers will not go to war to help the Poles.

Such indications as the fact that hostilities have not broken out so far in Eastern Europe, the signing of the Anglo-Polish agreement, and the reported journey of the British Ambassador at Berlin to London give the impression today that the position is somewhat less tense than it was yesterday.

[signed] F.T. Cremins

No. 352 NAI DFA Paris Embassy P19/34A

Confidential report from the Irish Legation in Paris[1]
to Joseph P. Walshe (Dublin)
(P.19/34 A) (Copy)

Paris, 30 August 1939

My telegram of this morning[2] will have informed you that looking at matters from here there was, at that time, no change in the situation which is still tense. For purposes of record, I should like to explain that official opinion here seems to regard the situation as tense so long as the conversations going on do not lead to a development which will mean finally either war or solid prospects of peace. What I have been able to gather from official circles, journalists and French newspapers would lend itself to the interpretation that France is resolved on this occasion to put an end to what is regarded as the more or less perpetual threat of German foreign policy. There is undoubtedly a feeling that Germany has been bluffing and that a sufficiently firm attitude on the part of France and her allies will lead to her modifying her demands.

[1] This report is an unsigned copy and it is not clear if it was sent by Seán Murphy or Con Cremin.
[2] Not printed.

It is even possible that the suggestions in some of the press to-day that the crisis is still acute are as a result of this belief, as, to convey the impression that France regards the crisis as acute, where German circles might expect a reaction of détente, would only serve to emphasise the firm attitude which France is observing. In the normal way, one would have expected a feeling of détente to prevail here to-day and it is quite probable that at bottom official circles do regard the situation as somewhat brighter. However, the manner in which M. Daladier chose to summarise the written reply he received from Herr Hitler on Sunday (i.e. by simply stating that 'Chancellor Hitler declared that he could not accept the proposal that M. Daladier had suggested') would seem to be symptomatic of the determination of the French Government to accept nothing less than a modification of the German attitude towards her problem with Poland (i.e. unconditional return without discussion of Danzig and the corridor as set out in Herr Hitler's reply). This determination may, of course, be based on a false appreciation of the factors of the problem and, in particular, it might be contended, of the prospects for France and her allies of a victory in the event of war. I think, however, that it must be taken to exist and it would be a mistake to assume that because a feeling of optimism prevails as a result of, or would seem to follow from, any particular development the possibility of war in the immediate future is diminished. The fact, for instance, of the continuation of preliminary 'conversations' and the apparent optimism to-day of some of the German press as to a pacific solution, which may be a consequence of that fact, have not led the Quai d'Orsay to alter its general verdict of the situation, viz, that it is still serious. I have the impression that France will have no hesitation in going to war if she considers that any apparent change in the policy of Germany is not likely to be permanent; and it is doubtful at this stage to what extent Great Britain, even if she should favour a compromise which would go further than the French are prepared to go, could influence this attitude of France.

There is a certain amount of attention being devoted to the attitude of various countries obviously with an eye to the way in which the attitude of such countries may influence the lines of German policy in conversations for peace or may effect Germany's chances in the event of war. I gather that the position in Japan and in Italy in particular preoccupies the Quai d'Orsay. The general public undoubtedly entertains considerable hopes that Japan will at least be neutral in the event of war and the impression is also general that Spain for the same reason as Japan (The German-Soviet pact) is lost to Germany.

No. 353 NAI DFA 219/6

Confidential report from Michael MacWhite to Joseph P. Walshe (Dublin)[1]
(Confidential)
ROME, 31 August 1939

The feeling still prevails in Italy that the Duce will be able to keep the country out of war. Some high military officers are of this opinion and it is generally believed that he has exercised a restraining influence on the Fuehrer. The Italian army is not pro-German and it is believed that a number of Generals have warned the Duce of the serious consequences that would follow if German generals were placed in commands over them. It is also stated on good authority that the most outstanding of the Italian army chiefs warned the Duce that Italian armaments were so inferior to modern requirements that it would be suicide to go to war. Perhaps it is for these reasons that Italy has not so far ordered a general mobilisation. The two classes recently called up got nine days notice as they will only join their units on next Monday. Some of these previously called up are in barracks, but have not yet been supplied with uniforms.

On the surface everything in Rome appeared normal until yesterday. There is no excitement. Crowds gather, however, around the Stores having loud speakers to hear the latest news. At seven o'clock every evening many go to the Piazza Venezia in the expectation of hearing a peace announcement from the Duce.

Last night we had a complete black out. The electricity supply to private houses was also cut off. From Sunday no private motor cars can run and from the same date the sale of coffee will be forbidden. Restaurants, Cafés, Cinemas, etc. are to close at 11 p.m. and food restrictions have been imposed. Circulars have been distributed to homes asking for information as to the qualifications for work of all women between the age of 14 and 70. Women and children and old persons are invited to leave the large cities and go to the country.

As a result of these regulations and precautions the people are being gradually accustomed to war conditions so that in case of general mobilisation everything will work smoothly.

[signed] M. MACWHITE

No. 354 NAI DFA 219/7

Confidential report from Francis T. Cremins to Joseph P. Walshe (Dublin)
(S. Gen 1.1) (Confidential)
GENEVA, 31 August 1939

With reference to previous minutes regarding the general situation, I have to state for the information of the Minister that while opinion here remains

---

[1] The marginal annotations on this document show that it was read by Joseph P. Walshe, Frederick H. Boland and Michael Rynne.

calm, there is no doubt that the situation is regarded today as being much more tense than during the past few days. The opinion is in fact freely expressed that war may break out now at any moment. This is more true for international circles than for Swiss circles – with the exception of course of official circles – which seem unwilling to believe that a way out of war will not be found. In the international circles, hope has almost reached vanishing point. I myself consider the situation as being extremely grave, the chief danger being that the position at Danzig may precipitate events in the pursuit of the Nazi-programme.

The emergency measures are in evidence here. Public buildings, railways, bridges, etc. are guarded by military. Columns of soldiers in full kit march undemonstrably through the town on the way to their stations. Certain essential foods and food products, such as sugar, rice, oatmeal, salt, etc. are temporarily off the market, and people are using the reserve stocks which, a few months ago, they were directed by the authorities to lay in. And today, for the first time for years, re-appeared five-franc notes instead of the ordinary silver five-franc pieces. All these measures bring home to the population the seriousness of the situation, but nevertheless some hope persists.

The international circles are for the most part simply waiting on events. The possibility of a settlement arising from the Hitler-Chamberlain communications is regarded now as slender in view of British-French commitments and of the unlikelihood of any appreciable climb down on the part of the dictator. There is also the feeling that more than the Danzig question is in play; that in fact the whole issue between the two sides is knit even though this may not appear explicitly in the correspondence. Some hope had been placed on Italy, but little reliance is now placed in that quarter. There is however the further offer from King Leopold and the Queen of the Netherlands which could still be seized upon as a way out and there remains of course the suggestion of a conference of five or six Powers. Events may however be precipitated if German restraint is not exercised in Danzig and the Corridor.

There is speculation here as to whether Italy would, at first at any rate, remain neutral, with the consent of Germany, if hostilities broke out, and whether such an attitude on the part of Italy would not practically render impossible the bringing of help to Poland. It is alleged by some that armed neutrality on the part of Italy might not be acceptable to Britain and France. The Bulgarian Minister tells me that it is the policy of his country to remain neutral, and he expresses the opinion also that Roumania would like to take up a similar position. It is stated that Roumania is one of the countries which is most disturbed by the German-Soviet pact, on account of the Bessarabian question which is still open between that country and Russia.

In certain Soviet circles here efforts are being made to explain the pact with Germany as a deliberate wedge driven by the Soviets into the anti-comintern pact, and therefore as a weakening of the totalitarian States. It is undoubtedly that, but it also seems to give Germany carte-blanche to act against Poland. The possible reactions of the pact are much discussed. It is stated that benefits to Germany in the shape of supplies could hardly be effective before six months, as communications would have to be organised.

Moreover, the position of Italy would be worsened through increased naval pressure in the Mediterranean if owing to Japanese irritation at the pact tension lessened for a time between Japan and Britain.

I presume that whether this present crisis is resolved peacefully or not, you will send me immediately instructions on the various points raised in my minutes of April and May last (e.g. disposal, if there was any danger of their getting out of my control, of confidential reports, and of code and cypher: also as regards funds for the Office, and, if it happened that the Office and flat had to be vacated, how furniture etc. should be disposed of).[1]

I mentioned in a previous minute that it is not now the intention of the Secretariat to take the initiative in moving from Switzerland in the event of war in Europe. It is stated here that the Swiss Government are fairly well satisfied that they would as in the last war succeed in maintaining their neutrality if war unhappily broke out between surrounding countries.

[signed] F.T. CREMINS
Permanent Delegate

No. 355 NAUK PREM 1/341

Message from Eamon de Valera to Neville Chamberlain sent via
John W. Dulanty
(Copy)

LONDON, 31 August 1939

The German Minister called on me to-day.

He informed me of the friendly attitude of the German Government towards Ireland and of their intention to respect Ireland's neutrality should Germany be engaged in a European conflict.

I replied that the Irish Government wished to remain at peace with Germany as with all other powers and I referred to my statement published in the press on the 20th February last that the aim of Irish Government policy was to maintain and preserve Ireland's neutrality in the event of war.

This information will probably appear in the press on Saturday morning.

No. 356 NAI DFA 219/6

Confidential report from Michael MacWhite to Joseph P. Walshe
(It/455/39)[2] (Copy)

ROME, 31 August 1939

During the past fourteen days, since the international situation became tense, this Legation has been kept extremely busy. The heads of Irish and other colleges having Irish students or professors, priests, nuns and other Irish

---

[1] This paragraph was drawn to the attention of Frederick H. Boland by Sheila Murphy and has been highlighted in the left-hand margin.
[2] Marginal annotation by Nicholas Nolan (Nioclás Ó Nualláin), Department of External Affairs: 'Original on 246/41'.

citizens in numbers have come to inquire about their situation in the case of a European war, if they should go or stay and if they remained how things would work out. All these people insist on seeing me or speaking to me over the telephone. Calls have been received from places as far apart as Stresa, Milan, Siena, Viareggio, Florence, Turin, etc. Others have written for advice and others again have come to exchange their English passports for Irish ones. For this purpose a woman travelled two days ago from Genoa, and yesterday I had two persons from Florence for the same purpose. The representatives of colleges and a number of priests either telephone or make personal daily calls with the result that I am beginning to suffer from the strain.

It seems that there are in Italy about four or five hundred Irish citizens all of whom depend on this Legation for advice and protection. To meet their demands in a thorough manner during the past fortnight would require the aid of two competent Secretaries of Legation. My son was able to help materially before his departure, my wife also lends a hand and Signora Benedetti is fully occupied. The making out of passports which has to be done by me is a most tedious business. As all my time is thus taken up with Consular work it is quite impossible for me to meet my colleagues or to glean any particular information on international matters. In fact I had only a moment last night to study the new code which seems very complicated and because of the advance in the slide for each word is liable to numerous errors in coding particularly when one is working under the pressure that happens to be my lot at present.

[unsigned]

No. 357 NAI DFA 241/89

Decode telegram from William Warnock to Department of External Affairs
(Dublin)
(Copy)
BERLIN, 9.45 am, 1 September 1939

33. Personal. German Government has informed me officially that neutral countries are requested to advise ships and aircraft to avoid Poland. Danzig, Gdynia blockaded – hostilities expected immediately.[1]

EIREANN

No. 358 NAI DFA 219/4

Confidential report from William Warnock to Joseph P. Walshe (Dublin)[2]
(43/33) (Copy)
BERLIN, 1 September 1939

I was notified this morning by the Foreign Office at 6 a.m. that the German Government wished neutral ships and aircraft to keep away from Danzig territory and Poland, as it was expected that hostilities would have

---

[1] Initialled: 'S.G.M.'.
[2] Marginal annotations: 'Secy'; 'file with A/Secy'; 'File with Dr Rynne'.

commenced by the time of receipt of this notice.[1] No doubt you received my telegrams.

I was asked by telephone to attend a meeting of the Reichstag at 10 a.m. I presume that you have seen the text of the Chancellor's speech in the newspapers. The Chancellor, as might be expected, looked very worn and worried, and the speech was not so brilliant as usual. He was obviously speaking with great emotion. The British Ambassador did not attend, but he was represented by Sir George Ogilvie-Forbes, the Counsellor of the Embassy. We were informed that direct action had already been taken against Poland. Herr Hitler enumerated all his efforts since he has come to power to obtain a peaceful settlement of Germany's claims, and endeavoured to show that it was only after repeated refusals of other powers to negotiate on a fair basis that he had been driven to assert Germany's rights by other means. He emphasised in a very moving passage that Germany could not regard the Treaty of Versailles as a law by which she was bound. At the end of his speech the Chancellor said that his whole political life had been given to the work of restoring Germany to its rightful place in the world and that now the testing time seemed to have come. In closing he hade a call for service and discipline, and said that he demanded no more from anybody than that which he would give himself.

After the speech it still remained uncertain whether or not a general war would break out, but the general opinion amongst my colleagues was that there seemed to be no alternative for Great Britain and France but to come in on Poland's side.

The Japanese Ambassador remained rather aloof, but I cannot say whether any particular significance may be attached to this.

Communication between the legation and Ireland will be extremely difficult if war breaks out. I am anxiously awaiting news from you as to how correspondence will be maintained. I have telegraphed to you concerning the codes at present in use. It seems to me that we shall have to devise a distinctive code of our own in that other codes will be no longer available.

A serious problem is that of currency and finance. I received an imprest from you this morning, and that will, I anticipate, suffice for at least a month. I take it that we shall have to deal in the currency of some neutral State.

So far as I am aware, all Irish who were here as tourists have succeeded in leaving the country. Since Friday, 25th August, I had advised Irish visitors to leave Germany. There are still some Irish people in the country, but with one exception, they have been living here for some years. The one exception is Mr. J.D.B. O'Toole, who is studying German engineering methods with Messrs. Siemens. Mr. O'Toole is a recent graduate of the engineering faculty in University College, Dublin. He is in constant communication with his parents, who have an address at Leinster Road, Rathmines, Dublin.

[stamped] W. WARNOCK

---

[1] See above No. 357.

Appendix 1
Destruction of files and documents dating from 1938 to 1940 by the Department of External Affairs

On 25 May 1940 Eamon de Valera ordered that files and documents that the Department of External Affairs feared would fall into German hands in the event of a German invasion of Ireland be 'confidentially destroyed' by officials in the Department of External Affairs. The files known to have been destroyed came from the 100-Series and 200-Series general registry files and the entries relating to these files in the departmental file registers were marked with 'CD 25/5/40' against their record. Details of these 'confidentially destroyed' files are given below. The files represent only a small portion of the 100-series and 200-series. There are also large gaps in the 100-series due to files migrating to the subsequent 200-series and from the 200-series into the later 300-series. It is clear from the titles and chronological scope of the destroyed files that they often contained extremely important material and material which is irreplaceable for the historian of Irish foreign policy.

Of these files the most significant are the confidential report files:

1	119/1	Confidential reports from Berlin	14 Jan. 1937-7 Dec. 1938
2	119/2	Confidential reports from Rome	12 Jan. 1937-30 Dec. 1938
3	119/5	Confidential reports from San Francisco	4 Jan. 1937-20 Dec. 1938
4	119/7	Confidential reports from Washington	12 July 1937-3 Jan. 1939
5	119/8	Confidential reports from Paris	18 July 1938-12 Jan. 1939
6	119/8A	Confidential reports from Paris	18 July 1938-12 Jan. 1939
7	119/10	Confidential reports from Geneva	4 Feb. 1937-28 June 1938
8	119/17	Confidential reports from St Jean de Luz	21 Aug. 1937-28 Nov. 1938
9	219/1	Confidential reports from Paris	1939

In many cases it has been possible to locate copies of the documents destroyed in the 'Embassies Series' records for the relevant Legation or in personal papers, but the destruction of the Irish Legation in Berlin during an Allied air raid in November 1943 and the previous destruction in May 1940 of confidential reports from Berlin for 1937 and 1938 has left a large gap in the material reproduced in this volume relating to Irish reporting on events in Germany during the war years. In an effort to partially overcome the loss of the material in file 119/1, section four below reproduces, as taken from the register of correspondence for file 119/1, the topics and subjects of confidential reports from Charles Bewley in Berlin for 1937 and 1938.

It seems likely that considerable portions of what are now known as the Secretary's 'S' Series files were also destroyed in 1940 or thereabouts. At the time these files were known as 'Secret' files and were kept in the custody of the Secretary of the Department of External Affairs and the Private Secretary to the Secretary.

The appendix below is divided into four sections:
1 100-Series (Sections 101-147). List of files destroyed on 25 May 1940.
2 200-Series (Sections 201-247). List of files destroyed on 25 May 1940.
3 Other collections of files known to have been destroyed in whole or in part.
4 Titles/Subjects of confidential reports by Charles Bewley contained in 100-Series file 119/1 and destroyed on 25 May 1940.

1 100-Series (Sections 101-147). List of files destroyed on 25 May 1940

1	101/64	Issue of British nationality certificates	1937-8
2	101/228	Proposed legislation dealing with public display or interference with foreign national flags	1938
3	101/324	Polish citizenship laws	1938
4	102/16	Non-recognition of Saorstát Éireann (SÉ) passports by British Consuls abroad	1937
5	102/19	Visa fees and regulations for aliens visiting Irish Free State (IFS)	unknown
6	102/30	Passports withheld for travel to Russia	1937
7	102/31	British suspect – Index list	1937
8	102/31A	British suspect – Index list	1937
9	102/31B	British suspect – Index list	1938-9
10	102/39	IFS citizens desiring British passports	1937-9
11	102/42	Passport and visa fees: Special list 1925-31	1925-31
12	102/55	Prolongation of stay in IFS of certain German nationals	1937-8
13	102/104	SÉ nationals in Germany and German nationals in SÉ	1937-8
14	102/129	Permission for Herr Klaus, German National to remain in SÉ	1937
15	102/205	Case of Abdul Hadi Bey: Palestinian national	1937
16	102/302	Visas: Ireland and Germany/Austria	1938
17	102/302A	Visas: Ireland and Germany/Austria	1938
18	102/302B	Visas: Ireland and Germany/Austria	1938
19	102/408	Case of individuals who arrived at Baldonnell from Austria	1938-9
20	102/427	Permission for German student to attend school in Waterford	1938
21	102/572	Naturalisation of German nationals as Irish citizens	1938-9
22	102/657	Visa to Dr Stefan Lendt	1939
23	105/3	Coronation of King George VI	1937
24	105/5	Coronation of King George VI	1937
25	105/17	Coronation of King George VI	1937
26	105/18	Germany's claim to Colonies	1937
27	105/27	Co-ordination of policy re exhibitions limited to members of the Commonwealth	1937

28	105/79	Visit to Paris of George VI	1938
29	105/83	Arrest and imprisonment of Eamon Donnelly	1938
30	106/13	Hydrographical services in SÉ	1937
31	106/19	Lands occupied by British forces in Ned's fort and vicinity	1937
32	106/20	Norwegian territorial waters	1937
33	106/22	Submarine cables in Cork harbour	1937
34	106/31	Inspection visit by British to SÉ coastal defences	1937
35	106/42	Repairs: Fort Carlisle	1937
36	106/48	Defence of Merchant Shipping	1938
37	106/49	Visit of foreign war vessels and aircraft to British ports	1938
38	111/3	Purchase of ammunition, guns etc from Britain	1937
39	111/4	London Naval Treaty: 1930	1937
40	111/6	Disarmament (Geneva)	1937-8
41	111/18	Small arms factory	1937
42	111/35	Torpedo aircraft	1938
43	115/100	Aircraft factory	1937
44	115/430	Aircraft fuel oil production	1938
45	115/460	Alleged campaign by Jews in Ireland to boycott German goods	11 Apr. 1938
46	116/95	Request for Foreign Office publication dealing with privilege of documents	May 1937
47	117/60	Irish-German political relations	5 Oct. 1938-12 Dec. 1938
48	119/1	Confidential reports from Berlin	14 Jan. 1937-7 Dec.1938
49	119/2	Confidential reports from Rome	12 Jan. 1937-30 Dec. 1938
50	119/5	Confidential reports from San Francisco	4 Jan. 1937-20 Dec. 1938
51	119/7	Confidential reports from Washington	12 July 1937-3 Jan. 1939
52	119/8	Confidential reports from Paris	18 July 1938-12 Jan. 1939
53	119/8A	Confidential reports from Paris	18 July 1938-12 Jan. 1939
54	119/10	Confidential reports from Geneva	4 Feb. 1937-28 June 1938
55	119/17	Confidential reports from St Jean de Luz	21 Aug. 1937-28 Nov. 1938
56	119/38	Bewley interview	17 Mar. 1937
57	119/41	British Consular instructions	20 Sept. 1937-12 Nov. 1937

58	119/47	Report on work of Berlin Legation 1937-38	4 Apr. 1938
59	119/52	Confidential reports from Rome (Quirinale)	16 May 1938- 19 Dec. 1938
60	119/59	Paris: Belgian Foreign policy	20 Oct. 1938- 10 Jan. 1939
61	121/20	German overflights of Irish territory	29 Jan. 1937- 5 May 1937
62	121/35	Irish Army officers attendance at RAF courses	19 Mar. 1937- 30 Apr. 1937
63	121/36	Lufthansa facilities in SÉ for transatlantic flight	1937
64	121/39	Permission for Zeppelin overflights	Mar. 1937
65	121/75	Experimental German transatlantic flights	15 July 1937- 12 Nov. 1937
66	121/180	Interdepartmental Committee on Air Raid precautions	Oct. 1938- July 1939
67	121/189	Permission for George Charles Avon to enlist in RAF	Dec. 1938
68	124/64	Re-occupation of the Rhineland	July- Dec. 1937
69	127/66	Blockade of Germany during 1914-18 War	13 July 1937
70	127/140	Agreements between Hungary and the Little Entente	24 Aug. 1938
71	127/145	Irish Friends of the Spanish republic: non-intervention	19 Oct. 1938
72	127/147	Germany's claim to Colonies	25 Oct. 1938
73	130/7	London: Electric Power invention of A. J. Haldane	17 Feb. 1937- 18 Mar. 1937
74	134/48	Communication from Mr Richard Monahan MD, Switzerland	10 Sept. 1937
75	134/58	Political situation in Germany (1938)	Feb. 1938
76	135/21	Important public functions in UK: measures to prevent landings of undesirable aliens	1937
77	138/50	Position of the Church in Germany	1937
78	138/221	Position of Dr Mahr, National Museum, in connection with his membership of the Nazi Party	Aug. 1938
79	141/14	General O'Duffy's Irish Brigade for Spain and other volunteers from Ireland	1937-8
80	141/70	Desertion of Private R. Stringer from Irish Army and charge for wearing British uniform	1938
81	141/71	Private Looby, Irish Army Reservist, application for enlistment in RAF	1938
82	141/74	Particulars of service of Private Thomas Franklin in Irish Army	1938

83	141/94	Enquiry of Commander K. Mitchell MVO re posts for ex RN officers in Irish services	Aug.-Nov. 1938
84	141/99	M. Hayes, RAF, position in event of war	1938
85	141/112	Communication re National Defence and Recruiting	Oct. 1938
86	144/7	Resolutions for release of Irish political prisoners in SÉ	1937-8
87	144/41	Enquiry re John Scanlon, former Flight Sergeant RAF	July 1938
88	144/49	Application of Civic Guard for post in Palestine Police	1938

2 200-Series (Sections 201-247). List of files destroyed on 25 May 1940

1	202/12	Permits for admission of German and Austrian nationals to Ireland
2	202/13	Issue of visas for Ireland by British consuls
3	202/19	British suspect list
4	202/19A	British suspect list
5	202/19B	British suspect list
6	202/50	Issue of passports by British representatives in countries where there are Irish representatives
7	202/71	Theft of passports from the Imperial Iranian Legation at Berlin
8	202/75	Siemens Ireland Ltd, employment of aliens
9	202/77	Copies of visas for the United Kingdom issued by British passport control officers, Paris, to Germans who will probably visit Ireland
10	202/89	Ernest Klaar: suspect false visa application
11	202/93	Mutual abolition of visas, agreement with Czechoslovakia
12	202/111	Palestinian visa regulations (original file destroyed)
13	202/118	Procedures regulating visas for alien refugees in Ireland who wish to proceed to Britain and dominions or colonies
14	202/135	Visa certificates of origin for Turkey
15	202/136	Passport visa requirements of foreign countries
16	202/149	Alien refugees: channel of enquiry
17	202/156	Iraqi visa and passport requirements
18	202/199	Helmut Joseph, visa application
19	202/53	Facilities for renewal of passports of Irish citizens
20	202/311	Alleged unauthorised issue of passports to persons desirous of leaving Germany
21	202/408	Alois Ludwig Rutter and Bertha Rutter, visa application
22	202/550	Transjordan nationals: visas and passports for Transjordan
23	202/709	Aliens employed by Irish Sugar Company
24	202/842	Reciprocal check between British and Irish authorities on the issue of visas to aliens
25	205/4	Press comments in Germany on Irish affairs

26	205/12	Messages of greeting to King George (first part confidentially destroyed)
27	205/77	Alleged meeting of protest of Irish republicans at Hotel Seville in New York, July 1935, against policy of government of Éire
28	206/39	Seaplane floats observed by *SS Hibernia* off Kish lightship
29	206/42	Fisheries vessel *Fort Rannoch*
30	206/59	Supply of Admiralty charts
31	206/61	Transfer to German ownership of MV *Sophia*
32	207/60	German-Romanian commercial agreement
33	208/76	Deportation from Ireland of Germans (some papers destroyed)
34	211/1A	Brandt mortar and ammunition, importation from France
35	214/8	Information re Irish affairs in German press
36	216/24	British government war establishment. Publications from Dept of Defence
37	218/31	Position of former consul and staff of Czechoslovak consulate in Dublin
38	219/1	Confidential Reports, Paris, 1939
39	219/1A	Anglo-American luncheon, Paris
40	219/1B	Germany's peace proposals
41	220/8	Customs facilities for Czechoslovak consul (papers prior to 25 May 1940 destroyed)
42	220/75	Entry duty free for Czechoslovak consul (papers prior to 25 May 1940 destroyed)
43	227/22	European situation: temporary file (first part confidentially destroyed)
44	232/77	International tobacco congress under auspices of International Federation of Technical Agriculturalists
45	233/13	Transfer of wireless stations from British to Irish government
46	241/1	Facilities in connection with visits of Irish Army officers to British Admiralty
47	241/8	Visits of officers of Dept of Defence to London in connection with purchase of gas masks and ARP equipment
48	241/18	Purchase of stores by Dept of Defence from British War Office
49	241/37	Course for gas detection officers
50	241/71	Direct correspondence on technical matters between Dept of Defence and Woolwich Inspection Officers
51	241/91	Position of civil servants and employees of local authorities who wish to join the Irish Defence Forces and also Reserves in the British Army
52	241/99	Visit of Irish Army officers to War Office
53	241/120	Enquiry by Commanding Officer Irish Guards re Michael McArdle

3 Other collections of files known to have been destroyed in whole or in part

1 S Series Secretary's Files (an unknown quantity of these files was destroyed)
2 Berlin Legation (RAF raid, Nov. 1943)
3 London High Commissioner's Office (shredding in the 1950s due to water damage)
4 Washington Legation (unknown reason)
5 Geneva Office (some confidential files for 1939-40 destroyed by Frank Cremins)

4 Titles/Subjects of confidential reports by Charles Bewley contained on file 119/1 and destroyed on 25 May 1940

Headquarters file reference	Date	Berlin Reference	Subject/Title
119/1	14 Jan. 1937	43/33	German troops in Spanish Morocco
119/1	26 Jan. 1937	43/33	Political report – European Situation
119/1	5 Feb. 1937	43/33	Reminders re letters of 14th and 26th January
119/1	8 Feb. 1937	43/33	Position of Ambassador von Ribbentrop
119/1	15 Feb. 1937	43/33	Reminder re letters of 26th January and 5th February – instructions re SÉ govt's position vis a vis Spanish Civil War
119/1	5 Mar. 1937	43/33	Instructions re SÉ govt's position vis a vis the Spanish Civil War
119/1	5 Mar. 1937	43/33	German claim for colonies
119/1	14 Apr. 1937	43/33	Relations between German govt and Catholic Church
119/1	25 May 1937	43/33	New govt in Valencia: English proposals for truce in Spain
119/1	4 June 1937	43/33	Germany's attitude to UK and France in connection with Spain
119/1	18 June 1937	43/33	Coronation picture shown under patronage of Ambassador of Great Britain and Ireland
119/1	23 June 1937	43/33	General political report
119/1	7 July 1937	43/33	Question of colonies and raw materials
119/1	23 Aug. 1937	43/33	Expulsion of an English journalist Mr Ebbuth from Germany
119/1	16 Sept. 1937	43/33	German Policy: Nuremberg Parteitag
119/1	20 Sept. 1937	43/33	General European situation
119/1	8 Oct. 1937	43/33	Reference to colonial question in Hitler's speech at harvest thanksgiving
119/1	11 Oct. 1937	43/33	Results of visit of Mussolini to Berlin: summing up of 'BZ am Mittag'
119/1	28 Oct. 1937	43/33	Political report

119/1	15 Nov. 1937	43/33	Adhesion of Italy to German-Japanese pact
119/1	13 Dec. 1937	43/33	Relations between Germany, Italy and Japan
119/1	31 Jan. 1938	43/33	Visit of Yugoslav Minister President Stojadanovic to Germany
119/1	7 Feb. 1938	43/33	Changes in German Army command, Govt and Diplomatic corps
119/1	14 Feb. 1938	43/33	Reports in Foreign Press re 'crisis' in Germany
119/1	21 Feb. 1938	43/33	Chancellor's Reichstag speech, Feb. '38
119/1	11 Mar. 1938	43/33	Announcement of plebiscite in Austria
119/1	14 Mar. 1938	43/33	Austria – intervention by Germany
119/1	18 Mar. 1938	43/33	Austria – report re
119/1	1 Apr. 1938	43/33	Austria – report re
119/1	13 Apr. 1938	43/33	Austria – report re result of plebiscite
119/1	25 Apr. 1938	43/33	Successful termination of English-Italian negotiations
119/1	3 May 1938	43/33	German–Czechoslovakia situation
119/1	1 June 1938	43/33	German–Czechoslovakia situation report re
119/1	2 June 1938	43/33	German–Czechoslovakia situation report re
119/1	28 June 1938	43/33	International situation
119/1	9 July 1938	43/33	German minority in Czechoslovakia – copy of 'Volkabund'
119/1	29 July 1938	43/33	Position of the Sudeten Germans
119/1	14 Sept. 1938	43/33	Check of false news disseminated by press: mention of Taoiseach
119/1	22 Sept. 1938	43/33	Article entitled 'Hitler's Germany provides work for them'
119/1	28 Sept. 1938	25/32	*City of Limerick* not landing its cargo at Bremen
119/1	12 Oct. 1938		Anti-Jewish feeling in Czechoslovakia
119/1	27 Oct. 1938	10/34.	Regulations governing admission of Jews into Germany
119/1	18 Nov. 1938	76/36	Anti-British article in Borsen-Zeitung ref. Black and Tan period in Ireland
119/1	30 Nov. 1938	13/38	German press on British atrocities in Palestine
119/1	7 Dec. 1938	Confid.	re dinner to Mr Pirow – report re
119/1	1 Feb. 1939	43/33	Hitler's speech in the Reichstag 30 Jan. 1937
119/1	1 Mar. 1939	43/33	General political report

Appendix 2

Months of the year in Irish and English

Irish	*English*
Eanair	January
Feabhra	February
Márta	March
Aibreán	April
Bealtaine	May
Meitheamh	June
Iúil	July
Lúnasa	August
Meán Fómhair	September
Deireadh Fómhair	October
Samhain	November
Mí na Nollag	December

Appendix 3

Glossary of Irish words and phrases

This list was compiled with the help of the Royal Irish Academy's Foclóir na
nua-Ghaeilge project. Details of the editorial conventions on the reproduction
of Irish language material are given in the introduction

Aire	Minister
Aire Lán-Chómhachtach	Minister Plenipotentiary
Ard-Fheis	Convention
A chara	Dear Sir/Madam (literally: Friend)
A chara dhílis	Dear Sir/Madam (literally: Dear friend)
a.s. Rúnaí (ar son Rúnaí)	p.p. Secretary
Do chara/Mise, do Chara	Yours sincerely (literally: Your friend)
Dáil	the Lower House of the Irish parliament
A dhíl/A dhílis	Dear (salutation)
Garda Síochána	Police (literally: Guardians of the Peace)
Le mór mheas/le meas mór	With much respect
Is Mise, le meas/Mise, le meas	With respect
Príomh-Aturnae	Attorney General
Rúnaí/Rúnaidhe	Secretary
Saorstát	Free State
Saorstát Éireann/An Saorstát	Irish Free State
Sinn Féin	Sinn Féin (political party) (literally: ourselves)
Teachta Dála (TD)	Dáil deputy
Uachtarán	President

Appendix 4
The Anglo-Irish Treaty (6 December 1921)

NAI DE 2/304/1

*Final text of the Articles of Agreement for a Treaty between
Great Britain and Ireland as signed.*
LONDON, 6 December 1921

1. Ireland shall have the same constitutional status in the Community of Nations known as the British Empire as the Dominion of Canada, the Commonwealth of Australia, the Dominion of New Zealand, and the Union of South Africa with a Parliament having powers to make laws for the peace order and good government of Ireland and an Executive responsible to that Parliament, and shall be styled and known as the Irish Free State.

2. Subject to the provisions hereinafter set out the position of the Irish Free State in relation to the Imperial Parliament and Government and otherwise shall be that of the Dominion of Canada, and the law, practice and constitutional usage governing the relationship of the Crown or the representative of the Crown and of the Imperial Parliament to the Dominion of Canada shall govern their relationship to the Irish Free State.

3. The representative of the Crown in Ireland shall be appointed in like manner as the Governor-General of Canada and in accordance with the practice observed in the making of such appointments.

4. The oath to be taken by Members of the Parliament of the Irish Free State shall be in the following form:-

> I .... do solemnly swear true faith and allegiance to the Constitution of the Irish Free State as by law established and that I will be faithful to H.M. King George V., his heirs and successors by law, in virtue of the common citizenship of Ireland with Great Britain and her adherence to and membership of the group of nations forming the British Commonwealth of Nations.

5. The Irish Free State shall assume liability for the service of the Public Debt of the United Kingdom as existing as the date hereof and towards the payment of War Pensions as existing at that date in such proportion as may be fair and equitable, having regard to any just claim on the part of Ireland by way of set-off or counter claim, the amount of such sums being determined in default of agreement by the arbitration of one or more independent persons being citizens of the British Empire.

6. Until an arrangement has been made between the British and Irish Governments whereby the Irish Free State undertakes her own coastal defence, the defence by sea of Great Britain and Ireland shall be undertaken by His Majesty's Imperial Forces, but this shall not prevent the construction or maintenance by the Government of the Irish Free State of such vessels as are necessary for the protection of the Revenue or the Fisheries. The foregoing

provisions of this article shall be reviewed at a conference of Representatives of the British and Irish governments, to be held at the expiration of five years from the date hereof with a view to the undertaking by Ireland of a share in her own coastal defence

7.   The Government of the Irish Free State shall afford to His Majesty's Imperial Forces

(a) In the time of peace such harbour and other facilities as are indicated in the Annex hereto, or such other facilities as may from time to time be agreed between the British Government and the Government of the Irish Free State; and

(b) In time of war or of strained relations with a Foreign Power such harbour and other facilities as the British Government may require for the purposes of such defence as aforesaid.

8.   With a view to securing the observance of the principle of international limitation of armaments, if the Government of the Irish Free State establishes and maintains a military defence force, the establishments thereof shall not exceed in size such proportion of the military establishes maintained in Great Britain as that which the population of Ireland bears to the population of Great Britain.

9.   The ports of Great Britain and the Irish Free State shall be freely open to the ships of the other country on payment of the customary port and other dues.

10. The Government of the Irish Free State agrees to pay fair compensation on terms not less favourable than those accorded by the Act of 1920 to judges, officials, members of Police Forces and other Public Servants who are discharged by it or who retire in consequence of the change of government effected in pursuance hereof.

Provided that this agreement shall not apply to members of the Auxiliary Police Force or to persons recruited in Great Britain for the Royal Irish Constabulary during the two years next preceding the date hereof. The British Government will assume responsibility for such compensation or pensions as may be payable to any of these excepted persons.

11. Until the expiration of one month from the passing of the Act of Parliament for the ratification of this instrument, the powers of the Parliament and the Government of the Irish Free State shall not be exercisable as respects Northern Ireland, and the provisions of the Government of Ireland Act 1920, shall, so far as they relate to Northern Ireland remain of full force and effect, and no election shall be held for the return of members to serve in the Parliament of the Irish Free State for constituencies in Northern Ireland, unless a resolution is passed by both Houses of the Parliament of Northern Ireland in favour of the holding of such elections before the end of the said month.

12. If before the expiration of the said month, an address is presented to His Majesty by both Houses of the Parliament of Northern Ireland to that effect, the powers of the Parliament and the Government of the Irish Free State shall no longer extend to Northern Ireland, and the provisions of the Government of Ireland Act, 1920, (including those relating to the Council of Ireland) shall

so far as they relate to Northern Ireland, continue to be of full force and effect, and this instrument shall have effect subject to the necessary modifications. Provided that if such an address is so presented a Commission consisting of three persons, one to be appointed by the Government of the Irish Free State, one to be appointed by the Government of Northern Ireland, and one who shall be Chairman to be appointed by the British Government shall determine in accordance with the wishes of the inhabitants, so far as may be compatible with economic and geographic conditions the boundaries between Northern Ireland and the rest of Ireland, and for the purposes of the Government of Ireland Act, 1920, and of this instrument, the boundary of Northern Ireland shall be such as may be determined by such Commission.

13. For the purpose of the last foregoing article, the powers of the Parliament of Southern Ireland under the Government of Ireland Act, 1920, to elect members of the Council of Ireland shall after the Parliament of the Irish Free State is constituted be exercised by that Parliament.

14. After the expiration of the said month, if no such address as is mentioned in Article 12 hereof is presented, the Parliament and Government of Northern Ireland shall continue to exercise as respects Northern Ireland the powers conferred on them by the Government of Ireland Act, 1920, but the Parliament and Government of the Irish Free State shall in Northern Ireland have in relation to matters in respect of which the Parliament of Northern Ireland has not the power to make laws under the Act (including matters which under the said Act are within the jurisdiction of the Council of Ireland) the same powers as in the rest of Ireland, subject to such other provisions as may be agreed in manner hereinafter appearing.

15. At any time after the date hereof the Government of Northern Ireland and the provisional Government of Southern Ireland hereinafter constituted may meet for the purpose of discussing the provisions subject to which the last foregoing Article is to operate in the event of no such address as is therein mentioned being presented and those provisions may include:-

(a) Safeguards with regard to patronage in Northern Ireland.

(b) Safeguards with regard to the collection of revenue in Northern Ireland.

(c) Safeguards with regard to import and export duties affecting the trade or industry of Northern Ireland.

(d) Safeguards for minorities in Northern Ireland.

(e) The settlement of the financial relations between Northern Ireland and the Irish Free State.

(f) The establishment and powers of a local militia in Northern Ireland and the relation of the Defence Forces of the Irish Free State and of Northern Ireland respectively,

and if at any such meeting provisions are agreed to, the same shall have effect as if they were included amongst the provisions subject to which the powers of the Parliament and the Government of the Irish Free State are to be exercisable in Northern Ireland under Article 14 hereof.

16. Neither the Parliament of the Irish Free State nor the Parliament of Northern Ireland shall make any law so as either directly or indirectly to endow any religion or prohibit or restrict the free exercise thereof or give any

preference or impose any disability on account of religious belief or religious status or affect prejudicially the right of any child to attend a school receiving public money without attending the religious instruction at the school or make any discrimination as respects State aid between schools under the management of different religious denominations or divert from any religious denomination or any educational institution any of its property except for public utility purposes and on payment of compensation.

17. By way of provisional arrangement for the administration of Southern Ireland during the interval which must elapse between the date hereof and the constitution of a Parliament and Government of the Irish Free State in accordance therewith, steps shall be taken forthwith for summoning a meeting of members of Parliament elected for constituencies in Southern Ireland since the passing of the Government of Ireland Act, 1920, and for constituting a provisional Government, and the British Government shall take the steps necessary to transfer to such provisional Government the powers and machinery requisite for the discharge of its duties, provided that every member of such provisional Government shall have signified in writing his or her acceptance of this instrument. But this arrangement shall not continue in force beyond the expiration of twelve months from the date hereof.

18. This instrument shall be submitted forthwith by His Majesty's Government for the approval of Parliament and by the Irish signatories to a meeting summoned for the purpose of the members elected to sit in the House of Commons of Southern Ireland and if approved shall be ratified by the necessary legislation.

(Signed)

On behalf of the British Delegation,	On behalf of the Irish Delegation.
D. LLOYD GEORGE.	ART Ó GRIOBHTHA.
AUSTEN CHAMBERLAIN.	MICHEÁL Ó COILEAIN.
BIRKENHEAD.	RIOBÁRD BARTÚN
WINSTON S. CHURCHILL.	E. S. Ó DUGAIN.
L. WORTHINGTON-EVANS.	SEÓRSA GHABHÁIN UÍ DHUBHTHAIGH
HAMAR GREENWOOD.	
GORDON HEWART.	

6th December, 1921.

ANNEX.

1. The following are the specific facilities required:-

Dockyard Port at Berehaven.

(a) Admiralty property and rights to be retained as at the date hereof. Harbour defences to remain in charge of British care and maintenance parties.

Queenstown.

(b) Harbour defences to remain in charge of British care and maintenance parties. Certain mooring buoys to be retained for use of His Majesty's ships.

Belfast Lough.

(c) Harbour defences to remain in charge of British care and maintenance parties.

Lough Swilly.
(d) Harbour defences to remain in charge of British care and maintenance parties.
AVIATION.
(e) Facilities in the neighbourhood of the above ports for coastal defence by air.
OIL FUEL STORAGE.
(f) Haulbowline   ) To be offered for sale to commercial
) companies under guarantee that purchasers
    Rathmullen   ) shall maintain a certain minimum stock for
) Admiralty purposes.
2. A Convention shall be made between the British Government and the Government of the Irish Free State to give effect to the following conditions :-
(a) That submarine cables shall not be landed or wireless stations for communication with places outside Ireland be established except by agreement with the British Government; that the existing cable landing rights and wireless concessions shall not be withdrawn except by agreement with the British Government; and that the British Government shall be entitled to land additional submarine cables or establish additional wireless stations for communication with places outside Ireland.
(b) That lighthouses, buoys, beacons, and any navigational marks or navigational aids shall be maintained by the Government of the Irish Free State as at the date hereof and shall not be removed or added to except by agreement with the British Government.
(c) That war signal stations shall be closed down and left in charge of care and maintenance parties, the Government of the Irish Free State being offered the option of taking them over and working them for commercial purposes subject to Admiralty inspection, and guaranteeing the upkeep of existing telegraphic communication therewith.
3. A Convention shall be made between the same Governments for the regulation of Civil Communication by Air.

Appendix 5
List of Irish Missions Abroad: 1937-1939

Britain
(opened 1922)
Occupant	*Post*	*Dates*
John W. Dulanty	High Commissioner	1930-49

League of Nations
(opened 1923)
Occupant	*Post*	*Dates*
Francis T. Cremins	Permanent Delegate to the League of Nations	1934-40

United States of America
Washington DC
(opened 1924)
Occupant	*Post*	*Dates*
Michael MacWhite	Minister Plenipotentiary and Envoy Extraordinary	1929-38
Robert Brennan	Minister Plenipotentiary and Envoy Extraordinary	1938-47

Boston
(opened 1929)
Occupant	*Post*	*Dates*
Percy Galwey-Foley	Consul General	1929-43

New York
(opened 1930)
Occupant	*Post*	*Dates*
Leo T. McCauley	Consul General	1934-46

San Francisco
(opened 1933)
Occupant	*Post*	*Dates*
Matthew Murphy	Consul General	1933-47

Chicago
(opened 1934)
Occupant	*Post*	*Dates*
Daniel McGrath	Consul General	1934-42

France
(opened 1929)

Occupant	Post	Dates
Art O'Brien	Minister Plenipotentiary and Envoy Extraordinary	1935-8
Seán Murphy	Minister Plenipotentiary and Envoy Extraordinary	1938-50

Holy See
(opened 1929)

Occupant	Post	Dates
William J.B. Macaulay	Minister Plenipotentiary and Envoy Extraordinary	1934-40

Germany
(opened 1929)

Occupant	Post	Dates
Charles Bewley	Minister Plenipotentiary and Envoy Extraordinary	1933-9
William Warnock	Chargé d'Affaires ad interim	1939-43

Spain
(opened 1935)

Occupant	Post	Dates
Leopold H. Kerney	Minister Plenipotentiary and Envoy Extraordinary	1935-46

Italy
(opened 1938)

Occupant	Post	Dates
Michael MacWhite	Minister Plenipotentiary and Envoy Extraordinary	1938-50

Appendix 6
Calendars for years 1937, 1938 and 1939

1937

January
S	M	Tu	W	Th	F	S
					1	2
3	4	5	6	7	8	9
10	11	12	13	14	15	16
17	18	19	20	21	22	23
24	25	26	27	28	29	30
31						

February
S	M	Tu	W	Th	F	S
	1	2	3	4	5	6
7	8	9	10	11	12	13
14	15	16	17	18	19	20
21	22	23	24	25	26	27
28						

March
S	M	Tu	W	Th	F	S
	1	2	3	4	5	6
7	8	9	10	11	12	13
14	15	16	17	18	19	20
21	22	23	24	25	26	27
28	29	30	31			

April
S	M	Tu	W	Th	F	S
				1	2	3
4	5	6	7	8	9	10
11	12	13	14	15	16	17
18	19	20	21	22	23	24
25	26	27	28	29	30	

May
S	M	Tu	W	Th	F	S
						1
2	3	4	5	6	7	8
9	10	11	12	13	14	15
16	17	18	19	20	21	22
23	24	25	26	27	28	29
30	31					

June
S	M	Tu	W	Th	F	S
		1	2	3	4	5
6	7	8	9	10	11	12
13	14	15	16	17	18	19
20	21	22	23	24	25	26
27	28	29	30			

July
S	M	Tu	W	Th	F	S
				1	2	3
4	5	6	7	8	9	10
11	12	13	14	15	16	17
18	19	20	21	22	23	24
25	26	27	28	29	30	31

August
S	M	Tu	W	Th	F	S
1	2	3	4	5	6	7
8	9	10	11	12	13	14
15	16	17	18	19	20	21
22	23	24	25	26	27	28
29	30	31				

September
S	M	Tu	W	Th	F	S
			1	2	3	4
5	6	7	8	9	10	11
12	13	14	15	16	17	18
19	20	21	22	23	24	25
26	27	28	29	30		

October
S	M	Tu	W	Th	F	S
					1	2
3	4	5	6	7	8	9
10	11	12	13	14	15	16
17	18	19	20	21	22	23
24	25	26	27	28	29	30
31						

November
S	M	Tu	W	Th	F	S
	1	2	3	4	5	6
7	8	9	10	11	12	13
14	15	16	17	18	19	20
21	22	23	24	25	26	27
28	29	30				

December
S	M	Tu	W	Th	F	S
			1	2	3	4
5	6	7	8	9	10	11
12	13	14	15	16	17	18
19	20	21	22	23	24	25
26	27	28	29	30	31	

1938

January
S	M	Tu	W	Th	F	S
						1
2	3	4	5	6	7	8
9	10	11	12	13	14	15
16	17	18	19	20	21	22
23	24	25	26	27	28	29
30	31					

February
S	M	Tu	W	Th	F	S
		1	2	3	4	5
6	7	8	9	10	11	12
13	14	15	16	17	18	19
20	21	22	23	24	25	26
27	28					

March
S	M	Tu	W	Th	F	S
		1	2	3	4	5
6	7	8	9	10	11	12
13	14	15	16	17	18	19
20	21	22	23	24	25	26
27	28	29	30	31		

April
S	M	Tu	W	Th	F	S
					1	2
3	4	5	6	7	8	9
10	11	12	13	14	15	16
17	18	19	20	21	22	23
24	25	26	27	28	29	30

May
S	M	Tu	W	Th	F	S
1	2	3	4	5	6	7
8	9	10	11	12	13	14
15	16	17	18	19	20	21
22	23	24	25	26	27	28
29	30	31				

June
S	M	Tu	W	Th	F	S
			1	2	3	4
5	6	7	8	9	10	11
12	13	14	15	16	17	18
19	20	21	22	23	24	25
26	27	28	29	30		

July
S	M	Tu	W	Th	F	S
					1	2
3	4	5	6	7	8	9
10	11	12	13	14	15	16
17	18	19	20	21	22	23
24	25	26	27	28	29	30
31						

August
S	M	Tu	W	Th	F	S
	1	2	3	4	5	6
7	8	9	10	11	12	13
14	15	16	17	18	19	20
21	22	23	24	25	26	27
28	29	30	31			

September
S	M	Tu	W	Th	F	S
				1	2	3
4	5	6	7	8	9	10
11	12	13	14	15	16	17
18	19	20	21	22	23	24
25	26	27	28	29	30	

October
S	M	Tu	W	Th	F	S
						1
2	3	4	5	6	7	8
9	10	11	12	13	14	15
16	17	18	19	20	21	22
23	24	25	26	27	28	29
30	31					

November
S	M	Tu	W	Th	F	S
		1	2	3	4	5
6	7	8	9	10	11	12
13	14	15	16	17	18	19
20	21	22	23	24	25	26
27	28	29	30			

December
S	M	Tu	W	Th	F	S
				1	2	3
4	5	6	7	8	9	10
11	12	13	14	15	16	17
18	19	20	21	22	23	24
25	26	27	28	29	30	31

1939

January
S	M	Tu	W	Th	F	S
1	2	3	4	5	6	7
8	9	10	11	12	13	14
15	16	17	18	19	20	21
22	23	24	25	26	27	28
29	30	31				

February
S	M	Tu	W	Th	F	S
			1	2	3	4
5	6	7	8	9	10	11
12	13	14	15	16	17	18
19	20	21	22	23	24	25
26	27	28				

March
S	M	Tu	W	Th	F	S
			1	2	3	4
5	6	7	8	9	10	11
12	13	14	15	16	17	18
19	20	21	22	23	24	25
26	27	28	29	30	31	

April
S	M	Tu	W	Th	F	S
						1
2	3	4	5	6	7	8
9	10	11	12	13	14	15
16	17	18	19	20	21	22
23	24	25	26	27	28	29
30						

May
S	M	Tu	W	Th	F	S
	1	2	3	4	5	6
7	8	9	10	11	12	13
14	15	16	17	18	19	20
21	22	23	24	25	26	27
28	29	30	31			

June
S	M	Tu	W	Th	F	S
				1	2	3
4	5	6	7	8	9	10
11	12	13	14	15	16	17
18	19	20	21	22	23	24
25	26	27	28	29	30	

July
S	M	Tu	W	Th	F	S
						1
2	3	4	5	6	7	8
9	10	11	12	13	14	15
16	17	18	19	20	21	22
23	24	25	26	27	28	29
30	31					

August
S	M	Tu	W	Th	F	S
		1	2	3	4	5
6	7	8	9	10	11	12
13	14	15	16	17	18	19
20	21	22	23	24	25	26
27	28	29	30	31		

September
S	M	Tu	W	Th	F	S
					1	2
3	4	5	6	7	8	9
10	11	12	13	14	15	16
17	18	19	20	21	22	23
24	25	26	27	28	29	30

October
S	M	Tu	W	Th	F	S
1	2	3	4	5	6	7
8	9	10	11	12	13	14
15	16	17	18	19	20	21
22	23	24	25	26	27	28
29	30	31				

November
S	M	Tu	W	Th	F	S
			1	2	3	4
5	6	7	8	9	10	11
12	13	14	15	16	17	18
19	20	21	22	23	24	25
26	27	28	29	30		

December
S	M	Tu	W	Th	F	S
					1	2
3	4	5	6	7	8	9
10	11	12	13	14	15	16
17	18	19	20	21	22	23
24	25	26	27	28	29	30
31						

Index

This volume is indexed by page number and should be used in conjunction with the list of documents reproduced (pp xxxii-xlix). The term 'Anglo-Irish', though now superseded by 'British-Irish', has been used in this volume. Note the following abbreviations: IFS, Irish Free State; TD, Teachta Dála (Member of Dáil Éireann).